Instructor's Manual

Solutions prepared by
Li Lee • Jordan Rosenthal • Maya Said • Greg Slabaugh

Matlab Links and Exam Problems Prepared by
John R. Buck

DISCRETE-TIME SIGNAL PROCESSING

SECOND EDITION

Alan V. Oppenheim
Ronald W. Schafer
John R. Buck

PRENTICE HALL, Upper Saddle River, NJ 07458

Publisher: Tom Robbins
Editorial Assistant: Dan DePasquale
Special Projects Manager: Barbara A. Murray
Production Editor: Shea Oakley
Supplement Cover Manager: Paul Gourhan
Supplement Cover Designer: PM Workshop Inc.
Manufacturing Buyer: Pat Brown

Printed in the United States of America

10 9 8 7 6 5 4 3 2 1

ISBN 0-13-085158-2

Prentice-Hall International (UK) Limited, London
Prentice-Hall of Australia Pty. Limited, Sydney
Prentice-Hall Canada, Inc., Toronto
Prentice-Hall Hispanoamericana, S.A., Mexico
Prentice-Hall of India Private Limited, New Delhi
Prentice-Hall (Singapore) Pte. Ltd.,
Prentice-Hall of Japan, Inc., Tokyo
Editora Prentice-Hall do Brazil, Ltda., Rio de Janeiro

Acknowledgement

The problems in the text and the solutions in this manual have been written by the authors and numerous teaching assistants over a period of over twenty years. Some are more polished than others, and inevitably, there will be errors in the problems and the solutions. We believe strongly that both the problems in the book and the solutions contained in this manual are greatly improved from the problems and solutions manual with the first edition of this book. Many of the solutions have been corrected or rewritten, and many of the figures have been improved as well. We hope you will find these improved solutions helpful.

We plan to remove errors in the problem statements in future printings of the text, and we intend to update this manual periodically by removing errors and improving the solutions. We welcome errata sent to John Buck at the address below.

This manual is primarily the work of the follow four people:

Li Lee
Jordan Rosenthal
Maya Said
Greg Slabaugh

They updated and corrected the previous version of this manual. They wrote new solutions to the new problems, and new solutions to the old problems where necessary. They drafted the greatly improved figures of this manual. Greg Slabaugh then undertook the task of integrating their individual efforts into a cohesive manuscript.

All of these efforts are indebted to the solutions manual for the first edition of this book. Specifically, that first solutions manual would not have existed without the efforts of Robert Bamberger, Joseph Bondaryk, Steven Eddins, Patrick Velardo, Larry Candell, Kay Gilstrap, Jon Maiara, Douglas Reynolds, Roz Picard, Lih-Bor Yinn. We express our sincere appreciation to all of the people named above and to the many other students and teaching assistants who have helped to shape these problems over the years.

John. R. Buck
ECE Dept., UMass Dartmouth
285 Old Westport Rd.
N. Dartmouth, Ma 02747-2300
jbuck@umassd.edu

Solutions – Chapter 2

Discrete-Time Signals and Systems

2.1. (a) $T(x[n]) = g[n]x[n]$

- Stable: Let $|x[n]| \leq M$ then $|T[x[n]| \leq |g[n]|M$. So, it is stable if $|g[n]|$ is bounded.
- Causal: $y_1[n] = g[n]x_1[n]$ and $y_2[n] = g[n]x_2[n]$, so if $x_1[n] = x_2[n]$ for all $n < n_0$, then $y_1[n] = y_2[n]$ for all $n < n_0$, and the system is causal.
- Linear:

$$\begin{aligned} T(ax_1[n] + bx_2[n]) &= g[n](ax_1[n] + bx_2[n] \\ &= ag[n]x_1[n] + bg[n]x_2[n] \\ &= aT(x_1[n]) + bT(x_2[n]) \end{aligned}$$

So this is linear.
- Not time-invariant:

$$\begin{aligned} T(x[n-n_0]) &= g[n]x[n-n_0] \\ &\neq y[n-n_0] = g[n-n_0]x[n-n_0] \end{aligned}$$

which is not TI.
- Memoryless: $y[n] = T(x[n])$ depends only on the nth value of x, so it is memoryless.

(b) $T(x[n]) = \sum_{k=n_0}^{n} x[k]$

- Not Stable: $|x[n]| \leq M \rightarrow |T(x[n])| \leq \sum_{k=n_0}^{n} |x[k]| \leq |n - n_0|M$. As $n \rightarrow \infty$, $T \rightarrow \infty$, so not stable.
- Not Causal: $T(x[n])$ depends on the future values of $x[n]$ when $n < n_0$, so this is not causal.
- Linear:

$$\begin{aligned} T(ax_1[n] + bx_2[n]) &= \sum_{k=n_0}^{n} ax_1[k] + bx_2[k] \\ &= a\sum_{k=n_0}^{n} x_1[n] + b\sum_{k=n_0}^{n} x_2[n] \\ &= aT(x_1[n]) + bT(x_2[n]) \end{aligned}$$

The system is linear.
- Not TI:

$$\begin{aligned} T(x[n-n_0]) &= \sum_{k=n_0}^{n} x[k-n_0] \\ &= \sum_{k=0}^{n-n_0} x[k] \\ &\neq y[n-n_0] = \sum_{k=n_0}^{n-n_0} x[k] \end{aligned}$$

The system is not TI.
- Not Memoryless: Values of $y[n]$ depend on past values for $n > n_0$, so this is not memoryless.

(c) $T(x[n]) \sum_{k=n-n_0}^{n+n_0} x[k]$

- Stable: $|T(x[n])| \leq \sum_{k=n-n_0}^{n+n_0} |x[k]| \leq \sum_{k=n-n_0}^{n+n_0} x[k]M \leq |2n_0 + 1|M$ for $|x[n]| \leq M$, so it is stable.
- Not Causal: $T(x[n])$ depends on future values of $x[n]$, so it is not causal.

- Linear:

$$\begin{aligned} T(ax_1[n]+bx_2[n]) &= \sum_{k=n-n_0}^{n+n_0} ax_1[k]+bx_2[k] \\ &= a\sum_{k=n-n_0}^{n+n_0} x_1[k]+b\sum_{k=n-n_0}^{n+n_0} x_2[k] = aT(x_1[n])+bT(x_2[n]) \end{aligned}$$

  This is linear.
- TI:

$$\begin{aligned} T(x[n-n_0] &= \sum_{k=n-n_0}^{n+n_0} x[k-n_0] \\ &= \sum_{k=n-n_0}^{n} x[k] \\ &= y[n-n_0] \end{aligned}$$

  This is TI.
- Not memoryless: The values of $y[n]$ depend on $2n_0$ other values of x, not memoryless.

(d) $T(x[n]) = x[n-n_0]$

- Stable: $|T(x[n])| = |x[n-n_0]| \leq M$ if $|x[n] \leq M$, so stable.
- Causality: If $n_0 \geq 0$, this is causal, otherwise it is not causal.
- Linear:

$$\begin{aligned} T(ax_1[n]+bx_2[n]) &= ax_1[n-n_0]+bx_2[n-n_0] \\ &= aT(x_1[n])+bT(x_2[n]) \end{aligned}$$

  This is linear.
- TI: $T(x[n-n_d] = x[n-n_0-n_d] = y[n-n_d]$. This is TI.
- Not memoryless: Unless $n_0 = 0$, this is not memoryless.

(e) $T(x[n]) = e^{x[n]}$

- Stable: $|x[n]| \leq M$, $|T(x[n])| = |e^{x[n]}| \leq e^{|x[n]|} \leq e^M$, this is stable.
- Causal: It doesn't use future values of $x[n]$, so it causal.
- Not linear:

$$\begin{aligned} T(ax_1[n]+bx_2[n]) &= e^{ax_1[n]+bx_2[n]} \\ &= e^{ax_1[n]}e^{bx_2[n]} \\ &\neq aT(x_1[n])+bT(x_2[n]) \end{aligned}$$

  This is not linear.
- TI: $T(x[n-n_0]) = e^{x[n-n_0]} = y[n-n_0]$, so this is TI.
- Memoryless: $y[n]$ depends on the nth value of x only, so it is memoryless.

(f) $T(x[n]) = ax[n]+b$

- Stable: $|T(x[n])| = |ax[n]+b| \leq a|M|+|b|$, which is stable for finite a and b.
- Causal: This doesn't use future values of $x[n]$, so it is causal.
- Not linear:

$$\begin{aligned} T(cx_1[n]+dx_2[n]) &= acx_1[n]+adx_2[n]+b \\ &\neq cT(x_1[n])+dT(x_2[n]) \end{aligned}$$

  This is not linear.

- TI: $T(x[n-n_0]) = ax[n-n_0] + b = y[n-n_0]$. It is TI.
- Memoryless: $y[n]$ depends on the nth value of $x[n]$ only, so it is memoryless.

(g) $T(x[n]) = x[-n]$

- Stable: $|T(x[n])| \leq |x[-n]| \leq M$, so it is stable.
- Not causal: For $n < 0$, it depends on the future value of $x[n]$, so it is not causal.
- Linear:

$$\begin{aligned} T(ax_1[n] + bx_2[n]) &= ax_1[-n] + bx_2x[-n] \\ &= aT(x_1[n]) + bT(x_2[n]) \end{aligned}$$

This is linear.
- Not TI:

$$\begin{aligned} T(x[n-n_0]) &= x[-n-n_0] \\ &\neq y[n-n_0] = x[-n+n_0] \end{aligned}$$

This is not TI.
- Not memoryless: For $n \neq 0$, it depends on a value of x other than the nth value, so it is not memoryless.

(h) $T(x[n]) = x[n] + u[n+1]$

- Stable: $|T(x[n])| \leq M + 3$ for $n \geq -1$ and $|T(x[n])| \leq M$ for $n < -1$, so it is stable.
- Causal: Since it doesn't use future values of $x[n]$, it is causal.
- Not linear:

$$\begin{aligned} T(ax_1[n] + bx_2[n]) &= ax_1[n] + bx_2[n] + 3u[n+1] \\ &\neq aT(x_1[n]) + bT(x_2[n]) \end{aligned}$$

This is not linear.
- Not TI:

$$\begin{aligned} T(x[n-n_0] &= x[n-n_0] + 3u[n+1] \\ &= y[n-n_0] \\ &= x[n-n_0] + 3u[n-n_0+1] \end{aligned}$$

This is not TI.
- Memoryless: $y[n]$ depends on the nth value of x only, so this is memoryless.

2.2. For an LTI system, the output is obtained from the convolution of the input with the impulse response of the system:

$$y[n] = \sum_{k=-\infty}^{\infty} h[k]x[n-k]$$

(a) Since $h[k] \neq 0$, for $(N_0 \leq n \leq N_1)$,

$$y[n] = \sum_{k=N_0}^{N_1} h[k]x[n-k]$$

The input, $x[n] \neq 0$, for $(N_2 \leq n \leq N_3)$, so

$$x[n-k] \neq 0, \text{ for } N_2 \leq (n-k) \leq N_3$$

Note that the minimum value of $(n-k)$ is N_2. Thus, the lower bound on n, which occurs for $k = N_0$ is

$$N_4 = N_0 + N_2.$$

Using a similar argument,

$$N_5 = N_1 + N_3.$$

Therefore, the output is nonzero for

$$(N_0 + N_2) \leq n \leq (N_1 + N_3).$$

(b) If $x[n] \neq 0$, for some $n_o \leq n \leq (n_o + N - 1)$, and $h[n] \neq 0$, for some $n_1 \leq n \leq (n_1 + M - 1)$, the results of part (a) imply that the output is nonzero for:

$$(n_o + n_1) \leq n \leq (n_o + n_1 + M + N - 2)$$

So the output sequence is $M + N - 1$ samples long. This is an important quality of the convolution for finite length sequences as we shall see in Chapter 8.

2.3. We desire the step response to a system whose impulse response is

$$h[n] = a^{-n}u[-n], \text{ for } 0 < a < 1.$$

The convolution sum:

$$y[n] = \sum_{k=-\infty}^{\infty} h[k]x[n-k]$$

The step response results when the input is the unit step:

$$x[n] = u[n] = \begin{cases} 1, & \text{for } n \geq 0 \\ 0, & \text{for } n < 0 \end{cases}$$

Substitution into the convolution sum yields

$$y[n] = \sum_{k=-\infty}^{\infty} a^{-k}u[-k]u[n-k]$$

For $n \leq 0$:

$$\begin{aligned} y[n] &= \sum_{k=-\infty}^{\infty} a^{-k} \\ &= \sum_{k=-n}^{\infty} a^{k} \\ &= \frac{a^{-n}}{1-a} \end{aligned}$$

For $n > 0$:

$$\begin{aligned} y[n] &= \sum_{k=-\infty}^{0} a^{-k} \\ &= \sum_{k=0}^{\infty} a^{k} \\ &= \frac{1}{1-a} \end{aligned}$$

2.4. The difference equation:

$$y[n] - \frac{3}{4}y[n-1] + \frac{1}{8}y[n-2] = 2x[n-1]$$

To solve, we take the Fourier transform of both sides.

$$Y(e^{j\omega}) - \frac{3}{4}Y(e^{j\omega})e^{-j\omega} + \frac{1}{8}Y(e^{j\omega})e^{-j2\omega} = 2 \cdot X(e^{j\omega})e^{-j\omega}$$

The system function is given by:

$$\begin{aligned} H(e^{j\omega}) &= \frac{Y(e^{j\omega})}{X(e^{j\omega})} \\ &= \frac{2e^{-j\omega}}{1 - \frac{3}{4}e^{-j\omega} + \frac{1}{8}e^{-j2\omega}} \end{aligned}$$

The impulse response (for $x[n] = \delta[n]$) is the inverse Fourier transform of $H(e^{j\omega})$.

$$H(e^{j\omega}) = \frac{-8}{1 + \frac{1}{4}e^{-j\omega}} + \frac{8}{1 - \frac{1}{2}e^{-j\omega}}$$

Thus,

$$h[n] = -8(\frac{1}{4})^n u[n] + 8(\frac{1}{2})^n u[n].$$

2.5. (a) The homogeneous difference equation:

$$y[n] - 5y[n-1] + 6y[n-2] = 0$$

Taking the Z-transform,

$$1 - 5z^{-1} + 6z^{-2} = 0$$
$$(1 - 2z^{-1})(1 - 3z^{-1}) = 0.$$

The homogeneous solution is of the form

$$y_h[n] = A_1(2)^n + A_2(3)^n.$$

(b) We take the z-transform of both sides:

$$Y(z)[1 - 5z^{-1} + 6z^{-2}] = 2z^{-1}X(z)$$

Thus, the system function is

$$\begin{aligned} H(z) &= \frac{Y(z)}{X(z)} \\ &= \frac{2z^{-1}}{1 - 5z^{-1} + 6z^{-2}} \\ &= \frac{-2}{1 - 2z^{-1}} + \frac{2}{1 - 3z^{-1}}, \end{aligned}$$

where the region of convergence is outside the outermost pole, because the system is causal. Hence the ROC is $|z| > 3$. Taking the inverse z-transform, the impulse response is

$$h[n] = -2(2)^n u[n] + 2(3)^n u[n].$$

(c) Let $x[n] = u[n]$ (unit step), then

$$X(z) = \frac{1}{1 - z^{-1}}$$

and

$$\begin{aligned} Y(z) &= X(z) \cdot H(z) \\ &= \frac{2z^{-1}}{(1 - z^{-1})(1 - 2z^{-1})(1 - 3z^{-1})}. \end{aligned}$$

Partial fraction expansion yields

$$Y(z) = \frac{1}{1 - z^{-1}} - \frac{4}{1 - 2z^{-1}} + \frac{3}{1 - 3z^{-1}}.$$

The inverse transform yields:

$$y[n] = u[n] - 4(2)^n u[n] + 3(3)^n u[n].$$

2.6. (a) The difference equation:

$$y[n] - \frac{1}{2} y[n-1] = x[n] + 2x[n-1] + x[n-2]$$

Taking the Fourier transform of both sides,

$$Y(e^{j\omega})[1 - \frac{1}{2} e^{-j\omega}] = X(e^{j\omega})[1 + 2e^{-j\omega} + e^{-j2\omega}].$$

Hence, the frequency response is

$$\begin{aligned} H(e^{j\omega}) &= \frac{Y(e^{j\omega})}{X(e^{j\omega})} \\ &= \frac{1 + 2e^{-j\omega} + e^{-j2\omega}}{1 - \frac{1}{2} e^{-j\omega}}. \end{aligned}$$

(b) A system with frequency response:

$$\begin{aligned} H(e^{j\omega}) &= \frac{1 - \frac{1}{2} e^{-j\omega} + e^{-j3\omega}}{1 + \frac{1}{2} e^{-j\omega} + \frac{3}{4} e^{-j2\omega}} \\ &= \frac{Y(e^{j\omega})}{X(e^{j\omega})} \end{aligned}$$

cross multiplying,

$$Y(e^{j\omega})[1 + \frac{1}{2} e^{-j\omega} + \frac{3}{4} e^{-j2\omega}] = X(e^{j\omega})[1 - \frac{1}{2} e^{-j\omega} + e^{-j3\omega}],$$

and the inverse transform gives

$$y[n] + \frac{1}{2} y[n-1] + \frac{3}{4} y[n-2] = x[n] - \frac{1}{2} x[n-1] + x[n-3].$$

2.7. $x[n]$ is periodic with period N if $x[n] = x[n+N]$ for some integer N.

(a) $x[n]$ is periodic with period 12:

$$e^{j(\frac{\pi}{6} n)} = e^{j(\frac{\pi}{6})(n+N)} = e^{j(\frac{\pi}{6} n + 2\pi k)}$$

$$\Longrightarrow 2\pi k = \frac{\pi}{6} N, \text{for integers } k, N$$

Making $k = 1$ and $N = 12$ shows that $x[n]$ has period 12.

(b) $x[n]$ is periodic with period 8:

$$e^{j(\frac{3\pi}{4}n)} = e^{j(\frac{3\pi}{4})(n+N)} = e^{j(\frac{3\pi}{4}n+2\pi k)}$$

$$\Longrightarrow 2\pi k = \frac{3\pi}{4}N, \text{for integers } k, N$$

$$\Longrightarrow N = \frac{8}{3}k, \text{for integers } k, N$$

The smallest k for which both k and N are integers are is 3, resulting in the period N being 8.

(c) $x[n] = [\sin(\pi n/5)]/(\pi n)$ is not periodic because the denominator term is linear in n.

(d) We will show that $x[n]$ is not periodic. Suppose that $x[n]$ is periodic for some period N:

$$e^{j(\frac{\pi}{\sqrt{2}}n)} = e^{j(\frac{\pi}{\sqrt{2}})(n+N)} = e^{j(\frac{\pi}{\sqrt{2}}n+2\pi k)}$$

$$\Longrightarrow 2\pi k = \frac{\pi}{\sqrt{2}}N, \text{for integers } k, N$$

$$\Longrightarrow N = 2\sqrt{2}k, \text{for some integers } k, N$$

There is no integer k for which N is an integer. Hence $x[n]$ is not periodic.

2.8. We take the Fourier transform of both $h[n]$ and $x[n]$, and then use the fact that convolution in the time domain is the same as multiplication in the frequency domain.

$$\begin{aligned}
H(e^{j\omega}) &= \frac{5}{1+\frac{1}{2}e^{-j\omega}} \\
Y(e^{j\omega}) &= H(e^{j\omega})X(e^{j\omega}) \\
&= \frac{5}{1+\frac{1}{2}e^{-j\omega}} \cdot \frac{1}{1-\frac{1}{3}e^{-j\omega}} \\
&= \frac{3}{1+\frac{1}{2}e^{-j\omega}} + \frac{2}{1-\frac{1}{3}e^{-j\omega}} \\
y[n] &= 2(\frac{1}{3})^n u[n] + 3(-\frac{1}{2})^n u[n]
\end{aligned}$$

2.9. (a) First the frequency response:

$$Y(e^{j\omega}) - \frac{5}{6}e^{-j\omega}Y(e^{j\omega}) + \frac{1}{6}e^{-2j\omega}Y(e^{j\omega}) = \frac{1}{3}e^{-2j\omega}X(e^{j\omega})$$

$$\begin{aligned}
H(e^{j\omega}) &= \frac{Y(e^{j\omega})}{X(e^{j\omega})} \\
&= \frac{\frac{1}{3}e^{-2j\omega}}{1-\frac{5}{6}e^{-j\omega}+\frac{1}{6}e^{-2j\omega}}
\end{aligned}$$

Now we take the inverse Fourier transform to find the impulse response:

$$\begin{aligned}
H(e^{j\omega}) &= \frac{-2}{1-\frac{1}{3}e^{-j\omega}} + \frac{2}{1-\frac{1}{2}e^{-j\omega}} \\
h[n] &= -2(\frac{1}{3})^n u[n] + 2(\frac{1}{2})^n u[n]
\end{aligned}$$

For the step response $s[n]$:

$$\begin{aligned} s[n] &= \sum_{k=-\infty}^{\infty} h[k]u[n-k] \\ &= \sum_{k=-\infty}^{n} h[k] \\ &= -2\frac{1-(1/3)^{n+1}}{1-1/3}u[n] + 2\frac{1-(1/2)^{n+1}}{1-1/2}u[n] \\ &= (1+(\frac{1}{3})^n - 2(\frac{1}{2})^n)u[n] \end{aligned}$$

(b) The homogeneous solution $y_h[n]$ solves the difference equation when $x[n] = 0$. It is in the form $y_h[n] = \sum A(c)^n$, where the c's solve the quadratic equation

$$c^2 - \frac{5}{6}c + \frac{1}{6} = 0$$

So for $c = 1/2$ and $c = 1/3$, the general form for the homogeneous solution is:

$$y_h[n] = A_1(\frac{1}{2})^n + A_2(\frac{1}{3})^n$$

(c) The total solution is the sum of the homogeneous and particular solutions, with the particular solution being the impulse response found in part (a):

$$\begin{aligned} y[n] &= y_h[n] + y_p[n] \\ &= A_1(\frac{1}{2})^n + A_2(\frac{1}{3})^n + -2(\frac{1}{3})^n u[n] + 2(\frac{1}{2})^n u[n] \end{aligned}$$

Now we use the constraint $y[0] = y[1] = 1$ to solve for A_1 and A_2:

$$\begin{aligned} y[0] &= A_1 + A_2 - 2 + 2 = 1 \\ y[1] &= A_1/2 + A_2/3 - 2/3 + 1 = 1 \\ A_1 + A_2 &= 1 \\ A_1/2 + A_2/3 &= 2/3 \end{aligned}$$

With $A_1 = 2$ and $A_2 = -1$ solving the simultaneous equations, we find that the impulse response is

$$y[n] = 2(\frac{1}{2})^n - (\frac{1}{3})^n + -2(\frac{1}{3})^n u[n] + 2(\frac{1}{2})^n u[n]$$

2.10. (a)

$$\begin{aligned} y[n] &= h[n] * x[n] \\ &= \sum_{k=-\infty}^{\infty} a^k u[-k-1]u[n-k] \\ &= \begin{cases} \sum_{k=-\infty}^{n} a^k, & n \leq -1 \\ \sum_{k=-\infty}^{-1} a^k, & n > -1 \end{cases} \\ &= \begin{cases} \dfrac{a^n}{1-1/a}, & n \leq -1 \\ \dfrac{1/a}{1-1/a}, & n > -1 \end{cases} \end{aligned}$$

(b) First, let us define $v[n] = 2^n u[-n-1]$. Then, from part (a), we know that

$$w[n] = u[n] * v[n] = \begin{cases} 2^{n+1}, & n \leq -1 \\ 1, & n > -1 \end{cases}$$

Now,

$$\begin{aligned} y[n] &= u[n-4] * v[n] \\ &= w[n-4] \\ &= \begin{cases} 2^{n-3}, & n \leq 3 \\ 1, & n > 3 \end{cases} \end{aligned}$$

(c) Given the same definitions for $v[n]$ and $w[n]$ from part(b), we use the fact that $h[n] = 2^{n-1}u[-(n-1)-1] = v[n-1]$ to reduce our work:

$$\begin{aligned} y[n] &= x[n] * h[n] \\ &= x[n] * v[n-1] \\ &= w[n-1] \\ &= \begin{cases} 2^{n}, & n \leq 0 \\ 1, & n > 0 \end{cases} \end{aligned}$$

(d) Again, we use $v[n]$ and $w[n]$ to help us.

$$\begin{aligned} y[n] &= x[n] * h[n] \\ &= (u[n] - u[n-10]) * v[n] \\ &= w[n] - w[n-10] \\ &= (2^{n+1}u[-(n+1)] + u[n]) - (2^{n-9}u[-(n-9)] + u[n-10]) \\ &= \begin{cases} 2^{(n+1)} - 2^{(n-9)}, & n \leq -2 \\ 1 - 2^{(n-9)}, & -1 \leq n \leq 8 \\ 0, & n \geq 9 \end{cases} \end{aligned}$$

2.11. First we re-write $x[n]$ as a sum of complex exponentials:

$$x[n] = \sin(\frac{\pi n}{4}) = \frac{e^{j\pi n/4} - e^{-j\pi n/4}}{2j}.$$

Since complex exponentials are eigenfunctions of LTI systems,

$$y[n] = \frac{H(e^{j\pi/4})e^{j\pi n/4} - H(e^{-j\pi/4})e^{-j\pi n/4}}{2j}$$

Evaluating the frequency response at $\omega = \pm\pi/4$:

$$\begin{aligned} H(e^{j\frac{\pi}{4}}) &= \frac{1 - e^{-j\pi/2}}{1 + 1/2e^{-j\pi}} = 2(1-j) = 2\sqrt{2}e^{-j\pi/4} \\ H(e^{-j\frac{\pi}{4}}) &= \frac{1 - e^{j\pi/2}}{1 + 1/2e^{j\pi}} = 2(1+j) = 2\sqrt{2}e^{j\pi/4} \end{aligned}$$

We get:

$$\begin{aligned} y[n] &= \frac{2\sqrt{2}e^{-j\pi/4}e^{j\pi n/4} - 2\sqrt{2}e^{j\pi/4}e^{-j\pi n/4}}{2j} \\ &= 2\sqrt{2}\sin(\pi n/4 - \pi/4). \end{aligned}$$

2.12. The difference equation:

$$y[n] = ny[n-1] + x[n]$$

Since the system is causal and satisfies initial-rest conditions, we may recursively find the response to any input.

(a) Suppose $x[n] = \delta[n]$:

$$y[n] = 0, \text{ for } n < 0$$
$$y[0] = 1$$
$$y[1] = 1$$
$$y[2] = 2$$
$$y[3] = 6$$
$$y[4] = 24$$

$$y[n] = h[n] = n!u[n]$$

(b) To determine if the system is linear, consider the input:

$$x[n] = a\delta[n] + b\delta[n]$$

performing the recursion,

$$y[n] = 0, \text{ for } n < 0$$
$$y[0] = a + b$$
$$y[1] = a + b$$
$$y[2] = 2(a + b)$$
$$y[3] = 6(a + b)$$
$$y[4] = 24(a + b)$$

Because the output of the superposition of two input signals is equivalent to the superposition of the individual outputs, the system is LINEAR.

(c) To determine if the system is time-invariant, consider the input:

$$x[n] = \delta[n-1]$$

the recursion yields

$$y[n] = 0, \text{ for } n < 0$$
$$y[0] = 0$$
$$y[1] = 1$$
$$y[2] = 2$$
$$y[3] = 6$$
$$y[4] = 24$$

Using $h[n]$ from part (a),

$$h[n-1] = (n-1)!u[n-1] \neq y[n]|_{x[n]=\delta[n-1]}$$

Conclude: NOT TIME INVARIANT.

2.13. Eigenfunctions of LTI systems are of the form α^n, so functions (a), (b), and (e) are eigenfunctions. Notice that part (d), $\cos(\omega_0 n) = .5(e^{j\omega_0 n} + e^{-j\omega_0 n})$ is a sum of two α^n functions, and is therefore not an eigenfunction itself.

2.14. (a) The information given shows that the system satisfies the eigenfunction property of exponential sequences for LTI systems for one particular eigenfunction input. However, we do not know the system response for any other eigenfunction. Hence, we can say that the system may be LTI, but we cannot uniquely determine it. $\Longrightarrow$ (iv).

(b) If the system were LTI, the output should be in the form of $A(1/2)^n$, since $(1/2)^n$ would have been an eigenfunction of the system. Since this is not true, the system cannot be LTI. $\Longrightarrow$ (i).

(c) Given the information, the system *may* be LTI, but does not have to be. For example, for any input other than the given one, the system may output 0, making this system non-LTI. $\Longrightarrow$ (iii). If it were LTI, its system function can be found by using the DTFT:

$$\begin{aligned} H(e^{j\omega}) &= \frac{Y(e^{j\omega})}{X(e^{j\omega})} \\ &= \frac{1}{1 - \frac{1}{2}e^{-j\omega}} \\ h[n] &= (\frac{1}{2})^n u[n] \end{aligned}$$

2.15. (a) No. Consider the following input/outputs:

$$x_1[n] = \delta[n] \Longrightarrow y_1[n] = (\frac{1}{4})^n u[n]$$
$$x_2[n] = \delta[n-1] \Longrightarrow y_2[n] = (\frac{1}{4})^{n-1} u[n]$$

Even though $x_2[n] = x_1[n-1]$, $y_2[n] \neq y_1[n-1] = (\frac{1}{4})^{n-1}u[n-1]$

(b) No. Consider the input/output pair $x_2[n]$ and $y_2[n]$ above. $x_2[n] = 0$ for $n < 1$, but $y_2[0] \neq 0$.

(c) Yes. Since $h[n]$ is stable and multiplication with $u[n]$ will not cause any sequences to become unbounded, the entire system is stable.

2.16. (a) The homogeneous solution $y_h[n]$ solves the difference equation when $x[n] = 0$. It is in the form $y_h[n] = \sum A(c)^n$, where the c's solve the quadratic equation

$$c^2 - \frac{1}{4}c + \frac{1}{8} = 0$$

So for $c = 1/2$ and $c = -1/4$, the general form for the homogeneous solution is:

$$y_h[n] = A_1(\frac{1}{2})^n + A_2(-\frac{1}{4})^n$$

(b) Taking the z-transform of both sides, we find that

$$Y(z)(1 - \frac{1}{4}z^{-1} - \frac{1}{8}z^{-2}) = 3X(z)$$

and therefore

$$\begin{aligned} H(z) &= \frac{Y(z)}{X(z)} \\ &= \frac{3}{1 - 1/4z^{-1} - 1/8z^{-2}} \\ &= \frac{3}{(1 + 1/4z^{-1})(1 - 1/2z^{-1})} \\ &= \frac{1}{1 + 1/4z^{-1}} + \frac{2}{1 - 1/2z^{-1}} \end{aligned}$$

The causal impulse response corresponds to assuming that the region of convergence extends outside the outermost pole, making

$$h_c[n] = ((-1/4)^n + 2(1/2)^n)u[n]$$

The anti-causal impulse response corresponds to assuming that the region of convergence is inside the innermost pole, making

$$h_{ac}[n] = -((-1/4)^n + 2(1/2)^n)u[-n-1]$$

(c) $h_c[n]$ is absolutely summable, while $h_{ac}[n]$ grows without bounds.

(d)

$$\begin{aligned}
Y(z) &= X(z)H(z) \\
&= \frac{1}{1-\frac{1}{2}z^{-1}} \cdot \frac{1}{(1+\frac{1}{4}z^{-1})(1-\frac{1}{2}z^{-1})} \\
&= \frac{1/3}{1+1/4z^{-1}} + \frac{2}{1-1/2z^{-1}} + \frac{2/3}{1-1/2z^{-1}} \\
y[n] &= \frac{1}{3}(\frac{1}{4})^n u[n] + 4(n+1)(\frac{1}{2})^{n+1}u[n+1] + \frac{2}{3}(\frac{1}{2})^n u[n]
\end{aligned}$$

2.17. (a) We have

$$r[n] = \begin{cases} 1, & \text{for } 0 \le n \le M \\ 0, & \text{otherwise} \end{cases}$$

Taking the Fourier transform

$$\begin{aligned}
R(e^{j\omega}) &= \sum_{n=0}^{M} e^{-j\omega n} \\
&= \frac{1-e^{-j\omega(M+1)}}{1-e^{-j\omega}} \\
&= e^{-j\frac{M}{2}\omega}\left(\frac{e^{j\frac{M+1}{2}\omega} - e^{-j\frac{M+1}{2}\omega}}{e^{j\omega} - e^{-j\omega}}\right) \\
&= e^{-j\frac{M}{2}\omega}\left(\frac{\sin(\frac{M+1}{2}\omega)}{\sin(\omega/2)}\right).
\end{aligned}$$

(b) We have

$$w[n] = \begin{cases} \frac{1}{2}(1+\cos(\frac{2\pi n}{M}), & \text{for } 0 \le n \le M \\ 0, & \text{otherwise} \end{cases}$$

We note that,

$$w[n] = r[n] \cdot \frac{1}{2}[1 + cos(\frac{2\pi n}{M})].$$

Thus,

$$\begin{aligned}
W(e^{j\omega}) &= R(e^{j\omega}) * \sum_{n=-\infty}^{\infty} \frac{1}{2}(1 + cos(\frac{2\pi n}{M}))e^{-j\omega n} \\
&= R(e^{j\omega}) * \sum_{n=-\infty}^{\infty} \frac{1}{2}(1 + \frac{1}{2}e^{j\frac{2\pi n}{M}} + \frac{1}{2}e^{-j\frac{2\pi n}{M}})e^{-j\omega} \\
&= R(e^{j\omega}) * (\frac{1}{2}\delta(\omega) + \frac{1}{4}\delta(\omega + \frac{2\pi}{M}) + \frac{1}{4}\delta(\omega - \frac{2\pi}{M}))
\end{aligned}$$

(c)

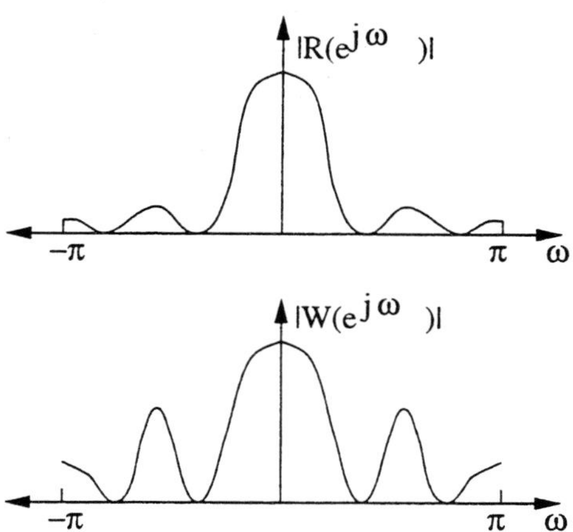

2.18. $h[n]$ is causal if $h[n] = 0$ for $n < 0$. Hence, (a) and (b) are causal, while (c), (d), and (e) are not.

2.19. $h[n]$ is stable if it is absolutely summable.

(a) Not stable because $h[n]$ goes to ∞ as n goes to ∞.

(b) Stable, because $h[n]$ is non-zero only for $0 \le n \le 9$.

(c) Stable.

$$\sum_n |h[n]| = \sum_{n=-\infty}^{-1} 3^n = \sum_{n=1}^{\infty} (1/3)^n = 1/2 < \infty$$

(d) Not stable. Notice that

$$\sum_{n=0}^{5} |\sin(\pi n/3)| = 2\sqrt{3}$$

and summing $|h[n]|$ over all positive n therefore grows to ∞.

(e) Stable. Notice that $|h[n]|$ is upperbounded by $(3/4)^{|n|}$, which is absolutely summable.

(f) Stable.

$$h[n] = \begin{cases} 2, & ,-5 \le n \le -1 \\ 1, & ,0 \le n \le 4 \\ 0, & ,\text{otherwise} \end{cases}$$

So $\sum |h[n]| = 15$.

2.20. (a) Taking the difference equation $y[n] = (1/a)y[n-1] + x[n-1]$ and assuming $h[0] = 0$ for $n < 0$:

$$\begin{aligned} h[0] &= 0 \\ h[1] &= 1 \\ h[2] &= 1/a \\ h[3] &= (1/a)^2 \\ &\vdots \\ h[n] &= (1/a)^{n-1}u[n-1] \end{aligned}$$

(b) $h[n]$ is absolutely summable if $|1/a| < 1$ or if $|a| > 1$

2.21. For an arbitrary linear system, we have

$$y[n] = T\{x[n]\},$$

Let $x[n] = 0$ for all n.

$$y[n] = T\{x[n]\}$$

For some arbitrary $x_1[n]$, we have

$$y_1[n] = T\{x_1[n]\}$$

Using the linearity of the system:

$$\begin{aligned} T\{x[n] + x_1[n]\} &= T\{x[n]\} + T\{x_1[n]\} \\ &= y[n] + y_1[n] \end{aligned}$$

Since $x[n]$ is zero for all n,

$$T\{x[n] + x_1[n]\} = T\{x_1[n]\} = y_1[n]$$

Hence, $y[n]$ must also be zero for all n.

2.22. We use the graphical approach to compute the convolution:

$$\begin{aligned} y[n] &= x[n] * h[n] \\ &= \sum_{k=-\infty}^{\infty} x[k]h[n-k] \end{aligned}$$

(a) $y[n] = x[n] * h[n]$

$$y[n] = \delta[n-1] * h[n] = h[n-1]$$

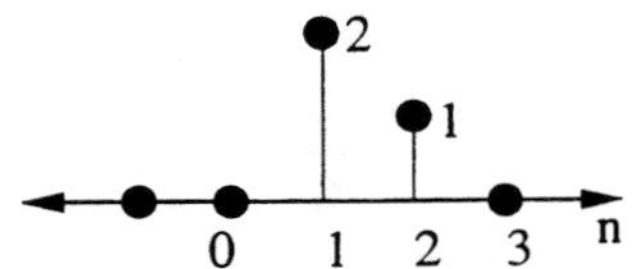

(b) $y[n] = x[n] * h[n]$

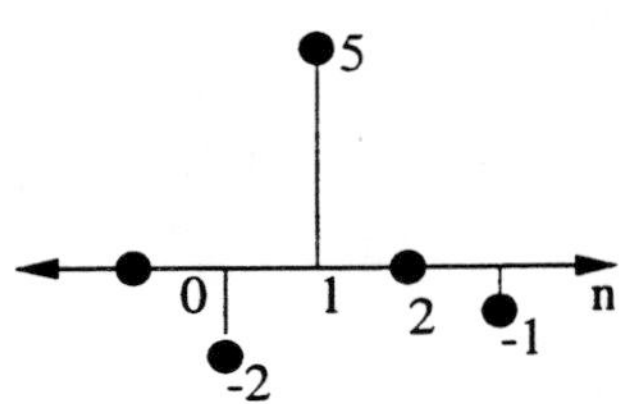

(c) $y[n] = x[n] * h[n]$

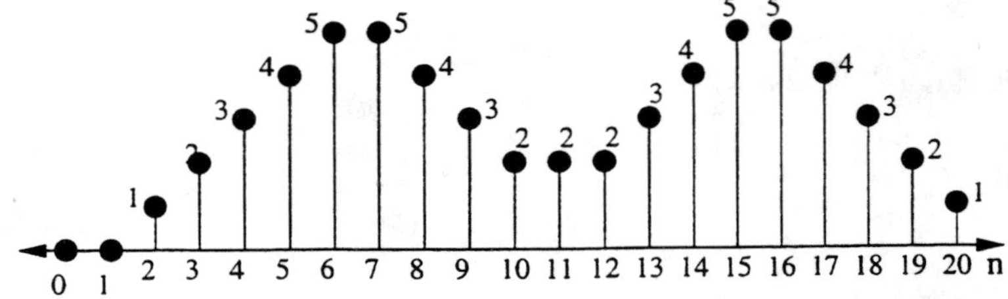

(d) $y[n] = x[n] * h[n]$

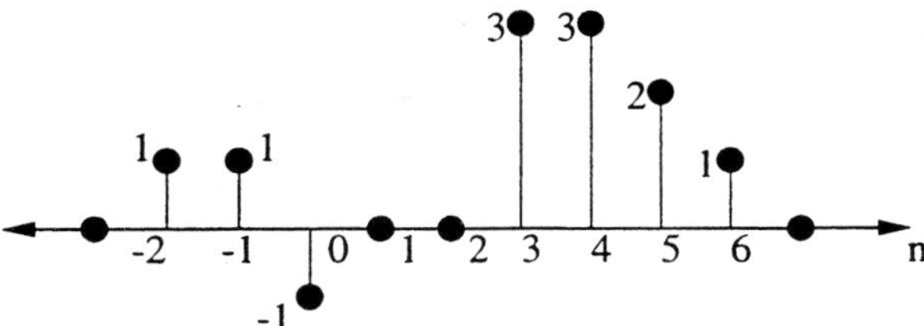

2.23. The ideal delay system:

$$y[n] = T\{x[n]\} = x[n - n_o]$$

Using the definition of linearity:

$$\begin{aligned} T\{ax_1[n] + bx_2[n]\} &= ax_1[n - n_o] + bx_2[n - n_o] \\ &= ay_1[n] + by_2[n] \end{aligned}$$

So, the ideal delay system is LINEAR.

The moving average system:

$$y[n] = Tx[n] = \frac{1}{M_1 + M_2 + 1} \sum_{k=-M_1}^{M_2} x[n - k]$$

by linearity:

$$\begin{aligned} T\{ax_1[n] + bx_2[n]\} &= \frac{1}{M_1 + M_2 + 1} \sum_{k=-M_1}^{M_2} (ax_1[n] + bx_2[n]) \\ &= \frac{1}{M_1 + M_2 + 1} \sum_{k=-M_1}^{M_2} ax_1[n] + \frac{1}{M_1 + M_2 + 1} \sum_{k=-M_1}^{M_2} bx_2[n] \\ &= ay_1[n] + by_2[n] \end{aligned}$$

Conclude, the moving average is LINEAR.

2.24. The response of the system to a delayed step:

$$\begin{aligned} y[n] &= x[n] * h[n] \\ &= \sum_{k=-\infty}^{\infty} x[k]h[n - k] \\ &= \sum_{k=-\infty}^{\infty} u[k - 4]h[n - k] \end{aligned}$$

$$y[n] = \sum_{k=4}^{\infty} h[n - k]$$

Evaluating the above summation:

For $n < 4$: $y[n] = 0$
For $n = 4$: $y[n] = h[0] = 1$
For $n = 5$: $y[n] = h[1] + h[0] = 2$
For $n = 6$: $y[n] = h[2] + h[1] + h[0] = 3$
For $n = 7$: $y[n] = h[3] + h[2] + h[1] + h[0] = 4$
For $n = 8$: $y[n] = h[4] + h[3] + h[2] + h[1] + h[0] = 2$
For $n \geq 9$: $y[n] = h[5] + h[4] + h[3] + h[2] + h[1] + h[0] = 0$

2.25. The output is obtained from the convolution sum:

$$\begin{aligned} y[n] &= x[n] * h[n] \\ &= \sum_{k=-\infty}^{\infty} x[k]h[n-k] \\ &= \sum_{k=-\infty}^{\infty} x[k]u[n-k] \end{aligned}$$

The convolution may be broken into five regions over the range of n:

$$y[n] = 0, \text{for } n < 0$$

$$\begin{aligned} y[n] &= \sum_{k=0}^{n} a^k \\ &= \frac{1-a^{(n+1)}}{1-a}, \text{for } 0 \le n \le N_1 \end{aligned}$$

$$\begin{aligned} y[n] &= \sum_{k=0}^{N_1} a^k \\ &= \frac{1-a^{(N_1+1)}}{1-a}, \text{ for } N_1 < n < N_2 \end{aligned}$$

$$\begin{aligned} y[n] &= \sum_{k=0}^{N_1} a^k + \sum_{k=N_2}^{n} a^{(k-N_2)} \\ &= \frac{1-a^{(N_1+1)}}{1-a} + \frac{1-a^{(n+1)}}{1-a} \\ &= \frac{2-a^{(N_1+1)} - a^{(n+1)}}{1-a}, \text{ for } N_2 \le n \le (N_1+N_2) \end{aligned}$$

$$\begin{aligned} y[n] &= \sum_{k=0}^{N_1} a^k + \sum_{k=N_2}^{N_1+N_2} a^{(k-N_2)} \\ &= \sum_{k=0}^{N_1} a^k + \sum_{m=0} N_1 a^m \\ &= 2\sum_{k=0}^{N_1} a^k \\ &= 2 \cdot \left(\frac{1-a^{(N_1+1)}}{1-a}\right), \text{ for } n > (N_1+N_2) \end{aligned}$$

2.26. Recall that an eigenfunction of a system is an input signal which appears at the output of the system scaled by a complex constant.

(a) $x[n] = 5^n u[n]$:

$$\begin{aligned} y[n] &= \sum_{k=-\infty}^{\infty} h[k]x[n-k] \\ &= \sum_{k=-\infty}^{\infty} h[k]5^{(n-k)}u[n-k] \\ &= 5^n \sum_{k=-\infty}^{n} h[k]5^{-k} \end{aligned}$$

Becuase the summation depends on n, $x[n]$ is NOT AN EIGENFUNCTION.

(b) $x[n] = e^{j2\omega n}$:

$$\begin{aligned} y[n] &= \sum_{k=-\infty}^{\infty} h[k]e^{j2\omega(n-k)} \\ &= e^{j2\omega n} \sum_{k=-\infty}^{\infty} h[k]e^{-j2\omega k} \\ &= e^{j2\omega n} \cdot H(e^{j2\omega}) \end{aligned}$$

YES, EIGENFUNCTION.

(c) $e^{j\omega n} + e^{j2\omega n}$:

$$\begin{aligned} y[n] &= \sum_{k=-\infty}^{\infty} h[k]e^{j\omega(n-k)} + \sum_{k=-\infty}^{\infty} h[k]e^{j2\omega(n-k)} \\ &= e^{j\omega n} \sum_{k=-\infty}^{\infty} h[k]e^{-j\omega k} + e^{j2\omega n} \sum_{k=-\infty}^{\infty} h[k]e^{-j2\omega k} \\ &= e^{j\omega n} \cdot H(e^{j\omega}) + e^{j2\omega n} \cdot H(e^{j2\omega}) \end{aligned}$$

Since the input cannot be extracted from the above expression, the sum of complex exponentials is NOT AN EIGENFUNCTION. (Although, separately the inputs are eigenfunctions. In general, complex exponential signals are always eigenfunctions of LTI systems.)

(d) $x[n] = 5^n$:

$$\begin{aligned} y[n] &= \sum_{k=-\infty}^{\infty} h[k]5^{(n-k)} \\ &= 5^n \sum_{k=-\infty}^{\infty} h[k]5^{-k} \end{aligned}$$

YES, EIGENFUNCTION.

(e) $x[n] = 5^n e^{j2\omega n}$:

$$\begin{aligned} y[n] &= \sum_{k=-\infty}^{\infty} h[k]5^{(n-k)}e^{j2\omega(n-k)} \\ &= 5^n e^{j2\omega n} \sum_{k=-\infty}^{\infty} h[k]5^{-k}e^{-j2\omega k} \end{aligned}$$

YES, EIGENFUNCTION.

2.27. • System A:

$$x[n] = (\frac{1}{2})^n$$

This input is an eigenfunction of an LTI system. That is, if the system is linear, the output will be a replica of the input, scaled by a complex constant.
Since $y[n] = (\frac{1}{4})^n$, System A is NOT LTI.

• System B:

$$x[n] = e^{jn/8}u[n]$$

The Fourier transform of $x[n]$ is

$$\begin{aligned} X(e^{j\omega}) &= \sum_{n=-\infty}^{\infty} e^{jn/8}u[n]e^{-j\omega n} \\ &= \sum_{n=0}^{\infty} e^{-j(\omega-\frac{1}{8})n} \\ &= \frac{1}{1-e^{-j(\omega-\frac{1}{8})}}. \end{aligned}$$

The output is $y[n] = 2x[n]$, thus

$$Y(e^{j\omega}) = \frac{2}{1-e^{-j(\omega-\frac{1}{8})}}.$$

Therefore, the frequency response of the system is

$$\begin{aligned} H(e^{j\omega}) &= \frac{Y(e^{j\omega})}{X(e^{j\omega})} \\ &= 2. \end{aligned}$$

Hence, the system is a linear amplifier. We conclude that System B is LTI, and unique.

• System C: Since $x[n] = e^{jn/8}$ is an eigenfunction of an LTI system, we would expect the output to be given by

$$y[n] = \gamma e^{jn/8},$$

where γ is some complex constant, if System C were indeed LTI. The given output, $y[n] = 2e^{jn/8}$, indicates that this is so.
Hence, System C is LTI. However, it is not unique, since the only constraint is that

$$H(e^{j\omega})|_{\omega=1/8} = 2.$$

2.28. $x[n]$ is periodic with period N if $x[n] = x[n+N]$ for some integer N.

(a) $x[n]$ is periodic with period 5:

$$e^{j(\frac{2\pi}{5}n)} = e^{j(\frac{2\pi}{5})(n+N)} = e^{j(\frac{2\pi}{5}n+2\pi k)}$$

$$\Longrightarrow 2\pi k = \frac{2\pi}{5}N, \text{for integers } k, N$$

Making $k = 1$ and $N = 5$ shows that $x[n]$ has period 5.

(b) $x[n]$ is periodic with period 38. Since the sin function has period of 2π:

$$x[n+38] = \sin(\pi(n+38)/19) = \sin(\pi n/19 + 2\pi) = x[n]$$

(c) This is not periodic because the linear term n is not periodic.

(d) This is again not periodic. $e^{j\omega}$ is periodic over period 2π, so we have to find k, N such that

$$x[n+N] = e^{j(n+N)} = e^{j(n+2\pi k)}$$

Since we can make k and N integers at the same time, $x[n]$ is not periodic.

2.29.

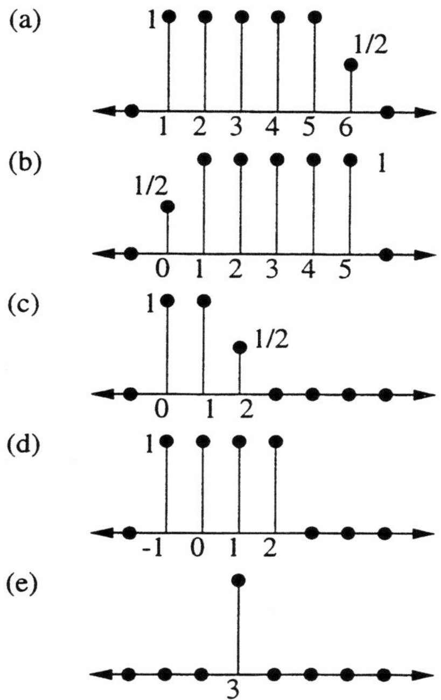

2.30. (a) Since $\cos(\pi n)$ only takes on values of +1 or -1, this transformation outputs the current value of $x[n]$ multiplied by either ± 1. $T(x[n]) = (-1)^n x[n]$.

- Hence, it is stable, because it doesn't change the magnitude of $x[n]$ and hence satisfies bounded-in/bounded-out stability.
- It is causal, because each output depends only on the current value of $x[n]$.
- It is linear. Let $y_1[n] = T(x_1[n]) = \cos(\pi n)x_1[n]$, and $y_2[n] = T(x_2[n]) = \cos(\pi n)x_2[n]$. Now

$$T(ax_1[n] + bx_2[n]) = \cos(\pi n)(ax_1[n] + bx_2[n]) = ay_1[n] + by_2[n]$$

- It is not time-invariant. If $y[n] = T(x[n]) = (-1)^n x[n]$, then $T(x[n-1]) = (-1)^n x[n-1] \neq y[n-1]$.

(b) This transformation simply "samples" $x[n]$ at location which can be expressed as k^2.

- The system is stable, since if $x[n]$ is bounded, $x[n^2]$ is also bounded.
- It is not causal. For example, $Tx[4] = x[16]$.
- It is linear. Let $y_1[n] = T(x_1[n]) = x_1[n^2]$, and $y_2[n] = T(x_2[n]) = x_2[n^2]$. Now

$$T(ax_1[n] + bx_2[n]) = ax_1[n^2] + bx_2[n^2]) = ay_1[n] + by_2[n]$$

- It is not time-invariant. If $y[n] = T(x[n]) = x[n^2]$, then $T(x[n-1]) = x[n^2-1] \neq y[n-1]$.

(c) First notice that

$$\sum_{k=0}^{\infty} \delta[n-k] = u[n]$$

So $T(x[n]) = x[n]u[n]$. This transformation is therefore stable, causal, linear, but not time-invariant.

To see that it is not time invariant, notice that $T(\delta[n]) = \delta[n]$, but $T(\delta[n+1]) = 0$.

(d) $T(x[n]) = \sum_{k=n-1}^{\infty} x[k]$

- This is not stable. For example, $T(u[n]) = \infty$ for all n ¿ 1.
- It is not causal, since it sums *forward* in time.
- It is linear, since

$$\sum_{k=n-1}^{\infty} ax_1[k] + bx_2[k] = a \sum_{k=n-1}^{\infty} x_1[k] + b \sum_{k=n-1}^{\infty} x_2[k]$$

- It is time-invariant. Let

$$y[n] = T(x[n]) = \sum_{k=n-1}^{\infty} x[k],$$

then

$$T(x[n-n_0]) = \sum_{k=n-n_0-1}^{\infty} x[k] = y[n-n_0]$$

2.31. (a) The homogeneous solution $y_h[n]$ solves the difference equation when $x[n] = 0$. It is in the form $y_h[n] = \sum A(c)^n$, where the c's solve the quadratic equation

$$c^2 + \frac{1}{15}c - \frac{2}{5} = 0$$

So for $c = 1/3$ and $c = -2/5$, the general form for the homogeneous solution is:

$$y_h[n] = A_1(\frac{1}{3})^n + A_2(-\frac{2}{5})^n$$

(b) We use the z-transform, and use different ROCs to generate the causal and anti-causal impulses responses:

$$H(z) = \frac{1}{(1-\frac{1}{3}z^{-1})(1+\frac{2}{5}z^{-1})} = \frac{5/11}{1-\frac{1}{3}z^{-1}} + \frac{6/11}{1+\frac{2}{5}z^{-1}}$$

$$h_c[n] = \frac{5}{11}(\frac{1}{3})^n u[n] + \frac{6}{11}(-\frac{2}{5})^n u[n]$$

$$h_{ac}[n] = -\frac{5}{11}(\frac{1}{3})^n u[-n-1] - \frac{6}{11}(-\frac{2}{5})^n u[-n-1]$$

(c) Since $h_c[n]$ is causal, and the two exponential bases in $h_c[n]$ are both less than 1, it is absolutely summable. $h_{ac}[n]$ grows without bounds as n approaches $-\infty$.

(d)

$$\begin{aligned} Y(z) &= X(z)H(z) \\ &= \frac{1}{1-\frac{3}{5}z^{-1}} \cdot \frac{1}{(1-\frac{1}{3}z^{-1})(1+\frac{2}{5}z^{-1})} \\ &= \frac{-25/44}{1-1/3z^{-1}} + \frac{55/12}{1+2/5z^{-1}} + \frac{27/20}{1-3/5z^{-1}} \\ y[n] &= \frac{-25}{44}(\frac{1}{3})^n u[n] + \frac{55}{12}(-\frac{2}{5})^n u[n] + \frac{27}{20}(\frac{3}{5})^n u[n] \end{aligned}$$

2.32. We first re-write the system function $H(e^{j\omega})$:

$$\begin{aligned} H(e^{j\omega}) &= e^{j\pi/4} \cdot e^{-j\omega} \left(\frac{1 + e^{-j2\omega} + 4e^{-j4\omega}}{1 + \frac{1}{2}e^{-j2\omega}} \right) \\ &= e^{j\pi/4} G(e^{j\omega}) \end{aligned}$$

Let $y_1[n] = x[n] * g[n]$, then

$$\begin{aligned} x[n] &= \cos(\frac{\pi n}{2}) = \frac{e^{j\pi n/2} + e^{-j\pi n/2}}{2} \\ y_1[n] &= \frac{G(e^{j\pi/2})e^{j\pi n/2} + G(e^{-j\pi/2})e^{-j\pi n/2}}{2} \end{aligned}$$

Evaluating the frequency response at $\omega = \pm\pi/2$:

$$\begin{aligned} G(e^{j\frac{\pi}{2}}) &= e^{-j\frac{\pi}{2}} \left(\frac{1 + e^{-j\pi} + 4e^{-j2\pi}}{1 + \frac{1}{2}e^{-j\pi}} \right) = 8e^{-j\pi/2} \\ G(e^{-j\frac{\pi}{2}}) &= 8e^{j\pi/2} \end{aligned}$$

Therefore,

$$y_1[n] = (8e^{j(\pi n/2 - \pi/2)} + 8e^{j(-\pi n/2 + \pi/2)})/2 = 8\cos(\frac{\pi}{2}n - \frac{\pi}{2})$$

and

$$y[n] = e^{j\pi/4} y_1[n] = 8e^{j\pi/4} \cos(\frac{\pi}{2}n - \frac{\pi}{2})$$

2.33. Since $H(e^{-j\omega}) = H^*(e^{j\omega})$, we can apply the results of Example 2.13 from the text,

$$y[n] = |H(e^{j\frac{3\pi}{2}})| \cos(\frac{3\pi}{2}n + \frac{\pi}{4} + \angle H(e^{j\frac{3\pi}{2}}))$$

To find $H(e^{j\frac{3\pi}{2}})$, we use the fact that $H(e^{j\omega})$ is periodic over 2π, so

$$H(e^{j\frac{3\pi}{2}}) = H(e^{-j\frac{\pi}{2}}) = e^{j\frac{2\pi}{3}}$$

Therefore,

$$y[n] = \cos(\frac{3\pi}{2}n + \frac{\pi}{4} + \frac{2\pi}{3}) = \cos(\frac{3\pi}{2}n + \frac{11\pi}{12})$$

2.34. (a) Notice that

$$x[n] = x_0[n-2] + 2x_0[n-4] + x_0[n-6]$$

Since the system is LTI,

$$y[n] = y_0[n-2] + 2y_0[n-4] + y_0[n-6],$$

and we get sequence shown here:

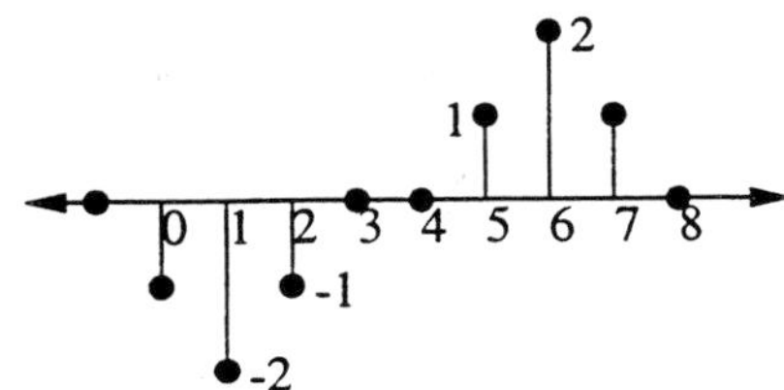

(b) Since

$$y_0[n] = -1x_0[n+1] + x_0[n-1] = x_0[n] * (-\delta[n+1] + \delta[n-1]),$$
$$h[n] = -\delta[n+1] + \delta[n-1]$$

2.35. (a) Notice that $x_1[n] = x_2[n] + x_3[n+4]$, so if $T\{\cdot\}$ is linear,

$$\begin{aligned} T\{x_1[n]\} &= T\{x_2[n]\} + T\{x_3[n+4]\} \\ &= y_2[n] + y_3[n+4] \end{aligned}$$

From Fig P2.4, the above equality is not true. Hence, the system is NOT LINEAR.
(b) To find the impulse response of the system, we note that

$$\delta[n] = x_3[n+4]$$

Therefore,

$$\begin{aligned} T\{\delta[n]\} &= y_3[n+4] \\ &= 3\delta[n+6] + 2\delta[n+5] \end{aligned}$$

(c) Since the system is known to be time-invariant and not linear, we cannot use choices such as:

$$\delta[n] = x_1[n] - x_2[n]$$

and

$$\delta[n] = \frac{1}{2}x_2[n+1]$$

to determine the impulse response. With the given information, we can only use shifted inputs.

2.36. (a) Suppose we form the impulse:

$$\delta[n] = \frac{1}{2}x_1[n] - \frac{1}{2}x_2[n] + x_3[n]$$

Since the system is linear,

$$L\{\delta[n]\} = \frac{1}{2}y_1[n] - \frac{1}{2}y_2[n] + y_3[n]$$

A shifted impulse results when:

$$\delta[n-1] = -\frac{1}{2}x_1[n] + \frac{1}{2}x_2[n]$$

The response to the shifted impulse

$$L\{\delta[n-1]\} = -\frac{1}{2}y_1[n] + \frac{1}{2}y_2[n]$$

Since,

$$L\{\delta[n]\} \neq L\{\delta[n-1]\}$$

The system is NOT TIME INVARIANT.

(b) An impulse may be formed:

$$\delta[n] = \frac{1}{2}x_1[n] - \frac{1}{2}x_2[n] + x_3[n]$$

since the system is linear,

$$\begin{aligned} L\{\delta[n]\} &= \frac{1}{2}y_1[n] - \frac{1}{2}y_2[n] + y_3[n] \\ &= h[n] \end{aligned}$$

from the figure,

$$y_1[n] = -\delta[n+1] + 3\delta[n] + 3\delta[n-1] + \delta[n-3]$$
$$y_2[n] = -\delta[n+1] + \delta[n] - 3\delta[n-1] - \delta[n-3]$$
$$y_3[n] = 2\delta[n+2] + \delta[n+1] - 3\delta[n] + 2\delta[n-2]$$

Combining:

$$\begin{aligned} h[n] &= 2\delta[n+2] + \delta[n+1] - 2\delta[n] + 3\delta[n-1] \\ &\quad +2\delta[n-2] + \delta[n-3] \end{aligned}$$

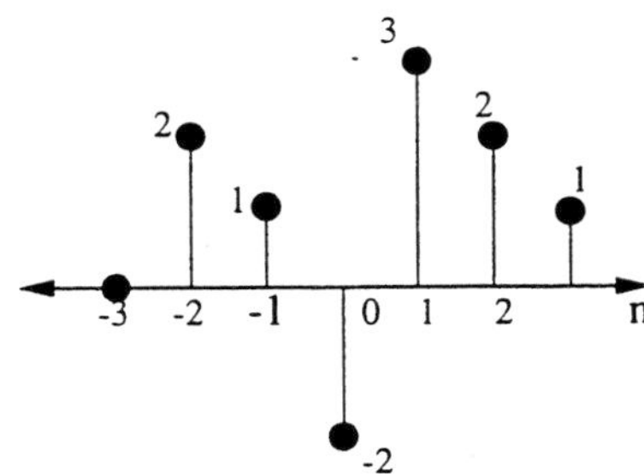

2.37. For an LTI system, we use the convolution equation to obtain the output:

$$y[n] = \sum_{k=-\infty}^{\infty} x[n-k]h[k]$$

Let $n = m + N$:

$$\begin{aligned} y[m+N] &= \sum_{k=-\infty}^{\infty} x[m+N-k]h[k] \\ &= \sum_{k=-\infty}^{\infty} x[(m-k)+N]h[k] \end{aligned}$$

Since $x[n]$ is periodic, $x[n] = x[n+rN]$ for any integer r. Hence,

$$\begin{aligned} y[m+N] &= \sum_{k=-\infty}^{\infty} x[m-k]h[k] \\ &= y[m] \end{aligned}$$

So, the output must also be periodic with period N.

2.38. (a) The homogeneous solution to the second order difference equation,

$$y[n] - \frac{3}{4}y[n-1] + \frac{1}{8}y[n-2] = 2x[n-1],$$

is obtained by setting the input (forcing term) to zero.

$$y[n] - \frac{3}{4}y[n-1] + \frac{1}{8}y[n-2] = 0$$

Solving,

$$1 - \frac{3}{4}z^{-1} + \frac{1}{8}z^{-2} = 0,$$

$$(1-\frac{1}{2}z^{-1})(1-\frac{1}{4}z^{-1})=0,$$

and the homogeneous solution takes the form

$$y_h[n]=A_1(\frac{1}{2})^n+A_2(\frac{1}{4})^n,$$

for the constants A_1 and A_2.

(b) Substituting the intial conditions,

$$y_h[-1]=A_1(\frac{1}{2})^{-1}+A_2(\frac{1}{4})^{-1}=1,$$

and

$$y_h[0]=A_1+A_2=0.$$

We have

$$2A_1+4A_2=1$$
$$A_1+A_2=0$$

Solving,

$$A_1=-1/2$$

and

$$A_2=1/2.$$

(c) Homogeneous equation:

$$y[n]-y[n-1]+\frac{1}{4}y[n-2]=0$$

Solving,

$$1-z^{-1}+\frac{1}{4}z^{-2}=0,$$
$$(1-\frac{1}{2}z^{-1})(1-\frac{1}{2}z^{-1})=0,$$

and the homogeneous solution takes the form

$$y_h[n]=A_1(\frac{1}{2})^n.$$

Invoking the intial conditions, we have

$$y_h[-1]=2A_1=1$$
$$y_h[0]=A_1=0$$

Evident from the above contradiction, the initial conditions cannot be met.

(d) The homogeneous difference equation:

$$y[n]-y[n-1]+\frac{1}{4}y[n-2]=0$$

Suppose the homogeneous solution is of the form

$$y_h[n]=A_1(\frac{1}{2})^n+nB_1(\frac{1}{2})^n,$$

substituting into the difference equation:

$$y_h[n]-y_h[n-1]+\frac{1}{4}y_h[n-2]=0$$

$$A_1(\frac{1}{2})^n+nB_1(\frac{1}{2})^n-A_1(\frac{1}{2})^{n-1}-(n-1)B_1(\frac{1}{2})^{n-1}$$
$$\frac{1}{4}A_1(\frac{1}{2})^{n-2}+\frac{1}{4}(n-2)B_1(\frac{1}{2})^{n-2}\quad=\quad 0.$$

(e) Using the solution from part (d):

$$y_h[n] = A_1(\frac{1}{2})^n + nB_1(\frac{1}{2})^n,$$

and the initial conditions

$$y_h[-1] = 1$$

and

$$y_h[0] = 0,$$

we solve for A_1 and B_1:

$$A_1 = 0$$
$$B_1 = -1/2.$$

2.39. (a) For $x_1[n] = \delta[n]$,

$$\begin{aligned} y_1[0] &= 1 \\ y_1[1] &= ay[0] = a \end{aligned}$$

For $x_2[n] = \delta[n-1]$,

$$\begin{aligned} y_2[0] &= 1 \\ y_2[1] &= ay[0] + x_2[1] = a + 1 \neq y_1[0] \end{aligned}$$

Even though $x_2[n] = x_1[n-1]$, $y_2[n] \neq y_2[n-1]$. Hence the system is NOT TIME INVARIANT.

(b) A linear system has the property that

$$T\{ax_1[n] + bx_2[n]\} = aT\{x_1[n]\} + bT\{x_2[n]\}\}$$

Hence, if the input is doubled, the output must also double at each value of n. Because $y[0] = 1$, always, the system is NOT LINEAR.

(c) Let $x_3 = \alpha x_1[n] + \beta x_2[n]$.
For $n \geq 0$:

$$\begin{aligned} y_3[n] &= x_3[n] + ay_3[n-1] \\ &= \alpha x_1[n] + \beta x_2[n] + a(x_3[n-1] + y_3[n-2]) \\ &= \alpha \sum_{k=0}^{n-1} a^k x_1[n-k] + \beta \sum_{k=0}^{n-1} a^k x_2[n-k] \\ &= \alpha(h[n] * x_1[n]) + \beta(h[n] * x_2[n]) \\ &= \alpha y_1[n] + \beta y_2[n]. \end{aligned}$$

For $n < 0$:

$$\begin{aligned} y_3[n] &= a^{-1}(y_3[n+1] - x_3[n]) \\ &= -\alpha \sum_{k=-1}^{n} a^k x_1[n-k] - \beta \sum_{k=-1}^{n} a^k x_2[n-k] \\ &= \alpha y_1[n] + \beta y_2[n]. \end{aligned}$$

For $n = 0$:

$$y_3[n] = y_1[n] = y_2[n] = 0.$$

Conclude,

$$y_3[n] = \alpha y_1[n] + \beta y_2[n], \text{ for all } n.$$

Therefore, the system is LINEAR. The system is still NOT TIME INVARIANT.

2.40. For the input

$$\begin{aligned} x[n] &= \cos(\pi n)u[n] \\ &= (-1)^n u[n], \end{aligned}$$

the output is

$$\begin{aligned} y[n] &= \sum_{k=-\infty}^{\infty} (j/2)^k u[k](-1)^{(n-k)} u[n-k] \\ &= (-1)^n \sum_{k=0}^{n} (j/2)^k (-1)^{-k} \\ &= (-1)^n \sum_{k=0}^{n} (-j/2)^k \\ &= (-1)^n \left(\frac{1-(-j/2)^{(n+1)}}{1+j/2} \right) \end{aligned}$$

For large n, $(-j/2)^{(n+1)} \to 0$. Thus, the steady-state response becomes

$$\begin{aligned} y[n] &= \frac{(-1)^n}{1+j/2} \\ &= \frac{\cos(\pi n)}{1+j/2}. \end{aligned}$$

2.41. The input sequence,

$$x[n] = \sum_{k=-\infty}^{\infty} \delta[n+16k],$$

has the Fourier representation

$$\begin{aligned} X(e^{j\omega}) &= \sum_{n=-\infty}^{\infty} \sum_{k=-\infty}^{\infty} \delta[n+16k] e^{-j\omega n} \\ &= \frac{1}{16} \sum_{k=-\infty}^{\infty} \delta(\omega + \frac{2\pi k}{16}). \end{aligned}$$

Therefore, the frequency representation of the input is also a periodic impulse train. There are 16 frequency impulses in the range $-\pi \leq \omega \leq \pi$.

We sketch the magnitudes of $X(e^{j\omega})$ and $H(e^{j\omega})$:

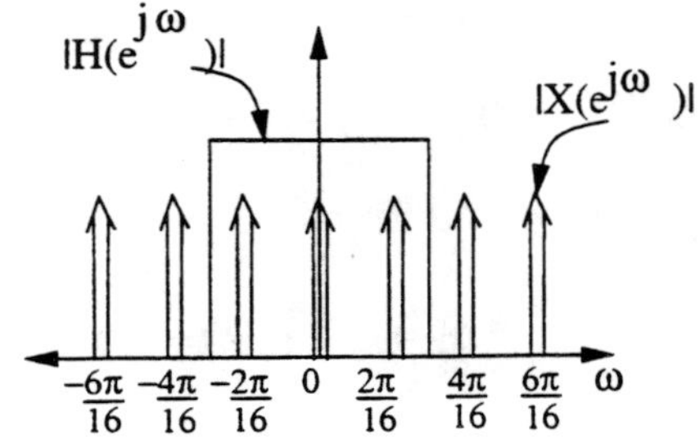

From the sketch, we observe that the LTI system is a lowpass filter which removes all but three of the frequency impulses. To these, it multiplies a phase factor $e^{-j3\omega}$.

The Fourier transform of the output is

$$\begin{aligned} Y(e^{j\omega}) &= \frac{1}{16}\delta(\omega) + \frac{1}{16}e^{-j\frac{6\pi}{16}}\delta(\omega - \frac{2\pi}{16}) \\ &\quad + \frac{1}{16}e^{j\frac{6\pi}{16}}\delta(\omega + \frac{2\pi}{16}) \end{aligned}$$

Thus the output sequence is

$$y[n] = \frac{1}{16} + \frac{1}{8}\cos(\frac{2\pi n}{16} + \frac{3\pi}{8}).$$

2.42. (a) From the figure,

$$\begin{aligned} y[n] &= (x[n] + x[n] * h_1[n]) * h_2[n] \\ &= (x[n] * (\delta[n] + h_1[n])) * h_2[n]. \end{aligned}$$

Let $h[n]$ be the impulse response of the overall system,

$$y[n] = x[n] * h[n].$$

Comparing with the above expression,

$$\begin{aligned} h[n] &= (\delta[n] + h_1[n]) * h_2[n] \\ &= h_2[n] + h_1[n] * h_2[n] \\ &= \alpha^n u[n] + \beta^{(n-1)}u[n-1]. \end{aligned}$$

(b) Taking the Fourier transform of $h[n]$ from part (a),

$$\begin{aligned} H(e^{j\omega}) &= \sum_{n=-\infty}^{\infty} h[n]e^{-j\omega n} \\ &= \sum_{n=-\infty}^{\infty} \alpha^n u[n]e^{-j\omega n} + \beta \sum_{n=-\infty}^{\infty} \alpha^{(n-1)}u[n-1]e^{-j\omega n} \\ &= \sum_{n=0}^{\infty} \alpha^n e^{-j\omega n} + \beta \sum_{\ell=0}^{\infty} \alpha^{(\ell-1)}e^{-j\omega \ell}, \end{aligned}$$

where we have used $\ell = (n-1)$ in the second sum.

$$\begin{aligned} H(e^{j\omega}) &= \frac{1}{1-\alpha e^{-j\omega}} + \frac{\beta e^{-j\omega}}{1-\alpha e^{-j\omega}} \\ &= \frac{1+\beta e^{-j\omega}}{1-\alpha e^{-j\omega}}, \text{ for } |\alpha| < 1. \end{aligned}$$

Note that the Fourier transform of $\alpha^n u[n]$ is well known, and the second term of $h[n]$ (see part (a)) is just a scaled and shifted version of $\alpha^n u[n]$. So, we could have used the properties of the Fourier transform to reduce the algebra.

(c) We have

$$\begin{aligned} H(e^{j\omega}) &= \frac{Y(e^{j\omega})}{X(e^{j\omega})} \\ &= \frac{1+\beta e^{-j\omega}}{1-\alpha e^{-j\omega}}, \end{aligned}$$

cross multiplying,

$$Y(e^{j\omega})[1-\alpha e^{-j\omega}] = X(e^{j\omega})[1+\beta e^{-j\omega}]$$

taking the inverse Fourier transform, we have

$$y[n]-\alpha y[n-1] = x[n]+\beta x[n-1].$$

(d) From part (a):

$$h[n]=0, \text{ for } n<0.$$

This implies that the system is CAUSAL.

If the system is stable, its Fourier transform exists. Therefore, the condition for stability is the same as the condition imposed on the frequency response of part (b). That is, STABLE, if $|\alpha|<1$.

2.43. For $(-1<a<0)$, we have

$$X(e^{j\omega}) = \frac{1}{1-ae^{-j\omega}}$$

(a) real part of $X(e^{j\omega})$:

$$\begin{aligned} X_R(e^{j\omega}) &= \frac{1}{2}\cdot[X(e^{j\omega})+X^*(e^{j\omega})] \\ &= \frac{1-a\cos(\omega)}{1-2a\cos(\omega)+a^2} \end{aligned}$$

(b) imaginary part:

$$\begin{aligned} X_I(e^{j\omega}) &= \frac{1}{2j}\cdot[X(e^{j\omega})-X^*(e^{j\omega})] \\ &= \frac{-a\sin(\omega)}{1-2a\cos(\omega)+a^2} \end{aligned}$$

(c) magnitude:

$$\begin{aligned} |X(e^{j\omega})| &= [X(e^{j\omega})X^*(e^{j\omega})]^{\frac{1}{2}} \\ &= \left(\frac{1}{1-2a\cos(\omega)+a^2}\right)^{\frac{1}{2}} \end{aligned}$$

(d) phase:

$$\angle X(e^{j\omega}) = \arctan\left(\frac{-a\sin(\omega)}{1-a\cos(\omega)}\right)$$

2.44. (a)

$$\begin{aligned} X(e^{j\omega})|_{\omega=0} &= \sum_{n=-\infty}^{\infty} x[n]e^{-j\omega n}|_{\omega=0} \\ &= \sum_{n=-\infty}^{\infty} x[n] \\ &= 6 \end{aligned}$$

(b)

$$\begin{aligned} X(e^{j\omega})|_{\omega=\pi} &= \sum_{n=-\infty}^{\infty} x[n]e^{-j\pi n} \\ &= \sum_{n=-\infty}^{\infty} x[n](-1)^n \\ &= 2 \end{aligned}$$

(c) Because $x[n]$ is symmetric about $n = 2$ this signal has linear phase.

$$X(e^{j\omega}) = A(\omega)e^{-j2\omega}$$

$A(\omega)$ is a zero phase (real) function of ω. Hence,

$$\angle X(e^{j\omega}) = -2\omega, \qquad -\pi \le \omega \le \pi$$

(d)

$$\int_{-\pi}^{\pi} X(e^{j\omega})e^{-j\omega n}d\omega = 2\pi x[n]$$

for $n = 0$:

$$\int_{-\pi}^{\pi} X(e^{j\omega})d\omega = 2\pi x[0] = 4\pi$$

(e) Let $y[n]$ be the unknown sequence. Then

$$\begin{aligned}
Y(e^{j\omega}) &= X(e^{-j\omega}) \\
&= \sum_n x[n]e^{j\omega n} \\
&= \sum_n x[-n]e^{-j\omega n} \\
&= \sum_n y[n]e^{-j\omega n}
\end{aligned}$$

Hence $y[n] = x[-n]$.

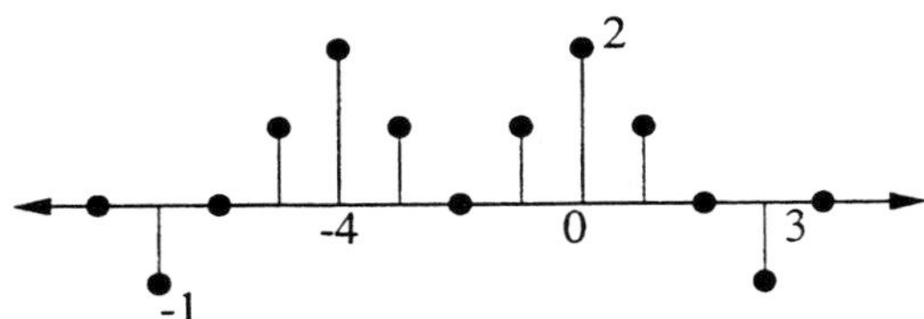

(f) We have determined that:

$$X(e^{j\omega}) = A(\omega)e^{-j2\omega}$$

$$\begin{aligned}
X_R(e^{j\omega}) &= \mathcal{R}e\{X(e^{j\omega})\} \\
&= A(\omega)\cos(2\omega) \\
&= \frac{1}{2}A(\omega)\left(e^{j2\omega} + e^{-j2\omega}\right)
\end{aligned}$$

Taking the inverse transform, we have

$$\frac{1}{2}a[n+2] + \frac{1}{2}a[n-2] = \frac{1}{2}x[n+4] + \frac{1}{2}x[n]$$

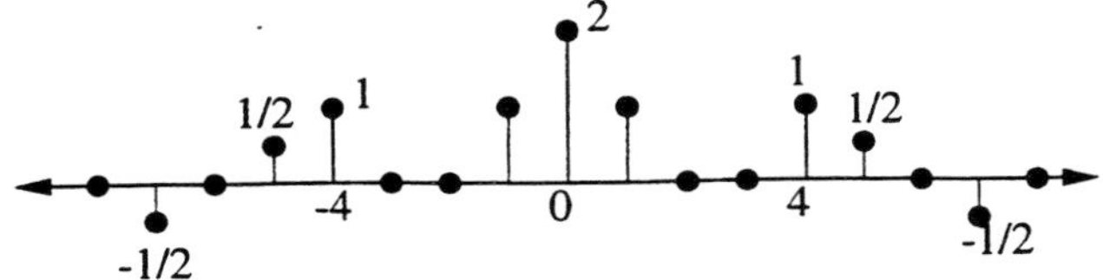

2.45. Let $x[n] = \delta[n]$, then

$$X(e^{j\omega}) = 1$$

The output of the ideal lowpass filter:

$$W(e^{j\omega}) = X(e^{j\omega})H(e^{j\omega}) = H(e^{j\omega})$$

The multiplier:

$$(-1)^n w[n] = e^{-j\pi n} w[n]$$

causes a shift in the frequency domain:

$$W(e^{j(\omega-\pi)}) = H(e^{j(\omega-\pi)})$$

The overall output:

$$y[n] = e^{-j\pi n} w[n] + w[n]$$
$$Y(e^{j\omega}) = H(e^{j(\omega-\pi)}) + H(e^{j\omega})$$

Noting that:

$$H(e^{j(\omega-\pi)}) = \begin{cases} 1, & \frac{\pi}{2} \le |\omega| \le \pi \\ 0, & |\omega| < \frac{\pi}{2} \end{cases}$$

$Y(e^{j\omega}) = 1$, thus $y[n] = \delta[n]$.

2.46. (a) We first perform a partial-fraction expansion of $X(e^{j\omega})$:

$$\begin{aligned} X(e^{j\omega}) &= \frac{1-a^2}{(1-ae^{-j\omega})(1-ae^{j\omega})} \\ &= \frac{1}{1-ae^{-j\omega}} + \frac{ae^{j\omega}}{1-ae^{j\omega}} \\ x[n] &= a^n u[n] + a^{-n} u[-n-1] \\ &= a^{|n|} \end{aligned}$$

(b)

$$\begin{aligned} \frac{1}{2\pi}\int_{-\pi}^{\pi} X(e^{j\omega})\cos(\omega)d\omega &= \frac{1}{2\pi}\int_{-\pi}^{\pi} X(e^{j\omega})\frac{e^{j\omega}+e^{-j\omega}}{2}d\omega \\ &= \frac{1}{2}\left(\frac{1}{2\pi}\int_{-\pi}^{\pi} X(e^{j\omega})e^{j\omega}d\omega + \frac{1}{2\pi}\int_{-\pi}^{\pi} X(e^{j\omega})e^{-j\omega}d\omega\right) \\ &= \frac{1}{2}(x[n-1] + x[n+1]) \\ &= \frac{1}{2}(a^{|n-1|} + a^{|n+1|}) \end{aligned}$$

2.47. (a)

$$\begin{aligned} y[n] &= x[n] + 2x[n-1] + x[n-2] \\ &= x[n] * h[n] \\ &= x[n] * (\delta[n] + 2\delta[n-1] + \delta[n-2]) \\ h[n] &= \delta[n] + 2\delta[n-1] + \delta[n-2] \end{aligned}$$

(b) Yes. $h[n]$ is finite-length and absolutely summable.

(c)

$$\begin{aligned}H(e^{j\omega}) &= 1 + 2e^{-j\omega} + e^{-2j\omega} \\ &= 2e^{-j\omega}(\frac{1}{2}e^{j\omega} + 1 + \frac{1}{2}e^{-j\omega}) \\ &= 2e^{-j\omega}(\cos(\omega) + 1)\end{aligned}$$

(d)

$$\begin{aligned}|H(e^{j\omega})| &= 2(\cos(\omega) + 1) \\ \angle H(e^{j\omega}) &= -\omega\end{aligned}$$

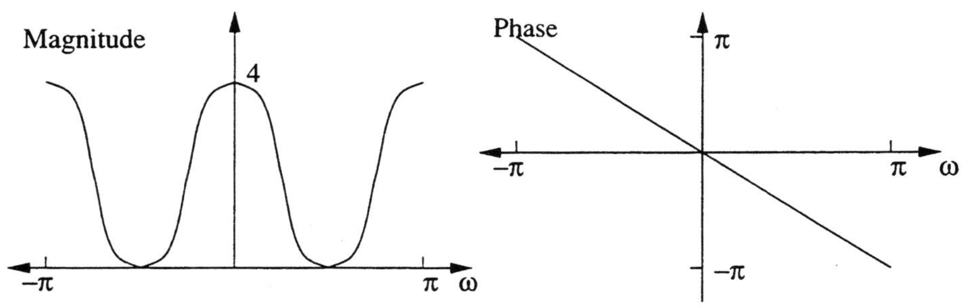

(e)

$$\begin{aligned}h_1[n] &= \frac{1}{2\pi}\int_{<2\pi>} H_1(e^{j\omega})e^{j\omega}d\omega \\ &= \frac{1}{2\pi}\int_{<2\pi>} H(e^{j(\omega+\pi)})e^{j\omega n}d\omega \\ &= \frac{1}{2\pi}\int_{<2\pi>} H(e^{j(\omega)})e^{j(\omega-\pi)n}d\omega \\ &= e^{-j\pi n}\frac{1}{2\pi}\int_{<2\pi>} H(e^{j(\omega)})e^{j\omega n}d\omega \\ &= -1^n h[n] \\ &= \delta[n] - 2\delta[n-1] + \delta[n-2]\end{aligned}$$

2.48. (a) Notice that

$$s[n] = 1 + \cos(\pi n) = 1 + (-1)^n$$

$$S(e^{j\omega}) = 2\pi\sum_k \delta(\omega - k\pi)$$

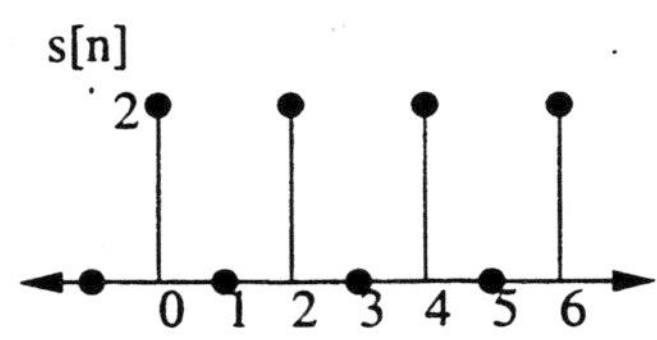

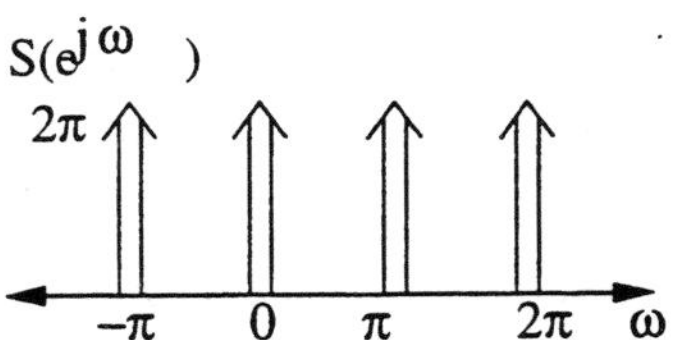

(b) Since $y[n] = x[n]s[n]$,

$$Y(e^{j\omega}) = \frac{1}{2\pi}\int_{-\pi}^{\pi} S(e^{j\theta})X(e^{j(\omega-\theta)})d\omega$$

$$
\begin{aligned}
&= \frac{1}{2\pi}\int_{-\pi}^{\pi} S(e^{j\theta})X(e^{j(\omega-\theta)})d\omega \\
&= X(e^{j\omega}) + X(e^{j(\omega-\pi)})
\end{aligned}
$$

$Y(e^{j\omega})$ contains copies of $X(e^{j\omega})$ replicated at intervals of π.

(c) Since $w[n] = y[n] + (1/2)(y[n+1] + y[n-1])$,

$$
\begin{aligned}
W(e^{j\omega}) &= Y(e^{j\omega}) + \frac{1}{2}\left(e^{j\omega}Y(e^{j\omega}) + e^{-j\omega}Y(e^{j\omega})\right) \\
&= Y(e^{j\omega})(1+\cos(\omega))
\end{aligned}
$$

(d) The following figure shows $X(e^{j\omega})$, $Y(e^{j\omega})$, and $W(e^{j\omega})$ for $a < 2$ and $a > 2$. Notice that

$$
X(e^{j\omega}) = \begin{cases} 1, & |\omega| \le \pi/a, \\ 0, & \pi/a \le |\omega| \ge \pi \end{cases}
$$

So, for $a > 2$, $Y(e^{j\omega})$ contains two non-overlapping replications of $X(e^{j\omega})$, whereas for $a < 2$, "aliasing" occurs. When there is aliasing, $W(e^{j\omega})$ is not at all close to $X(e^{j\omega})$. Hence, a must be greater than 2 for $w[n]$ to be "close" to $x[n]$.

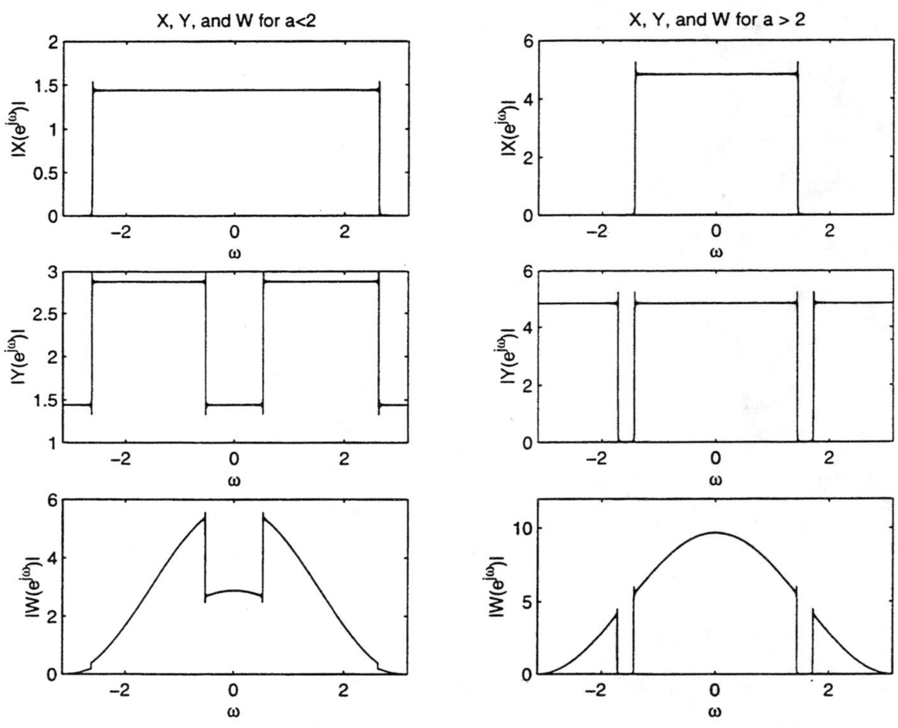

2.49. (a) We start by interpreting each clue.

(i) The system is causal implies

$$h[n] = 0 \text{ for } n \le 0.$$

(ii) The Fourier transform is conjugate symmetric implies $h[n]$ is real.

(iii) The DTFT of the sequence $h[n+1]$ is real implies $h[n+1]$ is even.

From the above observations, we deduce that $h[n]$ has length 3, therefore it has finite duration.

(b) From part (a) we know that $h[n]$ is length 3 with even symmetry around $h[1]$. Let $h[0] = h[2] = a$ and $h[1] = b$, from (iv) and using Parseval's theorem, we have

$$2a^2 + b^2 = 2.$$

From (v), we also have

$$2a - b = 0.$$

Solving the above equations, we get

$$\begin{aligned} h[0] &= \frac{1}{\sqrt{3}} \\ h[1] &= \frac{2}{\sqrt{3}} \\ h[2] &= \frac{1}{\sqrt{3}} \end{aligned}$$

or

$$\begin{aligned} h[0] &= -\frac{1}{\sqrt{3}} \\ h[1] &= -\frac{2}{\sqrt{3}} \\ h[2] &= -\frac{1}{\sqrt{3}}. \end{aligned}$$

2.50. (a) Carrying out the convolution sum, we get the following sequence $q[n]$:

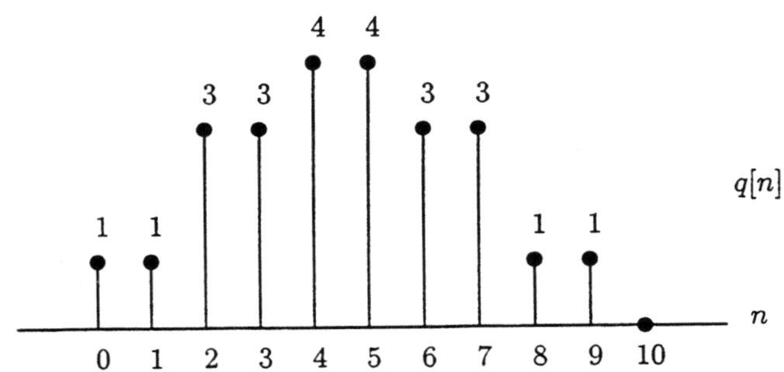

(b) Again carrying out the convolution sum, we get the following sequence $r[n]$:

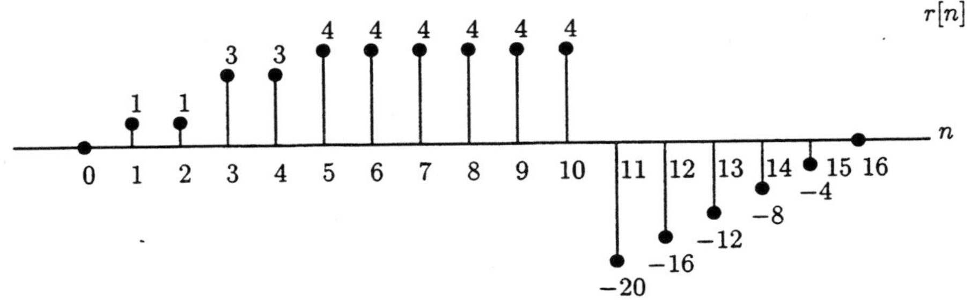

(c) Let $a[n] = v[-n]$ and $b[n] = w[-n]$, then:

$$\begin{aligned} a[n] * b[n] &= \sum_{k=-\infty}^{+\infty} a[k]b[n-k] \\ &= \sum_{k=-\infty}^{+\infty} v[-k]w[k-n] \\ &= \sum_{r=-\infty}^{+\infty} v[r]w[-n-r] \text{ where } r = -k \\ &= q[-n]. \end{aligned}$$

We thus conclude that $q[-n] = v[-n] * w[-n]$.

2.51. For $(-1 < a < 0)$, we have

$$X(e^{j\omega}) = \frac{1}{1 - ae^{-j\omega}}$$

(a) real part of $X(e^{j\omega})$:

$$\begin{aligned} X_R(e^{j\omega}) &= \frac{1}{2} \cdot [X(e^{j\omega}) + X^*(e^{j\omega})] \\ &= \frac{1 - a\cos(\omega)}{1 - 2a\cos(\omega) + a^2} \end{aligned}$$

(b) imaginary part:

$$\begin{aligned} X_I(e^{j\omega}) &= \frac{1}{2j} \cdot [X(e^{j\omega}) - X^*(e^{j\omega})] \\ &= \frac{-a\sin(\omega)}{1 - 2a\cos(\omega) + a^2} \end{aligned}$$

(c) magnitude:

$$\begin{aligned} |X(e^{j\omega})| &= [X(e^{j\omega})X^*(e^{j\omega})]^{\frac{1}{2}} \\ &= \left(\frac{1}{1 - 2acos(\omega) + a^2}\right)^{\frac{1}{2}} \end{aligned}$$

(d) phase:

$$\angle X(e^{j\omega}) = \arctan\left(\frac{-a\sin(\omega)}{1 - a\cos(\omega)}\right)$$

2.52. $x[n]$ can be rewritten as:

$$\begin{aligned} x[n] &= cos(\frac{5\pi n}{2}) \\ &= cos(\frac{\pi n}{2}) \\ &= \frac{e^{j\frac{\pi n}{2}}}{2} + \frac{e^{-j\frac{\pi n}{2}}}{2}. \end{aligned}$$

We now use the fact that complex exponentials are eigenfunctions of LTI systems, we get:

$$\begin{aligned} y[n] &= e^{-j\frac{\pi}{8}}\frac{e^{j\frac{\pi n}{2}}}{2} + e^{j\frac{\pi}{8}}\frac{e^{-j\frac{\pi n}{2}}}{2} \\ &= \frac{e^{j(\frac{\pi n}{2}-\frac{\pi}{8})}}{2} + \frac{e^{-j(\frac{\pi n}{2}-\frac{\pi}{8})}}{2} \\ &= cos(\frac{\pi}{2}(n-\frac{1}{4})). \end{aligned}$$

2.53. First $x[n]$ goes through a lowpass filter with cutoff frequency 0.5π. Since the cosine has a frequency of 0.6π, it will be filtered out. The delayed impulse will be filtered to a delayed sinc and the constant will remain unchanged. We thus get:

$$w[n] = 3\frac{sin(0.5\pi(n-5))}{\pi(n-5)} + 2.$$

$y[n]$ is then given by:

$$y[n] = 3\frac{sin(0.5\pi(n-5))}{\pi(n-5)} - 3\frac{sin(0.5\pi(n-6))}{\pi(n-6)}.$$

2.54.

$$\begin{aligned} x[n] &= \cos(\frac{15\pi n}{4} - \frac{\pi}{3}) \\ &= \cos(-\frac{\pi n}{4} - \frac{\pi}{3}) \\ &= \cos(\frac{\pi n}{4} + \frac{\pi}{3}) \\ &= \frac{e^{j\frac{\pi}{3}}e^{j\frac{\pi n}{4}}}{2} + \frac{e^{-j\frac{\pi}{3}}e^{-j\frac{\pi n}{4}}}{2}. \end{aligned}$$

Using the fact that complex exponentials are eigenfunctions of LTI systems, we get:

$$\begin{aligned} y[n] &= e^{-j\frac{3\pi}{8}}\frac{e^{j\frac{\pi}{3}}e^{j\frac{\pi n}{4}}}{2} + e^{-j\frac{\pi}{8}}\frac{e^{-j\frac{\pi}{3}}e^{-j\frac{\pi n}{4}}}{2} \\ &= \frac{e^{-j\frac{\pi}{24}}e^{j\frac{\pi n}{4}}}{2} + \frac{e^{-j\frac{11\pi}{24}}e^{-j\frac{\pi n}{4}}}{2} \\ &= e^{-j\frac{\pi}{4}}(\frac{e^{j\frac{5\pi}{24}}e^{j\frac{\pi n}{4}}}{2} + \frac{e^{-j\frac{5\pi}{24}}e^{-j\frac{\pi n}{4}}}{2}) \\ &= e^{-j\frac{\pi}{4}}\cos(\frac{\pi n}{4} + \frac{5\pi}{24}). \end{aligned}$$

2.55. Since system 1 is memoryless, it is time invariant. The input, $x[n]$ is periodic in ω, therefore $w[n]$ will also be periodic in ω. As a consequence, $y[n]$ is periodic in ω and so is A.

2.56. (a)

$$\begin{aligned} y[n] &= h[n] * (e^{-j\omega_0 n}x[n]) \\ &= \sum_{k=-\infty}^{+\infty} e^{-j\omega_0 k}x[k]h[n-k]. \end{aligned}$$

Let $x[n] = ax_1[n] + bx_2[n]$, then:

$$\begin{aligned} y[n] &= h[n] * (e^{-j\omega_0 n}(ax_1[n] + bx_2[n])) \\ &= \sum_{k=-\infty}^{+\infty} e^{-j\omega_0 k}(ax_1[k] + bx_2[k])h[n-k] \\ &= a\sum_{k=-\infty}^{+\infty} e^{-j\omega_0 k}x_1[k]h[n-k] + b\sum_{k=-\infty}^{+\infty} e^{-j\omega_0 k}x_2[k]h[n-k] \\ &= ay_1[n] + by_2[n] \end{aligned}$$

where $y_1[n]$ and $y_2[n]$ are the responses to $x_1[n]$ and $x_2[n]$ respectively. We thus conclude that system S is linear.

(b) Let $x_2[n] = x[n - n_0]$, then:

$$\begin{aligned} y_2[n] &= h[n] * (e^{-j\omega_0 n}x_2[n]) \\ &= \sum_{k=-\infty}^{+\infty} e^{-j\omega_0(n-k)}x_2[n-k]h[k] \\ &= \sum_{k=-\infty}^{+\infty} e^{-j\omega_0(n-k)}x[n-n_0-k]h[k] \\ &\neq y[n-n_0]. \end{aligned}$$

We thus conclude that system S is not time invariant.

(c) Since the magnitude of $e^{-j\omega_0 n}$ is always bounded by 1 and $h[n]$ is stable, a bounded input $x[n]$ will always produce a bounded input to the stable LTI system and therefore the output $y[n]$ will be bounded. We thus conclude that system S is stable.

(d) We can rewrite $y[n]$ as:

$$\begin{aligned} y[n] &= h[n] * (e^{-j\omega_0 n}x[n]) \\ &= \sum_{k=-\infty}^{+\infty} e^{-j\omega_0(n-k)}x[n-k]h[k] \\ &= \sum_{k=-\infty}^{+\infty} e^{-j\omega_0 n}e^{j\omega_0 k}x[n-k]h[k] \\ &= e^{-j\omega_0 n}\sum_{k=-\infty}^{+\infty} e^{j\omega_0 k}x[n-k]h[k]. \end{aligned}$$

System C should therefore be a multiplication by $e^{-j\omega_0 n}$.

2.57. (a) $H_1(e^{j\omega})$ corresponds to a frequency shifted version of $H(e^{j\omega})$, specifically:

$$H_1(e^{j\omega}) = H(e^{j(\omega-\pi)}).$$

We thus have:

$$H_1(e^{j\omega}) = \begin{cases} 0 & , \quad |\omega| < 0.8\pi \\ 1 & , \quad 0.8\pi \le |\omega| \le \pi. \end{cases}$$

This is a highpass filter.

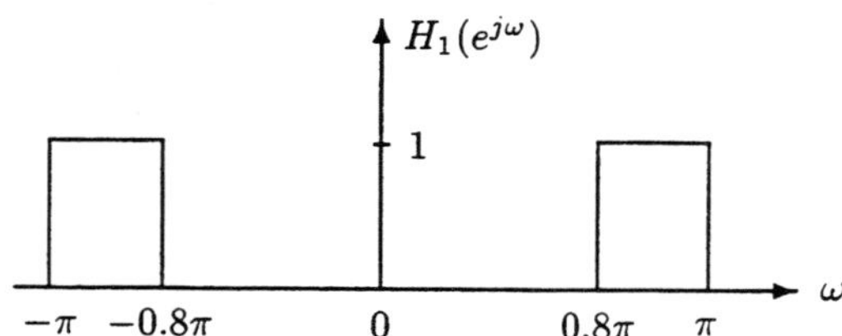

(b) $H_2(e^{j\omega})$ corresponds to a frequency modulated version of $H(e^{j\omega})$, specifically:

$$H_2(e^{j\omega}) = H(e^{j\omega}) * (\delta(\omega - 0.5\pi) + \delta(\omega + 0.5\pi)) \qquad \text{where } |\omega| \le \pi.$$

We thus have:

$$H_2(e^{j\omega}) = \begin{cases} 0 & , \quad |\omega| < 0.3\pi \\ 1 & , \quad 0.3\pi \le |\omega| \le 0.7\pi \\ 0 & , \quad 0.7\pi < |\omega| \le \pi. \end{cases}$$

This is a bandpass filter.

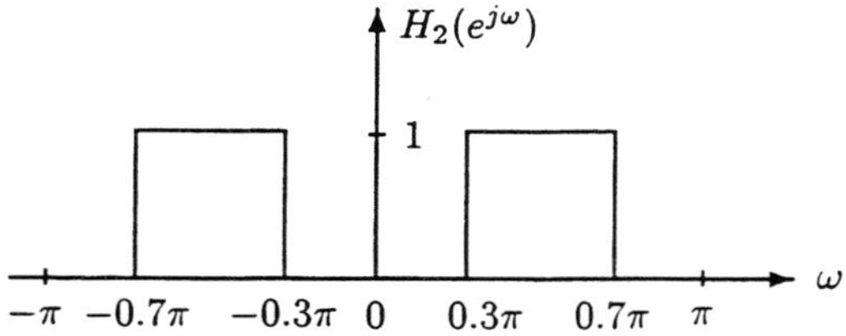

(c) $H_3(e^{j\omega})$ corresponds to a periodic convolution of $H_{lp}(e^{j\omega})$ with another lowpass filter, specifically:

$$H_3(e^{j\omega}) = \frac{1}{2\pi} \int_{-\pi}^{\pi} H(e^{j\theta}) H_{lp}(e^{j\omega - \theta})\, d\theta$$

where $H(e^{j\omega})$ is given by:

$$H(e^{j\omega}) = \begin{cases} 1 & , \quad |\omega| < 0.1\pi \\ 0 & , \quad 0.1\pi \le |\omega| \le \pi \end{cases}$$

Carrying out the convolution, we get:

$$H_3(e^{j\omega}) = \begin{cases} 0.1 & , \quad |\omega| < 0.1\pi \\ -\frac{|\omega|}{2\pi} + 0.15 & , \quad 0.1\pi \le |\omega| \le 0.3\pi \\ 0 & , \quad 0.3\pi < |\omega| \le \pi. \end{cases}$$

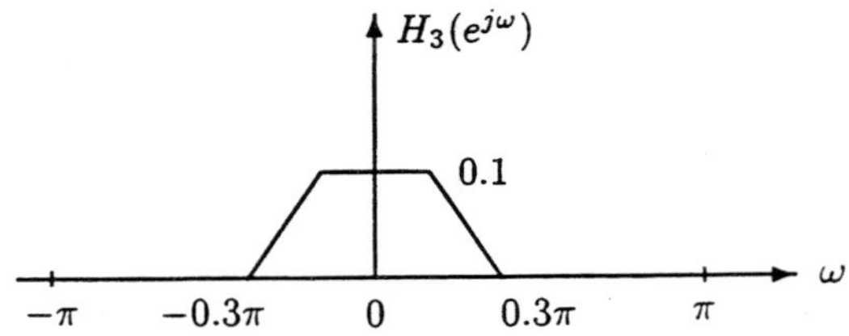

2.58. Note that $X(e^{j\omega})$ is real, and $Y(e^{j\omega})$ is given by:

$$Y(e^{j\omega}) = \begin{cases} -jX(e^{j\omega}) & , \quad 0 < \omega < \pi \\ +jX(e^{j\omega}) & , \quad -\pi < \omega < 0. \end{cases}$$

$w[n] = x[n] + jy[n]$, therefore:

$$W(e^{j\omega}) = X(e^{j\omega}) + jY(e^{j\omega}).$$

Using the above, we get:

$$jY(e^{j\omega}) = \begin{cases} X(e^{j\omega}) & , \quad 0 < \omega < \pi \\ -X(e^{j\omega}) & , \quad -\pi < \omega < 0. \end{cases}$$

We thus conclude:

$$W(e^{j\omega}) = \begin{cases} 2X(e^{j\omega}) & , \quad 0 < \omega < \pi \\ 0 & , \quad -\pi < \omega < 0. \end{cases}$$

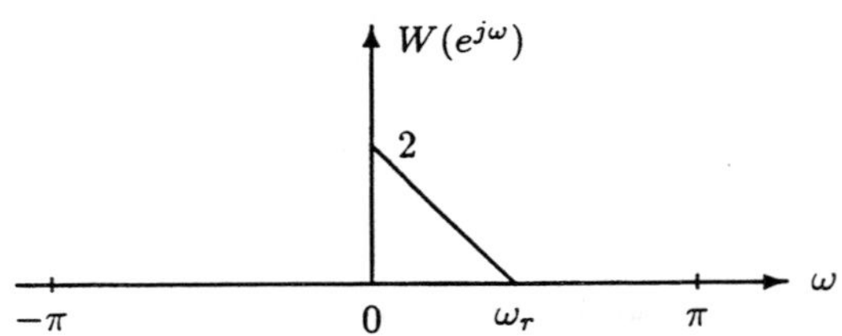

2.59. (a) Using the change of variable: $r = -k$, we can rewrite $R_x[n]$ as:

$$R_x[n] = \sum_{r=-\infty}^{\infty} x^*[-r]x[n-r] = x^*[-n] * x[n].$$

We therefore have:

$$g[n] = x^*[-n].$$

(b) The Fourier transform of $x^*[-n]$ is $X^*(e^{j\omega})$, therefore:

$$R_x(e^{j\omega}) = X^*(e^{j\omega})X(e^{j\omega}) = |X(e^{j\omega})|^2.$$

2.60. (a) Note that $x_2[n] = -\sum_{k=0}^{k=4} x[n-k]$. Since the system is LTI, we have:

$$y_2[n] = -\sum_{k=0}^{k=4} y[n-k].$$

(b) By carrying out the convolution, we get:

$$h[n] = \begin{cases} -1 & , \quad n = 0, n = 2 \\ -2 & , \quad n = 1 \\ 0 & , \quad \text{o.w.} \end{cases}$$

2.61. The system is not stable, any bounded input that excites the zero input response will result in an unbounded output.

The solution to the difference equation is given by:

$$y[n] = y_{zir}[n] + y_{zsr}[n]$$

where $y_{zir}[n]$ is the zero input response and $y_{zsr}[n]$ is the zero state response, the response to zero initial conditions:

$$\begin{aligned} y_{zir}[n] &= a(\frac{1}{2})^n \qquad \text{where } a \text{ is a constant determined by the initial condition.} \\ y_{zsr}[n] &= (\frac{1}{2})^n u[n] * x[n]. \end{aligned}$$

An example of a bounded input that results in an unbounded output is:

$$x[n] = \delta[n+1].$$

The output is unbounded and given by:

$$y[n] = (\frac{1}{2})^{n+1} u[n+1] - \frac{1}{2}(\frac{1}{2})^n.$$

2.62. The definition of causality implies that the output of a causal LTI system may only be derived from past and present inputs.

The convolution sum:

$$\begin{aligned} y[n] &= \sum_{k=-\infty}^{\infty} h[k]x[n-k] \\ &= \sum_{k=-\infty}^{-1} h[k]x[n-k] + \sum_{k=0}^{\infty} h[k]x[n-k] \end{aligned}$$

Note that the first summation represents a weighted sum of future values of the input. Thus, if the system is causal,

$$\sum_{k=-\infty}^{-1} h[k]x[n-k] = 0.$$

This can only be guaranteed if $h[k] = 0$ for $n < 0$.

Using reverse logic, we can show that if $h[n] = 0$ for $n < 0$,

$$y[n] = \sum_{k=0}^{\infty} h[k]x[n-k].$$

Since the convolution sum specifies that the input is formed from past and present input values, the system is, by definition, causal.

2.63. The system could be LTI. A possible impulse response is:

$$\begin{aligned} h[n] &= (\delta[n] - \frac{1}{4}\delta[n-1]) * (\frac{1}{2})^n \\ &= (\frac{1}{2})^n - \frac{1}{4}(\frac{1}{2})^{n-1}. \end{aligned}$$

2.64. Let the input be $x[n] = \delta[n-1]$, if the system is causal then the output, $y[n]$, should be zero for $n < 1$. Let's evaluate $y[0]$:

$$\begin{aligned} y[0] &= \frac{1}{2\pi}\int_{-\pi}^{+\pi} Y(e^{j\omega})\,d\omega \\ &= \frac{1}{2\pi}\int_{-\pi}^{+\pi} e^{-j\omega}e^{-j\omega/2}\,d\omega \\ &= -\frac{2}{3\pi} \\ &\neq 0. \end{aligned}$$

This proves that the system is not causal.

2.65. $x_1[n]$ is even-symmetric around $n = 1.5$, furthermore since $\sum x_1[n] < 0$ and we want $A_1(0) \geq 0$, we need to include a π factor in the phase. An appropriate choice for $\theta_1(\omega)$ is therefore:

$$\theta_1(\omega) = -\frac{3}{2}\omega + \pi \qquad |\omega| < \pi.$$

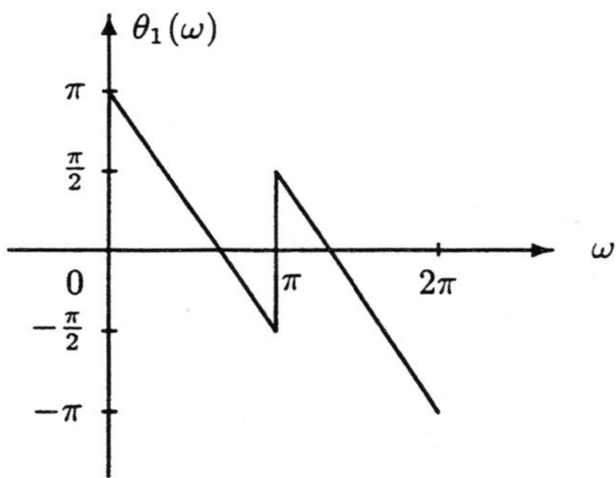

$x_2[n]$ is odd-symmetric around $n = 3$, therefore:

$$\theta_2(\omega) = -3\omega + \frac{\pi}{2} \qquad |\omega| < \pi.$$

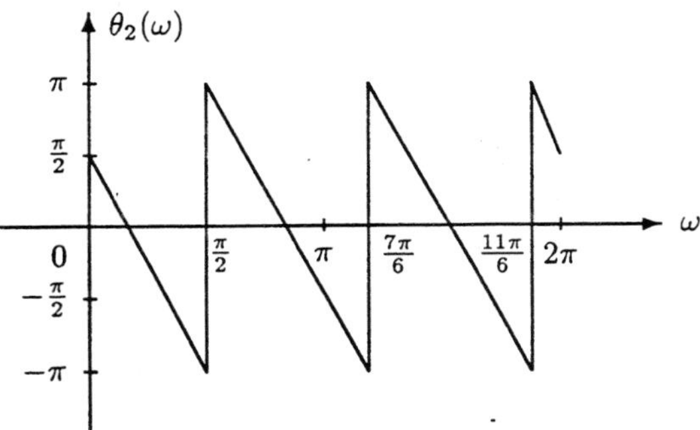

2.66. (a)

$$\begin{aligned} E(e^{j\omega}) &= H_1(e^{j\omega})X(e^{j\omega}) \\ F(e^{j\omega}) &= E(e^{-j\omega}) \\ &= H_1(e^{-j\omega})X(e^{-j\omega}) \\ G(e^{j\omega}) &= H_1(e^{j\omega})F(e^{j\omega}) \\ &= H_1(e^{j\omega})H_1(e^{-j\omega})X(e^{-j\omega}) \\ Y(e^{j\omega}) &= G(e^{-j\omega}) \\ &= H_1(e^{-j\omega})H_1(e^{j\omega})X(e^{j\omega}). \end{aligned}$$

(b) Since:

$$Y(e^{j\omega}) = H_1(e^{-j\omega})H_1(e^{j\omega})X(e^{j\omega}),$$

We get:

$$H(e^{j\omega}) = H_1(e^{-j\omega})H_1(e^{j\omega}).$$

(c) Taking the inverse transform of $H(e^{j\omega})$, we get:

$$h[n] = h_1[-n] * h_1[n].$$

2.67. (a) Using the properties of the Fourier transform and the fact that $(-1)^n = e^{j\pi n}$, we get:

$$\begin{aligned} V(e^{j\omega}) &= X(e^{j(\omega+\pi)}) \\ W(e^{j\omega}) &= H_1(e^{j\omega})V(e^{j\omega}) \\ &= H_1(e^{j\omega})X(e^{j(\omega+\pi}) \\ Y(e^{j\omega}) &= W(e^{j(\omega-\pi)}) \\ &= H_1(e^{j(\omega-\pi)})X(e^{j\omega}) \end{aligned}$$

$H(e^{j\omega})$ is thus given by:

$$H(e^{j\omega}) = H_1(e^{j(\omega-\pi)}).$$

(b)

$$H(e^{j\omega}) = H_1(e^{j(\omega-\pi)}).$$

With the given choice of $H_1(e^{j\omega})$,

$$H(e^{j\omega}) = \begin{cases} 0 \quad , & |\omega| < \pi - \omega_c \\ 1 \quad , & \pi - \omega_c < |\omega| \le \pi. \end{cases}$$

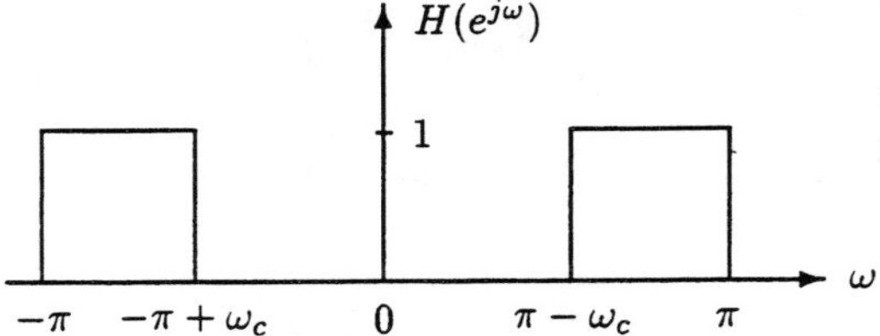

2.68. If $x_1[n] = x_2[n]$, $w_1[n]$ and $w_2[n]$ will not be necessarily equal.

$$\begin{aligned} w_1[n] &= x_1[-n-2] \\ w_2[n] &= x_2[-n+2] \\ &\neq x_2[-n-2] \end{aligned}$$

A simple counterexample is $x_1[n] = x_2[n] = \delta[n]$. Then:

$$\begin{aligned} w_1[n] &= \delta[n+2] \\ w_2[n] &= \delta[n-2]. \end{aligned}$$

2.69. (a) The overall system is not guaranteed to be an LTI system. A simple counterexample is:

$$\begin{aligned} y_1[n] &= x[n] \\ y_2[n] &= x[n] \\ y[n] &= y_1[n]y_2[n] = x^2[n] \end{aligned}$$

which is not a linear system, therefore the system is not LTI.

(b)

$$\begin{aligned} Y_1(e^{j\omega}) &= H_1(e^{j\omega})X(e^{j\omega}) \\ Y_2(e^{j\omega}) &= H_2(e^{j\omega})X(e^{j\omega}) \\ Y(e^{j\omega}) &= Y_1(e^{j\omega}) * Y_2(e^{j\omega}). \end{aligned}$$

Using the above relationships, we get:

$$Y(e^{j\omega}) = \begin{cases} \text{unspecified} \quad , & 0 < |\omega| < 0.6\pi \\ 0 \quad , & 0.6\pi \le |\omega| \le \pi. \end{cases}$$

2.70. The first difference:

$$y[n] = \nabla(x[n]) = x[n] - x[n-1].$$

(a) To determine if the system is linear:

$$\begin{aligned}\nabla(ax_1[n] + bx_2[n]) &= ax_1[n] + bx_2[n] - ax_1[n-1] - bx_2[n-1] \\ &= a(x_1[n] - x_1[n-1]) + b(x_2[n] - x_2[n-1]) \\ &= \nabla(ax_1[n]) + \nabla(ax_2[n]).\end{aligned}$$

Therefore, the system is LINEAR.

To determine if the first difference is time invariant:

$$\begin{aligned}\nabla(x_1[n-1]) &= x[n-1] - x[n-2] \\ &= y[n-1].\end{aligned}$$

The system is TIME INVARIANT.

(b) The impulse response is obtained by setting the input to $x[n] = \delta[n]$,

$$y[n] = h[n] = \delta[n] - \delta[n-1]$$

(c) Taking the Fourier transform of the result of part (b), we find that the system function is

$$H(e^{j\omega}) = 1 - e^{-j\omega}.$$

Thus the magnitude of the frequency response is

$$\begin{aligned}|H(e^{j\omega})| &= \sqrt{(1-e^{-j\omega})(1-e^{-j\omega})} \\ &= \sqrt{2 - 2\cos(\omega)}.\end{aligned}$$

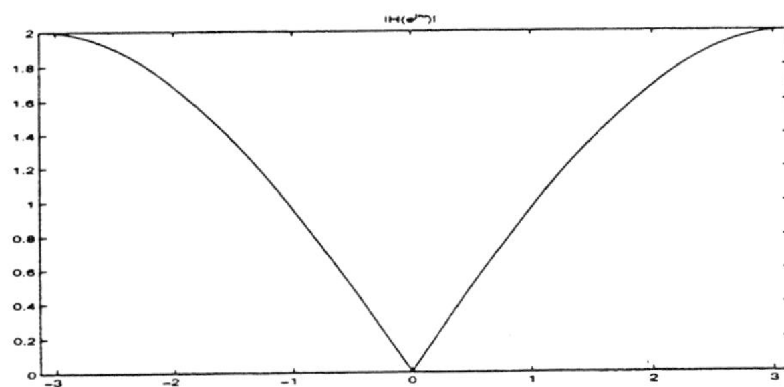

We calculate the phase of the frequency response:

$$H(e^{j\omega}) = (1 - \cos(\omega)) + j\sin(\omega)$$

Thus,

$$\angle H(e^{j\omega}) = \arctan\left(\frac{\sin(\omega)}{1-\cos(\omega)}\right)$$

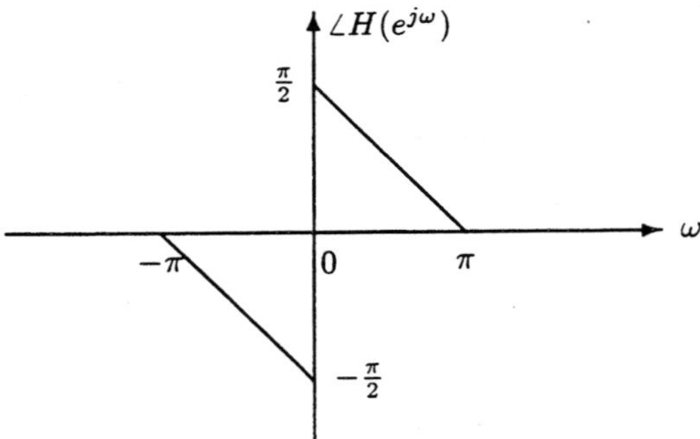

(d) In general,

$$\begin{aligned}\nabla(x[n]) &= x[n] * (\delta[n] - \delta[n-1]) \\ &= x[n] - x[n-1].\end{aligned}$$

So, for $x[n] = f[n] * g[n]$,

$$\begin{aligned}\nabla(x[n]) &= f[n] * g[n] * (\delta[n] - \delta[n-1]) \\ &= f[n] * \nabla(g[n]) \\ &= \nabla(f[n]) * g[n].\end{aligned}$$

Where we have used the commutivity of the convolution operator to obtain the last two equalities.

(e) We desire the inverse system, $h_i[n]$, such that

$$h_i[n] * \nabla(x[n]) = x[n]$$

The inverse system must satisfy:

$$h_i[n] * h[n] = \delta[n],$$

in the frequency domain,

$$H_i(e^{j\omega})H(e^{j\omega}) = 1.$$

Recall from part (c),

$$H(e^{j\omega}) = 1 - e^{-j\omega}.$$

So,

$$H_i(e^{j\omega}) = \frac{1}{1 - e^{-j\omega}},$$

and

$$h_i[n] = u[n].$$

Hence, the unit step is the inverse system for the first difference.

2.71. For impulse response $h[n]$, the frequency response of an LTI system is given by

$$H(e^{j\omega}) = \sum_{n=-\infty}^{\infty} h[n]e^{-j\omega n}$$

(a) Suppose the impulse response is $h^*[n]$,

$$\begin{aligned}\sum_{n=-\infty}^{\infty} h^*[n]e^{-j\omega n} &= \left(\sum_{n=-\infty}^{\infty} h[n]e^{j\omega n}\right)^* \\ &= H^*(e^{-j\omega}).\end{aligned}$$

(b) We have

$$\begin{aligned} H^*(e^{j\omega}) &= \left(\sum_{n=-\infty}^{\infty} h[n]e^{-j\omega n}\right)^* \\ &= \sum_{n=-\infty}^{\infty} h^*[n]e^{j\omega n}. \end{aligned}$$

If $h[n]$ is real,

$$\begin{aligned} H^*(e^{j\omega}) &= \sum_{n=-\infty}^{\infty} h[n]e^{j\omega n} \\ &= H(e^{-j\omega}). \end{aligned}$$

Hence, the frequency response is conjugate symmetric.

2.72. The analysis equation for the Fourier transform:

$$X(e^{j\omega}) = \sum_{n=-\infty}^{\infty} x[n]e^{-j\omega n}$$

(a) The Fourier transform of $x^*[n]$,

$$\begin{aligned} \sum_{n=-\infty}^{\infty} x^*[n]e^{-j\omega n} &= \left(\sum_{n=-\infty}^{\infty} x[n]e^{j\omega n}\right)^* \\ &= X^*(e^{-j\omega n}). \end{aligned}$$

(b) The Fourier transform of $x^*[-n]$,

$$\begin{aligned} \sum_{n=-\infty}^{\infty} x^*[-n]e^{-j\omega n} &= \sum_{l=-\infty}^{\infty} x^*[l]e^{j\omega l} \\ &= \left(\sum_{l=-\infty}^{\infty} x[l]e^{-j\omega l}\right)^* \\ &= X^*(e^{j\omega}). \end{aligned}$$

2.73. From property 1:

$$X^*(e^{-j\omega}) = \sum_{n=-\infty}^{\infty} x^*[n]e^{-j\omega n}$$

for $x[n]$ real, $x[n] = x^*[n]$, so

$$\begin{aligned} X^*(e^{-j\omega}) &= \sum_{n=-\infty}^{\infty} x[n]e^{-j\omega n} \\ &= X(e^{j\omega}). \end{aligned}$$

Thus, the Fourier transform of a real input is conjugate symmetric.

$$X(e^{j\omega}) = X_R(e^{j\omega}) + jX_I(e^{j\omega})$$

$$X^*(e^{-j\omega}) = X_R(e^{-j\omega}) - jX_I(e^{j\omega})$$

From property 7, $X(e^{j\omega}) = X^*(e^{-j\omega})$ for $x[n]$ real. Thus,

$$X_R(e^{j\omega}) + jX_I(e^{j\omega}) = X_R(e^{-j\omega}) - jX_I(e^{-j\omega}).$$

We may infer

$$\begin{array}{ll} \text{property 8:} & X_R(e^{j\omega}) = X_R(e^{-j\omega}) \\ \text{property 9:} & X_I(e^{j\omega}) = -X_I(e^{-j\omega}) \end{array}$$

$$X(e^{j\omega}) = |X(e^{j\omega})|e^{j\angle X(e^{j\omega})}$$

$$X^*(e^{-j\omega}) = |X(e^{-j\omega})|e^{-j\angle X(e^{-j\omega})}$$

From property 7:

$$X(e^{j\omega}) = X^*(e^{-j\omega}).$$

So,

$$\begin{array}{ll} \text{property 10:} & |X(e^{j\omega})| = |X(e^{-j\omega})| \\ \text{property 11:} & \angle X(e^{j\omega}) = -\angle X(e^{-j\omega}). \end{array}$$

2.74. Theorem 1:

$$\begin{aligned} \sum_{n=-\infty}^{\infty} (ax_1[n] + bx_2[n])e^{-j\omega n} &= \sum_{n=-\infty}^{\infty} ax_1[n]e^{-j\omega n} + \sum_{n=-\infty}^{\infty} bx_2[n]e^{-j\omega n} \\ &= aX_1(e^{j\omega}) + bX_2(e^{j\omega}) \end{aligned}$$

Theorem 2:

$$\begin{aligned} \sum_{n=-\infty}^{\infty} x[n-n_d]e^{-j\omega n} &= \sum_{\ell=-\infty}^{\infty} x[\ell]e^{-j\omega(\ell-n_d)} \\ &= e^{j\omega n_d} \sum_{\ell=-\infty}^{\infty} x[\ell]e^{-j\omega\ell} \\ &= e^{j\omega n_d} X(e^{j\omega}) \end{aligned}$$

Theorem 3:

$$\begin{aligned} \sum_{n=-\infty}^{\infty} x[n]e^{j\omega_0 n}e^{-j\omega n} &= \sum_{n=-\infty}^{\infty} x[n]e^{-j(\omega-\omega_0)n} \\ &= X(e^{j(\omega-\omega_0)}) \end{aligned}$$

Theorem 4:

$$\begin{aligned} \sum_{n=-\infty}^{\infty} x[-n]e^{-j\omega n} &= \sum_{\ell=-\infty}^{\infty} x[\ell]e^{j\omega\ell} \\ &= X(e^{-j\omega}) \end{aligned}$$

Theorem 5:

$$\begin{aligned} \sum_{n=-\infty}^{\infty} nx[n]e^{-j\omega n} &= -\frac{1}{j}\frac{d}{d\omega}\left(\sum_{n=-\infty}^{\infty} x[n]e^{-j\omega n}\right) \\ &= j\frac{d}{d\omega}(X(e^{j\omega})) \end{aligned}$$

2.75. The output of an LTI system is obtained by the convolution sum,

$$y[n] = \sum_{k=-\infty}^{\infty} x[k]h[n-k].$$

Taking the Fourier transform,

$$\begin{aligned} Y(e^{j\omega}) &= \sum_{n=-\infty}^{\infty} \left(\sum_{k=-\infty}^{\infty} x[k]h[n-k] \right) e^{-j\omega n} \\ &= \sum_{k=-\infty}^{\infty} x[k] \left(\sum_{n=-\infty}^{\infty} h[n-k]e^{-j\omega n} \right) \\ &= \sum_{k=-\infty}^{\infty} x[k]e^{-j\omega k} \left(\sum_{n=-\infty}^{\infty} h[n-k]e^{-j\omega(n-k)} \right) \end{aligned}$$

Hence,

$$Y(e^{j\omega}) = X(e^{j\omega})H(e^{j\omega}).$$

2.76. The Modulation theorem:

$$Y(e^{j\omega}) = \frac{1}{2\pi} \int_{-\pi}^{\pi} X(e^{j\theta})W(e^{j(\omega-\theta)})\, d\theta$$

the time-domain representation,

$$\begin{aligned} y[n] &= \frac{1}{(2\pi)^2} \int_{-\pi}^{\pi} d\theta \int_{-\pi}^{\pi} d\omega\, X(e^{j\theta})W(e^{j(\omega-\theta)})e^{j\omega n} \\ &= \frac{1}{2\pi} \int_{-\pi}^{\pi} d\theta\, X(e^{j\theta})w[n]e^{j\theta n} \\ &= x[n]w[n] \end{aligned}$$

2.77. (a) The Fourier transform of $y^*[-n]$ is $Y^*(e^{j\omega})$, and $X(e^{j\omega})Y(e^{j\omega})$ forms a transform pair with $x[n] * y[n]$. So

$$G(e^{j\omega}) = X(e^{j\omega})Y^*(e^{j\omega})$$

and

$$g[n] = x[n] * y^*[-n]$$

form a transform pair.

(b)

$$\begin{aligned} \frac{1}{2\pi} \int_{-\pi}^{\pi} X(e^{j\omega})Y^*(e^{j\omega})e^{j\omega n} d\omega &= \sum_{n=-\infty}^{\infty} (x[n] * y^*[-n])\, e^{-j\omega n} \\ &= \sum_{n=-\infty}^{\infty} \sum_{k=-\infty}^{\infty} x[k]y^*[k-n]e^{-j\omega n} \end{aligned}$$

for $n = 0$:

$$\frac{1}{2\pi} \int_{-\infty}^{\infty} X(e^{j\omega})Y^*(e^{j\omega})d\omega = \sum_{k=-\infty}^{\infty} x[k]y^*[k]$$

(c) Using the result from part (b):

$$x[n] = \frac{\sin(\pi n/4)}{2\pi n}$$
$$y^*[n] = \frac{\sin(\pi n/6)}{5\pi n}$$

We recognize each sequence to be a pulse in the frequency domain:

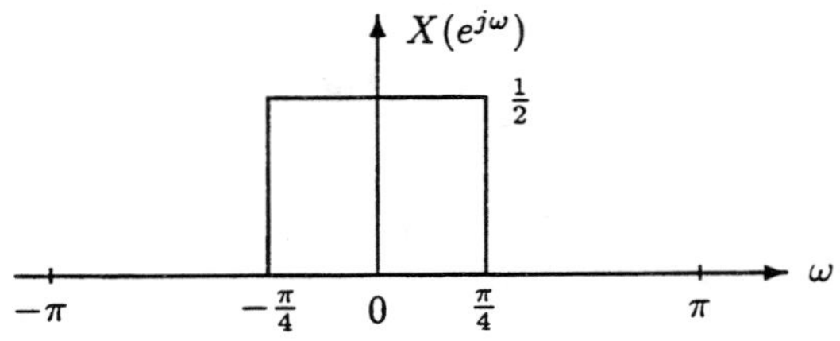

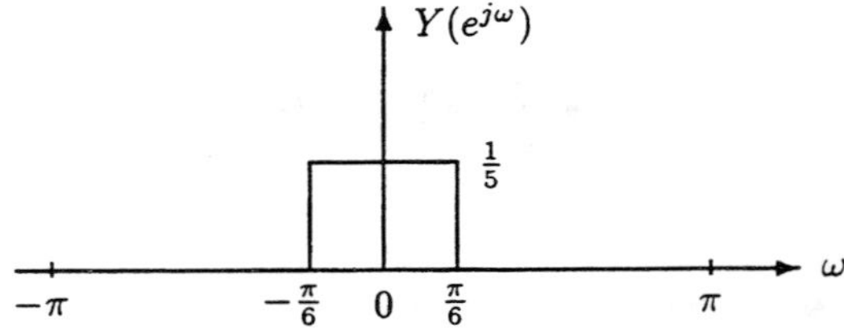

Substituting into Eq. (P2.77-1):

$$\begin{aligned}
\sum_{n=-\infty}^{\infty} x[n]y^*[n] &= \frac{1}{2\pi}\int_{-\pi}^{\pi} X(e^{j\omega})Y^*(e^{j\omega})d\omega \\
&= \frac{1}{2\pi}\left[(\frac{1}{2})(\frac{1}{5})(\frac{2\pi}{6})\right] \\
&= \frac{1}{60}
\end{aligned}$$

2.78. $X(e^{j\omega})$ is given by:

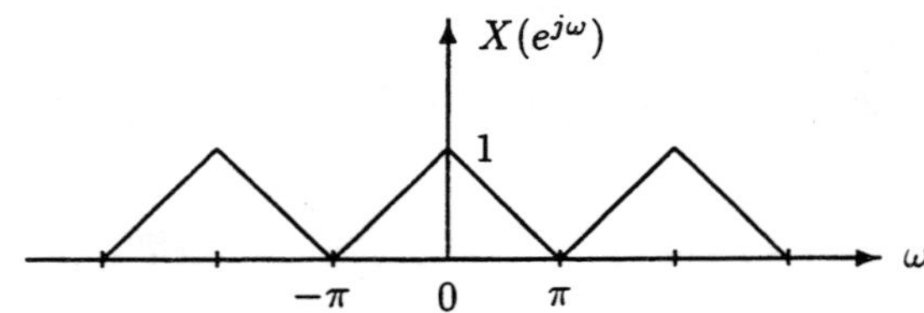

(a)

$$\begin{aligned}
y_s[n] &= \begin{cases} x[n], & n \text{ even} \\ 0, & n \text{ odd} \end{cases} \\
&= \frac{1}{2}\left(1 + e^{j\pi n}\right) x[n]
\end{aligned}$$

which transforms to

$$Y_s(e^{j\omega}) = \frac{1}{2}\left[X(e^{j\omega}) + X(e^{j(\omega+\pi)})\right]$$

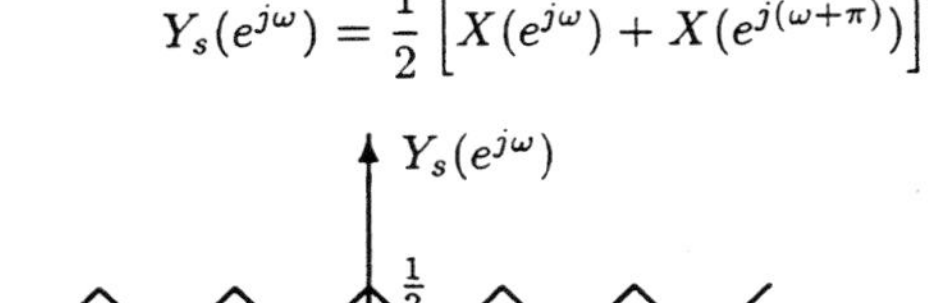
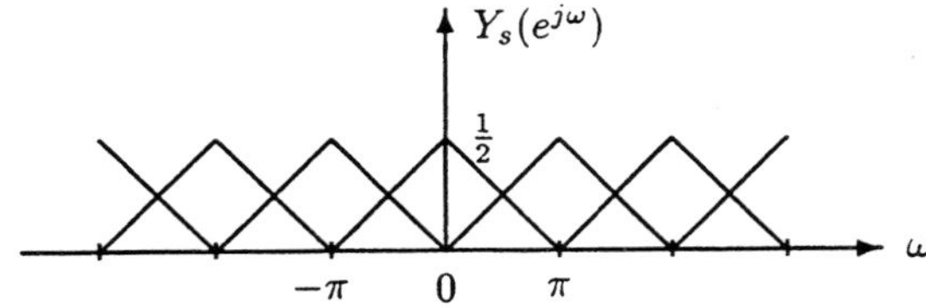

(b)

$$y_d[n] = x[2n]$$

$$\begin{aligned} Y_d(e^{j\omega}) &= \frac{1}{2}\left[X(e^{j\frac{\omega}{2}}) + X(e^{j(\frac{\omega}{2}+\pi)})\right] \\ &= Y_s(e^{j\frac{\omega}{2}}) \end{aligned}$$

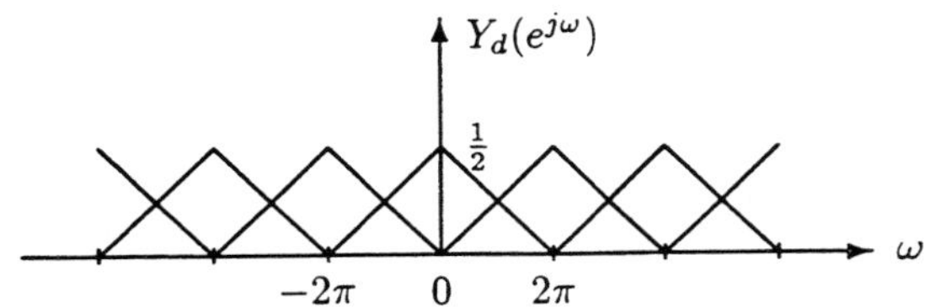

(c)

$$y_e[n] = \begin{cases} x[n/2], & n \text{ even} \\ 0, & n \text{ odd} \end{cases}$$

$$Y_e(e^{j\omega}) = X(e^{j2\omega})$$

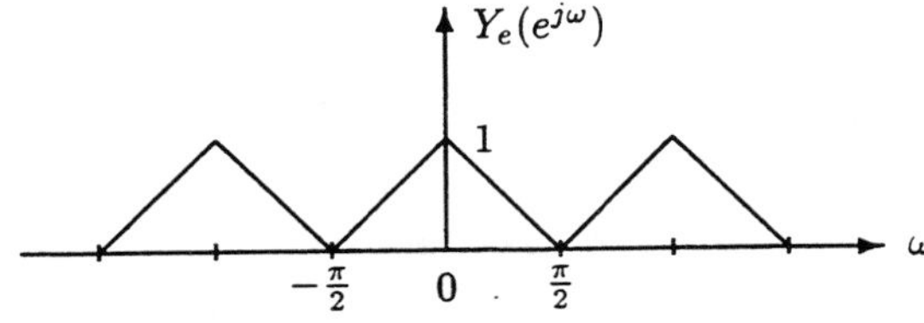

2.79. (a)

$$\begin{aligned} \Phi_x(-N,-\omega) &= \sum_{n=-\infty}^{\infty} x[n-N]x^*[n+N]e^{j\omega n}. \\ \Phi_x^*(N,\omega) &= \left(\sum_{n=-\infty}^{\infty} x[n+N]x^*[n-N]e^{-j\omega n}\right)^* \end{aligned}$$

$$
\begin{aligned}
&= \sum_{n=-\infty}^{\infty} (x[n+N]x^*[n-N]e^{-j\omega n})^* \\
&= \sum_{n=-\infty}^{\infty} x^*[n+N]x[n-N]e^{j\omega n} \\
&= \Phi_x(-N,-\omega).
\end{aligned}
$$

(b)

$$
\begin{aligned}
\Phi_x(N,\omega) &= \sum_{n=-\infty}^{\infty} Aa^{n+N}u[n+N]Aa^{n-N}u[n-N]e^{-j\omega n} \\
&= A^2 \sum_{n=N}^{\infty} a^{2n}e^{-j\omega n} \\
&= A^2 \sum_{n=N}^{\infty} (a^2e^{-j\omega})^n \\
&= A^2 \frac{(a^2e^{-j\omega})^N}{1-a^2e^{-j\omega}} \\
&= A^2 \frac{a^{2N}e^{-j\omega N}}{1-a^2e^{-j\omega}}.
\end{aligned}
$$

(c)

$$
\begin{aligned}
X(e^{j(v+(\omega/2))}) &= \sum_{n=-\infty}^{\infty} x[n]e^{-j(v+\omega/2)n}. \\
X^*(e^{j(v-(\omega/2))}) &= \sum_{n=-\infty}^{\infty} x^*[n]e^{j(v-\omega/2)n}.
\end{aligned}
$$

Let $S = \frac{1}{2\pi}\int_{-\pi}^{\pi} X(e^{j(v+(\omega/2))})X^*(e^{j(v-(\omega/2))})e^{j2vN}\,dv$, then:

$$
\begin{aligned}
S &= \frac{1}{2\pi}\int_{-\pi}^{\pi} \sum_{n=-\infty}^{\infty} x[n]e^{-j(v+\omega/2)n} \sum_{k=-\infty}^{\infty} x^*[k]e^{j(v-\omega/2)k}e^{j2vN}\,dv \\
&= \frac{1}{2\pi}\sum_{n=-\infty}^{\infty}\sum_{k=-\infty}^{\infty} x[n]x^*[k]e^{-j\frac{\omega(n+k)}{2}} \int_{-\pi}^{\pi} e^{j(k-n+2N)}\,dv \\
&= \frac{1}{2\pi}\sum_{n=-\infty}^{\infty}\sum_{k=-\infty}^{\infty} x[n]x^*[k]e^{-j\frac{\omega(n+k)}{2}} \frac{2\sin(\pi(k-n+2N))}{k-n+2N} \\
&= \sum_{n=-\infty}^{\infty} x[n]x^*[n-2N]e^{-j\frac{\omega(2n-2N)}{2}} \\
&= \sum_{n=-\infty}^{\infty} x[n+N]x^*[n-N]e^{-j\omega n} \\
&= \Phi_x(N,\omega).
\end{aligned}
$$

We thus conclude that:

$$
\Phi_x(N,\omega) = \frac{1}{2\pi}\int_{-\pi}^{\pi} X(e^{j(v+(\omega/2))})X^*(e^{j(v-(\omega/2))})e^{j2vN}\,dv.
$$

2.80.

$$w[n] = x[n] + y[n]$$

The mean of $w[n]$:

$$\begin{aligned} m_w &= E\{w[n]\} \\ &= E\{x[n] + y[n]\} \\ &= E\{x[n]\} + E\{y[n]\} \\ &= m_x + m_y \end{aligned}$$

The variance of $w[n]$:

$$\begin{aligned} \sigma_w^2 &= E\{(w[n] - m_w)^2\} \\ &= E\{w^2[n]\} - m_w^2 \\ &= E\{(x[n] + y[n])^2\} - m_w^2 \\ &= E\{x^2[n]\} + 2E\{x[n]y[n]\} + E\{y^2[n]\} - m_x^2 - 2m_x m_y - m_y^2 \end{aligned}$$

If $x[n]$ and $y[n]$ are uncorrelated:

$$\begin{aligned} \sigma_w^2 &= E\{x^2[n]\} - m_x^2 + E\{y^2[n]\} - m_y^2 \\ &= \sigma_x^2 + \sigma_y^2 \end{aligned}$$

2.81. Let $e[n]$ be a white noise sequence and $E\{s[n]e[m]\} = 0$ for all n and m.

$$\begin{aligned} E\{y[n]y[n+m]\} &= E\{s[n]e[n]s[n+m]e[n+m]\} \\ &= E\{s[n]s[n+m]e[n]e[n+m]\} \end{aligned}$$

Since $s[n]$ is uncorrelated with $e[n]$:

$$\begin{aligned} E\{y[n]y[n+m]\} &= E\{s[n]s[n+m]\}E\{e[n]e[n+m]\} \\ &= \sigma_s^2 \sigma_e^2 \delta[m] \end{aligned}$$

2.82. (a)

$$\begin{aligned} \phi_{xx}[m] &= E(x[n]x[n+m]) \\ &= E((s[n] + e[n])(s[n+m] + e[n+m])) \\ &= E(s[n]s[n+m]) + E(e[n]e[n+m]) + E(s[n]e[n+m]) + E(e[n]s[n+m]) \\ &= \phi_{ss}[m] + \phi_{ee}[m] + 2E(e[n])E(s[n]) \quad \text{since } s[n] \text{ and } e[n] \text{ are independent and stationary.} \\ &= \phi_{ss}[m] + \phi_{ee}[m] \qquad \text{where we assumed } e[n] \text{ has zero mean.} \end{aligned}$$

Taking the Fourier transform of the above equation, we get:

$$\Phi_{xx}(e^{j\omega}) = \Phi_{ss}(e^{j\omega}) + \Phi_{ee}(e^{j\omega}).$$

(b)

$$\begin{aligned} \phi_{xe}[m] &= E(x[n]e[n+m]) \\ &= E((s[n] + e[n])e[n+m]) \\ &= E(s[n])E(e[n]) + \phi_{ee}[m] \qquad \text{since } s[n] \text{ and } e[n] \text{ are independent and stationary.} \\ &= \phi_{ee}[m] \qquad \text{where we assumed } e[n] \text{ has zero mean.} \end{aligned}$$

Taking the Fourier transform of the above equation, we get:

$$\Phi_{xe}(e^{j\omega}) = \Phi_{ee}(e^{j\omega}).$$

(c)

$$\begin{aligned}\phi_{xs}[m] &= E(x[n]s[n+m]) \\ &= E((s[n]+e[n])s[n+m]) \\ &= \phi_{ss}[m] + E(e[n])E(s[n]) \quad \text{since } s[n] \text{ and } e[n] \text{ are independent and stationary.} \\ &= \phi_{ss}[m] \quad \text{where we assumed } e[n] \text{ has zero mean.}\end{aligned}$$

Taking the Fourier transform of the above equation, we get:

$$\Phi_{xs}(e^{j\omega}) = \Phi_{ss}(e^{j\omega}).$$

2.83. (Throughout this problem, we will assume $|a| < 1$.)

(a)

$$\phi_{hh}[m] = h[m] * h[-m].$$

Taking the Fourier transform, we get:

$$\begin{aligned}\Phi_{hh}(e^{j\omega}) &= H(e^{j\omega})H(e^{-j\omega}) \\ &= \frac{1}{(1-ae^{-j\omega})}\frac{1}{(1-ae^{j\omega})} \\ &= \frac{1}{1-a^2}\left(\frac{1}{1-ae^{-j\omega}} + \frac{1}{1-ae^{j\omega}}\right).\end{aligned}$$

Taking the Inverse Fourier transform, we get:

$$\phi_{hh}[m] = \frac{a^{|n|}}{1-a^2}.$$

(b) Using part (a), we get:

$$\begin{aligned}|H(e^{j\omega})|^2 &= H(e^{j\omega})H^*(e^{j\omega}) \\ &= H(e^{j\omega})H(e^{-j\omega}) \text{ since } h[n] \text{ is real} \\ &= \Phi_{hh}(e^{j\omega}) \\ &= \frac{1}{(1-ae^{-j\omega})}\frac{1}{(1-ae^{j\omega})} \\ &= \frac{1}{1-a^2}\left(\frac{1}{1-ae^{-j\omega}} + \frac{1}{1-ae^{j\omega}}\right).\end{aligned}$$

(c) Using Parseval's theorem:

$$\begin{aligned}\frac{1}{2\pi}\int_{-\pi}^{\pi} |H(e^{j\omega})|^2\, d\omega &= \sum_{n=-\infty}^{+\infty} |h[n]|^2 \\ &= \sum_{n=-\infty}^{+\infty} |a|^{2n}u[n] \\ &= \sum_{n=0}^{+\infty}(|a|^2)^n \\ &= \frac{1}{1-|a|^2}.\end{aligned}$$

2.84. The first-backward-difference system is given by:

$$y[n] = x[n] - x[n-1].$$

(a)

$$\begin{aligned}
\phi_{yy}[m] &= E(y[n]y[n+m]) \\
&= E((x[n]-x[n-1])(x[n+m]-x[n+m-1])) \\
&= E(x[n]x[n+m]) - E(x[n]x[n+m-1]) - E(x[n-1]x[n+m]) \\
&\quad +E(x[n-1]x[n+m-1]) \\
&= \phi_{xx}[m] - \phi_{xx}[m-1] - \phi_{xx}[m+1] + \phi_{xx}[m] \\
&= 2\phi_{xx}[m] - \phi_{xx}[m-1] - \phi_{xx}[m+1] \\
&= 2\sigma_x^2\delta[m] - \sigma_x^2\delta[m-1] - \sigma_x^2\delta[m+1].
\end{aligned}$$

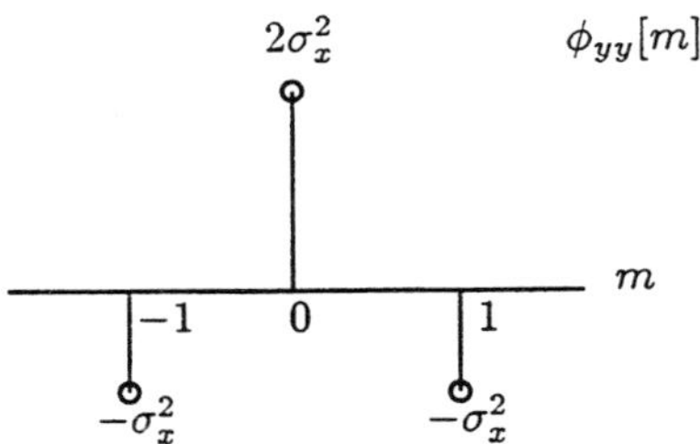

To get the power spectrum, we take the Fourier transform of the autocorrelation function:

$$\begin{aligned}
\Phi_{yy}(e^{j\omega}) &= 2\sigma_x^2 - \sigma_x^2 e^{-j\omega} - \sigma_x^2 e^{j\omega} \\
&= 2\sigma_x^2 - 2\sigma_x^2 cos(\omega) \\
&= 2\sigma_x^2(1 - cos(\omega)).
\end{aligned}$$

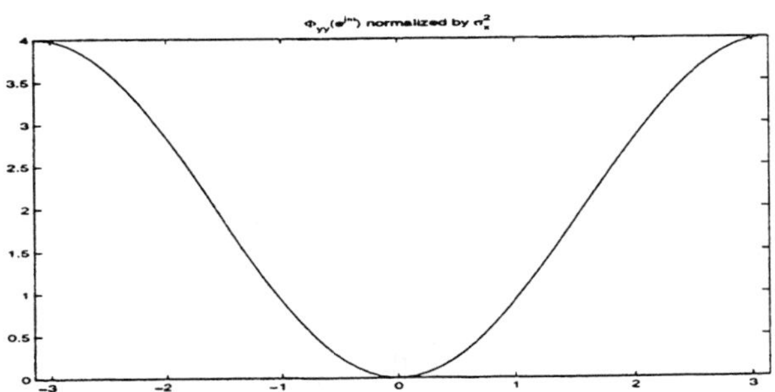

(b) The average power of the output of the system is given by $\phi_{yy}[0]$:

$$\phi_{yy}[0] = 2\sigma_x^2.$$

(c) The noise power increased by going through the first-backward-difference system. This tells us that the first backward difference amplifies the noise of a signal.

2.85. (a)

$$\begin{aligned} E\{x[n]y[n]\} &= E\{x[n] \sum_{k=-\infty}^{\infty} h[n]x[n-k]\} \\ &= \sum_{k=-\infty}^{\infty} h[k]E\{x[n]x[n-k]\} \\ &= \sum_{k=-\infty}^{\infty} h[k]\phi_{xx}[k] \end{aligned}$$

Because $x[n]$ is a real, stationary white noise process:

$$\phi_{xx}[n] = \sigma_x^2\delta[n].$$

Therefore,

$$\begin{aligned} E\{x[n]y[n]\} &= \sigma_x^2 \sum_{k=-\infty}^{\infty} h[k]\delta[k] \\ &= \sigma_x^2 h[0]. \end{aligned}$$

(b) The variance of the output:

$$\begin{aligned} \sigma_y^2 &= E\{(y[n]-m_y)^2\} \\ &= E\{y^2[n]\} - m_y^2. \end{aligned}$$

When a zero-mean random process is input to a determistic LTI system, the output is also zero-mean:

$$\begin{aligned} y[n] &= x[n] * h[n] \\ &= \sum_{k=-\infty}^{\infty} x[k]h[n-k]. \end{aligned}$$

Taking the expected value of both sides:

$$\begin{aligned} m_y &= \sum_{k=-\infty}^{\infty} E\{x[n]\}h[n-k] \\ m_y &= 0, \quad \text{if } m_x = 0. \end{aligned}$$

So,

$$\begin{aligned} \sigma_y^2 &= E\{y^2[n]\} \\ &= E\left\{ \sum_{m=-\infty}^{\infty} h[m]x[n-m] \sum_{k=-\infty}^{\infty} h[k]x[n-k] \right\} \\ &= \sum_{m=-\infty}^{\infty} \sum_{k=-\infty}^{\infty} h[m]h[k]E\{x[n-m]x[n-k]\} \\ &= \sigma_x^2 \sum_{m=-\infty}^{\infty} \sum_{k=-\infty}^{\infty} h[m]h[k]\delta[m-k] \\ \sigma_y^2 &= \sigma_x^2 \sum_{m=-\infty}^{\infty} h^2[m]. \end{aligned}$$

2.86. Using the solution to problem 2.85:

(a)

$$\sigma_y^2 = \sigma_x^2 \sum_{k=-\infty}^{\infty} h_1^2[k]$$

this statement is TRUE, because $x[n]$ is a white noise sequence.

(b) Since $y[n]$ is not a white noise sequence, this statement is FALSE.

(c) Let

$$\begin{aligned} h_1[n] &= a^n u[n] \\ h_2[n] &= b^n u[n]. \end{aligned}$$

These systems are cascaded:

$$\begin{aligned} h[n] &= h_1[n] * h_2[n] \\ &= \sum_{k=0}^{n} a^k b^{n-k}, \qquad n \geq 0 \\ &= b^n \left(\frac{1-(a/b)^{n+1}}{1-(a/b)} \right) u[n] \end{aligned}$$

$$w[n] = x[n] * h[n].$$

Since $x[n]$ is zero-mean, $m_w = 0$ also.

$$\begin{aligned} \sigma_w^2 &= E\{w^2[n]\} \\ &= \sigma_x^2 \sum_{k=0}^{\infty} h^2[k]. \end{aligned}$$

2.87. (a) x[n] is a stationary white noise process.

$$y[n] = \sum_{k=-\infty}^{\infty} h[k]x[n-k], \qquad n \geq 0$$

$$\begin{aligned} E\{y[n]\} &= E\left\{ \sum_{k=-\infty}^{n} h[k]x[n-k] \right\}, \qquad n \geq 0 \\ &= \sum_{k=-\infty}^{n} h[k]E\{x[n-k]\} \\ &= \begin{cases} m_x \sum_{k=-\infty}^{n} h[k], & n \geq 0 \\ 0, & n < 0 \end{cases} \end{aligned}$$

(b)

$$\begin{aligned} \phi_{yy}[n_1, n_2] &= E\{y[n_1]y[n_2]\}. \\ &= E\left\{ \sum_{k=-\infty}^{n_1} h[k]x[n_1-k] \sum_{m=-\infty}^{n_2} h[m]x[n_2-m] \right\}, \qquad n \geq 0 \\ &= \sum_{k=-\infty}^{n_1} \sum_{m=-\infty}^{n_2} h[k]h[m]E\{x[n_1-k]x[n_2-m]\} \\ &= \sum_{k=-\infty}^{n_1} \sum_{m=-\infty}^{n_2} h[k]h[m]\phi_{xx}[n_1-k, n_2-m]. \end{aligned}$$

(c)

$$\lim_{n\to\infty} m_x \sum_{k=-\infty}^{n} h[k] = m_x \sum_{k=-\infty}^{\infty} h[k] = m_y.$$

$$\lim_{n_1,n_2\to\infty} \sum_{k=-\infty}^{n_1} \sum_{m=-\infty}^{n_2} h[k]h[m]\phi_{xx}[n_1-k,n_2-m] = \sum_{k=-\infty}^{\infty} \sum_{m=-\infty}^{\infty} h[k]h[m]\phi_{xx}[k,m].$$

(d)

$$h[n] = a^n u[n]$$

$$E\{y[n]\} = m_x \sum_{k=-\infty}^{\infty} a^n u[n] = \frac{m_x}{1-a}.$$

2.88. (a) No, the system is not linear. In the expression of $y[n]$, we have nonlinear terms such as $x^2[n]$ and divisions by $x[n]$, $x[n-1]$ and $x[n+1]$.

(b) Yes, the system is shift invariant. If we shift the input by n_0, $m_x[n]$ shifts by n_0 as well as $\sigma_x^2[n]$ and $\sigma_s^2[n]$, therefore $y[n]$ shifts by n_0 and the system is thus shift invariant.

(c) If $x[n]$ is bounded, $m_x[n]$ is bounded so is $\sigma_x^2[n]$ and $\sigma_s^2[n]$. As a result, $y[n]$ is bounded and therefore the system is stable.

(d) No, the system is not causal. Values of the output at time n depend on values of the input at time $n+1$ (through $\sigma_x^2[n]$ and $m_x[n]$). Since present values of the ouput depend of future values of the input, the system cannot be causal.

(e) When $\sigma_w^2[n]$ is very large, $\sigma_s^2[n]$ is zero, therefore:

$$y[n] = m_x[n] = \frac{1}{3}\sum_{k=n-1}^{n+1} x[k]$$

which is the average of the previous, present and next value of the input.

When $\sigma_w^2[n]$ is very small (approximately zero), then:

$$y[n] = x[n].$$

$y[n]$ makes sense for these extreme cases, because in very small noise power, the ouput is equal to the input since the noise is negligible. On the other hand, in very large noise power, the input is too noisy and so the output is an average of the input.

2.89. (a)

$$E\{x[n]x[n]\} = \phi_{xx}[0].$$

(b)

$$\begin{aligned}\Phi_{xx}(e^{j\omega}) &= X(e^{j\omega})X^*(e^{j\omega}) \\ &= W(e^{j\omega})H(e^{j\omega})W^*(e^{j\omega})H^*(e^{j\omega}) \\ &= \Phi_{ww}(e^{j\omega})|H(e^{j\omega})|^2 \\ &= \sigma_w^2 \frac{1}{1-\cos(\omega)+1/4}.\end{aligned}$$

(c)

$$\begin{aligned}\phi_{xx}[n] &= \phi_{ww}[n] * h[n] * h[-n] \\ &= \sigma_w^2 \left(\left(\frac{1}{2}\right)^n u[n] * \left(\frac{1}{2}\right)^{-n} u[-n] \right) \\ &= \sigma_w^2 \phi_{hh}[n].\end{aligned}$$

2.90. (a)

$$\begin{aligned}\phi_{yz}[n] &= E\{y[k]z[k-n]\} \\ &= E\left\{ \sum_{r=-\infty}^{\infty} h[r]x[k-r] \sum_{m=-\infty}^{\infty} h[m]v[k-n-m] \right\}\end{aligned}$$

Note that $\phi_{xv}[n] = E\{x[p]v[p-\ell]\}$, therefore:

$$\begin{aligned}\phi_{yz}[n] &= \sum_{r=-\infty}^{\infty} \sum_{m=-\infty}^{\infty} h[r]h[m]E\{x[p]v[p-(n+\ell-s)]\} \\ &= h[-n] * h[n] * \phi_{xv}[n].\end{aligned}$$

$$\Phi_{yz}(e^{j\omega}) = |H(e^{j\omega})|^2 \Phi_{xv}(e^{j\omega}).$$

(b) No, consider $x[n]$ white and

$$\begin{aligned}v[n] &= -x[n] \\ \phi_{xv}[n] &= -\sigma_x^2 \delta[n] \\ \Phi_{xv}(e^{j\omega}) &= -\sigma_x^2.\end{aligned}$$

Noting that $|H(e^{j\omega})|^2$ is positive,

$$\Phi_{yz}(e^{j\omega}) = -\sigma_x^2 |H(e^{j\omega})|^2$$

Hence, the cross power spectrum can be negative.

2.91. (a) Since $f[n] = e[n] - e[n-1]$,

$$H_1(e^{j\omega}) = 1 - e^{-j\omega}.$$

$\Phi_{ff}(e^{j\omega})$ is given by:

$$\begin{aligned}\Phi_{ff}(e^{j\omega}) &= H_1(e^{j\omega})H_1(e^{-j\omega})\Phi_{ee}(e^{j\omega}) \\ &= (1 - e^{-j\omega})(1 - e^{j\omega})\sigma_e^2 \\ &= \sigma_e^2(2 - e^{j\omega} - e^{-j\omega}) \\ &= \sigma_e^2(2 - 2\cos(\omega)).\end{aligned}$$

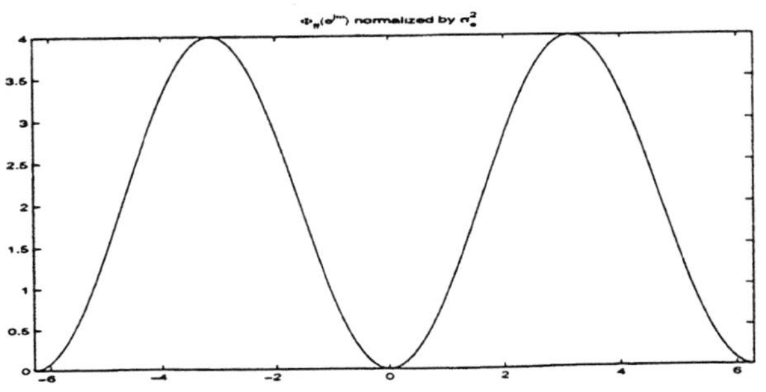

(b) $\phi_{ff}[m]$ is the inverse Fourier transform of $\Phi_{ff}(e^{j\omega})$. Using part (a), we get:

$$\phi_{ff}[m] = \sigma_e^2(2\delta[m] - \delta[m+1] - \delta[m-1]).$$

(c)

$$\begin{aligned}\Phi_{gg}(e^{j\omega}) &= H_2(e^{j\omega})H_2(e^{-j\omega})\Phi_{ff}(e^{j\omega}) \\ &= \begin{cases} \sigma_e^2(2 - 2\cos(\omega)) &, \quad |\omega| < \omega_c \\ 0 &, \quad \omega_c < |\omega| \le \pi. \end{cases}\end{aligned}$$

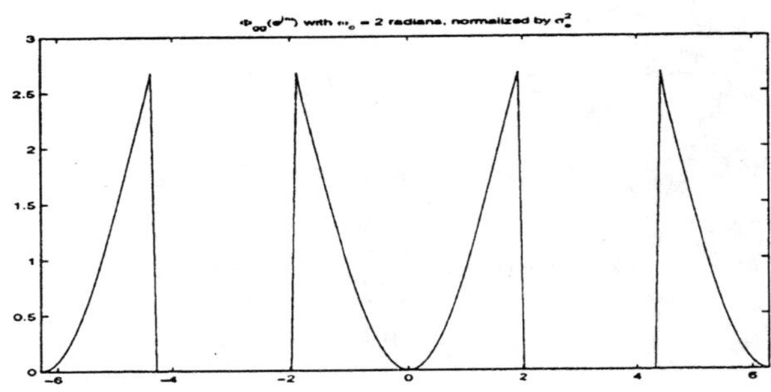

(d)

$$\begin{aligned}\sigma_g^2 &= \frac{1}{2\pi}\int_{-\pi}^{\pi} \Phi_{gg}(e^{j\omega})\, d\omega \\ &= \frac{1}{2\pi}\int_{-\omega_c}^{\omega_c} \sigma_e^2(2 - 2\cos(\omega))\, d\omega \\ &= \frac{2\sigma_e^2}{\pi}(\omega_c - \sin(\omega_c)).\end{aligned}$$

Solutions – Chapter 3

The z-Transform

3.1. (a)

$$\mathcal{Z}\left[\left(\frac{1}{2}\right)^n u[n]\right] = \sum_{n=0}^{\infty}\left(\frac{1}{2}\right)^n z^{-n} = \sum_{n=0}^{\infty}\left(\frac{1}{2z}\right)^n = \frac{1}{1-\frac{1}{2}z^{-1}} \qquad |z| > \frac{1}{2}$$

(b)

$$\begin{aligned}\mathcal{Z}\left[-\left(\frac{1}{2}\right)^n u(-n-1)\right] &= -\sum_{n=-\infty}^{-1}\left(\frac{1}{2}\right)^n z^{-n} = -\sum_{n=1}^{\infty}(2z)^n \\ &= -\frac{2z}{1-2z} = \frac{1}{1-\frac{1}{2}z^{-1}} \qquad |z| < \frac{1}{2}\end{aligned}$$

(c)

$$\mathcal{Z}\left[\left(\frac{1}{2}\right)^n u[-n]\right] = \sum_{n=-\infty}^{0}(2z)^n = \frac{1}{1-2z} \qquad |z| < \frac{1}{2}$$

(d)

$$\mathcal{Z}[\delta[n]] = z^0 = 1 \qquad \text{all } z$$

(e)

$$\mathcal{Z}[\delta[n-1]] = z^{-1} \qquad |z| > 0$$

(f)

$$\mathcal{Z}[\delta[n+1]] = z^{+1} \qquad 0 \le |z| < \infty$$

(g)

$$\mathcal{Z}\left[\left(\frac{1}{2}\right)^n (u[n]-u[n-10])\right] = \sum_{n=0}^{9}\left(\frac{1}{2z}\right)^n = \frac{1-(2z)^{-10}}{1-(2z)^{-1}} \qquad |z| > 0$$

3.2.

$$x[n] = \begin{cases} n, & 0 \le n \le N-1 \\ N, & N \le n \end{cases} = n\,u[n] - (n-N)u[n-N]$$

$$\begin{aligned} n\,x[n] &\Leftrightarrow -z\frac{d}{dz}X(z) \Rightarrow n\,u[n] \Leftrightarrow -z\frac{d}{dz}\frac{1}{1-z^{-1}} \quad |z| > 1 \\ n\,u[n] &\Leftrightarrow \frac{z^{-1}}{(1-z^{-1})^2} \quad |z| > 1 \\ x[n-n_0] &\Leftrightarrow X(z)\cdot z^{-n_0} \Rightarrow (n-N)u[n-N] \Leftrightarrow \frac{z^{-N-1}}{(1-z^{-1})^2} \quad |z| > 1 \end{aligned}$$

therefore

$$X(z) = \frac{z^{-1}-z^{-N-1}}{(1-z^{-1})^2} = \frac{z^{-1}(1-z^{-N})}{(1-z^{-1})^2}$$

3.3. (a)

$$x_a[n] = \alpha^{|n|} \qquad 0 < |\alpha| < 1$$

$$\begin{aligned} X_a(z) &= \sum_{n=-\infty}^{-1} \alpha^{-n} z^{-n} + \sum_{n=0}^{\infty} \alpha^n z^{-n} \\ &= \sum_{n=1}^{\infty} \alpha^n z^n + \sum_{n=0}^{\infty} \alpha^n z^{-n} \\ &= \frac{\alpha z}{1-\alpha z} + \frac{1}{1-\alpha z^{-1}} = \frac{z(1-\alpha^2)}{(1-\alpha z)(z-\alpha)}, \qquad |\alpha| < |z| < \frac{1}{|\alpha|} \end{aligned}$$

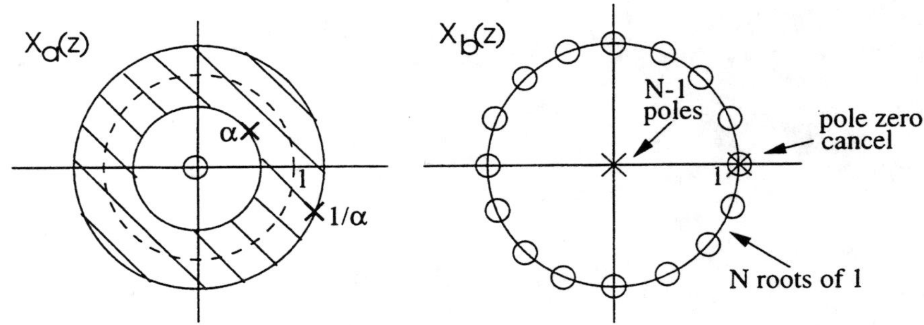

(b)

$$x_b = \begin{cases} 1, & 0 \le n \le N-1 \\ 0, & N \le n \\ 0, & n < 0 \end{cases} \Rightarrow X_b(z) = \sum_{n=0}^{N-1} z^{-n} = \frac{1-z^{-N}}{1-z^{-1}} = \frac{z^N - 1}{z^{N-1}(z-1)} \qquad z \ne 0$$

(c)

$$x_c[n] = x_b[n-1] * x_b[n] \Leftrightarrow X_c(z) = z^{-1} X_b(z) \cdot X_b(z)$$

$$X_c(z) = z^{-1} \left(\frac{z^N - 1}{z^{N-1}(z-1)} \right)^2 = \frac{1}{z^{2N-1}} \left(\frac{z^N - 1}{z-1} \right)^2 \qquad z \ne 0, 1$$

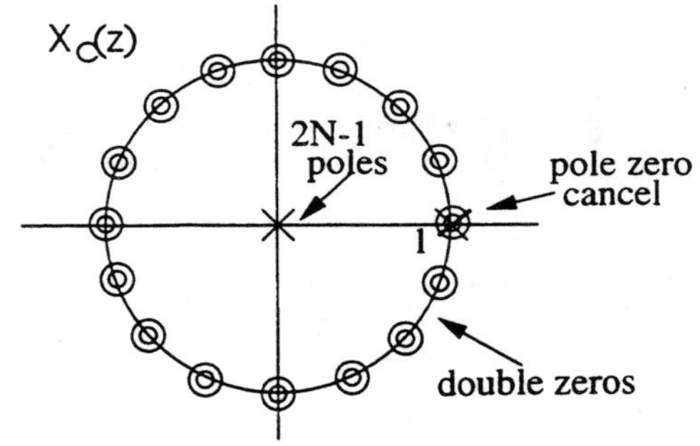

3.4. The pole-zero plot of $X(z)$ appears below.

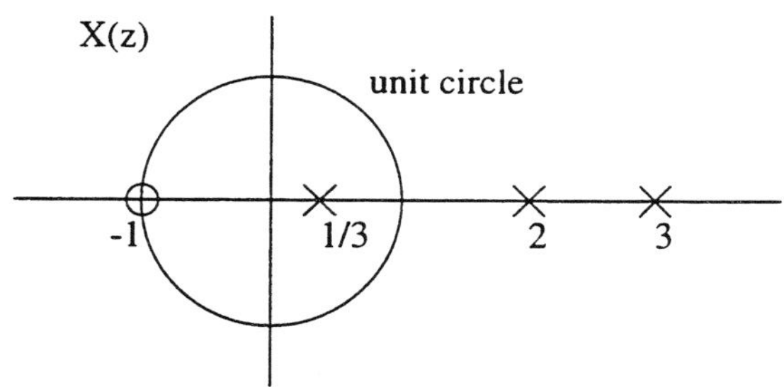

(a) For the Fourier transform of $x[n]$ to exist, the z-transform of $x[n]$ must have an ROC which includes the unit circle, therefore, $|\frac{1}{3}| < |z| < |2|$.
Since this ROC lies outside $\frac{1}{3}$, this pole contributes a right-sided sequence. Since the ROC lies inside 2 and 3, these poles contribute left-sided sequences. The overall $x[n]$ is therefore two-sided.

(b) Two-sided sequences have ROC's which look like washers. There are two possibilities. The ROC's corresponding to these are: $|\frac{1}{3}| < |z| < |2|$ and $|2| < |z| < |3|$.

(c) The ROC must be a connected region. For stability, the ROC must contain the unit circle. For causality the ROC must be outside the outermost pole. These conditions cannot be met by any of the possible ROC's of this pole-zero plot.

3.5.

$$\begin{aligned} X(z) &= (1+2z)(1+3z^{-1})(1-z^{-1}) \\ &= 2z + 5 - 4z^{-1} - 3z^{-2} \\ &= \sum_{n=-\infty}^{\infty} x[n]z^{-n} \end{aligned}$$

Therefore,

$$x[n] = 2\delta[n+1] + 5\delta[n] - 4\delta[n-1] - 3\delta[n-2]$$

3.6. (a)

$$X(z) = \frac{1}{1+\frac{1}{2}z^{-1}} \quad |z| > \frac{1}{2}$$

Partial fractions: one pole $\rightarrow$ inspection, $x[n] = (-\frac{1}{2})^n u[n]$

Long division:

$$\begin{array}{r|llll} & 1 & -\frac{1}{2}z^{-1} & +\frac{1}{4}z^{-2} & +\ \dots \\ \hline 1+\frac{1}{2}z^{-1} & 1 & & & \\ & 1 & +\frac{1}{2}z^{-1} & & \\ \hline & & -\frac{1}{2}z^{-1} & & \\ & & -\frac{1}{2}z^{-1} & -\frac{1}{4}z^{-2} & \\ \hline & & & +\frac{1}{4}z^{-2} & \\ & & & +\frac{1}{4}z^{-2} & +\frac{1}{8}z^{-3} \\ \hline \end{array}$$

$$\Longrightarrow x[n] = \left(-\frac{1}{2}\right)^n u[n]$$

(b)

$$X(z) = \frac{1}{1+\frac{1}{2}z^{-1}} \quad |z| < \frac{1}{2}$$

Partial Fractions: one pole $\rightarrow$ inspection, $x[n] = -(-\frac{1}{2})^n u[-n-1]$

Long division:

$$\begin{array}{r|l}
 & 2z \quad -4z^2 \quad +8z^3 \quad + \ldots \\
\hline
\frac{1}{2}z^{-1}+1 & 1 \\
 & 1 \quad +2z \\
\hline
 & \quad -2z \\
 & \quad -2z \quad -4z^2 \\
\hline
 & \quad\quad +4z^2 \\
 & \quad\quad +4z^2 \quad +8z^3 \\
\hline
\end{array}$$

$$\Longrightarrow x[n] = -\left(-\frac{1}{2}\right)^n u[-n-1]$$

(c)

$$X(z) = \frac{1-\frac{1}{2}z^{-1}}{1+\frac{3}{4}z^{-1}+\frac{1}{8}z^{-2}} \quad |z| > \frac{1}{2}$$

Partial Fractions:

$$\begin{aligned}
X(z) &= \frac{-3}{1+\frac{1}{4}z^{-1}} + \frac{4}{1+\frac{1}{2}z^{-1}} \quad |z| > \frac{1}{2} \\
x[n] &= \left[-3\left(-\frac{1}{4}\right)^n + 4\left(-\frac{1}{2}\right)^n\right] u[n]
\end{aligned}$$

Long division:

$$\begin{array}{r|llll}
 & 1 & +(-\frac{3}{4}-\frac{1}{2})z^{-1} & +(-\frac{3}{16}+1)z^{-2} & + \ldots \\
\hline
1+\frac{3}{4}z^{-1}+\frac{1}{8}z^{-2} & 1 & -\frac{1}{2}z^{-1} & & \\
 & 1 & +\frac{3}{4}z^{-1} & +\frac{1}{8}z^{-2} & \\
\hline
 & & (-\frac{3}{4}-\frac{1}{2})z^{-1} & -\frac{1}{8}z^{-2} & \\
 & & (-\frac{3}{4}-\frac{1}{2})z^{-1} & +\frac{3}{4}(-\frac{3}{4}-\frac{1}{2})z^{-2} & +\frac{1}{8}(-\frac{3}{4}-\frac{1}{2})z^{-3} \\
\hline
 & & & [-\frac{1}{8}+\frac{3}{4}(\frac{3}{4}+\frac{1}{2})]z^{-2} & +\frac{1}{8}(\frac{3}{4}+\frac{1}{2})z^{-3}
\end{array}$$

$$\Longrightarrow x[n] = \left[-3(\left(-\frac{1}{4}\right)^n + \left(-\frac{1}{2}\right)^{n-2}\right] u[n]$$

(d)

$$X(z) = \frac{1-\frac{1}{2}z^{-1}}{1-\frac{1}{4}z^{-2}} \quad |z| > \frac{1}{2}$$

Partial Fractions:

$$\begin{aligned}
X(z) &= \frac{1-\frac{1}{2}z^{-1}}{1-\frac{1}{4}z^{-2}} = \frac{1}{1+\frac{1}{2}z^{-1}} \quad |z| > \frac{1}{2} \\
x[n] &= \left(-\frac{1}{2}\right)^n u[n]
\end{aligned}$$

Long division: see part (i) above.

(e)

$$X(z) = \frac{1 - az^{-1}}{z^{-1} - a} \qquad |z| > |a^{-1}|$$

Partial Fractions:

$$X(z) = -a - \frac{a^{-1}(1 - a^2)}{1 - a^{-1}z^{-1}} \qquad |z| > |a^{-1}|$$

$$x[n] = -a\delta[n] - (1 - a^2)a^{-(n+1)}u[n]$$

Long division:

$$\begin{array}{r|l} & -\frac{1}{a} \quad - (\frac{a^{-1}-a}{a})z^{-1} \quad - (\frac{a^{-1}-a}{a^2})z^{-2} \quad + \ldots \\ \hline -a + z^{-1} & 1 \qquad - az^{-1} \\ & 1 \qquad - az^{-1} \\ \hline & (a^{-1} - a)z^{-1} \qquad \ldots \end{array}$$

$$\Longrightarrow \qquad x[n] = -a\delta[n] - (1 - a^2)a^{-(n+1)}u[n]$$

3.7. (a)

$$x[n] = u[-n-1] + \left(\frac{1}{2}\right)^n u[n]$$

$$\Rightarrow \qquad X(z) = \frac{-1}{1 - z^{-1}} + \frac{1}{1 - \frac{1}{2}z^{-1}} \qquad \frac{1}{2} < |z| < 1$$

Now to find $H(z)$ we simply use $H(z) = Y(z)/X(z)$; i.e.,

$$H(z) = \frac{Y(z)}{X(z)} = \frac{-\frac{1}{2}z^{-1}}{(1 - \frac{1}{2}z^{-1})(1 + z^{-1})} \cdot \frac{(1 - z^{-1})(1 - \frac{1}{2}z^{-1})}{-\frac{1}{2}z^{-1}} = \frac{1 - z^{-1}}{1 + z^{-1}}$$

$H(z)$ causal $\Rightarrow$ ROC $|z| > 1$.

(b) Since one of the poles of $X(z)$, which limited the ROC of $X(z)$ to be less than 1, is cancelled by the zero of $H(z)$, the ROC of $Y(z)$ is the region in the z-plane that satisfies the remaining two constraints $|z| > \frac{1}{2}$ and $|z| > 1$. Hence $Y(z)$ converges on $|z| > 1$.

(c)

$$Y(z) = \frac{-\frac{1}{3}}{1 - \frac{1}{2}z^{-1}} + \frac{\frac{1}{3}}{1 + z^{-1}} \qquad |z| > 1$$

Therefore,

$$y[n] = -\frac{1}{3}\left(\frac{1}{2}\right)^n u[n] + \frac{1}{3}(-1)^n u[n]$$

3.8. The causal system has system function

$$H(z) = \frac{1 - z^{-1}}{1 + \frac{3}{4}z^{-1}}$$

and the input is $x[n] = \left(\frac{1}{3}\right)^n u[n] + u[-n-1]$. Therefore the z-transform of the input is

$$X(z) = \frac{1}{1 - \frac{1}{3}z^{-1}} - \frac{1}{1 - z^{-1}} = \frac{-\frac{2}{3}z^{-1}}{(1 - \frac{1}{3}z^{-1})(1 - z^{-1})} \qquad \frac{1}{3} < |z| < 1$$

(a) $h[n]$ causal $\Rightarrow$

$$h[n] = \left(-\frac{3}{4}\right)^n u[n] - \left(-\frac{3}{4}\right)^{n-1} u[n-1]$$

(b)

$$\begin{aligned} Y(z) &= X(z)H(z) = \frac{-\frac{2}{3}z^{-1}}{(1-\frac{1}{3}z^{-1})(1+\frac{3}{4}z^{-1})} \qquad \frac{3}{4} < |z| \\ &= \frac{-\frac{8}{13}}{1-\frac{1}{3}z^{-1}} + \frac{\frac{8}{13}}{1+\frac{3}{4}z^{-1}} \end{aligned}$$

Therefore the output is

$$y[n] = -\frac{8}{13}\left(\frac{1}{3}\right)^n u[n] + \frac{8}{13}\left(-\frac{3}{4}\right)^n u[n]$$

(c) For $h[n]$ to be causal the ROC of $H(z)$ must be $\frac{3}{4} < |z|$ which includes the unit circle. Therefore, $h[n]$ absolutely summable.

3.9.

$$H(z) = \frac{1+z^{-1}}{(1-\frac{1}{2}z^{-1})(1+\frac{1}{4}z^{-1})} = \frac{2}{(1-\frac{1}{2}z^{-1})} - \frac{1}{(1+\frac{1}{4}z^{-1})}$$

(a) $h[n]$ causal $\Rightarrow$ ROC outside $|z| = \frac{1}{2} \Rightarrow |z| > \frac{1}{2}$.

(b) ROC includes $|z| = 1 \Rightarrow$ stable.

(c)

$$\begin{aligned} y[n] &= -\frac{1}{3}\left(-\frac{1}{4}\right)^n u[n] - \frac{4}{3}(2)^n u[-n-1] \\ Y(z) &= \frac{-\frac{1}{3}}{1+\frac{1}{4}z^{-1}} + \frac{\frac{4}{3}}{1-2z^{-1}} \\ &= \frac{1+z^{-1}}{(1+\frac{1}{4}z^{-1})(1-2z^{-1})} \qquad \frac{1}{4} < |z| < 2 \\ X(z) &= \frac{Y(z)}{H(z)} = \frac{(1-\frac{1}{2}z^{-1})}{(1-2z^{-1})} \qquad |z| < 2 \\ x[n] &= -(2)^n u[-n-1] + \frac{1}{2}(2)^{n-1}u[-n] \end{aligned}$$

(d)

$$h[n] = 2\left(\frac{1}{2}\right)^n u[n] - \left(-\frac{1}{4}\right)^n u[n]$$

3.10. (a)

$$\begin{aligned} x[n] &= \left(\frac{1}{2}\right)^n u[n-10] + \left(\frac{3}{4}\right)^n u[n-10] \\ &= \left(\frac{1}{2}\right)^n u[n] + \left(\frac{3}{4}\right)^n u[n] \\ &\quad - \left[\left(\left(\frac{1}{2}\right)^n + \left(\frac{3}{4}\right)^n\right)(u[n] - u[n-11])\right] \end{aligned}$$

The last term is finite length and converges everywhere except at $z = 0$. Therefore, ROC outside largest pole $\frac{3}{4} < |z|$.

(b)

$$x[n] = \begin{cases} 1, & -10 \le n \le 10 \\ 0, & \text{otherwise} \end{cases}$$

Finite length but has positive and negative powers at z in its $X(z)$. Therefore the ROC is $0 < |z| < \infty$.

(c)

$$\begin{aligned} x[n] &= 2^n u[-n] = \left(\frac{1}{2}\right)^{-n} u[-n] \\ x[-n] &\leftrightarrow X(1/z) \\ \left(\frac{1}{2}\right)^{n} u[n] &\Rightarrow \text{ROC is} \quad |z| > \frac{1}{2} \\ \left(\frac{1}{2}\right)^{-n} u[-n] &\Rightarrow \text{ROC is} \quad |z| < 2 \end{aligned}$$

(d)

$$x[n] = \left[\left(\frac{1}{4}\right)^{n+4} - (e^{j\pi/3})^n\right] u[n-1]$$

$x[n]$ is right-sided, so its ROC extends outward from the outermost pole $e^{j\pi/3}$. But since it is non-zero at $n = -1$, the ROC does not include ∞. So the ROC is $1 < |z| < \infty$.

(e)

$$\begin{aligned} x[n] &= u[n+10] - u[n+5] \\ &= \begin{cases} 1, & -10 \le n \le -6 \\ 0, & \text{otherwise} \end{cases} \end{aligned}$$

$x[n]$ is finite-length and has only positive powers of z in its $X(z)$. So the ROC is $|z| < \infty$.

(f)

$$x[n] = \left(\frac{1}{2}\right)^{n-1} u[n] + (2+3j)^{n-2} u[-n-1]$$

$x[n]$ is two-sided, with two poles. Its ROC is the ring between the two poles: $\frac{1}{2} < |z| < \left|\frac{1}{2+3j}\right|$, or $\frac{1}{2} < |z| < \frac{1}{\sqrt{13}}$.

3.11.

$$x[n] \text{ causal} \Rightarrow X(z) = \sum_{n=0}^{\infty} x[n] z^{-n}$$

which means this summation will include *no* positive powers of z. This means that the closed form of $X(z)$ must converge at $z = \infty$, i.e., $z = \infty$ must be in the ROC of $X(z)$, or $\lim_{z\to\infty} X(z) \neq \infty$.

(a)

$$\lim_{z\to\infty} \frac{(1-z^{-1})^2}{(1-\frac{1}{2}z^{-1})} = 1 \qquad \text{could be causal}$$

(b)

$$\lim_{z\to\infty} \frac{(z-1)^2}{(z-\frac{1}{2})} = \infty \qquad \text{could not be causal}$$

(c)

$$\lim_{z\to\infty} \frac{(z-\frac{1}{4})^5}{(z-\frac{1}{2})^6} = 0 \qquad \text{could be causal}$$

(d)

$$\lim_{z\to\infty} \frac{(z-\frac{1}{4})^6}{(z-\frac{1}{2})^5} = \infty \qquad \text{could not be causal}$$

3.12. (a)

$$X_1(z) = \frac{1-\frac{1}{2}z^{-1}}{1+2z^{-1}}$$

The pole is at -2, and the zero is at 1/2.

(b)

$$X_2(z) = \frac{1-\frac{1}{3}z^{-1}}{(1+\frac{1}{2}z^{-1})(1-\frac{2}{3}z^{-1})}$$

The poles are at -1/2 and 2/3, and the zero is at 1/3. Since $x_2[n]$ is causal, the ROC is extends from the outermost pole: $|z| > 2/3$.

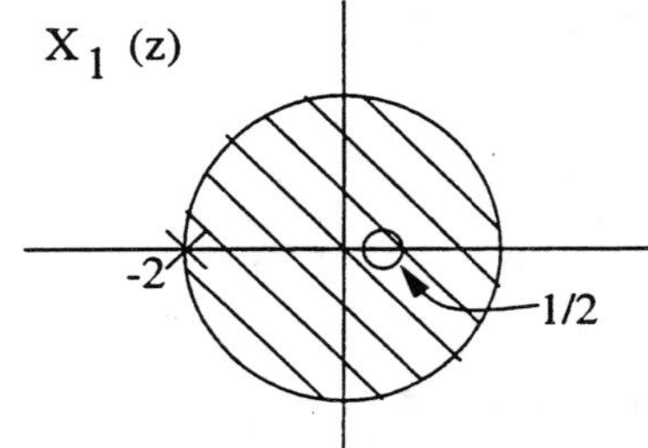

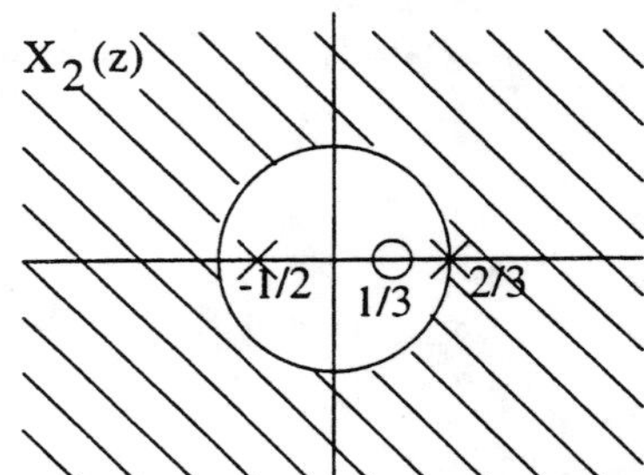

(c)

$$X_3(z) = \frac{1+z^{-1}-2z^{-2}}{1-\frac{13}{6}z^{-1}+z^{-2}}$$

The poles are at 3/2 and 2/3, and the zeros are at 1 and -2. Since $x_3[n]$ is absolutely summable, the ROC must include the unit circle: $2/3 < |z| < 3/2$.

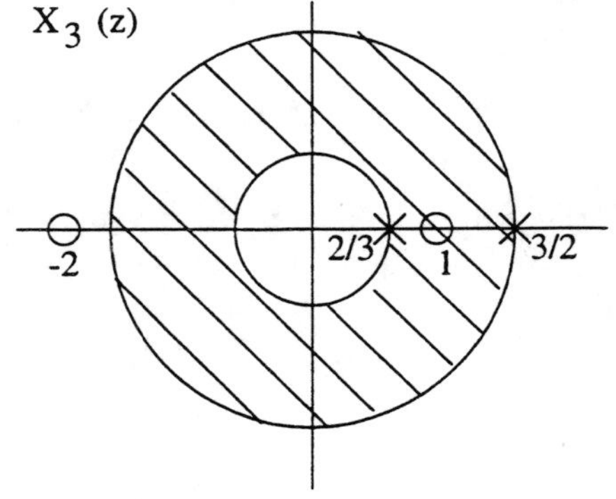

3.13.

$$\begin{aligned} G(z) &= \sin(z^{-1})(1+3z^{-2}+2z^{-4}) \\ &= (z^{-1} - \frac{z^{-3}}{3!} + \frac{z^{-5}}{5!} - \frac{z^{-7}}{7!})(1+3z^{-2}+2z^{-4}) \\ &= \sum_n g[n]z^{-n} \end{aligned}$$

$g[11]$ is simply the coefficient in front of z^{-11} in this power series expansion of $G(z)$:

$$g[11] = -\frac{1}{11!} + \frac{3}{9!} - \frac{2}{11!}.$$

3.14.

$$\begin{aligned} H(z) &= \frac{1}{1-\frac{1}{4}z^{-2}} \\ &= \frac{1}{(1-\frac{1}{2}z^{-1})(1+\frac{1}{2}z^{-1})} \\ &= \frac{0.5}{1-\frac{1}{2}z^{-1}} + \frac{0.5}{1+\frac{1}{2}z^{-1}} \end{aligned}$$

Taking the inverse z-Transform:

$$h[n] = \frac{1}{2}(\frac{1}{2})^n u[n] + \frac{1}{2}(-\frac{1}{2})^n u[n]$$

So,

$$A_1 = \frac{1}{2}; \qquad \alpha_1 = \frac{1}{2}; \qquad A_2 = \frac{1}{2}; \qquad \alpha_2 = -\frac{1}{2};$$

3.15. Using long division, we get

$$\begin{aligned} H(z) &= \frac{1-\frac{1}{1024}z^{-10}}{1-\frac{1}{2}z^{-1}} \\ &= \sum_{n=0}^{n=9} (\frac{1}{2})^n z^{-n} \end{aligned}$$

Taking the inverse z-transform,

$$h[n] = \begin{cases} (\frac{1}{2})^n, & n = 0, 1, 2, \ldots, 9 \\ 0, & \text{otherwise} \end{cases}$$

Since $h[n]$ is 0 for $n < 0$, the system is causal.

3.16. (a) To determine $H(z)$, we first find $X(z)$ and $Y(z)$:

$$\begin{aligned} X(z) &= \frac{1}{1-\frac{1}{3}z^{-1}} - \frac{1}{1-2z^{-1}} \\ &= \frac{-\frac{5}{3}z^{-1}}{(1-\frac{1}{3}z^{-1})(1-2z^{-1})}, \qquad \frac{1}{3} < |z| < 2 \end{aligned}$$

$$
\begin{aligned}
Y(z) &= \frac{5}{1-\frac{1}{3}z^{-1}} - \frac{5}{1-\frac{2}{3}z^{-1}} \\
&= \frac{-\frac{5}{3}z^{-1}}{(1-\frac{1}{3}z^{-1})(1-\frac{2}{3}z^{-1})}, \qquad |z| > \frac{2}{3}
\end{aligned}
$$

Now

$$
\begin{aligned}
H(z) &= \frac{Y(z)}{X(z)} \\
&= \frac{1-2z^{-1}}{1-\frac{2}{3}z^{-1}} \qquad |z| > \frac{2}{3}
\end{aligned}
$$

The pole-zero plot of $H(z)$ is plotted below.

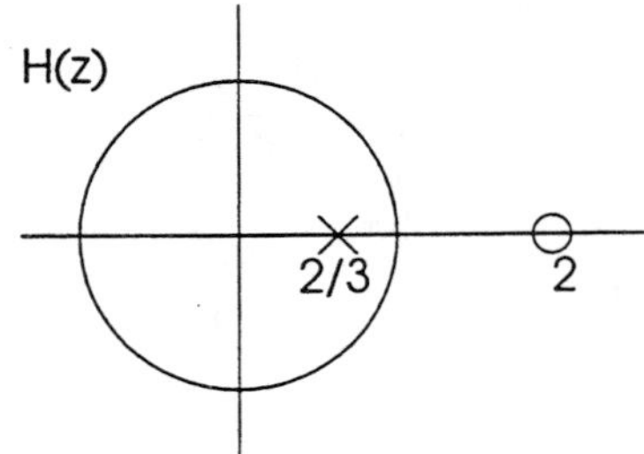

(b) Taking the inverse z-transform of $H(z)$, we get

$$
\begin{aligned}
h[n] &= (\frac{2}{3})^n u[n] - 2(\frac{2}{3})^{n-1} u[n-1] \\
&= (\frac{2}{3})^n (u[n] - 3u[n-1])
\end{aligned}
$$

(c) Since

$$
H(z) = \frac{Y(z)}{X(z)} = \frac{1-2z^{-1}}{1-\frac{2}{3}z^{-1}},
$$

we can write

$$
Y(z)(1-\frac{2}{3}z^{-1}) = X(z)(1-2z^{-1}),
$$

whose inverse z-transform leads to

$$
y[n] - \frac{2}{3}y[n-1] = x[n] - 2x[n-1]
$$

(d) The system is stable because the ROC includes the unit circle. It is also causal since the impulse response $h[n] = 0$ for $n < 0$.

3.17. We solve this problem by finding the system function $H(z)$ of the system, and then looking at the different impulse responses which can result from our choice of the ROC.

Taking the z-transform of the difference equation, we get

$$
Y(z)(1-\frac{5}{2}z^{-1}+z^{-2}) = X(z)(1-z^{-1}),
$$

and thus

$$
H(z) = \frac{Y(z)}{X(z)} = \frac{1-z^{-1}}{1-\frac{5}{2}z^{-1}+z^{-2}}
$$

$$\begin{aligned} &= \frac{1-z^{-1}}{(1-2z^{-1})(1-\frac{1}{2}z^{-1})} \\ &= \frac{2/3}{1-2z^{-1}} + \frac{1/3}{1-\frac{1}{2}z^{-1}} \end{aligned}$$

If the ROC is

(a) $|z| < \frac{1}{2}$:

$$h[n] = -\frac{2}{3}2^n u[-n-1] - \frac{1}{3}(\frac{1}{2})^n u[-n-1]$$
$$\Longrightarrow \quad h[0] = 0.$$

(b) $\frac{1}{2} < |z| < 2$:

$$h[n] = -\frac{2}{3}2^n u[-n-1] + \frac{1}{3}(\frac{1}{2})^n u[n]$$
$$\Longrightarrow \quad h[0] = \frac{1}{3}.$$

(c) $|z| > 2$:

$$h[n] = \frac{2}{3}2^n u[n] + \frac{1}{3}(\frac{1}{2})^n u[n]$$
$$\Longrightarrow \quad h[0] = 1.$$

(d) $|z| > 2$ or $|z| < \frac{1}{2}$:

$$h[n] = \frac{2}{3}2^n u[n] - \frac{1}{3}(\frac{1}{2})^n u[n-1]$$
$$\Longrightarrow \quad h[0] = \frac{2}{3}.$$

3.18. (a)

$$\begin{aligned} H(z) &= \frac{1+2^z-1+z^{-2}}{(1+\frac{1}{2}z^{-1})(1-z^{-1})} \\ &= -2 + \frac{\frac{1}{3}}{1+\frac{1}{2}z^{-1}} + \frac{\frac{8}{3}}{1-z^{-1}} \end{aligned}$$

Taking the inverse z-transform:

$$h[n] = -2\delta[n] + \frac{1}{3}(-\frac{1}{2})^n u[n] + \frac{8}{3}u[n].$$

(b) We use the eigenfunction property of the input:

$$y[n] = H(e^{j\pi/2})x[n],$$

where

$$\begin{aligned} H(e^{j\pi/2}) &= -2 + \frac{\frac{1}{3}}{1+\frac{1}{2}e^{-j\pi/2}} + \frac{\frac{8}{3}}{1-e^{-j\pi/2}} \\ &= -2 + \frac{\frac{1}{3}}{1-\frac{1}{2}j} + \frac{\frac{8}{3}}{1+j} \\ &= \frac{-2j}{\frac{3}{2}+\frac{j}{2}}. \end{aligned}$$

Putting it together,

$$y[n] = \frac{-2j}{\frac{3}{2}+\frac{j}{2}} e^{j(\pi/2)n}.$$

3.19. The ROC($Y(z)$) includes the intersection of ROC($H(z)$) and ROC($X(z)$).

(a)

$$Y(z) = \frac{1}{(1+\frac{1}{2}z^{-1})(1-\frac{1}{4}z^{-1})}$$

The intersection of ROCs of $H(z)$ and $X(z)$ is $|z| > \frac{1}{2}$. So the ROC of $Y(z)$ is $|z| > \frac{1}{2}$.

(b) The ROC of $Y(z)$ is exactly the intersection of ROCs of $H(z)$ and $X(z)$: $\frac{1}{3} < |z| < 2$.

(c)

$$Y(z) = \frac{1}{(1-\frac{1}{5}z^{-1})(1+\frac{1}{3}z^{-1})}$$

The ROC is $|z| > \frac{1}{3}$.

3.20. In both cases, the ROC of $H(z)$ has to be chosen such that ROC($Y(z)$) includes the intersection of ROC($H(z)$) and ROC($X(z)$).

(a)

$$H(z) = \frac{1-\frac{3}{4}z^{-1}}{1+\frac{2}{3}z^{-1}}$$

The ROC is $|z| > \frac{2}{3}$.

(b)

$$H(z) = \frac{1}{1-\frac{1}{6}z^{-1}}$$

The ROC is $|z| > \frac{1}{6}$.

3.21. (a)

$$\begin{aligned}
y[n] &= 0 \qquad n < 0 \\
y[n] &= \sum_{k=0}^{n} x[k]h[n-k] = \sum_{k=0}^{n} a^{n-k} = a^n \frac{1-a^{-(n+1)}}{1-a^{-1}} = \frac{1-a^{n+1}}{1-a} \qquad 0 \le n < N-1 \\
y[n] &= \sum_{k=0}^{N-1} x[k]h[n-k] = \sum_{k=0}^{N-1} a^{n-k} = a^n \frac{1-a^{-N}}{1-a^{-1}} = a^{n+1}\frac{1-a^{-N}}{a-1}, \qquad n \ge N
\end{aligned}$$

(b)

$$\begin{aligned}
H(z) &= \sum_{n=0}^{\infty} a^n z^{-n} = \frac{1}{1-az^{-1}} \qquad |z| > |a| \\
X(z) &= \sum_{n=0}^{N-1} z^{-n} = \frac{1-z^{-N}}{1-z^{-1}} \qquad |z| > 0
\end{aligned}$$

Therefore,

$$Y(z) = \frac{1-z^{-N}}{(1-az^{-1})(1-z^{-1})} = \frac{1}{(1-az^{-1})(1-z^{-1})} - \frac{z^{-N}}{(1-az^{-1})(1-z^{-1})} \qquad |z| > |a|$$

Now,

$$\frac{1}{(1-az^{-1})(1-z^{-1})} = \frac{\frac{1}{1-a^{-1}}}{1-az^{-1}} + \frac{\frac{1}{1-a}}{1-z^{-1}} = \left(\frac{1}{1-a}\right)\left(\frac{1}{1-z^{-1}} - \frac{a}{1-az^{-1}}\right)$$

So

$$\begin{aligned}
y[n] &= \left(\frac{1}{1-a}\right)\left[u[n] - a^{n+1}u[n] - u[n-N] - a^{n-N+1}u[n-N]\right] \\
&= \frac{1-a^{n+1}}{1-a}u[n] - \frac{1-a^{n-N+1}}{1-a}u[n-N]
\end{aligned}$$

$$y[n] = \begin{cases} 0 & n < 0 \\ \frac{1-a^{n+1}}{1-a} & 0 \le n \le N-1 \\ a^{n+1}\left(\frac{1-a^{-N}}{a-1}\right) & n \ge N \end{cases}$$

3.22. (a)

$$\begin{aligned}
y[n] &= \sum_{k=-\infty}^{\infty} h[k]x[n-k] \\
&= \sum_{k=-\infty}^{\infty} \left(3\left(-\frac{1}{3}\right)^k u[k]\right) u[n-k] \\
&= \sum_{k=0}^{n} 3\left(-\frac{1}{3}\right)^k \\
&= \begin{cases} \frac{9}{4}\left(1-\left(-\frac{1}{3}\right)^{n+1}\right), & n \ge 0 \\ 0, & \text{otherwise} \end{cases}
\end{aligned}$$

(b)

$$\begin{aligned}
Y(z) &= H(z)X(z) \\
&= \frac{3}{1+\frac{1}{3}z^{-1}}\frac{1}{1-z^{-1}} \\
&= \frac{\frac{3}{4}}{1+\frac{1}{3}z^{-1}} + \frac{\frac{9}{4}}{1-z^{-1}} \\
y[n] &= \frac{3}{4}\left(-\frac{1}{3}\right)^n u[n] + \frac{9}{4}u[n] \\
&= \frac{9}{4}\left(1+\frac{1}{3}\left(-\frac{1}{3}\right)^n\right)u[n] \\
&= \frac{9}{4}\left(1-\left(-\frac{1}{3}\right)^{n+1}\right)u[n]
\end{aligned}$$

3.23. (a)

$$\begin{aligned}
H(z) &= \frac{1-\frac{1}{2}z^{-2}}{(1-\frac{1}{2}z^{-1})(1-\frac{1}{4}z^{-1})} \\
&= -4 + \frac{5+\frac{7}{2}z^{-1}}{1-\frac{3}{4}z^{-1}+\frac{1}{8}z^{-2}} \\
&= -4 - \frac{2}{1-\frac{1}{2}z^{-1}} + \frac{7}{1-\frac{1}{4}z^{-1}} \\
h[n] &= -4\delta[n] - 2\left(\frac{1}{2}\right)^n u[n] + 7\left(\frac{1}{4}\right)^n u[n]
\end{aligned}$$

(b)

$$y[n] - \frac{3}{4}y[n-1] + \frac{1}{8}y[n-2] = x[n] - \frac{1}{2}x[n-2]$$

3.24. The plots of the sequences are shown below.

(a) Let

$$a[n] = \sum_{k=-\infty}^{\infty} \delta[n-4k],$$

Then

$$A(z) = \sum_{k=-\infty}^{\infty} z^{-4n}$$

(b)

$$\begin{aligned}
b[n] &= \frac{1}{2}\left[e^{j\pi n} + \cos\left(\frac{\pi}{2}n\right) + \sin\left(\frac{\pi}{2} + 2\pi n\right)\right]u[n] \\
&= \frac{1}{2}\left[(-1)^n + \cos\left(\frac{\pi}{2}n\right) + 1\right]u[n] \\
&= \begin{cases} \frac{3}{2}, & n = 4k,\ k \geq 0 \\ \frac{1}{2}, & n = 4k+2,\ k \geq 0 \\ 0, & \text{otherwise} \end{cases} \\
B(z) &= \sum_{n=0}^{\infty} \frac{3}{2} z^{-4n} + \sum_{n=0}^{\infty} \frac{1}{2} z^{-(4n+2)} \\
&= \frac{3/2 + 1/2z^{-2}}{1 - z^{-4}}, \qquad |z| > 1
\end{aligned}$$

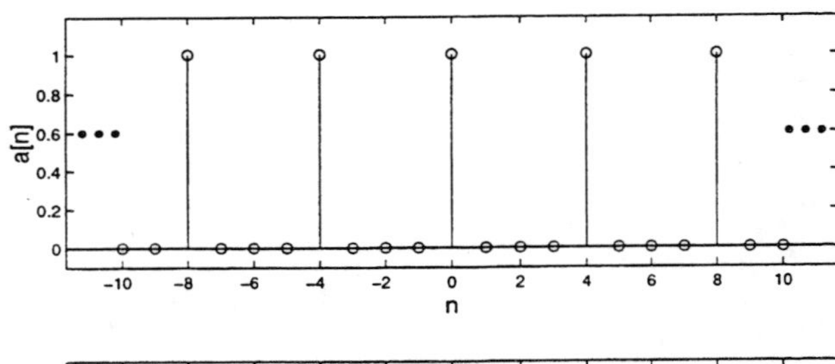

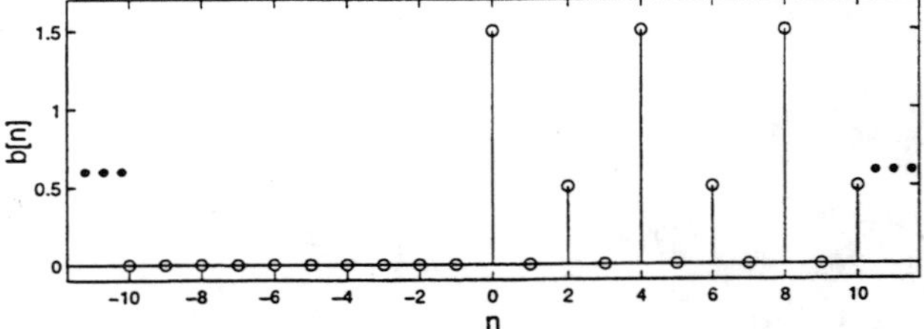

3.25.

$$X(z) = \frac{z^2}{(z-a)(z-b)} = \frac{z^2}{z^2 - (a+b)z + ab}$$

Obtain a proper fraction:

$$\begin{array}{r|l} & 1 \\ z^2-(a+b)z+ab & z^2 \\ & \underline{z^2 \quad -(a+b)z \quad +ab} \\ & \quad (a+b)z \quad -ab \end{array}$$

$$\begin{aligned} X(z) &= 1+\frac{(a+b)z-ab}{(z-a)(z-b)} = 1+\frac{\frac{(a+b)a-ab}{a-b}}{z-a}+\frac{\frac{(a+b)b-ab}{b-a}}{z-b} \\ &= 1+\frac{\frac{a^2}{a-b}}{z-a}-\frac{\frac{b^2}{a-b}}{z-b} = 1+\frac{1}{a-b}\left(\frac{a^2z^{-1}}{1-az^{-1}}-\frac{b^2z^{-1}}{1-bz^{-1}}\right) \\ x[n] &= \delta[n]+\frac{a^2}{a-b}a^{n-1}u[n-1]-\frac{b^2}{a-b}b^{n-1}u[n-1] \\ &= \delta[n]+\left(\frac{1}{a-b}\right)(a^{n+1}-b^{n+1})u[n-1] \end{aligned}$$

3.26. (a) $x[n]$ is right-sided and

$$X(z)=\frac{1-\frac{1}{3}z^{-1}}{1+\frac{1}{3}z^{-1}}$$

Long division:

$$\begin{array}{r|l} & 1 \quad -\frac{2}{3}z^{-1} \quad +\frac{2}{9}z^{-2} \quad +\ldots \\ 1+\frac{1}{3}z^{-1} & 1 \quad -\frac{1}{3}z^{-1} \\ & \underline{1 \quad -\frac{1}{3}z^{-1}} \\ & \quad -\frac{2}{3}z^{-1} \\ & \underline{\quad -\frac{2}{3}z^{-1} \quad -\frac{2}{9}z^{-2}} \\ & \quad\quad +\frac{2}{9}z^{-2} \end{array}$$

Therefore, $x[n]=2(-\frac{1}{3})^n u[n]-\delta[n]$

(b)

$$X(z)=\frac{3}{z-\frac{1}{4}-\frac{1}{8}z^{-1}}=\frac{3z^{-1}}{(1-\frac{1}{2}z^{-1})(1+\frac{1}{4}z^{-1})}=\frac{4}{1-\frac{1}{2}z^{-1}}-\frac{4}{1-\frac{1}{4}z^{-1}}$$

Poles at $\frac{1}{2}$, and $-\frac{1}{4}$. $x[n]$ stable, $\Rightarrow |z|>\frac{1}{2}$ $\Rightarrow$ causal.
Therefore,

$$x[n]=4\left(\frac{1}{2}\right)^n u[n]-4\left(-\frac{1}{4}\right)^n u[n]$$

(c)

$$\begin{aligned} X(z) &= \ln(1-4z) \qquad |z|<\frac{1}{4} \\ &= -\sum_{i=1}^{\infty}\frac{(4z)^i}{i} = -\sum_{\ell=-\infty}^{-1}\frac{1}{\ell}(4z)^{-\ell} \end{aligned}$$

Therefore,

$$x[n]=\frac{1}{n}(4)^{-n}u[-n-1]$$

(d)

$$X(z) = \frac{1}{1 - \frac{1}{3}z^{-3}} \qquad |z| > (3)^{-\frac{1}{3}} \Rightarrow \text{causal}$$

By long division:

$$\begin{array}{r|l} & 1 \quad + \frac{1}{3}z^{-3} \quad + \frac{1}{9}z^{-6} \quad + \ldots \\ \hline 1 - \frac{1}{3}z^{-3} & 1 \\ & 1 \quad - \frac{1}{3}z^{-3} \\ \hline & \quad + \frac{1}{3}z^{-3} \\ & \quad + \frac{1}{3}z^{-3} \quad - \frac{1}{9}z^{-6} \\ \hline & \quad\quad + \frac{1}{9}z^{-6} \end{array}$$

$$\Longrightarrow \qquad x[n] = \begin{cases} \left(\frac{1}{3}\right)^{\frac{n}{3}}, & n = 0, 3, 6, \ldots \\ 0, & \text{otherwise} \end{cases}$$

3.27. (a)

$$\begin{aligned} X(z) &= \frac{1}{(1 + \frac{1}{2}z^{-1})^2(1 - 2z^{-1})(1 - 3z^{-1})} \qquad \frac{1}{2} < |z| < 2 \\ &= \frac{\frac{1}{35}}{(1 + \frac{1}{2}z^{-2})^2} + \frac{\frac{88}{1225}}{(1 + \frac{1}{2}z^{-1})} - \frac{\frac{1568}{1225}}{(1 - 2z^{-1})} + \frac{\frac{2700}{1225}}{(1 - 3z^{-1})} \end{aligned}$$

Therefore,

$$x[n] = \frac{1}{35}(n+1)\left(\frac{-1}{2}\right)^{n+1} u[n+1] + \frac{58}{(35)^2}\left(\frac{-1}{2}\right)^n u[n] + \frac{1568}{(35)^2}(2)^n u[-n-1] - \frac{2700}{(35)^2}(3)^n u[-n-1]$$

(b)

$$X(z) = e^{z^{-1}} = 1 + z^{-1} + \frac{z^{-2}}{2!} + \frac{z^{-3}}{3!} + \frac{z^{-4}}{4!} + \ldots$$

Therefore, $x[n] = \frac{1}{n!}u[n]$.

(c)

$$X(z) = \frac{z^3 - 2z}{z - 2} = z^2 + 2z + \frac{2}{1 - 2z^{-1}} \qquad |z| < 2$$

Therefore,

$$x[n] = \delta[n + 2] + 2\delta[n + 1] - 2(2)^n u[-n - 1]$$

3.28. (a)

$$nx[n] \Leftrightarrow -z\frac{d}{dx}X(z)$$

$$x[n - n_0] \Leftrightarrow z^{-n_0}X(z)$$

$$X(z) = \frac{3z^{-3}}{(1 - \frac{1}{4}z^{-1})^2} = 12z^{-2}\left[-z\frac{d}{dz}\left(\frac{1}{1 - \frac{1}{4}z^{-1}}\right)\right]$$

$x[n]$ is left-sided. Therefore, $X(z)$ corresponds to:

$$x[n] = -12(n - 2)\left(\frac{1}{4}\right)^{n-2} u[-n + 1]$$

(b)

$$X(z) = \sin(z) = \sum_{k=0}^{\infty} \frac{(-1)^k}{(2k+1)!} z^{2k+1} \qquad \text{ROC includes } |z| = 1$$

Therefore,

$$x[n] = \sum_{k=0}^{\infty} \frac{(-1)^k}{(2k+1)!} \delta[n + 2k + 1]$$

Which is stable.

(c)

$$X(z) = \frac{z^7 - 2}{1 - z^{-7}} = z^7 - \frac{1}{1 - z^{-7}} \qquad |z| > 1$$

$$X(z) = z^7 - \sum_{n=0}^{\infty} z^{-7n}$$

Therefore,

$$x[n] = \delta[n+7] - \sum_{n=0}^{\infty} \delta[n - 7k]$$

3.29.

$$X(z) = e^z + e^{1/z} \quad z \neq 0$$

$$X(z) = \sum_{n=0}^{\infty} \frac{1}{n!} z^n + \sum_{n=0}^{\infty} \frac{1}{n!} \left(\frac{1}{z}\right)^n = \sum_{n=-\infty}^{0} \frac{1}{(-n)!} z^{-n} + \sum_{n=0}^{\infty} \frac{1}{n!} z^{-n} \Longrightarrow x[n] = \frac{1}{|n|!} + \delta[n]$$

3.30.

$$X(z) = \log_2(\frac{1}{2} - z) \qquad |z| < \frac{1}{2}$$

(a)

$$X(z) = \log(1 - 2z) = -\sum_{i=1}^{\infty} \frac{(2z)^i}{i} = -\sum_{\ell=-\infty}^{-1} \frac{1}{-\ell} (2z)^{-\ell} = \sum_{\ell=-\infty}^{1} \frac{1}{\ell} \left(\frac{1}{2}\right)^{\ell} z^{-\ell}$$

Therefore,

$$x[n] = \frac{1}{n} \left(\frac{1}{2}\right)^n u[-n-1]$$

(b)

$$\begin{aligned} nx[n] \quad &\Leftrightarrow \quad -z\frac{d}{dz}\log(1-2z) = -z\left(\frac{1}{1-2z}\right)(-2) = z^{-1}\left(\frac{-1}{1-\frac{1}{2}z^{-1}}\right), \qquad |z| < \frac{1}{2} \\ nx[n] \quad &= \quad \left(\frac{1}{2}\right)^n u[-n-1] \\ x[n] \quad &= \quad \frac{1}{n}\left(\frac{1}{2}\right)^n u[-n-1] \end{aligned}$$

3.31. (a)

$$
\begin{aligned}
x[n] &= a^n u[n] + b^n u[n] + c^n u[-n-1] & |a| < |b| < |c| \\
X(z) &= \frac{1}{1-az^{-1}} + \frac{1}{1-bz^{-1}} - \frac{1}{1-cz^{-1}} & |b| < |z| < |c| \\
X(z) &= \frac{1 - 2cz^{-1} + (bc + ac - ab)z^{-2}}{(1-az^{-1})(1-bz^{-1})(1-cz^{-1})} & |b| < |z| < |c|
\end{aligned}
$$

Poles: a, b, c,
Zeros: z_1, z_2, ∞ where z_1 and z_2 are roots of numerator quadratic.

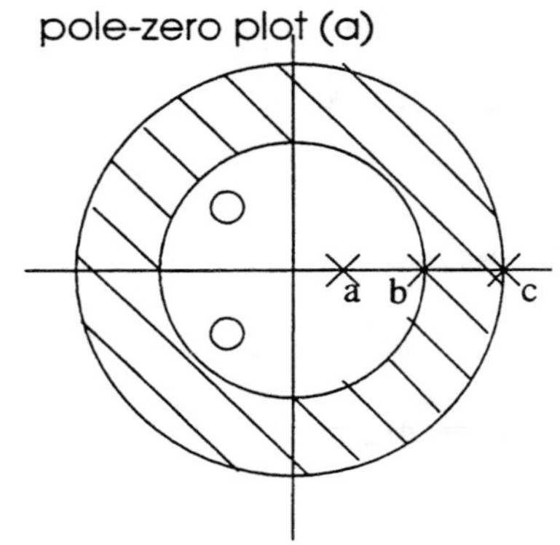

(b)

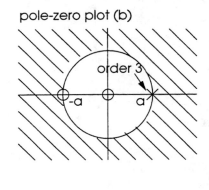

$$
\begin{aligned}
x[n] &= n^2 a^n u[n] \\
x_1[n] &= a^n u[n] \Leftrightarrow X_1(z) = \frac{1}{1-az^{-1}} \quad |z| > a \\
x_2[n] = nx_1[n] &= na^n u[n] \Leftrightarrow X_2(z) = -z\frac{d}{dz}X_1(z) = \frac{az^{-1}}{(1-az^{-1})^2} \quad |z| > a \\
x[n] = nx_2[n] &= n^2 a^n u[n] \Leftrightarrow -z\frac{d}{dz}X_2(z) = -z\frac{d}{dz}\left(\frac{az^{-1}}{(1-az^{-1})^2}\right) \quad |z| > a \\
X(z) &= \frac{-az^{-1}(1+az^{-1})}{(1-az^{-1})^3} \quad |z| > a
\end{aligned}
$$

(c)

$$
\begin{aligned}
x[n] &= e^{n^4}\left(\cos\frac{\pi}{12}n\right)u[n] - e^{n^4}\left(\cos\frac{\pi}{12}n\right)u[n-1] \\
&= e^{n^4}\left(\cos\frac{\pi}{12}n\right)(u[n] - u[n-1]) = \delta[n]
\end{aligned}
$$

Therefore, $X(z) = 1$ for all $|z|$.

3.32. From the pole-zero diagram

$$
X(z) = \frac{z}{(z^2 - z + \frac{1}{2})(z + \frac{3}{4})} \qquad |z| > \frac{3}{4}
$$

$$
\begin{aligned}
y[n] &= x[-n+3] = x[-(n-3)] \\
&\Rightarrow \; Y(z) = z^{-3}X(z^{-1}) = \frac{z^{-3}z^{-1}}{(z^{-2} - z^{-1} + \frac{1}{2})(z^{-1} + \frac{3}{4})} \\
&= \frac{8/3}{z(2 - 2z + z^2)(\frac{4}{3} + z)}
\end{aligned}
$$

Poles at $0, -\frac{4}{3}, 1 \pm j$, zeros at ∞

$x[n]$ causal $\Rightarrow x[-n+3]$ is left-sided $\Rightarrow$ ROC is $0 < |z| < 4/3$.

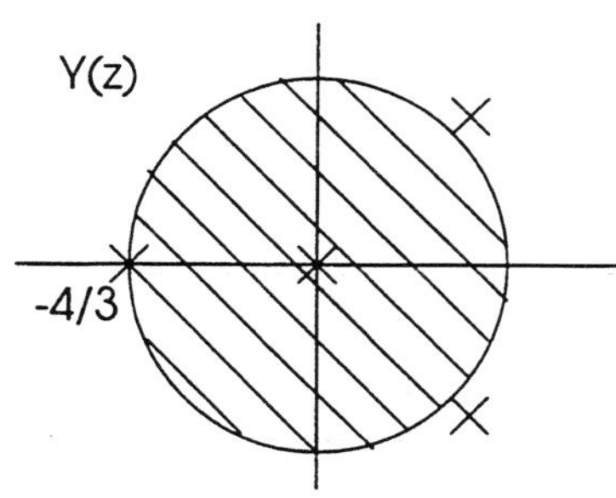

3.33. From pole-zero diagram

$$X(z) = \frac{z^2+1}{z-\frac{1}{2}}$$

(a)

$$y[n] = \left(\frac{1}{2}\right)^n x[n] \Rightarrow Y(z) = X(2z) = \frac{4z^2+1}{2z-\frac{1}{2}}$$

zeros $\pm\frac{1}{2}j$
poles $\frac{1}{4}, \infty$

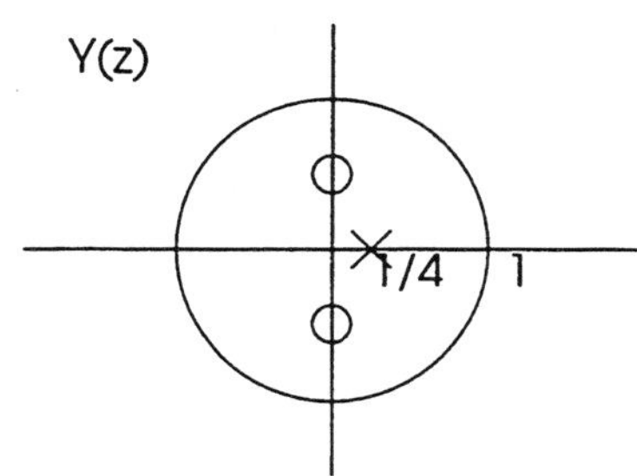

(b)

$$w[n] = \cos\left(\frac{\pi n}{2}\right) x[n] = \frac{1}{2}(e^{j\pi n/2} + e^{-j\pi n/2})x[n]$$

$$W(z) = \frac{1}{2}X(e^{-j\pi/2}z) + \frac{1}{2}X(e^{j\pi/2}z) = \frac{1}{2}X(-jz) + \frac{1}{2}X(jz)$$

$$W(z) = \frac{1}{2}\left(\frac{-z^2+1}{-jz-\frac{1}{2}}\right) + \frac{1}{2}\left(\frac{-z^2+1}{jz-\frac{1}{2}}\right) = \frac{z^2-1}{2(z^2+\frac{1}{4})}$$

poles at $\pm\frac{1}{2}j$
zeros at ± 1

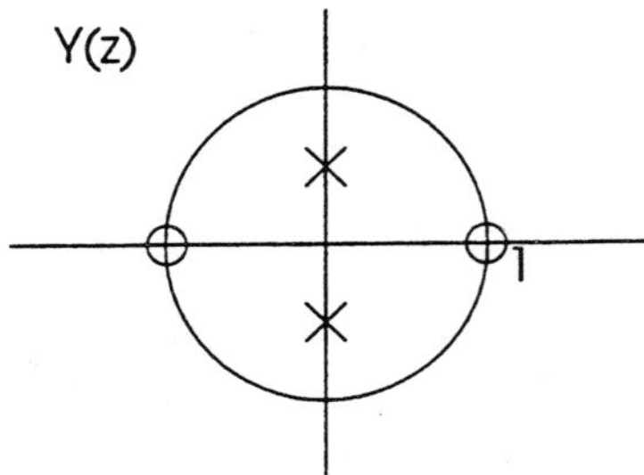

3.34.

$$H(z) = \frac{3 - 7z^{-1} + 5z^{-2}}{1 - \frac{5}{2}z^{-1} + z^{-2}} = 5 + \frac{1}{1 - 2z^{-1}} - \frac{3}{1 - \frac{1}{2}z^{-1}}$$

$$h[n] \text{ stable } \Rightarrow h[n] = 5\delta[n] - 2^n u[-n-1] - 3\left(\frac{1}{2}\right)^n u[n]$$

(a)

$$\begin{aligned}
y[n] &= h[n] * x[n] = \sum_{k=-\infty}^{n} h[k] \\
&= \begin{cases} -\sum_{k=-\infty}^{n} 2^k = -2^{n+1} & n < 0 \\ -\sum_{k-\infty}^{-1} 2^k + 5 - \sum_{k=0}^{n} 3\left(\frac{1}{2}\right)^k = 4 - 3\frac{1-(\frac{1}{2})^{n+1}}{1-\frac{1}{2}} = -2 + 3\left(\frac{1}{2}\right)^n & n \geq 0 \end{cases} \\
&= -2u[n] + 3\left(\frac{1}{2}\right)^n u[n] - 2^{n+1}u[-n-1]
\end{aligned}$$

(b)

$$\begin{aligned}
Y(z) &= \frac{1}{1-z^{-1}}H(z) = -2\frac{1}{1-z^{-1}} + 2\frac{1}{1-2z^{-1}} + 3\frac{1}{1-\frac{1}{2}z^{-1}}, \qquad \frac{1}{2} < |z| < 2 \\
y[n] &= -2u[n] - 2(2)^n u[-n-1] + 3\left(\frac{1}{2}\right)^n u[n]
\end{aligned}$$

3.35.

$$\begin{aligned}
H(z) &= \frac{1-z^3}{1-z^4} = z^{-1}\left(\frac{1-z^{-3}}{1-z^{-4}}\right) \qquad |z| > 1 \\
u[n] &\Leftrightarrow \frac{1}{1-z^{-1}} = \frac{z}{z-1} \qquad |z| > 1 \\
U(z)H(z) &= \frac{z^{-1} - z^{-4}}{(1-z^{-4})(1-z^{-1})} \\
&= \frac{z^{-1}}{1-z^{-1}} - \frac{z^{-4}}{1-z^{-4}} \qquad |z| > 1 \\
u[n] * h[n] &= u[n-1] - \sum_{k=0}^{\infty} \delta[n-4-4k]
\end{aligned}$$

3.36.

$$x[n] = u[n] \Leftrightarrow X(z) = \frac{1}{1 - z^{-1}} \qquad |z| > 1$$

$$y[n] = \left(\frac{1}{2}\right)^{n-1} u[n+1] = 4\left(\frac{1}{2}\right)^{n+1} u[n+1] \Leftrightarrow Y(z) = \frac{4z}{1 - \frac{1}{2}z^{-1}} \qquad |z| > \frac{1}{2}$$

(a)

$$H(z) = \frac{Y(z)}{X(Z)} = \frac{4z(1 - z^{-1})}{1 - \frac{1}{2}z^{-1}} \qquad |z| > \frac{1}{2}$$

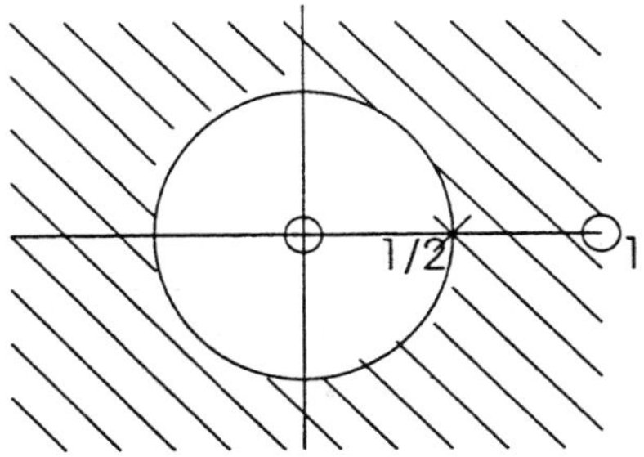

(b)

$$\begin{aligned} H(z) &= \frac{4z}{1 - \frac{1}{2}z^{-1}} - \frac{4}{1 - \frac{1}{2}z^{-1}} \qquad |z| > \frac{1}{2} \\ h[n] &= 4\left(\frac{1}{2}\right)^{n+1} u[n+1] - 4\left(\frac{1}{2}\right)^{n} u[n] \\ &= 4\delta[n+1] - 2\left(\frac{1}{2}\right)^{n} u[n] \end{aligned}$$

(c) The ROC of $H(z)$ includes $|z| = 1 \Rightarrow$ stable.

(d) From part (b) we see that $h[n]$ starts at $n = -1 \Rightarrow$ not causal

3.37.

$$X(z) = \frac{\frac{1}{3}}{1 - \frac{1}{2}z^{-1}} + \frac{\frac{1}{4}}{1 - 2z^{-1}}$$

has poles at $z = \frac{1}{2}$ and $z = 2$.

Since the unit circle is in the region of convergence $X(z)$ and $x[n]$ have both a causal and an anticausal part. The causal part is "outside" the pole at $\frac{1}{2}$. The anticausal part is "inside" the pole at 2, therefore, $x[0]$ is the sum of the two parts

$$x[0] = \lim_{z\to\infty} \frac{\frac{1}{3}}{1 - \frac{1}{2}z^{-1}} + \lim_{z\to 0} \frac{\frac{1}{4}z}{z - 2} = \frac{1}{3} + 0 = \frac{1}{3}$$

3.38.

$$Y(z) = \frac{z^{-1} + z^{-2}}{(1 - \frac{1}{2}z^{-1})(1 + \frac{1}{3}z^{-1})} \cdot \frac{2}{1 - z^{-1}} \qquad |z| > 1$$

Therefore using a contour C that lies outside of $|z| = 1$ we get

$$\begin{aligned} y[1] &= \frac{1}{2\pi j}\oint_C \frac{2(z+1)z^n dz}{(z-\frac{1}{2})(z+\frac{1}{3})(z-1)} \\ &= \frac{2(\frac{1}{2}+1)(\frac{1}{2})}{(\frac{1}{2}+\frac{1}{3})(\frac{1}{2}-1)} + \frac{2(-\frac{1}{3}+1)(-\frac{1}{3})}{(-\frac{1}{3}-\frac{1}{2})(-\frac{1}{3}-1)} + \frac{2(1+1)(1)}{(1-\frac{1}{2})(1+\frac{1}{3})} \\ &= -\frac{18}{5} - \frac{2}{5} + 6 = 2 \end{aligned}$$

3.39. (a)

$$X(z) = \frac{z^{10}}{(z-\frac{1}{2})(z-\frac{3}{2})^{10}(z+\frac{3}{2})^2(z+\frac{5}{2})(z+\frac{7}{2})}$$

Stable $\Rightarrow$ ROC includes $|z| = 1$. Therefore, the ROC is $\frac{1}{2} < |z| < \frac{3}{2}$.

(b) $x[-8] = \Sigma$[residues of $X(z)z^{-9}$ inside C], where C is contour in ROC (say the unit circle).

$$x[8] = \Sigma\left[\text{residues of } \frac{z}{(z-\frac{1}{2})(z-\frac{3}{2})^{10}(z+\frac{3}{2})^2(z+\frac{5}{2})(z+\frac{7}{2})} \text{ inside unit circle}\right]$$

First order pole at $z = \frac{1}{2}$ is only one inside the unit circle. Therefore

$$x[-8] = \frac{\frac{1}{2}}{(\frac{1}{2}-\frac{3}{2})^{10}(\frac{1}{2}+\frac{3}{2})^2(\frac{1}{2}+\frac{5}{2})(\frac{1}{2}+\frac{7}{2})} = \frac{1}{96}$$

3.40. (a) After writing the following equalities:

$$\begin{aligned} V(z) &= X(z) - W(z) \\ W(z) &= V(z)H(z) + E(z) \end{aligned}$$

we solve for W(z):

$$W(z) = \frac{H(z)}{1+H(z)}X(z) + \frac{1}{1+H(z)}E(z)$$

(b)

$$\begin{aligned} H_1(z) &= \frac{H(z)}{1+H(z)} = \frac{\frac{z^{-1}}{1-z^{-1}}}{1+\frac{z^{-1}}{1-z^{-1}}} = z^{-1} \\ H_2(z) &= \frac{1}{1+\frac{z^{-1}}{1-z^{-1}}} = 1 - z^{-1} \end{aligned}$$

(c) $H(z)$ is not stable due to its pole at $z = 1$, but $H_1(z)$ and $H_2(z)$ are.

3.41. (a) Yes, $h[n]$ is BIBO stable if its ROC includes the unit circle. Hence, the system is stable if $r_{min} < 1$ and $r_{max} > 1$.

(b) Let's consider the system step by step.

(i) First, $v[n] = \alpha^{-n}x[n]$. By taking the z-transform of both sides, $V(z) = X(\alpha z)$.

(ii) Second, $v[n]$ is filtered to get $w[n]$. So $W(z) = H(z)V(z) = H(z)X(\alpha z)$.

(iii) Finally, $y[n] = \alpha^n w[n]$. In the z-transform domain, $Y(z) = W(z/\alpha) = H(z/\alpha)X(z)$.

In conclusion, the system is LTI, with system function $G(z) = H(z/\alpha)$ and $g[n] = \alpha^n h[n]$.

(c) The ROC of $G(z)$ is $\alpha r_{min} < |z| < \alpha r_{max}$. We want $r_{min} < 1/\alpha$ and $r_{max} > 1/\alpha$ for the system to be stable.

3.42. (a) $h[n]$ is the response of the system when $x[n] = \delta[n]$. Hence,

$$h[n] + \sum_{k=1}^{10} \alpha_k h[n-k] = \delta[n] + \beta\delta[n-1],$$

Further, since the system is causal, $h[n] = 0$ for $n < 0$. Therefore,

$$h[0] + \sum_{k=1}^{10} \alpha_k h[-k] = h[0] = \delta[0] = 1.$$

(b) At $n = 1$,

$$h[1] + \alpha_1 h[0] = \delta[1] + \beta\delta[0] \qquad \Longrightarrow \alpha_1 = \frac{\beta - h[1]}{h[0]} = \beta - h[1]$$

(c) How can we extend h[n] for $n > 10$ and still have it compatible with the difference equation for S? Note that the difference equation can describe systems up to order 10. If we choose

$$h[n] = (0.9)^n \cos(\frac{\pi}{4}n)u[n],$$

we only need a second order difference equation:

$$\alpha_3 = \alpha_4 = \alpha_5 = \alpha_6 = \alpha_7 = \alpha_8 = \alpha_9 = \alpha_{10} = 0.$$

The z-transform of $h[n]$ can be found from the z-transform table:

$$H(z) = \frac{1 - \frac{0.9}{\sqrt{2}}}{(1 - 0.9e^{j\pi/4}z^{-1})(1 - 0.9e^{-j\pi/4}z^{-1})}$$

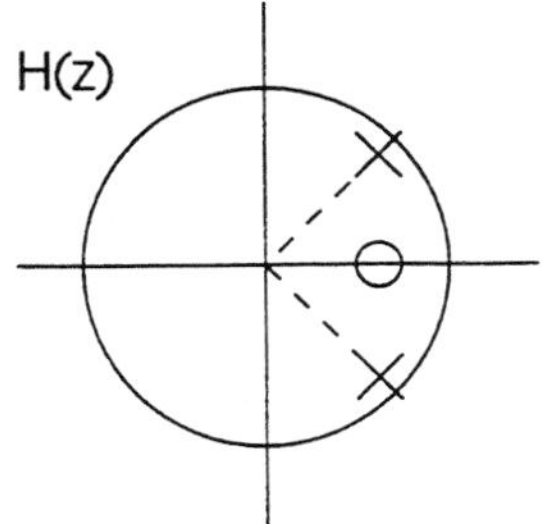

3.43. (a)

$$X(z) = \frac{1}{1 - \frac{1}{2}z^{-1}} - \frac{1}{1 - 2z^{-1}}, \qquad \frac{1}{2} < |z| < 2$$

$$Y(z) = \frac{6}{1 - \frac{1}{2}z^{-1}} - \frac{6}{1 - \frac{3}{4}z^{-1}}, \qquad |z| > \frac{3}{4}$$

$$\begin{aligned} H(z) &= \frac{Y(z)}{X(z)} = \frac{\frac{-\frac{3}{2}z^{-1}}{(1-\frac{1}{2}z^{-1})(1-\frac{3}{4}z^{-1})}}{\frac{-\frac{3}{2}z^{-1}}{(1-\frac{1}{2}z^{-1})(1-2z^{-1})}} \\ &= \frac{1 - 2z^{-1}}{1 - \frac{3}{4}z^{-1}}, \qquad |z| > \frac{3}{4} \end{aligned}$$

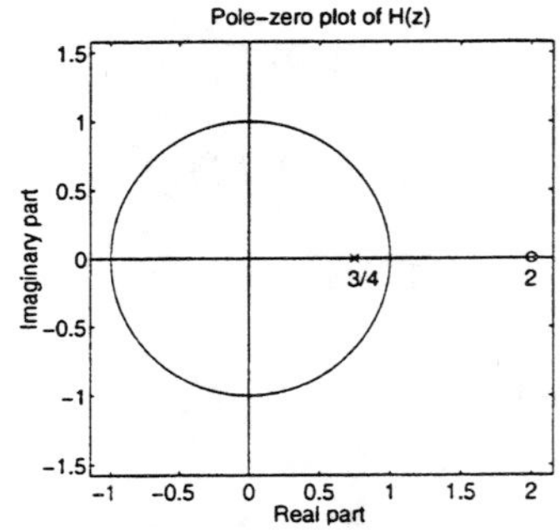

(b)

$$h[n] = \left(\frac{3}{4}\right)^n u[n] - 2\left(\frac{3}{4}\right)^{n-1} u[n-1]$$

(c)

$$y[n] - \frac{3}{4}y[n-1] = x[n] - 2x[n-1]$$

(d) The system is stable because the ROC includes the unit circle. It is also causal since $h[n] = 0$ for $n < 0$.

3.44. (a)

$$X(z) = \frac{-\frac{1}{3}}{1 - \frac{1}{2}z^{-1}} + \frac{\frac{4}{3}}{1 - 2z^{-1}}$$

The ROC is $\frac{1}{2} < |z| < 2$.

(b) The following figure shows the pole-zero plot of $Y(z)$. Since $X(z)$ has poles at 0.5 and 2, the poles at 1 and -0.5 are due to $H(z)$. Since $H(z)$ is causal, its ROC is $|z| > 1$. The ROC of $Y(z)$ must contain the intersection of the ROC of $X(z)$ and the ROC of $H(z)$. Hence the ROC of $Y(z)$ is $1 < |z| < 2$.

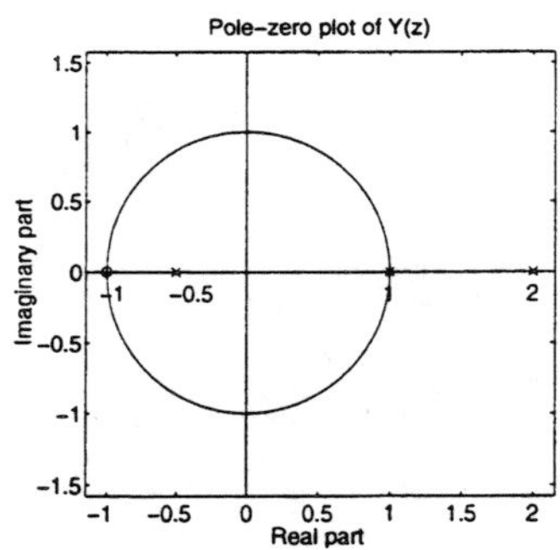

(c)

$$\begin{aligned} H(z) &= \frac{Y(z)}{X(z)} \\ &= \frac{\frac{1+z^{-1}}{(1-z^{-1})(1+\frac{1}{2}z^{-1})(1-2z^{-1})}}{\frac{1}{(1-12z^{-1})(1-2z^{-1})}} \end{aligned}$$

$$
\begin{aligned}
&= \frac{(1+z^{-1})(1-\frac{1}{2}z^{-1})}{(1-z^{-1})(1-\frac{1}{2}z^{-1})} \\
&= 1+\frac{\frac{2}{3}}{1-z^{-1}}+\frac{-\frac{2}{3}}{1+\frac{1}{2}z^{-1}}
\end{aligned}
$$

Taking the inverse z-transform, we find

$$
h[n] = \delta[n] + \frac{2}{3}u[n] - \frac{2}{3}(-\frac{1}{2})^n u[n]
$$

(d) Since $H(z)$ has a pole on the unit circle, the system is not stable.

3.45. (a)

$$
\begin{aligned}
ny[n] &= x[n] \\
-z\frac{dY(z)}{dz} &= X(z) \\
Y(z) &= -\int z^{-1}X(z)dz
\end{aligned}
$$

(b) To apply the results of part (a), we let $x[n] = u[n-1]$, and $w[n] = y[n]$.

$$
\begin{aligned}
W(z) &= -\int z^{-1}\frac{z^{-1}}{1-z^{-1}}dz \\
&= -\int \frac{1}{z(z-1)}dz \\
&= -\int \frac{-1}{z}+\frac{1}{z-1}dz \\
&= \ln(z) - \ln(z-1)
\end{aligned}
$$

3.46. (a) Since $y[n]$ is stable, its ROC contains the unit-circle. Hence, $Y(z)$ converges for $\frac{1}{2} < |z| < 2$.

(b) Since the ROC is a ring on the z-plane, $y[n]$ is a two-sided sequence.

(c) $x[n]$ is stable, so its ROC contains the unit-circle. Also, it has a zero at ∞ so the ROC includes ∞. ROC: $|z| > \frac{3}{4}$.

(d) Since the ROC of $x[n]$ includes ∞, $X(z)$ contains no positive powers of z, and so $x[n] = 0$ for $n < 0$. Therefore $x[n]$ is causal.

(e)

$$
\begin{aligned}
x[0] &= X(z)|_{z=\infty} \\
&= \frac{A(1-\frac{1}{4}z^{-1})}{(1+\frac{3}{4}z^{-1})(1-\frac{1}{2}z^{-1})}|_{z=\infty} \\
&= 0
\end{aligned}
$$

(f) $H(z)$ has zeros at -.75 and 0, and poles at 2 and ∞. Its ROC is $|z| < 2$.

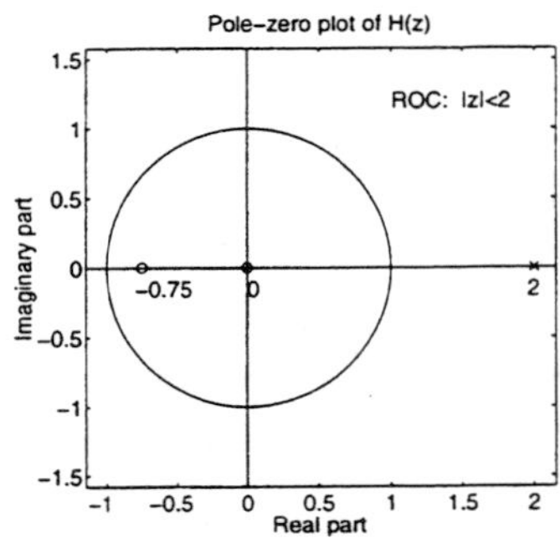

(g) Since the ROC of $h[n]$ includes 0, $H(z)$ contains no negative powers of z, which implies that $h[n] = 0$ for $n > 0$. Therefore $h[n]$ is anti-causal.

3.47. (a)

$$\begin{aligned} X(z) &= \sum_{n=0}^{\infty} x[n]z^{-n} \\ X(\infty) &= \lim_{z\to\infty} \sum_{n=0}^{\infty} x[n]z^{-n} = x[0] \end{aligned}$$

Therefore, $X(\infty) = x[0] \neq 0$ and finite by assumption. Thus, $X(z)$ has neither a pole nor a zero at $z = \infty$.

(b) Suppose $X(z)$ has finite numbers of poles and zeros in the finite z-plane. Then the most general form for $X(z)$ is

$$X(z) = \sum_{n=0}^{\infty} x[n]z^{-n} = Kz^L \frac{\prod_{k=1}^{M}(z - c_k)}{\prod_{K=1}^{N}(z - d_k)}$$

where K is a constant and M and N are finite positive integers and L is a finite positive or negative integer representing the net number of poles ($L < 0$) or zeros ($L > 0$) at $z = 0$. Clearly, since $X(\infty) = x[0] \neq 0$ and $< \infty$ we must have $L + M = N$; i.e., the total number of zeros in the finite z-plane must equal the total number of poles in the finite z-plane.

3.48.

$$X(z) = \frac{P(z)}{Q(z)}$$

where $P(z)$ and $Q(z)$ are polynomials in z. Sequence is absolutely summable $\Rightarrow$ ROC contains $|z| = 1$ and roots of $Q(z)$ inside $|z| = 1$.

These conditions do not necessarily imply that $x[n]$ is causal. A shift of a causal sequence would only add more zeros at $z = 0$ to $P(z)$. For example, consider

$$\begin{aligned} X(z) &= \frac{z^2}{z - \frac{1}{2}} \quad |z| > \frac{1}{2} \\ &= \frac{z}{z - \frac{1}{2}} = z \cdot \frac{1}{1 - \frac{1}{2}z^{-1}} \\ \Rightarrow \quad x[n] &= \left(\frac{1}{2}\right)^{n+1} u[n+1] \Rightarrow \text{ right-sided but non-causal.} \end{aligned}$$

3.49.

$$\begin{aligned} x[n] &= \delta[n] + a\delta(n-N) \quad |a|<1 \\ X(z) &= 1 + az^{-N} \\ \hat{X}(z) &= \log X(z) = \log(1+az^{-N}) = az^{-N} - \frac{a^2z^{-2N}}{2} + \frac{a^3z^{-3N}}{3} - \ldots \end{aligned}$$

Therefore,

$$\hat{x}[n] = \sum_{k=1}^{\infty} \frac{(-1)^{k+1}}{k} a^k \delta[n-kN]$$

3.50. (a)

$$x[n] = x[-n] \Longrightarrow X(z) = X\left(\frac{1}{z}\right)$$

Therefore,

$$X(z_0) = 0 = X\left(\frac{1}{z_0}\right)$$

i.e., $1/z_0$ is also a zero of $X(z)$.

(b)

$$x[n] \text{ real} \Longrightarrow x[n] = x^*[n] \Longrightarrow X(z) = X^*(z^*)$$

Therefore

$$X(z_0) = 0 = X(z_0^*)$$

i.e., z_0^* is also a zero and by part (a) so is $1/z_0^*$.

3.51. (a)

$$\mathcal{Z}[x^*[n]] = \sum_{n=-\infty}^{\infty} X^*[n]z^{-n} = \left(\sum_{n=-\infty}^{\infty} x[n](z^*)^{-n}\right)^* = X^*(z^*)$$

(b)

$$\mathcal{Z}[x[-n]] = \sum_{n=-\infty}^{\infty} x[-n]z^{-n} = \sum_{n=-\infty}^{\infty} x[n](z^{-1})^{-n} = X(z^{-1})$$

(c)

$$\mathcal{Z}[\mathcal{R}e\{x[n]\}] = \mathcal{Z}\left[\frac{x[n]+x^*[n]}{2}\right] = \frac{1}{2}\left[X(z) + X^*(z^*)\right]$$

(d)

$$\mathcal{Z}[\mathcal{I}m\{x[n]\}] = \mathcal{Z}\left[\frac{x[n]-x^*[n]}{2j}\right] = \frac{1}{2j}\left[X(z) - X^*(z^*)\right]$$

3.52.

$$x_1(n) = (-1)^n x(n) \Rightarrow X_1(z) = \sum_{n=-\infty}^{\infty} (-1)^n x(n) z^{-n} = X(-z)$$

The poles and zeros are rotated 180 degrees about the origin.

3.53. (a)

$$\theta_x(\omega) = \tan^{-1}\left(\frac{\mathcal{Im}\{X(e^{j\omega})\}}{\mathcal{Re}\{X(e^{j\omega})\}}\right) \Longrightarrow \tan\theta_x(\omega) = \frac{-\sum_{n=0}^{N-1} x[n]\sin(n\omega)}{\sum_{n=0}^{N-1} x[n]\cos(n\omega)}$$

$$\tan\theta_x(\omega)\sum_{n=0}^{N-1} x[n]\cos(\omega n) = -\sum_{n=1}^{N-1} x[n]\sin(n\omega)$$

$$\tan\theta_x(\omega)x[0] + \sum_{n=1}^{N-1} x[n](\tan\theta_x(\omega)\cos(n\omega) + \sin(n\omega)) = 0$$

$$\tan\theta_x(\omega_k) + \frac{1}{x[0]}\sum_{n=1}^{N-1} x[n](\tan\theta_x(\omega_k)\cos(n\omega_k) + \sin(n\omega_k)) = 0$$

for $N-1$ values of ω_k in the range $0 < \omega_k < \pi$.

(b) $x[n] = \delta[n] + 2\delta[n-1] + 3\delta[n-2] \Longrightarrow X(z) = 1 + 2z^{-1} + 3z^{-2}$

$$\theta_x(\omega) = \tan^{-1}\left(\frac{-2\sin(\omega) - 3\sin(2\omega)}{1 + 2\cos(\omega) + 3\cos(2\omega)}\right)$$

Consider the values $\theta_x\left(\frac{\pi}{2}\right) = \frac{5\pi}{4}$ and $\theta_x\left(\frac{2\pi}{3}\right) = \frac{5\pi}{6}$, which give the equations

$$\begin{aligned}
\tan\theta_x\left(\frac{\pi}{2}\right) &+ \frac{1}{x[0]}\left[x[1]\left(\tan\theta_x\left(\frac{\pi}{2}\right)\cos\frac{\pi}{2} + \sin\frac{\pi}{2}\right)\right. \\
&+ \left. x[2]\left(\tan\theta_x\left(\frac{\pi}{2}\right)\cos\pi + \sin\pi\right)\right] = 0 \\
\tan\theta_x\left(\frac{2\pi}{3}\right) &+ \frac{1}{x_0}\left[x[1]\left(\tan\theta_x\left(\frac{2\pi}{3}\right)\cos\frac{2\pi}{3} + \sin\frac{2\pi}{3}\right)\right. \\
&+ \left. x[2]\left(\tan\theta_x\left(\frac{2\pi}{3}\right)\cos\frac{4\pi}{3} + \sin\frac{4\pi}{3}\right)\right] = 0
\end{aligned}$$

$$\begin{aligned}
1 + \frac{1}{x[0]}(x[1]\cdot 1 + x[2]\cdot -1) &= 0 \\
-\frac{1}{\sqrt{3}} + \frac{1}{x[0]}\left(x[1] + \frac{1}{2\sqrt{3}} + \frac{\sqrt{3}}{2}\right) + x[2]\left(\frac{1}{2\sqrt{3}} - \frac{\sqrt{3}}{2}\right) &= 0
\end{aligned}$$

$$\left.\begin{aligned}
x[0] + x[1] - x[2] &= 0 \\
-x[0] + 2x[1] - x[2] &= 0
\end{aligned}\right\} \Longrightarrow \left\{\begin{aligned}
x[1] &= 2x[0] \\
x[2] &= 3x[0]
\end{aligned}\right.$$

Therefore

$$x[n] = x[0](\delta[n] + 2\delta[n-1] + 3\delta[n-2])$$

where $x[0]$ is undetermined.

3.54. $x[n] = 0$ for $n < 0$ implies:

$$\lim_{z\to\infty} X(z) = \lim_{z\to\infty}\sum_{n=0}^{\infty} x[n]z^{-n} = x[0] + \lim_{z\to\infty}\sum_{n=1}^{\infty} x[n]z^{-n} = x[0]$$

For the case $x[n] = 0$ for $n > 0$,

$$\lim_{z\to 0} X(z) = \lim_{z\to 0} \sum_{n=-\infty}^{0} x[n]z^{-n} = x[0] + \lim_{z\to 0} \sum_{n=1}^{\infty} x[-n]z^{n} = x[0]$$

3.55. (a)

$$c_{xx}[n] = \sum_{k=-\infty}^{\infty} x[k]x[n+k] = \sum_{k=-\infty}^{\infty} x[-k]x[n-k] = x[-n] * x[n]$$

$$C_{xx}(z) = X(z^{-1})X(z) = X(z)X(z^{-1})$$

$X(z)$ has ROC: $r_R < |z| < r_L$ and therefore $X(z^{-1})$ has ROC: $r_L^{-1} < |z| < r_R^{-1}$. Therefore $C_{xx}(z)$ has ROC: $\max[r_L^{-1}, r_R] < |z| < \min[r_R^{-1}, r_L]$

(b) $x[n] = a^n u[n]$ is stable if $|a| < 1$. In this case

$$X(z) = \frac{1}{1 - az^{-1}} \qquad |a| < |z| \quad \text{and} \quad X(z^{-1}) = \frac{1}{1 - az} \qquad |z| < |a^{-1}|$$

Therefore

$$\begin{aligned} C_{xx}(z) &= \frac{1}{1 - az^{-1}} \frac{1}{1 - az} = \frac{-az^{-1}}{(1 - az^{-1})(1 - a^{-1}z^{-1})} \\ &= \frac{\frac{1}{1-a^2}}{1 - az^{-1}} - \frac{\frac{1}{1-a^2}}{1 - a^{-1}z^{-1}} \qquad |a| < |z| < |a^{-1}| \end{aligned}$$

This implies that

$$c_{xx}[n] = \frac{1}{1 - a^2}\left[a^n u[n] + a^{-n} u[-n-1]\right]$$

Thus, in summary, the poles are at a and a^{-1}; the zeros are at 0 and ∞; and the ROC of $C_{xx}(z)$ is $|a| < |z| < |a^{-1}|$.

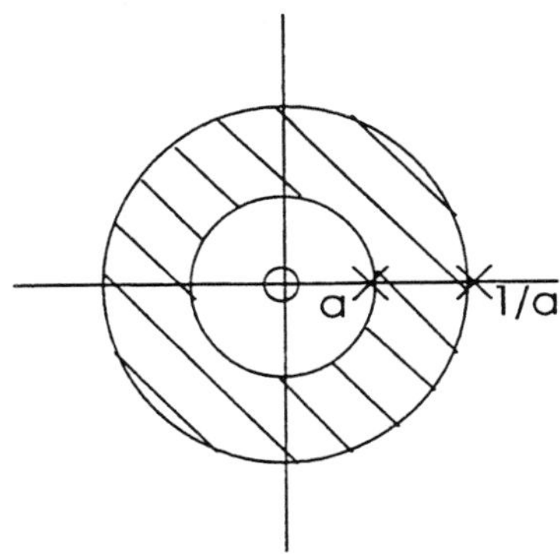

(c) Clearly, $x_1[n] = x[-n]$ will have the same autocorrelation function. For example,

$$X_1(z) = \frac{1}{1 - az} \qquad |z| < |a^{-1}| \Longrightarrow C_{x_1x_1}(z) = \frac{1}{1 - az}\frac{1}{1 - az^{-1}} = C_{xx}(z)$$

(d) Also, any delayed version of $x[n]$ will have the same autocorrelation function; e.g., $x_2[n] = x[n-m]$ implies

$$X_2(z) = \frac{z^{-m}}{1 - az^{-1}} \qquad |a| < |z| \Longrightarrow C_{x_2x_2}(z) = \frac{z^{-m}}{1 - az^{-1}}\frac{z^{m}}{1 - az} = C_{xx}(z)$$

3.56. In order to be a z-transform, $X(z)$ must be analytic in some annular region of the z-plane. To determine if $X(z) = z^*$ is analytic we examine the existence of $X'(z)$ by the Cauchy Riemann conditions. If

$$X(z) = X(x + jy) = u(x, y) + jv(x, y)$$

then for the derivative to exist at z, we must have

$$\frac{\partial u}{\partial x} = \frac{\partial v}{\partial y} \quad \text{and} \quad \frac{\partial u}{\partial y} = -\frac{\partial v}{\partial x}$$

In our case,

$$X(x + jy) = x - jy$$

and thus,

$$\frac{\partial u}{\partial x} = 1 \neq \frac{\partial v}{\partial y} = -1$$

unless x and y are zero. Thus, $X'(z)$ exists only at $z = 0$. $X(z)$ is not analytic anywhere. Therefore,

$$x[n] = \frac{1}{2\pi j} \oint X(z) z^{n-1} dz \quad \text{does not exist.}$$

3.57. If $X(z)$ has a pole at $z = z_0$ then $A(z)$ can be expressed as a Taylor's series about $z = z_0$.

$$A(z) = A(z_0) + \sum_{n=1}^{\infty} \frac{A^n(z_0)}{n!}(z - z_0)^n$$

where $A(z_0) = 0$. Thus

$$\begin{aligned}
\text{Res } [X(z) \text{ at } z = z_0] &= X(z)(z - z_0)|_{z=z_0} = \left.\frac{B(z)}{A(z)}\right|_{z=z_0} \\
&= \left.\frac{B(z)(z - z_0)}{\sum_{n=1}^{\infty} \frac{A^n(z_0)}{n!}(z - z_0)^n}\right|_{z=z_0} \\
&= \left.\frac{B(z)}{A'(z_0) + \sum_{n=2}^{\infty} \frac{A^n(z_0)}{n!}(z - z_0)^{n-1}}\right|_{z=z_0} = \frac{B(z_0)}{A'(z_0)}
\end{aligned}$$

Solutions – Chapter 4

Sampling of Continuous-Time Signals

4.1.

$$\begin{aligned} x[n] &= x_c(nT) \\ &= \sin\left(2\pi(100)n\frac{1}{400}\right) \\ &= \sin\left(\frac{\pi}{2}n\right) \end{aligned}$$

4.2. The discrete-time sequence

$$x[n] = \cos(\frac{\pi n}{4})$$

results by sampling the continuous-time signal

$$x_c(t) = \cos(\Omega_o t).$$

Since $\omega = \Omega T$ and $T = 1/1000$ seconds, the signal frequency could be:

$$\Omega_o = \frac{\pi}{4} \cdot 1000 = 250\pi$$

or possibly:

$$\Omega_o = (2\pi + \frac{\pi}{4}) \cdot 1000 = 2250\pi.$$

4.3. (a) Since $x[n] = x_c(nT)$,

$$\begin{aligned} \frac{\pi n}{3} &= 4000\pi n T \\ T &= \frac{1}{12000} \end{aligned}$$

(b) No. For example, since

$$\cos(\frac{\pi}{3}n) = \cos(\frac{7\pi}{3}n),$$

T can be 7/12000.

4.4. (a) Letting $T = 1/100$ gives

$$\begin{aligned} x[n] &= x_c(nT) \\ &= \sin\left(20\pi n\frac{1}{100}\right) + \cos\left(40\pi n\frac{1}{100}\right) \\ &= \sin\left(\frac{\pi n}{5}\right) + \cos\left(\frac{2\pi n}{5}\right) \end{aligned}$$

(b) No, another choice is $T = 11/100$:

$$\begin{aligned} x[n] &= x_c(nT) \\ &= \sin\left(20\pi n\frac{11}{100}\right) + \cos\left(40\pi n\frac{11}{100}\right) \\ &= \sin\left(\frac{11\pi n}{5}\right) + \cos\left(\frac{22\pi n}{5}\right) \\ &= \sin\left(\frac{\pi n}{5}\right) + \cos\left(\frac{2\pi n}{5}\right) \end{aligned}$$

4.5. A plot of $H(e^{j\omega})$ appears below.

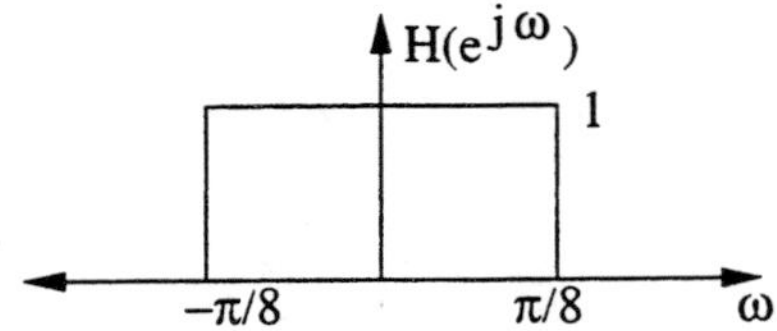

(a)

$$x_c(t) = 0, \quad , |\Omega| \geq 2\pi \cdot 5000$$

The Nyquist rate is 2 times the highest frequency. $\Rightarrow T = \frac{1}{10{,}000}$ sec. This avoids all aliasing in the C/D converter.

(b)

$$\begin{aligned} \frac{1}{T} &= 10kHz \\ \omega &= T\Omega \\ \frac{\pi}{8} &= \frac{1}{10,000}\Omega_c \\ \Omega_c &= 2\pi \cdot 625\text{rad/sec} \\ f_c &= 625Hz \end{aligned}$$

(c)

$$\begin{aligned} \frac{1}{T} &= 20kHz \\ \omega &= T\Omega \\ \frac{\pi}{8} &= \frac{1}{20,000}\Omega_c \\ \Omega_c &= 2\pi \cdot 1250\text{rad/sec} \\ f_c &= 1250Hz \end{aligned}$$

4.6. (a) The Fourier transform of the filter impulse response

$$\begin{aligned} H_c(j\Omega) &= \int_{-\infty}^{\infty} h_c(t)e^{-j\Omega t}\,dt \\ &= \int_{0}^{\infty} a^{-at}e^{-j\Omega t}\,dt \\ &= \frac{1}{a+j\Omega} \end{aligned}$$

So, we take the magnitude

$$|H_c(j\Omega)| = \left(\frac{1}{a^2+\Omega^2}\right)^{\frac{1}{2}}.$$

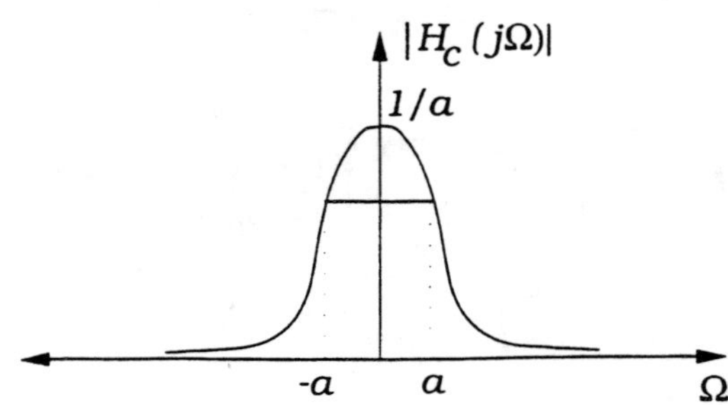

(b) Sampling the filter impulse response in (a), the discrete-time filter is described by

$$\begin{aligned} h_d[n] &= Te^{-anT}u[n] \\ H_d(e^{j\omega}) &= \sum_{n=0}^{\infty} Te^{-anT}e^{-j\omega n} \\ &= \frac{T}{1-e^{-aT}e^{-j\omega}} \end{aligned}$$

Taking the magnitude of this response

$$|H_d(e^{j\omega})| = \frac{T}{(1-2e^{-aT}\cos(\omega)+e^{-2aT})^{\frac{1}{2}}}.$$

Note that the frequency response of the discrete-time filter is periodic, with period 2π.

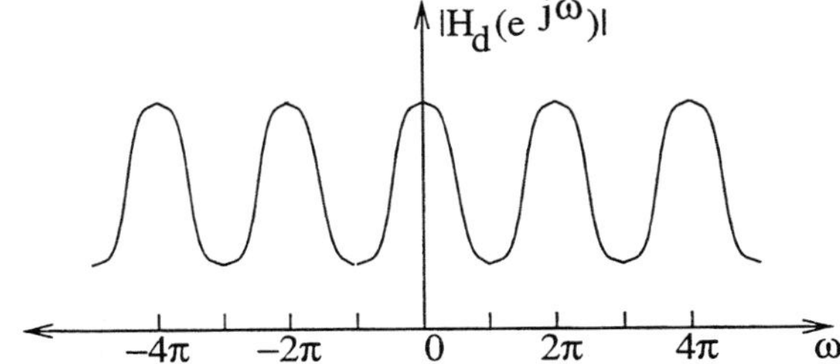

(c) The minimum occurs at $\omega = \pi$. The corresponding value of the frequency response magnitude is

$$\begin{aligned} |H_d(e^{j\pi})| &= \frac{T}{(1+2e^{-aT}+e^{-2aT})^{\frac{1}{2}}} \\ &= \frac{T}{1+e^{-aT}}. \end{aligned}$$

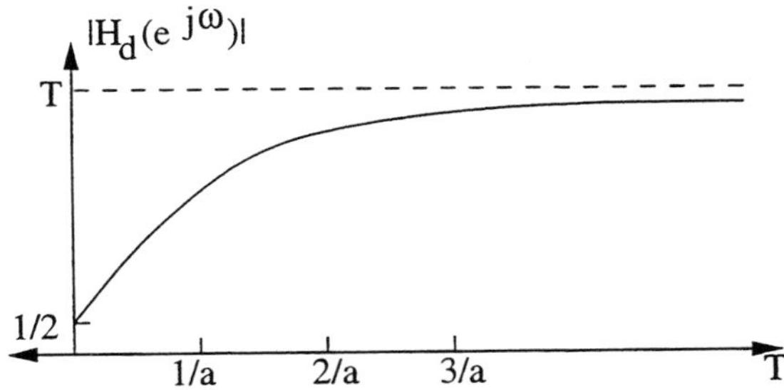

4.7. The continuous-time signal contains an attenuated replica of the original signal with a delay of τ_d.

$$x_c(t) = s_c(t) + \alpha s_c(t-\tau_d)$$

(a) Taking the Fourier transform of the analog signal:

$$X_c(j\Omega) = S_c(j\Omega)\cdot(1+\alpha e^{-j\tau_d\Omega})$$

Note that $X_c(j\Omega)$ is zero for $|\Omega| > \pi/T$. Sampling the continuous-time signal yields the discrete-time sequence, $x[n]$. The Fourier transform of the sequence is

$$\begin{aligned} X(e^{j\omega}) &= \frac{1}{T}\sum_{r=-\infty}^{\infty} S_c(\frac{j\omega}{T}+j\frac{2\pi r}{T}) \\ &+ \frac{\alpha}{T}\sum_{r=-\infty}^{\infty} S_c(\frac{j\omega}{T}+j\frac{2\pi r}{T})e^{-j\tau_d(\frac{\omega}{T}+\frac{2\pi r}{T})}. \end{aligned}$$

(b) The desired response:

$$H(j\Omega) = \begin{cases} 1 + \alpha e^{-j\tau_d \Omega}, & \text{for } |\Omega| \leq \frac{\pi}{T} \\ 0, & \text{otherwise} \end{cases}$$

Using $\omega = \Omega T$, we obtain a discrete-time system which simulates the above response:

$$H(e^{j\omega}) = 1 + \alpha e^{-j\frac{\tau_d \omega}{T}}$$

(c) We need to take the inverse Fourier transform of the discrete-time impulse response of part (b).

$$\begin{aligned} h[n] &= \frac{1}{2\pi} \int_{-\pi}^{\pi} H(e^{j\omega}) e^{j\omega n}\, d\omega \\ &= \frac{1}{2\pi} \int_{-\pi}^{\pi} (1 + \alpha e^{-j\frac{\tau_d \omega}{T}}) e^{j\omega n}\, d\omega \end{aligned}$$

(i) Consider the case when $\tau_d = T$:

$$\begin{aligned} h[n] &= \frac{1}{2\pi} \int_{-\pi}^{\pi} (e^{j\omega n} + \alpha e^{j\omega(n-1)})\, d\omega \\ &= \frac{\sin(\pi n)}{\pi n} + \frac{\alpha \sin[\pi(n-1)]}{\pi(n-1)} \\ &= \delta[n] + \alpha\delta[n-1] \end{aligned}$$

(ii) For $\tau_d = T/2$:

$$\begin{aligned} h[n] &= \frac{1}{2\pi} \int_{-\pi}^{\pi} (e^{j\omega n} + \alpha e^{j\omega(n-\frac{1}{2})})\, d\omega \\ &= \frac{\sin(\pi n)}{\pi n} + \frac{\alpha \sin[\pi(n-\frac{1}{2})]}{\pi(n-\frac{1}{2})} \\ &= \delta[n] + \frac{\alpha \sin[\pi(n-\frac{1}{2})]}{\pi(n-\frac{1}{2})} \end{aligned}$$

4.8. A plot of $X_c(j\Omega)$ appears below.

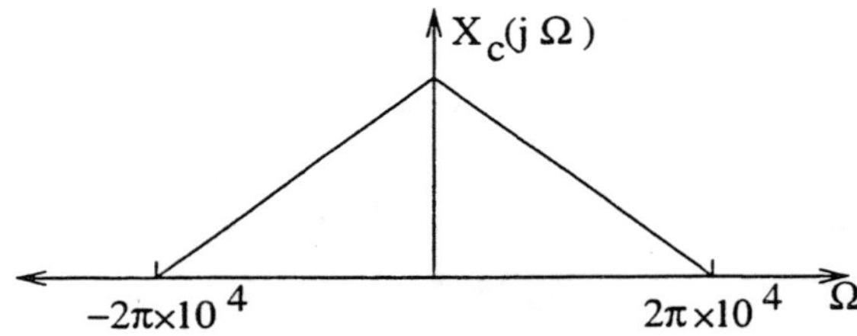

(a) For $x_c(t)$ to be recoverable from $x[n]$, the transform of the discrete signal must have no aliasing. When sampling, the radian frequency is related to the analog frequency by

$$\omega = \Omega T.$$

No aliasing will occur if the sampling interval satisfies the Nyquist Criterion. Thus, for the band-limited signal, $x_c(t)$, we should select T as:

$$T \leq \frac{1}{2 \times 10^4}.$$

(b) Assuming that the system is linear and time-invariant, the convolution sum describes the input-output relationship.

$$y[n] = \sum_{k=-\infty}^{\infty} x[k]h[n-k]$$

We are given

$$\begin{aligned} y[n] &= T \sum_{k=-\infty}^{n} x[k] \\ &= T \sum_{k=-\infty}^{\infty} x[k]u[n-k] \end{aligned}$$

Hence, we may infer that the impulse response of the system

$$h[n] = T \cdot u[n].$$

(c) We use the expression for $y[n]$ as given and examine the limit

$$\begin{aligned} \lim_{n\to\infty} y[n] &= \lim_{n\to\infty} T \cdot \sum_{k=-\infty}^{n} x[k] \\ &= T \cdot \sum_{k=-\infty}^{\infty} x[k] \end{aligned}$$

Recall the analysis equation for the Fourier transform:

$$X(e^{j\omega}) = \sum_{n=-\infty}^{\infty} x[n]e^{-j\omega n}$$

Hence,

$$\lim_{n\to\infty} y[n] = T \cdot X(e^{j\omega})|_{\omega=0}$$

(d) We use the result from part (c). Noting that

$$X(e^{j\omega}) = \frac{1}{T} \sum_{r=-\infty}^{\infty} X_c(\frac{j\omega}{T} + \frac{j2\pi r}{T}).$$

Thus, we have

$$T \cdot X(e^{j\omega})|_{\omega=0} = \sum_{r=-\infty}^{\infty} X_c(\frac{j2\pi r}{T})$$

From the given information, we seek a value of T such that:

$$\begin{aligned} \sum_{r=-\infty}^{\infty} X_c(\frac{j2\pi r}{T}) &= \int_{-\infty}^{\infty} x_c(t)\,dt \\ &= X_c(j\Omega)|_{\Omega=0} \end{aligned}$$

For the final equality to be true, there must be no contribution from the terms for which $r \neq 0$. That is, we require no aliasing at $\Omega = 0$. Since we are only interested in preserving the spectral component at $\Omega = 0$, we may sample at a rate which is lower than the Nyquist rate. The maximum value of T to satisfy these conditions is

$$T \leq \frac{1}{1 \times 10^4}.$$

4.9. (a) Since $X(e^{j\omega}) = X(e^{j(\omega-\pi)})$, $X(e^{j\omega})$ is periodic with period π.

(b) Using the inverse DTFT,

$$\begin{aligned} x[n] &= \frac{1}{2\pi}\int_{\langle 2\pi\rangle} X(e^{j\omega})e^{j\omega n}d\omega \\ &= \frac{1}{2\pi}\int_{\langle 2\pi\rangle} X(e^{j(\omega-\pi)})e^{j\omega n}d\omega \\ &= \frac{1}{2\pi}\int_{\langle 2\pi\rangle} X(e^{j\omega})e^{j(\omega+\pi)n}d\omega \\ &= \frac{1}{2\pi}e^{j\pi n}\int_{\langle 2\pi\rangle} X(e^{j\omega})e^{j\omega n}d\omega \\ &= (-1)^n x[n]. \end{aligned}$$

All odd samples of $x[n] = 0$, because $x[n] = -x[n]$. Hence $x[3] = 0$.

(c) Yes, $y[n]$ contains all even samples of $x[n]$, and all odd samples of $x[n]$ are 0.

$$x[n] = \begin{cases} y[n/2], & n \text{ even} \\ 0, & \text{otherwise} \end{cases}$$

4.10. Use $x[n] = x_c(nT)$, and simplify:

(a) $x[n] = \cos(2\pi n/3)$.

(b) $x[n] = \sin(4\pi n/3) = -\sin(2\pi n/3)$

(c) $x[n] = \frac{\sin(2\pi n/5)}{\pi n/5000}$

4.11. (a) Pick T such that

$$x[n] = x_c(nT) = \sin(10\pi nT) = \sin(\pi n/4) \qquad \Longrightarrow T = 1/40$$

There are other choices. For example, by realizing that $\sin(\pi n/4) = \sin(9\pi n/4)$, we find $T = 9/40$.

(b) Choose $T = 1/20$ to make $x[n] = x_c(nT)$. This is unique.

4.12. (a) Notice first that $H(e^{j\omega}) = 10j\omega, -\pi \leq \omega < \pi$.

(i) After sampling,

$$\begin{aligned} x[n] &= \cos(\frac{3\pi}{5}n), \\ y[n] &= |H(e^{j\frac{3\pi}{5}})|\cos(\frac{3\pi}{5}n + \angle H(e^{j\frac{3\pi}{5}})) \\ &= 6\pi\cos(\frac{3\pi}{5}n + \frac{\pi}{2}) \\ &= -6\pi\sin(\frac{3\pi}{5}n) \\ y_c(t) &= -6\pi\sin(6\pi t). \end{aligned}$$

(ii) After sampling, $x[n] = \cos(\frac{7\pi}{5}n) = \cos(\frac{3\pi}{5}n)$, so again, $y_c(t) = -6\pi\sin(6\pi t)$.

(b) $y_c(t)$ is what you would expect from a differentiator in the first case but not in the second case. This is because aliasing has occurred in the second case.

4.13. (a)

$$\begin{aligned} x_c(t) &= \sin(\frac{\pi}{20}t) \\ y_c(t) &= \sin(\frac{\pi}{20}(t-5)) \\ &= \sin(\frac{\pi}{20}t - \frac{\pi}{4}) \\ y[n] &= \sin(\frac{\pi n}{2} - \frac{\pi}{4}) \end{aligned}$$

(b) We get the same result as before:

$$\begin{aligned} x_c(t) &= \sin(\frac{\pi}{10}t) \\ y_c(t) &= \sin(\frac{\pi}{10}(t-2.5)) \\ &= \sin(\frac{\pi}{10}t - \frac{\pi}{4}) \\ y[n] &= \sin(\frac{\pi n}{2} - \frac{\pi}{4}) \end{aligned}$$

(c) The sampling period T is not limited by the continuous time system $h_c(t)$.

4.14. There is no loss of information if $X(e^{j\omega/2})$ and $X(e^{j(\omega/2-\pi)})$ do not overlap. This is true for (b), (d), (e).

4.15. The output $x_r[n] = x[n]$ if no aliasing occurs as result of downsampling. That is, $X(e^{j\omega}) = 0$ for $\pi/3 \leq |\omega| \leq \pi$.

(a) $x[n] = \cos(\pi n/4)$. $X(e^{j\omega})$ has impulses at $\omega = \pm\pi/4$, so there is no aliasing. $x_r[n] = x[n]$.

(b) $x[n] = \cos(\pi n/2)$. $X(e^{j\omega})$ has impulses at $\omega = \pm\pi/2$, so there is aliasing. $x_r[n] \neq x[n]$.

(c) A sketch of $X(e^{j\omega})$ is shown below. Clearly there will be no aliasing and $x_r[n] = x[n]$.

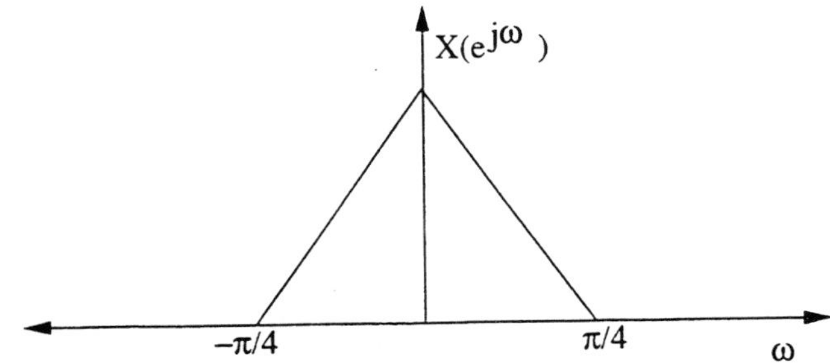

4.16. (a) In the frequency domain, we have

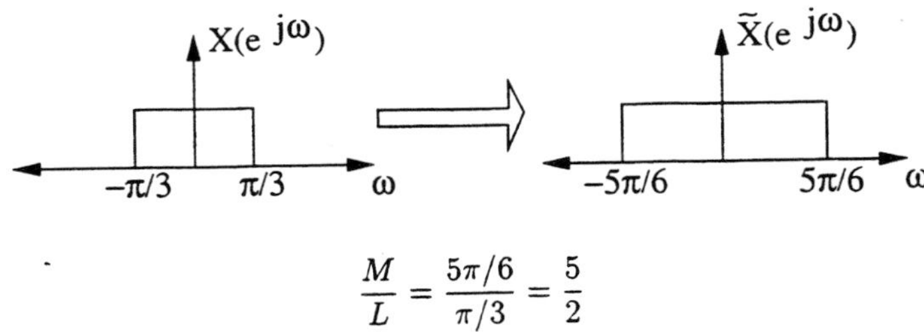

$$\frac{M}{L} = \frac{5\pi/6}{\pi/3} = \frac{5}{2}$$

This is unique.

(b) One choice is

$$\frac{M}{L} = \frac{\pi/2}{3\pi/4} = \frac{2}{3}$$

However, this is not unique. We can also write $\tilde{x}_d[n] = \cos(\frac{5\pi}{2}n)$, so another choice is

$$\frac{M}{L} = \frac{5\pi/2}{3\pi/4} = \frac{10}{3}$$

4.17. (a) In the frequency domain,

$$X(e^{j\omega}) = \begin{cases} 1, & |\omega| < 2\pi/3 \\ 0, & 2\pi/3 < |\omega| < \pi \end{cases}$$

After the sampling rate change,

$$\tilde{X}_d(e^{j\omega}) = \begin{cases} 4/3, & |\omega| < \pi/2 \\ 0, & \pi/2 < |\omega| < \pi \end{cases},$$

which leads to

$$x[n] = \frac{4}{3}\frac{\sin(\pi n/2)}{\pi n}$$

(b) Upsampling by 3 and low-pass filtering $x[n] = \sin(3\pi n/4)$ results in $\sin(\pi n/4)$. Downsampling by 5 gives us $\tilde{x}_d[n] = \sin(5\pi n/4) = -\sin(3\pi n/4)$.

4.18. For the condition to be satisfied, we have to ensure that $\omega_0/L \leq \min(\pi/L, \pi/M)$, so that the lowpass filtering does not cut out part of the spectrum.

(a) $\omega_0/2 \leq \pi/3 \Longrightarrow \omega_{0,max} = 2\pi/3$.

(b) $\omega_0/3 \leq \pi/5 \Longrightarrow \omega_{0,max} = 3\pi/5$.

(c) Since $L > M$, there is no chance of aliasing. Hence $\omega_{0,max} = \pi$.

4.19. The nyquist sampling property must be satisfied: $T \leq \pi/\Omega_0$.

4.20. (a) The Nyquist sampling property must be satisfied: $T \leq \pi/\Omega_0 \Longrightarrow F_s \geq 2000$.

(b) We'd have to sample so that $X(e^{j\omega})$ lies between $|\omega| < \pi/2$. So $F_s \geq 4000$.

4.21. (a) Keeping in mind that after sampling, $\omega = \Omega T$, the Fourier transform of $x[n]$ is

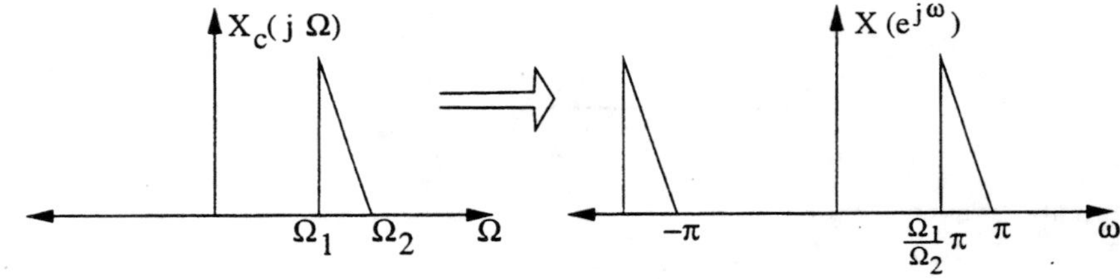

(b) A straight-forward application of the Nyquist criterion would lead to an incorrect conclusion that the sampling rate is at least twice the maximum frequency of $x_c(t)$, or $2\Omega_2$. However, since the spectrum is bandpass, we only need to ensure that the replications in frequency which occur as a result of sampling do not overlap with the original. (See the following figure of $X_s(j\Omega)$.) Therefore, we only need to ensure

$$\Omega_2 - \frac{2\pi}{T} < \Omega_1 \Longrightarrow T < \frac{2\pi}{\Delta\Omega}$$

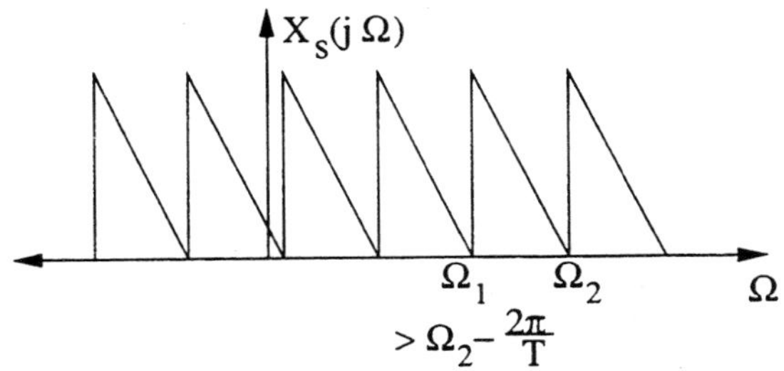

(c) The block diagram along with the frequency response of $h(t)$ is shown here:

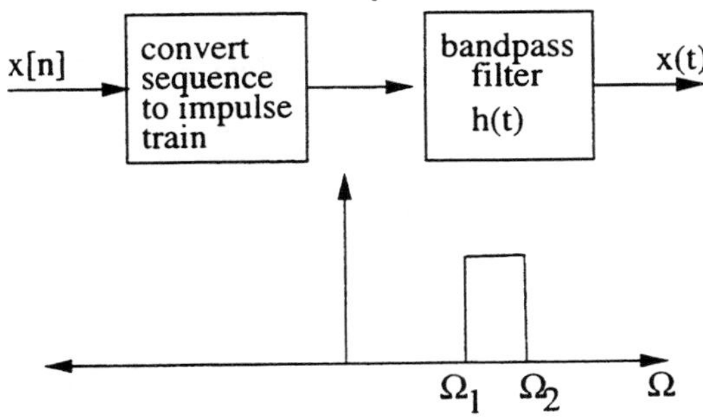

4.22. (a)

$$\omega = \Omega T, \qquad T = \frac{2\pi}{\Omega_0}$$

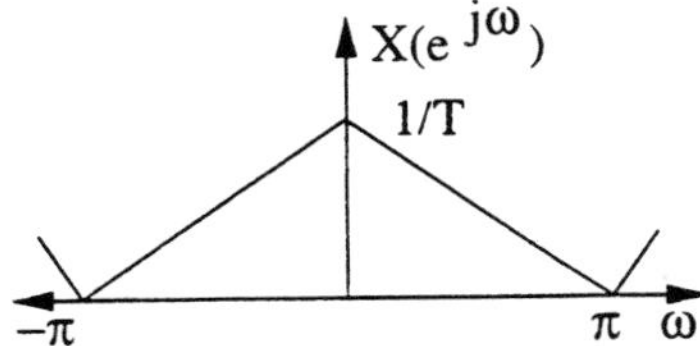

(b) To recover simply filter out the undesired parts of $X(e^{j\omega})$.

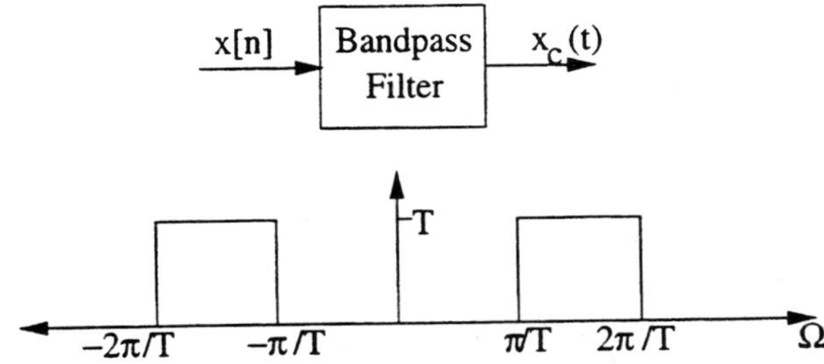

(c)

$$T \leq \frac{2\pi}{\Omega_0}$$

4.23. In the frequency domain, we have

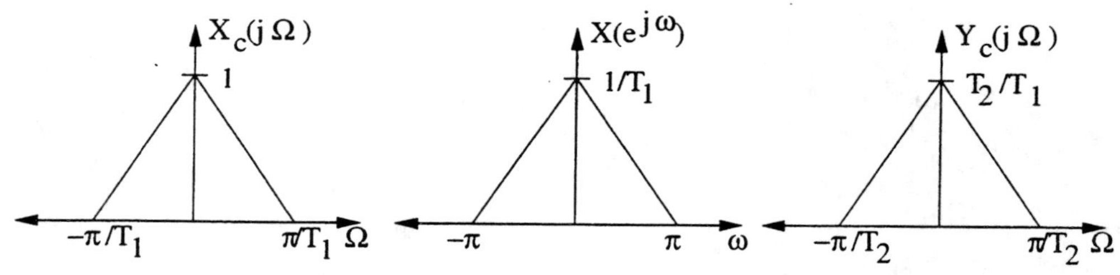

$$x_c(t) = 0, \qquad |\Omega| \geq \frac{\pi}{T_1}$$

Therefore, since we are sampling this $x_c(t)$ at the Nyquist frequency $x[n]$ will be full band and unaliased.

$$x[n] = x_c(nT_1)$$

$y_c(t)$ is a band-limited interpolation of $x[n]$ at a different period. Since no aliasing occurs at $x[n]$, the spectrum of $y_c(t)$ will be a frequency axis scaling of the spectrum of $x_c(t)$ for $T_1 > T_2$ or $T_1 < T_2$. As we show in the figure,

$$y_c(t) = \frac{T_2}{T_1} x_c\left(\frac{T_2}{T_1} t\right)$$

4.24. The Fourier transform of $y_c(t)$ is sketched below for each case.

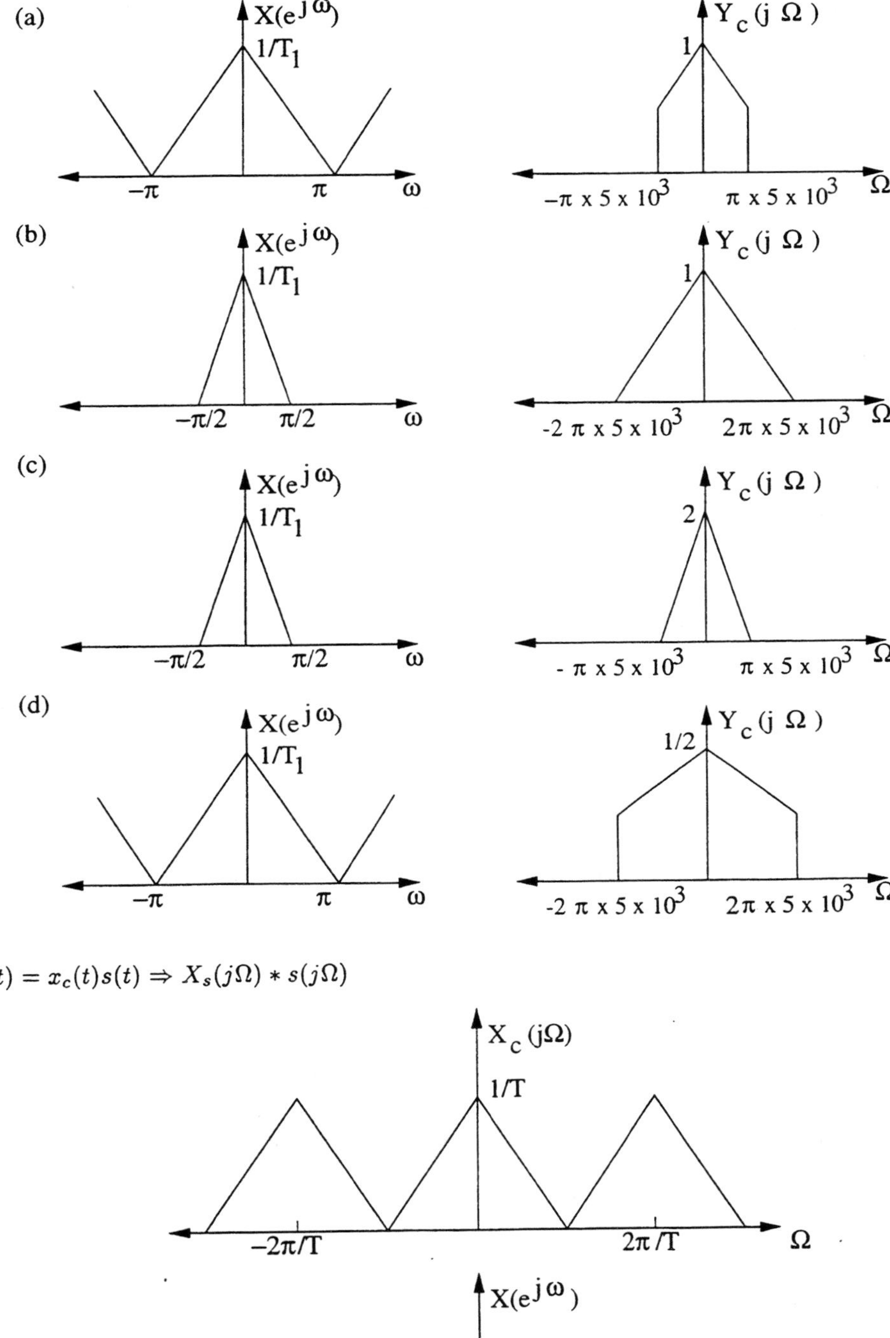

4.25. (a) $x_s(t) = x_c(t)s(t) \Rightarrow X_s(j\Omega) * s(j\Omega)$

(b) Since $H_d(e^{j\omega})$ is an ideal lowpass filter with $\omega_c = \frac{\pi}{4}$, we don't care about any signal aliasing that occurs in the region $\frac{\pi}{4} \leq \omega \leq \pi$. We require:

$$\begin{aligned} \frac{2\pi}{T} - 2\pi \cdot 10000 &\geq \frac{\pi}{4T} \\ \frac{1}{T} &\geq \frac{8}{7} \cdot 10000 \\ T &\leq \frac{7}{8} \times 10^{-4}\text{sec} \end{aligned}$$

Also, once all of the signal lies in the range $|\omega| \leq \frac{\pi}{4}$, the filter will be ineffective, i.e., $\frac{\pi}{4} \leq T(2\pi \times 10^4)$. So, $T \geq 12.5\mu$sec.

(c)

$$\Omega = \frac{\omega}{T} \Rightarrow \Omega_c = \frac{\pi}{4T}$$

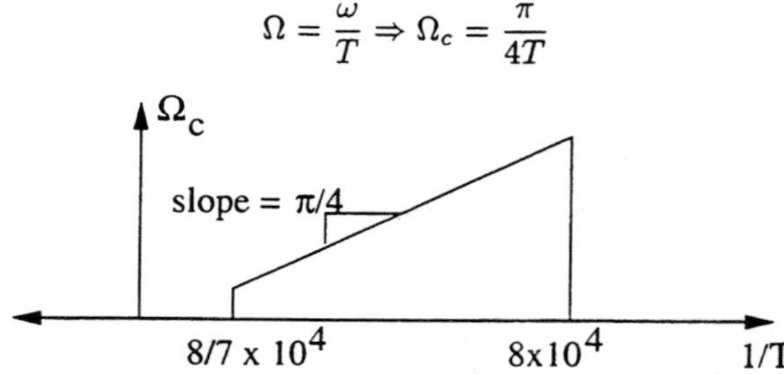

4.26. First we show that $X_s(e^{j\omega})$ is just a sum of shifted versions of $X(e^{j\omega})$:

$$\begin{aligned} x_s[n] &= \begin{cases} x[n], & n = Mk, \quad k = 0, \pm 1, \pm 2 \\ 0, & \text{otherwise} \end{cases} \\ &= \left(\frac{1}{M} \sum_{k=0}^{M-1} e^{j(2\pi kn/M)} \right) x[n] \\ X_s(e^{j\omega}) &= \sum_{n=-\infty}^{\infty} x_s[n] e^{-j\omega n} \\ &= \sum_{n=-\infty}^{\infty} \frac{1}{M} \sum_{k=0}^{M-1} x[n] e^{j(2\pi kn/M)} e^{-j\omega n} \\ &= \frac{1}{M} \sum_{k=0}^{M-1} \sum_{n=-\infty}^{\infty} x[n] e^{-j[\omega - (2\pi k/M)]n} \\ &= \frac{1}{M} \sum_{k=0}^{M-1} X\left(e^{j[\omega - (2\pi k/M)]}\right) \end{aligned}$$

Additionally, $X_d(e^{j\omega})$ is simply $X_s(e^{j\omega})$ with the frequency axis expanded by a factor of M:

$$\begin{aligned} X_d(e^{j\omega}) &= \sum_{n=-\infty}^{\infty} X_s[Mn] e^{-j\omega n} \\ &= \sum_{l=-\infty}^{\infty} x_s[l] e^{-j(\omega/M)l} \\ &= X_s\left(e^{j(\omega/M)}\right) \end{aligned}$$

(a) (i) $X_s(e^{j\omega})$ and $X_d(e^{j\omega})$ are sketched below for $M = 3$, $\omega_H = \pi/2$.

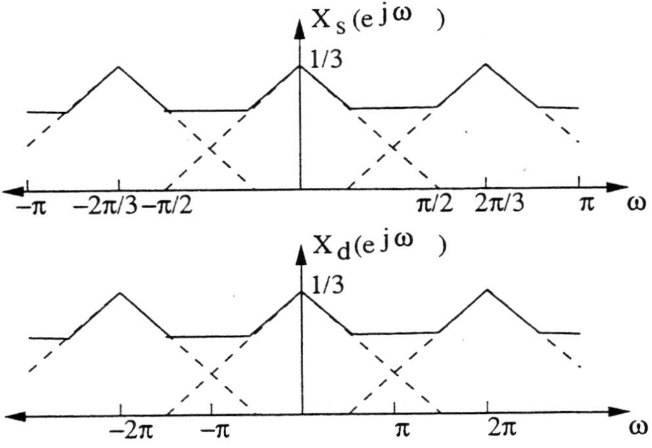

(ii) $X_s(e^{j\omega})$ and $X_d(e^{j\omega})$ are sketched below for $M = 3$, $\omega_H = \pi/4$.

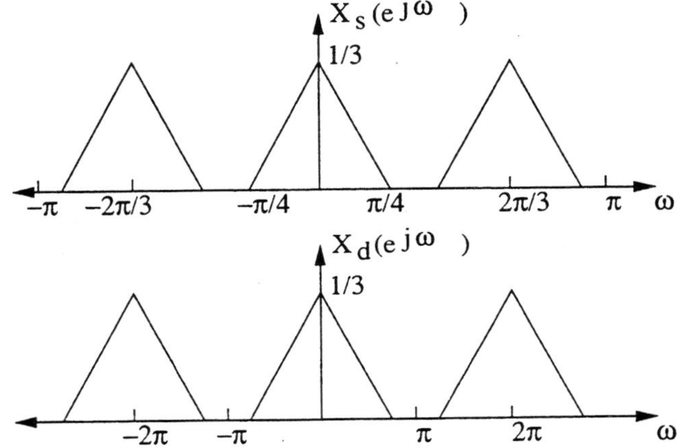

(b) From the definition of $X_s(e^{j\omega})$, we see that there will be no aliasing if the signal is bandlimited to π/M. In this problem, $M = 3$. Thus the maximum value of ω_H is $\pi/3$.

4.27. Parseval's Theorem:

$$\sum_{n=-\infty}^{\infty} |x[n]|^2 = \frac{1}{2\pi}\int_{-\pi}^{\pi} |X(e^{j\omega})|^2 d\omega$$

When we upsample, the added samples are zeros, so the upsampled signal $x_u[n]$ has the same energy as the original $x[n]$:

$$\sum_{n=-\infty}^{\infty} |x[n]|^2 = \sum_{n=-\infty}^{\infty} |x_u[n]|^2,$$

and by Parseval's theorem:

$$\frac{1}{2\pi}\int_{-\pi}^{\pi} |X(e^{j\omega})|^2 d\omega = \frac{1}{2\pi}\int_{-\pi}^{\pi} |X_u(e^{j\omega})|^2 d\omega.$$

Hence the amplitude of the Fourier transform does not change.

When we downsample, the downsampled signal $x_d[n]$ has less energy than the original $x[n]$ because some samples are discarded. Hence the amplitude of the Fourier transform will change after downsampling.

4.28. (a) Yes, the system is linear because each of the subblocks is linear. The C/D step is defined by $x[n] = x_c(nT)$, which is clearly linear. The DT system is an LTI system. The D/C step consists of converting the sequence to impulses and of CT LTI filtering, both of which are linear.

(b) No, the system is not time-invariant.
For example, suppose that $h[n] = \delta[n]$, $T = 5$ and $x_c(t) = 1$ for $-1 \le t \le 1$. Such a system would result in $x[n] = \delta[n]$ and $y_c(t) = \text{sinc}(\pi/5)$. Now suppose we delay the input to be $x_c(t-2)$. Now $x[n] = 0$ and $y_c(t) = 0$.

4.29. We can analyze the system in the frequency domain:

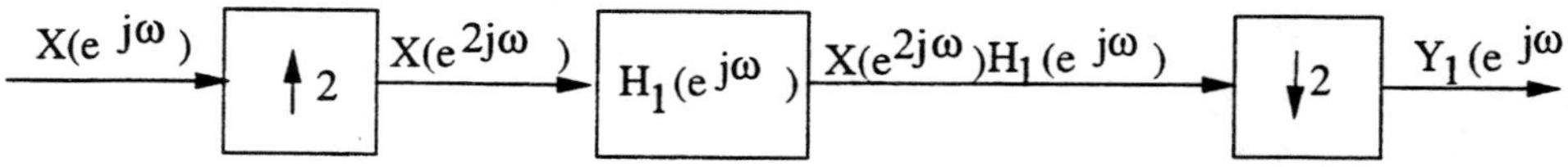

$X(e^{j\omega}) \rightarrow \boxed{\uparrow 2} \xrightarrow{X(e^{2j\omega})} \boxed{H_1(e^{j\omega})} \xrightarrow{X(e^{2j\omega})H_1(e^{j\omega})} \boxed{\downarrow 2} \rightarrow Y_1(e^{j\omega})$

$Y_1(e^{j\omega})$ is $X(e^{2j\omega})H_1(e^{j\omega})$ downsampled by 2:

$$\begin{aligned}
Y_1(e^{j\omega}) &= \frac{1}{2}\left\{X(e^{2j\omega/2})H_1(e^{j\omega/2}) + X(e^{(2j(\omega-2\pi)/2)})H_1(e^{j(\omega-2\pi)/2})\right\} \\
&= \frac{1}{2}\left\{X(e^{j\omega})H_1(e^{j\omega/2}) + X(e^{j(\omega-2\pi)})H_1(e^{j(\frac{\omega}{2}-\pi)})\right\} \\
&= \frac{1}{2}\left\{H_1(e^{j\omega/2}) + H_1(e^{j(\frac{\omega}{2}-\pi)})\right\} X(e^{j\omega}) \\
&= H_2(e^{j\omega})X(e^{j\omega}) \\
H_2(e^{j\omega}) &= \frac{1}{2}\left\{H_1(e^{j\omega/2}) + H_1(e^{j(\frac{\omega}{2}-\pi)})\right\}
\end{aligned}$$

4.30.

$$\begin{aligned}
&X_c(j\Omega) = 0 && |\Omega| \ge 4000\pi \\
&Y(j\Omega) = |\Omega| X_c(j\Omega), && 1000\pi \le |\Omega| \le 2000\pi
\end{aligned}$$

Since only half the frequency band of $X_c(j\Omega)$ is needed, we can alias everything past $\Omega = 2000\pi$. Hence, $T = 1/3000$ s.

Now that T is set, figure out $H(e^{j\omega})$ band edges.

$$\begin{aligned}
\omega_1 = \Omega_1 T \quad &\Rightarrow \omega_1 = 2\pi \cdot 500 \cdot \tfrac{1}{3000} \quad \Rightarrow \omega_1 = \frac{\pi}{3} \\
\omega_2 = \Omega_2 T \quad &\Rightarrow \omega_2 = 2\pi \cdot 1000 \cdot \tfrac{1}{3000} \quad \Rightarrow \omega_2 = \frac{2\pi}{3}
\end{aligned}$$

$$H(e^{j\omega}) = \begin{cases} |\omega| & \frac{\pi}{3} \le |\omega| \le \frac{2\pi}{3} \\ 0 & 0 \le |\omega| < \frac{\pi}{3},\ \frac{2\pi}{3} < |\omega| \le \pi \end{cases}$$

4.31.

$$X_c(j\Omega) = 0, \qquad |\Omega| > \frac{\pi}{T}$$

$$y_r(t) = \int_{-\infty}^{t} x_c(\tau)d\tau \Longrightarrow H_c(j\Omega) = \frac{1}{j\Omega}$$

In discrete-time, we want

$$H(e^{j\omega}) = \begin{cases} \frac{1}{j\omega}, & -\pi \le \omega \le \pi \\ 0, & \text{otherwise} \end{cases}$$

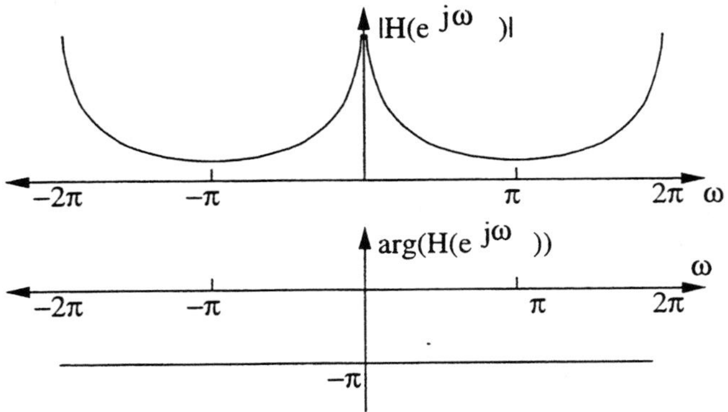

4.32. (a) The highest frequency is $\pi/T = \pi \times 10000$.

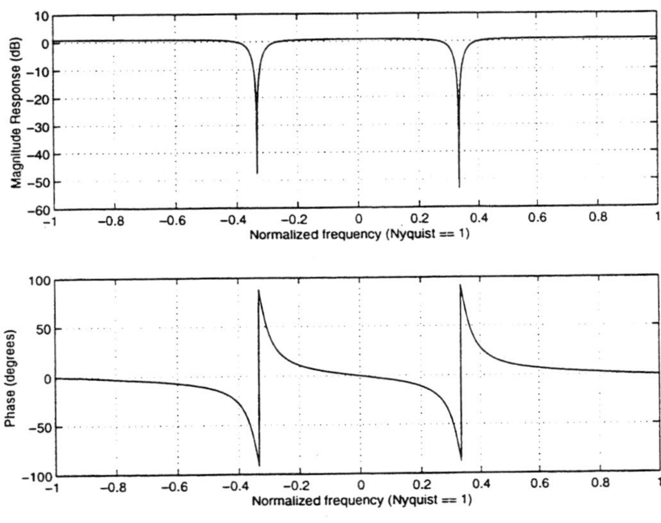

(b)

(c) To filter the 60Hz out,

$$\omega_0 = T\Omega = \frac{1}{10,000} \cdot 2\pi \cdot 60 = \frac{3\pi}{250}$$

4.33.

$$\begin{aligned} y[n] &= x^2[n] \\ Y(e^{j\omega}) &= X(e^{j\omega}) * X(e^{j\omega}) \end{aligned}$$

therefore, $Y(e^{j\omega})$ will occupy twice the frequency band that $X(e^{j\omega})$ does if no aliasing occurs. If $Y(e^{j\omega}) \neq 0, \quad -\pi < \omega < \pi$, then $X(e^{j\omega}) \neq 0, \quad -\frac{\pi}{2} < \omega < \frac{\pi}{2}$ and so $X(j\Omega) = 0, \quad |\Omega| \geq 2\pi(1000)$. Since $\omega = \Omega T$,

$$\begin{aligned} \frac{\pi}{2} &\geq T \cdot 2\pi(1000) \\ T &\leq \frac{1}{4000} \end{aligned}$$

4.34. (a) Since there is no aliasing involved in this process, we may choose T to be any value. Choose $T = 1$ for simplicity. $X_c(j\Omega) = 0, |\Omega| \geq \pi/T$. Since $Y_c(j\Omega) = H_c(j\Omega)X_c(j\Omega)$, $Y_c(j\Omega) = 0, |\Omega| \geq \pi/T$. Therefore, there will be no aliasing problems in going from $y_c(t)$ to $y[n]$.
Recall the relationship $\omega = \Omega T$. We can simply use this in our system conversion:

$$\begin{aligned} H(e^{j\omega}) &= e^{-j\omega/2} \\ H(j\Omega) &= e^{-j\Omega T/2} \\ &= e^{-j\Omega/2}, \quad T = 1 \end{aligned}$$

Note that the choice of T and therefore $H(j\Omega)$ is not unique.

(b)

$$\begin{aligned} \cos\left(\frac{5\pi}{2}n - \frac{\pi}{4}\right) &= \frac{1}{2}\left[e^{j(\frac{5\pi}{2}n-\frac{\pi}{4})} + e^{-j(\frac{5\pi}{2}n-\frac{\pi}{4})}\right] \\ &= \frac{1}{2}e^{-j(\pi/4)}e^{j(5\pi/2)n} + \frac{1}{2}e^{j(\pi/4)}e^{-j(5\pi/2)n} \end{aligned}$$

Since $H(e^{j\omega})$ is an LTI system, we can find the response to each of the two eigenfunctions separately.

$$y[n] = \frac{1}{2}e^{-j(\pi/4)}H\left(e^{j(5\pi/2)}\right)e^{j(5\pi/2)n} + \frac{1}{2}e^{j(\pi/4)}H\left(e^{-j(5\pi/2)}\right)e^{-j(5\pi/2)n}$$

Since $H(e^{j\omega})$ is defined for $0 \leq |\omega| \leq \pi$ we must evaluate the frequency at the baseband, i.e., $5\pi/2 \Rightarrow 5\pi/2 - 2\pi = \pi/2$. Therefore,

$$\begin{aligned} y[n] &= \frac{1}{2}e^{-j(\pi/4)}H\left(e^{j(5\pi/2)}\right)e^{j(5\pi/2)n} + \frac{1}{2}e^{j(\pi/4)}H\left(e^{-j(5\pi/2)}\right)e^{-j(5\pi/2)n} \\ &= \frac{1}{2}\left(e^{j[(5\pi/2)n-(\pi/2)]} + e^{-j[(5\pi/2)n-(\pi/2)]}\right) \\ &= \cos\left(\frac{5\pi}{2}n - \frac{\pi}{2}\right). \end{aligned}$$

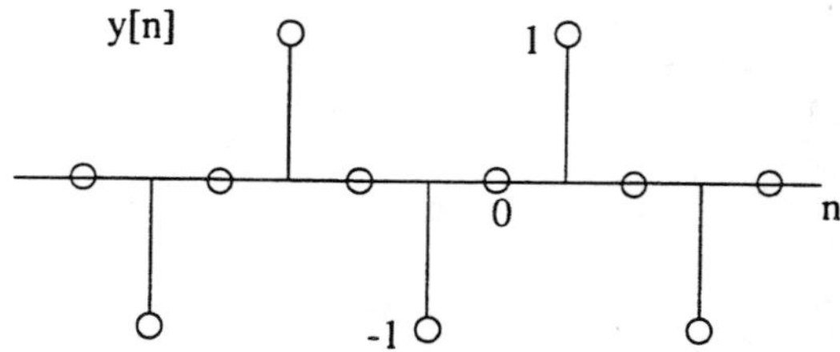

4.35. The frequency response $H(e^{j\omega}) = H_c(j\Omega/T)$. Finding that

$$H_c(j\Omega) = \frac{1}{(j\Omega)^2 + 4(j\Omega) + 3},$$

$$\begin{aligned} H(e^{j\omega}) &= \frac{1}{(10j\omega)^2 + 4(10j\omega) + 3} \\ &= \frac{1}{-100\omega^2 + 3 + 40j\omega} \end{aligned}$$

4.36. (a) Since $\Omega T = \omega$, $\quad (2\pi \cdot 100)T = \frac{\pi}{2} \Rightarrow T = \frac{1}{400}$

(b) The downsampler has $M = 2$. Since $x[n]$ is bandlimited to $\frac{\pi}{M}$, there will be no aliasing. The frequency axis simply expands by a factor of 2.
For $y_c(t) = x_c(t) \Leftrightarrow Y_c(j\Omega) = X_c(j\Omega)$.
Therefore $\Omega T' \Rightarrow 2\pi \cdot 100T' \Rightarrow T' = \frac{1}{200}$.

4.37. In both systems, the speech was filtered first so that the subsequent sampling results in no aliasing. Therefore, going $s[n]$ to $s_1[n]$ basically requires changing the sampling rate by a factor of 3kHz/5kHz = 3/5. This is done with the following system:

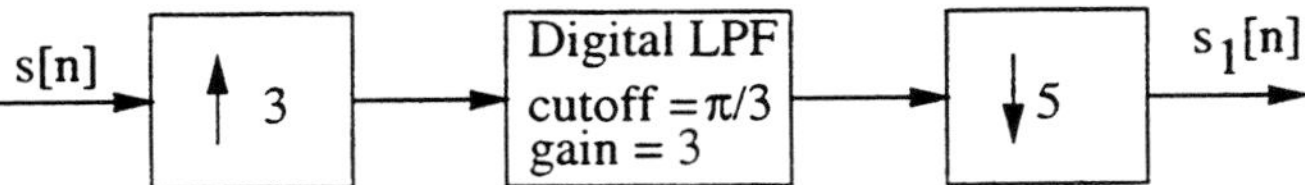

4.38. $X_c(j\Omega)$ is drawn below.

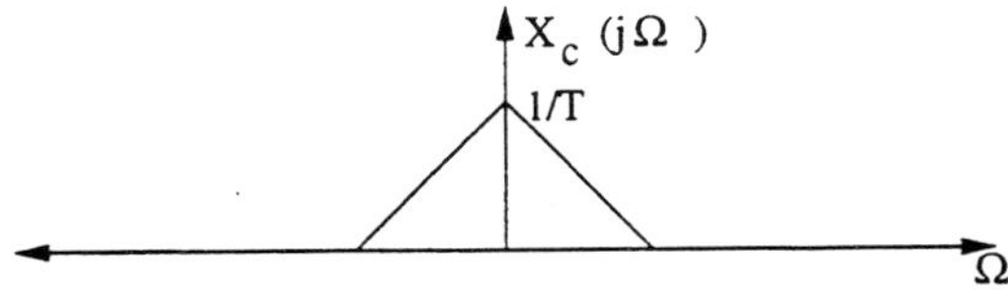

$x_c(t)$ is sampled at sampling period T, so there is no aliasing in $x[n]$.

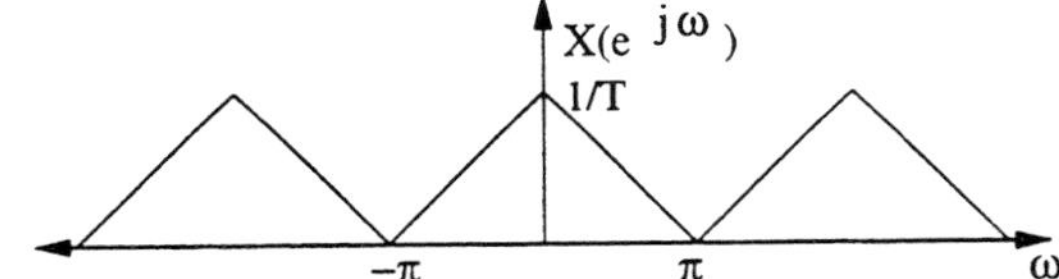

Inserting $L-1$ zeros between samples compresses the frequency axis.

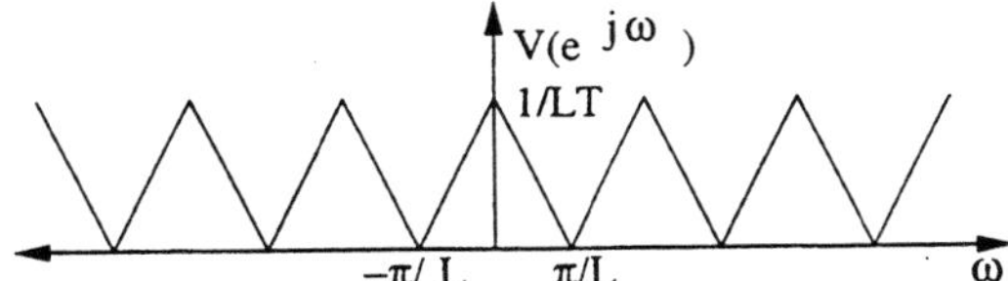

The filter $H(e^{j\omega})$ removes frequency components between π/L and π.

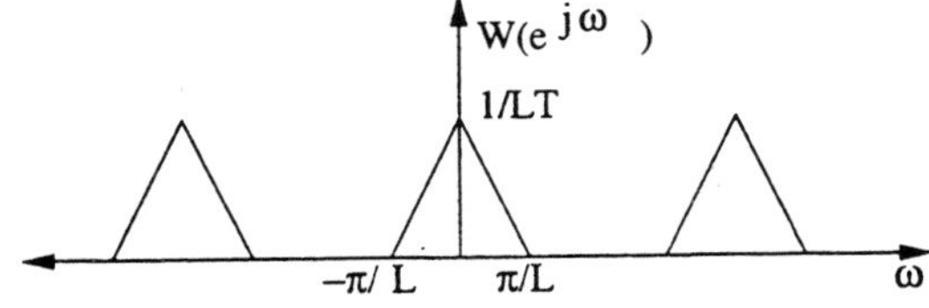

The multiplication by $(-1)^n$ shifts the center of the frequency band from 0 to π.

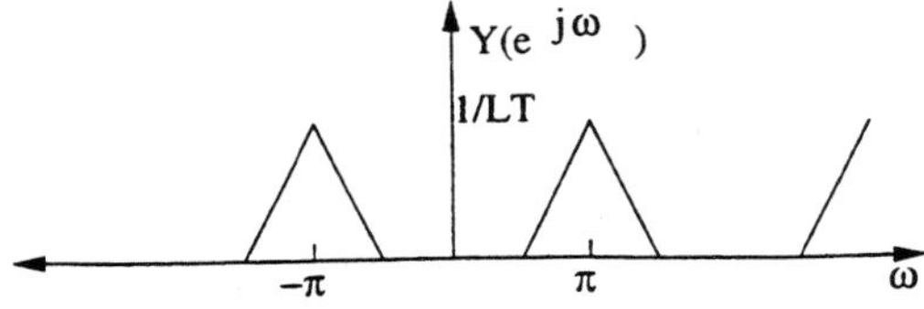

The D/C conversion maps the range $-\pi$ to π to the range $-\pi/T$ to π/T.

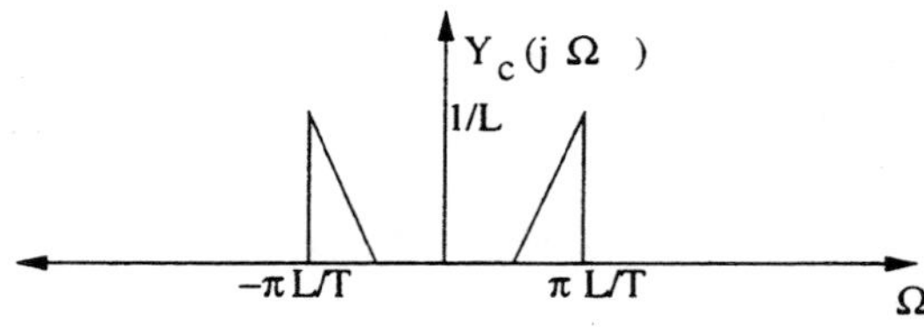

4.39. (a)

$$h[n] = 0, \qquad |n| > (RL-1)$$

Therefore, for causal system delay by $RL-1$ samples.

(b) General interpolator condition:

$$\begin{aligned} h[0] &= 1 \\ h[kL] &= 0, \qquad k = \pm 1, \pm 2, \ldots \end{aligned}$$

(c)

$$y[n] = \sum_{k=-(RL-1)}^{(RL-1)} h[k]v[n-k] = h[0]v[n] + \sum_{k=1}^{RL-1} h[n](v[n-k] + v[n+k])$$

This requires only RL-1 multiplies, (assuming $h[0] = 1$.)

(d)

$$y[n] = \sum_{k=n-(RL-1)}^{n+(RL-1)} v[k]h[n-k]$$

If $n = mL$ (m an integer), then we don't have any multiplications since $h[0] = 1$ and the other non-zero samples of $v[k]$ hit at the zeros $h[n]$. Otherwise the impulse response spans $2RL-1$ samples of $v[n]$, but only $2R$ of these are non-zero. Therefore, there are $2R$ multiplies.

4.40. Split $H(e^{j\omega})$ into a lowpass and a delay.

$$\begin{aligned} H(e^{j\omega}) &= H_{LP}(e^{j\omega})e^{-j\omega} \\ H_{LP}(e^{j\omega}) &= \begin{cases} 1, & |\omega| < \frac{\pi}{L} \\ 0, & \frac{\pi}{L} < |\omega| \le \pi \end{cases} \end{aligned}$$

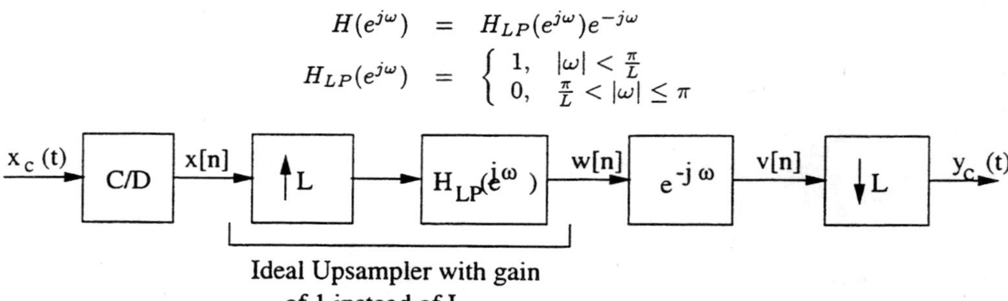

Then we analyze the system as follows:

$$\begin{aligned} x[n] &= x_c(nT) \qquad \text{no aliasing assumed} \\ w[n] &= \frac{1}{L}x_c(n\frac{T}{L}) \qquad \text{rate change} \\ v[n] &= w[n-1] = \frac{1}{L}x_c\left(n\frac{T}{L} - \frac{T}{L}\right), \qquad \text{delay at higher rate} \\ y[n] &= v[nL] = \frac{1}{L}x_c\left(nT - \frac{T}{L}\right) \end{aligned}$$

4.41. (a) See figures below.

(b) From part(a), we see that

$$Y_c(j\Omega) = X_c(j(\Omega - \frac{2\pi}{T})) + X_c(j(\Omega + \frac{2\pi}{T}))$$

Therefore,

$$y_c(t) = 2x_c(t)\cos(\frac{2\pi}{T}t)$$

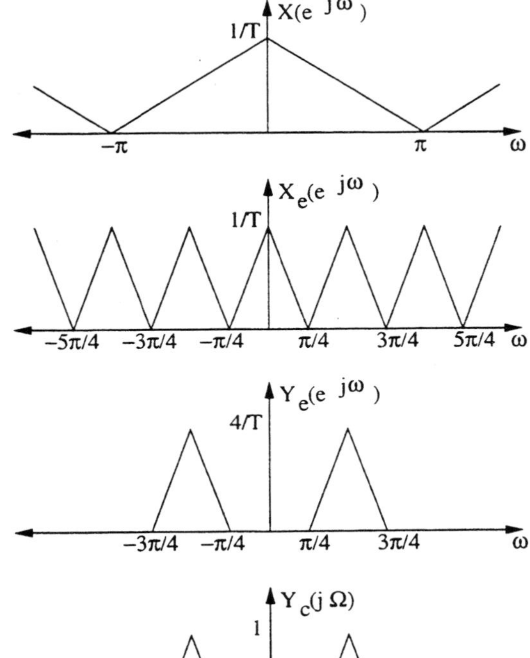

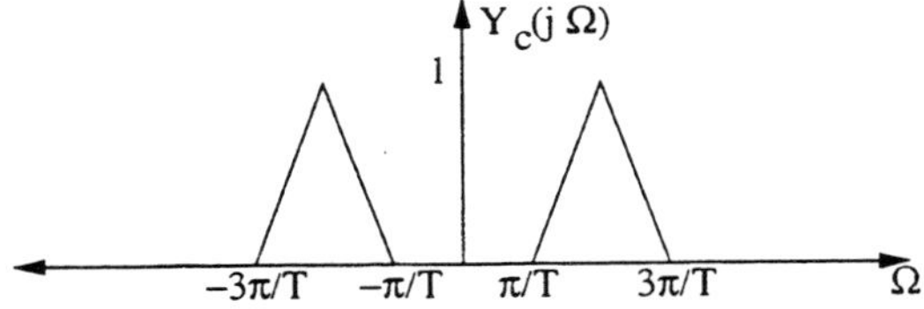

4.42. (a) The Nyquist criterion states that $x_c(t)$ can be recovered as long as

$$\frac{2\pi}{T} \geq 2 \times 2\pi(250) \Longrightarrow T \leq \frac{1}{500}.$$

In this case, $T = 1/500$, so the Nyquist criterion is satisfied, and $x_c(t)$ can be recovered.

(b) Yes. A delay in time does not change the bandwidth of the signal. Hence, $y_c(t)$ has the same bandwidth and same Nyquist sampling rate as $x_c(t)$.

(c) Consider first the following expressions for $X(e^{j\omega})$ and $Y(e^{j\omega})$:

$$\begin{aligned}
X(e^{j\omega}) &= \frac{1}{T}X_c(j\Omega)\mid_{\Omega=\frac{\omega}{T}} = \frac{1}{500}X_c(j500\omega) \\
Y(e^{j\omega}) &= \frac{1}{T}Y_c(j\Omega)\mid_{\Omega=\frac{\omega}{T}} = \frac{1}{T}e^{-j\Omega/1000}X_c(j\Omega)\mid_{\Omega=\frac{\omega}{T}} \\
&= \frac{1}{500}e^{-j\omega/2}X_c(j500\omega) \\
&= e^{-j\omega/2}X(e^{j\omega})
\end{aligned}$$

Hence, we let

$$H(e^{j\omega}) = \begin{cases} 2e^{-j\omega}, & |\omega| < \frac{\pi}{2} \\ 0, & \text{otherwise} \end{cases}$$

Then, in the following figure,

$$\begin{aligned} R(e^{j\omega}) &= X(e^{j2\omega}) \\ W(e^{j\omega}) &= \begin{cases} 2e^{-j\omega}X(e^{j2\omega}), & |\omega| < \frac{\pi}{2} \\ 0, & \text{otherwise} \end{cases} \\ Y(e^{j\omega}) &= e^{-j\omega/2}X(e^{j\omega}) \end{aligned}$$

x[n] → [↑2] → r[n] → [H] → w[n] → [↓2] → y[n]

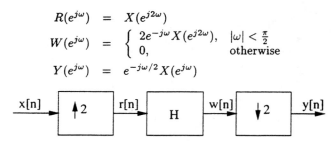

(d) Yes, from our analysis above,

$$H_2(e^{j\omega}) = e^{-j\omega/2}$$

4.43. (a) Notice first that

$$X_c(j\Omega) = \begin{cases} F_c(j\Omega)|H_{aa}(j\Omega)|e^{-j\Omega^3}, & |\Omega| \leq 400\pi \\ E_c(j\Omega)|H_{aa}(j\Omega)|e^{-j\Omega^3}, & 400\pi \leq |\Omega| \leq 800\pi \\ 0, & \text{otherwise} \end{cases}$$

For the given $T = 1/800$, there is no aliasing from the C/D conversion. Hence, the equivalent CT transfer function $H_c(j\Omega)$ can be written as

$$H_c(j\Omega) = \begin{cases} H(e^{j\omega})|_{\omega=\Omega T}, & |\Omega| \leq \pi/T \\ 0, & \text{otherwise} \end{cases}$$

Furthermore, since $Y_c(j\Omega) = H_c(j\Omega)X_c(j\Omega)$, the desired tranfer function is

$$H_c(j\Omega) = \begin{cases} e^{j\Omega^3}, & |\Omega| \leq 400\pi \\ 0, & \text{otherwise} \end{cases}$$

Combining the two previous equations, we find

$$H(e^{j\omega}) = \begin{cases} e^{j(800\omega)^3}, & |\omega| \leq \pi/2 \\ 0, & \pi/2 \leq |\omega| \leq \pi \end{cases}$$

(b) Some aliasing will occur if $2\pi/T < 1600\pi$. However, this is fine as long as the aliasing affects only $E_c(j\Omega)$ and not $F_c(j\Omega)$, as we show below:

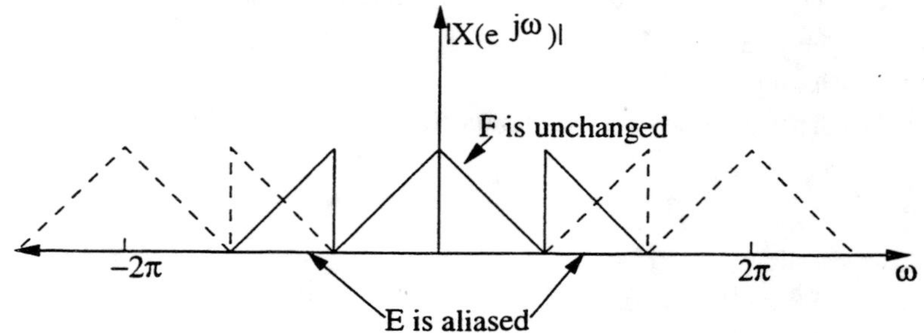

In order for the aliasing to not affect $F_c(j\Omega)$, we require

$$\frac{2\pi}{T} - 800\pi \geq 400\pi \Longrightarrow \frac{2\pi}{T} \geq 1200\pi$$

The minimum $\frac{2\pi}{T}$ is 1200π. For this choice, we get

$$H(e^{j\omega}) = \begin{cases} e^{j(600\omega)^3}, & |\omega| \leq 2\pi/3 \\ 0, & 2\pi/3 \leq |\omega| \leq \pi \end{cases}$$

4.44. (a) See the following figure:

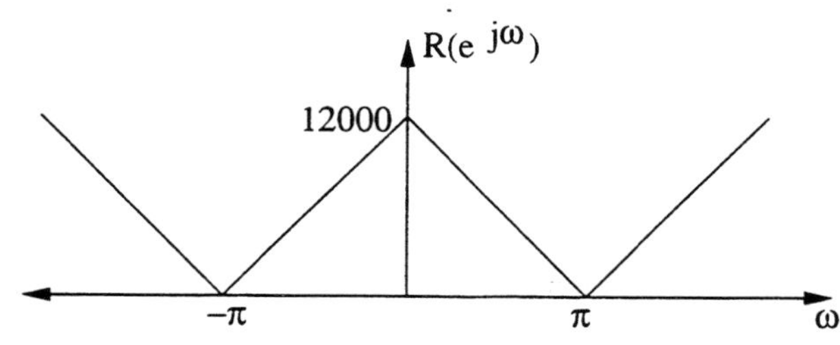

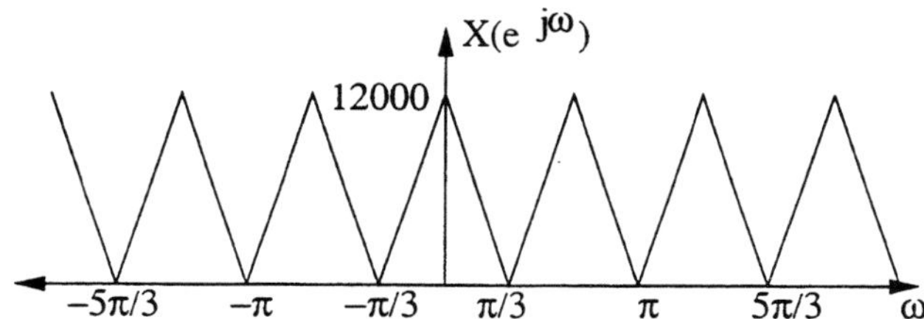

(b) For this to be true, $H(e^{j\omega})$ needs to filter out $X(e^{j\omega})$ for $\pi/3 \leq |\omega| \leq \pi$. Hence let $\omega_0 = \pi/3$. Furthermore, we want

$$\frac{\pi/2}{T_2} = 2\pi(1000) \Longrightarrow T_2 = 1/6000$$

(c) Matching the following figure of $S(e^{j\omega})$ with the figure for $R_c(j\Omega)$, and remembering that $\Omega = \omega/T$, we get $T_3 = (2\pi/3)/(2000\pi) = 1/3000$.

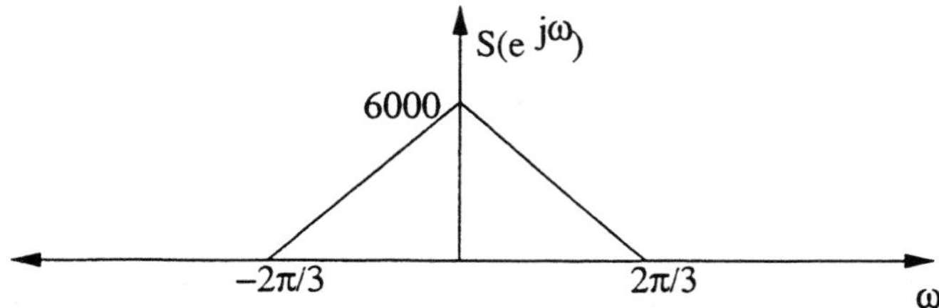

4.45. Notice first that since $x_c(t)$ is time-limited,

$$A = \int_0^{10} x_c(t)dt = \int_{-\infty}^{\infty} x_c(t)dt = X_c(j\Omega)|_{\Omega=0}.$$

To estimate $X_c(j \cdot 0)$ by DT processing, we need to sample only fast enough so that $X_c(j \cdot 0)$ is not aliased. Hence, we pick

$$2\pi/T = 2\pi \times 10^4 \Longrightarrow T = 10^{-4}.$$

The resulting spectrum satisfies

$$X(e^{j\cdot 0}) = \frac{1}{T}X_c(j\cdot 0)$$

Further,

$$X(e^{j\cdot 0}) = \sum_{n=-\infty}^{\infty} x[n].$$

Therefore, we pick $h[n] = Tu[n]$, which makes the system an accumulator. Our estimate $\hat{A}$ is the output $y[n]$ at $n = 10/(10^{-4}) = 10^5$, when all of the non-zero samples of $x[n]$ have been added-up. This is an *exact* estimate given our assumption of both band- and time-limitedness. Since the assumption can never be exactly satisfied, however, this method only gives an approximate estimate for actual signals.

The overall system is as follows:

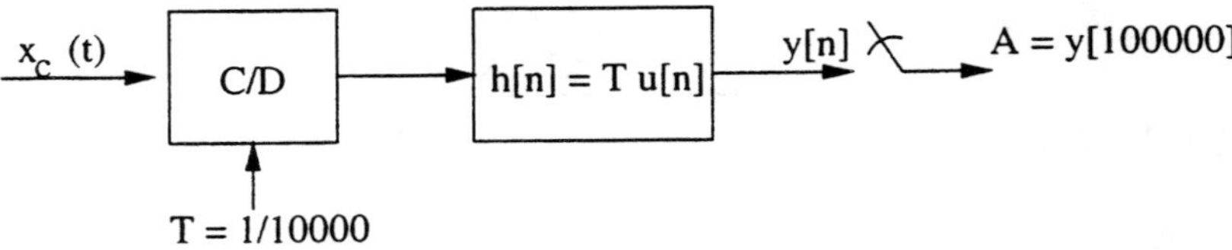

4.46. (a) Notice that

$$\begin{aligned} y_0[n] &= x[3n] \\ y_1[n] &= x[3n+1] \\ y_2[n] &= x[3n+2], \end{aligned}$$

and therefore,

$$x[n] = \begin{cases} y_0[n/3], & n = 3k \\ y_1[(n-1)/3], & n = 3k+1 \\ y_2[(n-2)/3], & n = 3k+2 \end{cases}$$

(b) Yes. Since the bandwidth of the filters are $2\pi/3$, there is no aliasing introduced by downsampling. Hence to reconstruct $x[n]$, we need the system shown in the following figure:

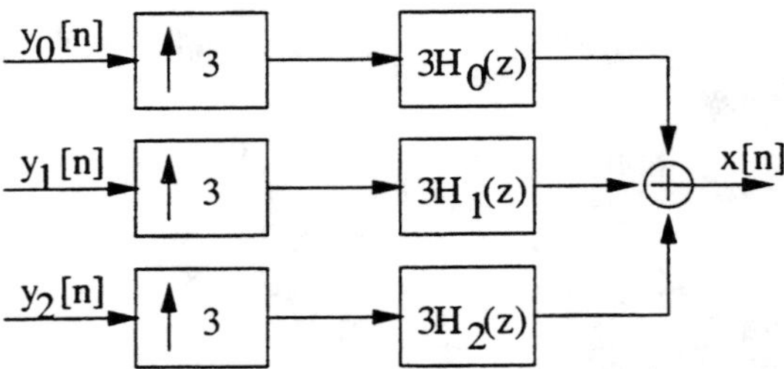

(c) Yes, $x[n]$ can be reconstructed from $y_3[n]$ and $y_4[n]$ as demonstrated by the following figure:

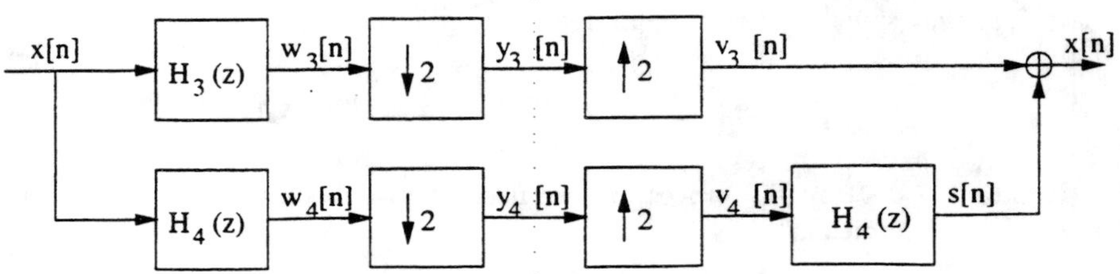

In the following discussion, let $x_e[n]$ denote the even samples of $x[n]$, and $x_o[n]$ denote the odd samples of $x[n]$:

$$\begin{aligned} x_e[n] &= \begin{cases} x[n], & n \text{ even} \\ 0, & n \text{ odd} \end{cases} \\ x_o[n] &= \begin{cases} 0, & n \text{ even} \\ x[n], & n \text{ odd} \end{cases} \end{aligned}$$

In the figure, $y_3[n] = x[2n]$, and hence,

$$\begin{aligned} v_3[n] &= \begin{cases} x[n], & n \text{ even} \\ 0, & n \text{ odd} \end{cases} \\ &= x_e[n] \end{aligned}$$

Furthermore, it can be verified using the IDFT that the impulse response $h_4[n]$ corresponding to $H_4(e^{j\omega})$ is

$$h_4[n] = \begin{cases} -2/(j\pi n), & n \text{ odd} \\ 0, & \text{otherwise} \end{cases}$$

Notice in particular that every other sample of the impulse response $h_4[n]$ is zero. Also, from the form of $H_4(e^{j\omega})$, it is clear that $H_4(e^{j\omega})H_4(e^{j\omega}) = 1$, and hence $h_4[n] * h_4[n] = \delta[n]$. Therefore,

$$\begin{aligned} v_4[n] &= \begin{cases} y_4[n/2], & n \text{ even} \\ 0, & n \text{ odd} \end{cases} \\ &= \begin{cases} w_4[n], & n \text{ even} \\ 0, & n \text{ odd} \end{cases} \\ &= \begin{cases} (x * h_4)[n], & n \text{ even} \\ 0, & n \text{ odd} \end{cases} \\ &= x_o[n] * h_4[n] \end{aligned}$$

where the last equality follows from the fact that $h_4[n]$ is non-zero only in the odd samples. Now, $s[n] = v_4[n] * h_4[n] = x_o[n] * h_4[n] * h_4[n] = x_o[n]$, and since $x[n] = x_e[n] + x_o[n]$, $s[n] + v_3[n] = x[n]$.

4.47. Sampling random processes

$$\phi_{x_c x_c}(\tau) = E(x_c(t)x_c^*(t+\tau)) \Leftrightarrow P_{x_c x_c}(\Omega) = \int_{-\infty}^{\infty} \phi_{x_c x_c}(\tau)e^{-j\Omega\tau}d\tau$$

(a)

$$\begin{aligned} \phi_{xx}[m] &= E(x[n]x^*[n+m]) = E(x_c(nT)x_c^*(nT+mT)) \\ &= \phi_{x_c x_c}(mT), \quad \text{i.e., sampled autocovariance} \end{aligned}$$

(b) Since $\phi_{xx}[m]$ is a sampled $\phi_{x_c x_c}(\tau)$

$$P_{xx}(\omega) = \frac{1}{T}\sum_{K=-\infty}^{\infty} P_{x_c x_c}\left(\frac{\omega}{T} + \frac{2\pi k}{T}\right)$$

(c) If

$$P_{x_c x_c} = 0, \text{ for } |\omega| \geq \pi$$

then

$$P_{xx}(\omega) = \frac{1}{T}P_{x_c x_c}\left(\frac{\omega}{T}\right), \quad |\omega| \leq \pi$$

4.48. (a)

$$\begin{aligned}\phi_{x_cx_c}(\tau) &= E(x_c(t)x_c(t+\tau))\\ \phi_{xx}[m] &= E(x[n]x[n+m]) = E(x_c(nT)x_c(nT+mT))\\ &= \phi_{x_cx_c}(mT)\end{aligned}$$

(b)

$$P_{xx}(\omega) = \frac{1}{T}\sum_{r=-\infty}^{\infty} P_{x_cx_c}\left(\frac{\omega}{T} + \frac{2\pi r}{T}\right)$$

Therefore, we require that $\frac{\pi}{T} \geq \Omega_0$.

(c) For the spectrum of Fig P3.8-2 it is clear that if $T = \frac{2\pi}{\Omega_0}$ then the discrete-time power spectrum will be white, as shown in the figure above.

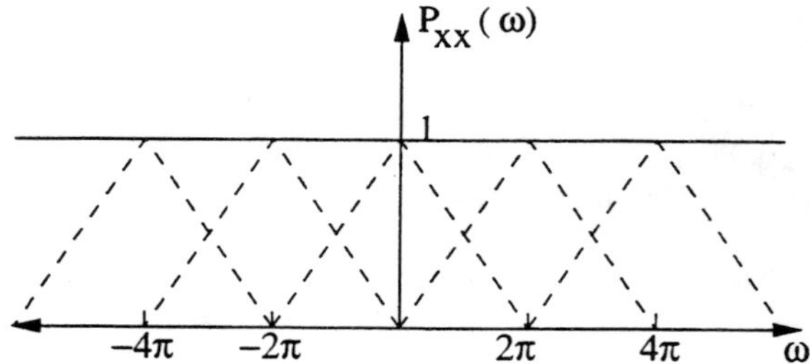

(d) For white discrete-time signal $\Rightarrow \phi_{xx}[m] = 0, \quad m \neq 0$ but $\phi_{xx}[m] = \phi_{x_cx_c}(mT)$. Therefore, any analog signal whose autocorrelation function has zeros equally spaced at intervals of T will yield a white discrete-time sequence is sampled with sampling period T. For example, for Fig P3.8-1:

$$\phi_{x_cx_c}(\tau) = \frac{\sin \Omega_0 T}{T\pi} \Rightarrow \phi_{xx}[m] = \frac{\sin \Omega_0 mT}{\pi mT}$$

$$\text{if } T = \frac{\pi}{\Omega_0} \qquad \phi_{xx}[m] = \frac{\sin \pi m}{\pi^2 m/\Omega_o} = 0, \qquad m \neq 0$$

4.49. (a) Consider the following plots.

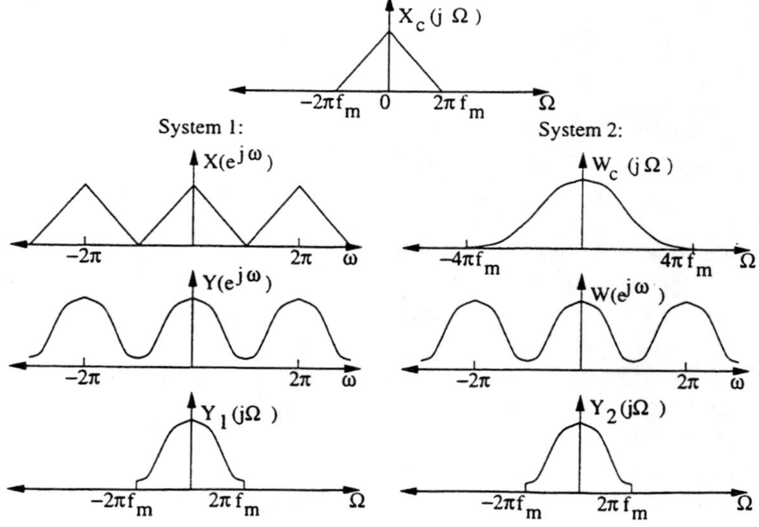

$y_1(t) = y_2(t)$: Convolution is a linear process. Aliasing is a linear process. Periodic convolution is equivalent to convolution followed by aliasing.
$y_1(t) \neq x^2(t)$: System 2 at Step 1 shows $X_c^2(j\Omega)$. This is clearly not $Y_1(j\Omega)$. $Y_1(j\Omega)$ is an aliased version of $X_c(j\Omega)$

(b) Now,

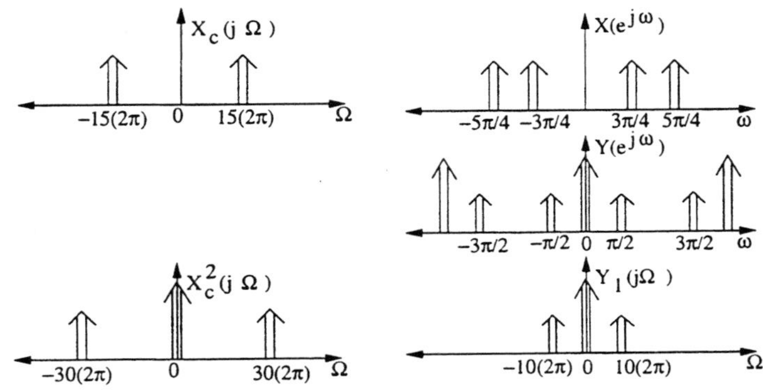

(c)

$$\begin{aligned} x(t) &= A\cos(30\pi t) \\ x^3(t) &= \frac{3}{4}A\cos(30\pi t) + \frac{1}{4}A\cos(3\cdot 30\pi t), \\ v[n] &= \frac{3}{4}A\cos\left(\frac{3}{4}\pi n\right) + \frac{1}{4}A\cos\left(\frac{1}{4}\pi n\right) \\ v[n] &= x^3[n] \\ y[n] &= x[n] \end{aligned}$$

We can see here that sometimes aliasing won't be destructive. When aliased sections do not overlap they can be reconstructed.

(d) This is the inverse to part (c). Since multiplication in time corresponds to convolution in frequency, a signal $x^2(t)$ has at most two times the bandwidth of $x(t)$. Therefore, $x^{1/2}$ will have at least $\frac{1}{2}$ the bandwidth of $x(t)$. If we run our signal through a box that will raise it to the $1/M$ power, then the sampling rate can be decreased by a factor of M.

4.50. (a)

$$\begin{aligned} x_i[n] &= x_u[n] * h_{zoh}[n] \\ h_{zoh}[n] &= \begin{cases} 1, & 0 \leq n \leq L-1 \\ 0, & \text{else} \end{cases} \end{aligned}$$

$$H_{zoh}(e^{j\omega}) = \frac{\sin(\omega L/2)}{\sin(\omega/2)} e^{-j(L-1)\omega/2}$$

(b) The impulse response $h_{lin}[n]$ corresponds to the convolution of two rectangular sequences, as shown below.

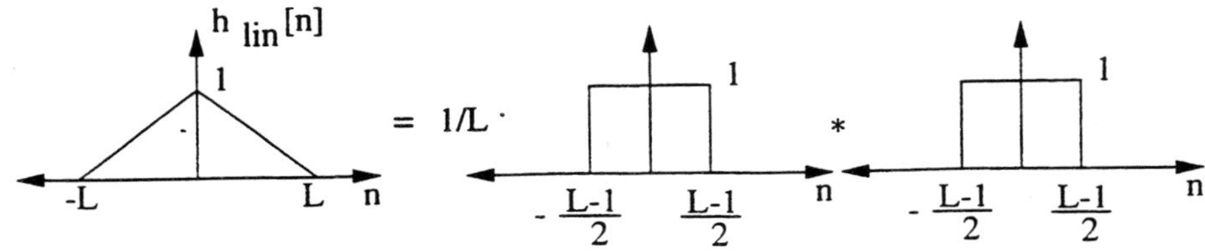

$$H_{lin}(e^{j\omega}) = \frac{1}{L}\left(\frac{\sin(\omega L/2)}{\sin(\omega/2)}\right)^2$$

(c) The frequency response of zero-order-hold is flatter in the region $[-\pi/L, \pi/L]$, but achieves less out-of-band attenuation.

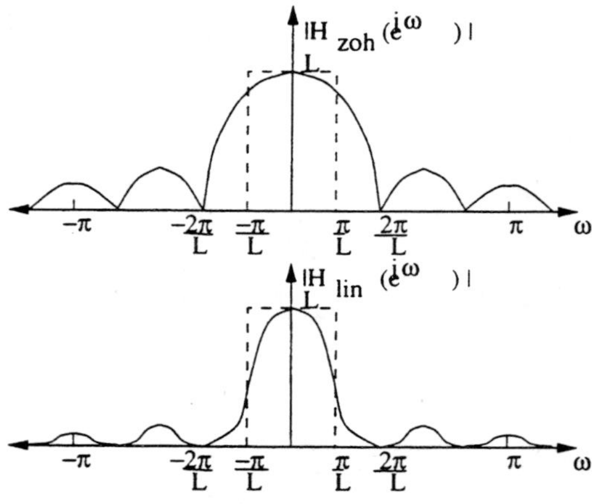

4.51.

$$\begin{aligned}
\phi_{xx}[n] &= x[n] * x[-n] \\
\Phi_{xx}(e^{j\omega}) &= X(e^{j\omega}) * X^*(e^{j\omega})
\end{aligned}$$

The bandwidth of $\Phi_{xx}(e^{j\omega})$ is no larger than the bandwidth of $X(e^{j\omega})$. Therefore, the outputs of the systems will be the same if $H_2(e^{j\omega})$ is an ideal lowpass filter with a cutoff of π/L.

4.52. The idea here is to exploit the fact that every other sample supplied to $h[n]$ in Fig 3.27-1 is zero. That is,

$$\begin{aligned}
y_1[n] &= h[n] * w[n] = \sum_{n=-\infty}^{\infty} w[n-k]h[k] \\
&= aw[n] + bw[n-1] + cw[n-2] + dw[n-3] + ew[n-4] \\
&= \begin{cases} ax[n/2] + cx[(n/2)-1] + e[(n/2)-2], & n \text{ even} \\ bx[(n/2)-(1/2)] + dx[(n/2)-(3/2)], & n \text{ odd} \end{cases}
\end{aligned}$$

$$\begin{aligned}
w_1[n] &= \begin{cases} h_1[n/2] * x[n/2], & n \text{ even} \\ 0, & n \text{ odd} \end{cases} \\
&= \begin{cases} h_1[0]x[n/2] + h_1[1]x[(n/2)-1] + h_1[2]x[(n/2)-2], & n \text{ even} \\ 0, & n \text{ odd} \end{cases}
\end{aligned}$$

$$\begin{aligned}
w_2[n] &= \begin{cases} h_2[n/2] * x[n/2], & n \text{ even} \\ 0, & n \text{ odd} \end{cases} \\
&= \begin{cases} h_2[0]x[n/2] + h_2[1]x[(n/2)-1] + h_2[2]x[(n/2)-2], & n \text{ even} \\ 0, & n \text{ odd} \end{cases}
\end{aligned}$$

Comparing $w_1[n], w_2[n]$ with $y_1[n]$ above:
$w[n]$ can give even samples if $h_1[0] = a, h_1[1] = c, h_2[2] = e$. Similarly, $w_2[n]$ can give the odd samples if $h_3[n]$ delays $w_2[n]$ by one sample, i.e., $h_3[0] = 0, h_3[1] = 0, h_3[2] = 0$. Thus

$$w_3[n] = \begin{cases} h_2[0]x[(n-1)/2] + h_2[1]x[(n-1)/2 - 1] + h_2[2]x[(n-1)/2 - 2], & n \text{ even} \\ 0, & n \text{ odd} \end{cases}$$

$$h_2[0] = b, \quad h_2[1] = d, \quad h_2[2] = 0$$

4.53. Sketches appear below.

(a) First, $X(e^{j\omega})$ is plotted.

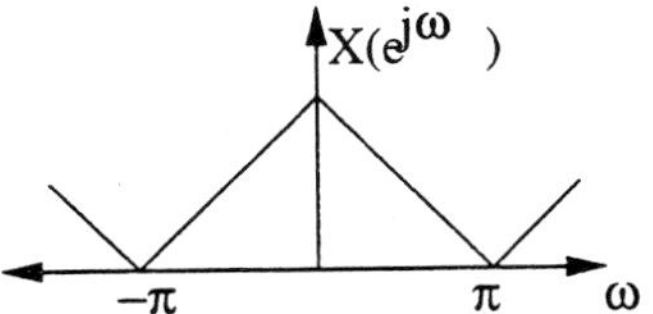

The lowpass filter cuts off at $\frac{\pi}{2}$.

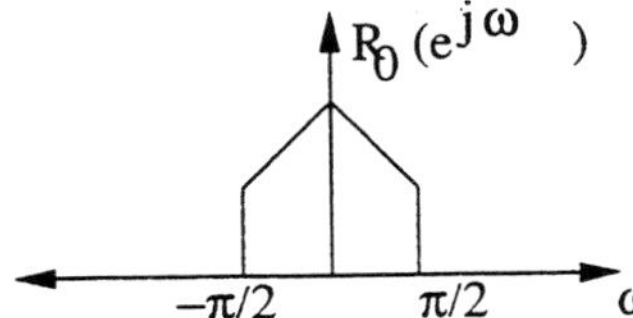

The downsampler expands the frequency axis. Since $R_0(e^{j\omega})$ is bandlimited to $\frac{\pi}{M}$, no aliasing occurs.

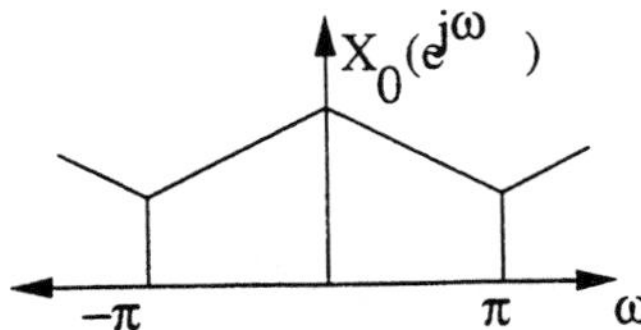

The upsampler compresses the frequency axis by a factor of 2.

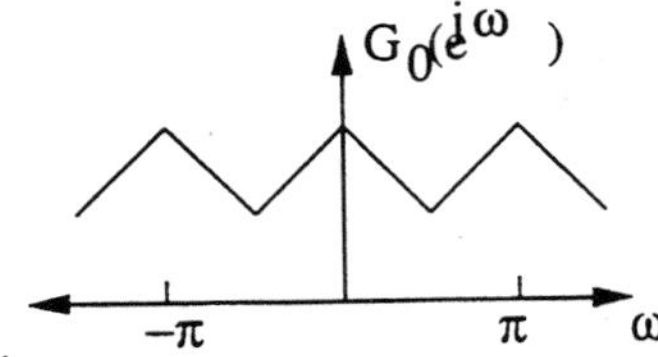

The lowpass filter cuts off at $\frac{\pi}{2} \Rightarrow Y_0(e^{j\omega}) = R_0(e^{j\omega})$ as sketched above.

(b) $G_0(e^{j\omega}) = \frac{1}{2}\left(X(e^{j\omega})H_0(e^{j\omega}) + X(e^{j(\omega+\pi)})H_0(e^{j(\omega+\pi)})\right)$

(c)

$$\begin{aligned}
Y_0(e^{j\omega}) &= \frac{1}{2}H_0(e^{j\omega})\left(X(e^{j\omega})H_0(e^{j\omega}) + X(e^{j(\omega+\pi)})H_0(e^{j(\omega+\pi)})\right)\\
Y_1(e^{j\omega}) &= \frac{1}{2}H_1(e^{j\omega})\left(X(e^{j\omega})H_1(e^{j\omega}) + X(e^{j(\omega+\pi)})H_1(e^{j(\omega+\pi)})\right)\\
Y(e^{j\omega}) &= Y_0(e^{j\omega}) - Y_1(e^{j\omega})\\
&= \frac{1}{2}X(e^{j\omega})\left[H_0^2(e^{j\omega}) - H_1^2(e^{j\omega})\right]\\
&\quad +\frac{1}{2}X(e^{j(\omega+\pi)})\underbrace{\left[H_0(e^{j\omega})H_0(e^{j(\omega+\pi)}) - H_1(e^{j\omega})H_1(e^{j(\omega+\pi)})\right]}_{=0}
\end{aligned}$$

The aliasing terms always cancel. $Y(e^{j\omega})$ is proportional to $X(e^{j\omega})$ if $[H_0^2(e^{j\omega}) - H_1^2(e^{j\omega})]$ is a constant.

$X(e^{j\omega}) = 0, \pi/3 \leq |\omega| \leq \pi$. $x[n]$ can be thought of as an oversampled signal. The approach is to determine whether n_0 is odd or even, then sample so that n_0 is avoided, upsampled and lowpass filter. This recovers $x[n_0]$.

4.54. (a) In the case where n_0 is not known, we determine whether it is even or odd as follows:

$$\begin{aligned}
\hat{x}[n] &= x[n] - A\delta[n-n_0]\\
\hat{X}(e^{j\omega}) &= X(e^{j\omega}) - Ae^{-j\omega n_0}\\
\hat{X}(e^{j\omega})|_{\omega=\frac{\pi}{2}} &= \sum_n x[n](-j)^n\\
\hat{X}(e^{j(\pi/2)}) &= -A(-j)^{n_0}
\end{aligned}$$

If the result is real, n_0 is even. If the result is imaginary, n_0 is odd.

(b) If n_0 is even, sample $\hat{x}[n]$ so that the even-numbered sequence values are set to zero. If n_0 is odd, sample so the odd-numbered samples are set to zero

(c) Filter the sampled sequence with a lowpass filter with cutoff frequency $\pi/3$, and gain 2. This is an exact procedure if ideal filters are used.

4.55. (a)

$$\begin{aligned}
w[n] &= \begin{cases} x_1[n/2], & n \text{ even}\\ x_2[(n-1)/2], & n \text{ odd}\end{cases}\\
x_1[n] &= w[2n]\\
x_2[n] &= w[2n+1]
\end{aligned}$$

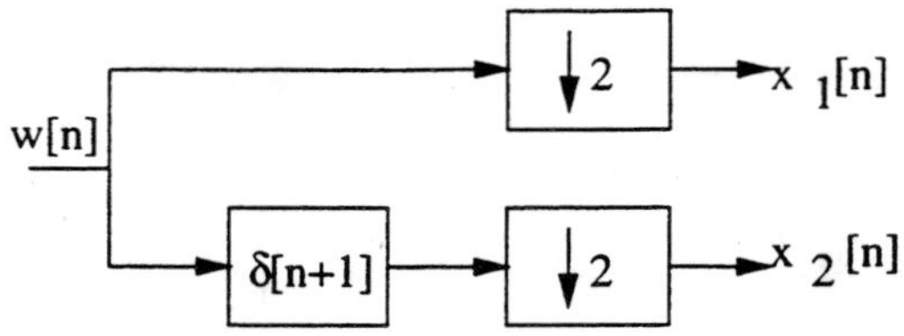

The system is linear, time-varying (due to downsampling), non-causal (due to $\delta[n+1]$), and stable.

(b)

$$T = \frac{\pi}{\Omega_N} = \frac{\pi}{2\pi \times 5000} = 10^{-4}\text{sec}, \qquad \frac{L\omega_1}{T} = 2\pi \times 10^5$$

To avoid aliasing in $y_c(t)$:

$$\begin{aligned} \frac{L\omega_1}{T} + \frac{2\pi}{T} &\leq \frac{L\pi}{T} \\ \omega_1 &= \frac{20\pi}{L} \\ 20\pi + 2\pi &= L\pi \end{aligned}$$

$$L = 22, \qquad \omega_1 = 2\pi(\frac{10}{22})$$

(c) The Fourier transforms are sketched below.

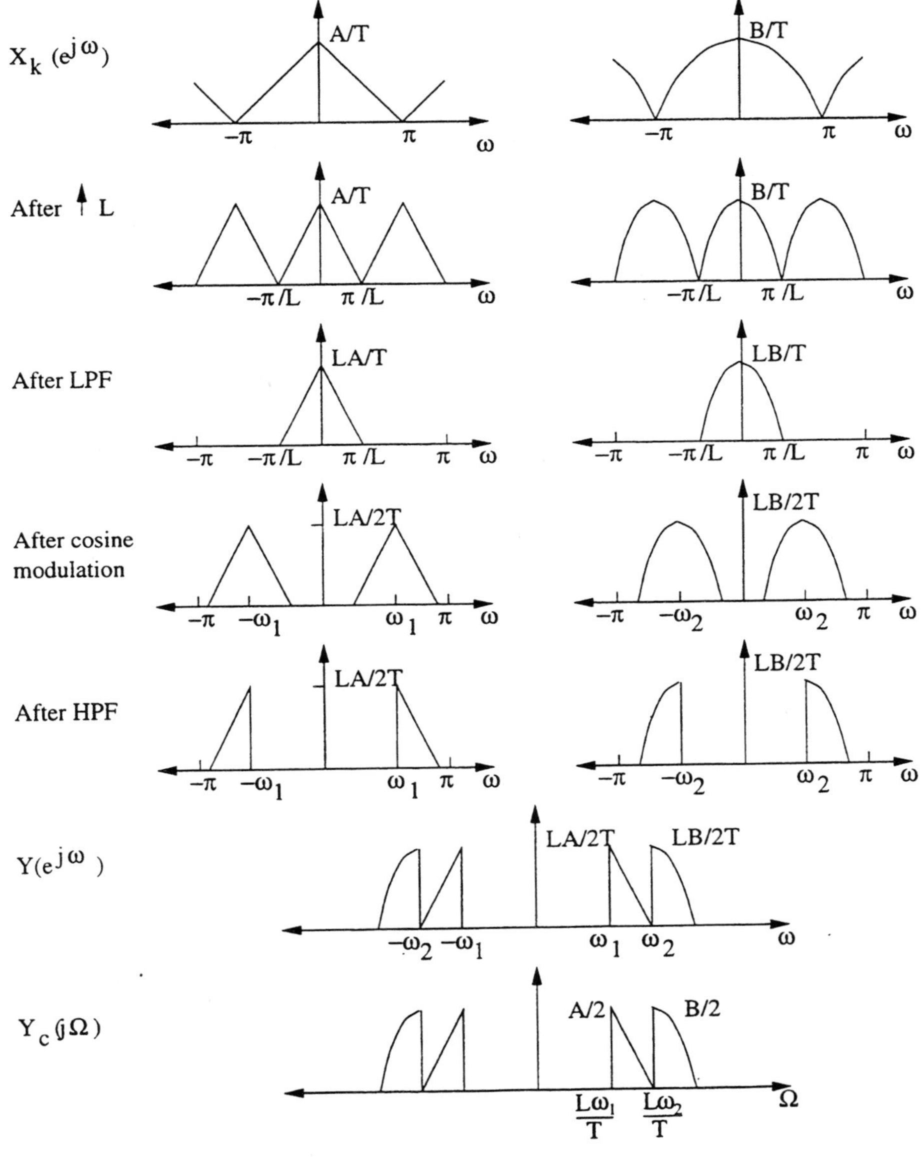

(d) To generalize for M channels, we would use the same modulators, but we would choose a larger value of L to make room for additional spectra above the lower frequency bound. If the lower

bound remained $2\pi \cdot 10^5$, L would become $L = 20 + M$ for M channels.
A branch of the TDM demultiplexing system would be:

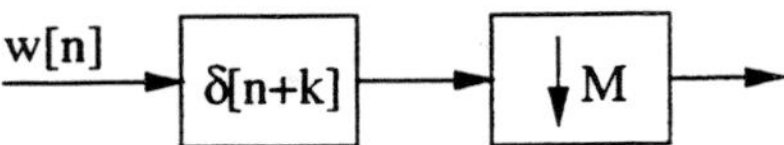

4.56. Since we want $W(e^{j\omega})$ to equal $X(e^{j\omega})$, then $H(e^{j\omega})$ must compensate for the drop offs in $H_{aa}(j\Omega)$.

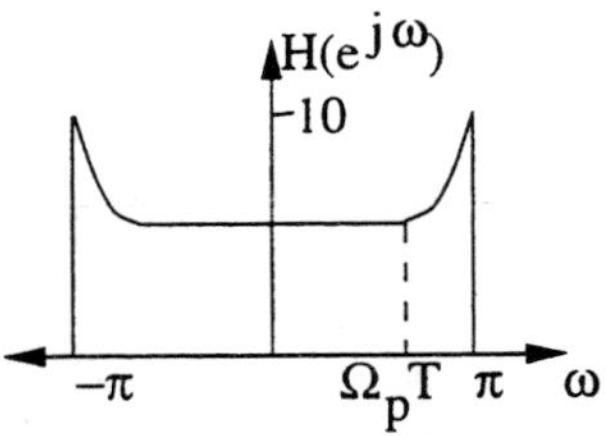

4.57. (a)

$$E(e) = \int ep(e)de = \frac{1}{\Delta}\int_{-\Delta/2}^{\Delta/2} ede = \frac{e^2}{2\Delta}\Big|_{-\Delta/2}^{\Delta/2} = 0$$

$$\sigma_e^2 = E(e^2 - 0) = \frac{1}{\Delta}\int_{-\Delta/2}^{\Delta/2} e^2 de = \frac{e^3}{3\Delta}\Big|_{-\Delta/2}^{\Delta/2} = \frac{\Delta^2}{12}$$

$$r[m,n] = E(e[m]e[n]) = \begin{cases} E(e[m])E(e[n]), & m \neq n \\ E(e^2[n]), & m = n \end{cases}$$

$$r[n,m] = r[n-m] = \frac{\Delta^2}{12}\delta[n-m]$$

(b)

$$\text{SNR} = \frac{\sigma_x^2}{\sigma_e^2} = \frac{12\sigma_x^2}{\Delta^2}$$

(c) Let $e_y[n]$ be the output noise.

$$\begin{aligned}
e_y[n] &= \sum_k h[k]e[n-k] \\
E(e_y^2[n]) &= E\left(\sum_k h[k]e[n-k]\sum_l h[l]e[n-l]\right) = \sum_k\sum_l h[k]h[l]\underbrace{E(e[n-k]e[n-l])}_{\sigma_e^2[k-l]} \\
\sigma_{e_y}^2 &= \sigma_e^2\sum_k h^2[k] \\
&= \sigma_e^2\sum_{k=0}^{\infty}\frac{1}{4}\left(a^k + (-a)^k\right)^2 = \frac{\sigma_e^2}{4}\sum_{k=0}^{\infty}\left(a^{2k} + 2a^k(-a)^k + (-a)^{2k}\right) \\
&= \frac{\sigma_e^2}{2}\left(\sum_{k=0}^{\infty}a^{2k} + \sum_{k=0}^{\infty}(-a^2)^k\right) = \frac{\sigma_e^2}{2}\left(\frac{1}{1-a^2} + \frac{1}{1+a^2}\right) \\
&= \sigma_e^2\left(\frac{1}{1-a^4}\right) = \frac{\Delta^2}{12(1-a^4)}
\end{aligned}$$

The variance of $x[n]$ is weighted similarly so the SNR does not change. $\text{SNR}_{\text{out}} = 12\frac{\sigma_x^2}{\Delta^2}$.

(d) $f[n] = x[n]e[n]$

$$E(f[n]) = E(x[n]e[n]) = E(x[n])E(e[n]) = 0$$

$$\sigma_f^2 = E(f^2[n]) = E(x^2[n]e^2[n]) = E(x^2[n])E(e^2[n]) = \sigma_x^2\sigma_e^2$$

$$r_f[n,m] = E(x[n]x[m]e[n]e[m]) = \underbrace{E(x[n]x[m])}_{\sigma_x^2\delta[n-m]} \cdot \underbrace{E(e[n]e[m])}_{\sigma_e^2\delta[n-m]}$$

(e)

$$\text{SNR} = \frac{\sigma_x^2}{\sigma_f^2} = \frac{\sigma_x^2}{\sigma_x^2\sigma_e^2} = \frac{1}{\sigma_e^2} = \frac{12}{\Delta^2}$$

(f) Using the results of part (c).

$$\sigma_{e_y}^2 = \sigma_f^2\left(\frac{1}{1-a^4}\right) = \frac{\sigma_x^2\sigma_e^2}{1-a^4}$$

Again, the variance of $x[n]$ is weighted by the same factor, so the SNR does not change.

$$\text{SNR}_{\text{out}} = \frac{12}{\Delta^2}.$$

4.58. First, notice that since $y_c(t) = x_1(t)x_2(t)$, $Y_c(j\Omega) = \frac{1}{2\pi}(X_1(j\Omega) * X_2(j\Omega))$, and so $Y_c(j\Omega) = 0$ for $|\Omega| \geq 11\pi/2 \times 10^4$. Hence the Nyquist rate $T = 1/55000$s.

Choose System A and B such that $w_1[n] = ax_1(nT)$ and $w_2[n] = bx_2(nT)$.

For System A, we need to resample such that

$$\frac{M}{L} = \frac{T}{T_1} = \frac{2\times 10^{-5}}{1/55000} = \frac{10}{11}$$

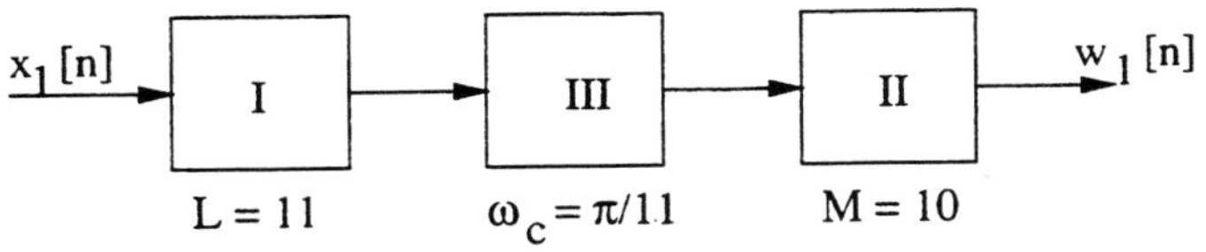

$x_1[n]$ → [I, $L = 11$] → [III, $\omega_c = \pi/11$] → [II, $M = 10$] → $w_1[n]$

For System B, we need to resample such that

$$\frac{M}{L} = \frac{T}{T_1} = \frac{2\times 10^{-4}}{1/55000} = \frac{1}{11}$$

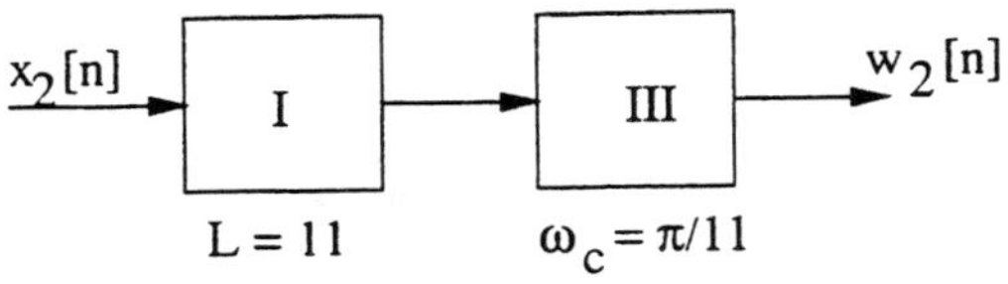

$x_2[n]$ → [I, $L = 11$] → [III, $\omega_c = \pi/11$] → $w_2[n]$

System C is simply the identity system.

4.59. The speech is first sampled at 44.1 kHz, and we wish to resample it so that the sampling rate is at 8 kHz. There are no aliasing effects anywhere in the system. Hence

$$\frac{L}{M} = \frac{44.1}{8} = \frac{441}{80}$$

We simply make $L = 441$, $M = 80$, and $\omega_c = \pi/441$.

4.60. Ω_p, and Ω_s has to be chosen such that

(a) The region $|\Omega| \leq \Omega_p$ maps to $|\omega| \leq \pi/4$:

$$\Omega_p T = \frac{\pi}{4} \Longrightarrow \Omega_p = 44\pi$$

(b) No aliasing occurs in the region $|\Omega| \leq \Omega_p$ during sampling:

$$\frac{2\pi}{T} - \Omega_s = \Omega_p \Longrightarrow \Omega_s = 2\pi(4 \cdot 44) - 44\pi = 308\pi$$

4.61. (a)

$$\begin{aligned} V(z) &= H_1(z)(X(z) - Y(z)) \\ U(z) &= H_2(z)(V(z) - Y(z)) \\ Y(z) &= U(z) + E(z) \\ &= \frac{H_1(z)H_2(z)}{1 + H_2(z)(1 + H_1(z))} X(z) + \frac{1}{1 + H_2(z)(1 + H_1(z))} E(z) \end{aligned}$$

Substituting $H_1(z) = 1/(1 - z^{-1})$ and $H_2(z) = z^{-1}/(1 - z^{-1})$, we find

$$\begin{aligned} H_{xy}(z) &= z^{-1} \\ H_{ey}(z) &= (1 - z^{-1})^2 \end{aligned}$$

Hence the difference equation is $y[n] = x[n-1] + f[n]$, where

$$f[n] = e[n] - 2e[n-1] + e[n-2].$$

(b)

$$\begin{aligned} P_{ff}(e^{j\omega}) &= \sigma_e^2 |H_{ey}(e^{j\omega})|^2 \\ &= \sigma_e^2 |(1 - e^{-j\omega})^2|^2 \\ &= \sigma_e^2 (1 - e^{-j\omega})^2 (1 - e^{j\omega})^2 \\ &= \sigma_e^2 (2 - 2\cos(\omega))^2 \\ &= \sigma_e^2 (4 \sin^2(\omega/2))^2 \\ &= 16\sigma_e^2 \sin^4(\omega/2) \end{aligned}$$

The total noise power σ_f^2 is the autocorrelation of $f[n]$ evaluated at 0:

$$\begin{aligned} \sigma_f^2 &= E[(e[n] - 2e[n-1] + e[n-2])^2] \\ &= E[e^2[n]] + E[-2e^2[n-1]] + E[e[n-2]^2] \\ &= 6\sigma_e^2, \end{aligned}$$

where we have used linearity of expectations, and the fact that since $e[n]$ is white, $E[e[n]e[n-k]] = 0$ for $k \neq 0$.

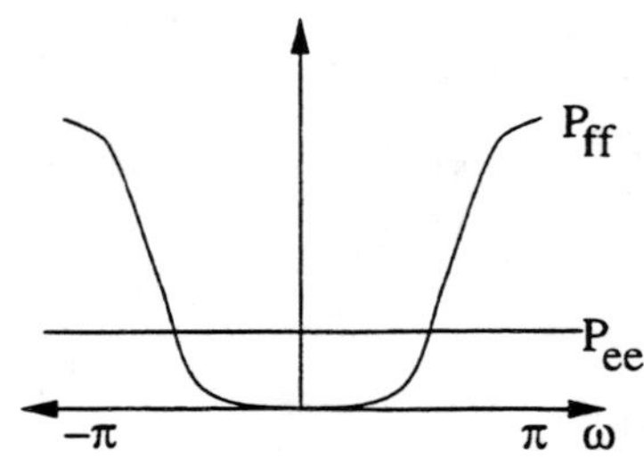

(c) Since $X(e^{j\omega})$ is bandlimited, $x[n] * h_3[n] = x[n]$. Hence,

$$w[n] = y[n] * h_3[n] = (x[n-1] + f[n]) * h_3[n] = x[n-1] + g[n],$$

where $g[n]$ is the quantization noise in the region $|\omega| < \pi/M$.

(d) For a small angle x, $\sin x \approx x$. Therefore,

$$\begin{aligned}
\sigma_g^2 &= \frac{1}{2\pi}\int_{\pi/M}^{\pi/M} \sigma_e^2 (2\sin\omega/2)^4 d\omega \\
&\approx \frac{1}{2\pi}\int_{\pi/M}^{\pi/M} \sigma_e^2 (2\omega/2)^4 d\omega \\
&= \frac{\sigma_e^2}{2\pi}\frac{\omega^5}{5}\Big|_{-\pi/M}^{\pi/M} \\
&= \frac{\sigma_e^2 \pi^4}{5M^5}
\end{aligned}$$

(e) $X_c(j\Omega)$ must be sufficiently bandlimited that $X(e^{j\omega}) = X_c(j\Omega T)$ is zero for $|\omega| > \pi/M$. Hence $X_c(j\Omega) = 0$ for $|\Omega| > \pi/MT$.
Assuming that is satisfied, $v_x[n] = x[Mn-1] = x_c(MTn - T)$.
Downsampling does not change the variance of the noise, and hence $\sigma_q^2 = \sigma_g^2$.

$$\begin{aligned}
P_{qq}(e^{j\omega}) &= P_{gg}(e^{j\omega/M}) \\
&= 16\sigma_e^2 \sin^4(\omega/2M)
\end{aligned}$$

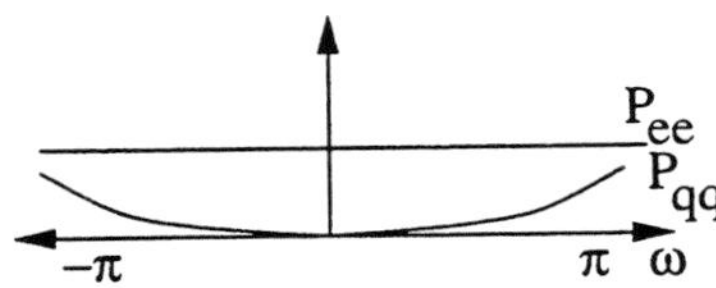

4.62. (a) (i) The transfer function from $x[n]$ to $y_x[n]$ is

$$H_{xy}(z) = \frac{\frac{z^{-1}}{1-z^{-1}}}{1 + \frac{z^{-1}}{1-z^{-1}}} = z^{-1}$$

Hence $y_x[n] = x[n-1]$.

(ii) The transfer function from $e[n]$ to $y_e[n]$ is

$$H_{ey}(z) = \frac{1}{1 + \frac{z^{-1}}{1-z^{-1}}} = 1 - z^{-1}$$

So

$$\begin{aligned}
P_{y_e}(\omega) &= P_e(\omega) H_{ey}(e^{j\omega}) H_{ey} e^{-j\omega} \\
&= \sigma_e^2 (1 - e^{-j\omega})(1 - e^{j\omega}) \\
&= \sigma_e^2 (2 - 2\cos(\omega))
\end{aligned}$$

(b) (i) $x[n]$ contributes only to $y_1[n]$, but not $y_2[n]$. Therefore

$$\begin{aligned}
y_{1x}[n] &= x[n-1] \\
r_x[n] &= x[n-2]
\end{aligned}$$

(ii) In part(a), the difference equation describing the sigma-delta noise-shaper is

$$y[n] = x[n-1] + e[n] - e[n-1].$$

So here we apply the difference equation to both sigma-delta modulators:

$$\begin{aligned}
y_{1e}[n] &= e_1[n] - e_1[n-1] \\
y_{2e}[n] &= e_1[n-1] + e_2[n] - e_2[n-1] \\
r_e[n] &= y_{1e}[n-1] - (y_{2e}[n] - y_{2e}[n-1]) \\
&= -e_2[n] + 2e_2[n-1] - e_w[n-2] \\
H_{e_2r}(z) &= -(1-z^{-1})^2 \\
P_{r_e}(\omega) &= \sigma_e^2(2 - 2\cos\omega)^2
\end{aligned}$$

Solutions – Chapter 5

Transform Analysis of Linear Time-Invariant Systems

5.1.

$$y[n] = \begin{cases} 1, & 0 \le n \le 10, \\ 0, & \text{otherwise} \end{cases}$$

Therefore,

$$Y(e^{j\omega}) = e^{-j5\omega} \frac{\sin \frac{11}{2}\omega}{\sin \frac{\omega}{2}}$$

This $Y(e^{j\omega})$ is full band. Therefore, since $Y(e^{j\omega}) = X(e^{j\omega})H(e^{j\omega})$, the only possible $x[n]$ and ω_c that could produce $y[n]$ is $x[n] = y[n]$ and $\omega_c = \pi$.

5.2. We have $y[n-1] - \frac{10}{3}y[n] + y[n+1] = x[n]$ or $z^{-1}Y(z) - \frac{10}{3}Y(z) + zY(z) = X(z)$. So,

$$\begin{aligned} H(z) &= \frac{1}{z^{-1} - \frac{10}{3} + z} \\ &= \frac{z}{(z-\frac{1}{3})(z-3)} \\ &= \frac{-\frac{1}{8}}{z-\frac{1}{3}} + \frac{\frac{9}{8}}{z-3} \end{aligned}$$

(a)

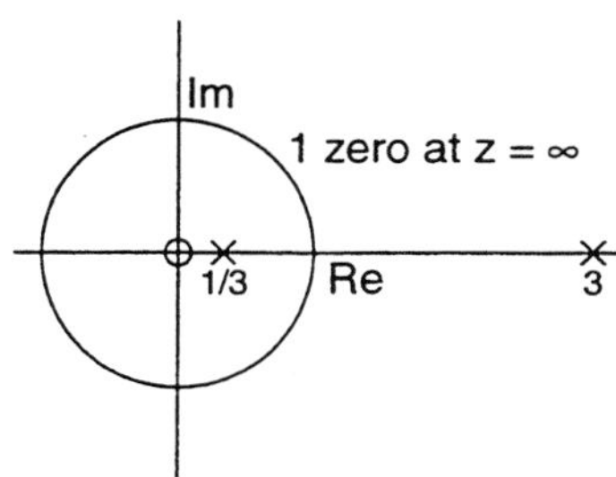

(b)

$$H(z) = \frac{-\frac{1}{8}z^{-1}}{1-\frac{1}{3}z^{-1}} + \frac{\frac{9}{8}z^{-1}}{1-3z^{-1}}$$

Stable $\Rightarrow$ ROC is $\frac{1}{3} \le |z| \le 3$. Therefore,

$$h[n] = -\frac{1}{8}\left(\frac{1}{3}\right)^{n-1} u[n-1] - \frac{9}{8}(3)^{n-1}u[-n]$$

5.3.

$$y[n-1] + \frac{1}{3}y[n-2] = x[n]$$

$$z^{-1}Y(z) + \frac{1}{3}z^{-2}Y(z) = X(z)$$

$$\begin{aligned} H(z) &= \frac{Y(z)}{X(z)} = \frac{1}{z^{-1} + \frac{1}{3}z^{-2}} \\ H(z) &= \frac{z}{1+\frac{1}{3}z^{-1}} \end{aligned}$$

i) $\frac{1}{3} < |z|$, $h[n] = (-\frac{1}{3})^{n+1}u[n+1] \Rightarrow$ answer (a)
ii) $\frac{1}{3} > |z|$,

$$\begin{aligned} h[n] &= -\left(-\frac{1}{3}\right)^{n+1} u[-n-2] \\ &= -\left(-\frac{1}{3}\right)\left(-\frac{1}{3}\right)^{n} u[-n-2] \\ &= \frac{1}{3}\left(-\frac{1}{3}\right)^{n} u[-n-2] \Rightarrow \text{answer (d)} \end{aligned}$$

5.4. (a)

$$x[n] = \left(\frac{1}{2}\right)^n u[n] + (2)^n u[-n-1]$$

$$X(z) = \frac{1}{1-\frac{1}{2}z^{-1}} - \frac{z}{z-2}, \qquad \frac{1}{2} < |z| < 2$$

$$y[n] = 6\left(\frac{1}{2}\right)^n u[n] - 6\left(\frac{3}{4}\right)^n u[n]$$

$$Y(z) = \frac{6}{1-\frac{1}{2}z^{-1}} - \frac{6}{1-\frac{3}{4}z^{-1}}, \qquad \frac{3}{4} < |z|$$

$$H(z) = \frac{Y(z)}{X(z)} = \frac{-\frac{3}{2}z^{-1}}{(1-\frac{1}{2}z^{-1})(1-\frac{3}{4}z^{-1})} \cdot \frac{(1-\frac{1}{2}z^{-1})(1-2z^{-1})}{-\frac{3}{2}z^{-1}} = \frac{1-2z^{-1}}{1-\frac{3}{4}z^{-1}}, \quad |z| > \frac{3}{4}$$

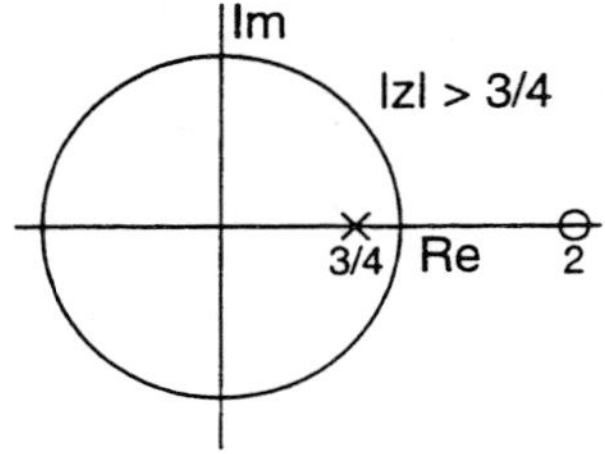

(b)

$$H(z) = \frac{1}{1-\frac{3}{4}z^{-1}} - \frac{2z^{-1}}{1-\frac{3}{4}z^{-1}}, \qquad |z| > \frac{3}{4}$$

$$h[n] = \left(\frac{3}{4}\right)^n u[n] - 2\left(\frac{3}{4}\right)^{n-1} u[n-1]$$

(c)

$$H(z) = \frac{Y(z)}{X(z)} = \frac{1-2z^{-1}}{1-\frac{3}{4}z^{-1}}$$

$$Y(z) - \frac{3}{4}z^{-1}Y(z) = X(z) - 2z^{-1}X(z)$$

$$y[n] - \frac{3}{4}y[n-1] = x[n] - 2x[n-1]$$

(d) The ROC is outside $|z| = \frac{3}{4}$, which includes the unit circle. Therefore the system is stable. The $h[n]$ we found in part (b) tells us the system is also causal.

5.5.

$$y[n] = \left(\frac{1}{3}\right)^n u[n] + \left(\frac{1}{4}\right)^n u[n] + u[n]$$

$$Y(z) = \frac{1}{1-\frac{1}{3}z^{-1}} + \frac{1}{1-\frac{1}{4}z^{-1}} + \frac{1}{1-z^{-1}}, \qquad |z| > 1$$

$$x[n] = u[n]$$

$$X(z) = \frac{1}{1-z^{-1}}, \qquad |z| > 1$$

$$H(z) = \frac{Y(z)}{X(z)} = \frac{3 - \frac{19}{6}z^{-1} + \frac{2}{3}z^{-2}}{1 - \frac{7}{12}z^{-1} + \frac{1}{12}z^{-2}}, \qquad |z| > \frac{1}{3}$$

(a) Cross multiplying and equating z^{-1} with a delay in time:

$$y[n] - \frac{7}{12}y[n-1] + \frac{1}{12}y[n-2] = 3x[n] - \frac{19}{6}x[n-1] + \frac{2}{3}x[n-2]$$

(b) Using partial fractions on $H(z)$ we get:

$$H(z) = \frac{1}{1-\frac{1}{3}z^{-1}} - \frac{z^{-1}}{1-\frac{1}{3}z^{-1}} + \frac{1}{1-\frac{1}{4}z^{-1}} - \frac{z^{-1}}{1-\frac{1}{4}z^{-1}} + 1, \qquad |z| > \frac{1}{3}$$

So,

$$h[n] = \left(\frac{1}{3}\right)^n u[n] - \left(\frac{1}{3}\right)^{n-1} u[n-1] + \left(\frac{1}{4}\right)^n u[n] - \left(\frac{1}{4}\right)^{n-1} u[n-1] + \delta[n]$$

(c) Since the ROC of $H(z)$ includes $|z| = 1$ the system is stable.

5.6. (a)

$$x[n] = -\frac{1}{3}\left(\frac{1}{2}\right)^n u[n] - \frac{4}{3}(2)^n u[-n-1]$$

$$X(z) = \frac{-\frac{1}{3}}{1-\frac{1}{2}z^{-1}} + \frac{\frac{4}{3}}{1-2z^{-1}} = \frac{1}{(1-\frac{1}{2}z^{-1})(1-2z^{-1})}, \qquad \frac{1}{2} < |z| < 2$$

(b)

$$Y(z) = \frac{1-z^{-2}}{(1-\frac{1}{2}z^{-1})(1-2z^{-1})}$$

This has the same poles as the input, therefore the ROC is still $\frac{1}{2} < |z| < 2$.

(c)

$$H(z) = \frac{Y(z)}{X(z)} = 1 - z^{-2} \Leftrightarrow h[n] = \delta[n] - \delta[n-2]$$

5.7. (a)

$$x[n] = 5u[n] \Leftrightarrow X(z) = \frac{5}{1 - z^{-1}}, \qquad |z| > 1$$

$$y[n] = \left(2\left(\frac{1}{2}\right)^n + 3\left(-\frac{3}{4}\right)^n\right)u[n] \Leftrightarrow Y(z) = \frac{2}{1 - \frac{1}{2}z^{-1}} + \frac{3}{1 + \frac{3}{4}z^{-1}}, \qquad |z| > \frac{3}{4}$$

$$H(z) = \frac{Y(z)}{X(z)} = \frac{1 - z^{-1}}{(1 - \frac{1}{2}z^{-1})(1 + \frac{3}{4}z^{-1})}, \qquad |z| > \frac{3}{4}$$

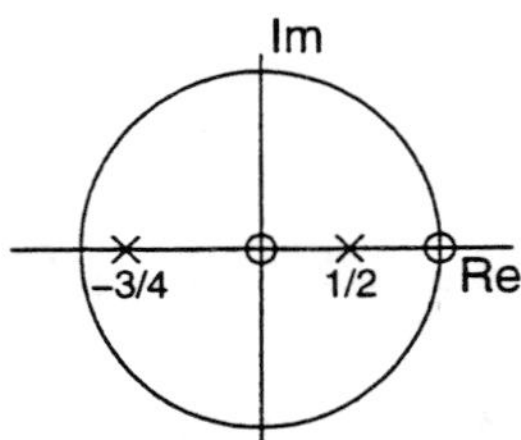

(b)

$$H(z) = \frac{1 - z^{-1}}{(1 - \frac{1}{2}z^{-1})(1 + \frac{3}{4}z^{-1})} = \frac{-\frac{2}{5}}{(1 - \frac{1}{2}z^{-1})} + \frac{\frac{7}{5}}{(1 + \frac{3}{4}z^{-1})}, \qquad |z| > \frac{3}{4}$$

$$h[n] = -\frac{2}{5}\left(\frac{1}{2}\right)^n u[n] + \frac{7}{5}\left(-\frac{3}{4}\right)^n u[n]$$

(c)

$$H(z) = \frac{Y(z)}{X(z)} = \frac{1 - z^{-1}}{1 + \frac{1}{4}z^{-1} - \frac{3}{8}z^{-2}}$$

$$Y(z) + \frac{1}{4}z^{-1}Y(z) - \frac{3}{8}z^{-2}Y(z) = X(z) - z^{-1}X(z)$$

$$y[n] + \frac{1}{4}y[n-1] - \frac{3}{8}y[n-2] = x[n] - x[n-1]$$

5.8. (a)

$$\begin{aligned} y[n] &= \frac{3}{2}y[n-1] + y[n-2] + x[n-1] \\ Y(z) &= \frac{3}{2}z^{-1}Y(z) + z^{-2}Y(z) + z^{-1}X(z) \end{aligned}$$

Therefore,

$$H(z) = \frac{Y(z)}{X(z)} = \frac{z^{-1}}{1 - \frac{3}{2}z^{-1} - z^{-2}} = \frac{z^{-1}}{(1 - 2z^{-1})(1 + \frac{1}{2}z^{-1})}, \qquad |z| > 2$$

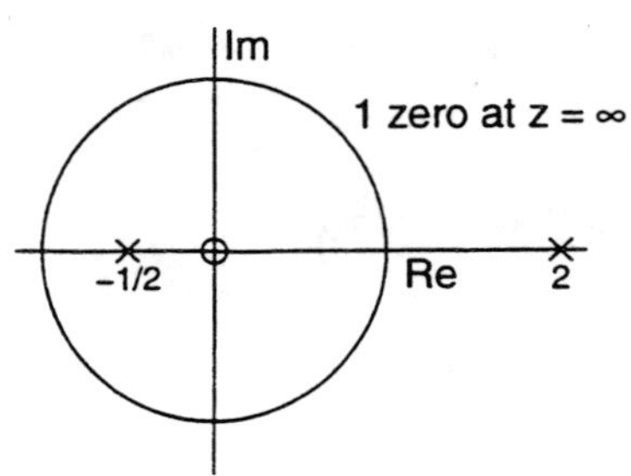

(b)

$$\begin{aligned}
H(z) &= \frac{z^{-1}}{(1-2z^{-1})(1+\frac{1}{2}z^{-1})} = \frac{A}{(1-2z^{-1})} + \frac{B}{(1+\frac{1}{2}z^{-1})}, \quad |z| > 2 \\
A &= \left.\frac{z^{-1}}{(1+\frac{1}{2}z^{-1})}\right|_{z^{-1}=\frac{1}{2}} = \frac{2}{5} \\
B &= \left.\frac{z^{-1}}{(1-2z^{-1})}\right|_{z^{-1}=-2} = -\frac{2}{5}
\end{aligned}$$

$$h[n] = \frac{2}{5}\left[(2)^n - \left(-\frac{1}{2}\right)^n\right]u[n]$$

(c) Use ROC of $\frac{1}{2} < |z| < 2$ since the ROC must include $|z| = 1$ for a stable system.

$$h[n] = -\frac{2}{5}(2)^n u[-n-1] - \frac{2}{5}\left(-\frac{1}{2}\right)^n u[n]$$

5.9.

$$y[n-1] - \frac{5}{2}y[n] + y[n+1] = x[n]$$

$$z^{-1}Y(z) - \frac{5}{2}Y(z) + zY(z) = X(z)$$

$$\begin{aligned}
H(z) &= \frac{Y(z)}{X(z)} \\
&= \frac{z^{-1}}{1-\frac{5}{2}z^{-1}+z^{-2}} \\
&= \frac{z^{-1}}{(1-2z^{-1})(1-\frac{1}{2}z^{-1})} \\
&= \frac{\frac{2}{3}}{1-2z^{-1}} - \frac{\frac{2}{3}}{1-\frac{1}{2}z^{-1}}
\end{aligned}$$

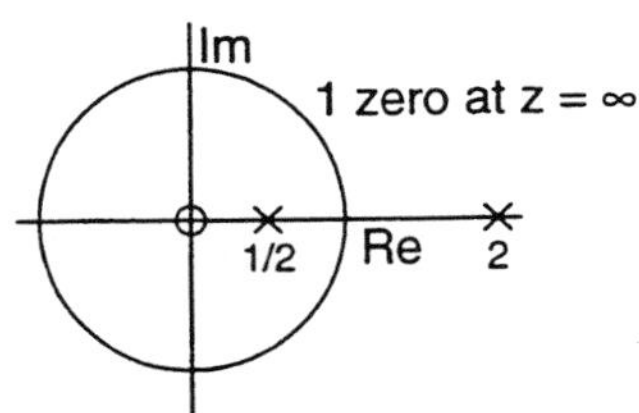

Three regions of convergence:

(a) $|z| < \frac{1}{2}$:

$$h[n] = -\frac{2}{3}(2)^n u[-n-1] + \frac{2}{3}\left(\frac{1}{2}\right)^n u[-n-1]$$

(b) $\frac{1}{2} < |z| < 2$:

$$h[n] = -\frac{2}{3}(2)^n u[-n-1] - \frac{2}{3}\left(\frac{1}{2}\right)^n u[n]$$

Includes $|z| = 1$, so this is stable.

(c) $|z| > 2$:

$$h[n] = \frac{2}{3}(2)^n u[n] - \frac{2}{3}\left(\frac{1}{2}\right)^n u[n]$$

ROC outside of largest pole, so this is causal.

5.10. Figure P5.16 shows two zeros and three poles inside the unit circle. Since the number of poles must equal the number of zeros, there must be an additional zero at $z = \infty$.

$H(z)$ is causal, so the ROC lies outside the largest pole and includes the unit circle. Therefore, the system is also stable.

The inverse system switches poles and zeros. The inverse system could have a ROC that includes $|z| = 1$, making it stable. However, the zero at $z = \infty$ of $H(z)$ is a pole for $H_i(z)$, so the system $H_i(z)$ cannot be causal.

5.11. (a) *It cannot be determined.* The ROC might or might not include the unit circle.

(b) *It cannot be determined.* The ROC might or might not include $z = \infty$.

(c) *False.* Given that the system is causal, we know that the ROC must be outside the outermost pole. Since the outermost pole is outside the unit circle, the ROC will not include the unit circle, and thus the system is not stable.

(d) *True.* If the system is stable, the ROC must include the unit circle. Because there are poles both inside and outside the unit circle, any ROC including the unit circle must be a ring. A ring-shaped ROC means that we have a two-sided system.

5.12. (a) *Yes.* The poles $z = \pm j(0.9)$ are inside the unit circle so the system is stable.

(b) First, factor $H(z)$ into two parts. The first should be minimum phase and therefore have all its poles and zeros inside the unit circle. The second part should contain the remaining poles and zeros.

$$H(z) = \underbrace{\frac{1+0.2z^{-1}}{1+0.81z^{-2}}}_{\text{minimum phase}} \cdot \underbrace{\frac{1-9z^{-2}}{1}}_{\substack{\text{poles \& zeros} \\ \text{outside unit circle}}}$$

Allpass systems have poles and zeros that occur in conjugate reciprocal pairs. If we include the factor $(1 - \frac{1}{9}z^{-2})$ in both parts of the equation above the first part will remain minimum phase and the second will become allpass.

$$\begin{aligned} H(z) &= \frac{(1+0.2z^{-1})(1-\frac{1}{9}z^{-2})}{1+0.81z^{-2}} \cdot \frac{1-9z^{-2}}{1-\frac{1}{9}z^{-2}} \\ &= H_1(z)H_{ap}(z) \end{aligned}$$

5.13. *An aside*: Technically, this problem is not well defined, since a pole/zero plot does not uniquely determine a system. That is, many system functions can have the same pole/zero plot. For example, consider the systems

$$\begin{aligned} H_1(z) &= z^{-1} \\ H_2(z) &= 2z^{-1} \end{aligned}$$

Both of these systems have the same pole/zero plot, namely a pole at zero and a zero at infinity. Clearly, the system $H_1(z)$ is allpass, as it passes all frequencies with unity gain (it is simply a unit delay). However, one could ask whether $H_2(z)$ is allpass. Looking at the standard definition of an allpass system provided in this chapter, the answer would be no, since the system does not pass all frequencies with *unity* gain.

A broader definition of an allpass system would be a system for which the system magnitude response $|H(e^{j\omega})| = a$, where a is a real constant. Such a system would pass all frequencies, and scale the output by a constant factor a. In a practical setting, this definition of an allpass system is satisfactory. Under this definition, both systems $H_1(z)$ and $H_2(z)$ would be considered allpass.

For this problem, it is assumed that none of the poles or zeros shown in the pole/zero plots are scaled, so this issue of using the proper definition of an allpass system does not apply. The standard definition of an allpass system is used.

Solution:

(a) Yes, the system is allpass, since it is of the appropriate form.

(b) No, the system is not allpass, since the zero does not occur at the conjugate reciprocal location of the pole.

(c) Yes, the system is allpass, since it is of the appropriate form.

(d) Yes, the system is allpass. This system consists of an allpass system in cascade with a pole at zero. The pole at zero is simply a delay, and does not change the magnitude spectrum.

5.14. (a) By the symmetry of $x_1[n]$ we know it has linear phase. The symmetry is around $n = 5$ so the continuous phase of $X_1(e^{j\omega})$ is $\arg[X_1(e^{j\omega})] = -5\omega$. Thus,

$$\text{grd}[X_1(e^{j\omega})] = -\frac{d}{d\omega}\{\arg[X_1(e^{j\omega})]\} = -\frac{d}{d\omega}\{-5\omega\} = 5$$

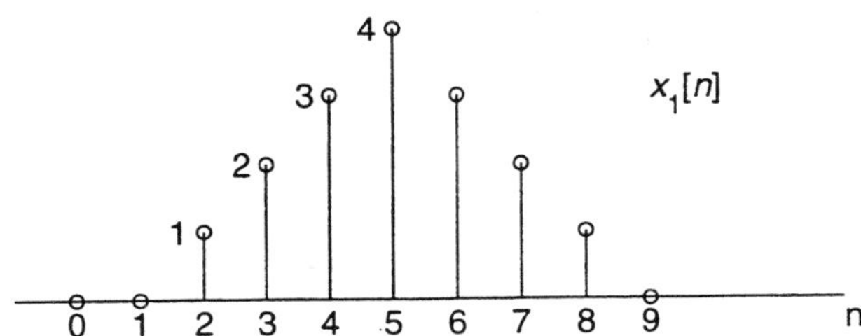

(b) By the symmetry of $x_2[n]$ we know it has linear phase. The symmetry is around $n = 1/2$ so we know the phase of $X_2(e^{j\omega})$ is $\arg[X_2(e^{j\omega}] = -\omega/2$. Thus,

$$\text{grd}[X_2(e^{j\omega})] = -\frac{d}{d\omega}\{\arg[X_2(e^{j\omega})]\} = -\frac{d}{d\omega}\left\{-\frac{\omega}{2}\right\} = \frac{1}{2}$$

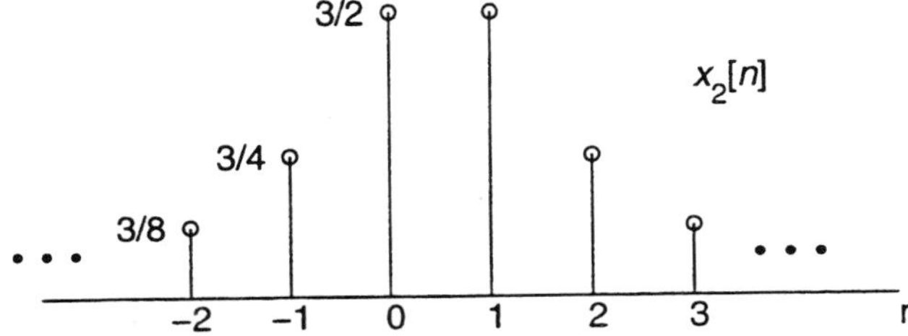

5.15. (a) $h[n]$ is symmetric about $n = 1$.

$$\begin{aligned} H(e^{j\omega}) &= 2 + e^{-j\omega} + 2e^{-2j\omega} \\ &= e^{-j\omega}(2e^{j\omega} + 1 + 2e^{-j\omega}) \\ &= (1 + 4\cos\omega)e^{-j\omega} \end{aligned}$$

$$A(\omega) = 1 + 4\cos\omega, \ \alpha = 1, \ \beta = 0$$

Generalized Linear phase but not Linear Phase since $A(\omega)$ is not always positive.

(b) This sequence has no even or odd symmetry, so it does not possess generalized linear phase.

(c) $h[n]$ is symmetric about $n = 1$.

$$\begin{aligned} H(e^{j\omega}) &= 1 + 3e^{-j\omega} + e^{-2j\omega} \\ &= e^{-j\omega}(e^{j\omega} + 3 + e^{-j\omega}) \\ &= (3 + 2\cos\omega)e^{-j\omega} \end{aligned}$$

$$A(\omega) = 3 + 2\cos\omega, \ \alpha = 1, \ \beta = 0$$

Generalized Linear phase & Linear Phase.

(d) $h[n]$ has even symmetry.

$$\begin{aligned} H(e^{j\omega}) &= 1 + e^{-j\omega} \\ &= e^{-j(1/2)\omega}(e^{j(1/2)\omega} + e^{-j(1/2)\omega}) \\ &= 2\cos(\omega/2)e^{-j(1/2)\omega} \end{aligned}$$

$$A(\omega) = 2\cos(\omega/2), \ \alpha = \frac{1}{2}, \ \beta = 0$$

Generalized Linear Phase but not Linear Phase since $A(\omega)$ is not always positive.

(e) $h[n]$ has odd symmetry.

$$\begin{aligned} H(e^{j\omega}) &= 1 - e^{-2j\omega} \\ &= e^{-j\omega}(e^{j\omega} - e^{-j\omega}) \\ &= e^{-j\omega}2j\sin\omega \\ &= (2\sin\omega)e^{-j\omega + j\frac{\pi}{2}} \end{aligned}$$

$$A(\omega) = 2\sin\omega, \ \alpha = 1, \ \beta = \frac{\pi}{2}$$

Generalized Linear Phase but not Linear Phase since $A(\omega)$ is not always positive.

5.16. The causality of the system cannot be determined from the figure. A causal system $h_1[n]$ that has a linear phase response $\angle H(e^{jw}) = -\alpha w$, is:

$$\begin{aligned} h_1[n] &= \delta[n] + 2\delta[n-1] + \delta[n-2] \\ H_1(e^{j\omega}) &= 1 + 2e^{-j\omega} + e^{-j2\omega} \\ &= e^{-j\omega}(e^{j\omega} + 2 + e^{-j\omega}) \\ &= e^{-j\omega}(2 + 2\cos(\omega)) \\ |H_1(e^{j\omega})| &= 2 + 2\cos(\omega) \\ \angle H_1(e^{j\omega}) &= -\omega \end{aligned}$$

An example of a non-causal system with the same phase response is:

$$\begin{aligned} h_2[n] &= \delta[n+1] + \delta[n] + 4\delta[n-1] + \delta[n-2] + \delta[n-3] \\ H_2(e^{j\omega}) &= e^{j\omega} + 1 + 4e^{-j\omega} + e^{-j2\omega} + e^{-j3\omega} \\ &= e^{-jw}(e^{j2\omega} + e^{j\omega} + 4 + e^{-j\omega} + e^{-j2\omega}) \\ &= e^{-j\omega}(4 + 2\cos(\omega) + 2\cos(2\omega)) \\ |H_2(e^{j\omega})| &= 4 + 2\cos(\omega) + 2\cos(2\omega) \\ \angle H_2(e^{j\omega}) &= -\omega \end{aligned}$$

Thus, both the causal sequence $h_1[n]$ and the non-causal sequence $h_2[n]$ have a linear phase response $\angle H(e^{j\omega}) = -\alpha\omega$, where $\alpha = 1$.

5.17. A minimum phase system is one which has all its poles and zeros inside the unit circle. It is causal, stable, and has a causal and stable inverse.

(a) $H_1(z)$ has a zero outside the unit circle at $z = 2$ so it is not minimum phase.

(b) $H_2(z)$ is minimum phase since its poles and zeros are inside the unit circle.

(c) $H_3(z)$ is minimum phase since its poles and zeros are inside the unit circle.

(d) $H_4(z)$ has a zero outside the unit circle at $z = \infty$ so it is not minimum phase. Moreover, the inverse system would not be causal due to the pole at infinity.

5.18. A minimum phase system with an equivalent magnitude spectrum can be found by analyzing the system function, and reflecting all poles are zeros that are outside the unit circle to their conjugate reciprocal locations. This will move them inside the unit circle. Then, all poles and zeros for $H_{min}(z)$ will be inside the unit circle. Note that a scale factor may be introduced when the pole or zero is reflected inside the unit circle.

(a) Simply reflect the zero at $z = 2$ to its conjugate reciprocal location at $z = \frac{1}{2}$. Then, determine the scale factor.

$$H_{min}(z) = 2\left(\frac{1 - \frac{1}{2}z^{-1}}{1 + \frac{1}{3}z^{-1}}\right)$$

(b) First, simply reflect the zero at $z = -3$ to its conjugate reciprocal location at $z = -\frac{1}{3}$. Then, determine the scale factor. This results in

$$H_{min}(z) = 3\frac{\left(1 + \frac{1}{3}z^{-1}\right)\left(1 - \frac{1}{2}z^{-1}\right)}{z^{-1}\left(1 + \frac{1}{3}z^{-1}\right)}$$

The $\left(1 + \frac{1}{3}z^{-1}\right)$ terms cancel, leaving

$$H_{min}(z) = 3\frac{\left(1 - \frac{1}{2}z^{-1}\right)}{z^{-1}}$$

Note that the term $\frac{1}{z^{-1}}$ does not affect the frequency response magnitude of the system. Consequently, it can be removed. Thus, the remaining term has a zero inside the unit circle, and is therefore minimum phase. As a result, we are left with the system

$$H_{min}(z) = 3\left(1 - \frac{1}{2}z^{-1}\right)$$

(c) Simply reflect the zero at 3 to its conjugate reciprocal location at $\frac{1}{3}$ and reflect the pole at $\frac{4}{3}$ to its conjugate reciprocal location at $\frac{3}{4}$. Then, determine the scale factor.

$$H_{min}(z) = \frac{9}{4}\frac{\left(1 - \frac{1}{3}z^{-1}\right)\left(1 - \frac{1}{4}z^{-1}\right)}{\left(1 - \frac{3}{4}z^{-1}\right)^2}$$

5.19. Due to the symmetry of the impulse responses, all the systems have generalized linear phase of $\arg[H(e^{j\omega})] = \beta - n_o\omega$ where n_o is the point of symmetry in the impulse response graphs. The group delay is

$$\text{grd}\left[H_i(e^{j\omega})\right] = -\frac{d}{d\omega}\left\{\arg\left[H_i(e^{j\omega})\right]\right\} = -\frac{d}{d\omega}\{\beta - n_o\omega\} = n_o$$

To find each system's group delay we need only find the point of symmetry n_o in each system's impulse response.

$$\begin{aligned} \text{grd}\left[H_1(e^{j\omega})\right] &= 2 & \text{grd}\left[H_4(e^{j\omega})\right] &= 3 \\ \text{grd}\left[H_2(e^{j\omega})\right] &= 1.5 & \text{grd}\left[H_5(e^{j\omega})\right] &= 3 \\ \text{grd}\left[H_3(e^{j\omega})\right] &= 2 & \text{grd}\left[H_6(e^{j\omega})\right] &= 3.5 \end{aligned}$$

5.20. (a) *Yes.* The system function could be a generalized linear phase system implemented by a linear constant-coefficient differential equation (LCCDE) with real coefficients. The zeros come in a set of four: a zero, its conjugate, and the two conjugate reciprocals. The pole-zero plot could correspond to a Type I FIR linear phase system.

(b) *No.* This system function could not be a generalized linear phase system implemented by a LCCDE with real coefficients. Since the LCCDE has real coefficients, its poles and zeros must come in conjugate pairs. However, the zeros in this pole-zero plot do not have corresponding conjugate zeros.

(c) *Yes.* The system function could be a generalized linear phase system implemented by a LCCDE with real coefficients. The pole-zero plot could correspond to a Type II FIR linear phase system.

5.21. $h_{lp}[n]$ is an ideal lowpass filter with $\omega_c = \frac{\pi}{4}$

(a) $y[n] = x[n] - x[n] * h_{lp}[n] \Rightarrow H(e^{j\omega}) = 1 - H_{lp}(e^{j\omega})$
This is a highpass filter.

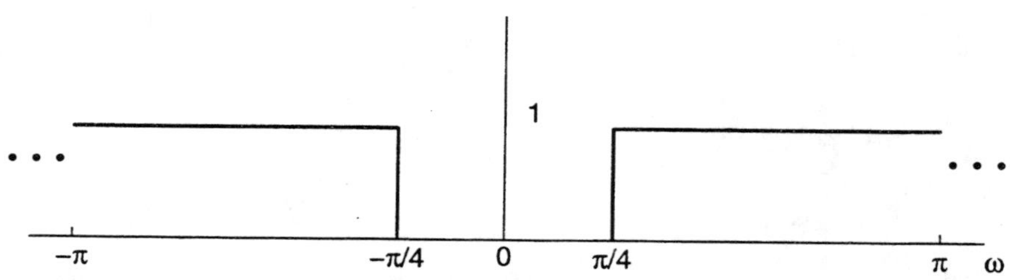

(b) $x[n]$ is first modulated by π, lowpass filtered, and demodulated by π. Therefore, $H_{lp}(e^{j\omega})$ filters the high frequency components of $X(e^{j\omega})$.
This is a highpass filter.

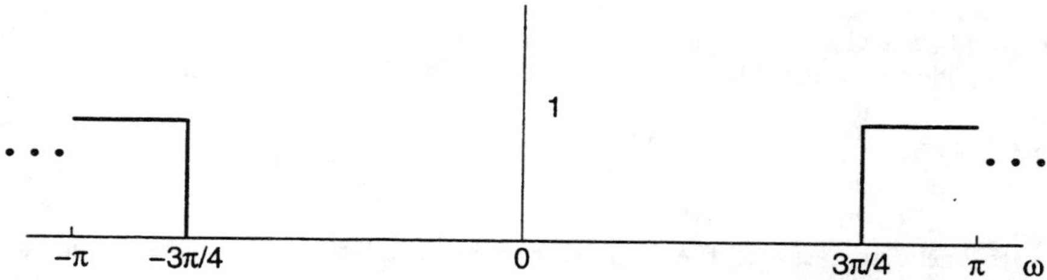

(c) $h_{lp}[2n]$ is a downsampled version of the filter. Therefore, the frequency response will be "spread out" by a factor of two, with a gain of $\frac{1}{2}$.
This is a lowpass filter.

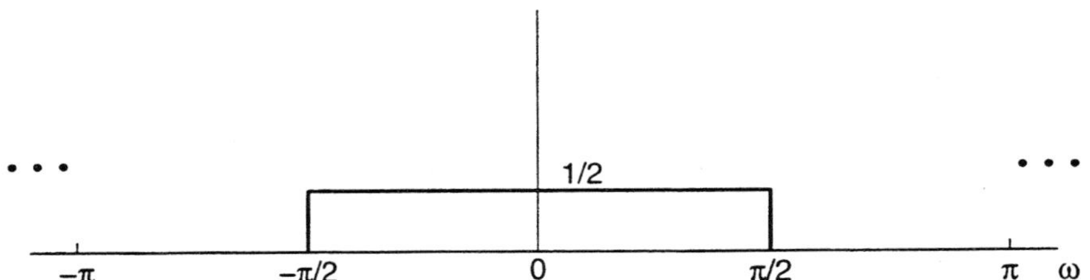

(d) This system upsamples $h_{lp}[n]$ by a factor of two. Therefore, the frequency axis will be compressed by a factor of two.
This is a bandstop filter.

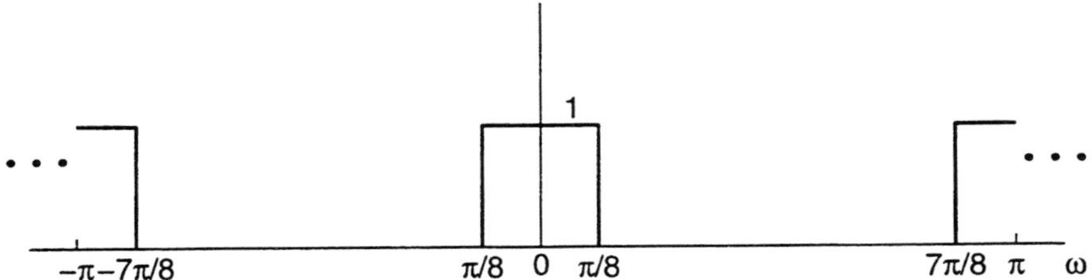

(e) This system upsamples the input before passing it through $h_{lp}[n]$. This effectively doubles the frequency bandwidth of $H_{lp}(e^{j\omega})$.
This is a lowpass filter.

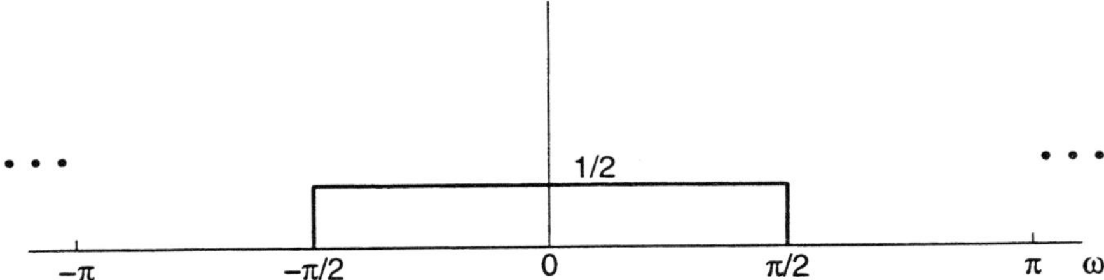

5.22.

$$H(z) = \frac{1 - a^{-1}z^{-1}}{1 - az^{-1}} = \frac{Y(z)}{X(z)}, \qquad \text{causal, so ROC is } |z| > a$$

(a) Cross multiplying and taking the inverse transform

$$y[n] - ay[n-1] = x[n] - \frac{1}{a}x[n-1]$$

(b) Since $H(z)$ is causal, we know that the ROC is $|z| > a$. For stability, the ROC must include the unit circle. So, $H(z)$ is stable for $|a| < 1$.

(c) $a = \frac{1}{2}$

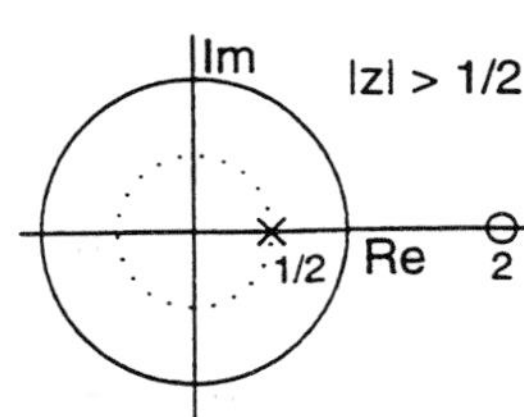

(d)

$$H(z) = \frac{1}{1-az^{-1}} - \frac{a^{-1}z^{-1}}{1-az^{-1}}, \qquad |z| > a$$

$$h[n] = (a)^n u[n] - \frac{1}{a}(a)^{n-1}u[n-1]$$

(e)

$$H(e^{j\omega}) = H(z)|_{z=e^{j\omega}} = \frac{1-a^{-1}e^{-j\omega}}{1-ae^{-j\omega}}$$

$$|H(e^{j\omega})|^2 = H(e^{j\omega})H^*(e^{j\omega}) = \frac{1-a^{-1}e^{-j\omega}}{1-ae^{-j\omega}} \cdot \frac{1-a^{-1}e^{j\omega}}{1-ae^{j\omega}}$$

$$\begin{aligned} |H(e^{j\omega})| &= \left(\frac{1+\frac{1}{a^2}-\frac{2}{a}\cos\omega}{1+a^2-2a\cos\omega}\right)^{\frac{1}{2}} \\ &= \frac{1}{a}\left(\frac{a^2+1-2a\cos\omega}{1+a^2-2a\cos\omega}\right)^{\frac{1}{2}} \\ &= \frac{1}{a} \end{aligned}$$

5.23. (a) Type I:

$$A(\omega) = \sum_{n=0}^{M/2} a[n]\cos\omega n$$

$\cos 0 = 1$, $\cos\pi = -1$, so there are no restrictions.

Type II:

$$A(\omega) = \sum_{n=1}^{(M+1)/2} b[n]\cos\omega\left(n-\frac{1}{2}\right)$$

$\cos 0 = 1$, $\cos\left(n\pi - \frac{\pi}{2}\right) = 0$. So $H(e^{j\pi}) = 0$.

Type III:

$$A(\omega) = \sum_{n=0}^{M/2} c[n]\sin\omega n$$

$\sin 0 = 0$, $\sin n\pi = 0$, so $H(e^{j0}) = H(e^{j\pi}) = 0$.

Type IV:

$$A(\omega) = \sum_{n=1}^{(M+1)/2} d[n]\sin\omega\left(n-\frac{1}{2}\right)$$

$\sin 0 = 0$, $\sin\left(n\pi - \frac{\pi}{2}\right) \neq 0$, so just $H(e^{j0}) = 0$.

(b)

	Type I	Type II	Type III	Type IV
Lowpass	Y	Y	N	N
Bandpass	Y	Y	Y	Y
Highpass	Y	N	N	Y
Bandstop	Y	N	N	N
Differentiator	Y	N	N	Y

5.24. (a) Taking the z-transform of both sides and rearranging

$$H(z) = \frac{Y(z)}{X(z)} = \frac{-\frac{1}{4} + z^{-2}}{1 - \frac{1}{4}z^{-2}}$$

Since the poles and zeros {2 poles at $z = \pm 1/2$, 2 zeros at $z = \pm 2$} occur in conjugate reciprocal pairs the system is allpass. This property is easy to recognize since, as in the system above, the coefficients of the numerator and denominator z-polynomials get reversed (and in general conjugated).

(b) It is a property of allpass systems that the output energy is equal to the input energy. Here is the proof.

$$\begin{aligned}
\sum_{n=0}^{N-1} |y[n]|^2 &= \sum_{n=-\infty}^{\infty} |y[n]|^2 \\
&= \frac{1}{2\pi}\int_{-\pi}^{\pi} \left|Y(e^{j\omega})\right|^2 d\omega && \text{(by Parseval's Theorem)} \\
&= \frac{1}{2\pi}\int_{-\pi}^{\pi} \left|H(e^{j\omega})X(e^{j\omega})\right|^2 d\omega \\
&= \frac{1}{2\pi}\int_{-\pi}^{\pi} \left|X(e^{j\omega})\right|^2 d\omega && (\left|H(e^{j\omega})\right|^2 = 1 \text{ since } h[n] \text{ is allpass}) \\
&= \sum_{n=-\infty}^{\infty} |x[n]|^2 && \text{(by Parseval's theorem)} \\
&= \sum_{n=0}^{N-1} |x[n]|^2 \\
&= 5
\end{aligned}$$

5.25. *The statement is false.* A non-causal system can indeed have a positive constant group delay. For example, consider the non-causal system

$$h[n] = \delta[n+1] + \delta[n] + 4\delta[n-1] + \delta[n-2] + \delta[n-3]$$

This system has the frequency response

$$\begin{aligned}
H(e^{j\omega}) &= e^{j\omega} + 1 + 4e^{-j\omega} + e^{-j2\omega} + e^{-j3\omega} \\
&= e^{-j\omega}(e^{j2\omega} + e^{j\omega} + 4 + e^{-j\omega} + e^{-j2\omega}) \\
&= e^{-j\omega}(4 + 2\cos(\omega) + 2\cos(2\omega)) \\
\left|H(e^{j\omega})\right| &= 4 + 2\cos(\omega) + 2\cos(2\omega) \\
\angle H(e^{j\omega}) &= -\omega \\
\text{grd}[H(e^{j\omega})] &= 1
\end{aligned}$$

5.26. (a) A labeled pole-zero diagram appears below.

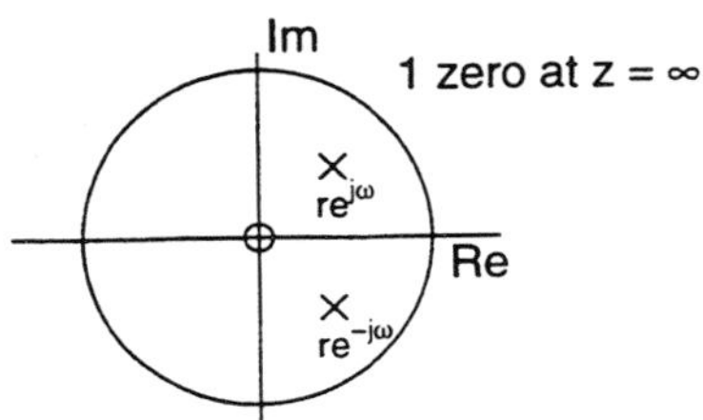

The table of common z-transform pairs gives us

$$(r^n \sin \omega_0 n)u[n] \longleftrightarrow \frac{(r \sin \omega_0)z^{-1}}{1-(2r\cos\omega_0)z^{-1}+r^2z^{-2}}, \quad |z|>r$$

which enables us to derive $h[n]$.

$$h[n] = \left(\frac{1}{\sin\omega_0}\right)(r^n \sin\omega_0 n)u[n]$$

(b) When $\omega_0 = 0$

$$H(z) = \frac{rz^{-1}}{1-(2r\cos\omega_0)z^{-1}+r^2z^{-2}} = \frac{rz^{-1}}{(1-rz^{-1})^2}, \quad |z|>r$$

Again, using a table lookup gives us

$$h[n] = nr^n u[n]$$

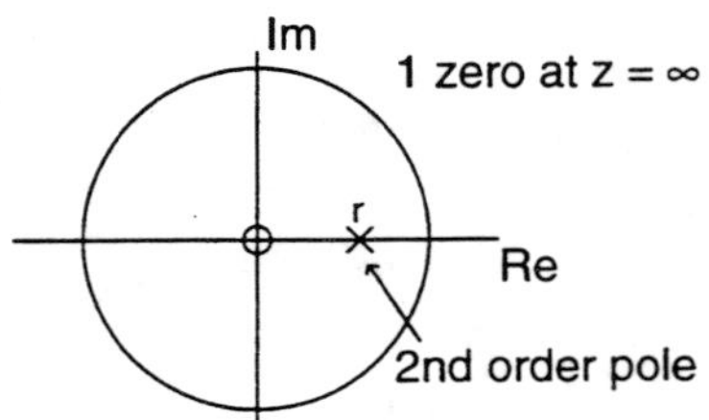

5.27. Making use of some DTFT properties can aide in the solution of this problem. First, note that

$$\begin{aligned} h_2[n] &= (-1)^n h_1[n] \\ h_2[n] &= e^{-j\pi n} h_1[n] \end{aligned}$$

Using the DTFT property that states that modulation in the time domain corresponds to a shift in the frequency domain,

$$H_2(e^{j\omega}) = H_1(e^{j(\omega+\pi)})$$

Consequently, $H_2(e^{j\omega})$ is simply $H_1(e^{j\omega})$ shifted by π. The ideal low pass filter has now become the ideal high pass filter, as shown below.

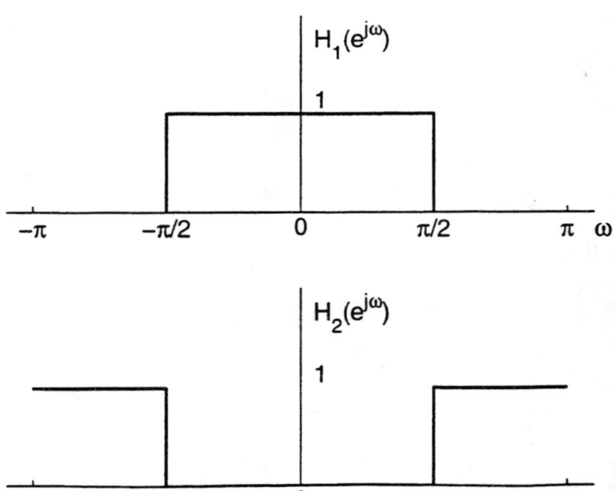

5.28. (a)

$$H(z) = \frac{A}{(1-\frac{1}{2}z^{-1})(1+\frac{1}{3}z^{-1})}, \qquad |z| > \frac{1}{2} \ h[n] \text{ causal}$$

$$H(1) = 6 \Rightarrow A = 4$$

(b)

$$\begin{aligned} H(z) &= \frac{4}{(1-\frac{1}{2}z^{-1})(1+\frac{1}{3}z^{-1})}, \qquad |z| > \frac{1}{2} \\ &= \frac{(\frac{12}{5})}{1-\frac{1}{2}z^{-1}} + \frac{(\frac{8}{5})}{1+\frac{1}{3}z^{-1}} \\ h[n] &= \frac{12}{15}\left(\frac{1}{2}\right)^n u[n] + \frac{8}{5}\left(-\frac{1}{3}\right)^n u[n] \end{aligned}$$

(c) (i)

$$x[n] = u[n] - \frac{1}{2}u[n-1] \Leftrightarrow X(z) = \frac{1-\frac{1}{2}z^{-1}}{1-z^{-1}}, \qquad |z| > 1$$

$$\begin{aligned} Y(z) &= X(z)H(z) \\ &= \frac{1-\frac{1}{2}z^{-1}}{1-z^{-1}} \cdot \frac{4}{(1-\frac{1}{2}z^{-1})(1+\frac{1}{3}z^{-1})}, \qquad |z| > 1 \\ &= \frac{4}{(1-z^{-1})(1+\frac{1}{3}z^{-1})} \\ &= \frac{3}{1-z^{-1}} + \frac{1}{1+\frac{1}{3}z^{-1}} \\ y[n] &= 3u[n] + \left(-\frac{1}{3}\right)^n u[n] \end{aligned}$$

(ii)

$$x(t) = 50 + 10\cos(20\pi t) + 30\cos(40\pi t)$$

$$T = \frac{1}{40} \qquad t = nT$$

$$\begin{aligned} x[n] &= 50 + 10\cos\frac{\pi}{2}n + 30\cos\pi n \\ &= 50 + 5e^{j(n\pi/2)} + 5e^{-j(n\pi/2)} + 15e^{jn\pi} + 15e^{-jn\pi} \end{aligned}$$

Using the eigenfunction property:

$$y[n] = 50H(e^{j0}) + 5e^{j(n\pi/2)}H(e^{j(\pi/2)}) + 5e^{-j(n\pi/2)}H(e^{-j(\pi/2)}) + 15e^{jn\pi}H(e^{j\pi}) + 15e^{-jn\pi}H(e^{-j\pi})$$

$$H(e^{j\omega}) = \frac{4}{1-\frac{1}{6}e^{-j\omega}-\frac{1}{6}e^{-j2\omega}}$$

$H(e^{j0}) = 6$, $H(e^{j(\pi/2)}) = 7\left(\frac{12}{25}\right) - j\frac{12}{25}$, $H(e^{-j(\pi/2)}) = 7\left(\frac{12}{25}\right) + j\frac{12}{25}$,
$H(e^{j\pi}) = 4$, $H(e^{-j\pi}) = 4$

$$y[n] = 300 + 24\sqrt{2}\cos\left(\frac{\pi}{2}n - \tan^{-1}\left(\frac{1}{7}\right)\right) + 120\cos\pi n$$

5.29.

$$\begin{aligned} H(z) &= \frac{21}{(1-\frac{1}{2}z^{-1})(1-2z^{-1})(1-4z^{-1})} \\ &= \frac{1}{1-\frac{1}{2}z^{-1}} - \frac{28}{1-2z^{-1}} + \frac{48}{1-4z^{-1}} \end{aligned}$$

Since we know the sequence is not stable, the ROC must not include $|z| = 1$, and since it is two-sided, the ROC must be a ring. This leaves only one possible choice: the ROC is $2 < |z| < 4$.

(a)

$$h[n] = \left(\frac{1}{2}\right)^n u[n] - 28(2)^n u[n] - 48(4)^n u[-n-1]$$

(b)

$$H_1(z) = \frac{1}{1-\frac{1}{2}z^{-1}} - \frac{28}{1-2z^{-1}}$$

$$H_2(z) = \frac{48}{1-4z^{-1}}$$

5.30. (a)

$$H(z) = \frac{(z+\frac{1}{2})(z-\frac{1}{2})}{z^M} = z^{-(M-2)}\left(1 - \frac{1}{4}z^{-2}\right)$$

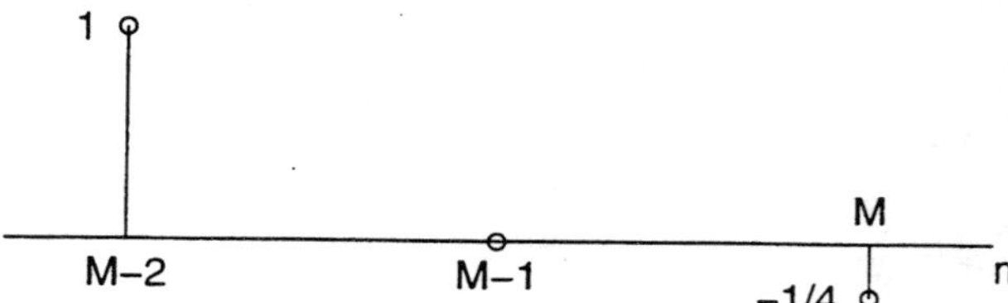

(b)

$$\begin{aligned} w[n] &= x[n-(M-2)] - \frac{1}{4}x[n-M] \\ y[n] &= w[2n] = x[2n-(M-2)] - \frac{1}{4}x[2n-M] \end{aligned}$$

Let $v[n] = x[2n]$,

$$y[n] = v[n-(M-2)/2] - \frac{1}{4}v[n-(M/2)]$$

Therefore,

$$g[n] = \delta[n-(M-2)/2] - \frac{1}{4}\delta[n-(M/2)], \qquad M \text{ even}$$

$$G(z) = z^{-(M-2)/2} - \frac{1}{4}z^{-M/2}$$

5.31. (a)

$$H(z) = \frac{z^{-2}}{(1-\frac{1}{2}z^{-1})(1-3z^{-1})}, \qquad \text{stable, so the ROC is } \tfrac{1}{2} < |z| < 3$$

$$x[n] = u[n] \Leftrightarrow X(z) = \frac{1}{1-z^{-1}}, \qquad |z| > 1$$

$$Y(z) = X(z)H(z) = \frac{\frac{4}{5}}{1-\frac{1}{2}z^{-1}} + \frac{\frac{1}{5}}{1-3z^{-1}} - \frac{1}{1-z^{-1}}, \qquad 1 < |z| < 3$$

$$y[n] = \frac{4}{5}\left(\frac{1}{2}\right)^n u[n] - \frac{1}{5}(3)^n u[-n-1] - u[n]$$

(b) ROC includes $z = \infty$ so $h[n]$ is causal. Since both $h[n]$ and $x[n]$ are 0 for $n < 0$, we know that $y[n]$ is also 0 for $n < 0$

$$H(z) = \frac{Y(z)}{X(z)} = \frac{z^{-2}}{1-\frac{7}{2}z^{-1}+\frac{3}{2}z^{-2}}$$

$$Y(z) - \frac{7}{2}z^{-1}Y(z) + \frac{3}{2}z^{-2}Y(z) = z^{-2}X(z)$$

$$y[n] = x[n-2] + \frac{7}{2}y[n-1] - \frac{3}{2}y[n-2]$$

Since $y[n] = 0$ for $n < 0$, recursion can be done:

$$y[0] = 0, \qquad y[1] = 0, \qquad y[2] = 1$$

(c)

$$H_i(z) = \frac{1}{H(z)} = z^2 - \frac{7}{2}z + \frac{3}{2}, \qquad \text{ROC: entire z-plane}$$

$$h_i[n] = \delta[n+2] - \frac{7}{2}\delta[n+1] + \frac{3}{2}\delta[n]$$

5.32. Since $H(e^{jw})$ has a zero on the unit circle, its inverse system will have a pole on the unit circle and thus is not stable.

5.33. (a)

$$X(z) = S(z)(1 - e^{-8\alpha}z^{-8})$$

$$H_1(z) = 1 - e^{-8\alpha}z^{-8}$$

There are 8 zeros at $z = e^{-\alpha}e^{j\frac{\pi}{4}k}$ for $k = 0, \ldots, 7$ and 8 poles at the origin.

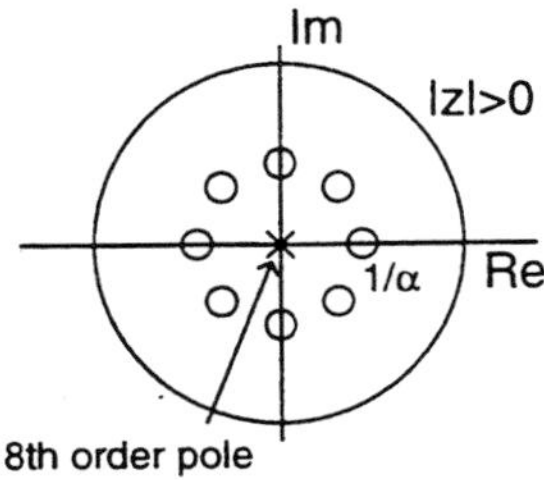

(b)

$$Y(z) = H_2(z)X(z) = H_2(z)H_1(z)S(z)$$

$$H_2(z) = \frac{1}{H_1(z)} = \frac{1}{1 - e^{-8\alpha}z^{-8}}$$

$|z| > e^{-\alpha}$ stable and causal, $\quad |z| < e^{-\alpha}$ not causal or stable

(c) Only the causal $h_2[n]$ is stable, therefore only it can be used to recover $s[n]$.

$$h[n] = \begin{cases} e^{-\alpha n}, & n = 0, 8, 16, \ldots \\ 0, & \text{otherwise} \end{cases}$$

(d)

$$s[n] = \delta[n] \Rightarrow x[n] = \delta[n] - e^{-8\alpha}\delta[n-8]$$

$$\begin{aligned} x[n] * h_2[n] &= \delta[n] - e^{-8\alpha}\delta[n-8] \\ &\quad + e^{-8\alpha}(\delta[n-8] - e^{-8\alpha}\delta[n-16]) \\ &\quad + e^{-16\alpha}(\delta[n-16] - e^{-8\alpha}\delta[n-32]) + \cdots \\ &= \delta[n] \end{aligned}$$

5.34.

$$h[n] = \left(\frac{1}{2}\right)^n u[n] + \left(\frac{1}{3}\right)^n u[n]$$

(a)

$$H(z) = \frac{1}{1 - \frac{1}{2}z^{-1}} + \frac{1}{1 - \frac{1}{3}z^{-1}} = \frac{2 - \frac{5}{6}z^{-1}}{1 - \frac{5}{6}z^{-1} + \frac{1}{6}z^{-2}}, \quad |z| > \frac{1}{2}$$

Since $h[n], x[n] = 0$ for $n < 0$ we can assume initial rest conditions.

$$y[n] = \frac{5}{6}y[n-1] - \frac{1}{6}y[n-2] + 2x[n] - \frac{5}{6}x[n-1]$$

(b)

$$h_1[n] = \begin{cases} h[n], & n \le 10^9 \\ 0, & n > 10^9 \end{cases}$$

(c)

$$H(z) = \frac{Y(z)}{X(z)} = \sum_{m=0}^{N-1} h[m]z^{-m}, \quad N = 10^9 + 1$$

$$y[n] = \sum_{m=0}^{N-1} h[m]x[n-m]$$

(d) For IIR, we have 4 multiplies and 3 adds per output point. This gives us a total of $4N$ multiplies and $3N$ adds. So, IIR grows with order N. For FIR, we have N multiplies and $N-1$ adds for the nth output point, so this configuration has order N^2.

5.35. (a)

$$20\log_{10}|H(e^{j(\pi/5)})| = \infty \Rightarrow \text{pole at } e^{j(\pi/5)}$$

$$20\log_{10}|H(e^{j(2\pi/5)})| = -\infty \Rightarrow \text{zero at } e^{j(2\pi/5)}$$

$$\text{Resonance at } \omega = \tfrac{3\pi}{5} \Rightarrow \text{pole inside unit circle here.}$$

Since the impulse response is real, the poles and zeros must be in conjugate pairs. The remaining 2 zeros are at zero (the number of poles always equals the number of zeros).

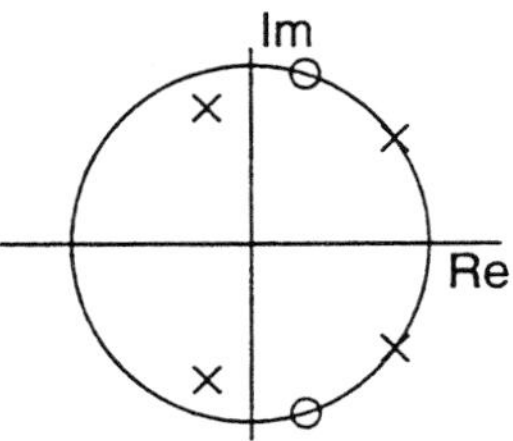

(b) Since $H(z)$ has poles, we know $h[n]$ is IIR.

(c) Since $h[n]$ is causal and IIR, it cannot be symmetric, and thus cannot have linear phase.

(d) Since there is a pole at $|z| = 1$, the ROC does not include the unit circle. This means the system is not stable.

5.36. (a)

$$\begin{aligned} H(z) &= \frac{(1 - 2z^{-1})(1 + \frac{1}{2}z^{-1})(1 + 0.9z^{-1})}{(1 - z^{-1})(1 + 0.7jz^{-1})(1 - 0.7jz^{-1})} \\ &= \frac{1 - 0.6z^{-1} - 2.35z^{-2} - 0.9z^{-3}}{1 - z^{-1} + 0.49z^{-2} - 0.49z^{-3}} \\ &= \frac{Y(z)}{X(z)} \end{aligned}$$

Cross multiplying and taking the inverse z-transform gives

$$y[n] - y[n-1] + 0.49y[n-2] - 0.49y[n-3] = x[n] - 0.6x[n-1] - 2.35x[n-2] - 0.9x[n-3]$$

(b)

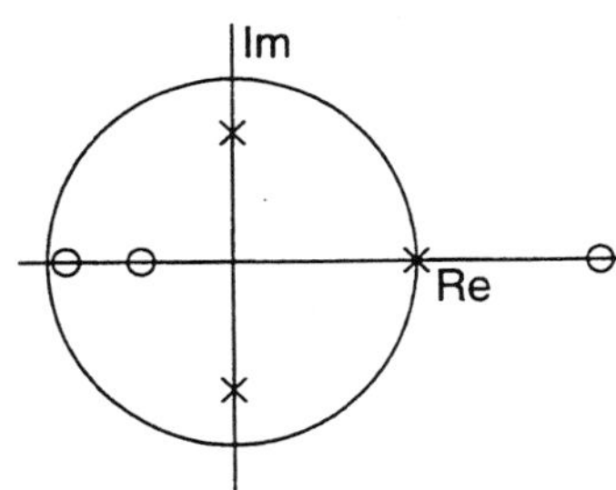

Note that since $h[n]$ is causal, ROC is $|z| > 1$.

(c)

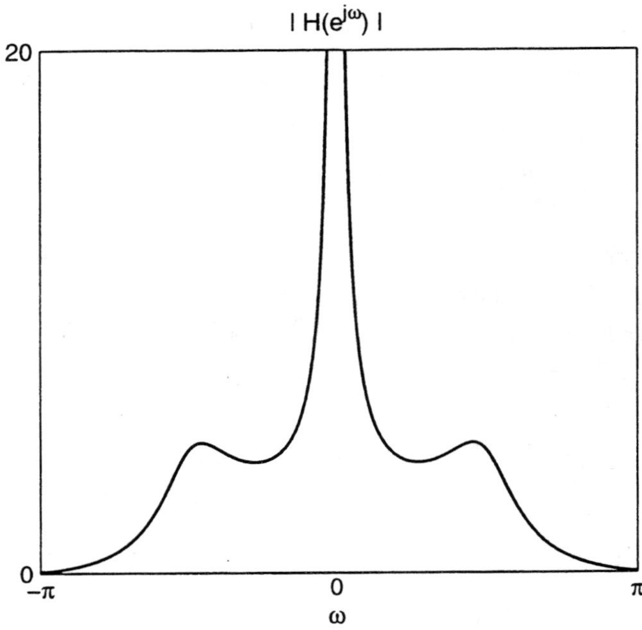

(d) (i) The system is not stable since the ROC does not include $|z| = 1$.

(ii) Because $h[n]$ is not stable, $h[n]$ does not approach a constant as $n \to \infty$.

(iii) We can see peaks at $\omega = \pm\frac{\pi}{2}$ in the graph of $|H(e^{j\omega})|$ shown in part (c), so this is false.

(iv) Swapping poles and zeros gives:

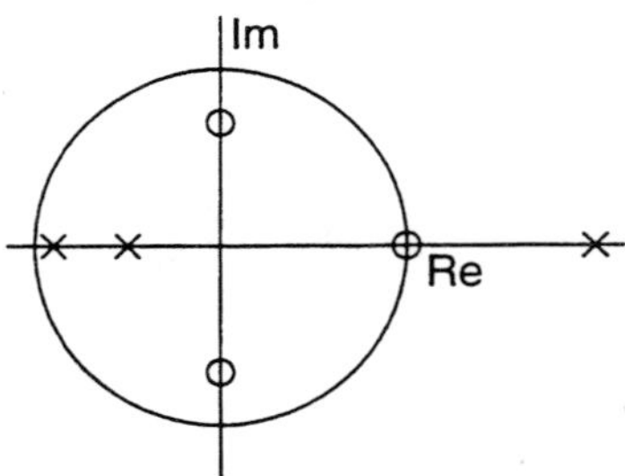

There is a ROC that includes the unit circle $(0.9 < |z| < 2)$. However, this stable system would be two sided, so we must conclude the statement is false.

5.37.

$$X(z) = \frac{(1 - \frac{1}{2}z^{-1})(1 - \frac{1}{4}z^{-1})(1 - \frac{1}{5}z)}{(1 - \frac{1}{6}z)} = \frac{6}{5}\frac{(1 - \frac{1}{2}z^{-1})(1 - \frac{1}{4}z^{-1})(1 - 5z^{-1})}{(1 - 6z^{-1})}$$

$$\alpha^n x[n] \Leftrightarrow X(\alpha^{-1}z) = \frac{6}{5}\frac{(1 - \frac{1}{2}\alpha z^{-1})(1 - \frac{1}{4}\alpha z^{-1})(1 - 5\alpha z^{-1})}{(1 - 6\alpha z^{-1})}$$

A minimum phase sequence has all poles and zeros inside the unit circle.

$$\begin{aligned} |\alpha/2| < 1 &\Rightarrow |\alpha| < 2 \\ |\alpha/4| < 1 &\Rightarrow |\alpha| < 4 \\ |5\alpha| < 1 &\Rightarrow |\alpha| < \frac{1}{5} \\ |6\alpha| < 1 &\Rightarrow |\alpha| < \frac{1}{6} \end{aligned}$$

Therefore, $\alpha^n x[n]$ is real and minimum phase iff α is real and $|\alpha| < \frac{1}{6}$.

5.38. (a) The causal systems have conjugate zero pairs inside or outside the unit circle. Therefore

$$\begin{aligned}
H(z) &= (1 - 0.9e^{j0.6\pi}z^{-1})(1 - 0.9e^{-j0.6\pi}z^{-1})(1 - 1.25e^{j0.8\pi}z^{-1})(1 - 1.25e^{-j0.8\pi}z^{-1}) \\
H_1(z) &= (0.9)^2(1.25)^2(1 - (10/9)e^{j0.6\pi}z^{-1})(1 - (10/9)e^{-j0.6\pi}z^{-1}) \cdot \\
&\quad (1 - 0.8e^{j0.8\pi}z^{-1})(1 - 0.8e^{-j0.8\pi}z^{-1}) \\
H_2(z) &= (0.9)^2(1 - (10/9)e^{j0.6\pi}z^{-1})(1 - (10/9)e^{-j0.6\pi}z^{-1})(1 - 1.25e^{j0.8\pi}z^{-1}) \cdot \\
&\quad (1 - 1.25e^{-j0.8\pi}z^{-1}) \\
H_3(z) &= (1.25)^2(1 - 0.9e^{j0.6\pi}z^{-1})(1 - 0.9e^{-j0.6\pi}z^{-1})(1 - 0.8e^{j0.8\pi}z^{-1}) \cdot \\
&\quad (1 - 0.8e^{-j0.8\pi}z^{-1})
\end{aligned}$$

$H_2(z)$ has all its zeros outside the unit circle, and is a maximum phase sequence. $H_3(z)$ has all its zeros inside the unit circle, and thus is a minimum phase sequence.

(b)

$$\begin{aligned}
H(z) &= 1 + 2.5788z^{-1} + 3.4975z^{-2} + 2.5074z^{-3} + 1.2656z^{-4} \\
h[n] &= \delta[n] + 2.5788\delta[n-1] + 3.4975\delta[n-2] + 2.5074\delta[n-3] + 1.2656\delta[n-4] \\
H_1(z) &= 1.2656 + 2.5074z^{-1} + 3.4975z^{-2} + 2.5788z^{-3} + z^{-4} \\
h_1[n] &= 1.2656\delta[n] + 2.5074\delta[n-1] + 3.4975\delta[n-2] + 2.5788\delta[n-3] + \delta[n-4] \\
H_2(z) &= 0.81 + 2.1945z^{-1} + 3.3906z^{-2} + 2.8917z^{-3} + 1.5625z^{-4} \\
h_2[n] &= 0.81\delta[n] + 2.1945\delta[n-1] + 3.3906\delta[n-2] + 2.8917\delta[n-3] + 1.5625\delta[n-4] \\
H_3(z) &= 1.5625 + 2.8917z^{-1} + 3.3906z^{-2} + 2.1945z^{-3} + 0.81z^{-4} \\
h_3[n] &= 1.5625\delta[n] + 2.8917\delta[n-1] + 3.3906\delta[n-2] + 2.1945\delta[n-3] + 0.81\delta[n-4]
\end{aligned}$$

(c)

n	$E(n)$	$E_1(n)$	$E_2(n)$	$E_3(n)$
0	1.0	1.6	0.7	2.4
1	7.7	7.9	5.5	10.8
2	19.9	20.1	17.0	22.3
3	26.2	26.8	25.3	27.1
4	27.8	27.8	27.8	27.8
5	27.8	27.8	27.8	27.8

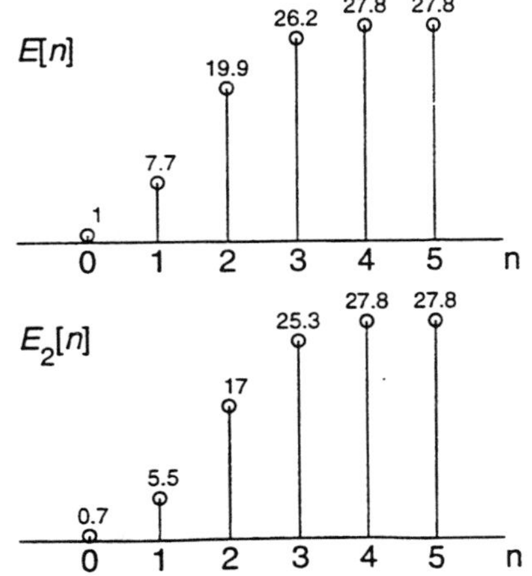

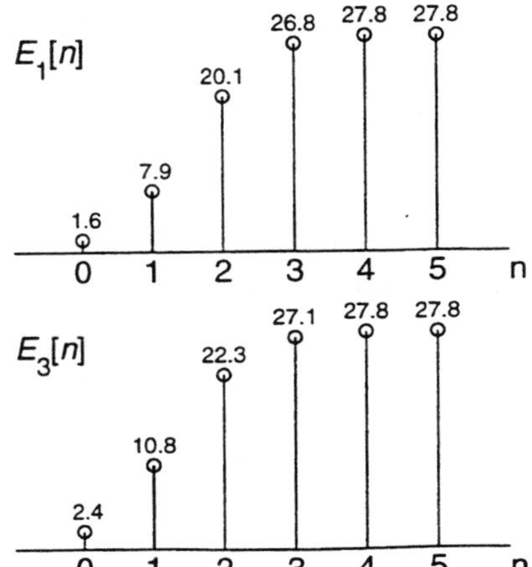

The plot of $E_3[n]$ corresponds to the minimum phase sequence.

5.39. All zeros inside the unit circle means the sequence is minimum phase. Since

$$\sum_{n=0}^{M} |h_{min}[n]|^2 \geq \sum_{n=0}^{M} |h[n]|^2$$

is true for all M, we can use $M = 0$ and just compute $h^2[0]$. The largest result will be the minimum phase sequence.

A	B	C	D	E	F	G	H
44.5	28.4	1.8	2.8	1.8	177.7	113.8	7.1

The answer is F.

5.40.

(i) A zero phase sequence has all its poles and zeros in conjugate reciprocal pairs. Generalized linear phase systems are zero phase systems with additional poles or zeros at $z = 0, \infty, 1$ or -1.

(ii) A stable system's ROC includes the unit circle.

(a) The poles are not in conjugate reciprocal pairs, so this does not have zero or generalized linear phase. $H_i(z)$ has a pole at $z = 0$ and perhaps $z = \infty$. Therefore, the ROC is $0 < |z| < \infty$, which means the inverse is stable. If the ROC includes $z = \infty$, the inverse will also be causal.

(b) Since the poles are not conjugate reciprocal pairs, this does not have zero or generalized linear phase either. $H_i(z)$ has poles inside the unit circle, so ROC is $|z| > \frac{2}{3}$ to match the ROC of $H(z)$. Therefore, the inverse is both stable and causal.

(c) The zeros occur in conjugate reciprocal pairs, so this is a zero phase system. The inverse has poles both inside and outside the unit circle. Therefore, a stable non-causal inverse exists.

(d) The zeros occur in conjugate reciprocal pairs, so this is a zero phase system. Since the poles of the inverse system are on the unit circle a stable inverse does not exist.

5.41. Convolving two symmetric sequences yields another symmetric sequence. A symmetric sequence convolved with an antisymmetric sequence gives an antisymmetric sequence. If you convolve two antisymmetric sequences, you will get a symmetric sequence.

$$A: \; h_1[n] * h_2[n] * h_3[n] = (h_1[n] * h_2[n]) * h_3[n]$$

$h_1[n] * h_2[n]$ is symmetric about $n = 3$, $\quad (-1 \leq n \leq 7)$
$(h_1[n] * h_2[n]) * h_3[n]$ is antisymmetric about $n = 3$, $\quad (-3 \leq n \leq 9)$

Thus, system A has generalized linear phase

$$B: \; (h_1[n] * h_2[n]) + h_3[n]$$

$h_1[n] * h_2[n]$ is symmetric about $n = 3$, as we noted above. Adding $h_3[n]$ to this sequence will destroy all symmtery, so this does not have generalized linear phase.

5.42. (a)

$$A(e^{j\omega}) = 1, \quad |\omega| < \pi$$
$$\phi(\omega) = -\alpha\omega, \quad |\omega| < \pi$$

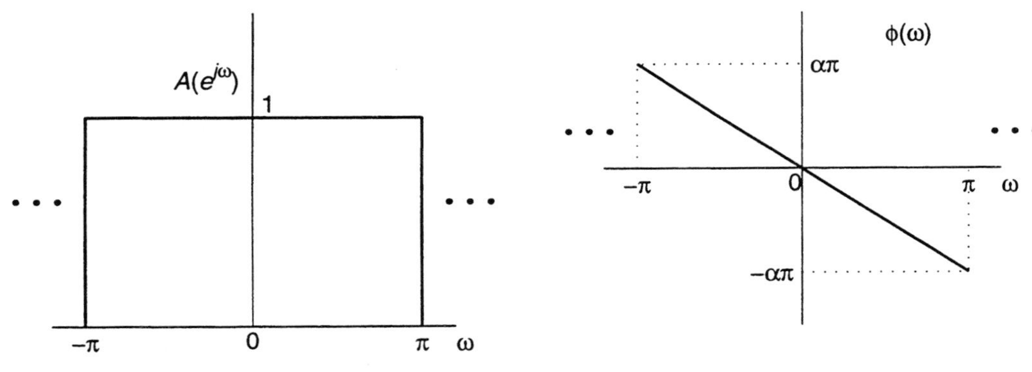

(b)

$$h[n] = \frac{1}{2\pi}\int_{-\pi}^{\pi} e^{-j\alpha\omega}e^{j\omega n}d\omega = \frac{\sin\pi(n-\alpha)}{\pi(n-\alpha)}$$

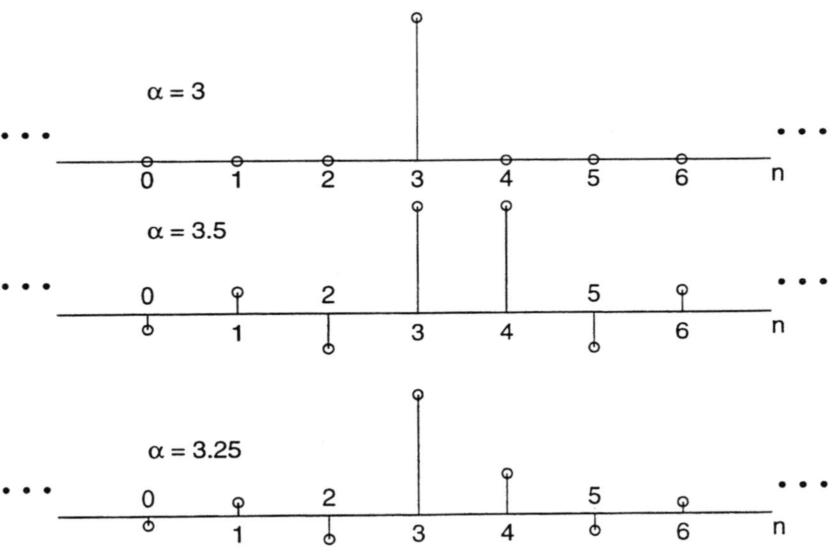

(c) If α is an integer, then $h[n]$ is symmetric about about the point $n = \alpha$. If $\alpha = \frac{M}{2}$, where M is odd, then $h[n]$ is symmetric about $\frac{M}{2}$, which is not a point of the sequence. For α in general, $h[n]$ will not be symmetric.

5.43. Type I: Symmetric, M Even, Odd Length

$$\begin{aligned}
H(e^{j\omega}) &= \sum_{n=0}^{M} h[n]e^{-j\omega n} \\
&= \sum_{n=0}^{(M-2)/2} h[n]e^{-j\omega n} + \sum_{n=(M+2)/2}^{M} h[n]e^{-j\omega n} + h[M/2]e^{-j\omega(M/2)} \\
&= \sum_{n=0}^{(M-2)/2} h[n]e^{-j\omega n} + \sum_{m=0}^{(M-2)/2} h[M-m]e^{-j\omega(M-m)} + h[M/2]e^{-j\omega(M/2)}
\end{aligned}$$

$$
\begin{aligned}
&= e^{-j\omega(M/2)}\left(\sum_{m=0}^{(M-2)/2} h[m]e^{j\omega((M/2)-m)} + \sum_{m=0}^{(M-2)/2} h[m]e^{-j\omega((M/2)-m)} + h[M/2]\right)\\
&= e^{-j\omega(M/2)}\left(\sum_{m=0}^{(M-2)/2} 2h[m]\cos\omega((M/2)-m) + h[M/2]\right)\\
&= e^{-j\omega(M/2)}\left(\sum_{n=1}^{M/2} 2h[(M/2)-n]\cos\omega n + h[M/2]\right)
\end{aligned}
$$

Let

$$
a[n] = \begin{cases} h[M/2], & n = 0\\ 2h[(M/2)-n], & n = 1,\ldots,M/2 \end{cases}
$$

Then

$$
H(e^{j\omega}) = e^{-j\omega(M/2)}\sum_{n=0}^{M/2} a[n]\cos\omega n
$$

and we have

$$
A(\omega) = \sum_{n=0}^{M/2} a[n]\cos(\omega n), \quad \alpha = \frac{M}{2}, \quad \beta = 0
$$

Type II: Symmetric, M Odd, Even Length

$$
\begin{aligned}
H(e^{j\omega}) &= \sum_{n=0}^{M} h[n]e^{-j\omega n}\\
&= \sum_{n=0}^{(M-1)/2} h[n]e^{-j\omega n} + \sum_{n=(M+1)/2}^{M} h[n]e^{-j\omega n}\\
&= \sum_{n=0}^{(M-1)/2} h[n]e^{-j\omega n} + \sum_{m=0}^{(M-1)/2} h[M-m]e^{-j\omega(M-m)}\\
&= e^{-j\omega(M/2)}\left(\sum_{m=0}^{(M-1)/2} h[m]e^{j\omega((M/2)-m)} + \sum_{m=0}^{(M-1)/2} h[m]e^{-j\omega((M/2)-m)}\right)\\
&= e^{-j\omega(M/2)}\left(\sum_{m=0}^{(M-1)/2} 2h[m]\cos\omega((M/2)-m)\right)\\
&= e^{-j\omega(M/2)}\left(\sum_{n=1}^{(M+1)/2} 2h[(M+1)/2-n]\cos\omega(n-(1/2))\right)
\end{aligned}
$$

Let

$$
b[n] = 2h[(M+1)/2-n], \quad n = 1,\ldots,(M+1)/2
$$

Then

$$
H(e^{j\omega}) = e^{-j\omega(M/2)}\sum_{n=1}^{(M+1)/2} b[n]\cos\omega(n-(1/2))
$$

and we have

$$
A(\omega) = \sum_{n=1}^{(M+1)/2} b[n]\cos\omega(n-(1/2)), \quad \alpha = \frac{M}{2}, \quad \beta = 0
$$

Type III: Antisymmetric, M Even, Odd Length

$$\begin{aligned}
H(e^{j\omega}) &= \sum_{n=0}^{M} h[n]e^{-j\omega n} \\
&= \sum_{n=0}^{(M-2)/2} h[n]e^{-j\omega n} + 0 + \sum_{(M+2)/2}^{M} h[n]e^{-j\omega n} \\
&= \sum_{n=0}^{(M-2)/2} h[n]e^{-j\omega n} + \sum_{m=0}^{(M-2)/2} h[M-m]e^{-j\omega(M-m)} \\
&= e^{-j\omega(M/2)} \left(\sum_{m=0}^{(M-2)/2} h[m]e^{j\omega((M/2)-m)} - \sum_{m=0}^{(M-2)/2} h[m]e^{-j\omega((M/2)-m)} \right) \\
&= e^{-j\omega(M/2)} \left(j \sum_{m=0}^{(M-2)/2} 2h[m]\sin\omega((M/2)-m) \right) \\
&= e^{-j\omega(M/2)} e^{j(\pi/2)} \left(\sum_{n=1}^{M/2} 2h[(M/2)-n]\sin\omega n \right)
\end{aligned}$$

Let

$$c[n] = h[(M/2)-n], \quad n = 1, \ldots, M/2$$

Then

$$H(e^{j\omega}) = e^{-j\omega(M/2)} e^{j(\pi/2)} \sum_{n=1}^{M/2} c[n]\sin\omega n$$

and we have

$$A(\omega) = \sum_{n=1}^{M/2} c[n]\sin(\omega n), \quad \alpha = \frac{M}{2}, \quad \beta = \frac{\pi}{2}$$

Type IV: Antisymmetric, M Odd, Even Length

$$\begin{aligned}
H(e^{j\omega}) &= \sum_{n=0}^{M} h[n]e^{-j\omega n} \\
&= \sum_{n=0}^{(M-1)/2} h[n]e^{-j\omega n} + \sum_{n=(M+1)/2}^{M} h[n]e^{-j\omega n} \\
&= \sum_{n=0}^{(M-1)/2} h[n]e^{-j\omega n} + \sum_{m=0}^{(M-1)/2} h[M-m]e^{-j\omega(M-m)} \\
&= e^{-j\omega(M/2)} \left(\sum_{m=0}^{(M-1)/2} h[m]e^{j\omega((M/2)-m)} - \sum_{m=0}^{(M-1)/2} h[m]e^{-j\omega((M/2)-m)} \right) \\
&= e^{-j\omega(M/2)} \left(j \sum_{m=0}^{(M-1)/2} 2h[m]\sin\omega((M/2)-m) \right) \\
&= e^{-j\omega(M/2)} e^{j(\pi/2)} \sum_{n=1}^{(M+1)/2} 2h[(M+1)/2-n]\sin\omega(n-(1/2))
\end{aligned}$$

Let

$$d[n] = 2h[(M+1)/2 - n], \quad n = 1, \ldots, (M+1)/2$$

Then

$$H(e^{j\omega}) = e^{-j\omega(M/2)} e^{j(\pi/2)} \sum_{n=1}^{(M+1)/2} d[n] \sin\omega(n - (1/2))$$

and we have

$$A(\omega) = \sum_{n=1}^{(M+1)/2} d[n] \sin\omega(n - (1/2)), \quad \alpha = \frac{M}{2}, \quad \beta = \frac{\pi}{2}$$

5.44. Filter Types II and III cannot be highpass filters since they both must have a zero at $z = 1$.

Type I $\to$ Type I could be highpass:

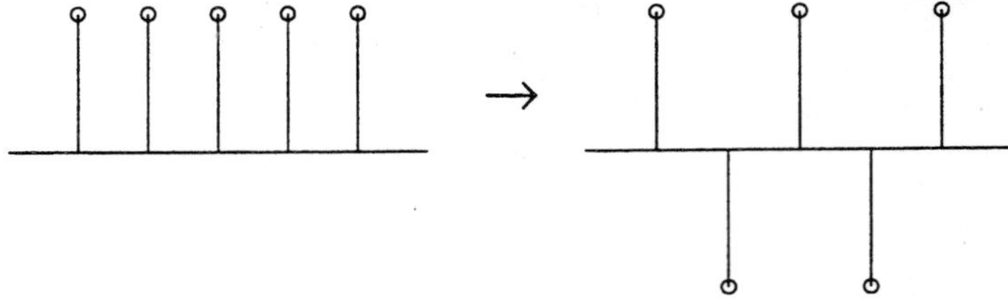

Type II $\to$ Type IV can be highpass:

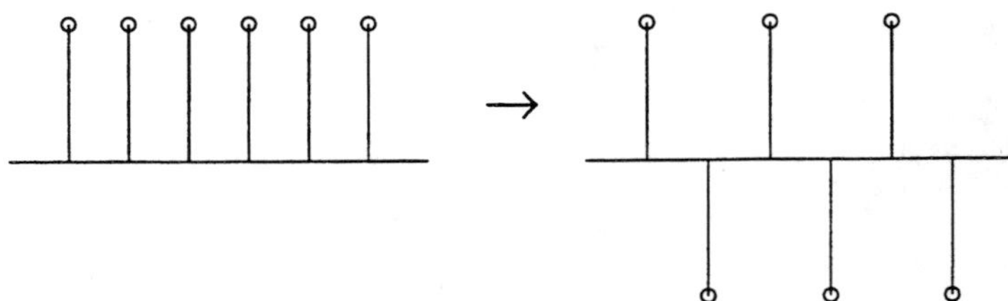

Type III $\to$ Type III cannot be highpass:

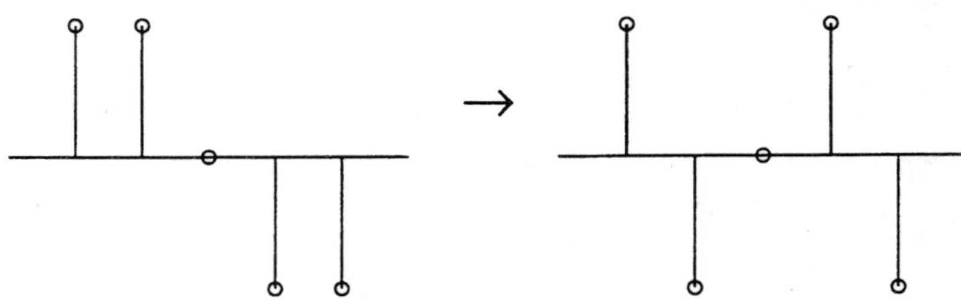

Type IV $\to$ Type II cannot be highpass:

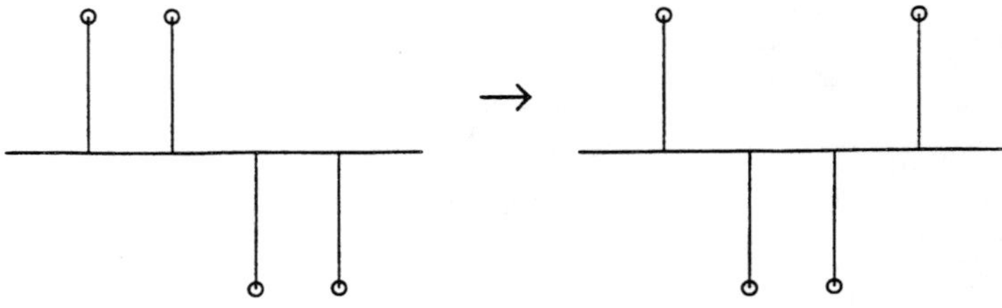

5.45.

$$H(z) = \frac{(1-0.5z^{-1})(1+2jz^{-1})(1-2jz^{-1})}{(1-0.8z^{-1})(1+0.8z^{-1})}$$

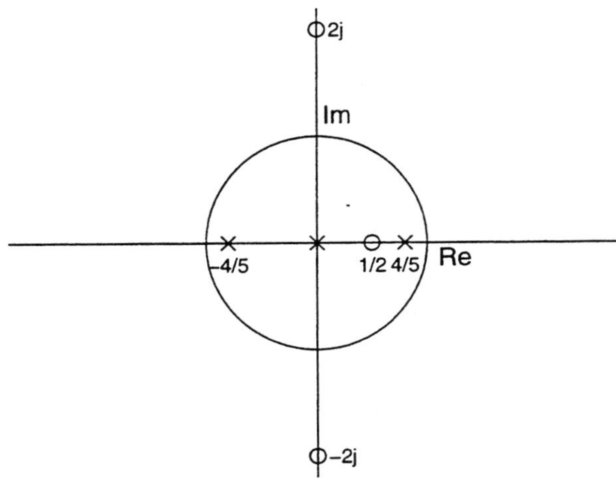

(a) A minimum phase system has all poles and zeros inside $|z| = 1$

$$H_1(z) = \frac{(1-0.5z^{-1})(1+\frac{1}{4}z^{-2})}{(1-0.64z^{-2})}$$

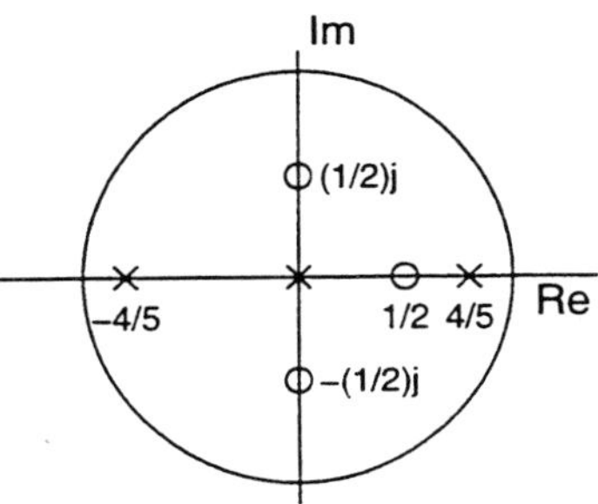

$$H_{ap}(z) = \frac{(1+4z^{-2})}{(1+\frac{1}{4}z^{-2})}$$

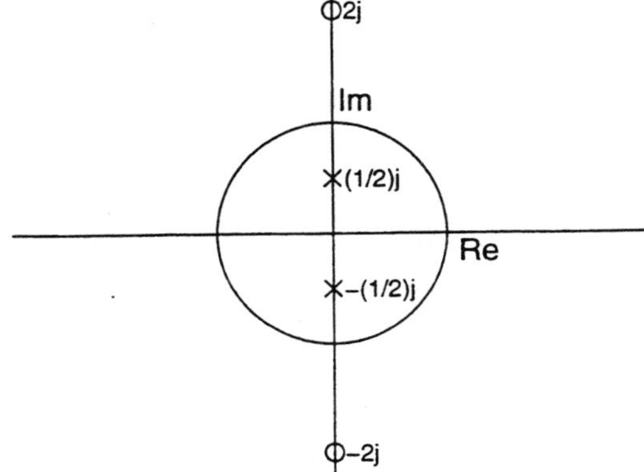

(b) A generalized linear phase system has zeros and poles at $z = 1, -1, 0$ or ∞ or in conjugate reciprocal pairs.

$$H_2(z) = \frac{(1 - 0.5z^{-1})}{(1 - 0.64z^{-2})(1 + \frac{1}{4}z^{-2})}$$

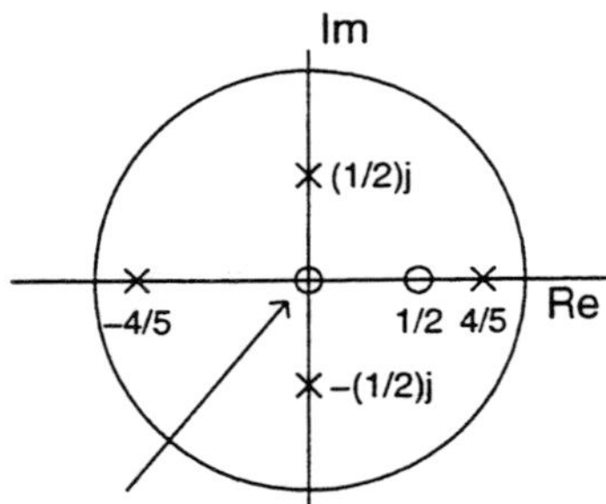

$$H_{lin}(z) = (1 + \tfrac{1}{4}z^{-2})(1 + 4z^{-2})$$

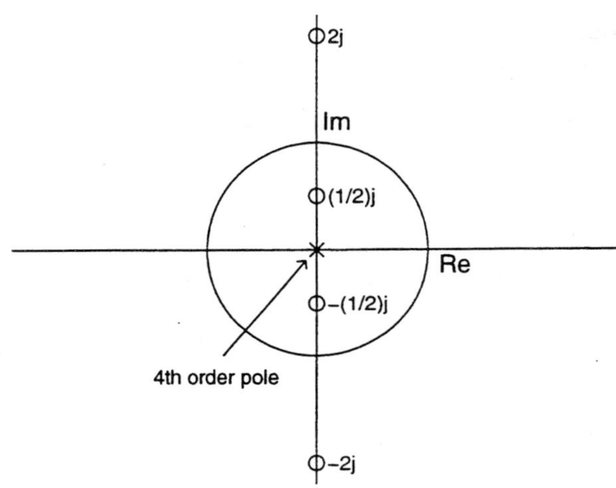

5.46. (a) Minimum phase systems have all poles and zeros inside $|z| = 1$. Allpass systems have pole-zero pairs at conjugate reciprocal locations. Generalized linear phase systems have pole pairs and zero pairs in conjugate reciprocal locations and at $z = 0, 1, -1$ and ∞. This implies that all the poles and zeros of $H_{min}(z)$ are second-order. When the allpass filter flips a pole or zero outside the unit circle, one is left in the conjugate reciprocal location, giving us linear phase.

(b) We know that $h[n]$ is length 8 and therefore has 7 zeros. Since it is an even length generalized linear phase filter with real coefficients and odd symmetry it must be a Type IV filter. It therefore has the property that its zeros come in conjugate reciprocal pairs stated mathematically as $H(z) = H(1/z^*)$. The zero at $z = -2$ implies a zero at $z = -\frac{1}{2}$, while the zero at $z = 0.8e^{j(\pi/4)}$ implies zeros at $z = 0.8e^{-j(\pi/4)}$, $z = 1.25e^{j(\pi/4)}$ and $z = 1.25e^{-j(\pi/4)}$. Because it is a IV filter, it also must have a zero at $z = 1$. Putting all this together gives us

$$\begin{aligned} H(z) &= (1 + 2z^{-1})(1 + 0.5z^{-1})(1 - 0.8e^{j(\pi/4)}z^{-1})(1 - 0.8e^{-j(\pi/4)}z^{-1}) \cdot \\ &\quad (1 - 1.25e^{j(\pi/4)}z^{-1})(1 - 1.25e^{-j(\pi/4)}z^{-1})(1 - z^{-1}) \end{aligned}$$

5.47. The input $x[n]$ in the frequency domain looks like

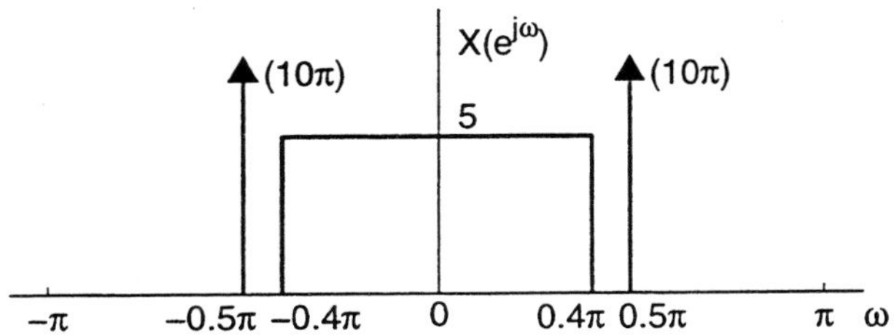

while the corresponding output $y[n]$ looks like

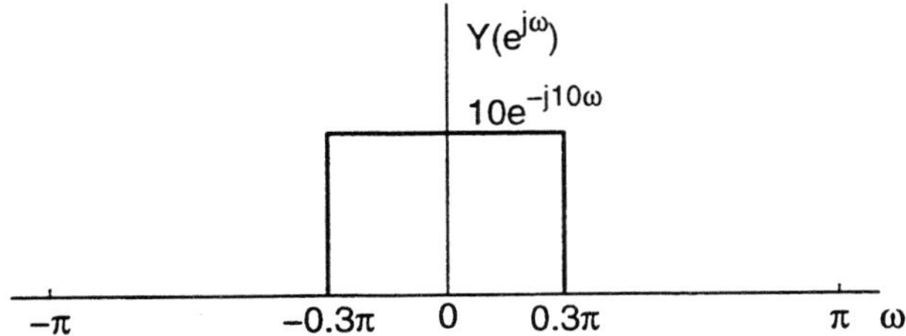

Therefore, the filter must be

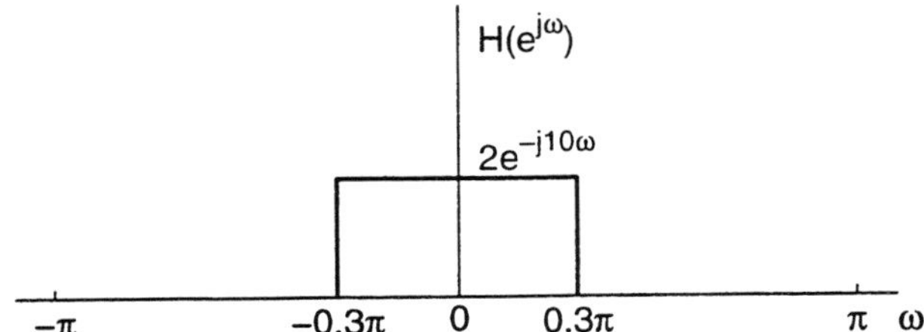

In the time domain this is

$$h[n] = \frac{2\sin[0.3\pi(n-10)]}{\pi(n-10)}$$

5.48. (a)

Property	Applies?	Comments
Stable	No	For a stable, causal system, all poles must be inside the unit circle.
IIR	Yes	The system has poles at locations other than $z = 0$ or $z = \infty$.
FIR	No	FIR systems can only have poles at $z = 0$ or $z = \infty$.
Minimum Phase	No	Minimum phase systems have all poles and zeros located inside the unit circle.
Allpass	No	Allpass systems have poles and zeros in conjugate reciprocal pairs.
Generalized Linear Phase	No	The causal generalized linear phase systems presented in this chapter are FIR.
Positive Group Delay for all w	No	This system is not in the appropriate form.

(b)

Property	Applies?	Comments
Stable	Yes	The ROC for this system function, $\lvert z\rvert > 0$, contains the unit circle. (Note there is 7th order pole at $z = 0$).
IIR	No	The system has poles only at $z = 0$.
FIR	Yes	The system has poles only at $z = 0$.
Minimum Phase	No	By definition, a minimum phase system must have all its poles and zeros located *inside* the unit circle.
Allpass	No	Note that the zeros on the unit circle will cause the magnitude spectrum to drop zero at certain frequencies. Clearly, this system is not allpass.
Generalized Linear Phase	Yes	This is the pole/zero plot of a type II FIR linear phase system.
Positive Group Delay for all w	Yes	This system is causal and linear phase. Consequently, its group delay is a positive constant.

(c)

Property	Applies?	Comments
Stable	Yes	All poles are inside the unit circle. Since the system is causal, the ROC includes the unit circle.
IIR	Yes	The system has poles at locations other than $z = 0$ or $z = \infty$.
FIR	No	FIR systems can only have poles at $z = 0$ or $z = \infty$.
Minimum Phase	No	Minimum phase systems have all poles and zeros located inside the unit circle.
Allpass	Yes	The poles inside the unit circle have corresponding zeros located at conjugate reciprocal locations.
Generalized Linear Phase	No	The causal generalized linear phase systems presented in this chapter are FIR.
Positive Group Delay for all w	Yes	Stable allpass systems have positive group delay for all w.

5.49. (a) *Yes.* By the region of convergence we know there are no poles at $z = \infty$ and it therefore must be causal. Another way to see this is to use long division to write $H_1(z)$ as

$$H_1(z) = \frac{1 - z^{-5}}{1 - z^{-1}} = 1 + z^{-1} + z^{-2} + z^{-3} + z^{-4}\ ,\ |z| > 0$$

(b) $h_1[n]$ is a causal rectangular pulse of length 5. If we convolve $h_1[n]$ with another causal rectangular pulse of length N we will get a triangular pulse of length $N + 5 - 1 = N + 4$. The triangular pulse is symmetric around its apex and thus has linear phase. To make the triangular pulse $g[n]$ have at least 9 nonzero samples we can choose $N = 5$ or let $h_2[n] = h_1[n]$.

Proof:

$$G(e^{j\omega}) \;=\; H_1(e^{j\omega})H_2(e^{j\omega}) = H_1^2(e^{j\omega})$$

$$
\begin{aligned}
&= \left[\frac{1-e^{-j5\omega}}{1-e^{-j\omega}}\right]^2 \\
&= \left[\frac{e^{-j\omega 5/2}\left(e^{j\omega 5/2}-e^{-j\omega 5/2}\right)}{e^{-j\omega/2}\left(e^{j\omega/2}-e^{-j\omega/2}\right)}\right]^2 \\
&= \frac{\sin^2(5\omega/2)}{\sin^2(\omega/2)} e^{-j4\omega}
\end{aligned}
$$

(c) The required values for $h_3[n]$ can intuitively be worked out using the flip and slide idea of convolution. Here is a second way to get the answer. Pick $h_3[n]$ to be the inverse system for $h_1[n]$ and then simplify using the geometric series as follows.

$$
\begin{aligned}
H_3(z) &= \frac{1-z^{-1}}{1-z^{-5}} \\
&= (1-z^{-1})\left[1+z^{-5}+z^{-10}+z^{-15}+\cdots\right] \\
&= 1-z^{-1}+z^{-5}-z^{-6}+z^{-10}-z^{-11}+z^{-15}-z^{-16}+\cdots
\end{aligned}
$$

This choice for $h_3[n]$ will make $q[n] = \delta[n]$ for all n. However, since we only need equality for $0 \le n \le 19$ truncating the infinite series will give us the desired result. The final answer is shown below.

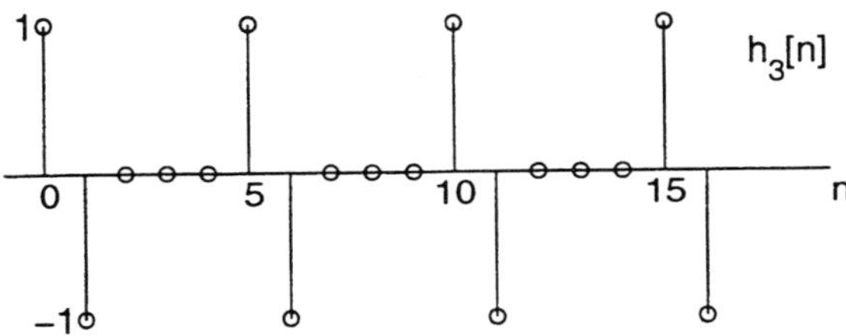

5.50. (a) This system does not necessarily have generalized linear phase. The phase response,

$$
G_1(e^{j\omega}) = \tan^{-1}\left(\frac{Im(H_1(e^{j\omega})+H_2(e^{j\omega}))}{Re(H_1(e^{j\omega})+H_2(e^{j\omega}))}\right)
$$

is not necessarily linear. As a counter-example, consider the systems

$$
\begin{aligned}
h_1[n] &= \delta[n]+\delta[n-1] \\
h_2[n] &= 2\delta[n]-2\delta[n-1] \\
g_1[n] &= h_1[n]+h_2[n] = 3\delta[n]-\delta[n-1] \\
G_1(e^{j\omega}) &= 3-e^{-j\omega} = 3-\cos\omega + j\sin\omega \\
\angle G_1(e^{j\omega}) &= \tan^{-1}\left(\frac{\sin\omega}{3-\cos\omega}\right)
\end{aligned}
$$

Clearly, $G_1(e^{j\omega})$ does not have linear phase.

(b) This system must have generalized linear phase.

$$
\begin{aligned}
G_2(e^{j\omega}) &= H_1(e^{j\omega})H_2(e^{j\omega}) \\
|G_2(e^{j\omega})| &= |H_1(e^{j\omega})|\,|H_2(e^{j\omega})| \\
\angle G_2(e^{j\omega}) &= \angle H_1(e^{j\omega}) + \angle H_2(e^{j\omega})
\end{aligned}
$$

The sum of two linear phase responses is also a linear phase response.

(c) This system does not necessarily have linear phase. Using properties of the DTFT, the circular convolution of $H_1(e^{jw})$ and $H_2(e^{jw})$ is related to the product of $h_1[n]$ and $h_2[n]$. Consider the systems

$$\begin{aligned} h_1[n] &= \delta[n] + \delta[n-1] \\ h_2[n] &= \delta[n] + 2\delta[n-1] + \delta[n-2] \\ g_3[n] &= h_1[n]h_2[n] = \delta[n] + 2\delta[n-1] \\ G_3(e^{j\omega}) &= 1 + 2e^{-j\omega} = 1 + 2\cos\omega - j2\sin\omega \\ \angle G_3(e^{j\omega}) &= \tan^{-1}\left(\frac{2\sin\omega}{1+2\cos\omega}\right) \end{aligned}$$

Clearly, $G_3(e^{j\omega})$ does not have linear phase.

5.51. *False.* Let $h[n]$ equal

$$h[n] = \frac{\sin\omega_c(n-4.3)}{\pi(n-4.3)} \longleftrightarrow H(e^{j\omega}) = \begin{cases} e^{-4.3\omega}, & |\omega| < \omega_c \\ 0, & \text{otherwise} \end{cases}$$

Proof: Although the group delay is constant (grd $\left[H(e^{j\omega})\right] = 4.3$) the resulting M is not an integer.

$$\begin{aligned} h[n] &= \pm h[M-n] \\ H(e^{j\omega}) &= \pm e^{jM\omega}H(e^{-j\omega}) \\ e^{-j4.3\omega} &= \pm e^{j(M+4.3)\omega}, \qquad |\omega| < \omega_c \\ M &= -8.6 \end{aligned}$$

5.52. The type II FIR system $H_{II}(z)$ has generalized linear phase. Therefore, it can be written in the form

$$H_{II}(e^{j\omega}) = A_e(e^{j\omega})e^{-j\omega M/2}$$

where M is an odd integer and $A_e(e^{j\omega})$ is a real, even, periodic function of ω. Note that the system $G(z) = (1 - z^{-1})$ is a type IV generalized linear phase system.

$$\begin{aligned} G(e^{j\omega}) &= 1 - e^{-j\omega} \\ &= e^{-j\omega/2}(e^{j\omega/2} - e^{-j\omega/2}) \\ &= e^{-j\omega/2}(2j\,\sin(\omega/2)) \\ &= 2\sin(\omega/2)e^{-j\omega/2+j\pi/2} \\ &= A_o(e^{j\omega})e^{-j\omega/2+j\pi/2} \\ A_o(e^{j\omega}) &= 2\sin(\omega/2) \\ \angle G(e^{j\omega}) &= -\frac{\omega}{2} + \frac{\pi}{2} \end{aligned}$$

The cascade of $H_{II}(z)$ with $G(z)$ results in a generalized linear phase system $H(z)$.

$$\begin{aligned} H(e^{j\omega}) &= A_e(e^{j\omega})A_o(e^{j\omega})e^{-j\omega M/2}e^{-j\omega/2+j\pi/2} \\ &= A'_o(e^{j\omega})e^{j\omega M'/2+j\pi/2} \end{aligned}$$

where $A'_o(e^{j\omega})$ is a real, odd, periodic function of ω and M' is an even integer.

Thus, the resulting system $H(e^{j\omega})$ has the form of a type III FIR generalized linear phase system. It is antisymmetric, has odd length (M is even), and has generalized linear phase.

5.53. For all of the following we know that the poles and zeros are real or occur in complex conjugate pairs since each impulse response is real. Since they are causal we also know that none have poles at infinity.

(a)
- Since $h_1[n]$ is real there are complex conjugate poles at $z = 0.9e^{\pm j\pi/3}$.
- If $x[n] = u[n]$

$$Y(z) = H_1(z)X(z) = \frac{H_1(z)}{1 - z^{-1}}$$

We can perform a partial fraction expansion on $Y(z)$ and find a term $(1)^n u[n]$ due to the pole at $z = 1$. Since $y[n]$ eventually decays to zero this term must be cancelled by a zero. Thus, the filter must have a zero at $z = 1$.

- The length of the impulse response is infinite.

(b)
- Linear phase and a real impulse response implies that zeros occur at conjugate reciprocal locations so there are zeros at $z = z_1, 1/z_1, z_1^*, 1/z_1^*$ where $z_1 = 0.8e^{j\pi/4}$.
- Since $h_2[n]$ is both causal and linear phase it must be a Type I, II, III, or IV FIR filter. Therefore the filter's poles only occur at $z = 0$.
- Since the $\arg\{H_2(e^{jw})\} = -2.5\omega$ we can narrow down the filter to a Type II or Type IV filter. This also tells us that the length of the impulse response is 6 and that there are 5 zeros. Since the number of poles always equal the number of zeros, we have 5 poles at $z = 0$.
- Since $20 \log |H_2(e^{j0})| = -\infty$ we must have a zero at $z = 1$. This narrows down the filter type even more from a Type II or Type IV filter to just a Type IV filter.

With all the information above we can determine $H_2(z)$ completely (up to a scale factor)

$$H_2(z) = A(1 - z^{-1})(1 - 0.8e^{j\pi/4}z^{-1})(1 - 0.8e^{-j\pi/4}z^{-1})(1 - 1.25e^{j\pi/4}z^{-1})(1 - 1.25e^{-j\pi/4}z^{-1})$$

(c) Since $H_3(z)$ is allpass we know the poles and zeros occur in conjugate reciprocal locations. The impulse response is infinite and in general looks like

$$H_3(z) = \frac{(z^{-1} - 0.8e^{j\pi/4})(z^{-1} - 0.8e^{-j\pi/4})}{(1 - 0.8e^{j\pi/4}z^{-1})(1 - 0.8e^{-j\pi/4}z^{-1})} H_{ap}(z)$$

5.54. (a) To be rational, X(z) must be of the form

$$X(z) = \frac{b_0}{a_0} \frac{\prod_{k=1}^{M}(1 - c_k z^{-1})}{\prod_{k=1}^{N}(1 - d_k z^{-1})}$$

Because x[n] is real, its zeros must appear in conjugate pairs. Consequently, there are two more zeros, at $z = \frac{1}{2}e^{-j\pi/4}$, and $z = \frac{1}{2}e^{-j3\pi/4}$. Since x[n] is zero outside $0 \leq n \leq 4$, there are only four zeros (and poles) in the system function. Therefore, the system function can be written as

$$X(z) = \left(1 - \frac{1}{2}e^{j\pi/4}z^{-1}\right)\left(1 - \frac{1}{2}e^{j3\pi/4}z^{-1}\right)\left(1 - \frac{1}{2}e^{-j\pi/4}z^{-1}\right)\left(1 - \frac{1}{2}e^{-j3\pi/4}z^{-1}\right)$$

Clearly, X(z) is rational.

(b) A sketch of the pole-zero plot for $X(z)$ is shown below. Note that the ROC for X(z) is $|z| > 0$.

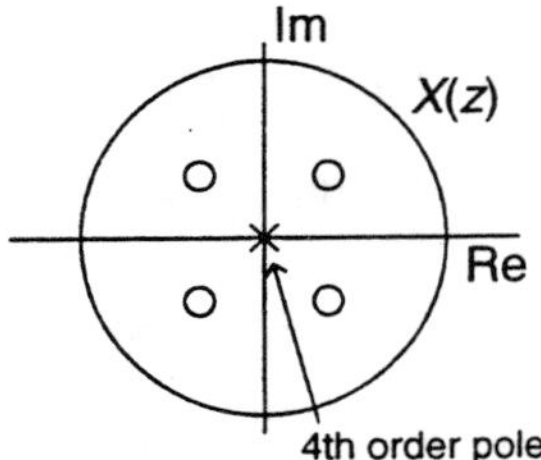

(c) A sketch of the pole-zero plot for $Y(z)$ is shown below. Note that the ROC for Y(z) is $|z| > \frac{1}{2}$.

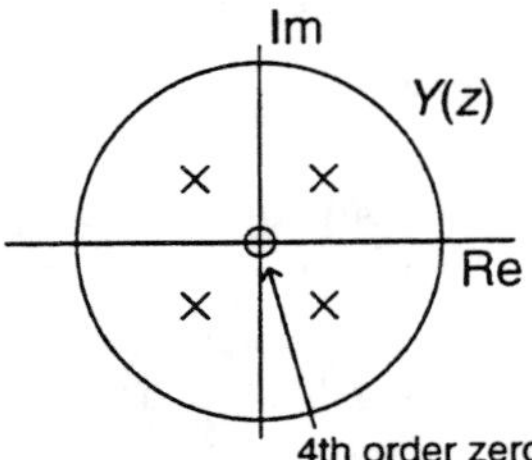

5.55.
- Since $x[n]$ is real the poles & zeros come in complex conjugate pairs.
- From (1) we know there are no poles except at zero or infinity.
- From (3) and the fact that $x[n]$ is finite we know that the signal has generalized linear phase.
- From (3) and (4) we have $\alpha = 2$. This and the fact that there are no poles in the finite plane except the five at zero (deduced from (1) and (2)) tells us the form of $X(z)$ must be

$$X(z) = x[-1]z + x[0] + x[1]z^{-1} + x[2]z^{-2} + x[3]z^{-3} + x[4]z^{-4} + x[5]z^{-5}$$

The phase changes by π at $\omega = 0$ and π so there must be a zero on the unit circle at $z = \pm 1$. The zero at $z = 1$ tells us $\sum x[n] = 0$. The zero at $z = -1$ tells us $\sum(-1)^n x[n] = 0$.
We can also conclude $x[n]$ must be a Type III filter since the length of $x[n]$ is odd and there is a zero at both $z = \pm 1$. $x[n]$ must therefore be antisymmetric around $n = 2$ and $x[2] = 0$.

- From (5) and Parseval's theorem we have $\sum |x[n]|^2 = 28$.
- From (6)

$$\begin{aligned} y[0] &= \frac{1}{2\pi}\int_{-\pi}^{\pi} Y(e^{j\omega})d\omega = 4 \\ &= x[n] * u[n]\,|_{n=0} = x[-1] + x[0] \end{aligned}$$

$$\begin{aligned} y[1] &= \frac{1}{2\pi}\int_{-\pi}^{\pi} Y(e^{j\omega})e^{jw}d\omega = 6 \\ &= x[n] * u[n]\,|_{n=1} = x[-1] + x[0] + x[1] \end{aligned}$$

- The conclusion from (7) that $\sum(-1)^n x[n] = 0$ we already derived earlier.
- Since the DTFT $\{x_e[n]\} = \mathcal{R}e\{X(e^{j\omega})\}$ we have

$$\begin{aligned} \frac{x[5] + x[-5]}{2} &= -\frac{3}{2} \\ x[5] &= -3 + x[-5] \\ x[5] &= -3 \end{aligned}$$

Summarizing the above we have the following (dependent) equations

(1) $x[-1]+x[0]+x[1]+x[2]+x[3]+x[4]+x[5]=0$
(2) $-x[-1]+x[0]-x[1]+x[2]-x[3]+x[4]-x[5]=0$
(3) $x[2]=0$
(4) $x[-1]=-x[5]$
(5) $x[0]=-x[4]$
(6) $x[1]=-x[3]$
(7) $x[-1]^2+x[0]^2+x[1]^2+x[2]^2+x[3]^2+x[4]^2+x[5]^2=28$
(8) $x[-1]+x[0]=4$
(9) $x[-1]+x[0]+x[1]=6$
(10) $x[5]=-3$

$x[n]$ is easily obtained from solving the equations in the following order: (3),(10),(4),(8),(5),(9), and (6).

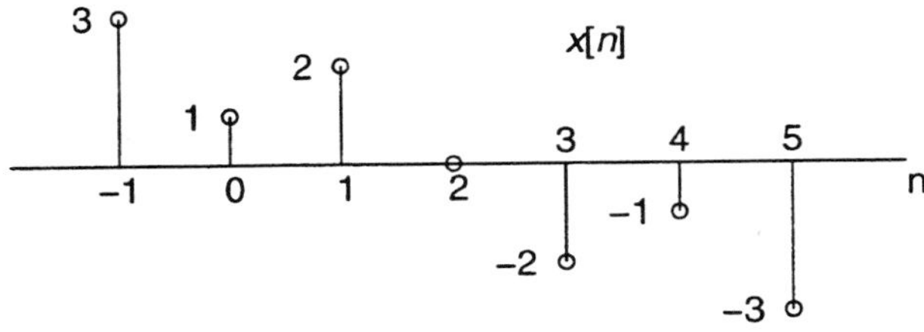

5.56. (a) The LTI system S_2 is characterized as a lowpass filter.
The z-transform of $h_1[n]$ is found below.

$$\begin{aligned} y[n]-y[n-1]+\frac{1}{4}y[n-2] &= x[n] \\ Y(z)-Y(z)z^{-1}+\frac{1}{4}Y(z)z^{-2} &= X(z) \\ Y(z)\left(1-z^{-1}+\frac{1}{4}z^{-2}\right) &= X(z) \end{aligned}$$

$$H_1(z)=\frac{1}{(1-z^{-1}+\frac{1}{4}z^{-2})}=\frac{1}{(1-\frac{1}{2}z^{-1})^2}$$

This system function has a second order pole at $z=\frac{1}{2}$. (There is also a second order zero at $z=0$). Evaluating this pole-zero plot on the unit circle yields a low pass filter, as the second order pole boosts the low frequencies.

Since

$$\begin{aligned} H_2(e^{j\omega}) &= H_1(-e^{j\omega}) \\ H_2(z) &= H_1(-z) \end{aligned}$$

If we replace all references to z in $H_1(z)$ with $-z$, we will get $H_2(z)$.

$$H_2(z)=\frac{1}{(1+\frac{1}{2}z^{-1})^2}$$

Consequently, $H_2(z)$ has two poles at $z=-\frac{1}{2}$. (There is also a second order zero at $z=0$). Evaluating this pole-zero plot on the unit circle yields a high pass filter, as the second order pole now boosts the high frequencies.

(b) The LTI system S_3 is characterized as a highpass filter. $H_3(e^{j\omega})$ is the inverse system of $H_1(e^{j\omega})$, since $H_3(e^{j\omega})H_1(e^{j\omega}) = 1$. Consequently, $H_3(z)H_1(z) = 1$.

As shown in part (a), $H_1(z)$ has a second order pole at $z = \frac{1}{2}$, and a second order zero at $z = 0$. Thus, $H_3(z)$ has a second order zero at $z = \frac{1}{2}$, and a second order pole at $z = 0$. Evaluating this pole-zero plot on the unit circle yields a high pass filter, as the second order zero attenuates the low frequencies.

S_3 is a minimum phase filter, since its poles and zeros are located inside the unit circle. However, because the zeros of S_3 do not occur in conjugate reciprocal pairs, S_3 cannot be classified as one of the four types of FIR filters with generalized linear phase.

(c) First, we compute the system function $H_4(z)$

$$
\begin{aligned}
y[n] + \alpha_1 y[n-1] + \alpha_2 y[n-2] &= \beta_0 x[n] \\
Y(z) + \alpha_1 Y(z)z^{-1} + \alpha_2 Y(z)z^{-2} &= \beta_0 X(z)
\end{aligned}
$$

$$
H_4(z) = \frac{\beta_0}{1 + \alpha_1 z^{-1} + \alpha_2 z^{-2}}
$$

S_4 is a stable and noncausal LTI system. Therefore, its poles must be located *outside* the unit circle, and its ROC must be an interior region that includes the unit circle. We place a second order pole at $z = 2$, which is the (conjugate) reciprocal location of the second order pole of $H_1(z)$ at $z = \frac{1}{2}$. This gives

$$
\begin{aligned}
H_4(z) &= \frac{\beta_0}{(1 - 2z^{-1})^2} \\
&= \frac{\beta_0}{(1 - 4z^{-1} + 4z^{-2})}
\end{aligned}
$$

In order for

$$
|H_4(e^{jw})| = |H_1(e^{jw})|
$$

an appropriate value of β_0 must be found. Consider the case when $z = 1$. Then,

$$
\begin{aligned}
\left|\frac{\beta_0}{(1 - 4z^{-1} + 4z^{-2})}\right| &= \left|\frac{1}{(1 - z^{-1} + \frac{1}{4}z^{-2})}\right| \\
\left|\frac{\beta_0}{(1 - 4 + 4)}\right| &= \left|\frac{1}{(1 - 1 + \frac{1}{4})}\right| \\
|\beta_0| &= 4
\end{aligned}
$$

The values $\alpha_1 = -4$, $\alpha_2 = 4$, and $\beta_0 = 4$ satisfy the criteria. Note that $\beta_0 = -4$ also is a valid solution.

(d) If $h_5[n] * h_1[n]$ is FIR, then the poles of $H_1(z)$ must be cancelled by zeros of $H_5(z)$. Thus, we expect a second order zero of $H_5(z)$ at $z = \frac{1}{2}$. Therefore, $H_5(z)$ will have the term $(1 - \frac{1}{2}z^{-1})^2$.

In order for the filter $h_5[n]$ to be zero phase, it must satisfy the symmetry property $h_5[n] = h_5^*[-n]$, which means that $H_5(z) = H_5^*(z)$. For this property to be satisfied, we need two more zeros located at $z = 2$. In addition, we want these zeros to correspond to a noncausal sequence. Therefore, $H_5(z)$ will also have the term $(1 - \frac{1}{2}z)^2$.

Combining these two results,

$$
\begin{aligned}
H_5(z) &= \left(1 - \frac{1}{2}z^{-1}\right)^2 \left(1 - \frac{1}{2}z\right)^2 \\
&= \left(1 - z^{-1} + \frac{1}{4}z^{-2}\right)\left(1 - z + \frac{1}{4}z^2\right) \\
&= \frac{1}{4}z^{-2} - \frac{5}{4}z^{-1} + \frac{33}{16} - \frac{5}{4}z + \frac{1}{4}z^2
\end{aligned}
$$

Taking the inverse z-transform yields

$$h_5[n] = \frac{1}{4}\delta[n-2] - \frac{5}{4}\delta[n-1] + \frac{33}{16}\delta[n] - \frac{5}{4}\delta[n+1] + \frac{1}{4}\delta[n+2]$$

5.57. (a)

$$x[n] = s[n]\cos\omega_0 n = \frac{1}{2}s[n]e^{j\omega_0 n} + \frac{1}{2}s[n]e^{-j\omega_0 n}$$

$$X(e^{j\omega}) = \frac{1}{2}S(e^{j(\omega-\omega_0)}) + \frac{1}{2}S(e^{j(\omega+\omega_0)})$$

$$Y(e^{j\omega}) = H(e^{j\omega})X(e^{j\omega}) = \frac{1}{2}e^{-j\phi_0}S(e^{j(\omega-\omega_0)}) + \frac{1}{2}e^{j\phi_0}S(e^{j(\omega+\omega_0)})$$

$$\begin{aligned} y[n] &= \frac{1}{2}s[n]e^{j(\omega_0 n-\phi_0)} + \frac{1}{2}s[n]e^{-j(\omega_0 n-\phi_0)} \\ &= s[n]\cos(\omega_0 n - \phi_0) \end{aligned}$$

(b) This time,

$$Y(e^{j\omega}) = H(e^{j\omega})X(e^{j\omega}) = \frac{1}{2}e^{-j\phi_0}e^{-j\omega n_d}S(e^{j(\omega-\omega_0)}) + \frac{1}{2}e^{j\phi_0}e^{-j\omega n_d}S(e^{j(\omega+\omega_0)})$$

$$\begin{aligned} y[n] &= \delta[n-n_d] * \left(\frac{1}{2}s[n]e^{j(\omega_0 n-\phi_0)} + \frac{1}{2}s[n]e^{-j(\omega_0 n-\phi_0)}\right) \\ &= \delta[n-n_d] * s[n]\cos(\omega_0 n - \phi_0) \\ &= s[n-n_d]\cos(\omega_0 n - \omega_0 n_d - \phi_0) \end{aligned}$$

Therefore, if $\phi_1 = \phi_0 + \omega_0 n_d$ then

$$y[n] = s[n-n_d]\cos(\omega_0 n - \phi_1)$$

for narrowband $s[n]$.

(c)

$$\begin{aligned} \tau_{gr} &= -\frac{d}{d\omega}arg[H(e^{j\omega})] = -\frac{d}{d\omega}[-\phi_0 - \omega n_d] = n_d \\ \tau_{ph} &= -\frac{1}{\omega}arg[H(e^{j\omega})] = -\frac{1}{\omega}[-\phi_0 - \omega n_d] = \frac{\phi_0}{\omega} - n_d \end{aligned}$$

$$y[n] = s[n - \tau_{gr}(\omega_0)]\cos[\omega_0(n - \tau_{ph}(\omega_0))]$$

(d) The effect would be the same as the following:

(i) Bandlimit interpolate the composite signal to a C–T signal with some rate T.

(ii) Delay the envelope by $T \cdot \tau_{gr}$, and delay the carrier by $T \cdot \tau_{ph}$.

(iii) Sample to a D–T signal at rate T

5.58. (a)

$$m_x = 0 \Rightarrow \phi_{yy}[m] = \Gamma_{yy}[m] \Leftrightarrow \Gamma_{yy}(z) = \Phi_{yy}(z)$$

$$\phi_{yy}[m] = y[n] * y[-n] = x[n] * x[-n] * h[n] * h[-n]$$

$$\Phi_{yy}(z) = X(z)X(z^{-1})H(z)H(z^{-1}) = \Phi_{xx}(z)H(z)H(z^{-1})$$

$$\phi_{xx}[m] = \sigma_x^2\delta[m] \Leftrightarrow \Phi_{xx}(z) = \sigma_x^2$$

$$y[n] = \sum_{k=1}^{N} a_k y[n-k] + \sum_{k=0}^{M} b_k x[n-k], \quad b_0 = 1$$

$$Y(z) = \sum_{k=1}^{N} a_k Y(z) z^{-k} + X(z) + \sum_{k=1}^{M} b_k X(z) z^{-k}$$

$$H(z) = \frac{1 + \sum_{k=1}^{M} b_k z^{-k}}{1 - \sum_{k=1}^{N} a_k z^{-k}} = A\frac{\prod_{k=1}^{M}(1 - c_k z^{-1})}{\prod_{k=1}^{N}(1 - d_k z^{-1})}$$

So,

$$\Gamma_{yy}(z) = \Phi_{xx}(z)H(z)H(z^{-1}) = \sigma_x^2 \frac{\left(1 + \sum_{k=1}^{M} b_k z^{-k}\right)\left(1 + \sum_{k=1}^{M} b_k z^{k}\right)}{\left(1 - \sum_{k=1}^{N} a_k z^{-k}\right)\left(1 - \sum_{k=1}^{N} a_k z^{k}\right)}$$

Or equivalently,

$$\Gamma_{yy}(z) = A^2\sigma_x^2 \frac{\prod_{k=1}^{M}(1 - c_k z^{-1})(1 - c_k z)}{\prod_{k=1}^{N}(1 - d_k z^{-1})(1 - d_k z)}$$

(b) To "whiten" the signal $y[n]$ we need a system:

$$H_w(z)H_w(z^{-1}) = \frac{1}{H(z)H(z^{-1})}$$

Therefore,

$$H_w(z)H_w(z^{-1}) = \frac{\prod_{k=1}^{N}(1 - d_k z^{-1})(1 - d_k z)}{\prod_{k=1}^{M}(1 - c_k z^{-1})(1 - c_k z)}$$

The poles of $H_w(z)$ are the zeros of $H(z)$ and the zeros of $H_w(z)$ are the poles of $H(z)$. We must now decide which N of the $2N$ zeros of $H_w(z)H_w(z^{-1})$ to associate with $H_w(z)$. The remaining N zeros and M poles will be reciprocals and will be associated with $H_w(z^{-1})$. In order for $H_w(z)$ to be stable, we must chose all its poles inside the unit circle. Thus for a pair c_k, c_k^{-1} we chose the one which is inside the unit circle.

(c) There is no real constraint on the zeros of $H_w(z)$, so we can select either d_k or d_k^{-1}. Thus, it is not unique.

5.59. (a)

$$H(e^{j\omega}) = \sum_{n=0}^{M-1} e^{-j\omega n} = \frac{1-e^{-j\omega M}}{1-e^{-j\omega}}$$

$$H_i(e^{j\omega}) = \frac{1-e^{-j\omega}}{1-e^{-j\omega M}} \Leftrightarrow h_i[n] = \sum_{k=0}^{\infty} \delta[n-kM] - \delta[n-kM-1]$$

1 1 1 ...
1 M+1 2M+1
0 M 2M n
−1 −1 −1

$h_i[n]$ has infinite length, so we can never get a result without infinite sums. Therefore, it is not a real time filter. We can use the transform approach but we must have all the input data available to do this.

(b) The proposed system is a windowed version of $h_i[n]$:

$$h_1[n] * h_2[n] = h_i[n]p[n]$$

Where

$$p[n] = \begin{cases} 1, & 0 \le n \le qM \\ 0, & \text{otherwise} \end{cases}$$

$$x[n] * h[n] * h_i[n]p[n] = w[n]$$

Therefore, if $x[n]$ is shorter than qM points, we can recover it by looking at $w[n]$ in the range $0 \le n \le qM-1$.

(c)

$$H_i(z) = \frac{1}{H(z)} = H_1(z)H_2(z)$$

$$h_1[n] = \sum_{k=0}^{q} \delta[n-kM] \Leftrightarrow H_1(z) = \frac{1-z^{-qM}}{1-z^{-M}}$$

Thus,

$$H_2(z) = \frac{1}{H(z)} \frac{1-z^{-M}}{1-z^{-qM}}$$

Note that

$$\frac{1-z^{-M}}{1-z^{-qM}}$$

has M zeros and qM poles. Since $H_2(z)$ is causal, there are no poles at $z=\infty$. If $H(z)$ has P poles and Z zeros:

$$Z + M \le P + qM$$

5.60. (a)

$$H(z) = z - \frac{1}{a} = \frac{az-1}{a} = \frac{a-z^{-1}}{az^{-1}}$$

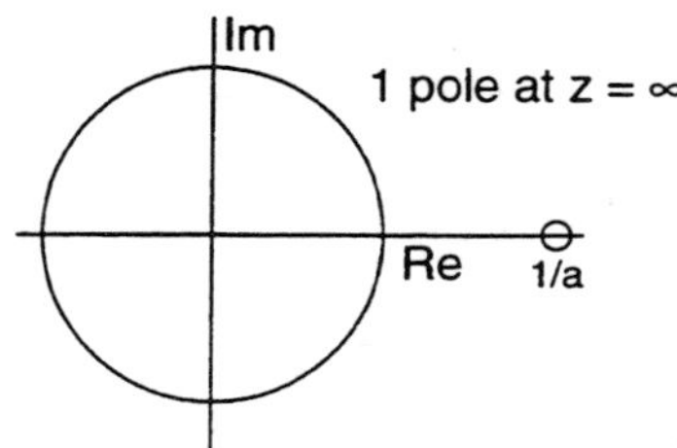

$$H(e^{j\omega}) = e^{j\omega} - \frac{1}{a} = \cos\omega + j\sin\omega - \frac{1}{a}$$

$$\arg[H(e^{j\omega})] = \tan^{-1}\left(\frac{\sin\omega}{\cos\omega - \frac{1}{a}}\right)$$

(b)

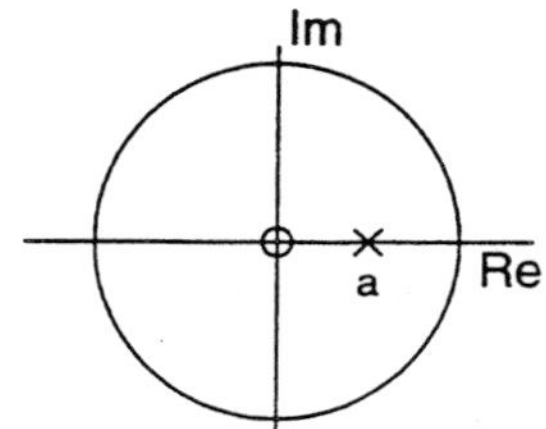

$$G(z) = \frac{z}{z-a} = \frac{1}{1-az^{-1}}$$

$$G(e^{j\omega}) = \frac{1}{1-ae^{-j\omega}} = \frac{1}{1-a\cos\omega + ja\sin\omega}$$

$$\begin{aligned}\arg[G(e^{j\omega})] &= -\tan^{-1}\left(\frac{a\sin\omega}{1-a\cos\omega}\right)\\ &= \tan^{-1}\left(\frac{a\sin\omega}{a\cos\omega - 1}\right)\\ &= \arg[H(e^{j\omega})]\end{aligned}$$

5.61. (a) Because $h_1[n], h_2[n]$ are minimum phase sequences, all poles and zeros of their transforms must be inside the unit circle.

$$h_1[n] * h_2[n] \leftrightarrow H_1(z)H_2(z)$$

Since $H_1(z)$ and $H_2(z)$ have all their poles and zeros inside the unit circle, their product will also.

(b)

$$h_1[n] + h_2[n] \leftrightarrow H_1(z) + H_2(z)$$

$$x_1[n] = \left(\frac{1}{2}\right)^n u[n] \longleftrightarrow \frac{1}{1-\frac{1}{2}z^{-1}} = X_1(z)$$

$$x_2[n] = 2\left(\frac{1}{2}\right)^n u[n] \longleftrightarrow \frac{2}{1-\frac{1}{2}z^{-1}} = X_2(z)$$

Both of these are minimum phase, with a zero at $z = 0$ and a pole at $z = \frac{1}{2}$.

$$X_1(z) + X_2(z) = \frac{3}{1-\frac{1}{2}z^{-1}}$$

This is minimum phase, with the same pole and zero as $X_1(z)$ and $X_2(z)$.

$$x_1[n] = 6\left(\frac{1}{2}\right)^n u[n] \longleftrightarrow \frac{6}{1-\frac{1}{2}z^{-1}} = X_1(z)$$

$$x_2[n] = -6\left(\frac{1}{3}\right)^n u[n] \longleftrightarrow \frac{-6}{1-\frac{1}{3}z^{-1}} = X_2(z)$$

$X_1(z)$ has a pole at $z = \frac{1}{2}$ and a zero at $z = 0$. $X_2(z)$ has a pole at $z = \frac{1}{3}$ and a zero at $z = 0$.

$$X_1(z) + X_2(z) = \frac{z^{-1}}{(1-\frac{1}{2}z^{-1})(1-\frac{1}{3}z^{-1})}$$

This has zeros at $z = 0, \infty$ and poles at $z = \frac{1}{2}, \frac{1}{3}$. Therefore, it is not minimum phase.

5.62. (a)

$$r[n] = \frac{4}{3}\left(\frac{1}{2}\right)^n u[n] + \frac{4}{3}(2)^n u[-n-1]$$

$$\begin{aligned} R(z) &= \frac{\frac{4}{3}}{1-\frac{1}{2}z^{-1}} - \frac{\frac{4}{3}}{1-2z^{-1}} \\ &= \frac{-2z^{-1}}{(1-\frac{1}{2}z^{-1})(1-2z^{-1})} \\ &= \frac{1}{(1-\frac{1}{2}z^{-1})(1-\frac{1}{2}z)}, \quad \text{ROC: } \tfrac{1}{2} < |z| < 2 \end{aligned}$$

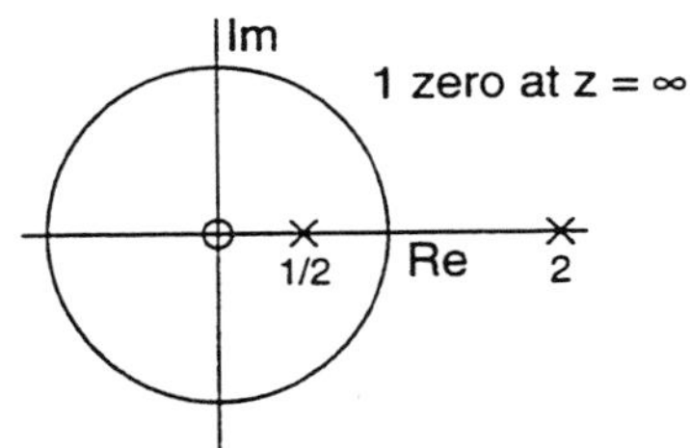

(b)

$$r[n] = h[n] * h[-n] \Leftrightarrow R(z) = H(z)H(z^{-1})$$

$$R(z) = \frac{1}{(1-\frac{1}{2}z^{-1})(1-\frac{1}{2}z)}$$

We have two choices from $H(z)$. Since $h[n]$ is minimum phase we need the one which has the pole at $z = \frac{1}{2}$, which is inside the unit circle.

$$H(z) = \frac{\pm 1}{(1-\frac{1}{2}z^{-1})}, \quad \text{ROC: } |z| > \tfrac{1}{2}$$

$$h[n] = \pm\left(\frac{1}{2}\right)^n u[n]$$

5.63. (a) Maximum phase systems are of the form

$$H(z) = \frac{\prod_{k=1}^{M}(z - c_k)}{\prod_{k=1}^{M}(z - d_k)}, \qquad |c_k|, |d_k| > 1$$

Since the poles are outside the unit circle, the only stable system will have a ROC of $|z| < \min|d_k|$. This implies the poles will all contribute to the $h[n]$ with terms of the form $-(d_k)^n u[-n-1]$, which are anticausal. The zeros are all positive powers of z, which means they are shifting to left, and $h[n]$ is still anticausal.

(b)

$$H_{min}(z) = h_{min}[0]\prod_{k=1}^{M}(1 - c_k z^{-1})$$

$$H_{max}(z) = h_{min}[0]\prod_{k=1}^{M}(1 - c_k z^{-1})\prod_{k=1}^{M}\left(\frac{z^{-1} - c_k^*}{1 - c_k z^{-1}}\right)$$

$$H_{ap}(z) = \prod_{k=1}^{M}\left(\frac{z^{-1} - c_k^*}{1 - c_k z^{-1}}\right)$$

(c)

$$\begin{aligned} H_{max}(z) &= h_{min}[0]\prod_{k=1}^{M}(1 - c_k z^{-1})\prod_{k=1}^{M}\left(\frac{z^{-1} - c_k^*}{1 - c_k z^{-1}}\right) \\ &= h_{min}[0]\prod_{k=1}^{M}(z^{-1} - c_k^*) \\ &= z^{-M} h_{min}[0]\prod_{k=1}^{M}(1 - c_k^* z) \\ &= z^{-M} H_{min}(z^{-1}) \end{aligned}$$

(d)

$$H_{max}(z) = z^{-M} H_{min}(z^{-1})$$

$$h_{max}[n] = \delta[n - M] * h_{min}[-n] = h_{min}[-n + M]$$

5.64. (a) We desire $|H(z)H_c(z)| = 1$, where $H_c(z)$ is stable and causal and $H(z)$ is not minimum phase. So,

$$|H_{ap}(z)H_{min}(z)H_c(z)| = 1$$

Since $|H_{ap}(z)| = 1$, we want

$$|H_{min}(z)H_c(z)| = 1$$

This means we have

$$H_c(z) = \frac{1}{H_{min}(z)}$$

which will be stable and causal since all the zeros of $H_{min}(z)$, which become the poles of $H_c(z)$, are inside the unit circle.

(b) Since

$$H_c(z) = \frac{1}{H_{min}(z)}$$

We have

$$G(z) = H_{ap}(z)$$

(c)

$$H(z) = (1 - 0.8e^{j0.3\pi}z^{-1})(1 - 0.8e^{-j0.3\pi}z^{-1})(1 - 1.2e^{j0.7\pi}z^{-1})(1 - 1.2e^{-j0.7\pi}z^{-1})$$

$$H_{min}(z) = (1.44)(1 - 0.8e^{j0.3\pi}z^{-1})(1 - 0.8e^{-j0.3\pi}z^{-1})(1 - (5/6)e^{j0.7\pi}z^{-1})(1 - (5/6)e^{-j0.7\pi}z^{-1})$$

$$H_c(z) = \frac{1}{(1.44)(1 - 0.8e^{j0.3\pi}z^{-1})(1 - 0.8e^{-j0.3\pi}z^{-1})(1 - (5/6)e^{j0.7\pi}z^{-1})(1 - (5/6)e^{-j0.7\pi}z^{-1})}$$

$$G(z) = H_{ap}(z) = \frac{(z^{-1} - (5/6)e^{-j0.7\pi})(z^{-1} - (5/6)e^{j0.7\pi})}{(1 - (5/6)e^{j0.7\pi}z^{-1})(1 - (5/6)e^{-j0.7\pi}z^{-1})}$$

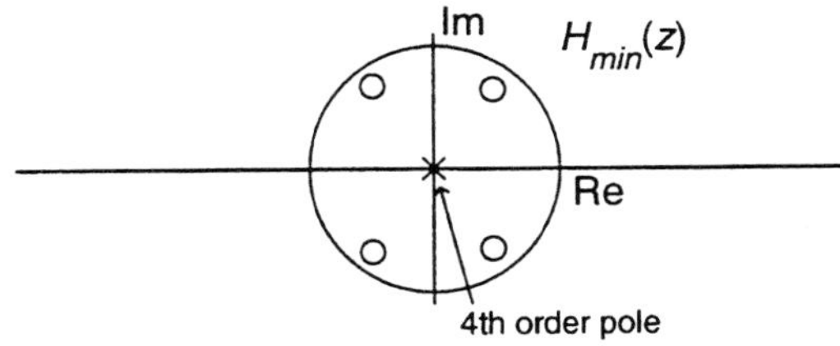

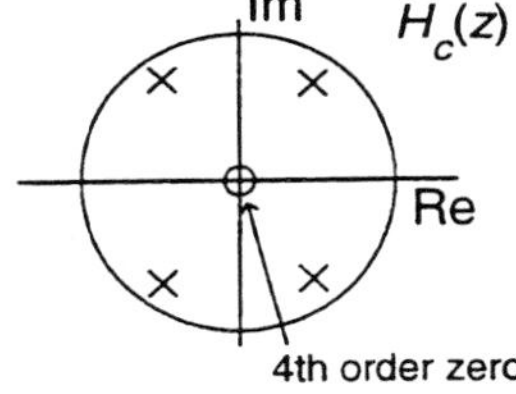

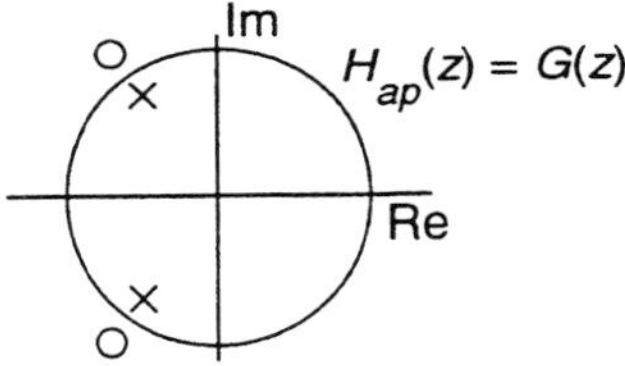

5.65.

$$H(z) = H_{min}(z)\frac{z^{-1} - a}{1 - az^{-1}}, \quad |a| < 1$$

Thus,

$$\lim_{z\to\infty} H_{min}(z) = \lim_{z\to\infty} \frac{1 - az^{-1}}{z^{-1} - a}H(z)$$

$$h_{min}[0] = -\frac{1}{a}h[0]$$

Therefore, $|h_{min}[0]| > |h[0]|$ since $|a| < 1$. This process can be repeated if more than one allpass system is cascaded. In each case, the factor for each will be larger than unity in the limit.

5.66. (a) We use the allpass principle and place a pole at $z = z_k$ and a zero at $z = \frac{1}{z_k^*}$.

$$\begin{aligned} H(z) &= H_{min}(z)\frac{z^{-1} - z_k^*}{1 - z_k z^{-1}} \\ &= Q(z)(z^{-1} - z_k^*) \end{aligned}$$

(b)

$$H(z) = Q(z)z^{-1} - z_k^* Q(z)$$

$$h[n] = q[n-1] - z_k^* q[n]$$

$$H_{min}(z) = Q(z) - z_k Q(z) z^{-1}$$

$$h_{min}[n] = q[n] - z_k q[n-1]$$

(c)

$$\begin{aligned}
\varepsilon &= \sum_{m=0}^{n} |h_{min}[m]|^2 - \sum_{m=0}^{n} |h[m]|^2 \\
&= \sum_{m=0}^{n} (|q[m]|^2 - z_k q[m-1]q^*[m] - z_k^* q^*[m-1]q[m] + |z_k|^2 |q[m-1]|^2) \\
&\quad - \sum_{m=0}^{n} (|q[m-1]|^2 - z_k^* q^*[m-1]q[m] - z_k q[m-1]q^*[m] + |z_k|^2 |q[m]|^2) \\
&= (1 - |z_k|^2) \sum_{m=0}^{n} (|q[m]|^2 - |q[m-1]|^2) \\
&= (1 - |z_k|^2)|q[n]|^2
\end{aligned}$$

(d)

$$\varepsilon = (1 - |z_k|^2)|q[n]|^2 \geq 0 \quad \forall n \text{ since } |z_k| < 1$$

Then

$$\sum_{m=0}^{n} |h_{min}[m]|^2 - \sum_{m=0}^{n} |h[m]|^2 \geq 0$$

$$\sum_{m=0}^{n} |h[m]|^2 \leq \sum_{m=0}^{n} |h_{min}[m]|^2 \quad \forall n$$

5.67. (a) $x[n]$ is real, minimum phase and $x[n] = 0$ for $n < 0$. Consider the system:

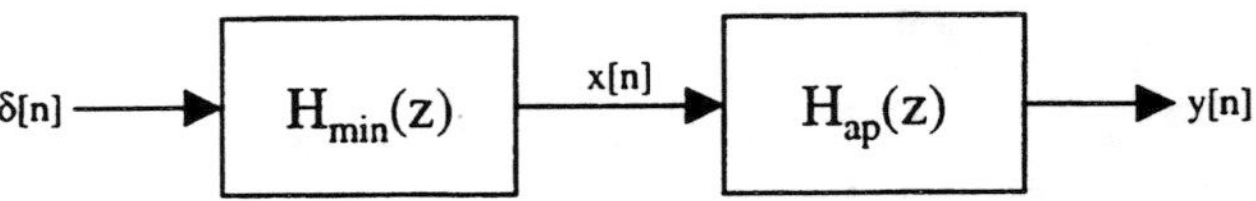

$x[n]$ is the impulse response of a minimum phase system. $y[n]$ is the impulse response of a system which has the same frequency response magnitude as that of $x[n]$ but it is not minimum phase. Therefore, the equation applies.

$$\sum_{k=0}^{n} |x[k]|^2 \geq \sum_{k=0}^{n} |y[k]|^2$$

Since $h_{ap}[n]$ is causal and $x[n]$ is causal, $y[n]$ is also causal, and these sums are meaningful.

(b) As discussed in the book, the group delay for a rational allpass system is always positive. That is,

$$\text{grd}[H_{ap}(e^{j\omega})] \geq 0$$

Therefore, filtering a signal $x[n]$ by such a system will delay the energy in the output $y[n]$. If we require that $x[n]$ is causal, then $y[n]$ will be causal as well, and the equation

$$\sum_{k=0}^{n} |x[k]|^2 \geq \sum_{k=0}^{n} |y[k]|^2$$

applies to the system.

5.68. (a)

$$\begin{aligned} g[n] &= x[n] * h[n] \\ r[n] &= g[-n] * h[n] \end{aligned}$$

$$s[n] = r[-n] = g[n] * h[-n] = x[n] * (h[n] * h[-n])$$

$$\begin{aligned} h_1[n] &= h[n] * h[-n] \\ H_1(e^{j\omega}) &= H(e^{j\omega})H^*(e^{j\omega}) = |H(e^{j\omega})|^2 \end{aligned}$$

Since $H_1(e^{j\omega})$ is real, it is zero phase.

(b)

$$\begin{aligned} g[n] &= x[n] * h[n] \\ r[n] &= x[-n] * h[n] \end{aligned}$$

$$y[n] = g[n] + r[-n] = x[n] * h[n] + x[n] * h[-n] = x[n] * (h[n] + h[-n])$$

$$\begin{aligned} h_2[n] &= h[n] + h[-n] \\ H_2(e^{j\omega}) &= H(e^{j\omega}) + H^*(e^{j\omega}) \\ &= 2\mathcal{R}e\{H(e^{j\omega})\} \end{aligned}$$

$H_2(e^{j\omega})$ is real, so it is also zero phase.

$$|H_2(e^{j\omega})| = 2|H(e^{j\omega})| \cos\left(\angle H(e^{j\omega})\right)$$

(c)

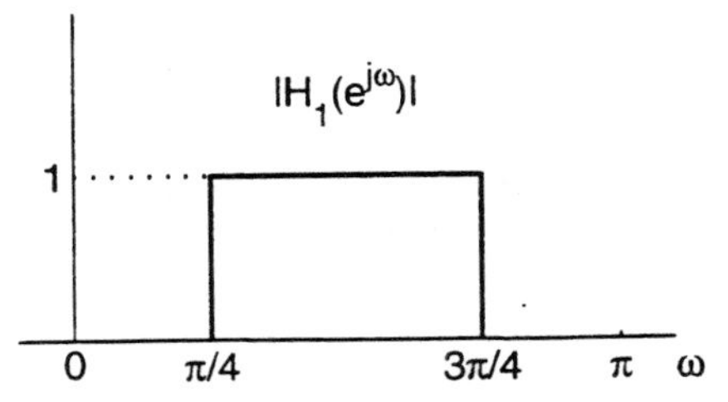

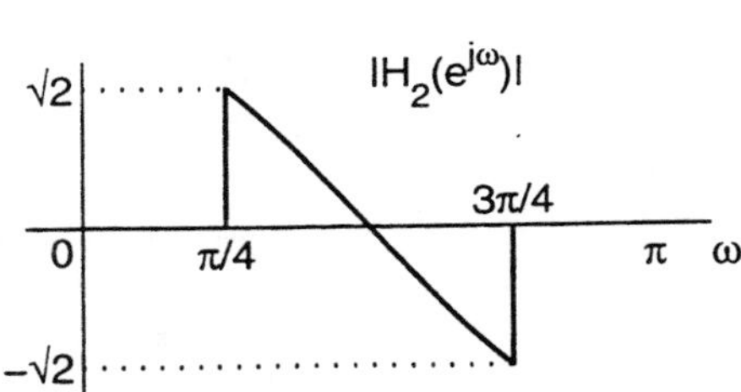

In general, method A is preferable since method B causes a magnitude distortion which is a function of the (possibly non-linear) phase of $h[n]$.

5.69. *False.* Consider

$$H(z) = \frac{1}{(1-\frac{1}{2}z^{-1})(1-2z^{-1})} = \frac{1}{1-\frac{5}{2}z^{-1}+z^{-2}}$$

This system function has poles at $z = 1/2$ and $z = 2$. However, as the following shows it is a generalized linear phase filter.

$$\begin{aligned} H(e^{j\omega}) &= \frac{1}{1-\frac{5}{2}e^{-j\omega}+e^{-j2\omega}} \\ &= \frac{e^{j\omega}}{e^{j\omega}-\frac{5}{2}+e^{-j\omega}} \\ &= \left(\frac{1}{2\cos w - \frac{5}{2}}\right)e^{j\omega} \end{aligned}$$

5.70. (a) Since $h[n]$ is a real causal linear phase filter the zeros must occur in sets of 4. Thus, if z_1 is a zero of $H(z)$ then $z_1^*, 1/z_1$ and $1/z_1^*$ must also be zeros. We can use this to find 4 zeros of $H(z)$ from the given information.

$$\begin{array}{rll} z_1, & \text{magnitude} = 0.5, & \text{angle} = 153 \text{ degrees} \\ z_1^*, & \text{magnitude} = 0.5, & \text{angle} = 207 \text{ degrees} \\ 1/z_1, & \text{magnitude} = 2, & \text{angle} = 207 \text{ degrees} \\ 1/z_1^*, & \text{magnitude} = 2, & \text{angle} = 153 \text{ degrees} \end{array}$$

(b) There are 24 zeros so the length of $h[n]$ is 25. Since it is a linear phase filter it has a delay of $(L-1)/2 = (25-1)/2 = 12$ samples. That corresponds to a time delay of

$$\left(0.5\ \frac{\text{ms}}{\text{sample}}\right)(12 \text{ samples}) = 6 \text{ ms}$$

(c) The zero locations used to create the following plot were estimated from the figure using a ruler and a protractor.

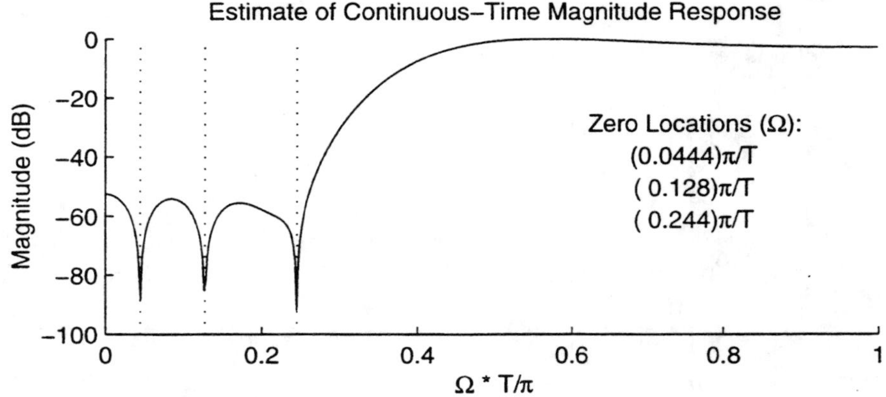

5.71. (a) There are many possible solutions to this problem. The idea behind any solution is to have $h[n]$ be an upsampled (by a factor of 2) version of $g[n]$. That is,

$$h[n] = \begin{cases} g[n/2], & n = 0, \pm 2, \pm 4, ... \\ 0, & \textit{otherwise} \end{cases}$$

Thus, $h[n]$ will process only the even-indexed samples. One such system would be described by

$$\begin{aligned} h[n] &= 1 + \delta[n-2] \\ g[n] &= 1 + \delta[n-1] \\ H(z) &= 1 + z^{-2} \\ G(z) &= 1 + z^{-1} \end{aligned}$$

(b) As in part a, there are many possible solutions to this problem. The idea behind any solution is to choose an $h[n]$ that cannot be an upsampled (by a factor of 2) version of $g[n]$. Clearly, choosing $h[n]$ to filter odd-indexed samples satisfies this criterion. One such $h[n]$ would be

$$\begin{aligned} h[n] &= 1 + \delta[n-1] + \delta[n-2] \\ H(z) &= 1 + z^{-1} + z^{-2} \end{aligned}$$

(c) In general, the odd-indexed samples of $h[n]$ must be zero, in order for a $g[n]$ to be found for which $r[n] = y[n]$. Thus, there must not be any odd powers of z^{-1} in $H(z)$.

(d) For the conditions determined in part c, $g[n]$ is a downsampled (by a factor of 2) version of $h[n]$. That is,

$$g[n] = h[2n]$$

5.72. (a) *No.* You cannot uniquely recover $h[n]$ from $c_{hh}[l]$.

$$\begin{aligned} c_{hh}[l] &= h[l] * h[-l] \\ C_{hh}(e^{j\omega}) &= H(e^{j\omega})H(e^{-j\omega}) = \left|H(e^{j\omega})\right|^2 \\ C_{hh}(z) &= H(z)H^*(1/z^*) \end{aligned}$$

Causality and stability put restrictions on the poles of $H(z)$ (they must be inside the unit circle) but not its zeros. We know the zeros of $C_{hh}(z)$ in general occur in sets of 4. Here is why. A complex conjugate pair of zeros occur in $H(z)$ due to the fact that $h[n]$ is real. These 2 zeros and their conjugate reciprocals occur in $C_{hh}(z)$ due to the formula above for a total of 4. Thus, $H(z)$ is not uniquely determined since we do not know which 2 out of these 4 zeros to factor into $H(z)$. This is illustrated with a simple example below.

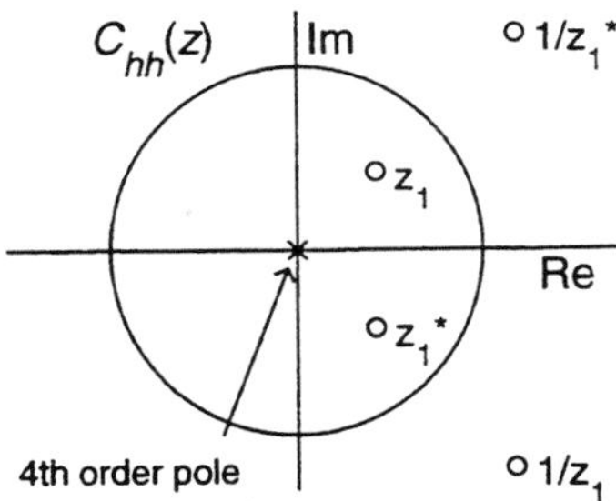

Let the above be the pole-zero diagram for $C_{hh}(z)$ and

$$\begin{aligned} H_1(z) &= \left(1 - z_1 z^{-1}\right)\left(1 - z_1^* z^{-1}\right) \\ H_2(z) &= \left(1 - \frac{1}{z_1} z^{-1}\right)\left(1 - \frac{1}{z_1^*} z^{-1}\right) \end{aligned}$$

Since

$$C_{hh}(z) = H_1(z)H_1^*(1/z^*) = H_2(z)H_2^*(1/z^*)$$

we cannot determine whether $h_1[n]$ or $h_2[n]$ generated $c_{hh}[l]$.

(b) *Yes.* The poles of $C_{hh}(z)$ must occur in sets of 4 for the same reasons outlined above for the zeros. However, since the poles of $h[n]$ must be inside the unit circle to be causal and stable we do not have any ambiguity in determining which poles to group into $h[n]$. We always choose the complex conjugate poles inside the unit circle. Here is an example

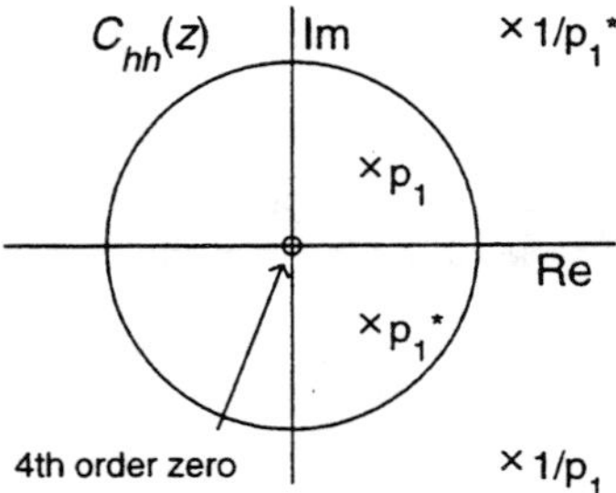

Let the above be the zero/pole diagram for $C_{hh}(z)$. Then, if $h[n]$ is to be real, causal, and stable $H(z)$ must equal

$$H(z) = \frac{1}{(1 - p_1 z^{-1})(1 - p_1^* z^{-1})}$$

5.73. As shown in the book, the most general form of the system function of an allpass system with a real-valued impulse response is

$$H(z) = \prod_{k=1}^{M_r} \frac{z^{-1} - d_k}{1 - d_k z^{-1}} \prod_{k=1}^{M_c} \frac{(z^{-1} - e_k^*)(z^{-1} - e_k)}{(1 - e_k z^{-1})(1 - e_k^* z^{-1})}, \quad |z| \in R_x$$

where R_x is the ROC which includes the unit circle. Correspondingly, the associated inverse system is

$$\begin{aligned} H_i(z) &= \frac{1}{H(z)} \\ &= \prod_{k=1}^{M_r} \frac{1 - d_k z^{-1}}{z^{-1} - d_k} \prod_{k=1}^{M_c} \frac{(1 - e_k z^{-1})(1 - e_k^* z^{-1})}{(z^{-1} - e_k^*)(z^{-1} - e_k)} \\ &= \prod_{k=1}^{M_r} \frac{z^{-1}(z - d_k)}{z^{-1} - d_k} \prod_{k=1}^{M_c} \frac{z^{-2}(z - e_k)(z - e_k^*)}{(z^{-1} - e_k^*)(z^{-1} - e_k)} \\ &= \prod_{k=1}^{M_r} \frac{z - d_k}{1 - d_k z} \prod_{k=1}^{M_c} \frac{(z - e_k)(z - e_k^*)}{(1 - e_k^* z)(1 - e_k z)} \\ &= H(1/z), \quad |z| \in \frac{1}{R_x} \end{aligned}$$

which in the time domain is

$$h_i[n] = h[-n]$$

5.74. We can model $g[n]$ as

$$g[n] = x[n] + \alpha\delta[n - n_0]$$

Now send the corrupted signal $g[n]$ through a highpass filter $h_{hpf}[n]$ with a cutoff of $w_c = \pi/2$.

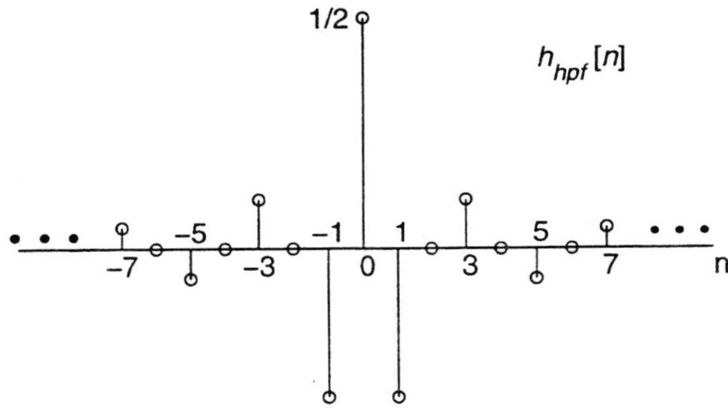

$$h_{hpf}[n] = (-1)^n \frac{\sin \frac{\pi}{2} n}{\pi n}$$

The highpass filter completely filters out the lowpass signal $x[n]$. The output $y[n]$ is

$$\begin{aligned} y[n] &= (x[n] + \alpha\delta[n - n_0]) * h_{hpf}[n] \\ &= \alpha h_{hpf}[n - n_0] \\ &= \alpha(-1)^{(n-n_0)} \frac{\sin \frac{\pi}{2}(n - n_0)}{\pi(n - n_0)} \end{aligned}$$

$y[n]$ looks similar to the picture of $h_{hpf}[n]$ above except that it is scaled by α and shifted to n_0. Thus,

$$\alpha = 2y[n_0]$$

$$x[n] = g[n] - 2y[n_0]\delta[n - n_0]$$

(a) When n_0 is odd, $y[n] = 0$ at all odd values of n except $n = n_0$. This leads to a procedure to find $x[n]$ from $g[n]$:
- Filter $g[n]$ with the highpass filter described above.
- Find the only nonzero value at an odd index in the output $y[n]$. This value is $y[n_0]$.
- $x[n] = g[n] - 2y[n_0]\delta[n - n_0]$

(b) The only time three consecutive nonzero samples occur in $y[n]$ is at $n = n_0$. The procedure to find $x[n]$ is
- Filter $g[n]$ with the highpass filter described above.
- Look for three consecutive nonzero output samples. The middle value is $y[n_0]$.
- $x[n] = g[n] - 2y[n_0]\delta[n - n_0]$

5.75. Looking at the z-transform of the FIR filter,

$$\begin{aligned} H(z) &= \sum_{n=0}^{\infty} h[n]z^{-n} \\ &= \sum_{n=0}^{N-1} h[N - 1 - n]z^{-n} \end{aligned}$$

Substituting $m = N - 1 - n$ into the summation gives

$$H(z) = \sum_{m=N-1}^{0} h[m]z^{m-N+1}$$

$$= \sum_{m=0}^{N-1} h[m] z^m z^{-N+1}$$

$$= z^{-N+1} \sum_{m=0}^{N-1} h[m] z^m$$

$$= z^{-N+1} H(z^{-1})$$

Thus, for such a filter,

$$H(1/z) = z^{N-1} H(z)$$

If z_0 is a zero of $H(z)$, then $H(z_0) = 0$, and

$$H(1/z_0) = z_0^{N-1} H(z_0) = 0$$

Consequently, even-symmetric linear phase FIR filters have zeros that are reciprocal images.

Solutions – Chapter 6

Structures for Discrete-Time Systems

6.1. We proceed by obtaining the transfer functions for each of the networks. For network 1,

$$Y(z) = 2r\cos\theta z^{-1}Y(z) - r^2z^{-2}Y(z) + X(z)$$

or

$$H_1(z) = \frac{Y(z)}{X(z)} = \frac{1}{1 - 2r\cos\theta z^{-1} + r^2z^{-2}}$$

For network 2, define $W(z)$ as in the figure below:

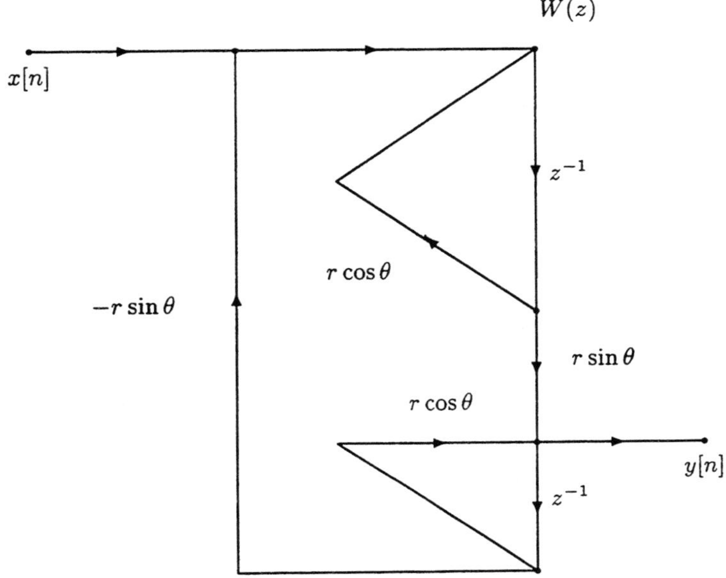

then

$$W(z) = X(z) - r\sin\theta z^{-1}Y(z) + r\cos\theta z^{-1}W(z)$$

and

$$Y(z) = r\sin\theta z^{-1}W(z) + r\cos\theta z^{-1}Y(z)$$

Eliminate $W(z)$ to get

$$H_2(z) = \frac{Y(z)}{X(z)} = \frac{r\sin\theta z^{-1}}{1 - 2r\cos\theta z^{-1} + r^2z^{-2}}$$

Hence the two networks have the same poles.

6.2. The only input to the $y[n]$ node is a unity branch connection from the $x[n]$ node. The rest of the network does not affect the input-output relationship. The difference equation is $y[n] = x[n]$.

6.3.

$$H(z) = \frac{2 + \frac{1}{4}z^{-1}}{1 + \frac{1}{4}z^{-1} - \frac{3}{8}z^{-2}}$$

System (d) is recognizable as a transposed direct form II implementation of $H(z)$.

6.4. (a) From the flow graph, we have:

$$Y(z) = 2X(z) + (\frac{1}{4}X(z) - \frac{1}{4}Y(z) + \frac{3}{8}Y(z)z^{-1})z^{-1}.$$

That is:

$$Y(z)(1+\frac{1}{4}z^{-1}-\frac{3}{8}z^{-2}) = X(z)(2+\frac{1}{4}z^{-1}).$$

The system function is thus given by:

$$H(z) = \frac{Y(z)}{X(z)} = \frac{2+\frac{1}{4}z^{-1}}{1+\frac{1}{4}z^{-1}-\frac{3}{8}z^{-2}}.$$

(b) To get the difference equation, we just inverse Z−transform the equation in a. We get:

$$y[n] + \frac{1}{4}y[n-1] - \frac{3}{8}y[n-2] = 2x[n] + \frac{1}{4}x[n-1].$$

6.5. The flow graph for this system is drawn below.

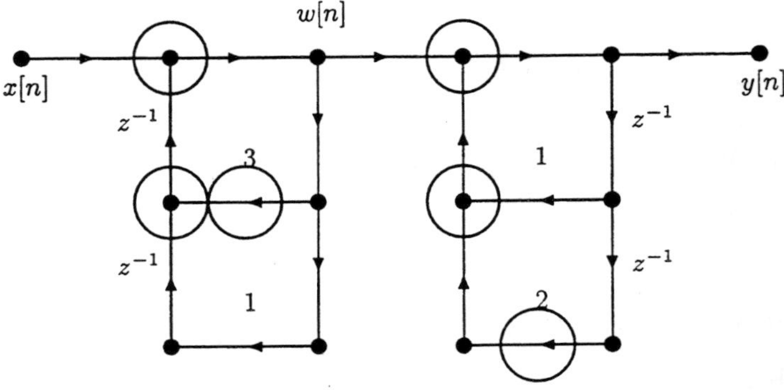

(a)

$$w[n] = x[n] + 3w[n-1] + w[n-2]$$

$$y[n] = w[n] + y[n-1] + 2y[n-2]$$

(b)

$$W(z) = X(z) + 3z^{-1}W(z) + z^{-2}W(z)$$

$$Y(z) = W(z) + z^{-1}Y(z) + 2z^{-2}Y(z)$$

So

$$\begin{aligned}\frac{Y(z)}{X(z)} &= H(z)\\ &= \frac{1}{(1-z^{-1}-2z^{-2})(1-3z^{-1}-z^{-2})}\\ &= \frac{1}{1-4z^{-1}+7z^{-3}+2z^{-4}}.\end{aligned}$$

(c) Adds and multiplies are circled above: 4 real adds and 2 real multiplies per output point.

(d) It is not possible to reduce the number of storage registers. Note that implementing $H(z)$ above in the canonical direct form II (minimum storage registers) also requires 4 registers.

6.6. The impulse responses of each system are shown below.

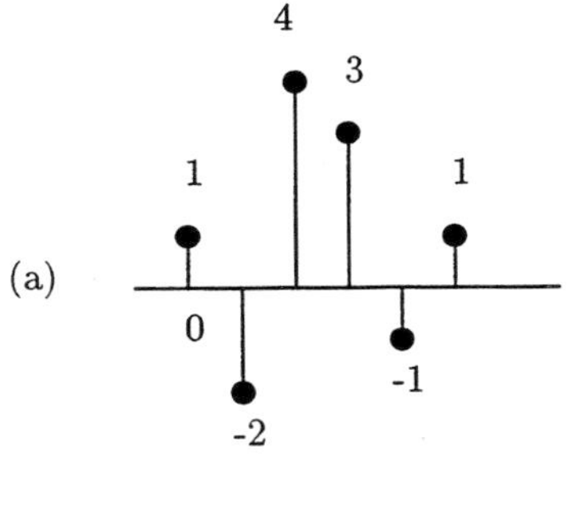

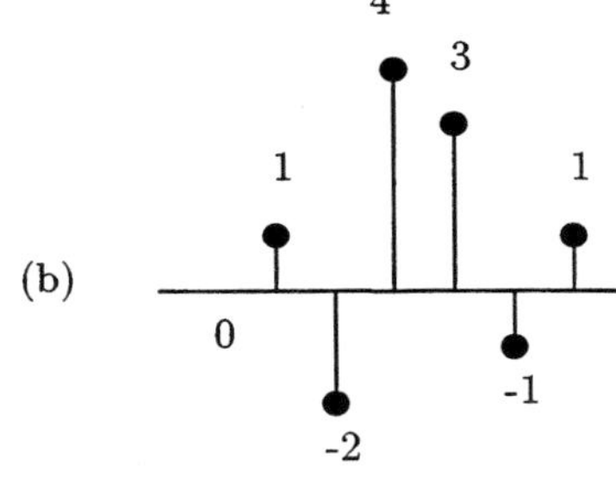

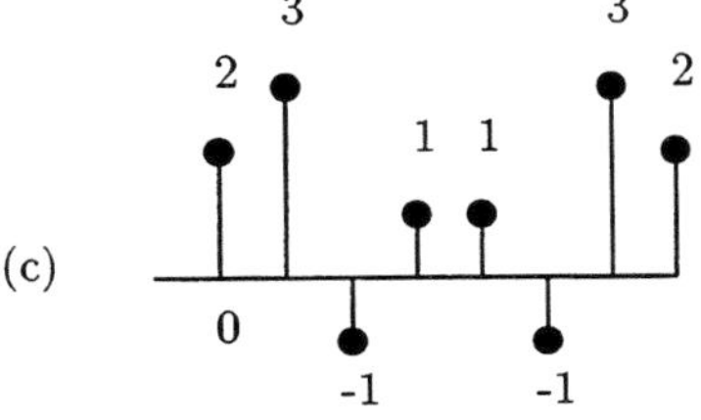

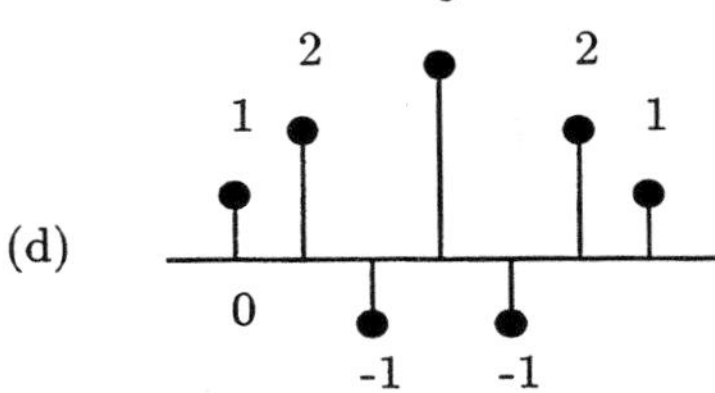

6.7. We have

$$H(z) = \frac{-\frac{1}{4} + z^{-2}}{1 - \frac{1}{4}z^{-2}}.$$

Therefore the direct form II is given by:

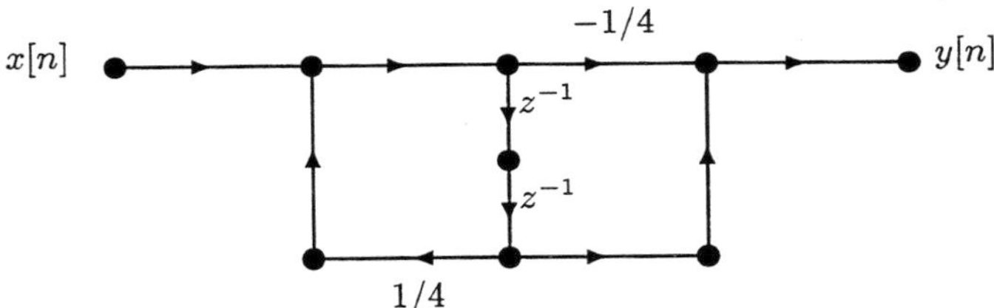

6.8. By looking at the graph, we get:

$$y[n] = 2y[n-2] + 3x[n-1] + x[n-2].$$

6.9. The signal flow graph for the system is:

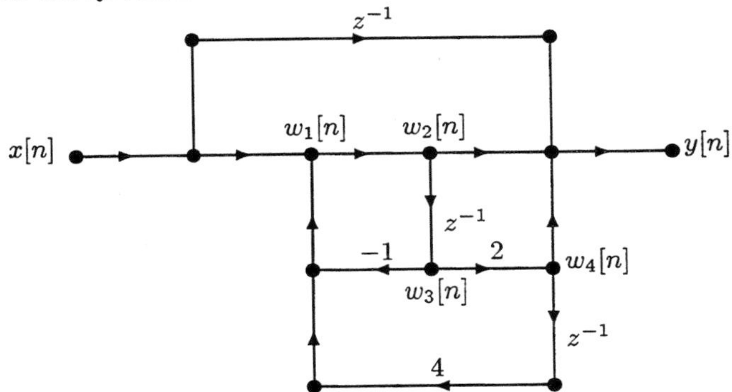

(a) First we need to determine the transfer function. We have

$$\begin{aligned} w_1[n] &= x[n] - w_3[n] + 4w_4[n-1] \\ w_2[n] &= w_1[n] \\ w_3[n] &= w_2[n-1] \\ w_4[n] &= 2w_3[n] \\ y[n] &= w_2[n] + x[n-1] + w_4[n]. \end{aligned}$$

Taking the $Z-$transform of the above equations, rearranging and substituting terms, we get:

$$H(z) = \frac{1 + 3z^{-1} + z^{-2} - 8z^{-3}}{1 + z^{-1} - 8z^{-2}}.$$

The difference equation is thus given by:

$$y[n] + y[n-1] - 8y[n-2] = x[n] + 3x[n-1] + x[n-2] - 8x[n-3].$$

The impulse response is the response to an impulse, therefore:

$$h[n] + h[n-1] - 8h[n-2] = \delta[n] + 3\delta[n-1] + \delta[n-2] - 8\delta[n-3].$$

From the above equation, we have:

$$\begin{aligned} &h[0] = 1 \\ &h[1] = 3 - h[0] = 2. \end{aligned}$$

(b) From part (a) we have:

$$y[n] + y[n-1] - 8y[n-2] = x[n] + 3x[n-1] + x[n-2] - 8x[n-3].$$

6.10. (a)

$$\begin{aligned} w[n] &= \frac{1}{2}y[n] + x[n] \\ v[n] &= \frac{1}{2}y[n] + 2x[n] + w[n-1] \\ y[n] &= v[n-1] + x[n]. \end{aligned}$$

(b) Using the $Z-$transform of the difference equations in part (a), we get the transfer function:

$$H(z) = \frac{Y(z)}{X(z)} = \frac{1 + 2z^{-1} + z^{-2}}{1 - \frac{1}{2}z^{-1} - \frac{1}{2}z^{-2}}.$$

We can rewrite it as :

$$H(z) = \frac{(1 + z^{-1})(1 + z^{-1})}{(1 + \frac{1}{2}z^{-1})(1 - z^{-1})}.$$

We thus get the following cascade form:

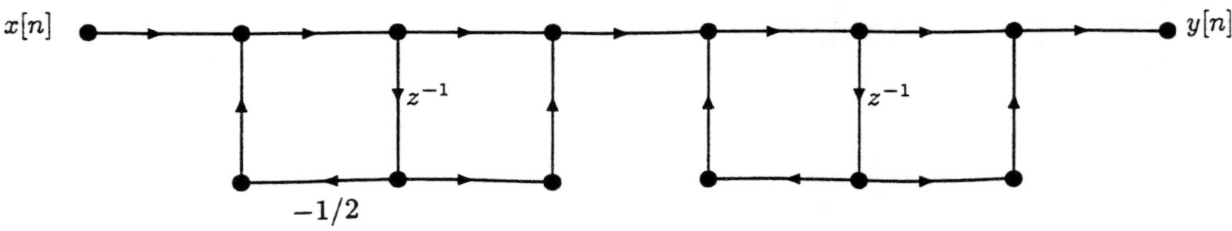

(c) The system function has poles at $z = -\frac{1}{2}$ and $z = 1$. Since the second pole is on the unit circle, the system is not stable.

6.11. (a) $H(z)$ can be rewritten as:

$$H(z) = \frac{z^{-1} - 6z^{-2} + 8z^{-3}}{1 - \frac{1}{2}z^{-1}}.$$

We thus get the following direct from II flow graph :

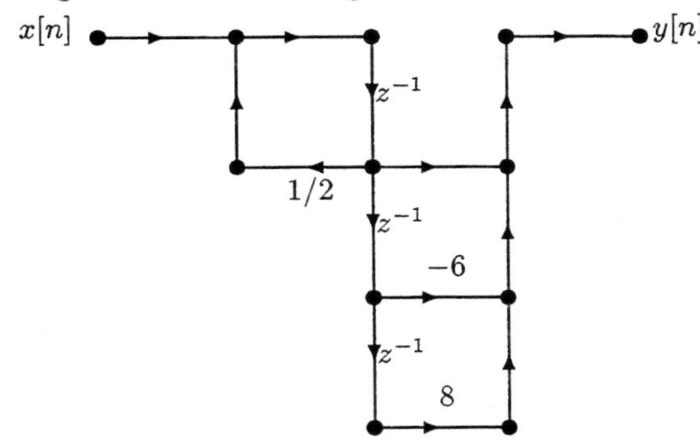

(b) To get the transposed form, we just reverse the arrows and exchange the input and the ouput. The graph can then be redrawn as:

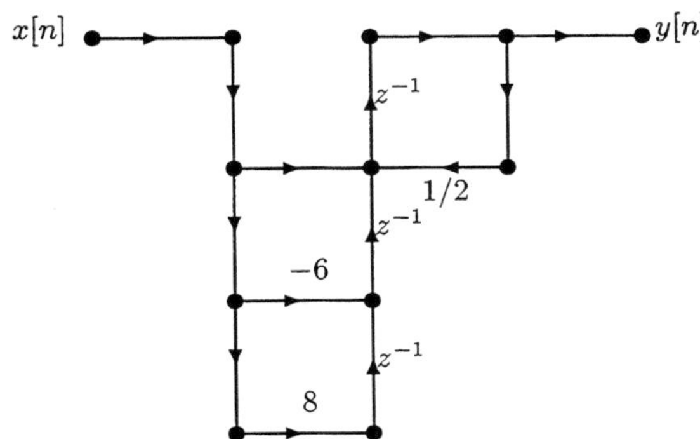

6.12. We define the intermediate variables $w_1[n]$, $w_2[n]$ and $w_3[n]$ as follows:

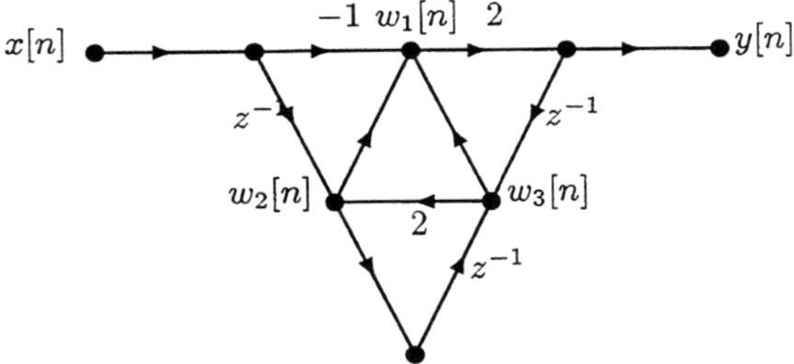

We thus have the following relationships:

$$\begin{aligned} w_1[n] &= -x[n] + w_2[n] + w_3[n] \\ w_2[n] &= x[n-1] + 2w_3[n] \\ w_3[n] &= w_2[n-1] + y[n-1] \\ y[n] &= 2w_1[n]. \end{aligned}$$

$Z-$transforming the above equations and rearranging and grouping terms, we get:

$$H(z) = \frac{Y(z)}{X(z)} = \frac{-2 + 6z^{-1} + 2z^{-2}}{1 - 8z^{-1}}.$$

Taking the inverse $Z-$transform, we get the following difference equation:

$$y[n] - 8y[n-1] = -2x[n] + 6x[n-1] + 2x[n-2].$$

6.13.

$$H(z) = \frac{1 - \frac{1}{2}z^{-2}}{1 - \frac{1}{4}z^{-1} - \frac{1}{8}z^{-2}}.$$

The direct form I implementation is:

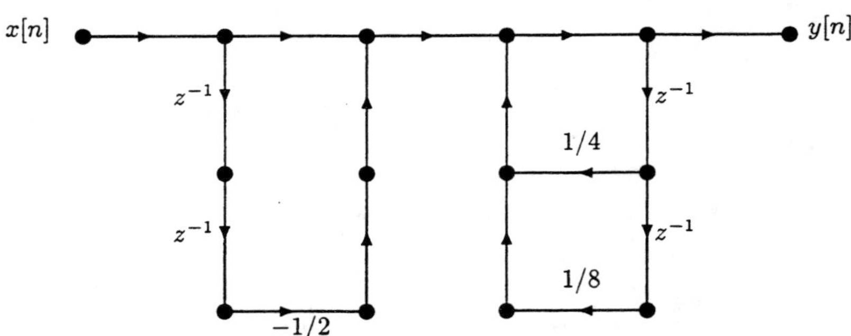

6.14.

$$H(z) = \frac{1 + \frac{5}{6}z^{-1} + \frac{1}{6}z^{-2}}{1 - \frac{1}{2}z^{-1} - \frac{1}{2}z^{-2}}.$$

The direct form II implementation is:

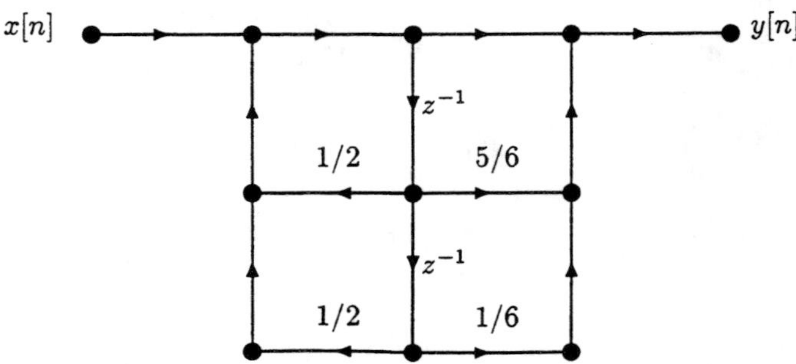

6.15.

$$H(z) = \frac{1 - \frac{7}{6}z^{-1} + \frac{1}{6}z^{-2}}{1 + z^{-1} + \frac{1}{2}z^{-2}}.$$

To get the transposed direct form II implementation, we first get the direct form II:

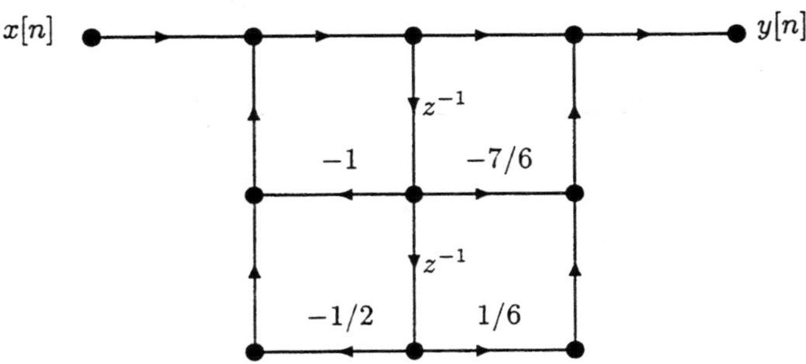

Now, we reverse the arrows and exchange the role of the input and the ouput to get the transposed direct form II:

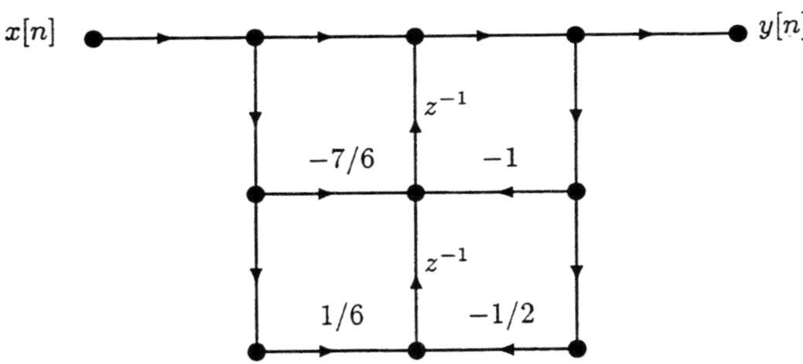

6.16. (a) We just reverse the arrows and reverse the role of the input and the output, we get:

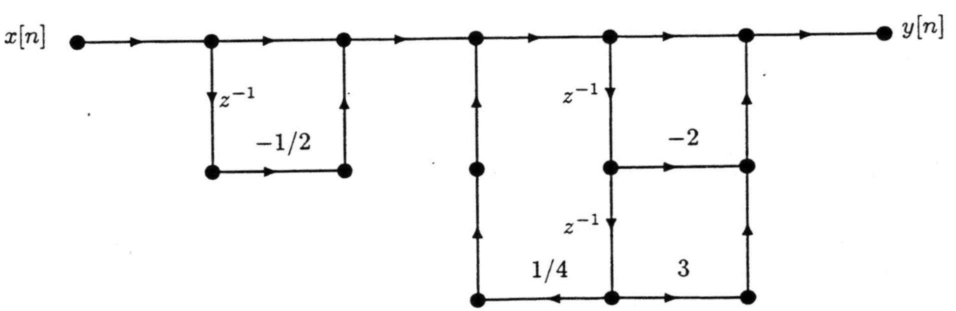

(b) The original system is the cascade of two transposed direct form II structures, therefore the system function is given by:

$$H(z) = \left(\frac{1 - 2z^{-1} + 3z^{-2}}{1 - \frac{1}{4}z^{-2}}\right)\left(1 - \frac{1}{2}z^{-1}\right).$$

The transposed graph, on the other hand, is the cascade of two direct form II structures, therefore the system function is given by:

$$H(z) = \left(1 - \frac{1}{2}z^{-1}\right)\left(\frac{1 - 2z^{-1} + 3z^{-2}}{1 - \frac{1}{4}z^{-2}}\right).$$

This confirms that both graphs have the same system function $H(z)$.

6.17.

$$H(z) = 1 - \frac{1}{3}z^{-1} + \frac{1}{6}z^{-2} + z^{-3}.$$

(a) Direct form implementation of this system:

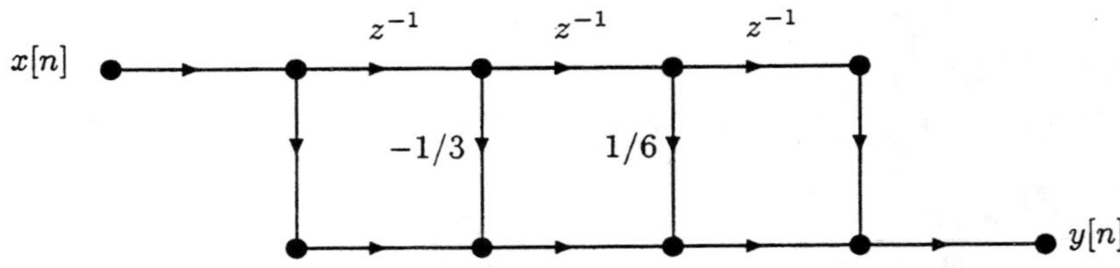

(b) Transposed direct form implementation of the system:

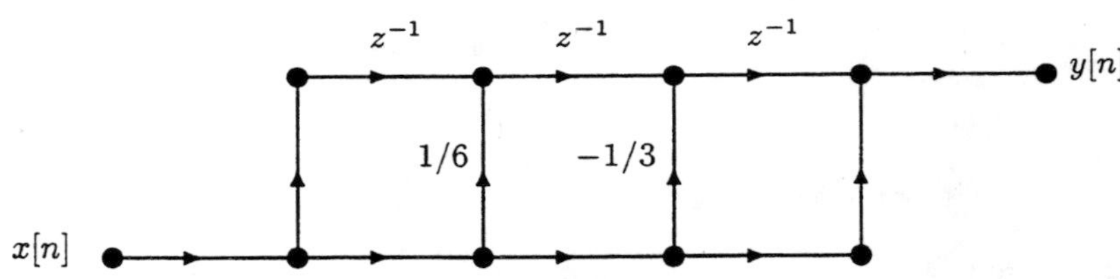

6.18. The flow graph is just a cascade of two transposed direct form II structures, the system function is thus given by:

$$H(z) = \left(\frac{1 + \frac{4}{3}z^{-1} - \frac{4}{3}z^{-2}}{1 + \frac{1}{4}z^{-1} - \frac{3}{8}z^{-2}}\right)\left(\frac{1}{1 - az^{-1}}\right).$$

Which can be rewritten as:

$$H(z) = \frac{(1+2z^{-1})(1-\frac{2}{3}z^{-1})}{(1+\frac{1}{4}z^{-1}-\frac{3}{8}z^{-2})(1-az^{-1})}.$$

In order to implement this system function with a second-order direct form II signal flow graph, a pole-zero cancellation has to occur, this happens if $a = \frac{2}{3}$, $a = -2$ or $a = 0$. If $a = \frac{2}{3}$, the overall system function is:

$$H(z) = \frac{1+2z^{-1}}{1+\frac{1}{4}z^{-1}-\frac{3}{8}z^{-2}}.$$

If $a = -2$, the overall system function is:

$$H(z) = \frac{1-\frac{2}{3}z^{-1}}{1+\frac{1}{4}z^{-1}-\frac{3}{8}z^{-2}}.$$

And finally if $a = 0$, the overall system function is:

$$H(z) = \frac{(1+2z^{-1})(1-\frac{2}{3}z^{-1})}{1+\frac{1}{4}z^{-1}-\frac{3}{8}z^{-2}}.$$

6.19. Using partial fraction expansion, the system function can be rewritten as:

$$H(z) = \frac{-8}{1-\frac{1}{3}z^{-1}} + \frac{1}{1+\frac{2}{3}z^{-1}} + 9.$$

Now we can draw the flow graph that implements this system as a parallel combination of first-order transposed direct form II sections:

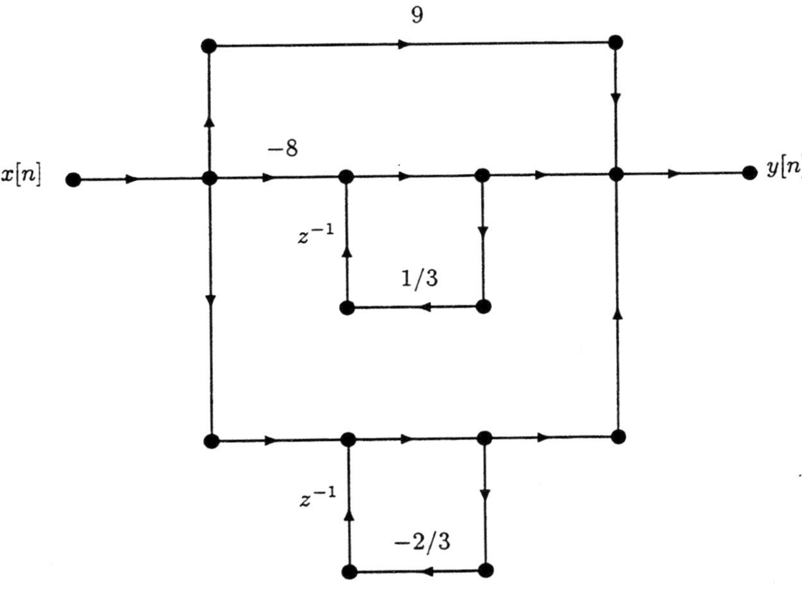

6.20. The transfer function can be rewritten as:

$$H(z) = \frac{(1+2z^{-1}+\frac{5}{4}z^{-2})}{(1+\frac{1}{4}z^{-2})(1-\frac{5}{2}z^{-1}+z^{-2})}$$

which can be implemented as the following cascade of second-order transposed direct form II sections:

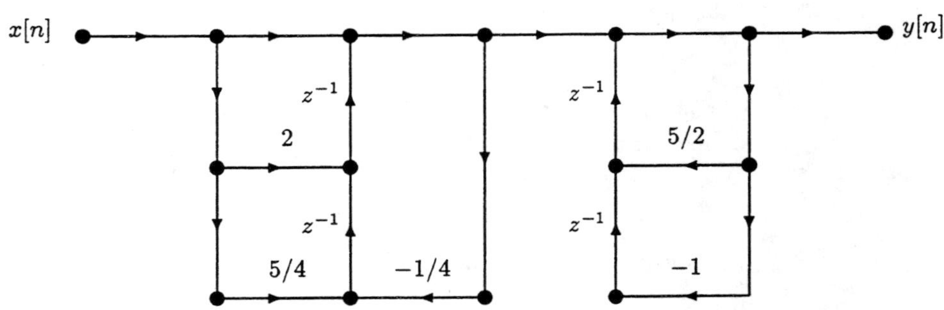

6.21.

$$h[n] = e^{j\omega_0 n}u[n] \longleftrightarrow H(z) = \frac{1}{1 - e^{j\omega_0}z^{-1}} = \frac{Y(z)}{X(z)}.$$

So $y[n] = e^{j\omega_0}y[n-1] + x[n]$. Let $y[n] = y_r[n] + jy_i[n]$. Then $y_r[n] + jy_i[n] = (\cos\omega_0 + j\sin\omega_0)(y_r[n-1] + jy_i[n-1]) + x[n]$. Separate the real and imaginary parts:

$$\begin{aligned} y_r[n] &= x[n] + \cos\omega_0 y_r[n-1] - \sin\omega_0 y_i[n-1] \\ y_i[n] &= \sin\omega_0 y_r[n-1] + \cos\omega_0 y_i[n-1]. \end{aligned}$$

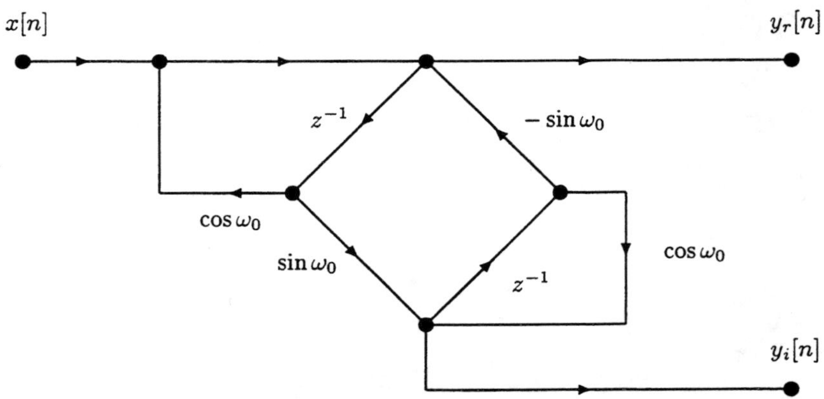

6.22.

$$H(z) = \frac{(1+z^{-1})^2}{(1-\frac{1}{4}z^{-1})(1-\frac{1}{2}z^{-1})}.$$

$$H(z) = \left(\frac{1+z^{-1}}{1-\frac{1}{4}z^{-1}}\right)\left(\frac{1+z^{-1}}{1-\frac{1}{2}z^{-1}}\right).$$

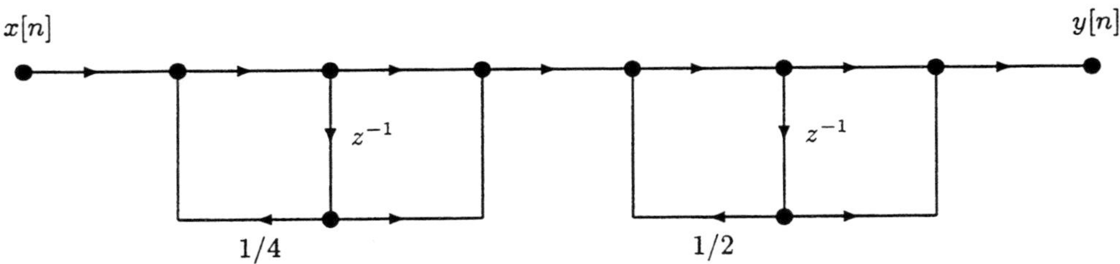

$$H(z) = \left(\frac{1+z^{-1}}{1-\frac{1}{2}z^{-1}}\right)\left(\frac{1+z^{-1}}{1-\frac{1}{4}z^{-1}}\right).$$

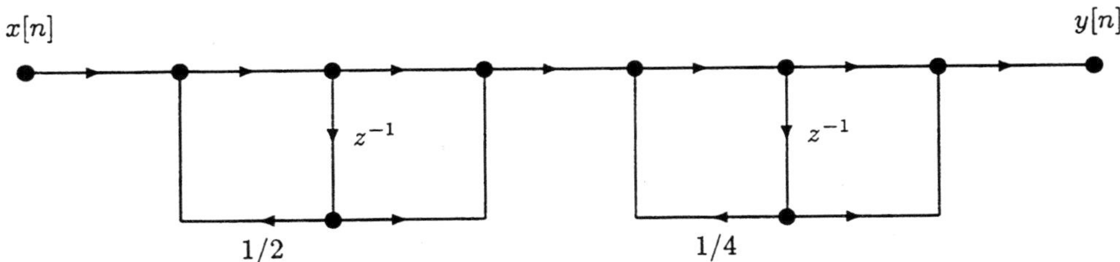

Plus 12 systems of this form:

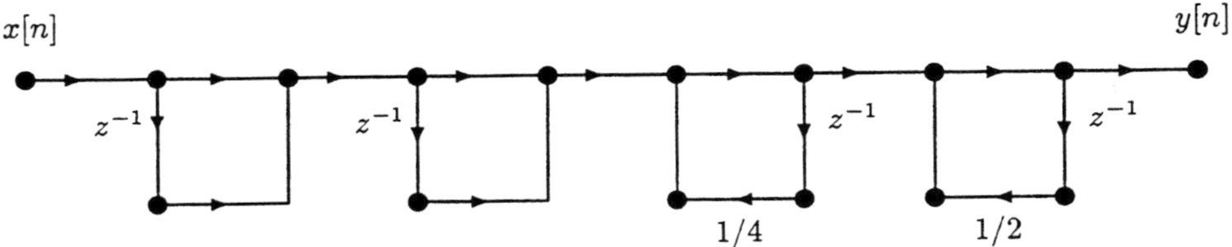

with the three types of 1st-order systems taken in various orders.

6.23. Causal LTI system with system function:

$$H(z) = \frac{1-\frac{1}{5}z^{-1}}{(1-\frac{1}{2}z^{-1}+\frac{1}{3}z^{-2})(1+\frac{1}{4}z^{-1})}.$$

(a) (i) Direct form I.

$$H(z) = \frac{1-\frac{1}{5}z^{-1}}{1-\frac{1}{4}z^{-1}+\frac{5}{24}z^{-2}+\frac{1}{12}z(-3)}$$

so

$$b_0 = 1\ ,\ b_1 = -\frac{1}{5} \text{ and } a_1 = \frac{1}{4}\ ,\ a_2 = -\frac{5}{24}\ ,\ a_3 = -\frac{1}{12}.$$

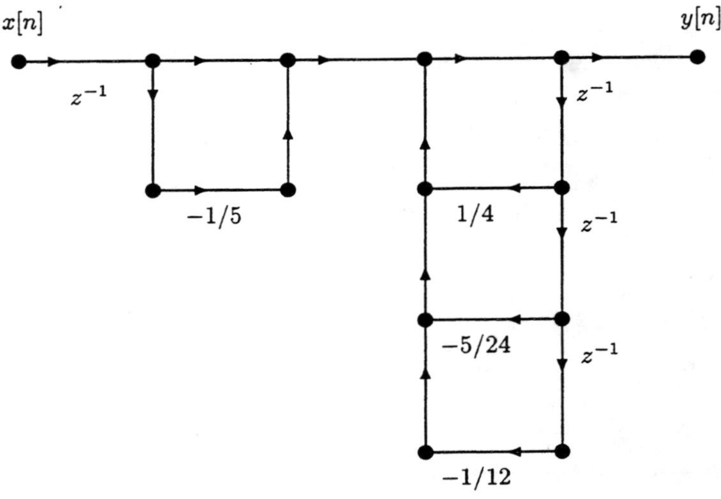

(ii) Direct form II.

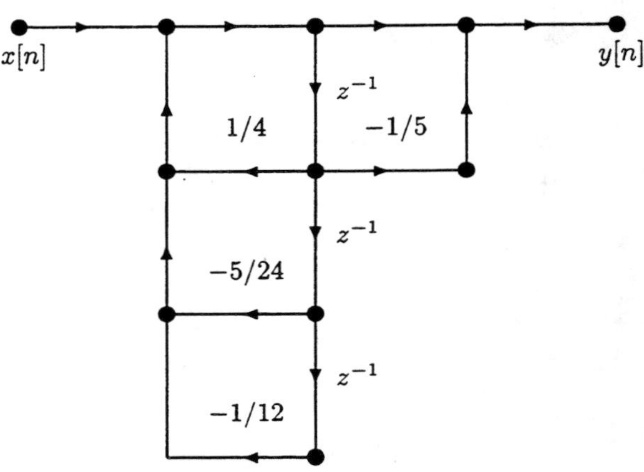

(iii) Cascade form using first and second order direct form II sections.

$$H(z) = (\frac{1 - \frac{1}{5}z^{-1}}{1 + \frac{1}{4}z^{-1}})(\frac{1}{1 - \frac{1}{2}z^{-1} + \frac{1}{3}z^{-2}}).$$

So

$$b_{01} = 1 \ , \ b_{11} = -\tfrac{1}{5} \ , \ b_{21} = 0 \ ,$$
$$b_{02} = 1 \ , \ b_{12} = 0 \ , \ b_{22} = 0 \text{ and}$$
$$a_{11} = -\tfrac{1}{4} \ , \ a_{21} = 0 \ , \ a_{12} = \tfrac{1}{2} \ , \ a_{22} = -\tfrac{1}{3}.$$

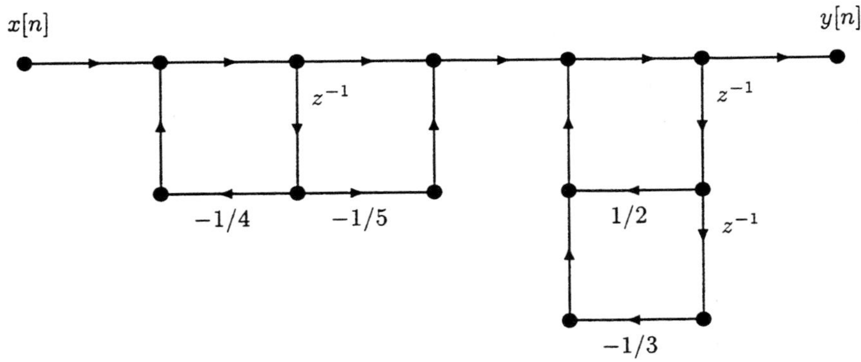

(iv) Parallel form using first and second order direct form II sections. We can rewrite the transfer function as:

$$H(z) = \frac{\frac{27}{125}}{1 + \frac{1}{4}z^{-1}} + \frac{\frac{98}{125} - \frac{36}{125}z^{-1}}{1 - \frac{1}{2}z^{-1} - \frac{1}{3}z^{-2}}.$$

So

$$e_{01} = \tfrac{27}{125} \ , \ e_{11} = 0 \ ,$$
$$e_{02} = \tfrac{98}{125} \ , \ e_{12} = -\tfrac{36}{125} \ , \ \text{ and}$$
$$a_{11} = -\tfrac{1}{4} \ , \ a_{21} = 0 \ , \ a_{12} = \tfrac{1}{2} \ , \ a_{22} = -\tfrac{1}{3}.$$

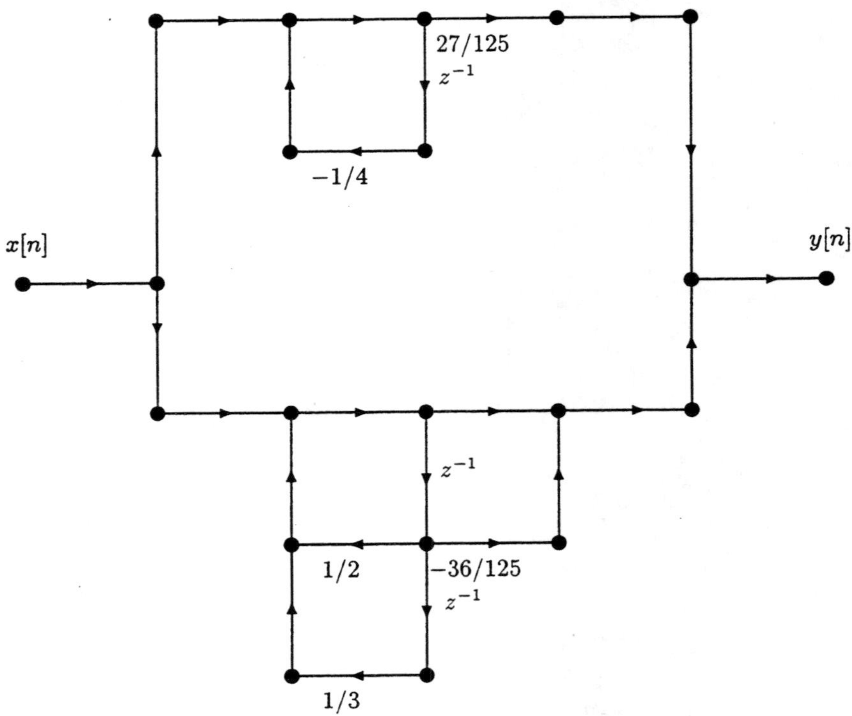

(v) Transposed direct form II
We take the direct form II derived in part (ii) and reverse the arrows as well as exchange the input and output. Then redrawing the flow graph, we get:

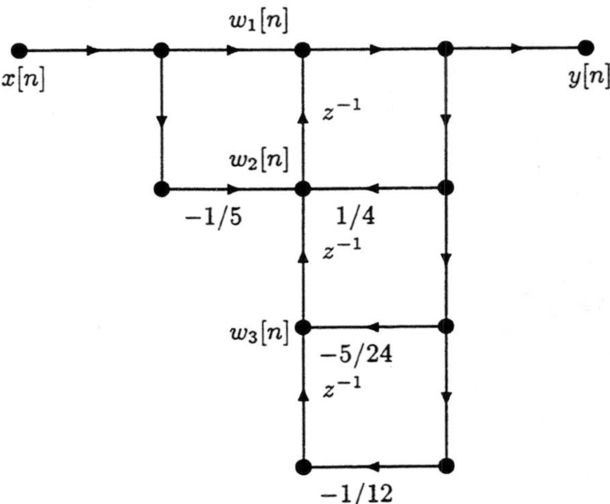

(b) To get the difference equation for the flow graph of part (v) in (a), we first define the intermediate variables: $w_1[n]$, $w_2[n]$ and $w_3[n]$. We have:

$$\begin{aligned}
(1)\ w_1[n] &= x[n] + w_2[n-1] \\
(2)\ w_2[n] &= \frac{1}{4}y[n] + w_3[n-1] - \frac{1}{5}x[n] \\
(3)\ w_3[n] &= -\frac{5}{24}y[n] - \frac{1}{12}y[n-1] \\
(4)\quad y[n] &= w_1[n].
\end{aligned}$$

Combining the above equations, we get:

$$y[n] - \frac{1}{4}y[n-1] + \frac{5}{24}y[n-2] + \frac{1}{12}y[n-3] = x[n] - \frac{1}{5}x[n-1].$$

Taking the Z-transform of this equation and combining terms, we get the following transfer function:

$$H(z) = \frac{1 - \frac{1}{5}z^{-1}}{1 - \frac{1}{4}z^{-1} + \frac{5}{24}z^{-2} + \frac{1}{12}z^{-3}}$$

which is equal to the initial transfer function.

6.24. (a)

$$H(z) = \frac{1}{1 - az^{-1}}$$

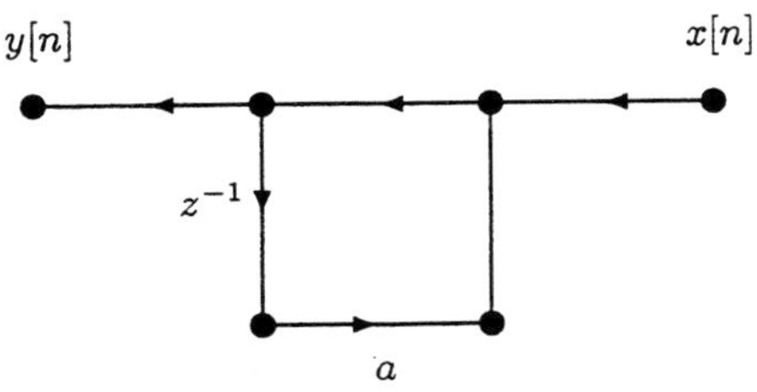

$$y[n] = x[n] + ay[n-1]$$

$$H_T(z) = \frac{1}{1 - az^{-1}} = H(z)$$

(b)

$$H(z) = \frac{1 + \frac{1}{4}z^{-1}}{1 - \frac{1}{2}z^{-1}}$$

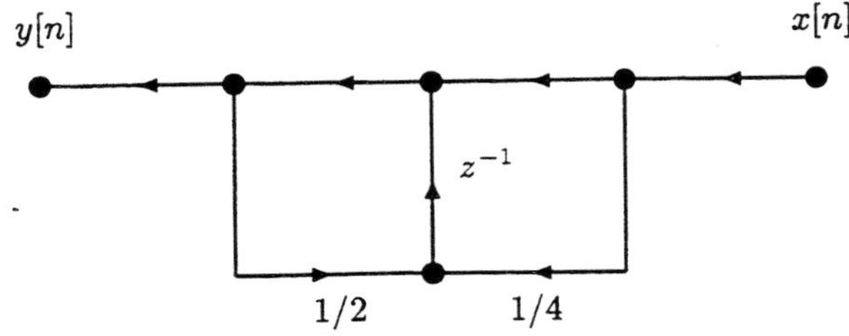

$$y[n] = x[n] + \frac{1}{4}x[n-1] + \frac{1}{2}y[n-1]$$

$$H_T(z) = \frac{1 + \frac{1}{4}z^{-1}}{1 - \frac{1}{2}z^{-1}} = H(z)$$

(c)

$$H(z) = a + bz^{-1} + cz^{-2}$$

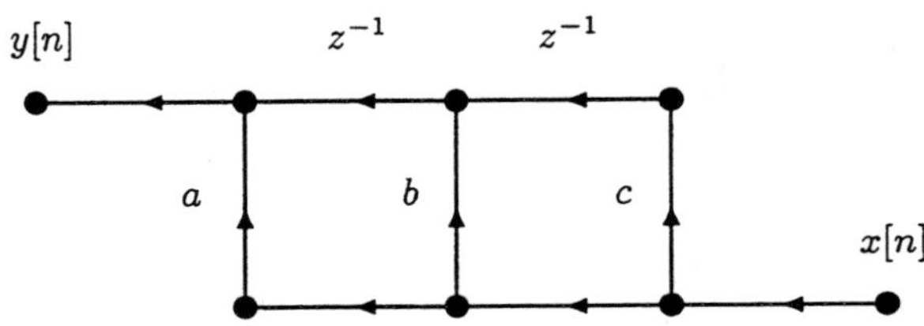

$$y[n] = ax[n] + bx[n-1] + cx[n-2]$$

$$H_T(z) = a + bz^{-1} + cz^{-2} = H(z)$$

(d)

$$H(z) = \frac{r \sin\theta z^{-1}}{1 - 2r\cos\theta z^{-1} + r^2 z^{-2}}$$

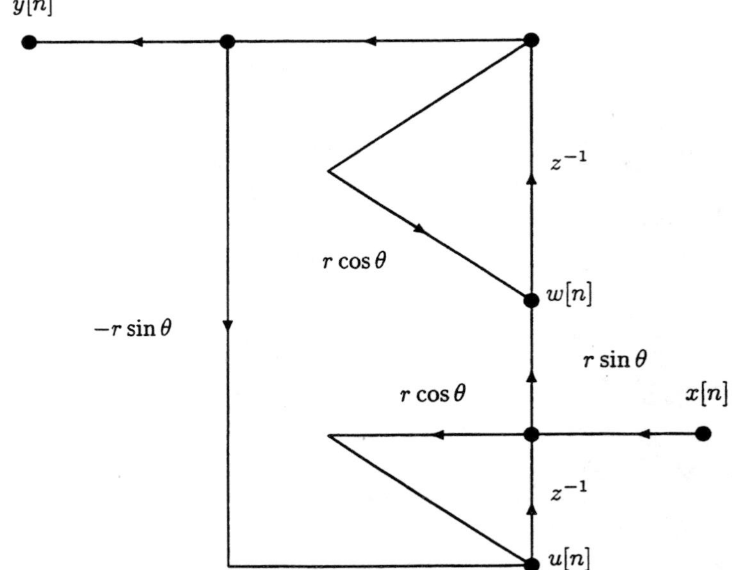

$$\begin{aligned}
V &= X + z^{-1}U \\
U &= r\cos\theta V - r\sin\theta Y \\
W &= r\sin\theta V + r\cos\theta z^{-1}W \\
Y &= z^{-1}W \\
\Longrightarrow \frac{Y}{X} &= H_T(z) \\
&= \frac{r\sin\theta z^{-1}}{1 - 2r\cos\theta z^{-1} + r^2 z^{-2}} \\
&= H(z)..
\end{aligned}$$

6.25. (a)

$$\begin{aligned}
H(z) &= \frac{1}{1-z^{-1}}\left[\frac{1-\frac{1}{2}z^{-1}}{1-\frac{3}{8}z^{-1}+\frac{7}{8}z^{-2}} + 1 + 2z^{-1} + z^{-2}\right] \\
&= \frac{2+\frac{9}{8}z^{-1}+\frac{9}{8}z^{-2}+\frac{11}{8}z^{-3}+\frac{7}{8}z^{-4}}{1-\frac{11}{8}z^{-1}+\frac{5}{4}z^{-2}-\frac{7}{8}z^{-3}}.
\end{aligned}$$

(b)

$$\begin{aligned}
y[n] &= 2x[n] + \frac{9}{8}x[n-1] + \frac{9}{8}x[n-2] + \frac{11}{8}x[n-3] + \frac{7}{8}x[n-4] \\
&+ \frac{11}{8}y[n-1] - \frac{5}{4}y[n-2] + \frac{7}{8}y[n-3].
\end{aligned}$$

(c) Use Direct Form II:

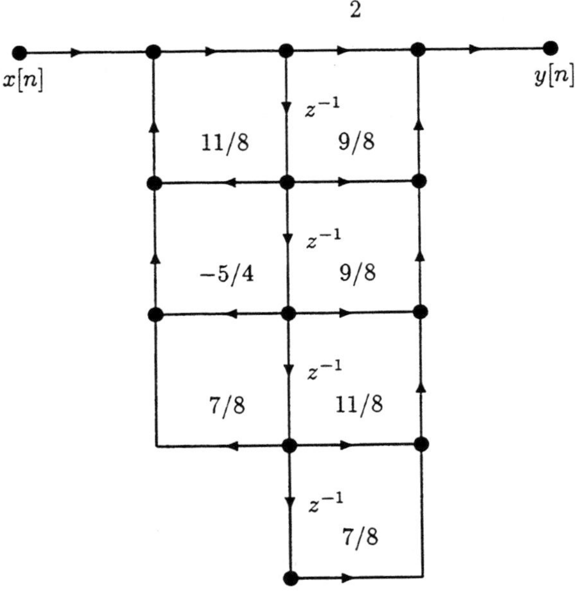

6.26. (a) We can rearrange $H(z)$ this way:

$$H(z) = \frac{(1+z^{-1})^2}{1-\frac{1}{2}z^{-1}+z^{-2}} \cdot \frac{(1+z^{-1})^2}{1+z^{-1}+\frac{1}{2}z^{-2}} \cdot (1+z^{-1})^2 \cdot \frac{1}{1-2z^{-1}+\frac{7}{8}z^{-2}} \cdot 0.2$$

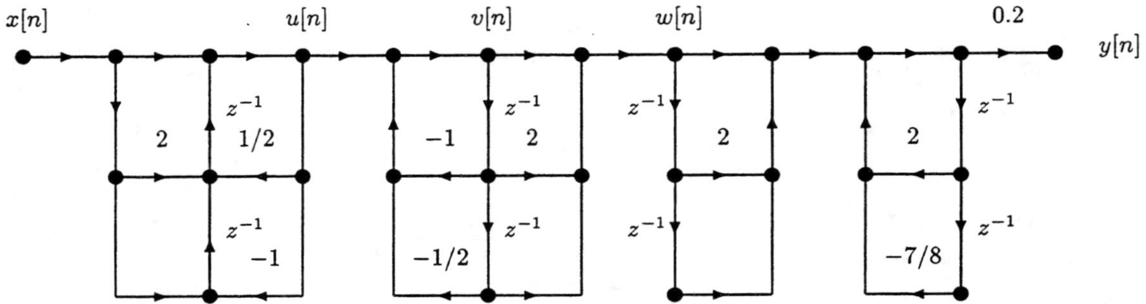

The solution is not unique; the order of the denominator 2nd-order sections may be rearranged.

(b)

$$
\begin{aligned}
u[n] &= x[n] + 2x[n-1] + x[n-2] + \frac{1}{2}u[n-1] - u[n-2] \\
v[n] &= u[n] - v[n-1] - \frac{1}{2}v[n-2] \\
w[n] &= v[n] + 2v[n-1] + v[n-2] \\
y[n] &= w[n] + 2w[n-1] + w[n-2] + 2y[n-1] - \frac{7}{8}y[n-2].
\end{aligned}
$$

6.27. (a) $H_1(e^{j\omega}) = H(e^{j(\omega+\pi)})$.

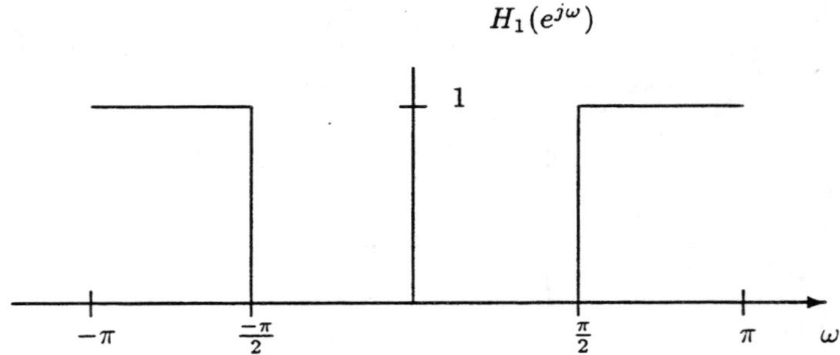

(b) For $H_1(z) = H(-z)$, replace each z^{-1} by $-z^{-1}$. Alternatively, replace each coefficient of an odd-delayed variable by its negative.

(c)

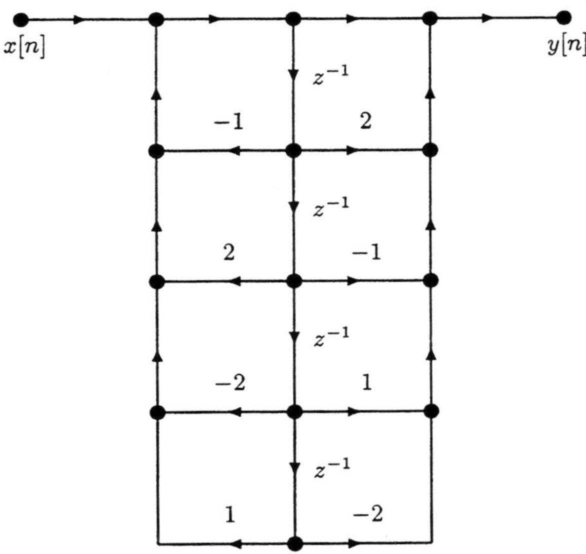

6.28.

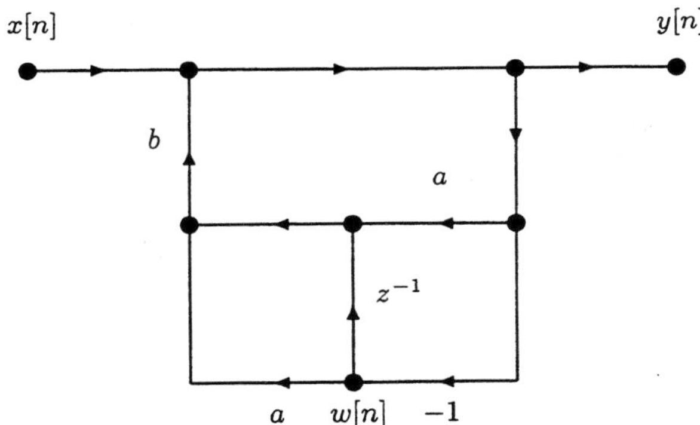

(a)

$$\begin{aligned} y[n] &= x[n] + abw[n] + bw[n-1] + aby[n] \\ w[n] &= -y[n]. \end{aligned}$$

Eliminate w[n]:

$$\begin{aligned} y[n] &= x[n] - aby[n] - by[n-1] + aby[n] \\ y[n] &= x[n] - by[n-1] \end{aligned}$$

So:

$$H(z) = \frac{1}{1 + bz^{-1}}.$$

(b)

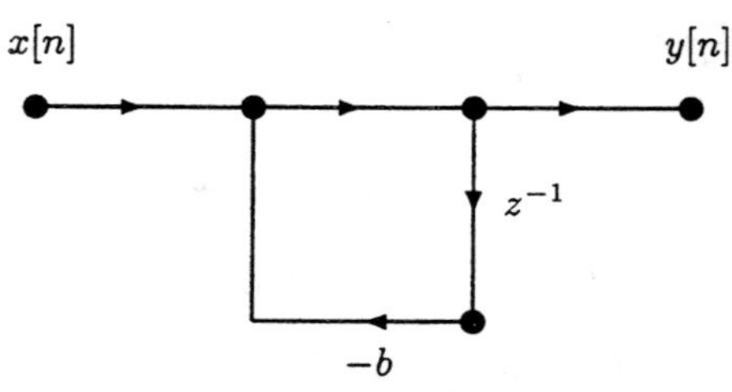

6.29. (a)

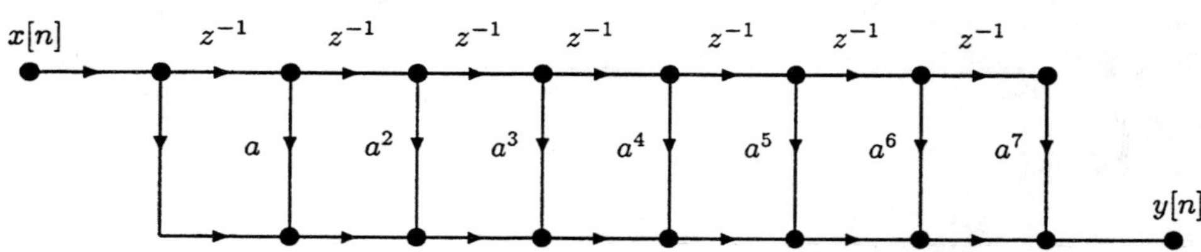

(b) From

$$\sum_{k=N_1}^{N_2} \alpha^k = \frac{\alpha^{N_1} - \alpha^{N_2+1}}{1-\alpha}$$

it follows that

$$\sum_{n=0}^{7} a^n z^{-n} = \frac{1 - a^8 z^{-8}}{1 - az^{-1}}.$$

(c)

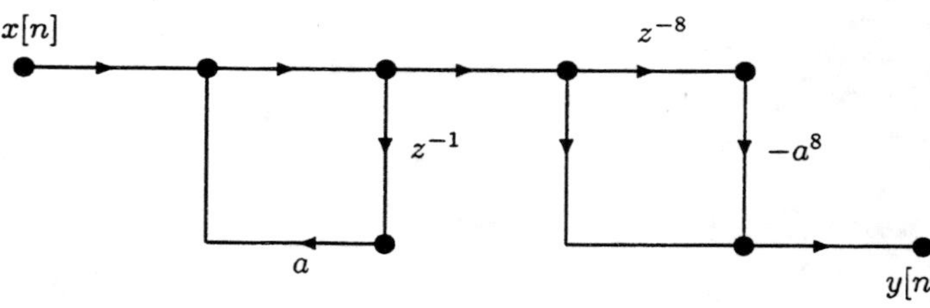

(d) (i) (c) has the most storage: 9 vs. 7.

(ii) (a) has the most arithmetic: 7 adds + 7 multiplies per sample, vs. 2 multiplies + 2 adds per sample.

6.30.

(a)

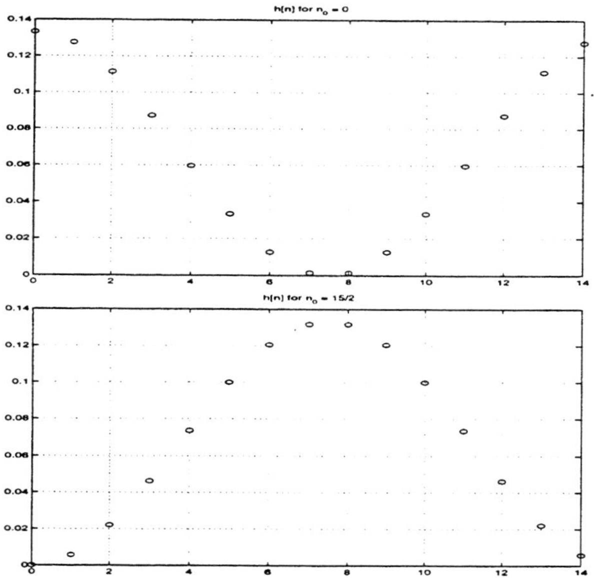

(b)

$$\begin{aligned}
H(z) &= \frac{1}{15}\sum_{n=0}^{14}\left[1+\cos\left(\frac{2\pi}{15}(n-n_0)\right)\right]z^{-n} \\
&= \frac{1}{15}\sum_{n=0}^{14}z^{-n}+\frac{1}{15}\sum_{n=0}^{14}\frac{1}{2}\left[e^{j\frac{2\pi}{15}(n-n_0)}+e^{-j\frac{2\pi}{15}(n-n_0)}\right]z^{-n} \\
&= \frac{1}{15}\frac{1-z^{-15}}{1-z^{-1}}+\frac{1}{15}\frac{1}{2}\frac{e^{-j\frac{2\pi}{15}n_0}[1-(e^{j\frac{2\pi}{15}}z^{-1})^{15}]}{1-e^{j\frac{2\pi}{15}}z^{-1}} \\
&\quad +\frac{1}{15}\frac{1}{2}\frac{e^{j\frac{2\pi}{15}n_0}[1-(e^{-j\frac{2\pi}{15}}z^{-1})^{15}]}{1-e^{-j\frac{2\pi}{15}}z^{-1}} \\
&= \frac{1}{15}(1-z^{-15})\left[\frac{1}{1-z^{-1}}+\frac{\frac{1}{2}e^{-j\frac{2\pi}{15}n_0}}{1-e^{j\frac{2\pi}{15}}z^{-1}}+\right. \\
&\quad \left.\frac{\frac{1}{2}e^{j\frac{2\pi}{15}n_0}}{1-e^{-j\frac{2\pi}{15}}z^{-1}}\right].
\end{aligned}$$

(c)

$$H(e^{j\omega})=\frac{1}{15}e^{-j7\omega}\left[\frac{\sin((15\omega)/2)}{\sin(\omega/2)}-\frac{1}{2}\frac{e^{-j\frac{\pi}{15}}\sin((15\omega)/2)}{\sin((\omega-\frac{2\pi}{15})/2)}-\frac{1}{2}\frac{e^{j\frac{\pi}{15}}\sin((15\omega)/2)}{\sin((\omega+(2\pi)/15)/2)}\right].$$

$$H(e^{j\omega})=\frac{1-e^{-j15\omega}}{15}\left[\frac{1}{1-e^{-j\omega}}+\frac{\frac{1}{2}e^{-j\frac{2\pi n_0}{15}}}{1-e^{j\frac{2\pi}{15}}e^{-j\omega}}+\frac{\frac{1}{2}e^{j\frac{2\pi n_0}{15}}}{1-e^{-j\frac{2\pi}{15}}e^{-j\omega}}\right]$$

When $n_0 = 15/2$, .

$$H(e^{j\omega}) = \frac{1}{15}\left[\frac{e^{j\frac{\omega}{2}}(1-e^{-j15\omega})}{e^{j\frac{\omega}{2}}-e^{-j\frac{\omega}{2}}}-\frac{\frac{1}{2}e^{j\frac{\omega-(2\pi/15)}{2}}(1-e^{-j15\omega})}{e^{j\frac{\omega-(2\pi/15)}{2}}-e^{-j\frac{\omega-(2\pi/15)}{2}}}-\right.$$

$$\left.\frac{\frac{1}{2}e^{j\frac{\omega+(2\pi/15)}{2}}(1-e^{-j15\omega})}{e^{j\frac{\omega+(2\pi/15)}{2}}-e^{-j\frac{\omega+(2\pi/15)}{2}}}\right]$$

$$= \frac{1}{15}\left[\frac{e^{-j\omega 7}(e^{j\omega\frac{15}{2}}-e^{-j\omega\frac{15}{2}})}{2j\sin\frac{\omega}{2}} - \right.$$

$$\frac{\frac{1}{2}e^{-j\omega 7}e^{-j\frac{\pi}{15}}(e^{j\omega\frac{15}{2}}-e^{-j\omega\frac{15}{2}})}{2j\sin\left(\frac{\omega-(2\pi/15)}{2}\right)} -$$

$$\left.\frac{\frac{1}{2}e^{-j\omega 7}e^{j\frac{\pi}{15}}(e^{j\frac{15}{2}\omega}-e^{-j\frac{15}{2}\omega})}{2j\sin\left(\frac{\omega+(2\pi/15)}{2}\right)}\right]$$

$$= \frac{e^{-j\omega 7}}{15}\left[\frac{\sin(15\omega/2)}{\sin(\omega/2)} - \frac{\frac{1}{2}e^{-j\frac{\pi}{15}}\sin(15\omega/2)}{\sin\left(\frac{\omega-(2\pi/15)}{2}\right)} - \right.$$

$$\left.\frac{\frac{1}{2}e^{j\frac{\pi}{15}}\sin(15\omega/2)}{\sin\left(\frac{\omega+(2\pi/15)}{2}\right)}\right]$$

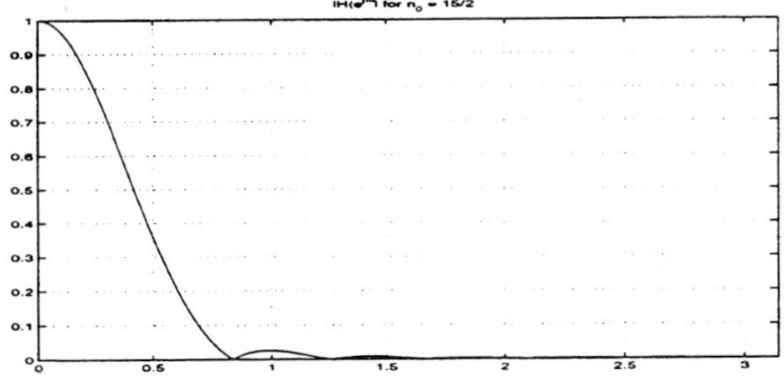

When $n_0 = 0$,

$$H(e^{j\omega}) = \frac{e^{-j\omega 7}}{15}\left[\frac{\sin(15\omega/2)}{\sin(\omega/2)} + \frac{\frac{1}{2}e^{-j\frac{\pi}{15}}\sin(15\omega/2)}{\sin\left(\frac{\omega-(2\pi/15)}{2}\right)} + \right.$$

$$\left.\frac{\frac{1}{2}e^{j\frac{\pi}{15}}\sin(15\omega/2)}{\sin\left(\frac{\omega+(2\pi/15)}{2}\right)}\right]$$

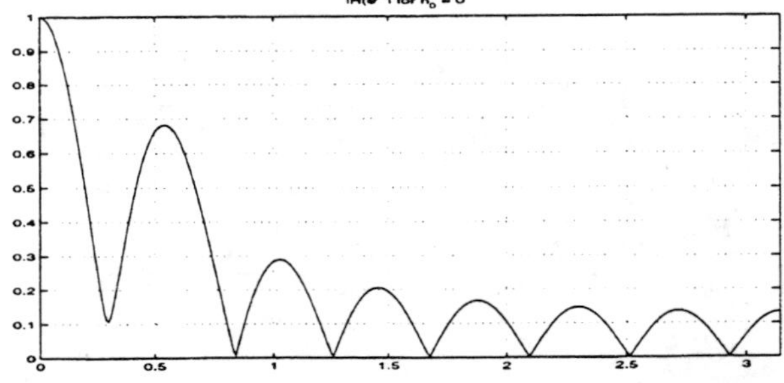

The system will have generalized linear phase if the impulse response has even symmetry (note it cannot have odd symmetry), or alternatively, if the frequency response can be expressed as:

$$H(e^{j\omega}) = e^{-jw7}A_e(e^{j\omega})$$

where $A_e(e^{j\omega})$ is a real, even, periodic function in ω. We thus conclude that the system will have generalized linear phase for $n_0 = \frac{15}{2}k$, where k is an odd integer.

(d) Rewrite $H(z)$ as

$$H(z) = \frac{1 - z^{-15}}{15}\left[\frac{1}{1 - z^{-1}} + \frac{\cos\frac{2\pi n_0}{15} - \cos\left(\frac{2\pi}{15} + \frac{2\pi n_0}{15}\right)z^{-1}}{1 - 2\cos\frac{2\pi}{15}z^{-1} + z^{-2}}\right].$$

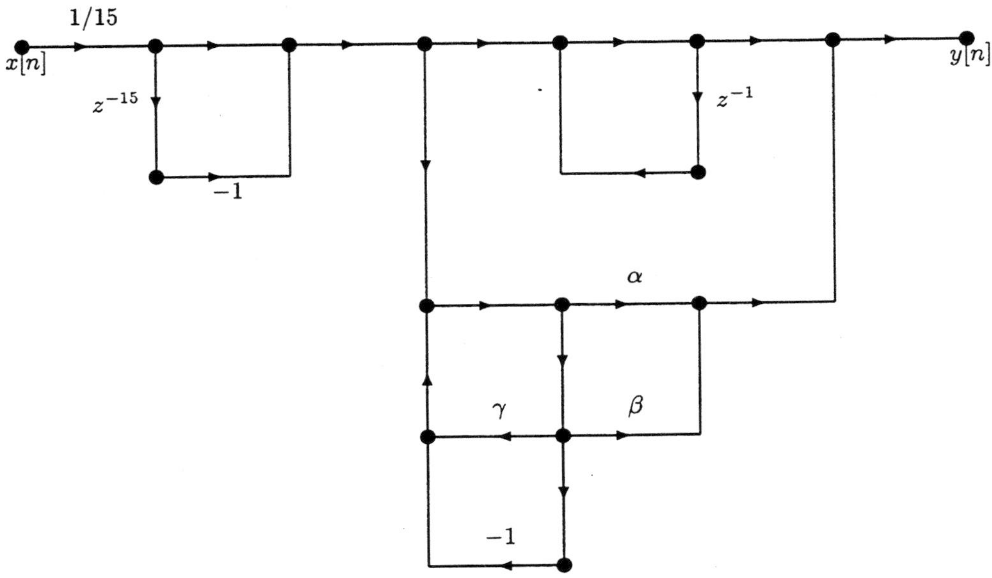

where $\alpha = \cos(2\pi n_0/15)$, $\beta = -\cos(2\pi(n_0 + 1)/15)$, and $\gamma = 2\cos(2\pi/15)$.

6.31. (a)

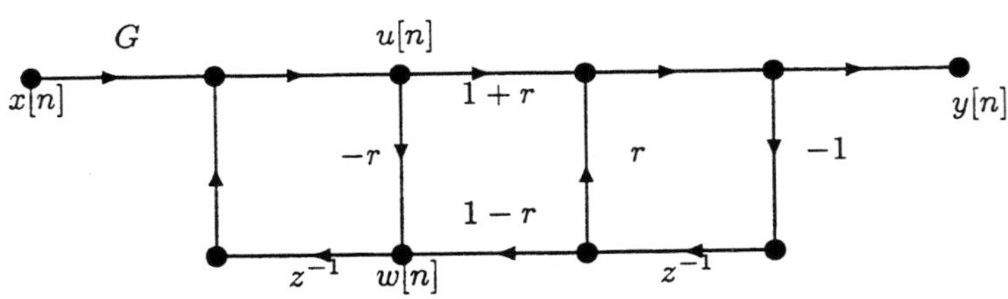

$$\begin{aligned}
u[n] &= Gx[n] + w[n-1] \\
w[n] &= -ru[n] - (1-r)y[n-1] \\
y[n] &= (1+r)u[n] - ry[n-1].
\end{aligned}$$

(b)

$$\begin{aligned}
U(z) &= GX(z) + z^{-1}W(z) \\
W(z) &= -ru(z) - (1-r)z^{-1}Y(z) \\
Y(z) &= (1+r)U(z) - rz^{-1}Y(z).
\end{aligned}$$

Solve for $U(z)$ in terms of $X(z)$ and $Y(z)$:

$$U(z) = \frac{GX(z) - (1-r)z^{-2}Y(z)}{1+rz^{-1}}$$

Then

$$Y(z) = (1+r)\left\{\frac{GX(z) - (1-r)z^{-2}Y(z)}{1+rz^{-1}}\right\} - rz^{-1}Y(z)$$

$$Y(z)(1+rz^{-1}) = G(1+r)X(z) - (1-r^2)z^{-2}Y(z) - rz^{-1}Y(z) - r^2z^{-2}Y(z)$$

$$Y(z)(1+2rz^{-1}+z^{-2}) = G(1+r)X(z)$$

$$H_1(z) = \frac{G(1+r)}{1+2rz^{-1}+z^{-2}}.$$

From the quadratic formula, the poles are at $(-r+j\sqrt{1-r^2})^{-1}$ and $(-r-j\sqrt{1-r^2})^{-1}$. The magnitude of each pole is 1. The angles are

$$-\tan^{-1}\left(\frac{\sqrt{1-r^2}}{r}\right) \quad \text{and} \quad \tan^{-1}\left(\frac{\sqrt{1-r^2}}{r}\right),$$

respectively.

(c) $U(z) = z^{-1}(GX(z) + W(z))$, $W(z) = -rU(z) - (1-r)Y(z)$, and $Y(z) = z^{-1}((1+r)U(z) - rY(z))$ lead to

$$H_2(z) = \frac{G(1+r)z^{-2}}{1+2rz^{-1}+z^{-2}} = z^{-2}H_1(z).$$

6.32. (a)

$$\begin{aligned} y_1[n] &= (1+r)x_1[n] + rx_2[n] \\ y_2[n] &= -rx_1[n] + (1-r)x_2[n]. \end{aligned}$$

(b)

$$\begin{aligned} y_1[n] &= (1+a)x_1[n] + dx_2[n] \quad (a = r = d) \\ y_2[n] &= (1+cd)x_2[n] + abx_1[n] \quad (c = d = -1). \end{aligned}$$

(c)

$$\begin{aligned} y_1[n] &= (1+e)x_1[n] + ex_2[n] \quad (e = r) \\ y_2[n] &= efx_1[n] + (1+ef)x_2[n] \quad (f = -1). \end{aligned}$$

(d) B and C preferred over A:

(i) coefficient quantization. If r is small, $1+r$ may not be precisely representable even in floating point. Also, network A has 4 multipliers that must be quantized, while B and C have only 1.

(ii) computational complexity. Networks B and C require fewer multiplications per output sample.

6.33.

$$H(z) = \frac{z^{-1} - 0.54}{1 - 0.54z^{-1}}.$$

(a)

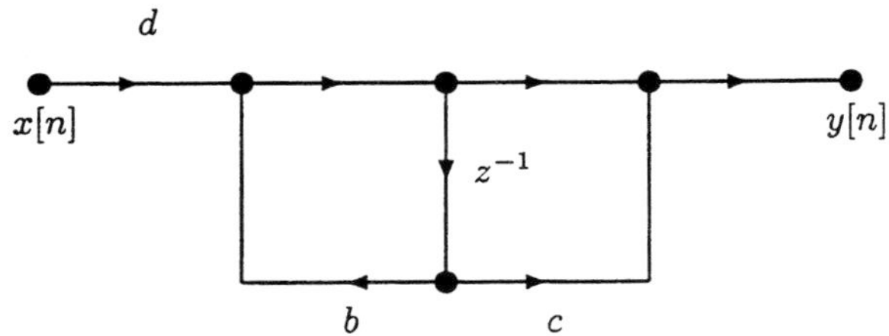

$$H(z) = \frac{cdz^{-1} + d}{1 - bz^{-1}}$$

so set $b = 0.54$, $c = -1.852$, and $d = -0.54$.

(b) With quantized coefficients $\hat{b}$, $\hat{c}$, and $\hat{d}$, $\hat{c}\hat{d} \neq 1$ and $\hat{d} \neq -\hat{b}$ in general, so the resulting system would not be allpass.

(c)

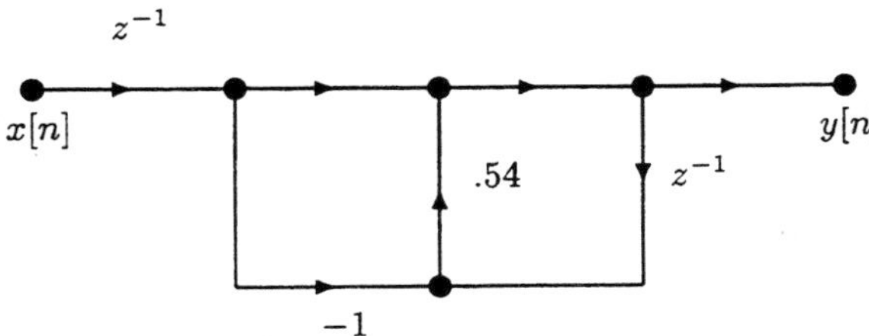

(d) Yes, since there is only one "0.54" to quantize.

(e)

$$H(z) = \left(\frac{z^{-1} - a}{1 - az^{-1}}\right)\left(\frac{z^{-1} - b}{1 - bz^{-1}}\right)$$

Cascading two sections like (c) gives

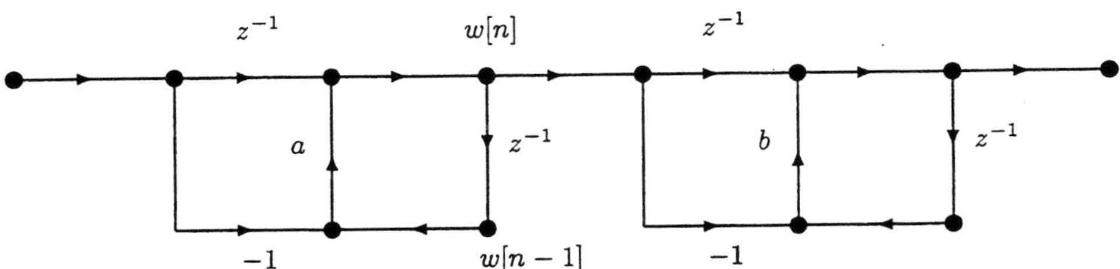

The first delay in the second section has output $w[n-1]$ so we can combine with the second delay of the first section:

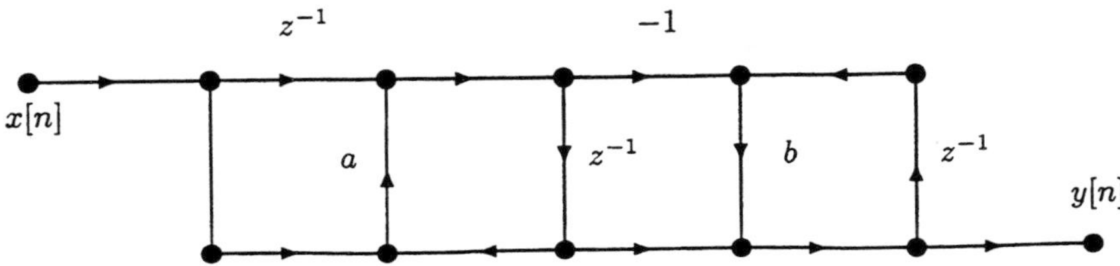

(f) Yes, same reason as part (d).

6.34. (a) We have:

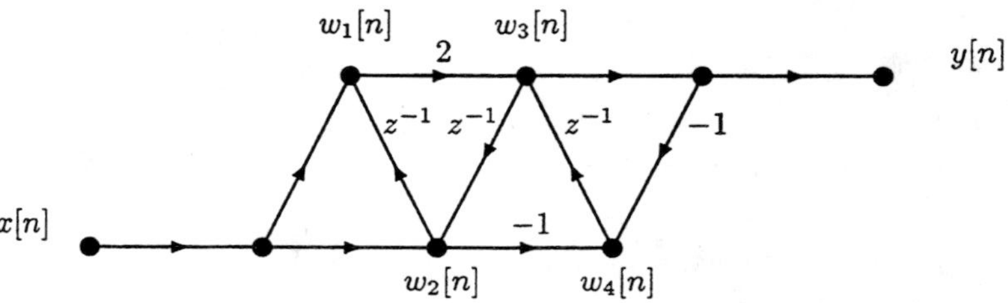

First, we find the system function, we have:

$$
\begin{aligned}
(1)\ w_1[n] &= x[n] + w_2[n-1] \\
(2)\ w_2[n] &= x[n] + w_3[n-1] \\
(3)\ w_3[n] &= 2w_1[n] + w_4[n-1] \\
(4)\ \ y[n] &= w_3[n] \\
(5)\ w_4[n] &= -y[n] - w_2[n]
\end{aligned}
$$

Taking the Z-transform of the above equations and combining terms, we get:

$$(1 - z^{-1})Y(z) + z^{-1}Y(z) = (2 + z^{-1})X(z).$$

The system function is thus given by:

$$H(z) = \frac{Y(z)}{X(z)} = \frac{2 + z^{-1}}{1 + z^{-1} - z^{-2}}$$

Since the system function is second order (highest order term is z^{-2}), we should be able to implement this system using only 2 delays, this can be done with a direct form II implementation. Therefore, the minimum number of delays required to implement an equivalent system is 2.

(b) Now we have:

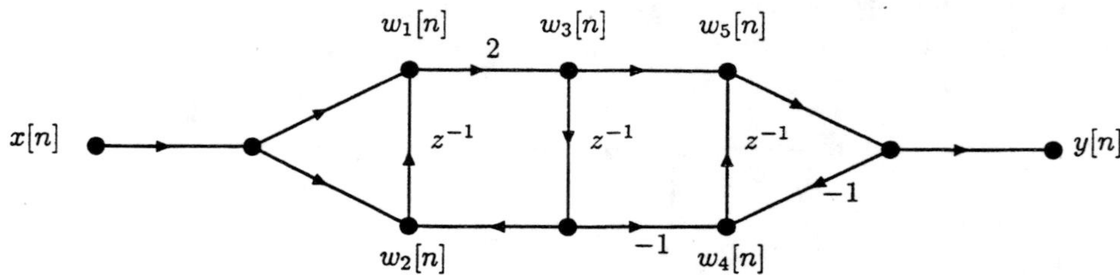

Let's find the transfer function, we have:

$$
\begin{aligned}
(1)\ w_1[n] &= x[n] + w_2[n-1] \\
(2)\ w_2[n] &= x[n] + w_3[n-1] \\
(3)\ w_3[n] &= 2w_1[n] \\
(4)\ w_4[n] &= -w_3[n-1] - y[n] \\
(5)\ w_5[n] &= w_3[n] + w_4[n-1] \\
(6)\quad y[n] &= w_5[n]
\end{aligned}
$$

Taking the Z-transform of the above equations and combining terms, we get:

$$(1+z^{-1})Y(z) = \frac{(1-z^{-2})(2+2z^{-1})}{1-2z^{-2}}X(z).$$

The system function is thus given by:

$$H(z) = \frac{Y(z)}{X(z)} = \frac{2(1+z^{-1})(1-z^{-1})}{1-2z^{-2}}.$$

Since the transfer function is not the same as the one in part a, we conclude that system B does not represent the same input-output relationship as system A. This should not be surprising since in system B we added two unidirectional wires and therefore changed the input-output relationship.

6.35.

$$H(z) = \frac{z^{-1} - \frac{1}{3}}{1 - \frac{1}{3}z^{-1}}.$$

(a) Direct form I:

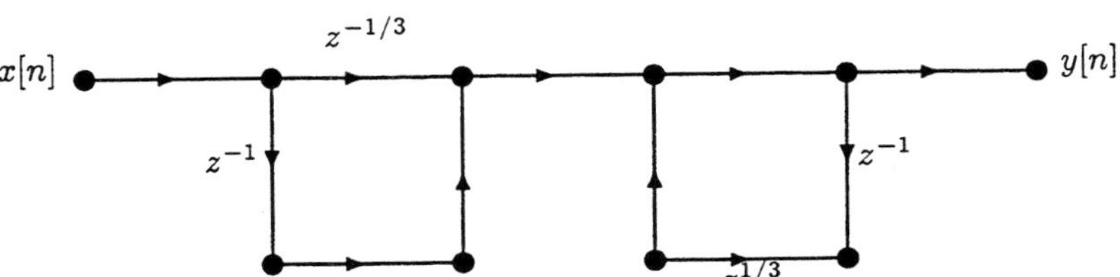

From the graph above, it is clear that 2 delays and 2 multipliers are needed.

(b)

$$(1 - \frac{1}{3}z^{-1})Y(z) = (-\frac{1}{3} + z^{-1})X(z)$$

Inverse $Z-$transforming, we get:

$$y[n] - \frac{1}{3}y[n-1] = -\frac{1}{3}x[n] + x[n-1]$$

$$y[n] = \frac{1}{3}(y[n-1] - x[n]) + x[n-1]$$

Which can be implemented with the following flow diagram:

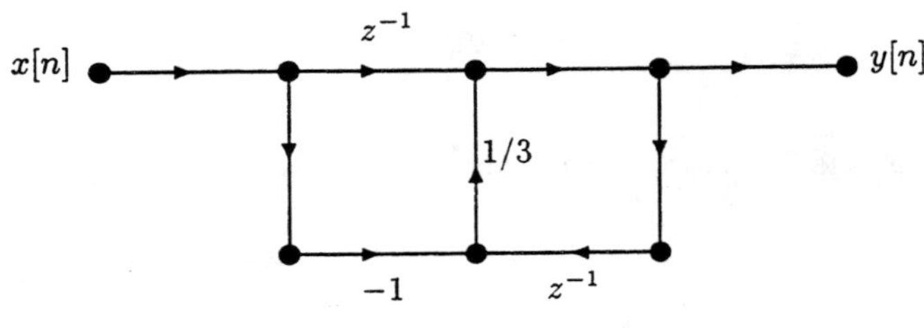

(c)

$$H(z) = \left(\frac{z^{-1} - \frac{1}{3}}{1 - \frac{1}{3}z^{-1}}\right)\left(\frac{z^{-1} - 2}{1 - 2z^{-1}}\right).$$

This can be implemented as the cascade of the flow graph in part (b) with the following flow graph:

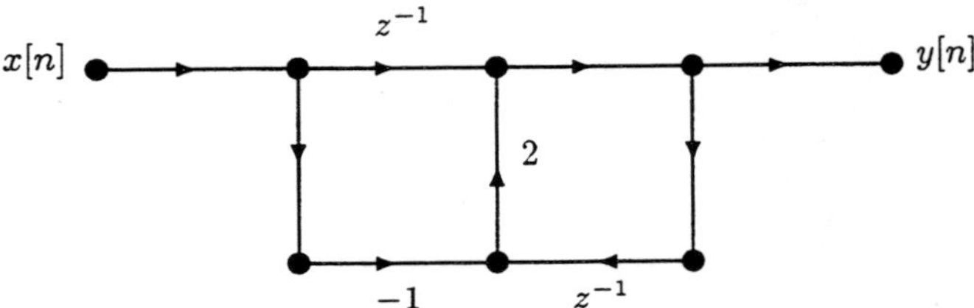

However the above flow graph can be redrawn as:

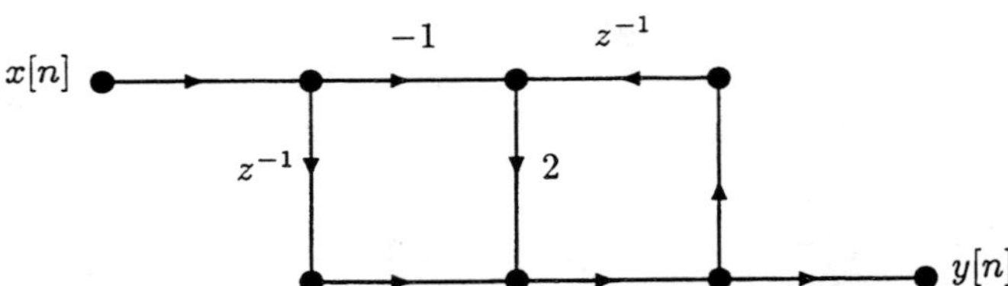

Now cascading the above flow graph with the one from part (b) and grouping the delay element we get the following system with two multipliers and three delays:

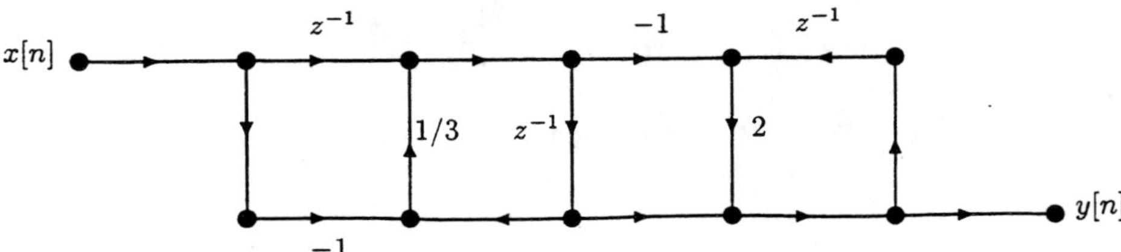

6.36. (a) Transpose = reverse arrows direction and reverse the input/output, we get:

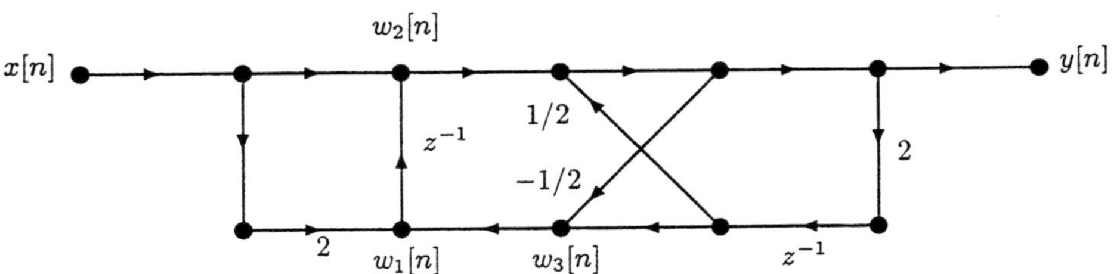

(b) From part (a), we have:

$$(1)\ w_1[n] = 2x[n] + w_3[n]$$
$$(2)\ w_2[n] = x[n] + w_1[n-1]$$
$$(3)\ w_3[n] = -\frac{1}{2}y[n] + 2y[n-1]$$
$$(4)\ y[n] = w_2[n] + y[n-1]$$

Taking the $Z-$transform of the above equations, substituting and rearranging terms, we get:

$$(1 - \frac{1}{2}z^{-1} - 2z^{-2})Y(z) = (2z^{-1} + 1)X(z).$$

Finally, inverse $Z-$transforming, we get the following difference equation:

$$y[n] - \frac{1}{2}y[n-1] - 2y[n-2] = x[n] + 2x[n-1].$$

(c) From part (b), the system function is given by:

$$H(z) = \frac{1 + 2z^{-1}}{1 - \frac{1}{2}z^{-1} - 2z^{-2}}.$$

It has poles at

$$z = -\frac{8}{1 - \sqrt{33}} \text{ and } z = -\frac{8}{1 + \sqrt{33}}$$

which are outside the unit circle, therefore the system is NOT BIBO stable.

(d)

$$y[2] = x[2] + 2x[1] + \tfrac{1}{2}y[1] + 2y[0]$$
$$y[0] = x[0] = 1$$
$$y[1] = x[1] + 2x[0] + \tfrac{1}{2}y[0] = \tfrac{1}{2} + 2 + \tfrac{1}{2} = 3$$

Therefore,

$$y[2] = \frac{1}{4} + 1 + \frac{3}{2} + 2 = \frac{19}{4}.$$

6.37. (a)

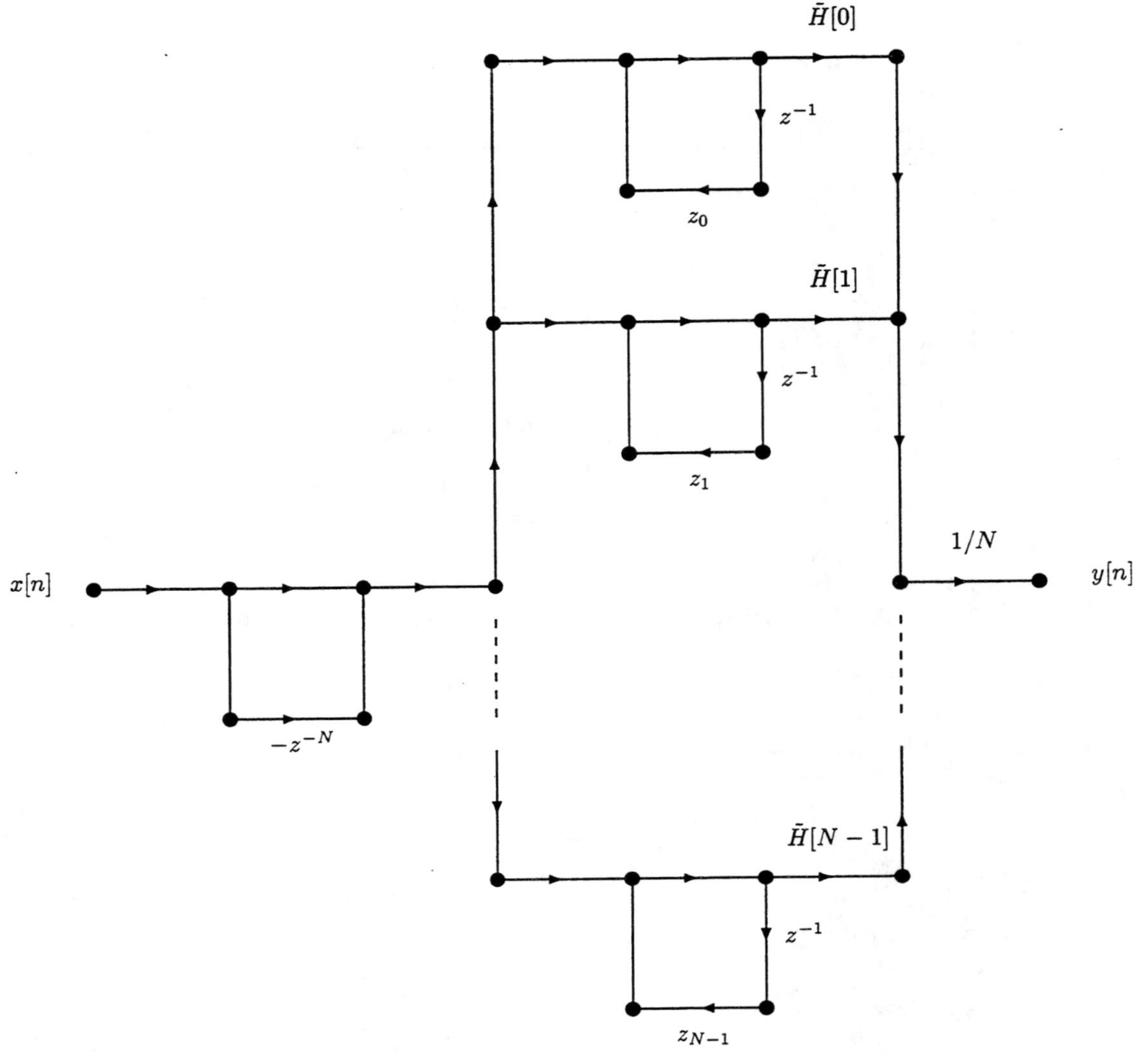

(b) Note that the z_k's are the zeros of $(1 - z^{-N})$. Then write $H(z)$ over a common denominator:

$$\begin{aligned} H(z) &= \frac{\prod_{\ell=0}^{N-1}(1 - z_\ell z^{-1}) \sum_{k=0}^{N-1} \frac{\tilde{H}[k]}{N} \prod_{\substack{i=0 \\ i \neq k}}^{N-1}(1 - z_i z^{-1})}{\prod_{k=0}^{N-1}(1 - z_k z^{-1})} \\ &= \sum_{k=0}^{N-1} \frac{\tilde{H}[k]}{N} \prod_{\substack{i=0 \\ i \neq k}}^{N-1} (1 - z_i z^{-1}). \end{aligned}$$

Therefore, $H(z)$ is the sum of polynomials in z^{-1} with degree $\leq N-1$. Hence, the system impulse response has length $\leq N$.

(c)

$$\mathcal{Z}^{-1}\left[(1 - z^{-N})\frac{\tilde{H}[k]/N}{1 - z_k z^{-1}}\right] = \frac{\tilde{H}[k]}{N}\mathcal{Z}^{-1}[1 - z^{-N}] * \mathcal{Z}^{-1}\left[\frac{1}{1 - z_k z^{-1}}\right]$$

$$
\begin{aligned}
&= \frac{\tilde{H}[k]}{N}(\delta[n] - \delta[n-N]) * (z_k^n u[n]) \\
&= \frac{\tilde{H}[k]}{N}[z_k^n u[n] - z_k^{n-N} u[n-N]] \\
&= \frac{\tilde{H}[k]}{N} z_k^n \{u[n] - u[n-N]\}.
\end{aligned}
$$

So

$$
h[n] = \left(\frac{1}{N} \sum_{k=0}^{N-1} \tilde{H}[k] e^{j\frac{2\pi}{N}kn} \right) (u[n] - u[n-N]).
$$

(d) Note that, since $(1 - z_m^{-N}) = 0$,

$$
\begin{aligned}
H(z_m) &= \left. \frac{(1 - z^{-N})\tilde{H}[m]/N}{1 - z_m z^{-1}} \right|_{z=z_m} \\
&= \frac{\frac{d}{dz}\{(1 - z^{-N})\tilde{H}[m]/N\}|_{z=z_m}}{\frac{d}{dz}\{1 - z_m z^{-1}\}|_{z=z_m}} \\
&= \frac{N z_m^{-N-1} \tilde{H}[m]/N}{z_m z_m^{-2}} \\
&= \tilde{H}[m] z_m^{-N} \\
&= \tilde{H}[m].
\end{aligned}
$$

(e) If $h[n]$ is real, $|H(e^{j\omega})| = |H(e^{j(2\pi-\omega)})|$, and $\angle H(e^{j\omega}) = -\angle H(e^{j(2\pi-\omega)})$. $H(e^{j2\pi k/N}) = \tilde{H}[k] = |\tilde{H}[k]| e^{j\tilde{\theta}[k]}$, so $|\tilde{H}[k]| = |\tilde{H}[N-k]|$ and $\tilde{\theta}[k] = -\tilde{\theta}[N-k]$, $k = 0, 1, \ldots, N-1$.

$$
\begin{aligned}
H(z) &= (1 - z^{-N}) \left[\frac{\tilde{H}[0]/N}{1 - z^{-1}} + \sum_{k=1}^{\frac{N}{2}-1} \frac{\tilde{H}[k]/N}{1 - z_k z^{-1}} + \frac{\tilde{H}[N/2]/N}{1 - z_{N/2} z^{-1}} + \sum_{\ell=\frac{N}{2}+1}^{N-1} \frac{\tilde{H}[\ell]/N}{1 - z_\ell z^{-1}} \right] \\
&= (1 - z^{-N}) \left[\frac{\tilde{H}[0]/N}{1 - z^{-1}} + \frac{\tilde{H}[N/2]/N}{1 + z^{-1}} + \sum_{k=1}^{\frac{N}{2}-1} \frac{\tilde{H}[k]/N}{1 - z_k z^{-1}} + \sum_{p=1}^{\frac{N}{2}-1} \frac{\tilde{H}[N-p]/N}{1 - z_{N-p} z^{-1}} \right] \\
&= (1 - z^{-N}) \left[\frac{\tilde{H}[0]/N}{1 - z^{-1}} + \frac{\tilde{H}[N/2]/N}{1 + z^{-1}} + \sum_{k=1}^{\frac{N}{2}-1} \left(\frac{\tilde{H}[k]/N}{1 - z_k z^{-1}} + \frac{\tilde{H}[N-k]/N}{1 - z_{-k} z^{-1}} \right) \right] \\
&= (1 - z^{-N}) \left[\frac{\tilde{H}[0]/N}{1 - z^{-1}} + \frac{\tilde{H}[N/2]/N}{1 + z^{-1}} + \right. \\
&\qquad \left. \frac{1}{N} \sum_{k=1}^{\frac{N}{2}-1} \frac{\tilde{H}[k](1 - z_{-k} z^{-1}) + \tilde{H}[N-k](1 - z_k z^{-1})}{(1 - z_k z^{-1})(1 - z_{-k} z^{-1})} \right] \\
&= (1 - z^{-N}) \left[\frac{\tilde{H}[0]/N}{1 - z^{-1}} + \frac{\tilde{H}[N/2]/N}{1 + z^{-1}} + \right. \\
&\qquad \left. \sum_{k=1}^{\frac{N}{2}-1} \frac{2|\tilde{H}[k]}{N} \cdot \frac{\cos(\tilde{\theta}[k]) - z^{-1}\cos(\tilde{\theta}[k] - 2\pi k/N)}{1 - 2\cos\frac{2\pi k}{N} z^{-1} + z^{-2}} \right]
\end{aligned}
$$

And since $\tilde{H}[0] = H(1)$, $\tilde{H}[N/2] = H(-1)$,

$$
H(z) = (1 - z^{-N}) \left[\frac{H(1)/N}{1 - z^{-1}} + \frac{H(-1)/N}{1 + z^{-1}} + \right.
$$

$$\sum_{k=1}^{\frac{N}{2}-1} \frac{2|H(e^{j\frac{2\pi}{N}k}|}{N} \cdot \frac{\cos[\theta(2\pi k/N)] - z^{-1}\cos[\theta(2\pi k/N) - 2\pi k/N]}{1 - 2\cos(2\pi k/N)z^{-1} + z^{-2}}\Bigg] .$$

If $\tilde{H}[14] = 0$,then $\tilde{H}[16-14] = \tilde{H}[2] = 0$ also.

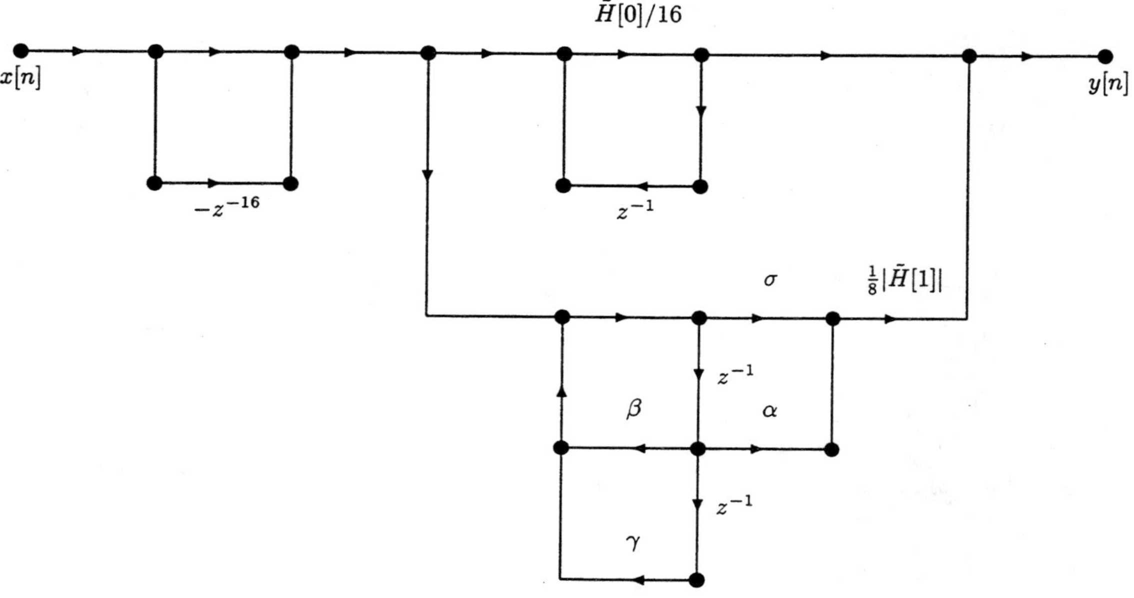

where $\sigma = \cos(\tilde{\theta}[1])$, $\alpha = -\cos(\tilde{\theta}[1] - (2\pi/16))$, $\beta = 2\cos(2\pi/16)$, and $\gamma = -1$.

6.38. (a)

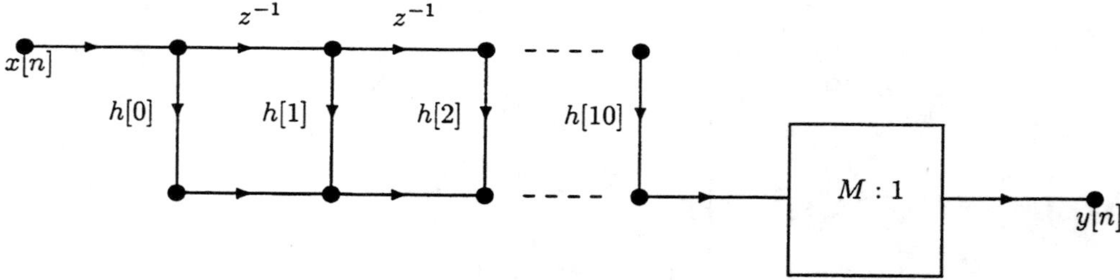

$M(N+1)$ multiplies per output sample; MN adds per output sample.

(b)

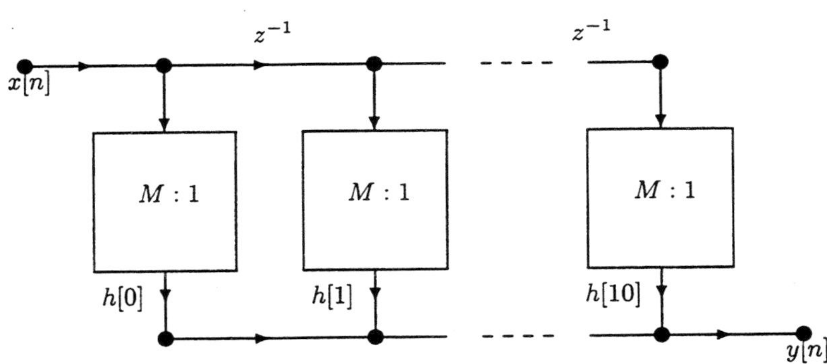

$N+1$ multiplies per output sample; N adds per output sample. The number of computations has been reduced by a factor of M in both adds and multiplies.

(c)

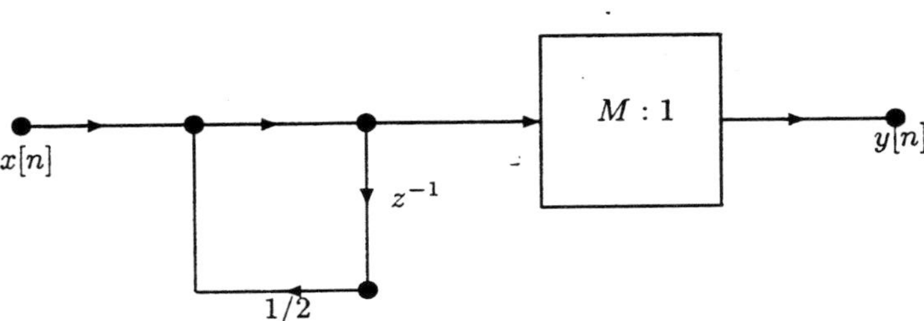

The total computation can not be reduced because to compute the value of any given output sample, the previous output value must be known.

(d)

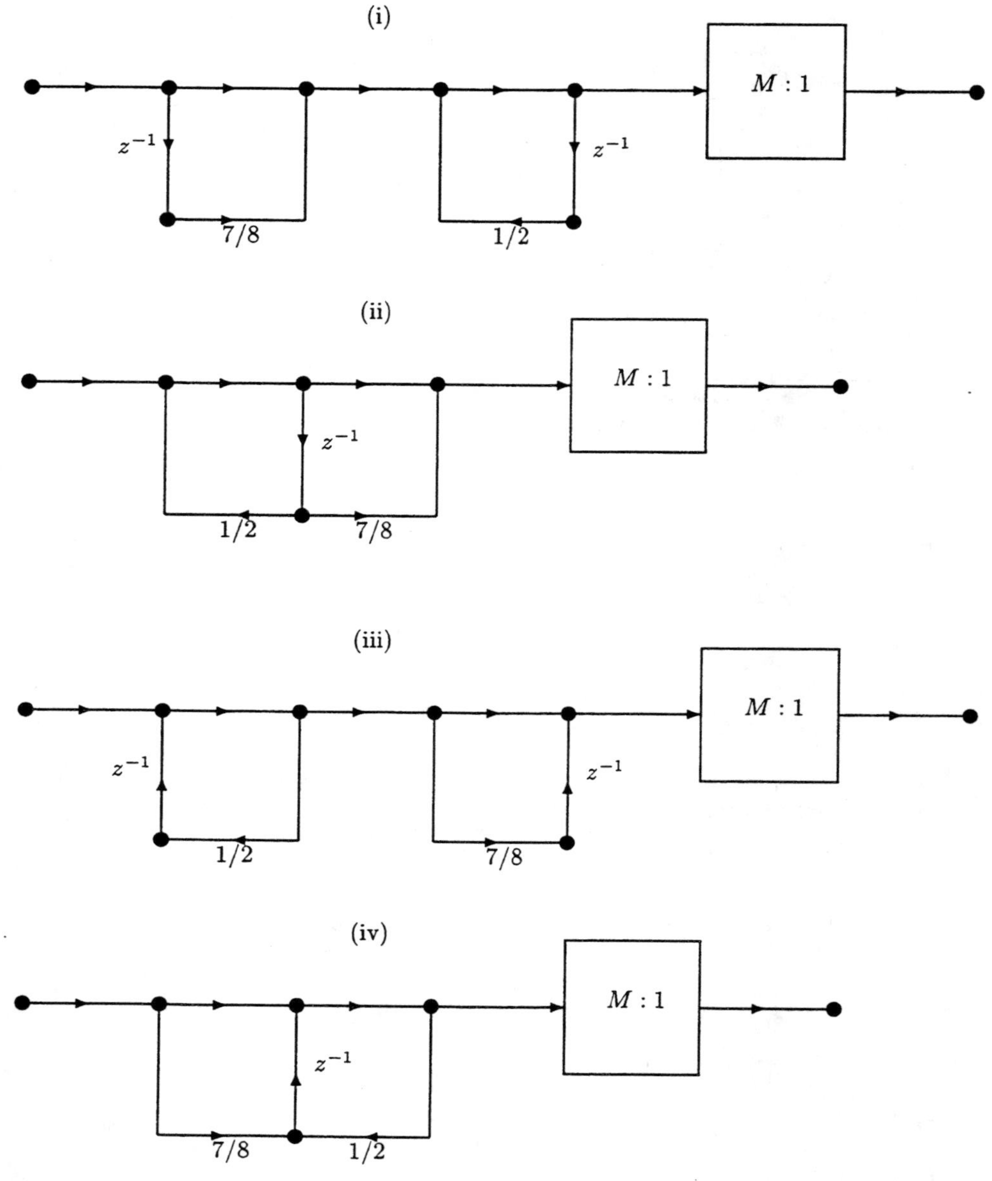

Only direct form II (ii) can be implemented more efficiently by commuting operations with the downsamplers.

6.39. Since each section is 3.4cm long, it takes

$$\frac{3.4\text{cm}}{3.4\frac{\text{cm}}{\text{sec}} \cdot 10^4} = 10^{-4}\text{sec}$$

to traverse one section. Since the sampling rate is 20kHz ($T_s = 0.5 \cdot 10^{-4}$sec), it takes two sampling intervals to traverse a section. The entire system is linear and so the forward going and backward going waves add at a boundary. Let

$$\alpha_{kn} = \frac{A_n - A_k}{A_n + A_k}$$

(from A_k into A_n); then $\alpha_{kn} = -\alpha_{nk}$ and we get:

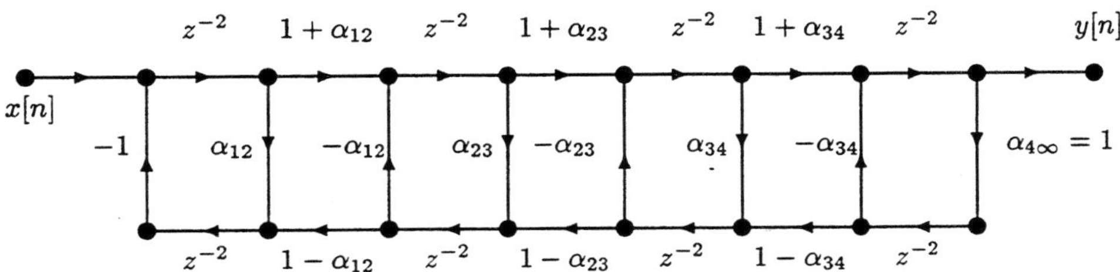

6.40. (a) For rounding:

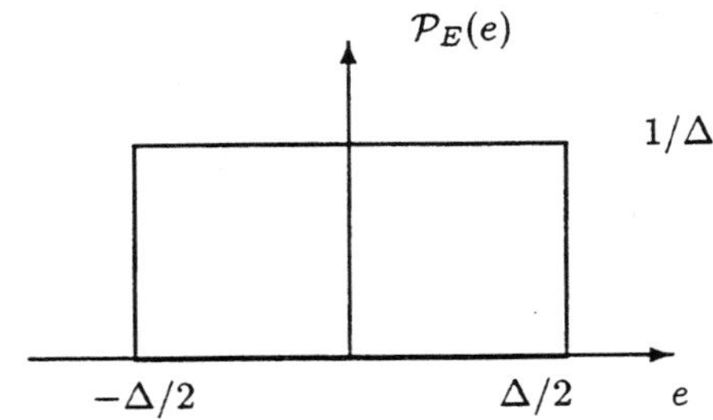

$$m_e = \frac{1}{\Delta}\int_{\frac{-\Delta}{2}}^{\frac{\Delta}{2}} e\,de = \frac{1}{\Delta}\frac{e^2}{2}\Big]_{\frac{-\Delta}{2}}^{\frac{\Delta}{2}} = 0$$

$$\sigma_e^2 = \frac{1}{\Delta}\int_{\frac{-\Delta}{2}}^{\frac{\Delta}{2}} e^2\,de = \frac{e^3}{3\Delta}\Big]_{\frac{-\Delta}{2}}^{\frac{\Delta}{2}} = \frac{\Delta^2}{12}.$$

(b) For truncation:

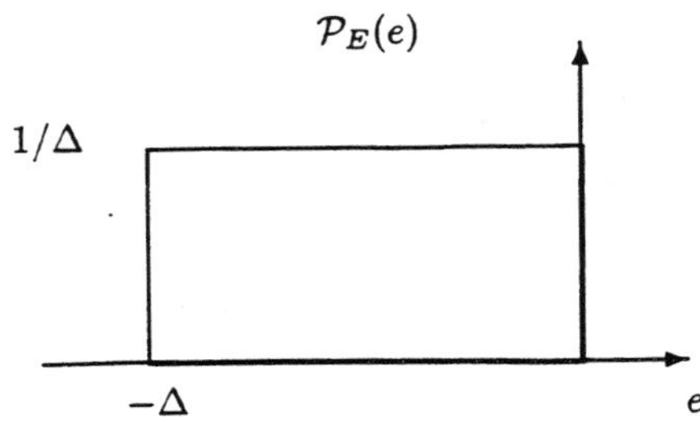

$$m_e = \frac{1}{\Delta}\int_{-\Delta}^{0} e\,de = \frac{1}{\Delta}\left.\frac{e^2}{2}\right]_{-\Delta}^{0} = \frac{-\Delta}{2}$$

$$\sigma_e^2 = \frac{1}{\Delta}\int_{-\Delta}^{0} e^2\,de - \frac{\Delta^2}{4} = \left.\frac{e^3}{3\Delta}\right]_{-\Delta}^{0} - \frac{\Delta^2}{4} = \frac{\Delta^2}{12}.$$

6.41. Since the system is linear, $y[n]$ is the sum of the outputs due to $x_1[n]$ and $x_2[n]$. Therefore

$$\begin{aligned} y[n] &= \sum_{k=-\infty}^{\infty} h_1[k]x_1[n-k] + \sum_{k=-\infty}^{\infty} h_2[k]x_2[n-k] \\ &= y_1[n] + y_2[n]. \end{aligned}$$

The correlation between $y_1[n]$ and $y_2[n]$ is

$$\begin{aligned} E\{y_1[m]y_2[n]\} &= E\left\{\sum_{\ell=-\infty}^{\infty} h_1[\ell]x_1[m-\ell] \cdot \sum_{k=-\infty}^{\infty} h_2[k]x_2[n-k]\right\} \\ &= \sum_{\ell=-\infty}^{\infty}\sum_{k=-\infty}^{\infty} h_1[\ell]h_2[k]E\{x_1[m-\ell]x_2[n-k]\} \end{aligned}$$

If $x_1[n]$ and $x_2[n]$ are uncorrelated, $E\{x_1[m-\ell]x_2[n-k]\} = 0$; hence, $E\{y_1[m]y_2[n]\} = 0$. Therefore, $y_1[n]$ and $y_2[n]$ are uncorrelated.

6.42. (a) The linear noise model for each system is drawn below.

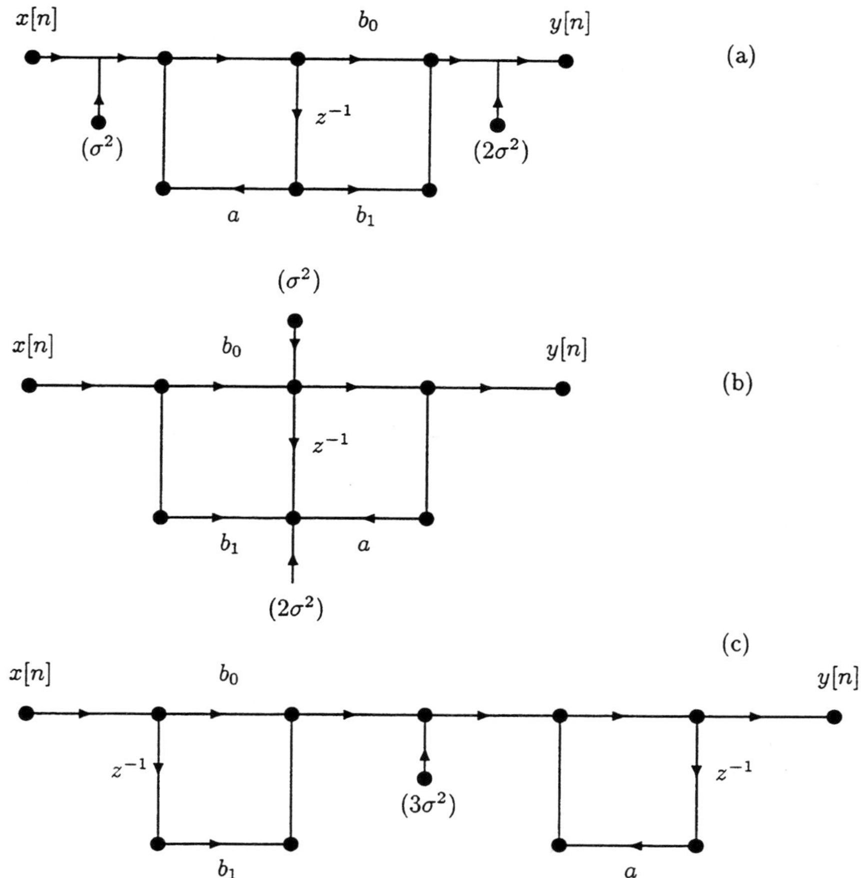

(b) Clearly (a) and (c) are different. Thus the answer is either (a) and (b) or (b) and (c). If we take (b) apart, we get

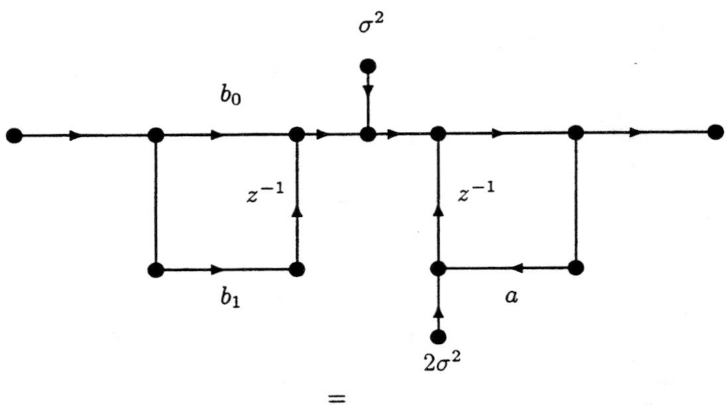

=

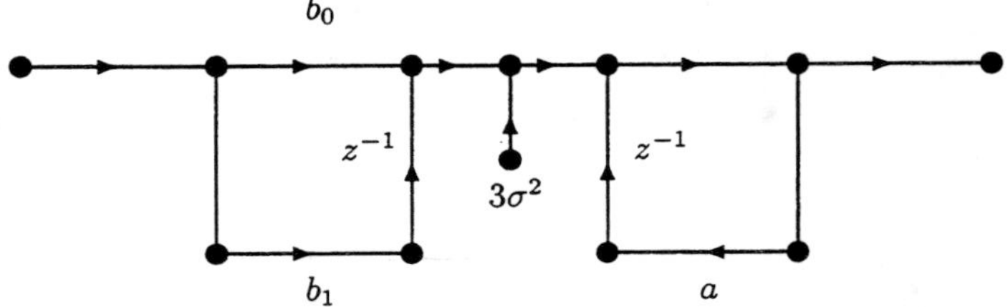

We see that the noise all goes through the poles. Note that the $1\sigma^2$ source sees a system function $(1 - az^{-1})^{-1}$ while the $2\sigma^2$ source sees $z^{-1}/(1 - az^{-1})$. However, the delay (z^{-1}) does not affect the average power. Hence, the answer is (b) and (c).

(c) For network (c),

$$\sigma_f^2 = 3\sigma^2 \sum_{n=0}^{\infty} (a^n)^2 = \frac{3\sigma^2}{1 - a^2},$$

or using the frequency domain formula,

$$\begin{aligned}
\sigma_f^2 &= 3\sigma^2 \frac{1}{2\pi j} \oint \frac{1}{1 - az^{-1}} \cdot \frac{1}{1 - az} \frac{dz}{z} \\
&= 3\sigma^2 \frac{1}{2\pi j} \oint \frac{dz}{(z - a)(1 - az)} \\
&= \frac{3\sigma^2}{1 - a^2}.
\end{aligned}$$

For network (a),

$$H(z) = \frac{b_0 + b_1 z^{-1}}{1 - az^{-1}}$$

$$h[n] = b_0 \delta[n] + (b_0 + \frac{b_1}{a}) a^n u[n]$$

- Time domain calculation:

$$\sigma_f^2 = 2\sigma^2 + \sigma^2 \sum_n h^2[n]$$

$$= \; 2\sigma^2 + \sigma^2 \left(b_0^2 + \left(b_0 + \frac{b_1}{a}\right)^2 \underbrace{\sum_{n=1}^{\infty} a^{2n}}_{\frac{a^2}{1-a^2}} \right)$$

$$= \; 2\sigma^2 + \sigma^2 \left(b_0^2 + \frac{(ab_0 + b_1)^2}{1-a^2} \right).$$

- Frequency domain calculation:

$$\sum_n h^2[n] \; = \; \frac{1}{2\pi j} \oint H(z)H(z^{-1}) \frac{dz}{z}$$

$$= \; \sum \left(\text{residues of } \frac{H(z)H(z^{-1})}{z} \text{inside unit circle} \right).$$

$$\frac{H(z)H(z^{-1})}{z} \; = \; \frac{(b_0 + b_1 z^{-1})(b_0 + b_1 z)}{(z-a)(1-az)} \frac{z}{z}$$

$$= \; \frac{(b_0 z + b_1)(b_0 + b_1 z)}{z(z-a)(1-az)}.$$

$$\text{residue } (z=0) = \frac{-b_1 b_0}{a}$$

$$\text{residue } (z=a) = \frac{(b_0 a + b_1)(b_0 + b_1 a)}{a(1-a^2)} = \frac{b_0^2 a + b_1^2 a + b_1 b_0 + b_1 b_0 a^2}{a(1-a^2)}.$$

$$\oint H(z)H(z^{-1}) \frac{dz}{z} \; = \; \frac{b_0^2 a + b_1^2 a + b_1 b_0 + b_1 b_0 a^2 - b_1 b_0 + b_1 b_0 a^2}{a(1-a^2)}$$

$$= \; \frac{b_0^2 + b_1^2 + 2b_0 b_1 a}{1-a^2}$$

$$= \; b_0^2 + \frac{(ab_0 + b_1)^2}{1-a^2}$$

6.43. (a)

$$y[n] = \frac{1}{4} y[n-1] + \frac{1}{2}, \quad n \geq 0$$

$$y[n] = \frac{1}{2} \sum_{i=0}^{n} \left(\frac{1}{4}\right)^i = \frac{1}{2} \frac{1 - \left(\frac{1}{4}\right)^{n+1}}{\frac{3}{4}}$$

For large n, $y[n] = (1/2)/(3/4) = 2/3$.

(b) Working from the difference equation and quantizating after multiplication, it is easy to see that, in the quantized case, $y[0] = 1/2$ and $y[n] = 5/8$ for $n \geq 1$. In the unquantized case, the output monotonically approaches $2/3$.

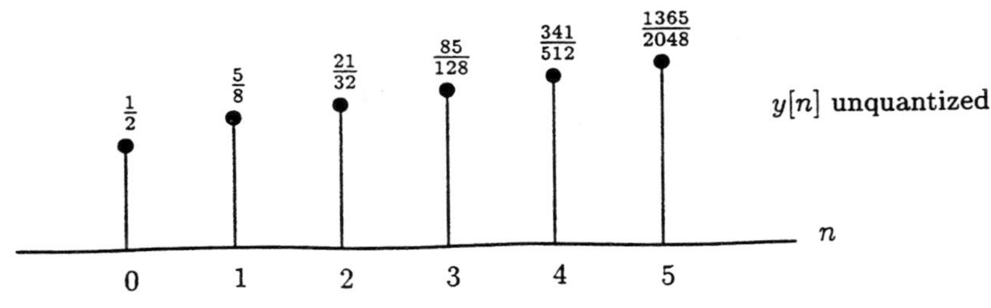

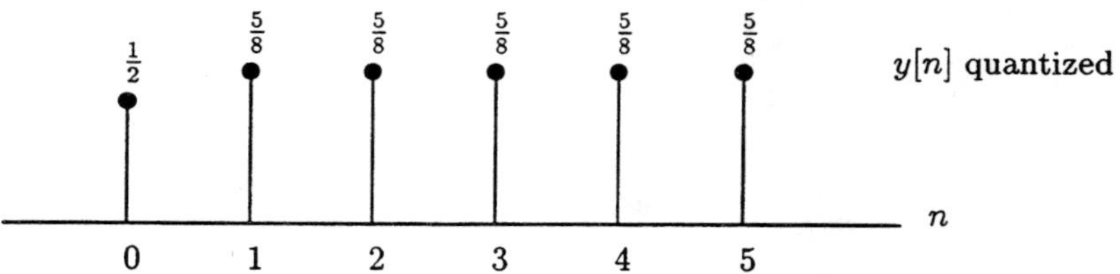

(c) The system diagram is direct form II:

$$H(e^{j\omega}) = \frac{1 + e^{-j\omega}}{1 - \frac{1}{4}e^{-j\omega}}$$

$$X(e^{j\omega}) = \frac{\frac{1}{2}}{1 + e^{-j\omega}}$$

So

$$Y(e^{j\omega}) = H(e^{j\omega})X(e^{j\omega}) = \frac{\frac{1}{2}}{1 - \frac{1}{4}e^{-j\omega}}$$

which implies that $y[n] = (1/2)(1/4)^n$, which approaches 0 as n grows large.
To find the quantized output (working from the difference equation): $y[0] = 1/2$, $y[1] = 1/8$, and $y[n] = 0$ for $n \geq 2$.

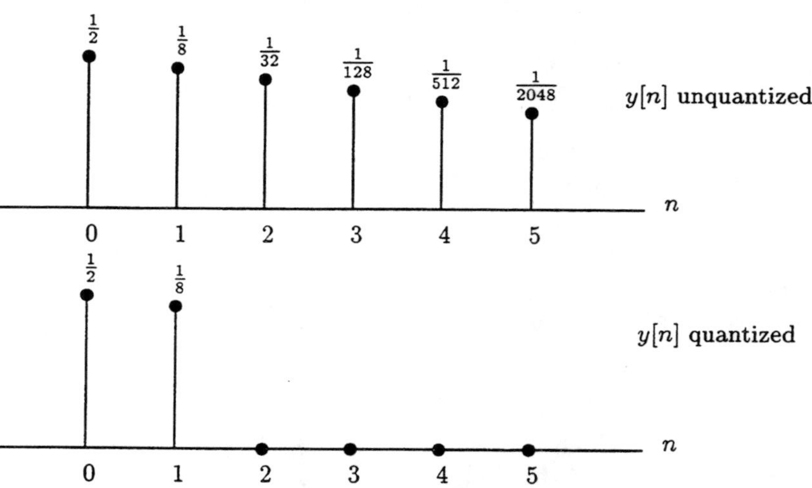

6.44. (a) To check for stability, we look at the poles location. The poles are located at

$$z \approx 0.52 + 0.84j \text{ and } z \approx 0.52 - 0.84j.$$

Note that

$$|z|^2 \approx 0.976 < 1.$$

The poles are inside the unit circle, therefore the system function is stable.

(b) If the coefficients are rounded to the nearest tenth, we have

$$1.04 \rightarrow 1.0 \text{ and } 0.98 \rightarrow 1.0.$$

Now the poles are at

$$z = \frac{1 - j\sqrt{3}}{2} \text{ and } z = \frac{1 - j\sqrt{3}}{2}.$$

Note that now,

$$|z|^2 = 1.$$

The poles are on the unit circle, therefore the system is not stable.

6.45. The flow graphs for networks 1 and 2 respectively are:

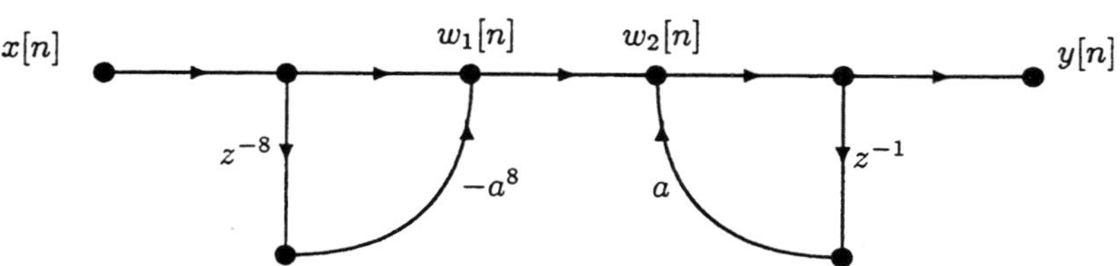

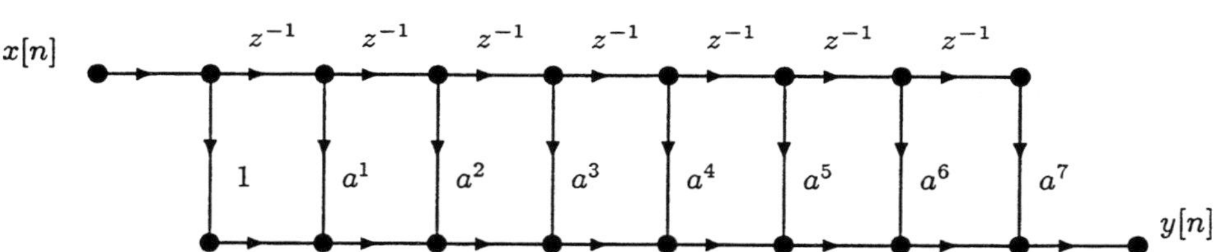

(a) For Network 1, we have:

$$\begin{aligned} w_1[n] &= x[n] - a^8 x[n-8] \\ w_2[n] &= ay[n-1] + w_1[n] \\ y[n] &= w_2[n] \end{aligned}$$

Taking the $Z-$transform of the above equations and combining terms, we get:

$$Y(z)(1 - az^{-1}) = (1 - a^8 z^{-8})X(z)$$

That is:

$$H(z) = \frac{1 - a^8 z^{-8}}{1 - az^{-1}}.$$

For Network 2, we have:

$$y[n] = x[n] + ax[n-1] + a^2 x[n-2] + ... + a^7 x[n-7].$$

Taking the $Z-$transform, we get:

$$Y(z) = (1 + az^{-1} + a^2z^{-2} + ... + a^7z^{-7})X(z).$$

So:

$$H(z) = 1 + az^{-1} + a^2z^{-2} + ... + a^7z^{-7} = \frac{1 - a^8z^{-8}}{1 - az^{-1}}.$$

(b) Network 1:

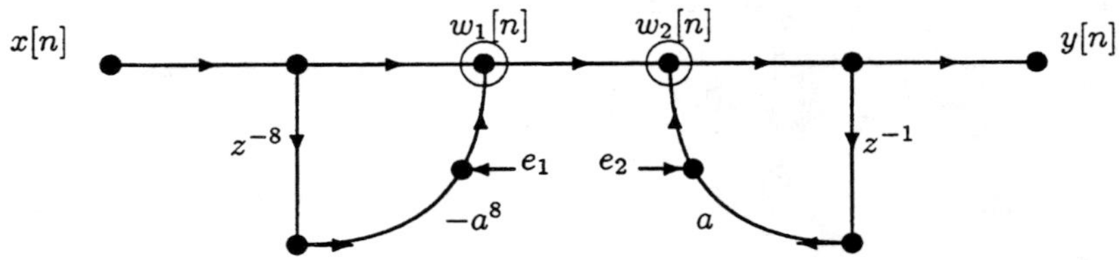

Network 2:

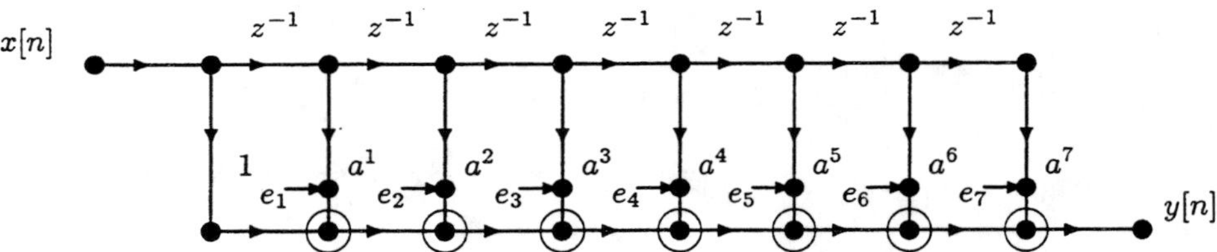

(c) The nodes are circled on the figures in part (b).

(d) In order to avoid overflow in the system, each node in the network must be constrained to have a magnitude less than 1. That is if $w_k[n]$ denotes the value of the kth node variable and $h_k[n]$ denotes the impulse response from the input $x[n]$ to the node variable $w_k[n]$, a sufficient condition for $|w_k[n]| < 1$ is

$$x_{max} < \frac{1}{\sum_{m=-\infty}^{\infty} |h_k[m]|}.$$

In this problem, we need to make sure overflow does not occur in each node, i.e. we need to take the tighter bound on x_{max}. For network 1, the impulse response from $w_2[n]$ to $y[n]$ is $a^n u[n]$, therefore the condition to avoid overflow from that node to the output is

$$w_{max} < 1 - |a|.$$

Where we assumed that $|a| < 1$. The transfer function from $x[n]$ to $w_1[n]$ is $1 - a^8z^{-8}$, therefore to avoid overflow at that node we need:

$$w_1[n] < x_{max}(1 - a^8) < 1 - |a|.$$

We thus conclude that to avoid overflow in network 1, we need:

$$x_{max} < \frac{1 - |a|}{1 - a^8}.$$

Now, for network 2, the transfer function from input to output is given by $\delta[n] + a\delta[n-1] + a^2\delta[n-2] + ... + a^7\delta[n-7]$, therefore to avoid overflow, we need:

$$x_{max} < \frac{1}{1 + |a| + a^2 + ... + |a|^7}.$$

(e) For network 1, the total noise power is $\frac{2\sigma_e^2}{1-|a|}$. For network 2, the total noise power is $7\sigma_e^2$. For network 1 to have less noise power than network 2, we need

$$\frac{2\sigma_e^2}{1 - |a|} < 7\sigma_e^2.$$

That is:

$$|a| < \frac{5}{7}.$$

The largest value of $|a|$ such that the noise in network 1 is less than network 2 is therefore $\frac{5}{7}$.

Solutions – Chapter 7

Filter Design Techniques

7.1. Using the partial fraction technique, we see

$$H_c(s) = \frac{s+a}{(s+a)^2+b^2} = \frac{0.5}{s+a+jb} + \frac{0.5}{s+a-jb}$$

Now we can use the Laplace transform pair

$$e^{-\alpha t}u(t) \longleftrightarrow \frac{1}{s+\alpha}$$

to get

$$h_c(t) = \frac{1}{2}\left(e^{-(a+jb)t} + e^{-(a-jb)t}\right)u(t).$$

(a) Therefore,

$$\begin{aligned} h_1[n] &= h_c(nT) = \frac{1}{2}\left[e^{-(a+jb)nT} + e^{-(a-jb)nT}\right]u[n] \\ H_1(z) &= \frac{0.5}{1-e^{-(a+jb)T}z^{-1}} + \frac{0.5}{1-e^{-(a-jb)T}z^{-1}}, \quad |z| > e^{-aT} \end{aligned}$$

(b) Since

$$s_c(t) = \int_{-\infty}^{t} h_c(\tau)d\tau \longleftrightarrow \frac{H_c(s)}{s} = S_c(s)$$

we get

$$S_c(s) = \frac{s+a}{s(s+a+jb)(s+a-jb)} = \frac{A_1}{s} + \frac{A_2}{s+a+jb} + \frac{A_2^*}{s+a-jb}$$

where

$$A_1 = \frac{a}{a^2+b^2}, \qquad A_2 = -\frac{0.5}{a+jb}$$

Though the system $h_2[n]$ is related by step invariance to $h_c(t)$, the signal $s_2[n]$ is related to $s_c(t)$ by impulse invariance. Therefore, we know the poles of the partial fraction expansion of $S_c(s)$ above must transform as $z_k = e^{s_k T}$, and we can find

$$S_2(z) = \frac{A_1}{1-z^{-1}} + \frac{A_2}{1-e^{-(a+jb)T}z^{-1}} + \frac{A_2^*}{1-e^{-(a-jb)T}z^{-1}}$$

Now, since the relationship between the step response and the impulse response is

$$s_2[n] = \sum_{k=-\infty}^{n} h_2[k] = \sum_{k=-\infty}^{\infty} h_2[k]u[n-k] = h_2[n] * u[n]$$

$$S_2(z) = \frac{H_2(z)}{1-z^{-1}}$$

We can finally solve for $H_2(z)$

$$\begin{aligned} H_2(z) &= S_2(z)(1-z^{-1}) \\ &= A_1 + A_2\frac{1-z^{-1}}{1-e^{-(a+jb)T}z^{-1}} + A_2^*\frac{1-z^{-1}}{1-e^{-(a-jb)T}z^{-1}}, \quad |z| > e^{-aT} \end{aligned}$$

where A_1 and A_2 are as given above.

(c)

$$\begin{aligned} s_1[n] &= \sum_{k=-\infty}^{n} h_1[k] = \frac{1}{2}\sum_{k=0}^{n}\left(e^{-(a+jb)kT} + e^{-(a-jb)kT}\right) \\ &= \frac{1}{2}\left[\frac{1-e^{-(a+jb)(n+1)T}}{1-e^{-(a+jb)T}} + \frac{1-e^{-(a-jb)(n+1)T}}{1-e^{-(a-jb)T}}\right]u[n] \\ &= \left[B_1 + B_2 e^{-(a+jb)Tn} + B_2^* e^{-(a-jb)Tn}\right]u[n] \end{aligned}$$

where

$$B_1 = \frac{1-e^{-aT}\cos bT}{1-2e^{-aT}\cos bT + e^{-2aT}}, \qquad B_2 = -\frac{e^{-(a+jb)T}}{1-e^{-(a+jb)T}}$$

¿From this we can see that

$$\begin{aligned} S_1(z) &= \frac{B_1}{1-z^{-1}} + \frac{B_2}{1-e^{-(a+jb)T}z^{-1}} + \frac{B_2^*}{1-e^{-(a-jb)T}z^{-1}} \\ &\neq S_2(z) \end{aligned}$$

since the partial fraction constants are different. Therefore, $s_1[n] \neq s_2[n]$, the two step responses are not equal.

Taking the inverse z-transform of $H_2(z)$

$$\begin{aligned} h_2[n] &= A_1\delta[n] + A_2\left[e^{-(a+jb)Tn}u[n] - e^{-(a+jb)T(n-1)}u[n-1]\right] \\ &\quad + A_2^*\left[e^{-(a-jb)Tn}u[n] - e^{-(a-jb)T(n-1)}u[n-1]\right] \end{aligned}$$

where A_1 and A_2 are as defined earlier. By comparing $h_1[n]$ and $h_2[n]$ one sees that $h_1[n] \neq h_2[n]$.

The overall idea this problem illustrates is that a filter designed with impulse invariance is different from a filter designed with step invariance.

7.2. Recall that $\Omega = \omega/T_d$.

(a) Then

$$\begin{aligned} &0.89125 \leq |H(j\Omega)| \leq 1, \quad 0 \leq |\Omega| \leq 0.2\pi/T_d \\ &|H(j\Omega)| \leq 0.17783, \qquad 0.3\pi/T_d \leq |\Omega| \leq \pi/T_d \end{aligned}$$

The plot of the tolerance scheme is

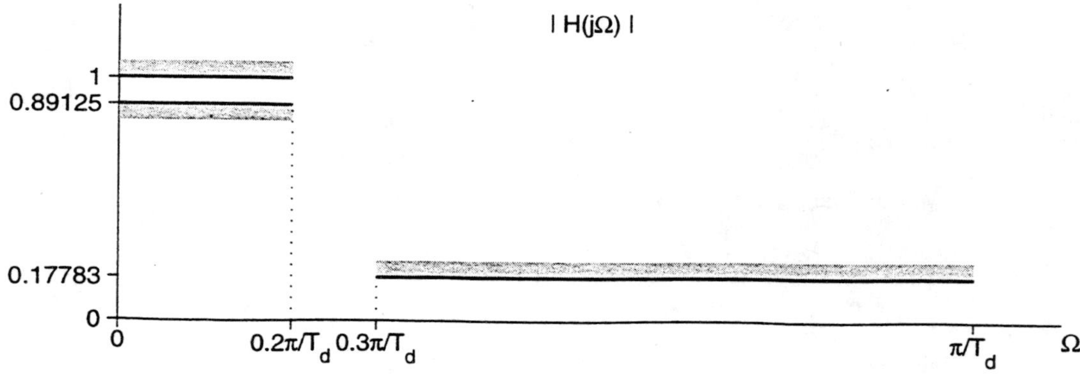

(b) As in the book's example, since the Butterworth frequency response is monotonic, we can solve

$$|H_c(j0.2\pi/T_d)|^2 = \frac{1}{1+\left(\dfrac{0.2\pi}{\Omega_c T_d}\right)^{2N}} = (0.89125)^2$$

$$|H_c(j0.3\pi/T_d)|^2 = \frac{1}{1+\left(\dfrac{0.3\pi}{\Omega_c T_d}\right)^{2N}} = (0.17783)^2$$

to get $\Omega_c T_d = 0.70474$ and $N = 5.8858$. Rounding up to $N = 6$ yields $\Omega_c T_d = 0.7032$ to meet the specifications.

(c) We see that the poles of the magnitude-squared function are again evenly distributed around a circle of radius 0.7032. Therefore, $H_c(s)$ is formed from the left half-plane poles of the magnitude-squared function, and the result is the same for any value of T_d. Correspondingly, $H(z)$ does not depend on T_d.

7.3. We are given the digital filter constraints

$$\begin{aligned} 1-\delta_1 \le |H(e^{j\omega})| \le 1+\delta_1, &\quad 0 \le |\omega| \le \omega_p \\ |H(e^{j\omega})| \le \delta_2, &\quad \omega_s \le |\omega| \le \pi \end{aligned}$$

and the analog filter constraints

$$\begin{aligned} 1-\hat{\delta}_1 \le |H_c(j\Omega)| \le 1, &\quad 0 \le |\Omega| \le \Omega_p \\ |H_c(j\Omega)| \le \hat{\delta}_2, &\quad \Omega_s \le |\Omega| \end{aligned}$$

(a) If we divide the digital frequency specifications by $(1+\delta_1)$ we get

$$\begin{aligned} 1-\hat{\delta}_1 &= \frac{1-\delta_1}{1+\delta_1} \\ \hat{\delta}_1 &= \frac{2\delta_1}{1+\delta_1} \\ \hat{\delta}_2 &= \frac{\delta_2}{1+\delta_1} \end{aligned}$$

(b) Solving the equations in Part (a) for δ_1 and δ_2, we find

$$\begin{aligned} \delta_1 &= \frac{\hat{\delta}_1}{2-\hat{\delta}_1} \\ \delta_2 &= \frac{2\hat{\delta}_2}{2-\hat{\delta}_1} \end{aligned}$$

In the example, we were given

$$\begin{aligned} \hat{\delta}_1 &= 1-0.89125 = 0.10875 \\ \hat{\delta}_2 &= 0.17783 \end{aligned}$$

Plugging in these values into the equations for δ_1 and δ_2, we find

$$\begin{aligned} \delta_1 &= 0.0575 \\ \delta_2 &= 0.1881 \end{aligned}$$

The filter $H'(z)$ satisfies the discrete-time filter specifications where $H'(z) = (1+\delta_1)H(z)$ and $H(z)$ is the filter designed in the example. Thus,

$$\begin{aligned} H'(z) &= 1.0575 \left[\frac{0.2871 - 0.4466z^{-1}}{1 - 1.2971z^{-1} + 0.6949z^{-2}} + \frac{-2.1428 + 1.1455z^{-1}}{1 - 1.0691z^{-1} + 0.3699z^{-2}} \right. \\ &\quad \left. + \frac{1.8557 - 0.6303z^{-1}}{1 - 0.9972z^{-1} + 0.2570z^{-2}} \right] \\ &= \frac{0.3036 - 0.4723z^{-1}}{1 - 1.2971z^{-1} + 0.6949z^{-2}} + \frac{-2.2660 + 1.2114z^{-1}}{1 - 1.0691z^{-1} + 0.3699z^{-2}} \\ &\quad + \frac{1.9624 - 0.6665z^{-1}}{1 - 0.9972z^{-1} + 0.2570z^{-2}} \end{aligned}$$

(c) Following the same procedure used in part (b) we find

$$\begin{aligned} H'(z) &= 1.0575 \left[\frac{0.0007378(1+z^{-1})^6}{(1 - 1.2686z^{-1} + 0.7051z^{-2})(1 - 1.0106z^{-1} + 0.3583z^{-2})} \right. \\ &\quad \left. \times \frac{1}{1 - 0.9044z^{-1} + 0.2155z^{-2}} \right] \\ &= \frac{0.0007802(1+z^{-1})^6}{(1 - 1.2686z^{-1} + 0.7051z^{-2})(1 - 1.0106z^{-1} + 0.3583z^{-2})} \\ &\quad \times \frac{1}{1 - 0.9044z^{-1} + 0.2155z^{-2}} \end{aligned}$$

7.4. (a) In the impulse invariance design, the poles transform as $z_k = e^{s_k T_d}$ and we have the relationship

$$\frac{1}{s+a} \longleftrightarrow \frac{T_d}{1 - e^{-aT_d}z^{-1}}$$

Therefore,

$$\begin{aligned} H_c(s) &= \frac{2/T_d}{s+0.1} - \frac{1/T_d}{s+0.2} \\ &= \frac{1}{s+0.1} - \frac{0.5}{s+0.2} \end{aligned}$$

The above solution is not unique due to the periodicity of $z = e^{j\omega}$. A more general answer is

$$H_c(s) = \frac{2/T_d}{s + \left(0.1 + j\frac{2\pi k}{T_d}\right)} - \frac{1/T_d}{s + \left(0.2 + j\frac{2\pi l}{T_d}\right)}$$

where k and l are integers.

(b) Using the inverse relationship for the bilinear transform,

$$z = \frac{1 + (T_d/2)s}{1 - (T_d/2)s}$$

we get

$$\begin{aligned} H_c(s) &= \frac{2}{1 - e^{-0.2}\left(\frac{1-s}{1+s}\right)} - \frac{1}{1 - e^{-0.4}\left(\frac{1-s}{1+s}\right)} \\ &= \frac{2(s+1)}{s(1+e^{-0.2}) + (1-e^{-0.2})} - \frac{(s+1)}{s(1+e^{-0.4}) + (1-e^{-0.4})} \\ &= \left(\frac{2}{1+e^{-0.2}}\right)\left(\frac{s+1}{s + \frac{1-e^{-0.2}}{1+e^{-0.2}}}\right) - \left(\frac{1}{1+e^{-0.4}}\right)\left(\frac{s+1}{s + \frac{1-e^{-0.4}}{1+e^{-0.4}}}\right) \end{aligned}$$

Since the bilinear transform does not introduce any ambiguity, the representation is unique.

7.5. (a) We must use the minimum specifications!

$$\begin{aligned}\delta &= 0.01\\ \Delta\omega &= 0.05\pi\\ \mathrm{A} &= -20\log_{10}\delta = 40\end{aligned}$$

$$M+1 = \frac{\mathrm{A}-8}{2.285\Delta\omega} + 1 = 90.2 \rightarrow 91$$

$$\beta = 0.5842(\mathrm{A}-21)^{0.4} + 0.07886(\mathrm{A}-21) = 3.395$$

(b) Since it is a linear phase filter with order 90, it has a delay of $90/2 = 45$ samples.

(c)

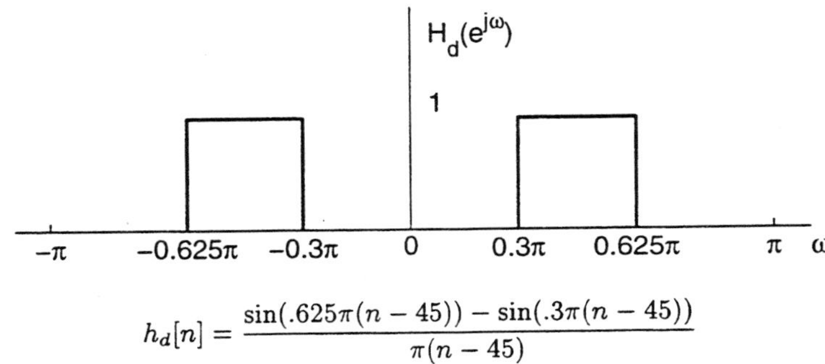

$$h_d[n] = \frac{\sin(.625\pi(n-45)) - \sin(.3\pi(n-45))}{\pi(n-45)}$$

7.6. (a) The Kaiser formulas say that a discontinuity of height 1 produces a peak error of δ. If a filter has a discontinuity of a different height the peak error should be scaled appropriately. This filter can be thought of as the sum of two filters. This first is a lowpass filter with a discontinuity of 1 and a peak error of δ. The second is a highpass filter with a discontinuity of 2 and a peak error of 2δ. In the region $0.3\pi \le |\omega| \le 0.475\pi$, the two peak errors add but must be less or equal to than 0.06.

$$\begin{aligned}\delta + 2\delta &\le 0.06\\ \delta_{\mathrm{max}} &= 0.02\end{aligned}$$

$$A = -20\log(0.02) = 33.9794$$

$$\beta = 0.5842(33.9794-21)^{0.4} + 0.07886(33.9794-21) = 2.65$$

(b) The transition width can be

$$\begin{aligned}\Delta\omega &= 0.3\pi - 0.2\pi\\ &= 0.1\pi \text{ rad}\end{aligned} \quad \textit{or} \quad \begin{aligned}\Delta\omega &= 0.525\pi - 0.475\pi\\ &= 0.05\pi \text{ rad}\end{aligned}$$

We must choose the smallest transition width so $\Delta\omega_{\mathrm{max}} = 0.05\pi$ rad. The corresponding value of M is

$$M = \frac{33.9794-8}{2.285(0.05\pi)} = 72.38 \rightarrow 73$$

7.7. Using the relation $\omega = \Omega T$, the passband cutoff frequency, ω_p, and the stopband cutoff frequency, ω_s, are found to be

$$\begin{aligned}\omega_p &= 2\pi(1000)10^{-4}\\ &= 0.2\pi \text{ rad}\\ \omega_s &= 2\pi(1100)10^{-4}\\ &= 0.22\pi \text{ rad}\end{aligned}$$

Therefore, the specifications for the discrete-time frequency response $H_d(e^{jw})$ are

$$\begin{aligned} 0.99 \le \left|H_d(e^{jw})\right| &\le 1.01, \qquad 0 \le |\omega| \le 0.20\pi \\ \left|H_d(e^{jw})\right| &\le 0.01, \qquad 0.22\pi \le |\omega| \le \pi \end{aligned}$$

7.8. Optimal Type I filters must have either $L+2$ or $L+3$ alternations. The filter is 9 samples long so its order is 8 and $L = M/2 = 4$. Thus, to be optimal, the filter must have either 6 or 7 alternations.

Filter 1:	6 alternations	Filter 2:	7 alternations
	Meets optimal conditions		Meets optimal conditions

7.9. Using the relation $\omega = \Omega T$, the cutoff frequency ω_c for the resulting discrete-time filter is

$$\begin{aligned} \omega_c &= \Omega_c T \\ &= [2\pi(1000)][0.0002] \\ &= 0.4\pi \text{ rad} \end{aligned}$$

7.10. Using the bilinear transform frequency mapping equation,

$$\begin{aligned} \omega_c &= 2\tan^{-1}\left(\frac{\Omega_c T}{2}\right) \\ &= 2\tan^{-1}\left(\frac{2\pi(2000)(0.4\times 10^{-3})}{2}\right) \\ &= 0.7589\pi \text{ rad} \end{aligned}$$

7.11. Using the relation $\omega = \Omega T$,

$$\begin{aligned} \Omega_c &= \frac{\omega_c}{T} \\ &= \frac{\pi/4}{0.0001} \\ &= 2500\pi \\ &= 2\pi(1250)\ \frac{\text{rad}}{\text{s}} \end{aligned}$$

7.12. Using the bilinear transform frequency mapping equation,

$$\begin{aligned} \Omega_c &= \frac{2}{T}\tan\left(\frac{\omega_c}{2}\right) \\ &= \frac{2}{0.001}\tan\left(\frac{\pi/2}{2}\right) \\ &= 2000\ \frac{\text{rad}}{\text{s}} \\ &= 2\pi(318.3)\ \frac{\text{rad}}{\text{s}} \end{aligned}$$

7.13. Using the relation $\omega = \Omega T$,

$$\begin{aligned} T &= \frac{\omega_c}{\Omega_c} \\ &= \frac{2\pi/5}{2\pi(4000)} \\ &= 50\ \mu\text{s} \end{aligned}$$

This value of T is unique. Although one can find other values of T that will alias the continuous-time frequency $\Omega_c = 2\pi(4000)$ rad/s to the discrete-time frequency $\omega_c = 2\pi/5$ rad, the resulting aliased filter will not be the ideal lowpass filter.

7.14. Using the bilinear transform frequency mapping equation,

$$\begin{aligned}\Omega_c &= \frac{2}{T}\tan\left(\frac{\omega_c + 2\pi k}{2}\right), \quad \text{k an integer} \\ &= \frac{2}{T}\tan\left(\frac{\omega_c}{2}\right)\end{aligned}$$

$$T = \frac{2}{2\pi(300)}\tan\left(\frac{3\pi/5}{2}\right) = 1.46 \text{ ms}$$

The only ambiguity in the above is the periodicity in ω. However, the periodicity of the tangent function "cancels" the ambiguity and so T is unique.

7.15. This filter requires a maximal passband error of $\delta_p = 0.05$, and a maximal stopband error of $\delta_s = 0.1$. Converting these values to dB gives

$$\begin{aligned}\delta p &= -26 \text{ dB} \\ \delta s &= -20 \text{ dB}\end{aligned}$$

This requires a window with a peak approximation error less than -26 dB. Looking in Table 7.1, the Hanning, Hamming, and Blackman windows meet this criterion.

Next, the minimum length L required for each of these filters can be found using the "approximate width of mainlobe" column in the table since the mainlobe width is about equal to the transition width. Note that the actual length of the filter is $L = M + 1$.

Hanning:

$$\begin{aligned}0.1\pi &= \frac{8\pi}{M} \\ M &= 80\end{aligned}$$

Hamming:

$$\begin{aligned}0.1\pi &= \frac{8\pi}{M} \\ M &= 80\end{aligned}$$

Blackman:

$$\begin{aligned}0.1\pi &= \frac{12\pi}{M} \\ M &= 120\end{aligned}$$

7.16. Since filters designed by the window method inherently have $\delta_1 = \delta_2$ we must use the smaller value for δ.

$$\begin{aligned}\delta &= 0.02 \\ A &= -20\log_{10}(0.02) = 33.9794\end{aligned}$$

$$\beta = 0.5842(33.9794 - 21)^{0.4} + 0.07886(33.9794 - 21) = 2.65$$

$$M = \frac{A - 8}{2.285\Delta\omega} = \frac{33.9794 - 8}{2.285(0.65\pi - 0.63\pi)} = 180.95 \rightarrow 181$$

7.17. Using the relation $\omega = \Omega T$, the specifications which should be used to design the prototype continuous-time filter are

$$\begin{aligned}-0.02 < H(j\Omega) < 0.02, &\quad 0 \le |\Omega| \le 2\pi(20) \\ 0.95 < H(j\Omega) < 1.05, &\quad 2\pi(30) \le |\Omega| \le 2\pi(70) \\ -0.001 < H(j\Omega) < 0.001, &\quad 2\pi(75) \le |\Omega| \le 2\pi(100)\end{aligned}$$

Note: Typically, a continuous-time filter's passband tolerance is between 1 and $1-\delta_1$ since historically most continuous-time filter approximation methods were developed for passive systems which have a gain less than one. If necessary, specifications using this convention can be obtained from the above specifications by scaling the magnitude response by $\frac{1}{1.05}$.

7.18. Using the bilinear transform frequency mapping equation,

$$\begin{aligned}\Omega_s &= \frac{2}{T}\tan\left(\frac{\omega_s}{2}\right) = \frac{2}{2\times 10^{-3}}\tan\left(\frac{0.2\pi}{2}\right) = 2\pi(51.7126)\ \frac{\text{rad}}{\text{s}} \\ \Omega_p &= \frac{2}{T}\tan\left(\frac{\omega_p}{2}\right) = \frac{2}{2\times 10^{-3}}\tan\left(\frac{0.3\pi}{2}\right) = 2\pi(81.0935)\ \frac{\text{rad}}{\text{s}}\end{aligned}$$

Thus, the specifications which should be used to design the prototype continuous-time filter are

$$\begin{aligned} |H_c(j\Omega)| < 0.04, &\qquad |\Omega| \leq 2\pi(51.7126) \\ 0.995 < |H_c(j\Omega)| < 1.005, &\qquad |\Omega| \geq 2\pi(81.0935)\end{aligned}$$

Note: Typically, a continuous-time filter's passband tolerance is between 1 and $1-\delta_1$ since historically most continuous-time filter approximation methods were developed for passive systems which have a gain less than one. If necessary, specifications using this convention can be obtained from the above specifications by scaling the magnitude response by $\frac{1}{1.005}$.

7.19. Using the relation $\omega = \Omega T$,

$$\begin{aligned} T &= \frac{\omega}{\Omega} \\ &= \frac{\pi/4}{2\pi(300)} \\ &= 417\ \mu\text{s}\end{aligned}$$

This choice of T is unique. It is possible to find other values of T that alias one of the given continuous-time band edges to its corresponding discrete-time band edge. However, this is the only value of T that maps both band edges correctly.

7.20. *True.* The bilinear transform is a frequency mapping. The value of $H(s)$ for a particular value of s gets mapped to $H(e^{j\omega})$ at a particular value of ω according to the mapping

$$s = \frac{2}{T_d}\left(\frac{1-e^{-j\omega}}{1+e^{-j\omega}}\right).$$

The continuous frequency axis gets warped onto the discrete-time frequency axis, but the magnitude values do not change. If $H(s)$ is constant for all s, then $H(e^{j\omega})$ must also be constant.

7.21. (a) Using the bilinear transform frequency mapping equation,

$$\Omega_p = \frac{2}{T_d}\tan\left(\frac{\omega_p}{2}\right)$$

we have

$$\begin{aligned} T_d &= \frac{2}{\Omega_p}\tan\left(\frac{\pi}{4}\right) \\ &= \frac{2}{\Omega_p}\end{aligned}$$

(b)

$$\omega_p = 2\tan^{-1}\left(\frac{\Omega_p T_d}{2}\right)$$

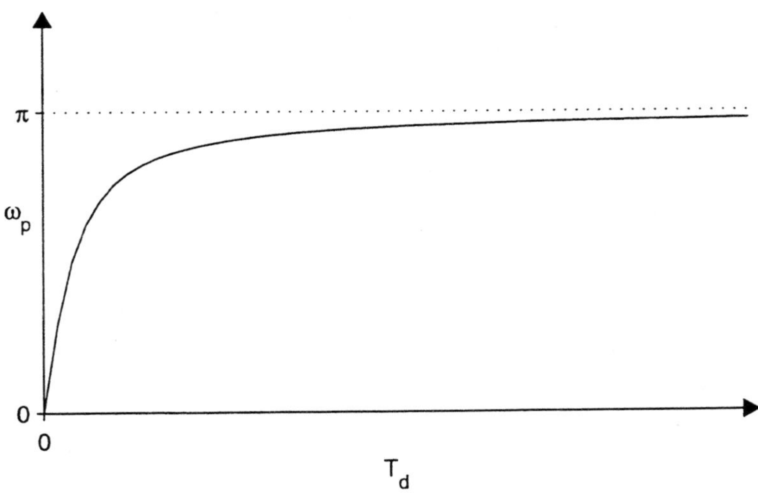

(c)

$$\begin{aligned} \omega_s &= 2\tan^{-1}\left(\frac{\Omega_s T_d}{2}\right) \\ \omega_p &= 2\tan^{-1}\left(\frac{\Omega_p T_d}{2}\right) \end{aligned}$$

$$\Delta\omega = \omega_s - \omega_p = 2\left[\tan^{-1}\left(\frac{\Omega_s T_d}{2}\right) - \tan^{-1}\left(\frac{\Omega_p T_d}{2}\right)\right]$$

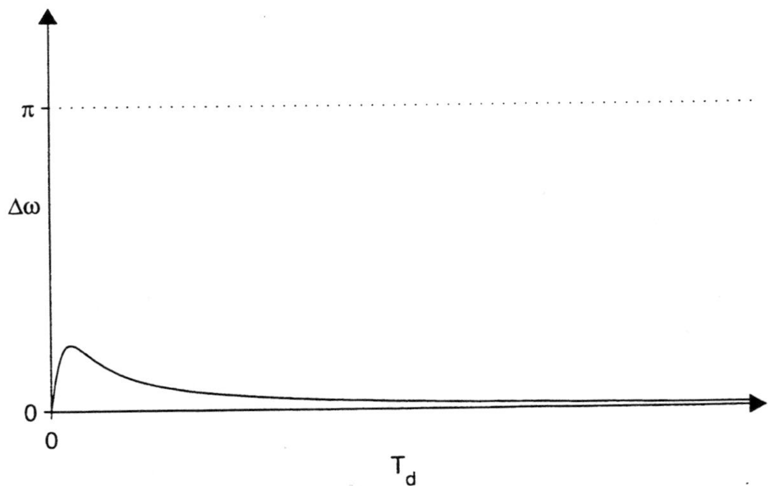

7.22. (a) Applying the bilinear transform yields

$$\begin{aligned} H(z) &= H_c(s)\,|_{s=\frac{2}{T_d}\left(\frac{1-z^{-1}}{1+z^{-1}}\right)} \\ &= \frac{T_d}{2}\left(\frac{1+z^{-1}}{1-z^{-1}}\right), \qquad |z|>1 \end{aligned}$$

which has the impulse response

$$h[n] = \frac{T_d}{2}\left(u[n] + u[n-1]\right)$$

(b) The difference equation is

$$y[n] = \frac{T_d}{2}(x[n] + x[n-1]) + y[n-1]$$

This system is not implementable since it has a pole on the unit circle and is therefore not stable.

(c) Since this system is not stable, it does not strictly have a frequency response. However, if we ignore this mathematical subtlety we get

$$\begin{aligned} H(e^{j\omega}) &= \frac{T_d}{2}\left(\frac{1+e^{-j\omega}}{1-e^{-j\omega}}\right) \\ &= \frac{T_d}{2}\left(\frac{e^{j\omega/2}+e^{-j\omega/2}}{e^{j\omega/2}-e^{-j\omega/2}}\right) \\ &= \frac{T_d}{2j}\cot(\omega/2) \end{aligned}$$

and since the Laplace transform evaluated along the $j\Omega$ axis is the continous-time Fourier transform we also have

$$H_c(j\Omega) = \frac{1}{j\Omega}$$

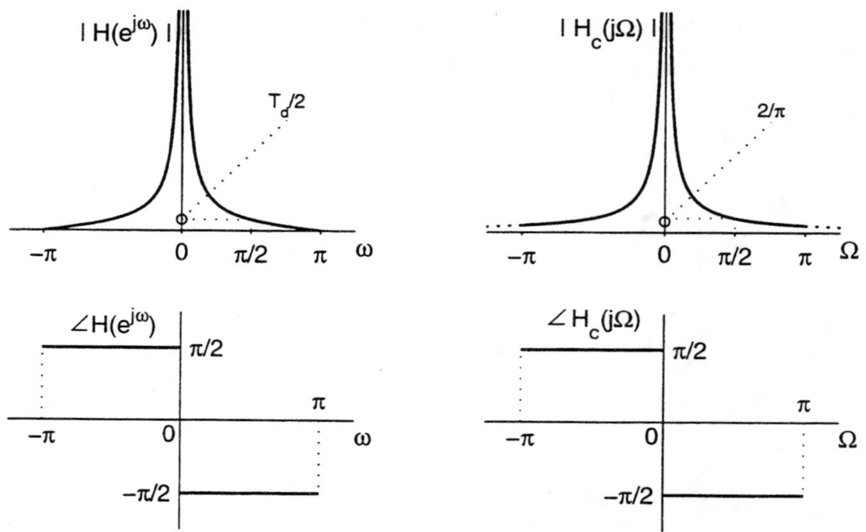

In general, we see that we will not be able to approximate the high frequencies, but we can approximate the lower frequencies if we choose $T_d = 4/\pi$.

(d) Applying the bilinear transform yields

$$\begin{aligned} G(z) &= H_c(s)\,|_{s=\frac{2}{T_d}\left(\frac{1-z^{-1}}{1+z^{-1}}\right)} \\ &= \frac{2}{T_d}\left[\frac{1-z^{-1}}{1+z^{-1}}\right], \qquad |z| > 1 \end{aligned}$$

which has the impulse response

$$\begin{aligned} g[n] &= \frac{2}{T_d}\left[(-1)^n u[n] - (-1)^{n-1}u[n-1]\right] \\ &= \frac{2}{T_d}\left[2(-1)^n u[n] - \delta[n]\right] \end{aligned}$$

(e) This system does not strictly have a frequency response either, due to the pole on the unit circle. However, ignoring this fact again we get

$$\begin{aligned} G(e^{j\omega}) &= \frac{2}{T_d}\left[\frac{1-e^{-j\omega}}{1+e^{-j\omega}}\right] \\ &= \frac{2}{T_d}\left(\frac{e^{j\omega/2}-e^{-j\omega/2}}{e^{j\omega/2}+e^{-j\omega/2}}\right) \\ &= \frac{2j}{T_d}\tan(\omega/2) \\ G(j\Omega) &= j\Omega \end{aligned}$$

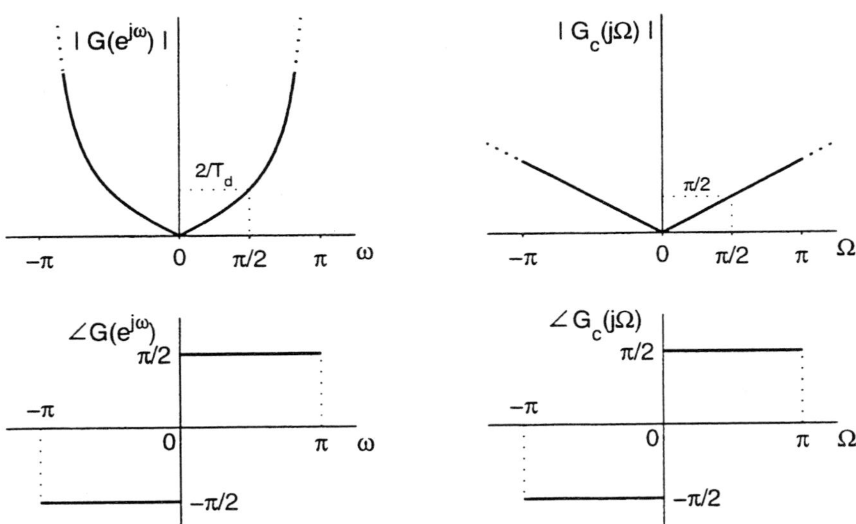

Again, we see that we will not be able to approximate the high frequencies, but we can approximate the lower frequencies if we choose $T_d = 4/\pi$.

(f) If the same value of T_d is used for each bilinear transform, then the two systems are inverses of each other, since then

$$H(e^{j\omega})G(e^{j\omega}) = 1$$

7.23. We start with $|H_c(j\Omega)|$,

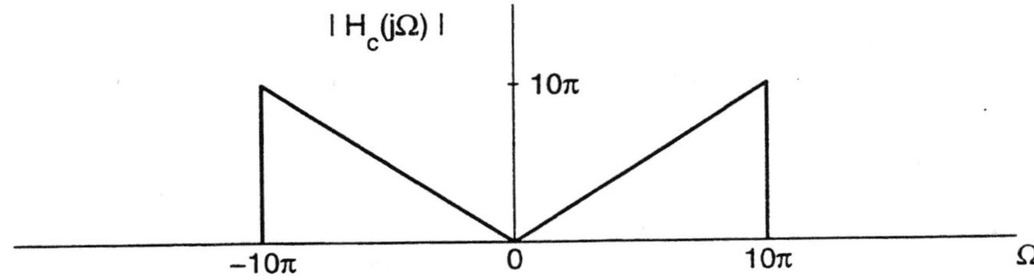

(a) By impulse invariance we scale the frequency axis by T_d to get

$$|H_1(e^{j\omega})| = \left|\sum_{k=-\infty}^{\infty} H_c\left(j\frac{\omega}{T_d} + j\frac{2\pi k}{T_d}\right)\right|$$

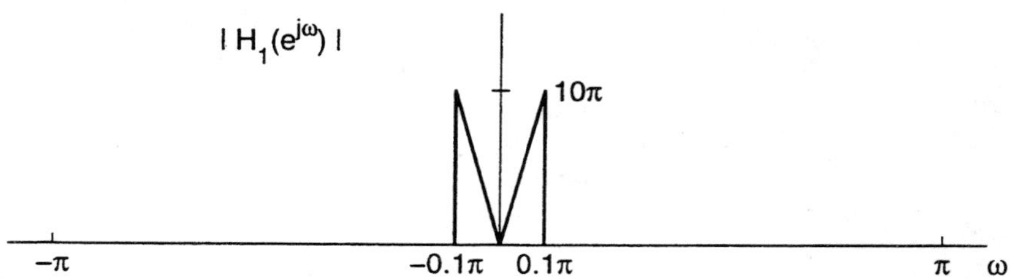

Then, to get the overall system response we scale the frequency axis by T and bandlimit the result according to the equation

$$|H_{\text{eff}_1}(j\Omega)| = \begin{cases} |H_1(e^{j\omega T})|, & |\Omega| < \frac{\pi}{T} \\ 0, & |\Omega| > \frac{\pi}{T} \end{cases}$$

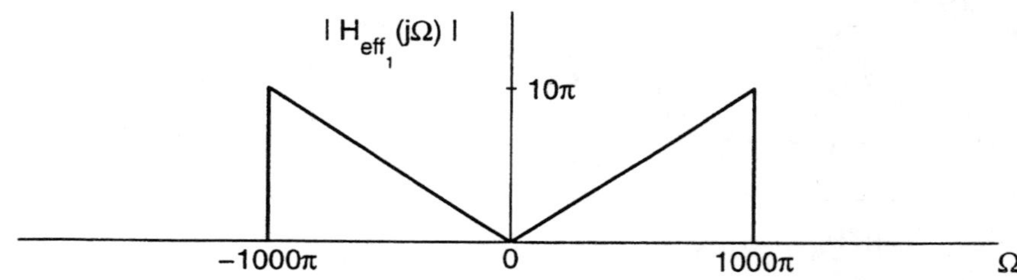

(b) Using the frequency mapping relationships of the bilinear transform,

$$\begin{aligned} \Omega &= \frac{2}{T_d} \tan\left(\frac{\omega}{2}\right), \\ \omega &= 2\tan^{-1}\left(\frac{\Omega T_d}{2}\right), \end{aligned}$$

we get

$$|H_2(e^{j\omega})| = \begin{cases} |\tan\left(\frac{\omega}{2}\right)|, & |\omega| < 2\tan^{-1}(10\pi) = 0.98\pi \\ 0, & \text{otherwise} \end{cases}$$

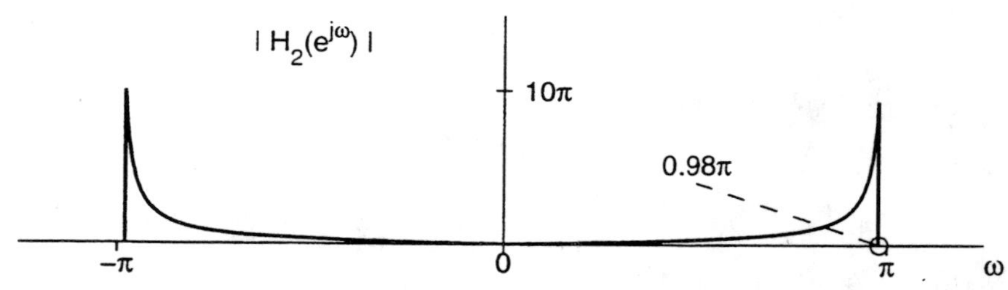

Then, to get the overall system response we scale the frequency axis by T and bandlimit the result according to the equation

$$|H_{\text{eff}_2}(j\Omega)| = \begin{cases} |H_2(e^{j\omega T})|, & |\Omega| < \frac{\pi}{T} \\ 0, & |\Omega| > \frac{\pi}{T} \end{cases}$$

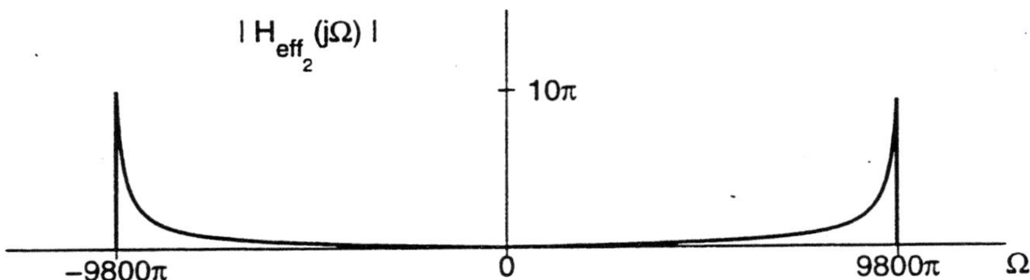

7.24. (a) Expanding the sum to see things more clearly, we get

$$\begin{aligned} H_c(s) &= \sum_{k=1}^{r} \frac{A_k}{(s-s_0)^k} + G_c(s) \\ &= \frac{A_1}{s-s_0} + \frac{A_2}{(s-s_0)^2} + \cdots + \frac{A_r}{(s-s_0)^r} + G_c(s) \end{aligned}$$

Now multiplying both sides by $(s-s_0)^r$ we get

$$(s-s_0)^r H_c(s) = A_1(s-s_0)^{r-1} + A_2(s-s_0)^{r-2} + \cdots + A_r + (s-s_0)^r G_c(s)$$

Evaluating both sides of the equal sign at $s = s_0$ gives us

$$A_r = (s-s_0)^r H_c(s)\,|_{s=s_0}$$

Note that $(s-s_0)^r G_c(s) = 0$ when $s = s_0$ because $G_c(s)$ has at most one pole at $s = s_0$.

Similarly, by taking the first derivative and evaluating at $s = s_0$ we get

$$\begin{aligned} \frac{d}{ds}\left[(s-s_0)^r H_c(s)\right] &= \sum_{k=1}^{r}(r-k)A_k(s-s_0)^{(r-k-1)} + \frac{d}{ds}\left[(s-s_0)^r G_c(s)\right] \\ &= (r-1)A_1(s-s_0)^{r-2} + (r-2)A_2(s-s_0)^{r-3} + \cdots + A_{r-1} + 0 + \frac{d}{ds}\left[(s-s_0)^r G_c(s)\right] \\ A_{r-1} &= \frac{d}{ds}\left[(s-s_0)^r H_c(s)\right]|_{s=s_0} \end{aligned}$$

This idea can be continued. By taking the $(r-k)$-th derivative and evaluating at $s = s_0$ we get the the general form

$$A_k = \frac{1}{(r-k)!}\left(\frac{d^{r-k}}{ds^{r-k}}\left[(s-s_0)^r H_c(s)\right]|_{s=s_0}\right)$$

(b) Using the following transform pair from a lookup table,

$$\frac{t^{k-1}}{(k-1)!}e^{-\alpha t}u(t) \longrightarrow \frac{1}{(s+\alpha)^k}, \quad \mathcal{R}e\{s\} > -\alpha$$

we get

$$\begin{aligned} h_c(t) &= \mathcal{L}^{-1}\{H_c(s)\} \\ &= \mathcal{L}^{-1}\left\{\sum_{k=1}^{r} \frac{A_k}{(s-s_0)^k} + G_c(s)\right\} \\ &= \sum_{k=1}^{r} A_k \frac{t^{k-1}}{(k-1)!}e^{s_0 t}u(t) + g_c(t) \end{aligned}$$

7.25. (a) **Answer:** Only the bilinear transform design will guarantee that a minimum phase discrete-time filter is created from a minimum phase continuous-time filter. For the following explanations remember that a discrete-time minimum phase system has all its poles and zeros inside the unit circle.

Impulse Invariance: Impulse invariance maps left-half s-plane poles to the interior of the z-plane unit circle. However, left-half s-plane zeros will *not necessarily* be mapped inside the z-plane unit circle. Consider:

$$H_c(s) = \sum_{k=1}^{N} \frac{A_k}{s - s_k} = \frac{\sum_{k=1}^{N} A_k \prod_{\substack{j=1 \\ j \neq k}}^{N} (s - s_j)}{\prod_{\ell=1}^{N} (s - s_\ell)}$$

$$H(z) = \sum_{k=1}^{N} \frac{T_d A_k}{1 - e^{s_k T_d} z^{-1}} = \frac{\sum_{k=1}^{N} T_d A_k \prod_{\substack{j=1 \\ j \neq k}}^{N} (1 - e^{s_j T_d} z^{-1})}{\prod_{\ell=1}^{N} (1 - e^{s_\ell T_d} z^{-1})}$$

If we define $\text{Poly}_k(z) = \prod_{\substack{j=1 \\ j \neq k}}^{N} \left(1 - e^{s_j T_d} z^{-1}\right)$, we can note that all the roots of $\text{Poly}_k(z)$ are inside the unit circle. Since the numerator of $H(z)$ is a sum of $A_k \text{Poly}_k(z)$ terms, we see that there are *no guarantees* that the roots of the numerator polynomial are inside the unit circle. In other words, the sum of minimum phase filters is not necessarily minimum phase. By considering the specific example of

$$H_c(s) = \frac{s + 10}{(s + 1)(s + 2)},$$

and using $T = 1$, we can show that a minimum phase filter is transformed into a non-minimum phase discrete time filter.

Bilinear Transform: The bilinear transform maps a pole or zero at $s = s_0$ to a pole or zero (respectively) at $z_0 = \frac{1 + \frac{T}{2} s_0}{1 - \frac{T}{2} s_0}$. Thus,

$$|z_0| = \left| \frac{1 + \frac{T}{2} s_0}{1 - \frac{T}{2} s_0} \right|$$

Since $H_c(s)$ is minimum phase, all the poles of $H_c(s)$ are located in the left half of the s-plane. Therefore, a pole $s_0 = \sigma + j\Omega$ must have $\sigma < 0$. Using the relation for s_0, we get

$$\begin{aligned} |z_0| &= \sqrt{\frac{(1 + \frac{T}{2}\sigma)^2 + (\frac{T}{2}\Omega)^2}{(1 - \frac{T}{2}\sigma)^2 + (\frac{T}{2}\Omega)^2}} \\ &< 1 \end{aligned}$$

Thus, all poles and zeros will be inside the z-plane unit circle and the discrete-time filter will be minimum phase as well.

(b) **Answer:** Only the bilinear transform design will result in an allpass filter.

Impulse Invariance: In the impulse invariance design we have

$$H(e^{j\omega}) = \sum_{k=-\infty}^{\infty} H_c\left(j\left(\frac{\omega}{T_d} + \frac{2\pi k}{T_d}\right)\right)$$

The aliasing terms can destroy the allpass nature of the continuous-time filter.

Bilinear Transform: The bilinear transform only warps the frequency axis. The magnitude response is not affected. Therefore, an allpass filter will map to an allpass filter.

(c) **Answer:** Only the bilinear transform will guarantee

$$H(e^{j\omega})|_{\omega=0} = H_c(j\Omega)|_{\Omega=0}$$

Impulse Invariance: Since impulse invariance may result in aliasing, we see that

$$H(e^{j0}) = H_c(j0)$$

if and only if

$$H(e^{j0}) = \sum_{k=-\infty}^{\infty} H_c\left(j\frac{2\pi k}{T_d}\right) = H_c(j0)$$

or equivalently

$$\sum_{\substack{k=-\infty \\ k\neq 0}}^{\infty} H_c\left(j\frac{2\pi k}{T_d}\right) = 0$$

which is generally not the case.

Bilinear Transform: Since, under the bilinear transformation, $\Omega = 0$ maps to $\omega = 0$,

$$H(e^{j0}) = H_c(j0)$$

for all $H_c(s)$.

(d) **Answer:** Only the bilinear transform design is guaranteed to create a bandstop filter from a bandstop filter.

If $H_c(s)$ is a bandstop filter, the bilinear transform will preserve this because it just warps the frequency axis; however aliasing (in the impulse invariance technique) can fill in the stop band.

(e) **Answer:** The property holds under the bilinear transform, but not under impulse invariance.

Impulse Invariance: Impulse invariance may result in aliasing. Since the order of aliasing and multiplication are not interchangeable, the desired identity does not hold. Consider $H_{a_1}(s) = H_{a_2}(s) = e^{-sT/2}$.

Bilinear Transform: By the bilinear transform,

$$\begin{aligned} H(z) &= H_c\left(\frac{2}{T_d}\left(\frac{1-z^{-1}}{1+z^{-1}}\right)\right) \\ &\equiv H_{c_1}\left(\frac{2}{T_d}\left(\frac{1-z^{-1}}{1+z^{-1}}\right)\right) H_{c_2}\left(\frac{2}{T_d}\left(\frac{1-z^{-1}}{1+z^{-1}}\right)\right) \\ &= H_1(z)H_2(z) \end{aligned}$$

(f) **Answer:** The property holds for both impulse invariance and the bilinear transform.

Impulse Invariance:

$$\begin{aligned} H(e^{j\omega}) &= \sum_{k=-\infty}^{\infty} H_c\left(j\left(\frac{\omega}{T_d} + \frac{2\pi}{T_d}k\right)\right) \\ &= \sum_{k=-\infty}^{\infty} H_{c1}\left(j\left(\frac{\omega}{T_d} + \frac{2\pi}{T_d}k\right)\right) + \sum_{k=-\infty}^{\infty} H_{c2}\left(j\left(\frac{\omega}{T_d} + \frac{2\pi}{T_d}k\right)\right) \\ &= H_1(e^{j\omega}) + H_2(e^{j\omega}) \end{aligned}$$

Bilinear Transform:

$$\begin{aligned}
H(z) &= H_c\left(\frac{2}{T_d}\left(\frac{1-z^{-1}}{1+z^{-1}}\right)\right) \\
&= H_{c_1}\left(\frac{2}{T_d}\left(\frac{1-z^{-1}}{1+z^{-1}}\right)\right) + H_{c2}\left(\frac{2}{T_d}\left(\frac{1-z^{-1}}{1+z^{-1}}\right)\right) \\
&= H_1(z) + H_2(z)
\end{aligned}$$

(g) **Answer:** Only the bilinear transform will result in the desired relationship.
Impulse Invariance: By impulse invariance,

$$\begin{aligned}
H_1\left(e^{j\omega}\right) &= \sum_{k=-\infty}^{\infty} H_{c_1}\left(j\left(\frac{\omega}{T_d}+\frac{2\pi k}{T_d}\right)\right) \\
H_2\left(e^{j\omega}\right) &= \sum_{k=-\infty}^{\infty} H_{c_2}\left(j\left(\frac{\omega}{T_d}+\frac{2\pi k}{T_d}\right)\right)
\end{aligned}$$

We can clearly see that due to the aliasing, the phase relationship is not guaranteed to be maintained.

Bilinear Transform: By the bilinear transform,

$$\begin{aligned}
H_1(e^{j\omega}) &= H_{c_1}\left(j\frac{2}{T_d}\tan(\omega/2)\right) \\
H_2(e^{j\omega}) &= H_{c_2}\left(j\frac{2}{T_d}\tan(\omega/2)\right)
\end{aligned}$$

therefore,

$$\frac{H_1(e^{j\omega})}{H_2(e^{j\omega})} = \frac{H_{c_1}\left(j\frac{2}{T_d}\tan(\omega/2)\right)}{H_{c_2}\left(j\frac{2}{T_d}\tan(\omega/2)\right)} = \begin{cases} e^{-j\pi/2}, & 0<\omega<\pi \\ e^{j\pi/2}, & -\pi<\omega<0 \end{cases}$$

7.26. (a) Since

$$H(e^{j\omega}) = \sum_{k=-\infty}^{\infty} H_c\left(j\left(\frac{\omega}{T_d}+\frac{2\pi k}{T_d}\right)\right)$$

and we desire

$$H(e^{j\omega})\mid_{\omega=0} = H_c(j\Omega)\mid_{\Omega=0},$$

we see that

$$H(e^{j\omega})|_{\omega=0} = \sum_{k=-\infty}^{\infty} H_c\left(j\left(\frac{\omega}{T_d}+\frac{2\pi k}{T_d}\right)\right)|_{\omega=0} = H_c(j\Omega)|_{\Omega=0}$$

requires

$$\sum_{\substack{k=-\infty \\ k\neq 0}}^{\infty} H_c\left(j\frac{2\pi k}{T_d}\right) = 0.$$

(b) Since the bilinear transform maps $\Omega=0$ to $\omega=0$, the condition will hold for any choice of $H_c(j\Omega)$.

7.27.

$$H(e^{j\omega}) = \begin{cases} 1, & |\omega|<\frac{\pi}{4} \\ 0, & \frac{\pi}{4}<|\omega|\leq\pi \end{cases}$$

(a)

$$\begin{aligned} h_1[n] &= h[2n] \\ H_1(e^{j\omega}) &= \sum_{n=-\infty}^{\infty} h[2n]e^{j\omega n} \\ &= \sum_{n \text{ even}} h[n]e^{\frac{j\omega n}{2}} \\ &= \sum_{n=-\infty}^{\infty} \frac{1}{2}\left[h[n] + (-1)^n h[n]\right] e^{j\frac{\omega n}{2}} \\ &= \frac{1}{2}H(e^{j\frac{\omega}{2}}) + \frac{1}{2}H\left(e^{j\frac{\omega+2\pi}{2}}\right) \end{aligned}$$

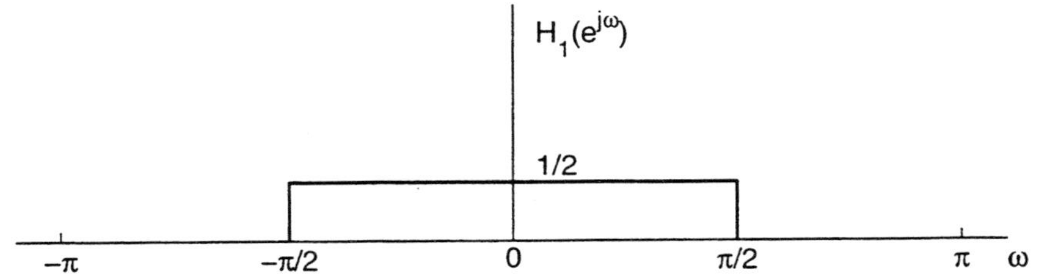

(b)

$$\begin{aligned} H_2(e^{j\omega}) &= \sum_{n \text{ even}} h[n/2]e^{-j\omega n} \\ &= \sum_{n=-\infty}^{\infty} h[n]e^{-j\omega 2n} \\ &= H\left(e^{j2\omega}\right) \end{aligned}$$

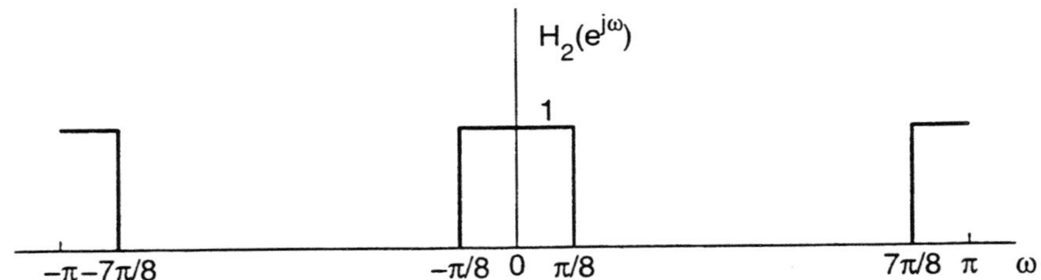

(c)

$$H_3(e^{j\omega}) = H\left(e^{j(\omega+\pi)}\right)$$

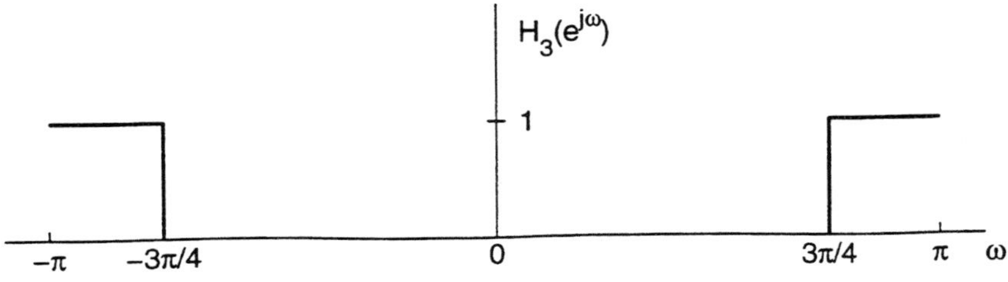

7.28. (a) We have

$$\begin{aligned} s &= \frac{1-z^{-1}}{1+z^{-1}} \\ j\Omega &= \frac{1-e^{-j\omega}}{1+e^{-j\omega}} \\ &= \frac{e^{j\omega/2}-e^{-j\omega/2}}{e^{j\omega/2}+e^{-j\omega/2}} \\ \Omega &= \tan\left(\frac{\omega}{2}\right) \end{aligned}$$

$$\Omega_p = \tan\left(\frac{\omega_{p_1}}{2}\right) \quad \longleftrightarrow \quad \omega_{p_1} = 2\tan^{-1}(\Omega_p)$$

(b)

$$\begin{aligned} s &= \frac{1+z^{-1}}{1-z^{-1}} \\ j\Omega &= \frac{1+e^{-j\omega}}{1-e^{-j\omega}} \\ &= \frac{e^{j\omega/2}+e^{-j\omega/2}}{e^{j\omega/2}-e^{-j\omega/2}} \\ \Omega &= -\cot\left(\frac{\omega}{2}\right) \\ &= \tan\left(\frac{\omega-\pi}{2}\right) \end{aligned}$$

$$\Omega_p = \tan\left(\frac{\omega_{p_2}-\pi}{2}\right) \quad \longleftrightarrow \quad \omega_{p_2} = \pi + 2\tan^{-1}(\Omega_p)$$

(c)

$$\tan\left(\frac{\omega_{p_2}-\pi}{2}\right) = \tan\left(\frac{\omega_{p_1}}{2}\right)$$

$$\Rightarrow \omega_{p_2} = \omega_{p_1} + \pi$$

(d)

$$H_2(z) = H_1(z)|_{z=-z}$$

The even powers of z do not get changed by this transformation, while the coefficients of the odd powers of z change sign.
Thus, replace $A, C, 2$ with $-A, -C, -2$.

7.29. (a) Substituting $Z = e^{j\theta}$ and $z = e^{j\omega}$ we get,

$$\begin{aligned} e^{j\theta} &= -e^{j2\omega} \\ &= e^{j(2\omega+\pi)} \end{aligned}$$

$$\theta = 2\omega + \pi \quad \longleftrightarrow \quad \omega = \frac{\theta-\pi}{2}$$

(b)

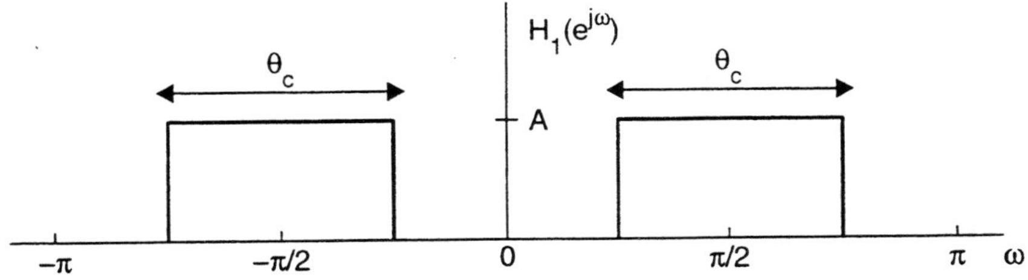

(c)

$$\begin{aligned} h[n] &\longleftrightarrow H(e^{j\theta}) \\ h_1[n] &\longleftrightarrow H\left(e^{j(2\omega+\pi)}\right) \end{aligned}$$

In the frequency domain, we first shift by π and then we upsample by 2. In the time domain, we can write that as

$$h_1[n] = \begin{cases} (-1)^{n/2}h[n/2], & \text{for } n \text{ even} \\ 0, & \text{for } n \text{ odd} \end{cases}$$

(d) In general, a filter

$$H(z) = \frac{b_0 + b_1 z^{-1} + b_2 z^{-2} + \cdots + b_{M-1}z^{M-1} + b_M z^{-M}}{a_0 + a_1 z^{-1} + a_2 z^{-2} + \cdots + a_{N-1}z^{N-1} + a_N z^{-N}}$$

will transform under $H_1(z) = H(-z^2)$ to

$$H_1(z) = \frac{b_0 - b_1 z^{-2} + b_2 z^{-4} + \cdots - b_{M-1}z^{2M-2} + b_M z^{-2M}}{a_0 - a_1 z^{-2} + a_2 z^{-4} + \cdots - a_{M-1}z^{2N-2} + a_N z^{-2N}}$$

where we are assuming here that M and N are even. All the delay terms increase by a factor of two, and the sign of the coefficient in front of any odd delay term is negated.
The given difference equations therefore become

$$\begin{aligned} g[n] &= x[n] + a_1 g[n-2] - b_1 f[n-4] \\ f[n] &= -a_2 g[n-2] - b_2 f[n-2] \\ y[n] &= c_1 f[n] + c_2 g[n-2] \end{aligned}$$

To avoid any possible confusion please note that the b_k and a_k in these difference equations are not the same b_k and a_k shown above for the general case.

7.30. We are given

$$H(z) = H_c(s)\mid_{s=\beta\left[\frac{1-z^{-\alpha}}{1+z^{-\alpha}}\right]}$$

where α is a nonzero integer and β is a real number.

(a) *It is true for* $\beta > 0$.
Proof:

$$\begin{aligned} s &= \beta\left[\frac{1-z^{-\alpha}}{1+z^{-\alpha}}\right] \\ s + sz^{-\alpha} &= \beta - \beta z^{-\alpha} \\ s - \beta &= -\beta z^{-\alpha} - sz^{-\alpha} \\ \beta - s &= z^{-\alpha}(\beta + s) \\ z^{-\alpha} &= \frac{\beta - s}{\beta + s} \\ z^{\alpha} &= \frac{\beta + s}{\beta - s} \end{aligned}$$

The poles s_k of a stable, causal, continuous-time filter satisfy the condition $\mathcal{R}e\,\{s\} < 0$. We want these poles to map to the points z_k in the z-plane such that $|z_k| < 1$. With $\alpha > 0$ it is also true that if $|z_k| < 1$ then $|z_k^\alpha| < 1$. Letting $s_k = \sigma + j\omega$ we see that

$$\begin{aligned} |z_k| &< 1 \\ |z_k^\alpha| &< 1 \\ |\beta + \sigma + j\Omega| &< |\beta - \sigma - j\Omega| \\ (\beta+\sigma)^2 + \Omega^2 &< (\beta-\sigma)^2 + \Omega^2 \\ 2\sigma\beta &< -2\sigma\beta \end{aligned}$$

But since the continuous-time filter is stable we have $\mathcal{R}e\{s_k\} < 0$ or $\sigma < 0$. That leads to

$$-\beta < \beta$$

This can only be true if $\beta > 0$.

(b) *It is true for* $\beta < 0$. The proof is similar to the last proof except now we have $|z^\alpha| > 1$.

(c) We have

$$\begin{aligned} z^2 &= \left.\frac{1+s}{1-s}\right|_{s=j\Omega} \\ |z^2| &= 1 \\ |z| &= 1 \end{aligned}$$

Hence, the $j\Omega$ axis of the s-plane is mapped to the unit circle of z-plane.

(d) First, find the mapping between Ω and ω.

$$\begin{aligned} j\Omega &= \frac{1-e^{-j2\omega}}{1+e^{-j2\omega}} \\ &= \frac{e^{j\omega} - e^{-j\omega}}{e^{j\omega} + e^{-j\omega}} \\ \Omega &= \tan(\omega) \\ \omega &= \tan^{-1}(\Omega) \end{aligned}$$

Therefore,

$$1 - \delta_1 \le |H(e^{j\omega})| \le 1 + \delta_1, \qquad \left\{|\omega| \le \frac{\pi}{4}\right\} \cup \left\{\frac{3\pi}{4} < |\omega| < \pi\right\}$$

Note that the highpass region $3\pi/4 \le |w| \le \pi$ is included because $\tan(\omega)$ is periodic with period π.

7.31. (a)

$$s = \frac{1+z^{-1}}{1-z^{-1}} \longleftrightarrow z = \frac{s+1}{s-1}$$

Now, we evaluate the above expressions along the $j\Omega$ axis of the s-plane

$$\begin{aligned} z &= \frac{j\Omega + 1}{j\Omega - 1} \\ |z| &= 1 \end{aligned}$$

(b) We want to show $|z| < 1$ if $\mathcal{R}e\{s\} < 0$.

$$\begin{aligned} z &= \frac{\sigma + j\Omega + 1}{\sigma + j\Omega - 1} \\ |z| &= \frac{\sqrt{(\sigma+1)^2 + \Omega^2}}{\sqrt{(\sigma-1)^2 + \Omega^2}} \end{aligned}$$

Therefore, if $|z| < 1$

$$\begin{aligned} (\sigma+1)^2 + \Omega^2 &< (\sigma-1)^2 + \Omega^2 \\ \sigma &< -\sigma \end{aligned}$$

it must also be true that $\sigma < 0$. We have just shown that the left-half s-plane maps to the interior of the z-plane unit circle. Thus, any pole of $H_c(s)$ inside the left-half s-plane will get mapped to a pole inside the z-plane unit circle.

(c) We have the relationship

$$\begin{aligned} j\Omega &= \frac{1 + e^{-j\omega}}{1 - e^{-j\omega}} \\ &= \frac{e^{j\omega/2} + e^{-j\omega/2}}{e^{j\omega/2} - e^{-j\omega/2}} \\ \Omega &= -\cot(\omega/2) \end{aligned}$$

$$\begin{aligned} |\Omega_s| &= |\cot(\pi/6)| = \sqrt{3} \\ |\Omega_{p_1}| &= |\cot(\pi/2)| = 0 \\ |\Omega_{p_2}| &= |\cot(\pi/4)| = 1 \end{aligned}$$

Therefore, the constraints are

$$\begin{aligned} 0.95 \le |H_c(j\Omega)| \le 1.05, &\quad 0 \le |\Omega| \le 1 \\ |H_c(j\Omega)| \le 0.01, &\quad \sqrt{3} \le |\Omega| \end{aligned}$$

7.32. (a) By using Parseval's theorem,

$$\begin{aligned} \epsilon^2 &= \frac{1}{2\pi} \int_{-\pi}^{\pi} |E(e^{j\omega})|^2 d\omega \\ &= \sum_{n=-\infty}^{\infty} |e[n]|^2 \end{aligned}$$

where

$$e[n] = \begin{cases} h_d[n], & n < 0, \\ h_d[n] - h[n], & 0 \le n \le M, \\ h_d[n], & n > M \end{cases}$$

(b) Since we only have control over $e[n]$ for $0 \le m \le M$, we get that ϵ^2 is minimized if $h[n] = h_d[n]$ for $0 \le n \le M$.

(c)

$$w[n] = \begin{cases} 1, & 0 \le n \le M, \\ 0, & \text{otherwise.} \end{cases}$$

which is a rectangular window.

7.33. (a)

$$H_d(e^{j\omega}) = [1 - 2u(\omega)]e^{j(\pi/2 - \tau\omega)} \quad \text{for} - \pi < \omega < \pi$$

$$|H_d(e^{j\omega})| = 1, \quad \forall \omega$$

$$\angle H_d(e^{j\omega}) = \begin{cases} \frac{\pi}{2} - \tau\omega, & -\pi < \omega < 0 \\ -\frac{\pi}{2} - \tau\omega, & 0 < \omega < \pi \end{cases}$$

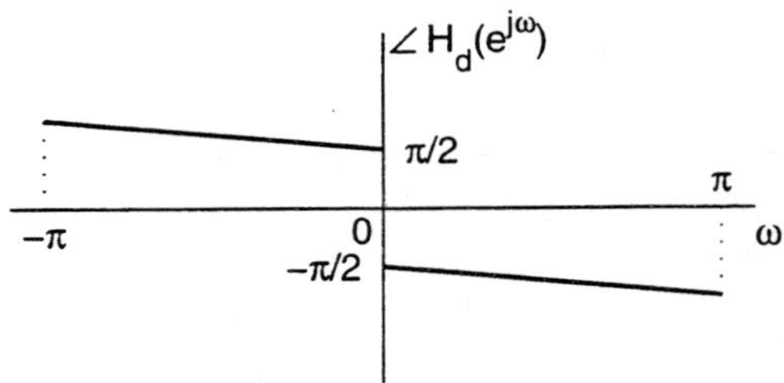

(b) A Hilbert transformer of this nature requires the filter to have a zero at $z = 0$ which introduces the 180° phase difference at that point. A zero at $z = 0$ means that the sum of the filter coefficients equals zero. Thus, only Types III and IV fulfill the requirements.

(c)

$$\begin{aligned} H_d(e^{j\omega}) &= [1 - 2u(\omega)]e^{j(\pi/2 - \omega\tau)} \\ h_d[n] &= \frac{1}{2\pi}\int_{-\pi}^{0} e^{j(\pi/2-\omega\tau)}e^{j\omega n}d\omega - \frac{1}{2\pi}\int_{0}^{\pi} e^{j(\pi/2-\omega\tau)}e^{j\omega n}d\omega \\ &= \frac{e^{j\frac{\pi}{2}}}{2\pi}\int_{-\pi}^{0} e^{j\omega(n-\tau)}d\omega - \frac{e^{j\frac{\pi}{2}}}{2\pi}\int_{0}^{\pi} e^{j\omega(n-\tau)}d\omega \\ &= \begin{cases} \frac{1-\cos[\pi(n-\tau)]}{\pi(n-\tau)}, & n \neq \tau \\ 0, & n = \tau \end{cases} \\ &= \begin{cases} \frac{2}{\pi}\frac{\sin^2[\pi(n-\tau)/2]}{(n-\tau)}, & n \neq \tau \\ 0, & n = \tau \end{cases} \end{aligned}$$

For the windowed FIR system to be linear phase it must be antisymmetric about $\frac{M}{2}$. Since the ideal Hilbert transformer $h_d[n]$ is symmetric about $n = \tau$ we should choose $\tau = \frac{M}{2}$.

(d) The delay is $M/2 = 21/2 = 10.5$ samples. It is therefore a Type IV system. Notice the mandatory zero at $\omega = 0$.

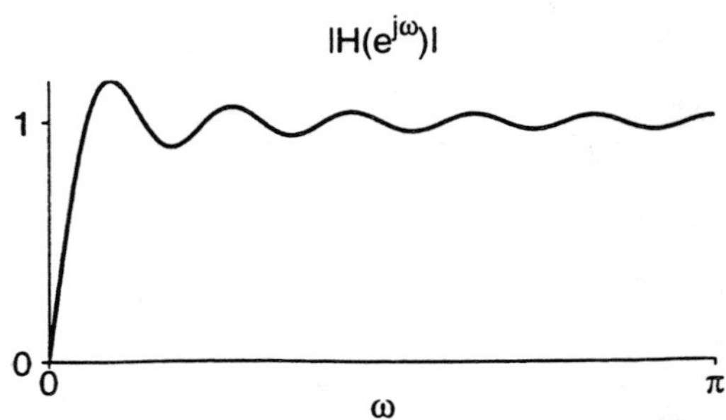

(e) The delay is $M/2 = 20/2 = 10$ samples. It is therefore a Type III system. Notice the mandatory zeros at $\omega = 0$ and π.

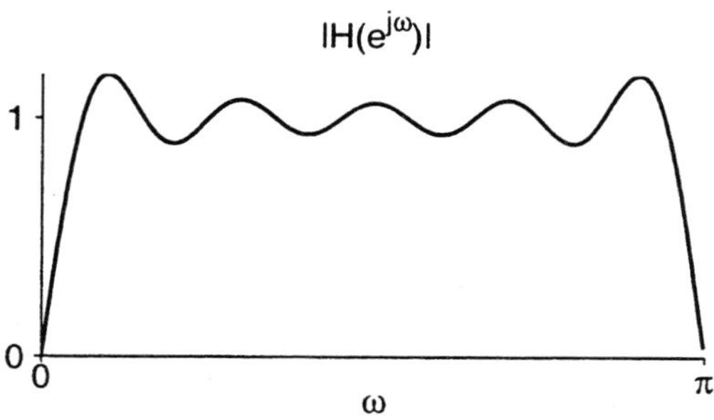

7.34. (a) It is well known that convolving two rectangular windows results in a triangular window. Specifically, to get the $(M+1)$ point Bartlett window for M even, we can convolve the following rectangular windows.

$$r_1[n] = \begin{cases} \sqrt{\frac{2}{M}}, & n = 0, \ldots, \frac{M}{2} - 1 \\ 0, & \text{otherwise} \end{cases}$$
$$r_2[n] = r_1[n-1]$$

Using the known transform of a rectangular window we have

$$W_{R_1}(e^{j\omega}) = \sqrt{\frac{2}{M}} \frac{\sin(\omega M/4)}{\sin(\omega/2)} e^{-j\omega(\frac{M}{4} - \frac{1}{2})}$$
$$W_{R_2}(e^{j\omega}) = \sqrt{\frac{2}{M}} \frac{\sin(\omega M/4)}{\sin(\omega/2)} e^{-j\omega(\frac{M}{4} + \frac{1}{2})}$$
$$W_B(e^{j\omega}) = W_{R_1}(e^{j\omega}) W_{R_2}(e^{j\omega})$$
$$= \frac{2}{M} \left(\frac{\sin(\omega M/4)}{\sin(\omega/2)} \right)^2 e^{-j\omega M/2}$$

Note: The Bartlett window as defined in the text is zero at $n = 0$ and $n = M$. These points are included in the $M + 1$ points.
For M odd, the Bartlett window is the convolution of

$$r_3[n] = \begin{cases} \sqrt{\frac{2}{M}}, & n = 0, \ldots, \frac{M-1}{2} \\ 0, & \text{otherwise} \end{cases}$$
$$r_4[n] = \begin{cases} \sqrt{\frac{2}{M}}, & n = 1, \ldots, \frac{M-1}{2} \\ 0, & \text{otherwise} \end{cases}$$

In the frequency domain we have

$$W_{R_3}(e^{j\omega}) = \sqrt{\frac{2}{M}} \frac{\sin(\omega(M+1)/4)}{\sin(\omega/2)} e^{-j\omega(\frac{M-1}{4})}$$
$$W_{R_4}(e^{j\omega}) = \sqrt{\frac{2}{M}} \frac{\sin(\omega(M-1)/4)}{\sin(\omega/2)} e^{-j\omega(\frac{M-3}{4}+1)}$$
$$W_B(e^{j\omega}) = W_{R_3}(e^{j\omega}) W_{R_4}(e^{j\omega})$$
$$= \frac{2}{M} \left(\frac{\sin[\omega(M+1)/2]}{\sin(\omega/2)} \right) \left(\frac{\sin[\omega(M-1)/2]}{\sin(\omega/2)} \right) e^{-j\omega M/2}$$

(b)

$$w[n] = \left[A + B\cos\left(\frac{2\pi n}{M}\right) + C\cos\left(\frac{4\pi n}{M}\right)\right] w_R[n]$$

$$\begin{aligned} W(e^{j\omega}) &= \left\{2\pi A\delta(\omega) + B\pi\left[\delta\left(\omega + \frac{2\pi}{M}\right) + \delta\left(\omega - \frac{2\pi}{M}\right)\right] + C\pi\left[\delta\left(\omega + \frac{4\pi}{M}\right) + \delta\left(\omega - \frac{4\pi}{M}\right)\right]\right\} \\ &\quad \frac{\otimes}{2\pi}\left\{\frac{\sin(\omega(M+1)/2))}{\sin(\omega/2)} e^{-j\omega M/2}\right\} \end{aligned}$$

where $\otimes$ denotes periodic convolution.

(c) For the Hanning window $A = 0.5$, $B = -0.5$, and $C = 0$.

$$\begin{aligned} w_{\text{Hanning}}[n] &= \left[0.5 - 0.5\cos\left(\frac{2\pi n}{M}\right)\right] w_r[n] \\ W_{\text{Hanning}}(e^{j\omega}) &= 0.5W_R(e^{j\omega}) - 0.25W_R(e^{j\omega}) \otimes \left[\delta\left(\omega + \frac{2\pi}{M}\right) + \delta\left(\omega - \frac{2\pi}{M}\right)\right] \\ &= 0.5W_R(e^{j\omega}) - 0.25\left[W_R(e^{j(\omega + \frac{2\pi}{M})}) + W_R(e^{j(\omega - \frac{2\pi}{M})})\right] \end{aligned}$$

where

$$W_R(e^{j\omega}) = \frac{\sin(\omega(M+1)/2))}{\sin(\omega/2)} e^{-j\omega M/2}$$

Below is a normalized sketch of the magnitude response in dB.

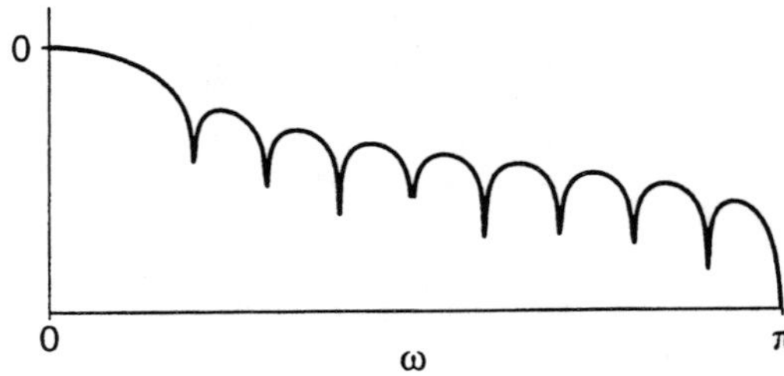

7.35. (a) The delay is $\frac{M}{2} = 24$.

(b)

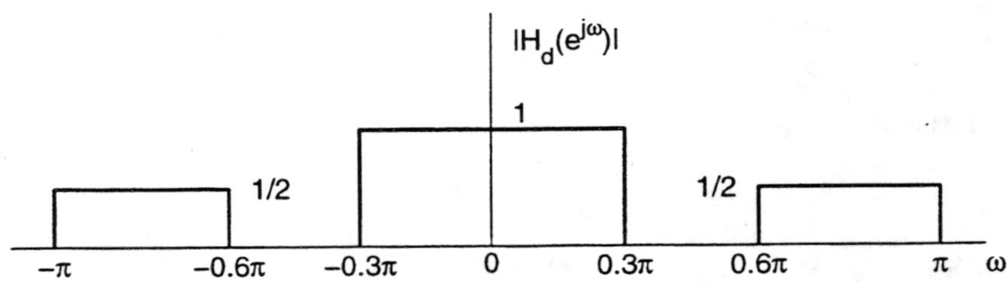

This can be viewed as the sum of two lowpass filters, one of which has been shifted in frequency (modulation in time-domain) to $\omega = \pi$. The linear phase factor adds a delay.

$$h_d[n] = \frac{\sin(0.3\pi(n-24))}{\pi(n-24)} + \frac{1}{2}(-1)^{(n-24)}\frac{\sin(0.4\pi(n-24))}{\pi(n-24)}$$

(c) To find the ripple values, which are all the same in this case since it is a Kaiser window design, we first need to determine A. Since we know β and A are related by

$$\beta = 3.68 = \begin{cases} 0.1102(A-8.7), & A > 50 \\ 0.5842(A-21)^{0.4} + 0.07886(A-21), & 21 \leq A \leq 50 \\ 0, & A < 21 \end{cases}$$

we can solve for A in the following manner:

1. We know $\beta = 3.68$. Therefore, from the formulas above, we see that $A \geq 21$.

2. If we assume $A > 50$ we find,

$$\begin{aligned} 3.68 &= 0.1102(A-8.7) \\ A &= 42.1 \end{aligned}$$

But, this contradicts our assumption that $A > 50$. Thus, $21 \leq A \leq 50$.

3. With $21 \leq A \leq 50$ we find,

$$\begin{aligned} 3.68 &= 0.5842(A-21)^{0.4} + 0.07886(A-21) \\ A &= 42.4256 \end{aligned}$$

With A, we can now calculate δ.

$$\begin{aligned} \delta &= 10^{-A/20} \\ &= 10^{-42.4256/20} \\ &= 0.0076 \end{aligned}$$

The discontinuity of 1 in the first passband creates a ripple of δ. The discontinuity of 1/2 in the second passband creates a ripple of $\delta/2$. The total ripple is $3\delta/2 = 0.0114$ and we therefore have

$$\delta_1 = \delta_2 = \delta_3 = 0.0114$$

Now using the relationship between M, A, and $\Delta\omega$

$$\begin{aligned} M &= \frac{A-8}{2.285\Delta\omega} \\ \Delta\omega &= \frac{42.4256-8}{2.285(48)} = 0.3139 \approx 0.1\pi \end{aligned}$$

Putting it all together with the information about $H_d(e^{j\omega})$ we arrive at our final answer.

$$\begin{aligned} 0.9886 \leq |H(e^{j\omega})| &\leq 1.0114, & 0 \leq \omega \leq 0.25\pi \\ |H(e^{j\omega})| &\leq 0.0114, & 0.35\pi \leq \omega \leq 0.55\pi \\ 0.4886 \leq |H(e^{j\omega})| &\leq 0.5114, & 0.65\pi \leq \omega \leq \pi \end{aligned}$$

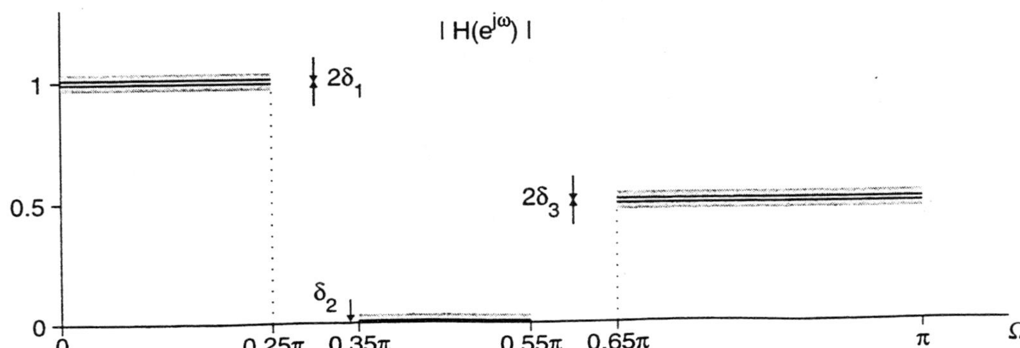

7.36. (a) Since $H(e^{j0}) \neq 0$ and $H(e^{j\pi}) \neq 0$, this must be a Type I filter.

(b) With the weighting in the stopband equal to 1, the weighting in the passband is $\frac{\delta_2}{\delta_1}$.

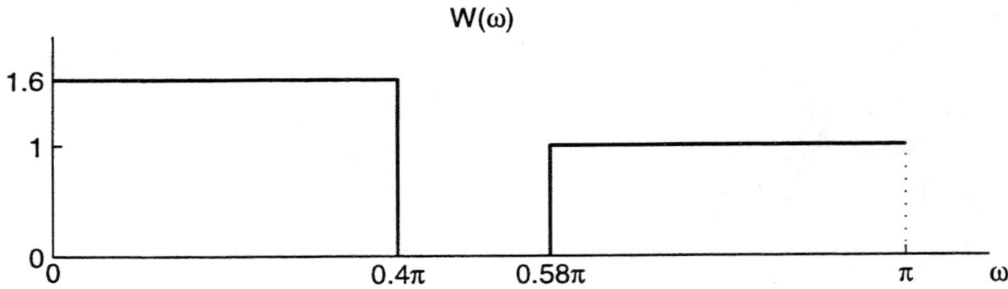

(c)

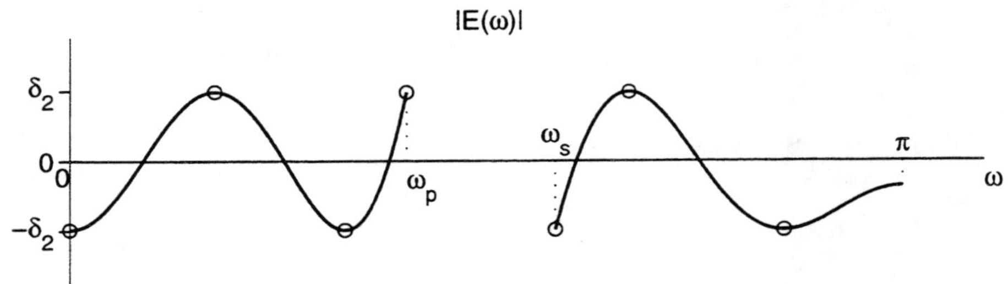

(d) An optimal (in the Parks-McClellan sense) Type I lowpass filter can have either $L+2$ or $L+3$ alternations. The second case is true only when an alternation occurs at all band edges. Since this filter does not have an alternation at $\omega = \pi$ it should only have $L+2$ alternations. From the figure, we see that there are 7 alternations so $L = 5$. Thus, the filter length is $2L+1 = 11$ samples long.

(e) Since the filter is 11 samples long, it has a delay of 5 samples.

(f) Note the zeroes off the unit circle are implied by the dips in the frequency response at the indicated frequencies.

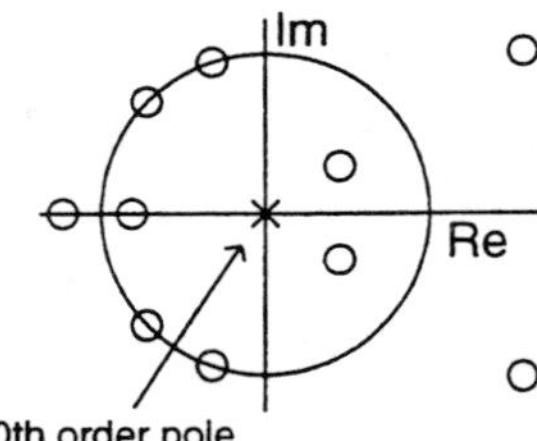

7.37. (a) The most straightforward way to find $h_d[n]$ is to recognize that $H_d(e^{j\omega})$ is simply the (periodic) convolution of two ideal lowpass filters with cutoff frequency $\omega_c = \pi/4$. That is,

$$H_d(e^{j\omega}) = \frac{1}{2\pi}\int_{-\pi}^{\pi} H_{lpf}(e^{j\theta})H_{lpf}(e^{j(\omega-\theta)})d\theta$$

where

$$H_{lpf}(e^{j\omega}) = \begin{cases} 1, & |\omega| \leq \frac{\pi}{4} \\ 0, & \text{otherwise} \end{cases}$$

Therefore, in the time domain, $h_d[n]$ is $(h_{lpf}[n])^2$, or

$$\begin{aligned} h_d[n] &= \left(\frac{\sin(\pi n/4)}{\pi n}\right)^2 \\ &= \frac{\sin^2(\pi n/4)}{\pi^2 n^2} \end{aligned}$$

(b) $h[n]$ must have even symmetry around $(N-1)/2$. $h[n]$ is a type-I FIR generalized linear phase system, since N is an odd integer, and $H(e^{j\omega}) \neq 0$ for $\omega = 0$. Type-I FIR generalized linear phase systems have even symmetry around $(N-1)/2$.

(c) Shifting the filter $h_d[n]$ by $(N-1)/2$ and applying a rectangular window will result in a causal $h[n]$ that minimizes the integral squared error ϵ. Consequently,

$$h[n] = \frac{\sin^2\left[\frac{\pi}{4}(n - \frac{N-1}{2})\right]}{\pi^2(n - \frac{N-1}{2})^2} w[n]$$

where

$$w[n] = \begin{cases} 1, & 0 \leq n \leq N-1 \\ 0, & \text{otherwise} \end{cases}$$

(d) The integral squared error ϵ

$$\epsilon = \frac{1}{2\pi} \int_{-\pi}^{\pi} \left|A(e^{j\omega}) - H_d(e^{j\omega})\right|^2 d\omega$$

can be reformulated, using Parseval's theorem, to

$$\epsilon = \sum_{-\infty}^{\infty} |a[n] - h_d[n]|^2$$

Since

$$a[n] = \begin{cases} h_d[n], & -\frac{N-1}{2} \leq n \leq \frac{N-1}{2} \\ 0, & \text{otherwise} \end{cases}$$

$$\begin{aligned} \epsilon &= \sum_{-\infty}^{-(N-1)/2-1} |a[n] - h_d[n]|^2 + \sum_{-(N-1)/2}^{(N-1)/2} |a[n] - h_d[n]|^2 + \sum_{(N-1)/2+1}^{\infty} |a[n] - h_d[n]|^2 \\ &= \sum_{-\infty}^{-(N-1)/2-1} |h_d[n]|^2 + 0 + \sum_{(N-1)/2+1}^{\infty} |h_d[n]|^2 \end{aligned}$$

By symmetry,

$$\epsilon = 2 \sum_{(N-1)/2+1}^{\infty} |h_d[n]|^2$$

7.38. (a) A Type-I lowpass filter that is optimal in the Parks-McClellan can have either $L+2$ or $L+3$ alternations. The second case is true only when an alternation occurs at all band edges. Since this filter does not have an alternation at $\omega = 0$ it only has $L+2$ alternations. From the figure we see there are 9 alternations so $L = 7$. Thus, $M = 2L = 2(7) = 14$.

(b) We have

$$\begin{aligned} h_{HP}[n] &= -e^{j\pi n} h_{LP}[n] \\ H_{HP}(e^{j\omega}) &= -H_{LP}(e^{j(\omega-\pi)}) \\ &= -A_e(e^{j(\omega-\pi)})e^{-j(\omega-\pi)\frac{M}{2}} \\ &= A_e(e^{j(\omega-\pi)})e^{-j\omega\frac{M}{2}} \\ &= B_e(e^{j\omega})e^{-j\omega\frac{M}{2}} \end{aligned}$$

where

$$B_e(e^{j\omega}) = A_e(e^{j(\omega-\pi)})$$

The fact that $M = 14$ is used to simplify the exponential term in the third line above.

(c)

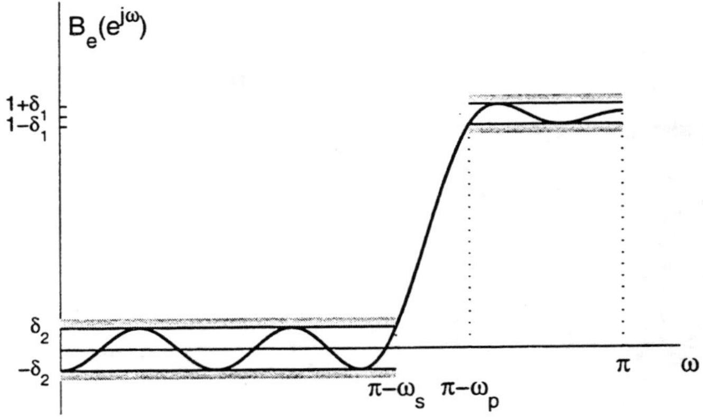

(d) *The assertion is correct.* The original amplitude function was optimal in the Parks-McClellan sense. The method used to create the new filter did not change the filter length, transition width, or relative ripple sizes. All it did was slide the frequency response along the frequency axis creating a new error function $E'(\omega) = E(\omega - \pi)$. Since translation does not change the Chebyshev error $(\max|E(\omega)|)$ the new filter is still optimal.

7.39. For this filter, $N = 3$, so the polynomial order L is

$$L = \frac{N-1}{2} = 1$$

Note that $h[n]$ must be a type-I FIR generalized linear phase filter, since it consists of three samples, and $H(e^{j\omega}) \neq 0$ for $\omega = 0$. $h[n]$ can therefore be written in the form

$$h[n] = a\delta[n] + b\delta[n-1] + a\delta[n-2]$$

Taking the DTFT of both sides gives

$$\begin{aligned} H(e^{j\omega}) &= a + be^{-j\omega} + ae^{-j2\omega} \\ &= e^{-j\omega}(ae^{j\omega} + b + ae^{-j\omega}) \\ &= e^{-j\omega}(b + 2a\cos w) \\ A(e^{j\omega}) &= b + 2a\cos w \end{aligned}$$

The filter must have at least $L+2=3$ alternations, but no more than $L+3=4$ alternations to satisfy the alternation theorem, and therefore be optimal in the minimax sense. Four alternations can be obtained if all four band edges are alternation frequencies such that the frequency response overshoots at $\omega=0$, undershoots at $\omega=\frac{\pi}{3}$, overshoots at $\omega=\frac{\pi}{2}$, and undershoots at $\omega=\pi$.

Let the error in the passband and the stopband be δ_p and δ_s. Then,

$$\begin{aligned} A(e^{j\omega})\,|_{\omega=0} &= 1+\delta_p \\ A(e^{j\omega})\,|_{\omega=\pi/3} &= 1-\delta_p \\ A(e^{j\omega})\,|_{\omega=\pi/2} &= \delta_s \\ A(e^{j\omega})\,|_{\omega=\pi} &= -\delta_s \end{aligned}$$

Using $A(e^{j\omega})=b+2a\cos w$,

$$\begin{aligned} A(e^{j\omega})\,|_{\omega=0} &= b+2a \\ A(e^{j\omega})\,|_{\omega=\pi/3} &= b+a \\ A(e^{j\omega})\,|_{\omega=\pi/2} &= b \\ A(e^{j\omega})\,|_{\omega=\pi} &= b-2a \end{aligned}$$

Solving these systems of equations for a and b gives

$$\begin{aligned} a &= \frac{2}{5} \\ b &= \frac{2}{5} \end{aligned}$$

Thus, the optimal (in the minimax sense) causal 3-point lowpass filter with the desired passband and stopband edge frequencies is

$$h[n]=\frac{2}{5}\delta[n]+\frac{2}{5}\delta[n-1]+\frac{2}{5}\delta[n-2]$$

7.40. *True.* Since filter C is a stable IIR filter it has poles in the left half plane. The bilinear transform maps the left half plane to the inside of the unit circle. Thus, the discrete filter B has to have poles and is therefore an IIR filter.

7.41. *No.* The resulting discrete-time filter would not have a constant group delay. The bilinear transformation maps the entire $j\Omega$ axis in the s-plane to one revolution of the unit circle in the z-plane. Consequently, the linear phase of the continuous-time filter will get nonlinearly warped via the bilinar transform, resulting in a nonlinear phase for the discrete-time filter. Thus, the group delay of the discrete-time filter will not be a constant.

7.42. (a) Using the fact that $H_c(s)=\frac{Y_c(s)}{X_c(s)}$ and cross multiplying we get

$$\begin{aligned} H_c(s)=\frac{Y_c(s)}{X_c(s)} &= \frac{A}{s+c} \\ (s+c)Y_c(s) &= AX_c(s) \\ \frac{dy_c(t)}{dt}+cy_c(t) &= Ax_c(t) \end{aligned}$$

(b)

$$\begin{aligned} \left.\frac{dy_c(t)}{dt}\right|_{t=nT} &= [Ax_c(t)-cy_c(t)]\,|_{t=nT} \\ &= Ax_c(nT)-cy_c(nT) \\ \frac{y_c(nT)-y_c(nT-T)}{T} &\approx Ax_c(nT)-cy_c(nT) \end{aligned}$$

(c)

$$\begin{aligned}
\frac{y[n]-y[n-1]}{T} &= Ax[n]-cy[n] \\
Ax[n] &= \left(c+\frac{1}{T}\right)y[n]-\frac{1}{T}y[n-1] \\
AX(z) &= \left(c+\frac{1}{T}\right)Y(z)-\frac{1}{T}Y(z)z^{-1} \\
H(z)=\frac{Y(z)}{X(z)} &= \frac{A}{c+\frac{1}{T}-\frac{1}{T}z^{-1}}
\end{aligned}$$

(d)

$$\begin{aligned}
H_c(s)\left.\right|_{s=\frac{1-z^{-1}}{T}} &= \left.\frac{A}{s+c}\right|_{s=\frac{1-z^{-1}}{T}} \\
&= \frac{A}{\frac{1-z^{-1}}{T}+c} \\
&= H(z)
\end{aligned}$$

(e) First solve for z

$$\begin{aligned}
s &= \frac{1-z^{-1}}{T} \\
z &= \frac{1}{1-sT}
\end{aligned}$$

and then substitute $s=\sigma+j\Omega$ to get

$$\begin{aligned}
z &= \frac{1}{1-(\sigma+j\Omega)T} \\
&= \frac{1}{\sqrt{(1-\sigma)^2+(\Omega T)^2}}e^{j\tan^{-1}\left(\frac{\Omega T}{1-\sigma}\right)}
\end{aligned}$$

If we let $\theta=\tan^{-1}\left(\frac{\Omega T}{1-\sigma}\right)$ we see that

$$\begin{aligned}
\frac{1}{\sqrt{(1-\sigma)^2+(\Omega T)^2}} &= \frac{\cos(\theta)}{1-\sigma} \\
&= \frac{1}{2(1-\sigma)}\left(e^{j\theta}+e^{-j\theta}\right)
\end{aligned}$$

and thus the s-plane maps to the z-plane in the following manner

$$\begin{aligned}
z &= \left[\frac{1}{2(1-\sigma)}\left(e^{j\theta}+e^{-j\theta}\right)\right]e^{j\theta} \\
&= \frac{1}{2(1-\sigma)}+\frac{1}{2(1-\sigma)}e^{j2\theta} \\
&= \frac{1}{2(1-\sigma)}+\frac{1}{2(1-\sigma)}e^{j2\tan^{-1}\left(\frac{\Omega T}{1-\sigma}\right)}
\end{aligned}$$

To find where the $j\Omega$ axis of the s-plane maps, we let $s=j\Omega$, i.e., $\sigma=0$ and find

$$z=\frac{1}{2}+\frac{1}{2}e^{j2\tan^{-1}(\Omega T)}$$

Therefore, the $j\Omega$-axis maps to a circle of radius 1/2 that is centered at 1/2 in the z-plane. We also see that the region $\sigma < 0$, i.e., the left half of the s-plane, maps to the interior of this circle.

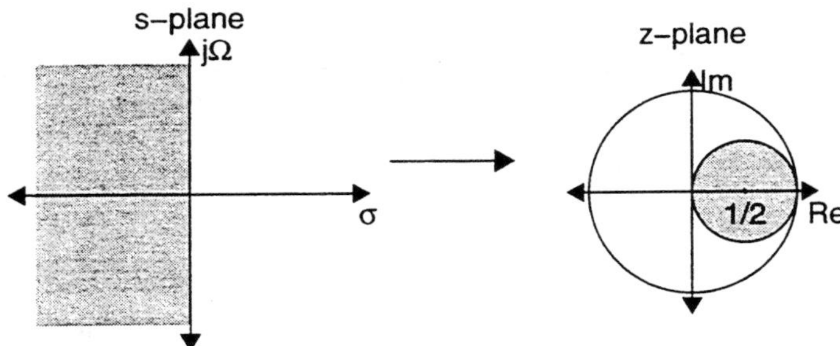

If the continuous-time system is stable, its poles are in the left half s-plane. As shown above, these poles map to the interior of the unit circle and so the discrete-time system will also be stable. The stability is independent of T.

Since the $j\Omega$-axis does not map to the unit circle, the discrete-time frequency response will not be a faithful reproduction of the continuous-time frequency response. As T gets smaller, i.e., as we oversample more, a larger portion of the $j\Omega$-axis gets mapped to the region close to the unit circle at $\omega = 0$. Although the frequency range becomes more compressed the shape of the two responses will look more similar. Thus, as T decreases we improve our approximation.

(f) Substituting for the first derivative in the differential equation obtained in part (a) we get

$$\begin{aligned}\frac{y_c(nT+T) - y_c(nT)}{T} + cy_c(nT) &= Ax_c(nT) \\ \frac{y[n+1] - y[n]}{T} + cy[n] &= Ax[n]\end{aligned}$$

$$H(z) = \frac{Y(z)}{X(z)} = \frac{A}{\frac{z-1}{T} + c} = H_c(s)\,|_{s=\frac{z-1}{T}}$$

$$\begin{aligned} s &= \frac{z-1}{T} \\ z &= 1 + sT \\ &= 1 + \sigma + j\Omega T \end{aligned}$$

To find where the $j\Omega$ axis of the s-plane maps, we let $s = j\Omega$, i.e., $\sigma = 0$ and find

$$z = 1 + j\Omega T$$

Therefore, the $j\Omega$-axis lies on the line $\mathcal{R}e\{z\} = 1$. We also see that the region $\sigma < 0$, i.e., the left half of the s=plane, maps to the left of this line.

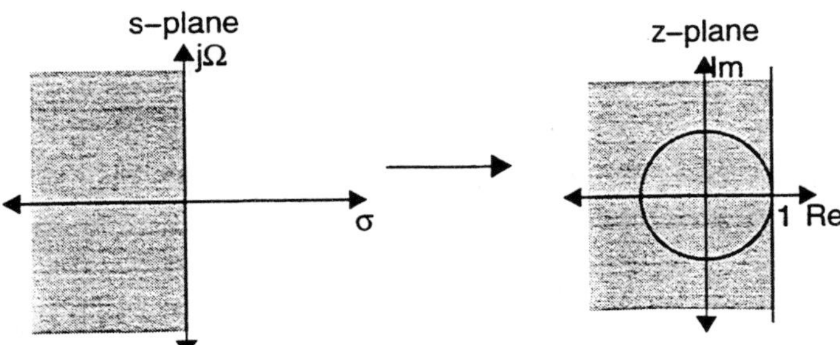

If the continuous-time system is stable, its poles are in the left half s-plane. As shown above, these poles can map to a point outside the unit circle and so the discrete-time system will not necessarily be stable. There are cases where varying T can turn an unstable system into a stable system, but it is not true for the general case.

Since the $j\Omega$-axis does not map to the unit circle, the discrete-time frequency response will not be a faithful reproduction of the continuous-time frequency response. However, as T gets smaller our approximation gets better for the same reasons outlined for the first backward difference.

7.43. (a) Just doing the integration reveals

$$\int_{nT-T}^{nT} \dot{y}_c(\tau)d\tau + y_c(nT-T) = y_c(\tau)|_{nT-T}^{nT} + y_c(nT-T) = y_c(nT)$$

Using the area in the trapezoidal region to replace the integral above, we get

$$\begin{aligned} y_c(nT) &= \int_{nT-T}^{nT} \dot{y}_c(\tau)d\tau + y_c(nT-T) \\ &\approx \left[\dot{y}_c(nT) + \dot{y}_c(nT-T)\right]\frac{T}{2} + y_c(nT-T) \end{aligned}$$

(b) Solving for $\dot{y}_c(nT)$ in the differential equation we get

$$\dot{y}_c(nT) = Ax_c(nT) - cy_c(nT)$$

Substituting this into the answer from part (a) yields

$$y_c(nT) = [Ax_c(nT) - cy_c(nT) + Ax_c(nT-T) - cy_c(nT-T)]\frac{T}{2} + y_c(nT-T)$$

(c) The difference equation is

$$y[n] = (Ax[n] - cy[n] + Ax[n-1] - cy[n-1])\frac{T}{2} + y[n-1]$$

$$y[n]\left(1 + c\frac{T}{2}\right) - y[n-1]\left(1 - c\frac{T}{2}\right) = A\frac{T}{2}(x[n] + x[n-1])$$

Therefore,

$$Y(z)\left[1 + c\frac{T}{2}\right] - Y(z)z^{-1}\left[1 - c\frac{T}{2}\right] = A\frac{T}{2}X(z)\left[1 + z^{-1}\right]$$

$$H(z) = \frac{Y(z)}{X(z)} = \frac{A\frac{T}{2}(1+z^{-1})}{1 + c\frac{T}{2} - z^{-1} + z^{-1}c\frac{T}{2}}$$

(d)

$$\begin{aligned} H_c(s)\,|_{s=\frac{2}{T}\left[\frac{1-z^{-1}}{1+z^{-1}}\right]} &= \left.\frac{A}{s+c}\right|_{s=\frac{2}{T}\left[\frac{1-z^{-1}}{1+z^{-1}}\right]} \\ &= \frac{\frac{T}{2}A(1+z^{-1})}{1 - z^{-1} + c\frac{T}{2}(1+z^{-1})} \\ &= H(z) \end{aligned}$$

7.44.

$$\begin{aligned} \Phi_c(j\Omega) &= H_c(j\Omega)H_c(-j\Omega) \\ \Phi(z) &= H(z)H(z^{-1}) \end{aligned}$$

(a) (i) Since $H_c(s)$ has poles at s_k, $H_c(-s)$ has poles at $-s_k$.

(ii) The material in this chapter shows that under impulse invariance

$$\frac{A_k}{s-s_k} \longleftrightarrow \frac{T_d A_k}{1-e^{s_k T_d} z^{-1}}.$$

Thus, going from step 1 to step 2 means that the autocorrelation of the discrete-time system is a sampled version of the autocorrelation of the continuous-time system.

(iii) Since $\Phi(z) = H(z)H(z^{-1})$ we can choose the poles and zeros of $H(z)$ to be all the poles inside the unit circle, and that choice leaves all the poles and zeros outside the unit circle for $H(z^{-1})$.

Consider the following example using $h_c(t) = e^{-\alpha t}u(t)$.

$$H_c(s) = \frac{1}{s+\alpha} \quad \text{and} \quad H_c(-s) = \frac{1}{-s+\alpha}$$

$$\begin{aligned}
\Phi_c(s) &= H_c(s)H_c(-s) \\
&= \left[\frac{1}{s+\alpha}\right]\left[\frac{1}{-s+\alpha}\right] \\
&= \frac{1/2\alpha}{s+\alpha} - \frac{1/2\alpha}{s-\alpha}
\end{aligned}$$

$$\begin{aligned}
\Phi(z) &= \frac{T_d/2\alpha}{1-e^{-\alpha T_d}z^{-1}} - \frac{T_d/2\alpha}{1-e^{\alpha T_d}z^{-1}} \\
&= \frac{T_d}{2\alpha}\frac{\left[1-e^{\alpha T_d}z^{-1} - 1 + e^{-\alpha T_d}z^{-1}\right]}{(1-e^{-\alpha T_d}z^{-1})(1-e^{\alpha T_d}z^{-1})} \\
&= \frac{T_d}{2\alpha}\frac{\left(e^{-\alpha T_d} - e^{\alpha T_d}\right)z^{-1}}{(1-e^{-\alpha T_d}z^{-1})(1-e^{\alpha T_d}z^{-1})} \\
&= \frac{T_d}{2\alpha}\frac{\left(e^{\alpha T_d} - e^{-\alpha T_d}\right)z^{-1}}{(1-e^{-\alpha T_d}z^{-1})(1-e^{-\alpha T_d}z)e^{\alpha T_d}z^{-1}} \\
&= \frac{T_d}{2\alpha}\frac{(1-e^{-2\alpha T_d})}{(1-e^{-\alpha T_d}z^{-1})(1-e^{-\alpha T_d}z)} \\
&= \left[\sqrt{\frac{T_d}{2\alpha}(1-e^{-2\alpha T_d})}\frac{1}{(1-e^{-\alpha T_d}z^{-1})}\right]\left[\sqrt{\frac{T_d}{2\alpha}(1-e^{-2\alpha T_d})}\frac{1}{(1-e^{-\alpha T_d}z)}\right]
\end{aligned}$$

if $\alpha > 0$, then

$$h[n] = \sqrt{\frac{T_d}{2\alpha}(1-e^{-2\alpha T_d})}\left(e^{-\alpha T_d}\right)^n u[n]$$

(b) Since $|H_c(j\Omega)|^2 = \Phi_c(j\Omega)$ and $\Phi(e^{j\omega}) = H(e^{j\omega})H(e^{-j\omega}) = |H(e^{j\omega})|^2$, we see that since $\phi[m] = T_d\phi_c(mT_d)$,

$$\Phi(e^{j\omega}) = \sum_{k=-\infty}^{\infty} \Phi_c\left(j\left(\frac{\omega}{T_d} + \frac{2\pi k}{T_d}\right)\right).$$

Therefore, if $\Phi_c(j\Omega) \simeq 0$ for $|\Omega| \geq \frac{\pi}{T_d}$, then $\Phi(e^{j\omega}) \simeq \Phi_c\left(j\frac{\omega}{T_d}\right)$ and $|H(e^{j\omega})|^2 \simeq \left|H_c\left(j\frac{\omega}{T_d}\right)\right|^2$.

(c) *No.* We could always cascade $H(z)$ with an allpass filter. The new filter is different, but has the same autocorrelation.

7.45. (a) Since the two flow diagrams are equivalent we have

$$\begin{aligned} Z^{-1} &= \frac{z^{-1}-\alpha}{1-\alpha z^{-1}} = \frac{1-\alpha z}{z-\alpha} \\ Z &= \frac{z-\alpha}{1-\alpha z} \end{aligned}$$

$$H(z) = H_{lp}(Z)|_{Z=\frac{z-\alpha}{1-\alpha z}} = H_{lp}\left(\frac{z-\alpha}{1-\alpha z}\right)$$

(b) Let $Z = e^{j\theta}$ and $z = e^{j\omega}$. Then

$$\begin{aligned} Z^{-1} &= \frac{z^{-1}-\alpha}{1-\alpha z^{-1}} \\ e^{-j\theta} &= \frac{e^{-j\omega}-\alpha}{1-\alpha e^{-j\omega}} \\ e^{-j\theta} - \alpha e^{-j\theta}e^{-j\omega} &= e^{-j\omega} - \alpha \\ e^{-j\omega}(1+\alpha e^{-j\theta}) &= e^{-j\theta} + \alpha \\ e^{-j\omega} &= \frac{e^{-j\theta}+\alpha}{1+\alpha e^{-j\theta}} \\ &= \frac{e^{-j\theta}+\alpha}{1+\alpha e^{-j\theta}} \cdot \frac{1+\alpha e^{j\theta}}{1+\alpha e^{j\theta}} \\ &= \frac{e^{-j\theta}+2\alpha+\alpha^2 e^{j\theta}}{1+2\alpha\cos\theta+\alpha^2} \end{aligned}$$

Using Euler's formula,

$$\begin{aligned} e^{-j\omega} &= \frac{\cos\theta - j\sin\theta + 2\alpha + \alpha^2\cos\theta + j\alpha^2\sin\theta}{1+2\alpha\cos\theta+\alpha^2} \\ &= \frac{2\alpha + (1+\alpha^2)\cos\theta + j[(\alpha^2-1)\sin\theta]}{1+2\alpha\cos\theta+\alpha^2} \end{aligned}$$

Noting that $-\omega = \tan^{-1}\left[\frac{Im\{\cdot\}}{Re\{\cdot\}}\right]$,

$$\begin{aligned} -\omega &= \tan^{-1}\left[\frac{(\alpha^2-1)\sin\theta}{2\alpha+(1+\alpha^2)\cos\theta}\right] \\ \omega &= \tan^{-1}\left[\frac{(1-\alpha^2)\sin\theta}{2\alpha+(1+\alpha^2)\cos\theta}\right] \end{aligned}$$

This relationship is plotted in the figure below for $\alpha = 0, \pm 0.5$.

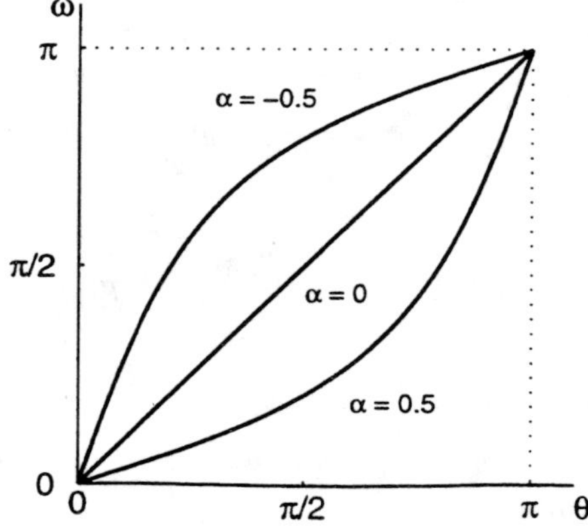

Although a warping of the frequency scale is evident in the figure, (except when $\alpha = 0$, which corresponds to $Z^{-1} = z^{-1}$), if the original system has a piecewise-constant lowpass frequency response with cutoff frequency θ_p, then the transformed system will likewise have a similar lowpass response with cutoff frequency ω_p determined by the choice of α.

$$\omega_p = \tan^{-1}\left[\frac{(1-\alpha^2)\sin(\theta_p)}{2\alpha + (1+\alpha^2)\cos(\theta_p)}\right]$$

(c)

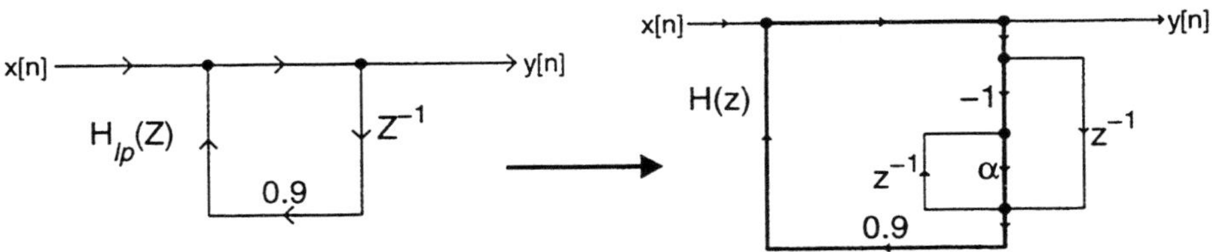

Looking at the flow graph for $H(z)$ we see a feedback loop with no delay. This effectively makes the current output, $y[n]$, a function of itself. Hence, there is no computable difference equation.

(d) *Yes*, the flow graph manipulation would lead to a computable difference equation. The flowgraph of an FIR filter has a path without delays leading from input to output, but this does not present any problems in terms of computation. Below is an example.

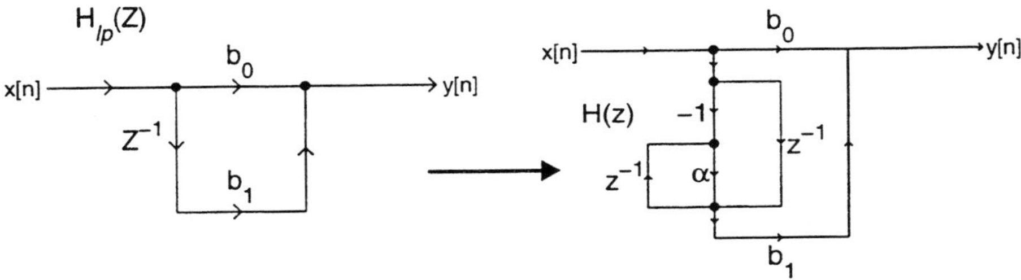

The transformation would destroy the linear phase of the FIR filter since the mapping between θ and ω is nonlinear. The only exception is the special case when $\alpha = 0$, i.e., when $\theta = \omega$.

Since there are feedback terms in the transformed filter, it must be an IIR filter. It therefore has an infinitely long impulse response.

(e) Since the two flow diagrams are equivalent we have

$$\begin{aligned} Z^{-1} &= z^{-1}\frac{z^{-1}-\alpha}{1-\alpha z^{-1}} = z^{-1}\frac{1-\alpha z}{z-\alpha} \\ Z &= z\frac{z-\alpha}{1-\alpha z} \end{aligned}$$

$$H(z) = H_{lp}(Z)|_{Z=z\frac{z-\alpha}{1-\alpha z}} = H_{lp}\left(z\frac{z-\alpha}{1-\alpha z}\right)$$

Letting $Z = e^{j\theta}$ and $z = e^{j\omega}$ we have,

$$\begin{aligned} e^{j\theta} &= e^{j\omega}\frac{e^{j\omega}-\alpha}{1-\alpha e^{j\omega}} \\ &= e^{j\omega}\frac{e^{j\omega}-\alpha}{1-\alpha e^{j\omega}}\cdot\frac{1-\alpha e^{-j\omega}}{1-\alpha e^{-j\omega}} \\ &= e^{j\omega}\frac{e^{j\omega}-2\alpha+\alpha^2 e^{-j\omega}}{1-2\alpha\cos\omega+\alpha^2} \end{aligned}$$

Using Euler's formula,

$$e^{j\theta} = e^{j\omega}\frac{(1+\alpha^2)\cos\omega - 2\alpha + j(1-\alpha^2)\sin\omega}{1 - 2\alpha\cos\omega + \alpha^2}$$

Noting that $\theta = \omega + \tan^{-1}\left[\frac{Im\{\cdot\}}{Re\{\cdot\}}\right]$,

$$\theta = \omega + \tan^{-1}\left[\frac{(1-\alpha^2)\sin\omega}{(1+\alpha^2)\cos\omega - 2\alpha}\right]$$

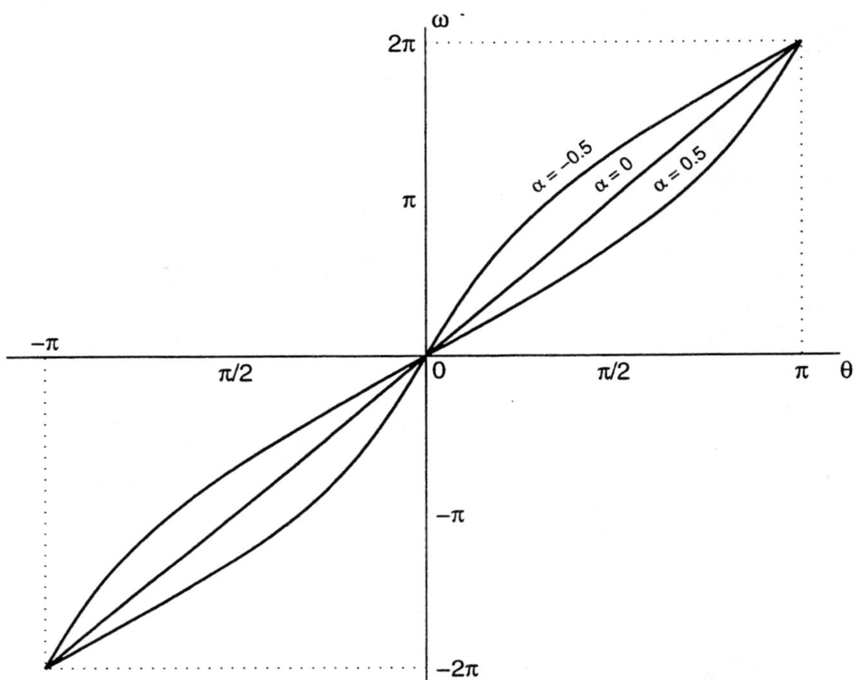

We see from the plot of ω versus θ that a lowpass filter will not always transform into a lowpass filter. Take, for example, the case when the original lowpass filter has a cutoff of $\theta = \pi/2$. With $\alpha = 0$ it would transform into an allpass filter.

7.46. (a) Since

$$\begin{aligned} y[n] &= (2x[n] - h[n] * x[n]) * h[n] \\ &= (2h[n] - h[n] * h[n]) * x[n] \end{aligned}$$

the new transfer function is

$$g[n] = 2h[n] - h[n] * h[n]$$

(i) It is FIR since the convolution of two finite length sequences results in a finite length sequence.

(ii) Note that the term $h[n] * h[n]$ is symmetric since it is the convolution of two symmetric sequences. Therefore, g[n] must be symmetric since it is the difference of two symmetric sequences.

(b) The frequency response for $G(e^{j\omega})$ is

$$G(e^{j\omega}) = 2H(e^{j\omega}) - H(e^{j\omega})H(e^{j\omega})$$

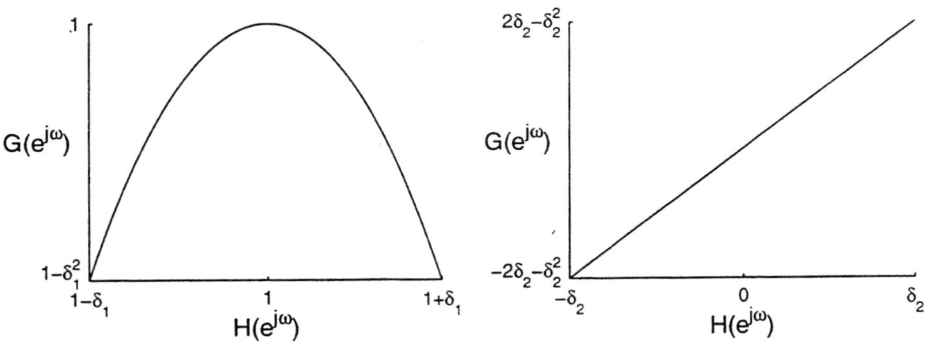

As shown above, if the passband of $H(e^{j\omega})$ is the region $[1-\delta_1, 1+\delta_1]$, then the passband of $G(e^{j\omega})$ is in the region $[1-\delta_1^2, 1]$ which is a smaller band. However, the stop band gets bigger since it maps to $[-2\delta_2-\delta_2^2, 2\delta_2-\delta_2^2]$.
Thus,

$$\begin{aligned} A &= (1-\delta_1^2) \\ B &= 1 \\ C &= -2\delta_2-\delta_2^2 \\ D &= 2\delta_2-\delta_2^2 \end{aligned}$$

If $\delta_1 \ll 1$ and $\delta_2 \ll 1$ then,

$$\begin{aligned} \text{Maximum passband approximation error} &\approx 0 \\ \text{Maximum stopband approximation error} &\approx 2\delta_2 \end{aligned}$$

(c) Since

$$\begin{aligned} y[n] &= (3x[n]-2x[n]*h[n])*h[n]*h[n] \\ &= (3h[n]*h[n]-2h[n]*h[n]*h[n])*x[n] \end{aligned}$$

the new transfer function is

$$h_{\text{sharp}}[n] = 3h[n]*h[n]-2h[n]*h[n]*h[n]$$

and so

$$H_{\text{sharp}}(e^{j\omega}) = 3H(e^{j\omega})^2-2H(e^{j\omega})^3$$

The new tolerance specifications can be found in a similar manner to the last section. We get,

$$\begin{aligned} A &= 1-3\delta_1^2-2\delta_1^3 \\ B &= 1 \\ C &= 0 \\ D &= 3\delta_2^2+2\delta_2^3 \end{aligned}$$

If $\delta_1 \ll 1$ and $\delta_2 \ll 1$ then,

$$\begin{aligned} \text{Maximum passband approximation error} &\approx 0 \\ \text{Maximum stopband approximation error} &\approx 0 \end{aligned}$$

(d) The order of the impulse response $h[n]$ is M. Since it is linear phase it must therefore have a delay of $\frac{M}{2}$ samples. To convert the two systems we must add a delay in the lower leg of each network to match the delay that was added by the first filter.

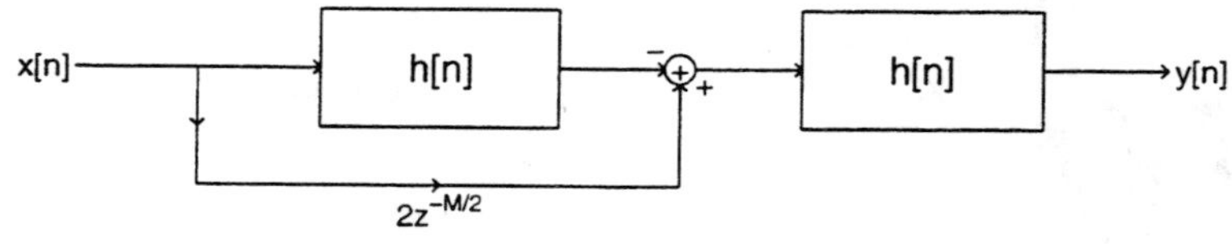

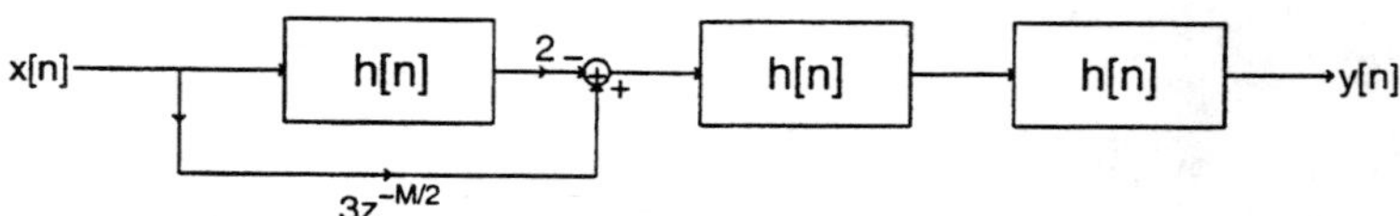

The restrictions on the filter that carry over from part (a) are that it have

(i) Even symmetry

(ii) Odd Length

Hence, Type I FIR filters can be used.

The length of $h[n]$ is $2L+1$. Since the term that is longest in the twicing system's impulse response is the $h[n]*h[n]$ term, the length of $g[n]$ is $4L+1$. Since the term that is longest in the sharpening system's impulse response is the $h[n]*h[n]*h[n]$ term, the length of $h_{\text{sharp}}[n]$ is $6L+1$.

7.47. We know that *any* system whose frequency response is of the form

$$A_e(e^{j\omega}) = \sum_{k=0}^{L} a_k(\cos(\omega))^k$$

can have at most $L-1$ local maxima and minima in the open interval $0 < \omega < \pi$ since it is in the form of a polynomial of degree L.

If we include all endpoints of the approximation region

$$\{0 \le |\omega| \le \omega_p\} \bigcup \{\omega_s \le |\omega| \le \pi\}$$

then we see we can have at most $L+3$ alternation frequencies.

If the transition band has two of the local minima or maxima of $A_e(e^{j\omega})$, then only $L-3$ can be in the approximation bands. Even with all four endpoints of the approximation region as alternation points, we can only have a maximum of $L+1$ alternation points. This does not satisfy the optimality condition of the Alternation Theorem which requires at least $L+2$ alternation points. It follows that the transition band cannot have more than two local minima or maxima of $A_e(e^{j\omega})$ either.

If the transition band only has one of the local minima or maxima of $A_e(e^{j\omega})$, then the error will not alternate between ω_p and ω_s and they cannot both be alternation frequencies. In this case, only $L-2$ of the local minima or maxima of $A_e(e^{j\omega})$ are in the approximation bands. If we add the maximum of three band edges to the total count of alternation frequencies we get $L+1$, which is again too low.

Therefore, the transition band cannot have any local minima or maxima and must be monotonic.

7.48. (a) $A_e(e^{j\omega})$ has 7 alternations of the error. If the approximation bands are of equal length and the weighting function is unity in both bands, why would the stopband have 1 extra alternation than the passband? The answer is that, if it were an optimal filter, it would not. The optimal filter for this set of specifications should have the *same* number of alternations in each band and therefore requires an *even* number of alternations. Since the optimal approximation is unique, the one shown in the figure cannot be optimal.

(b) A polynomial of degree L can have at most $L-1$ local minima or maxima in an open interval. Since $A_e(e^{j\omega})$ has three local extrema in the interval from $0 < \omega < \pi$, we know $L \geq 4$.

Note that the *optimal* filter is half wave anti-symmetric if you lower its frequency response by one half, i.e.,

$$A_{hw}(e^{j\omega}) = -A_{hw}\left(e^{j(\pi-\omega)}\right)$$

where $A_{hw}(e^{j\omega}) = H_{opt}(e^{j\omega}) - 1/2$. Another way of saying this is to say that the optimal filter is anti-symmetric around $\omega = \pi/2$ after lowering the response by $1/2$. This property holds because the optimal filter has symmetric bands with the same number of alternations. Plugging in $A_{hw}(e^{j\omega}) = H_{opt}(e^{j\omega}) - 1/2$ into the above expression gives

$$\begin{aligned} H_{opt}(e^{j\omega}) - 1/2 &= -\left[H_{opt}\left(e^{j(\pi-\omega)}\right) - 1/2\right] \\ H_{opt}(e^{j\omega}) &= -H_{opt}\left(e^{j(\pi-\omega)}\right) + 1 \\ h_{opt}[n] &= -(-1)^n h_{opt}[-n] + \delta[n] \end{aligned}$$

This condition implies that

$$h_{opt}[n] = \begin{cases} h_{opt}[-n], & n \text{ odd} \\ 0, & n \text{ even, n} \neq 0 \\ 0.5, & n = 0 \end{cases}$$

A sample plot of $h_{opt}[n]$ appears below, for $L = 6$.

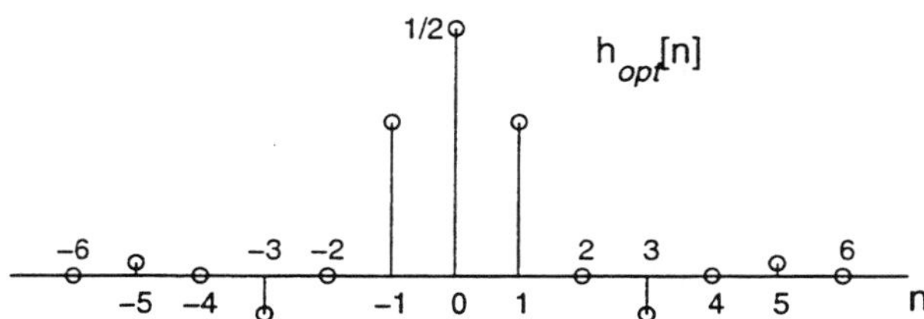

Note that because $h_{opt}[n] = 0$ for n even, $n \neq 0$, a plot of $h_{opt}[n]$ for $L = 5$ would have the same nonzero samples, and therefore be equivalent. So the optimal filter with $L = 6$ is really the same filter as the case of $L = 5$, just as the optimal filter with $L = 4$ is the same filter as the case with $L = 3$.

We know the filter non-optimal filter has 7 alternations. The optimal filter should be able to meet the same specifications, but with a lower order. From part (a), we know the number of alternations must be even. Thus, the optimal filter for these specifications will have 6 alternations.

An optimal lowpass filter has either $L+2$ or $L+3$ alternations which means $L = 4$ or $L = 3$. However, we showed above that these are really the same filter. Since the optimal filter has $L = 4$, the filter shown in the problem cannot have $L = 4$.

Putting it all together we find $L > 4$ for the filter shown in the figure.

7.49. (a)

$$\begin{aligned} H_{\text{eff}}(j\Omega) &= \frac{1}{T}H(e^{j\Omega T})H_0(j\Omega)H_r(j\Omega) \\ &= \begin{cases} \dfrac{2\sin\left(\frac{\Omega T}{2}\right)}{\Omega T}H\left(e^{j\Omega T}\right)e^{-j\frac{\Omega T}{2}}, & |\Omega| < \frac{\pi}{T} \\ 0, & \text{otherwise} \end{cases} \end{aligned}$$

(b) The delay of the linear phase system is $51/2 = 25.5$ samples since it is a linear phase system of order 51. Therefore, the total delay is

$$\begin{aligned}\text{Delay} &= \overbrace{25.5T}^{H(e^{j\Omega T})} + \overbrace{0.5T}^{H_0(j\Omega)} \\ &= 26T \\ &= 2.6 \text{ ms}\end{aligned}$$

(c) $H(e^{j\Omega T})$ should cancel the effects of $H_0(j\Omega)$. However, to cancel the effects of the delay introduced by $H_0(j\Omega)$ would require a noncausal filter which is not practical in this situation. Using the relation $\omega = \Omega T$,

$$H_d(e^{j\omega}) = \begin{cases} \dfrac{\frac{\omega}{2}}{\sin\left(\frac{\omega}{2}\right)}, & |\omega| \leq 0.2\pi \\ 0, & 0.4\pi \leq |\omega| \leq \pi \end{cases}$$

To obtain equiripple behavior in $H_{\text{eff}}(j\Omega)$, we need to weight the error so that the ripples grow with $H_d(e^{j\omega})$. Then when we multiply by $H_0(j\Omega)$ the ripples will be decreased to an equal size. Therefore, we need

$$W(\omega) = \begin{cases} \dfrac{\sin\left(\frac{\omega}{2}\right)}{\frac{\omega}{2}}, & |\omega| \leq 0.2\pi \\ 1, & 0.4\pi \leq |\omega| \leq \pi \end{cases}$$

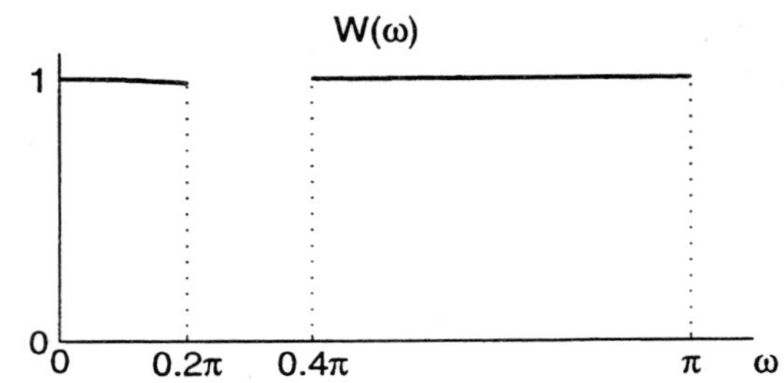

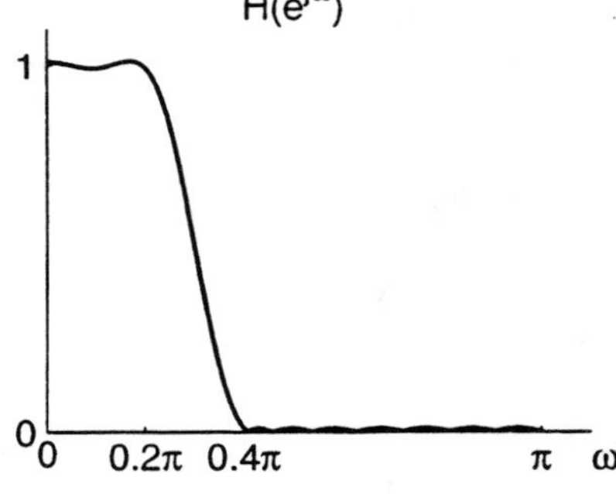

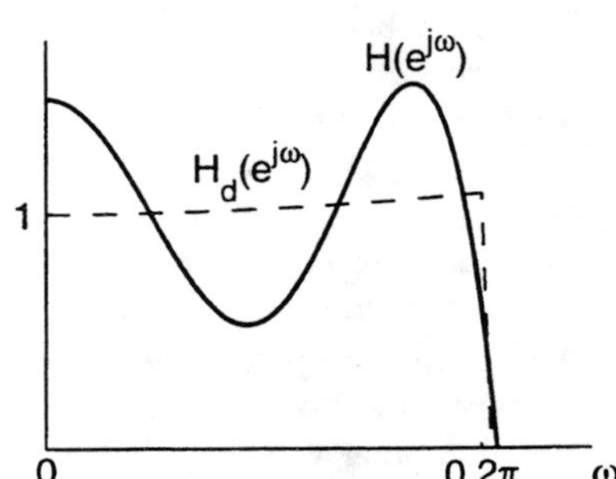

(d) If $H_r(j\Omega)$ is also sloping across the band, $|\Omega| < \pi/T$, we would combine its effects with those of $H_0(j\Omega)$ and compensate as in part (c), i.e.,

$$H_d(e^{j\omega}) = \begin{cases} \dfrac{\frac{\omega}{2}}{\sin\left(\frac{\omega}{2}\right)} \dfrac{1}{|H_r\left(j\frac{\omega}{T}\right)|}, & |\omega| < 0.2\pi \\ 0, & 0.4\pi \leq |\omega| \leq \pi \end{cases}$$

This would take care of the distortion due to $|H_r(j\Omega)|$ but not of any phase distortion. The weighting function will change in a similar manner.

7.50. (a) To avoid aliasing, we require

$$\begin{aligned} M\omega_s &\leq \pi \\ M &\leq \frac{\pi}{\omega_s} \end{aligned}$$

So the maximum allowable decimation factor is

$$M\text{max} = \frac{\pi}{\omega_s}$$

(b)

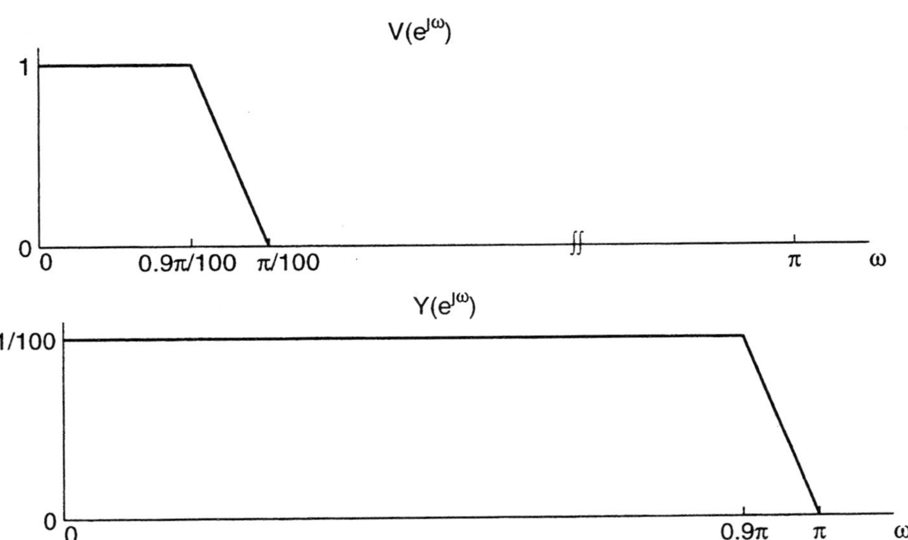

(c)

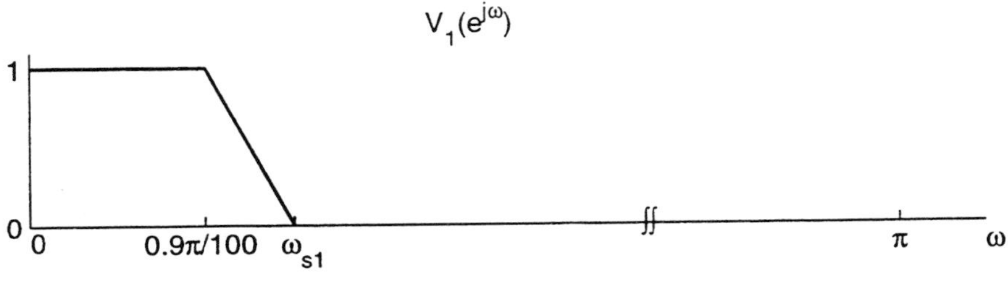

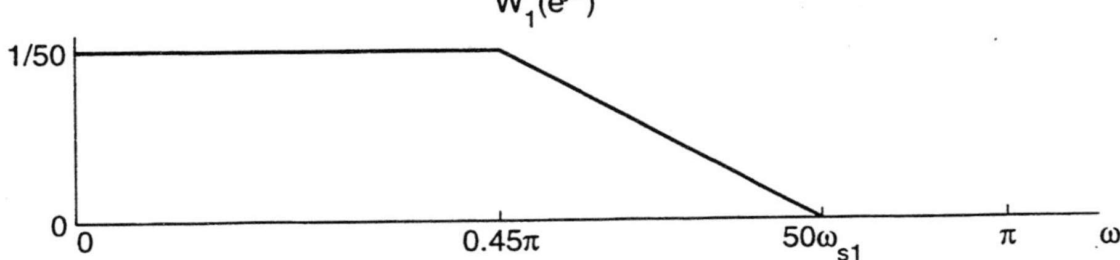

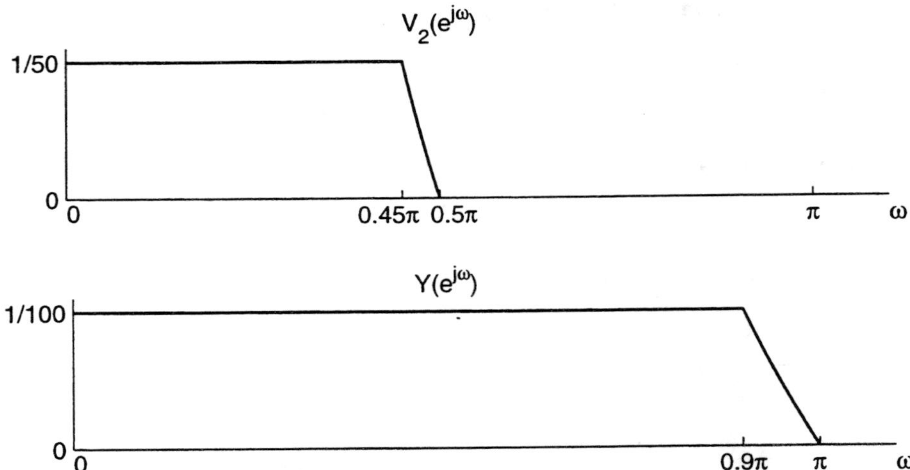

(d) After the first decimation by 50 is performed, $W_1(e^{j\omega})$ should look like the following:

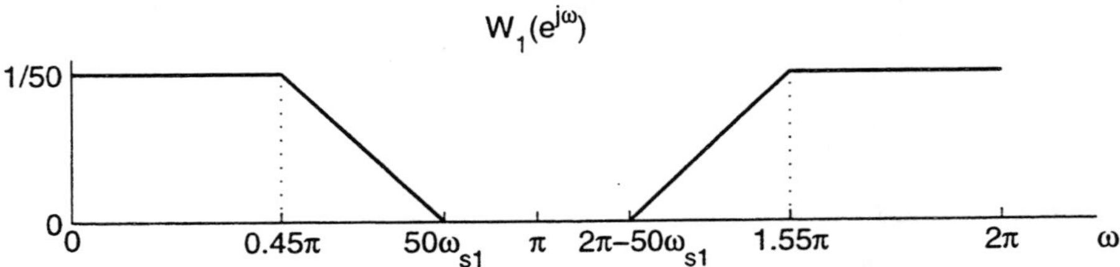

Since we allow aliasing to occur in the transition bands, we have

$$
\begin{aligned}
50\omega_{s_1} &\leq 1.55\pi \\
\omega_{s_1} &\leq 0.031\pi
\end{aligned}
$$

(e) Using $\delta_p = 0.01$, $\delta_s = 0.001$, $\Delta\omega = 0.001\pi$ we get

$$
\begin{aligned}
N &= \frac{-10\log_{10}(0.01 \times 0.001) - 13}{2.324(0.001\pi)} + 1 \\
&\simeq 5069
\end{aligned}
$$

In general, the number of multiplies required to compute a single output sample is just N. For a linear phase filter, however, the symmetry in the coefficients allow us to cut the number of multiplies (roughly) in half if implementing the filter with a difference equation. The following is an example of how this is accomplished using the simple Type I linear phase filter $h[n] = 0.25\delta[n] + \delta[n-1] + 0.25\delta[n-2]$.

$$
\begin{aligned}
y[n] &= 0.25x[n] + x[n-1] + 0.25x[n-2] \quad \text{(2 multiplies)} \\
&= x[n-1] + 0.25(x[n] + x[n-2]) \quad \text{(1 multiply)}
\end{aligned}
$$

The procedure is similar for the other types of linear phase filters.

Thus, we need 2535 multiplies to compute each sample of the output.

(f) We have

$$
N_1 = \frac{-10\log_{10}(0.01 \times 0.001) - 13}{2.324(0.031\pi - 0.009\pi)} + 1
$$

$$
\begin{aligned}
&\simeq 232 \\
N_2 &= \frac{-10\log_{10}(0.01 \times 0.001) - 13}{2.324(0.5\pi - 0.45\pi)} + 1 \\
&\simeq 103
\end{aligned}
$$

If we again use linear phase filters we find

116	multiplies to get each sample of $v_1[n]$
0	multiplies to get each sample of $w_1[n]$ from $v_1[n]$
52	multiplies to get each sample of $v_2[n]$ from $w_1[n]$
0	multiplies to get each sample of $y[n]$ from $v_2[n]$

The total number of multiplies is 168.

(g) We have

$$
\begin{aligned}
N_1 &= \frac{-10\log_{10}(0.005 \times 0.001) - 13}{2.324(0.022\pi)} + 1 \\
&\simeq 251 \\
N_2 &= \frac{-10\log_{10}(0.005 \times 0.001) - 13}{2.324(0.05\pi)} + 1 \\
&\simeq 111
\end{aligned}
$$

Therefore, we have a total of $126 + 56 = 182$ multiplies per output point.

(h) *No.* Since $\delta_s \ll 1$ we have $\delta_s^2 < \delta_s$ which means the stopband ripple is getting smaller. Thus, we could actually increase the specifications.

(i) Performing a similar analysis on the other possibilities yields

M_1	M_2	Multiplies per output
50	2	182
25	4	156
20	5	172
10	10	291
5	20	557
4	25	693
2	50	1375

Thus, the choice $M_1 = 25$ and $M_2 = 4$ yields the minimum number of multiplications for this example.

7.51. (a)

$$
\begin{aligned}
h_1[n] &= h[n] + \delta_2\delta[n - n_0] \\
H_1(e^{j\omega}) &= H(e^{j\omega}) + \delta_2 e^{-j\omega n_0} \\
&= A_e(e^{j\omega})e^{-j\omega n_0} + \delta_2 e^{-j\omega n_0} \\
&= \underbrace{\left[A_e(e^{j\omega}) + \delta_2\right]}_{H_3(e^{j\omega})} e^{-j\omega n_0}
\end{aligned}
$$

$H_3(e^{j\omega})$ is real since $A_e(e^{j\omega})$ is real and δ_2 is real. It is nonnegative since $A_e(e^{j\omega}) \geq -\delta_2$. Note that $H_3(e^{j\omega})$ is an even function of ω and is a zero-phase filter.

(b) $H_3(e^{j\omega})$ is a zero-phase filter with real coefficients. Thus, a zero at z_k implies there must also be zeros at z_k^*, $1/z_k$, and $1/z_k^*$. In addition, a zero on the unit circle must be a double zero because both its value and its derivative is zero. Note that this last property is true for $H_3(e^{j\omega})$ but not for $A_e(e^{j\omega})$. We can write $H_3(z)$ as

$$H_3(z) = H_2(z)H_2(1/z)$$

where $H_2(z)$ contains all the complex conjugate zero pairs inside the unit circle and $H_2(1/z)$ contains the corresponding complex conjugate zero pairs outside the unit circle. We factor one of the double zeros on the unit circle and its complex conjugate zero into $H_2(z)$. The other pair on the unit circle goes into $H_2(1/z)$.

Since $H_2(z)$ has its zeros on or inside the unit circle it is minimum phase (we allow minimum phase systems to have zeros on the unit circle in this problem). Since the zeros occur in complex conjugate pairs, $h_2[n]$ is real.

(c)

$$\begin{aligned} |H_{min}(e^{j\omega})|^2 &= \frac{H_2(e^{j\omega})H_2^*(e^{j\omega})}{a^2} \\ &= \frac{A_e(e^{j\omega}) + \delta_2}{a^2} \end{aligned}$$

where $a = \frac{\sqrt{1+\delta_1+\delta_2}+\sqrt{1-\delta_1+\delta_2}}{2}$. Since $1 - \delta_1 \leq A_e(e^{j\omega}) \leq 1 + \delta_1$ in the passband and $-\delta_2 \leq A_e(e^{j\omega}) \leq \delta_2$ in the stopband, we have

$$\frac{\sqrt{1-\delta_1+\delta_2}}{a} \leq |H_{min}(e^{j\omega})| \leq \frac{\sqrt{1+\delta_1+\delta_2}}{a}, \qquad \omega \in \text{passband}$$

$$0 \leq |H_{min}(e^{j\omega})| \leq \sqrt{\frac{2\delta_2}{1+\delta_2}}, \qquad \omega \in \text{stopband}$$

Therefore,

$$\begin{aligned} \delta_1' &= \frac{1}{2}\left[\frac{\sqrt{1+\delta_1+\delta_2}}{a} - \frac{\sqrt{1-\delta_1+\delta_2}}{a}\right] \\ &= \frac{1-b}{1+b}, \quad b = \sqrt{\frac{1-\delta_1+\delta_2}{1+\delta_1+\delta_2}} \\ \delta_2' &= \sqrt{\frac{2\delta_2}{1+\delta_2}} \end{aligned}$$

The original filter $h[n]$ has order M. Therefore, $h_1[n]$ also has order M, but $h_2[n]$ has order $M/2$ due to the spectral factorization. Since $h_{min}[n]$ has the same order as $h_2[n]$ we find that the length of $h_{min}[n]$ is $M/2 + 1$.

(d) *No.* If we remove the linear phase constraint, then the zeros of $H_3(z)$ are not distributed in conjugate reciprocal quads. It then becomes impossible to express

$$H_3(z) = H_2(z)H_2(z^{-1})$$

where $H_2(z)$ is a minimum phase filter.

No. It will not work with a Type II linear phase filter. In this case $n_0 = M/2$ is not an integer.

7.52. (a)

$$H(e^{j\omega}) = \sum_{n=0}^{M} h[n]e^{-j\omega n}$$

$$\begin{aligned}
&= \sum_{n=0}^{(M-1)/2} h[n]e^{-j\omega n} + \sum_{n=(M+1)/2}^{M} h[n]e^{-j\omega n} \\
&= \sum_{n=0}^{(M-1)/2} h[n]e^{-j\omega n} + \sum_{m=0}^{(M-1)/2} h[M-m]e^{-j\omega M}e^{j\omega m} \\
&= e^{-j\omega M/2}\left[\sum_{n=0}^{(M-1)/2} h[n]e^{j\omega(M/2-n)} + \sum_{n=0}^{(M-1)/2} h[n]e^{-j\omega(M/2-n)}\right] \\
&= e^{-j\omega M/2}\sum_{n=0}^{(M-1)/2} 2h[n]\cos\omega(M/2-n) \\
&= e^{-j\omega M/2}\sum_{n=1}^{(M+1)/2} 2h[\tfrac{M+1}{2}-n]\cos\omega(n-\tfrac{1}{2})
\end{aligned}$$

Then

$$H(e^{j\omega}) = e^{-j\omega M/2}\sum_{n=1}^{(M+1)/2} b[n]\cos\omega(n-1/2)$$

where $b[n] = 2h[(M+1)/2-n]$ for $n = 1, \ldots, (M+1)/2$.

(b) Using the trigonometric identity

$$\cos\alpha\cos\beta = \frac{1}{2}\cos(\alpha+\beta) + \frac{1}{2}\cos(\alpha-\beta)$$

we get

$$\begin{aligned}
\cos(\omega/2)\sum_{n=0}^{\frac{M-1}{2}} \tilde{b}[n]\cos\omega n &= \frac{1}{2}\sum_{n=0}^{\frac{M-1}{2}} \tilde{b}[n]\cos\omega(n+\tfrac{1}{2}) + \frac{1}{2}\sum_{n=0}^{\frac{M-1}{2}} \tilde{b}[n]\cos\omega(n-\tfrac{1}{2}) \\
&= \frac{1}{2}\sum_{n=1}^{\frac{M+1}{2}} \tilde{b}[n-1]\cos\omega(n-\tfrac{1}{2}) + \frac{1}{2}\sum_{n=1}^{\frac{M+1}{2}} \tilde{b}[n]\cos\omega(n-\tfrac{1}{2}) \\
&\quad + \frac{1}{2}\tilde{b}[0]\cos\omega/2 - \frac{1}{2}\tilde{b}[\tfrac{M+1}{2}]\cos\omega M/2 \\
&= \frac{1}{2}\sum_{n=1}^{\frac{M+1}{2}} \left(\tilde{b}[n]+\tilde{b}[n-1]\right)\cos\omega(n-\tfrac{1}{2}) + \tfrac{1}{2}\tilde{b}[0]\cos\omega/2 - \tfrac{1}{2}\tilde{b}[\tfrac{M+1}{2}]\cos\omega M/2
\end{aligned}$$

Since this last expression must equal

$$\sum_{n=1}^{\frac{M+1}{2}} b[n]\cos\omega(n-\tfrac{1}{2})$$

we can just match up the multipliers in front of the cosine terms of the two expressions. We get

$$b[n] = \begin{cases} \dfrac{\tilde{b}[1]+2\tilde{b}[0]}{2}, & n=1 \\[2ex] \dfrac{\tilde{b}[n]+\tilde{b}[n-1]}{2}, & 2 \le n \le \frac{M-1}{2} \\[2ex] \dfrac{\tilde{b}[\frac{M-1}{2}]}{2}, & n = \frac{M+1}{2} \end{cases}$$

(c) Consider

$$\begin{aligned}
W(\omega)\left[H_d(e^{j\omega}) - A(e^{j\omega})\right] &= W(\omega)\left[H_d(e^{j\omega}) - \sum_{n=1}^{\frac{M+1}{2}} b[n]\cos\omega\left(n-\frac{1}{2}\right)\right] \\
&= W(\omega)\left[H_d(e^{j\omega}) - \cos(\omega/2)\sum_{n=0}^{\frac{M-1}{2}} \tilde{b}[n]\cos\omega n\right] \\
&= \tilde{W}(\omega)\left[\tilde{H}_d(e^{j\omega}) - \sum_{n=0}^{\tilde{L}} \tilde{b}[n]\cos\omega n\right]
\end{aligned}$$

where we have defined

$$\begin{aligned}
\tilde{L} &= \frac{M-1}{2} \\
\tilde{H}_d(e^{j\omega}) &= \frac{H_d(e^{j\omega})}{\cos(\omega/2)} \\
\tilde{W}(\omega) &= W(\omega)\cos(\omega/2)
\end{aligned}$$

We also see that

$$\min_{\tilde{b}[n]}\left\{\max_{\omega\in\tilde{F}}\{\cdot\}\right\} \Longleftrightarrow \min_{b[n]}\left\{\max_{\omega\in F}\{\cdot\}\right\}$$

(d) **Type III filters:**

$$\begin{aligned}
H(e^{j\omega}) &= \sum_{n=0}^{M} h[n]e^{-j\omega n} \\
&= \sum_{n=0}^{M/2-1} h[n]e^{-j\omega n} + 0 + \sum_{n=M/2+1}^{M} h[n]e^{-j\omega n} \\
&= \sum_{n=0}^{M/2-1} h[n]e^{-j\omega n} - \sum_{m=0}^{M/2-1} h[m]e^{-j\omega(M-m)} \\
&= e^{-j\omega M/2}\sum_{n=0}^{M/2-1} h[n]\left(e^{-j\omega(n-M/2)} - e^{j\omega(n-M/2)}\right) \\
&= e^{-j\omega M/2}\sum_{n=0}^{M/2-1} (-2j)h[n]\sin\omega(n-M/2) \\
&= e^{-j\omega M/2}\sum_{m=1}^{M/2} 2jh[M/2-m]\sin\omega m
\end{aligned}$$

Then

$$H(e^{j\omega}) = e^{-j\omega M/2}\sum_{n=1}^{M/2} c[n]\sin\omega n$$

where $c[n] = 2jh[M/2-n]$ for $n = 1,\ldots,M/2$.
If we follow a similar analysis as the one in part (b) we get

$$\sin\omega\sum_{n=0}^{\frac{M}{2}-1}\tilde{c}[n]\cos\omega n = \frac{1}{2}\sum_{n=0}^{\frac{M}{2}-1}\tilde{c}[n]\sin\omega(n+1) - \frac{1}{2}\sum_{n=0}^{\frac{M}{2}-1}\tilde{c}[n]\sin\omega(n-1)$$

$$
\begin{aligned}
&= \frac{1}{2}\sum_{n=1}^{\frac{M}{2}} \tilde{c}[n-1]\sin\omega n - \frac{1}{2}\sum_{n=1}^{\frac{M}{2}} \tilde{c}[n]\sin\omega n \\
&\quad + \frac{1}{2}\tilde{c}[0]\sin\omega + \frac{1}{2}\tilde{c}[\tfrac{M}{2}]\sin\omega M/2 \\
&= \frac{1}{2}\sum_{n=1}^{\frac{M}{2}} (\tilde{c}[n-1]-\tilde{c}[n])\sin\omega n + \frac{1}{2}\tilde{c}[0]\sin\omega + \frac{1}{2}\tilde{c}[\tfrac{M}{2}]\sin\omega M/2
\end{aligned}
$$

Matching terms we get

$$
c[n] = \begin{cases} \dfrac{2\tilde{c}[0]-\tilde{c}[1]}{2}, & n = 1 \\ \dfrac{\tilde{c}[n-1]-\tilde{c}[n]}{2}, & 2 \le n \le \frac{M}{2}-1 \\ \dfrac{\tilde{c}[\frac{M}{2}-1]}{2}, & n = \frac{M}{2} \end{cases}
$$

In a manner similar to that of part (c) we can find

$$
\begin{aligned}
\tilde{L} &= \frac{M}{2} - 1 \\
\tilde{H}_d(e^{j\omega}) &= \frac{H_d(e^{j\omega})}{\sin\omega} \\
\tilde{W}(\omega) &= W(\omega)\sin\omega \\
\tilde{F} &= F
\end{aligned}
$$

Type IV filters:

$$
\begin{aligned}
H(e^{j\omega}) &= \sum_{n=0}^{M} h[n]e^{-j\omega n} \\
&= \sum_{n=0}^{(M-1)/2} h[n]e^{-j\omega n} + \sum_{n=(M+1)/2}^{M} h[n]e^{-j\omega n} \\
&= \sum_{n=0}^{(M-1)/2} h[n]e^{-j\omega n} - \sum_{m=0}^{(M-1)/2} h[m]e^{-j\omega(M-m)} \\
&= e^{-j\omega M/2} \sum_{n=0}^{(M-1)/2} h[n]\left(e^{-j\omega(n-M/2)} - e^{j\omega(n-M/2)}\right) \\
&= e^{-j\omega M/2} \sum_{n=0}^{(M-1)/2} (-2j)h[n]\sin\omega(n-M/2) \\
&= e^{-j\omega M/2} \sum_{m=1}^{(M+1)/2} 2jh[(M+1)/2-m]\sin\omega(m-1/2)
\end{aligned}
$$

Then

$$
H(e^{j\omega}) = e^{-j\omega M/2} \sum_{n=1}^{(M+1)/2} d[n]\sin\omega(n-1/2)
$$

where $d[n] = 2jh[(M+1)/2 - n]$ for $n = 1, \ldots, (M+1)/2$. We can find

$$d[n] = \begin{cases} \dfrac{2\tilde{d}[0] - \tilde{d}[1]}{2}, & n = 1 \\ \dfrac{\tilde{d}[n-1] - \tilde{d}[n]}{2}, & 2 \le n \le \frac{M-1}{2} \\ \dfrac{\tilde{d}[\frac{M-1}{2}]}{2}, & n = \frac{M+1}{2} \end{cases}$$

$$\begin{aligned} \tilde{L} &= \frac{M-1}{2} \\ \tilde{H}_d(e^{j\omega}) &= \frac{H_d(e^{j\omega})}{\sin \omega/2} \\ \tilde{W}(\omega) &= W(\omega)\sin\omega/2 \\ \tilde{F} &= F \end{aligned}$$

7.53. (a) The flow graph for $A_e(z)$ looks like

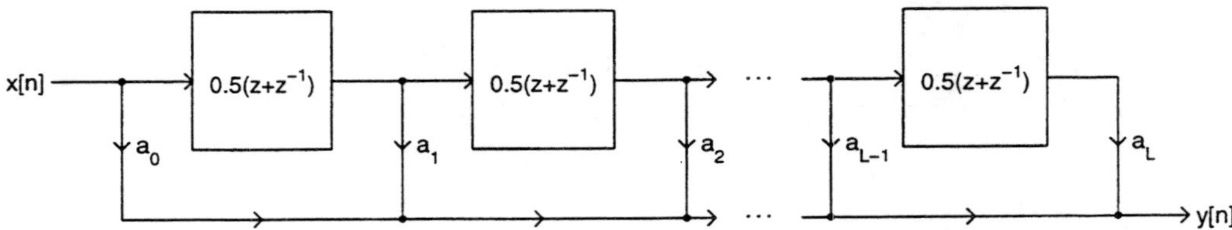

(b) The filter length is $2L+1$. The causal version of the flow graph looks like

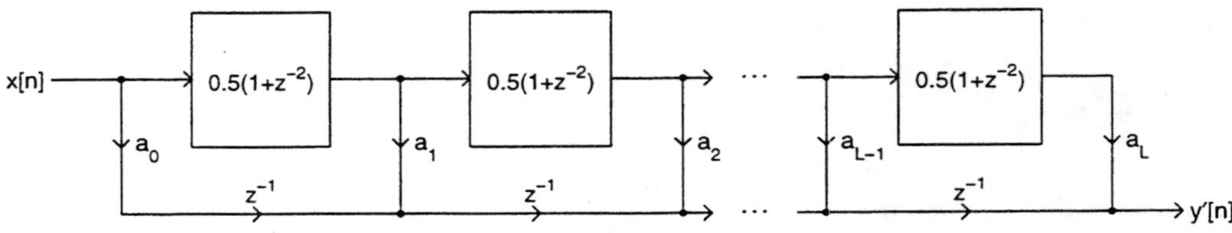

(c) The flow graph for $B_e(z)$ looks like

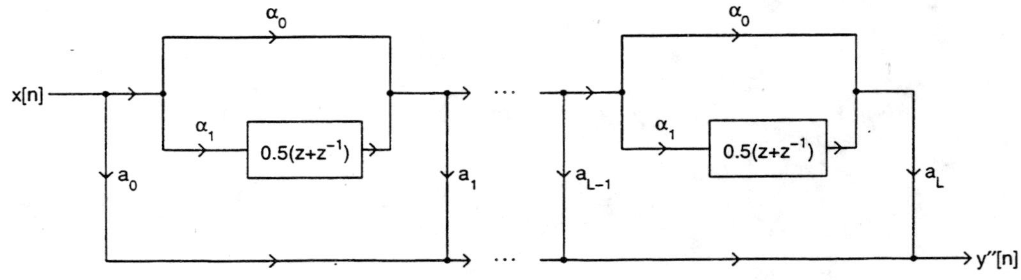

The filter length is still $2L+1$. The modified flow graph looks like

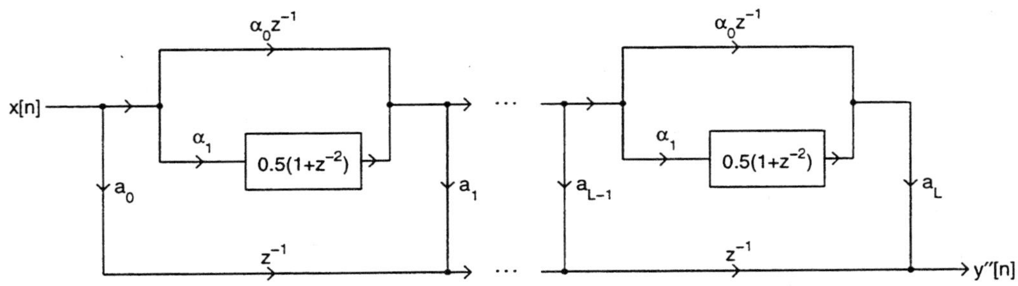

(d) Because $Z = e^{j\theta}$ and $z = e^{j\omega}$ we have

$$
\begin{aligned}
\frac{e^{j\theta} + e^{-j\theta}}{2} &= \alpha_0 + \alpha_1 \left[\frac{e^{j\omega} + e^{-j\omega}}{2}\right] \\
\cos\theta &= \alpha_0 + \alpha_1 \cos\omega \\
\cos\omega &= \frac{\cos\theta - \alpha_0}{\alpha_1} \\
\omega &= \cos^{-1}\left(\frac{\cos\theta - \alpha_0}{\alpha_1}\right), \quad \text{for } \left|\frac{\cos\theta - \alpha_0}{\alpha_1}\right| \leq 1
\end{aligned}
$$

(e)

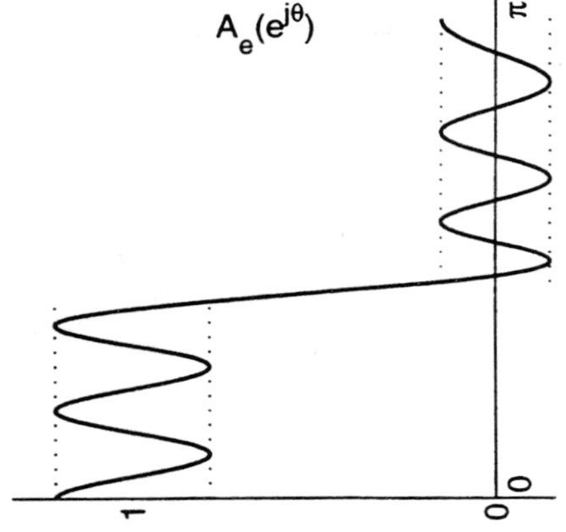

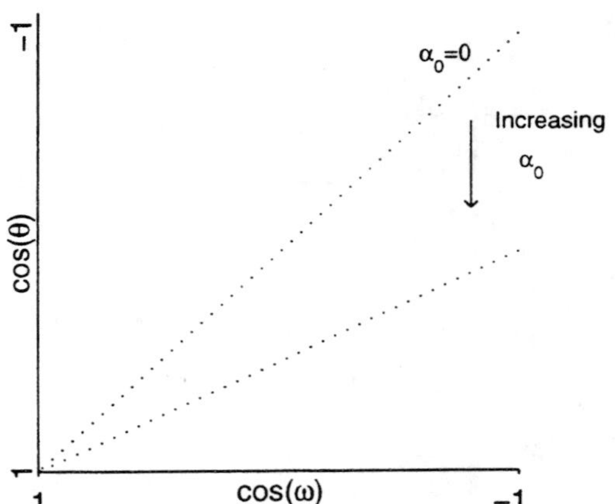

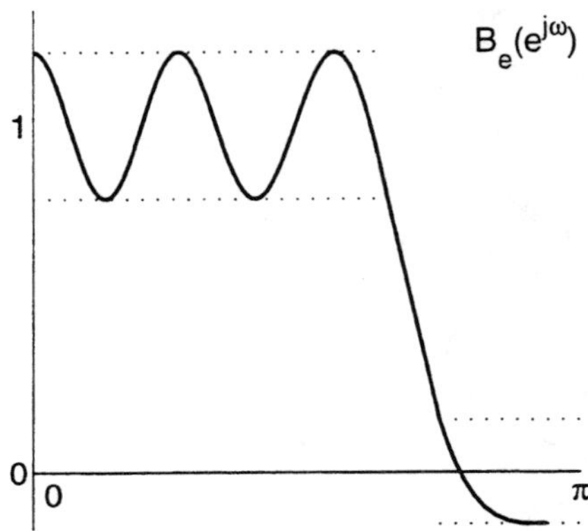

The picture above shows the mapping for α_0 somewhere between 0 and 1. The top right plot is the mapping of

$$\cos\theta = \alpha_0 + (1 - \alpha_0)\cos\omega$$

We see that as α_0 increases, the transformation pushes the new passband further towards π. The new filter is not generally an optimal filter since we lose ripples or alternations while keeping L fixed. (Note that some of the original filter does not map anywhere in the new filter).

(f) In a similar manner, this choice of α_0 will cause the new passband to decrease with decreasing α_0.

7.54. (a) Let $D_k(z)$ be the z-transform of $\Delta^{(k)}\{x[n]\}$. Then

$$\begin{aligned}
D_0(z) &= \mathcal{Z}\left\{\Delta^0\{x[n]\}\right\} = X(z) \\
D_1(z) &= \mathcal{Z}\left\{\Delta^1\{x[n]\}\right\} = (z - z^{-1})X(z) \\
D_2(z) &= \mathcal{Z}\left\{\Delta^2\{x[n]\}\right\} = (z - z^{-1})^2X(z) \\
&\vdots \\
D_k(z) &= \mathcal{Z}\left\{\Delta^k\{x[n]\}\right\} = (z - z^{-1})^kX(z)
\end{aligned}$$

(b) By taking the transform of both sides of the continuous-time differential equation one gets (assuming initial rest conditions)

$$\sum_{k=0}^{N} a_k s^k Y(s) = \sum_{r=0}^{M} b_r s^r X(s)$$

Solving for $H_c(s)$

$$H_c(s) = \frac{Y(s)}{X(s)} = \frac{\sum_{r=0}^{M} b_r s^r}{\sum_{k=0}^{N} a_k s^k}$$

Similarly,

$$\sum_{k=0}^{N} a_k (z - z^{-1})^k Y(z) = \sum_{r=0}^{M} b_r (z - z^{-1})^r X(z)$$

$$\begin{aligned} H_d(z) &= \frac{Y(z)}{X(z)} = \frac{\sum_{r=0}^{M} b_r (z - z^{-1})^r}{\sum_{k=0}^{N} a_k (z - z^{-1})^k} \\ &= H_c(s)|_{s=z-z^{-1}} \end{aligned}$$

$$\Rightarrow m(z) = z - z^{-1}$$

(c) First, map the continuous-time cutoff frequency into discrete-time and then make the sketch.

$$s = z - z^{-1}$$

$$j\Omega = e^{j\omega} - e^{-j\omega}$$

$$\Omega = \frac{e^{j\omega} - e^{-j\omega}}{j} = 2\sin(\omega) = 1$$

$$\omega = \frac{\pi}{6}$$

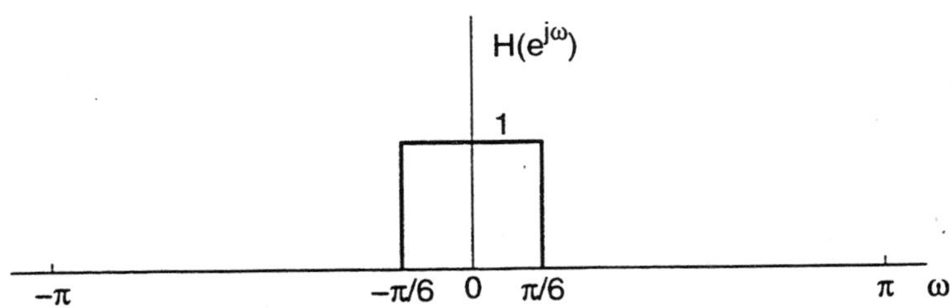

7.55. (a) Using DTFT properties,

$$\begin{aligned} h_1[n] &= h[-n] \\ H_1(e^{j\omega}) &= H(e^{-j\omega}) \end{aligned}$$

Since $H(e^{j\omega})$ is symmetric about $\omega = 0$, $H(e^{-j\omega}) = H(e^{j\omega})$. Thus, $H_1(e^{j\omega}) = H(e^{-j\omega}) = H(e^{j\omega})$. $H(e^{j\omega})$ is optimal in the minimax sense, so $H_1(e^{j\omega})$ is optimal in minimax sense as well.

$$H_d(e^{j\omega}) = \begin{cases} 1, & 0 \le \omega \le \omega_p \\ 0, & \omega_s \le \omega \le \pi \end{cases}$$

$$W(e^{j\omega}) = \begin{cases} \delta_2/\delta_1, & 0 \le \omega \le \omega_p \\ 1, & \omega_s \le \omega \le \pi \end{cases}$$

(b) Using DTFT properties,

$$\begin{aligned} h_2[n] &= (-1)^n h[n] \\ &= (e^{-j\pi})^n h[n] \\ H_2(e^{j\omega}) &= H(e^{j(\omega+\pi)}) \end{aligned}$$

$H_2(e^{j\omega})$ is a high pass filter obtained by shifting $H(e^{j\omega})$ by π along the frequency axis. $H_2(e^{j\omega})$ satisfies the alternation thereom, and is therefore optimal in the minimax sense.

$$H_d(e^{j\omega}) = \begin{cases} 0, & 0 \le \omega \le \pi - \omega_s \\ 1, & \pi - \omega_p \le \omega \le \pi \end{cases}$$

$$W(e^{j\omega}) = \begin{cases} 1, & 0 \le \omega \le \pi - \omega_s \\ \delta_2/\delta_1, & \pi - \omega_p \le \omega \le \pi \end{cases}$$

(c) Using DTFT properties,

$$\begin{aligned} h_3[n] &= h[n] * h[n] \\ H_3(e^{j\omega}) &= H(e^{j\omega})H(e^{j\omega}) \end{aligned}$$

In the passband, $H_3(e^{j\omega})$ alternates about $1 + \delta_1^2$ with a maximal error of $2\delta_1^2$. In the stopband, $H_3(e^{j\omega})$ alternates about $\delta_2^2/2$ with a maximal error of $\delta_2^2/2$. At first glance, it may appear that $H_3(e^{j\omega})$ is optimal. However, this is not the case. Counting alternations, we find that the original filter $H(e^{j\omega})$ has 8 alternations.
We know that since $H(e^{j\omega})$ is optimal, it must have at least $L+2$ alternations. It is also possible that $H(e^{j\omega})$ has $L+3$ alternations, if it corresponds to the extraripple case. So L is either 5 or 6 for this filter. Consequently, the filter length of $h[n]$, denoted as N, is either 11 or 13.

The filter $h_3[n]$ is the convolution of two length N sequences. Therefore, the length of $h_3[n]$, denoted as N', is $2N-1$. Since N is either 11 or 13, N' must be either 21 or 25. It follows that the polynomial order for $h_3[n]$, denoted as L', is either 10 or 12. For $h_3[n]$ to be optimal in the minimax sense, it must have at least $L'+2$ alternations. Thus, $h_3[n]$ must exhibit at least 12 alternations, for the non-extraripple case, or at least 14 alternations in the extraripple case to be optimal.

A simple counting of the alternations in $H_3(e^{j\omega})$ reveals that there are 11 alternations, consisting of the 8 alternations that were in $H(e^{j\omega})$ plus 3 where $H(e^{j\omega}) = 0$. These are too few to satisfy either the non-extraripple case or the extraripple case. As a result, this filter is not optimal in the minimax sense.

(d)

$$\begin{aligned} h_4[n] &= h[n] - K\delta[n] \\ H_4(e^{j\omega}) &= H(e^{j\omega}) - K \end{aligned}$$

This filter is simply $H(e^{j\omega})$ shifted down by K along the $H_4(e^{j\omega})$ axis. Consequently, this filter satisfies the alternation theorem, and is optimal in the minimax sense.

$$H_d(e^{j\omega}) = \begin{cases} 1-K, & 0 \le \omega \le \omega_p \\ -K, & \omega_s \le \omega \le \pi \end{cases}$$

$$W(e^{j\omega}) = \begin{cases} \delta_2/\delta_1, & 0 \le \omega \le \omega_p \\ 1, & \omega_s \le \omega \le \pi \end{cases}$$

(e) $h_5[n]$ is $h[n]$ upsampled by a factor of 2. In the frequency domain, upsampling by a factor of 2 will cause the frequency axis to get scaled by a factor of 1/2. Consequently, $H_5(e^{j\omega})$ will be a bandstop filter that satisfies the alternation theorem, with twice as many alternations as $H(e^{j\omega})$. This filter is optimal in the minimax sense.

$$H_d(e^{j\omega}) = \begin{cases} 1, & 0 \le \omega \le \omega_p/2 \\ 0, & \omega_s/2 \le \omega \le \pi - \omega_s/2 \\ 1, & \pi - \omega_p/2 \le \omega \le \pi \end{cases}$$

$$W(e^{j\omega}) = \begin{cases} \delta_2/\delta_1, & 0 \le \omega \le \omega_p/2 \\ 1, & \omega_s/2 \le \omega \le \pi - \omega_s/2 \\ \delta_2/\delta_1, & \pi - \omega_p/2 \le \omega \le \pi \end{cases}$$

7.56. We have an odd length causal linear phase filter with values from $n = 0, \dots, 24$. It must therefore be either a Type I or Type III filter.

(a) *True.* We know either

$$\begin{array}{ccc} \text{Type I} & & \text{Type III} \\ h[m] = h[24-m] & \textit{or} & h[m] = -h[24-m] \end{array}$$

for $-\infty < m < \infty$ since the filter has linear phase. Substituting $m = n + 12$ we get

$$h[n+12] = h[12-n] \quad \textit{or} \quad h[n+12] = -h[12-n]$$

(b) *False.* Since the filter is linear phase it either has zeros both inside and outside the unit circle or it has zeros only on the unit circle.
If the filter has zeros both inside and outside the unit circle, its inverse has poles both inside and outside the unit circle. The only region of convergence that would correspond to a stable inverse would be the ring that includes the unit circle. The inverse would therefore be two-sided and not causal.
If the filter only has zeros on the unit circle, its inverse has poles on the unit circle and is therefore unstable.

(c) *Insufficient Information.* If it is a Type III filter it would have a zero at $z = -1$ but if it is a Type I filter this is not necessarily true.

(d) *True.* To minimize the maximum weighted approximation error is the goal of the Parks-McClellan algorithm.

(e) *True.* The filter is FIR so there are no feedback paths in the signal flow graph.

(f) *True.* The filter has linear phase and

$$\arg\left[H(e^{j\omega})\right] = \beta - 12\omega$$

where $\beta = 0, \pi$ for a Type I filter or $\beta = \pi/2, 3\pi/2$ for a Type III filter. The group delay is

$$\begin{aligned} \text{grd}\left[H(e^{j\omega})\right] &= -\frac{d}{d\omega}\left\{\arg\left[H(e^{j\omega})\right]\right\} \\ &= 12 \\ &> 0 \end{aligned}$$

7.57. (a) The desired tolerance scheme is

$$H_d(e^{j\omega}) = \begin{cases} 0, & 0 \leq |\omega| \leq \omega_1 \\ 1, & \omega_2 \leq |\omega| \leq \omega_3 \\ 0, & \omega_4 \leq |\omega| \leq \pi \end{cases}$$

(b)

$$W(\omega) = \begin{cases} 1 & \left(\text{or } \frac{\delta_2}{\delta_1}\right) & \left(\text{or } \frac{\delta_3}{\delta_1}\right) & 0 \leq |\omega| \leq \omega_1 \\ \frac{\delta_1}{\delta_2} & (\text{or } 1) & \left(\text{or } \frac{\delta_3}{\delta_2}\right) & \omega_2 \leq |\omega| \leq \omega_3 \\ \frac{\delta_1}{\delta_3} & \left(\text{or } \frac{\delta_2}{\delta_3}\right) & (\text{or } 1) & \omega_4 \leq |\omega| \leq \pi \end{cases}$$

(c) From the Alternation Theorem, the minimum number of alternations is $L + 2$.

(d) The trigonometric polynomial (of degree L) can have at most $L - 1$ points of local minima or maxima in the open interval between 0 and π. If these are all alternation points and, in addition, all the band edges are alternation points, we find the maximum number of alternations is

$$L - 1 + 6 = L + 5$$

(e) If $M = 14$, then $L = M/2 = 7$. The maximum number of alternations is therefore $7 + 5 = 12$.

Typical $E(\omega)$ looks like :

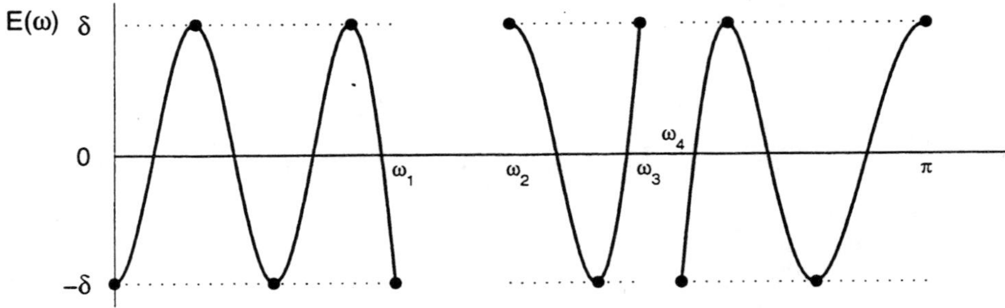

(f) As will be shown in part (g), the 3 band case can have maxima and minima in the transition regions. It follows that we do not have to have an extremal frequency at ω_4. Therefore, if we started with an optimal maximal ripple filter and just slid ω_4 over we may move a local minimum or maximum into the transition region, but there will still be enough alternations left to satisfy the alternation theorem. Thus, the maximum approximation error does not have to decrease.

(g) (i) If a point in the transition region has a local minimum or maximum then there is the possibility that the surrounding points of maximum error do not alternate. Thus, we might lower the number of alternations by two. However, if we started with $L + 5$ alternations this reduction does not drop the number of alternations below the lower limit of $L + 2$ set by the Alternation Theorem. Therefore, local maxima and minima of $A_e(e^{j\omega})$ can occur in the transition regions. Note that this is not true in the 2 band case.

(ii) If a point in the approximation bands is a local minimum or maximum, the surrounding points of maximum error do not alternate. Thus, a local minimum or maximum in the approximation bands implies that the total number of alternations is reduced by two. However, if we started with $L + 5$ alternations this reduction does not drop the number of alternations below the lower limit of $L + 2$ set by the Alternation Theorem. Therefore, we can have a local maximum or minimum in the approximation bands. Note that in the 2-band case we drop from $L + 3$ to $L + 1$ which violates the Alternation Theorem.

7.58. (a) In order for condition 3 to hold, $G(z^{-1})$ must be an allpass system, since

$$\begin{aligned} Z^{-1} &= G(z^{-1}) \\ e^{-j\theta} &= G(e^{-j\omega}) \\ &= \left|G(e^{-j\omega})\right| e^{j\angle G(e^{-j\omega})} \end{aligned}$$

Clearly, $\left|G(e^{-j\omega})\right|$ must equal unity to map the unit circle of the Z-plane onto the unit circle of the z-plane.

(b) Consider one allpass term in the product, and note that α_k is real.

$$Z^{-1} = \frac{z^{-1} - \alpha_k}{1 - \alpha_k z^{-1}}$$

The inside of the unit circle of the Z-plane is

$$0 \leq |Z| < 1$$

Or equivalently,

$$1 < \left|Z^{-1}\right| < \infty$$

Substituting the allpass term for Z^{-1} gives

$$\begin{aligned} 1 &< \left|\frac{z^{-1} - \alpha_k}{1 - \alpha_k z^{-1}}\right| \\ (1 - \alpha_k z^{-1})(1 - \alpha_k z^{*-1}) &< (z^{-1} - \alpha_k)(z^{*-1} - \alpha_k) \\ 1 - \alpha_k z^{-1} - \alpha_k z^{*-1} + \alpha_k^2 z^{-1} z^{*-1} &< z^{-1} z^{*-1} - \alpha_k z^{*-1} - \alpha_k z^{-1} + \alpha_k^2 \\ (1 - \alpha_k^2) &< z^{-1} z^{*-1}(1 - \alpha_k^2) \end{aligned}$$

If $(1 - \alpha_k^2) < 0$, then

$$\begin{aligned} 1 &> z^{-1} z^{*-1} \\ 1 &> \frac{1}{|z|^2} \\ |z| &> 1 \end{aligned}$$

The inside of the unit circle of the Z-plane maps to the *outside* of the unit circle of the z-plane. This is not the desired result. However, if $(1 - \alpha_k^2) > 0$, then

$$\begin{aligned} 1 &< z^{-1} z^{*-1} \\ 1 &< \frac{1}{|z|^2} \\ |z| &< 1 \end{aligned}$$

The inside of the unit circle of the Z-plane maps to the *inside* of the unit circle of the z-plane. This is the desired result. Thus, for condition 2 to be satisfied,

$$\begin{aligned} 1 - \alpha_k^2 &> 0 \\ |\alpha_k|^2 &< 1 \\ |\alpha_k| &< 1 \end{aligned}$$

This condition holds for the general case as well since the general case is just a product of the simpler allpass terms.

(c) First, it is shown that $G(z^{-1})$ produces the desired mapping for some value of α. Starting with $G(z^{-1})$,

$$
\begin{aligned}
Z^{-1} &= \frac{z^{-1}-\alpha}{1-\alpha z^{-1}} \\
e^{-j\theta} &= \frac{e^{-j\omega}-\alpha}{1-\alpha e^{-j\omega}} \\
e^{-j\theta}-\alpha e^{-j\theta}e^{-j\omega} &= e^{-j\omega}-\alpha \\
e^{-j\omega}(1+\alpha e^{-j\theta}) &= e^{-j\theta}+\alpha \\
e^{-j\omega} &= \frac{e^{-j\theta}+\alpha}{1+\alpha e^{-j\theta}} \\
&= \frac{e^{-j\theta}+\alpha}{1+\alpha e^{-j\theta}} \cdot \frac{1+\alpha e^{j\theta}}{1+\alpha e^{j\theta}} \\
&= \frac{e^{-j\theta}+2\alpha+\alpha^2 e^{j\theta}}{1+2\alpha\cos\theta+\alpha^2}
\end{aligned}
$$

Using Euler's formula,

$$
\begin{aligned}
e^{-j\omega} &= \frac{\cos\theta - j\sin\theta + 2\alpha + \alpha^2\cos\theta + j\alpha^2\sin\theta}{1+2\alpha\cos\theta+\alpha^2} \\
&= \frac{2\alpha + (1+\alpha^2)\cos\theta + j[(\alpha^2-1)\sin\theta]}{1+2\alpha\cos\theta+\alpha^2}
\end{aligned}
$$

Noting that $-\omega = \tan^{-1}\left[\frac{Im\{\cdot\}}{Re\{\cdot\}}\right]$,

$$
\begin{aligned}
-\omega &= \tan^{-1}\left[\frac{(\alpha^2-1)\sin\theta}{2\alpha+(1+\alpha^2)\cos\theta}\right] \\
\omega &= \tan^{-1}\left[\frac{(1-\alpha^2)\sin\theta}{2\alpha+(1+\alpha^2)\cos\theta}\right]
\end{aligned}
$$

This relationship is plotted in the figure below for different values of α. Although a warping of the frequency scale is evident in the figure, (except when $\alpha = 0$, which corresponds to $Z^{-1} = z^{-1}$), if the original system has a piecewise-constant lowpass frequency response with cutoff frequency θ_p, then the transformed system will likewise have a similar lowpass response with cutoff frequency ω_p determined by the choice of α.

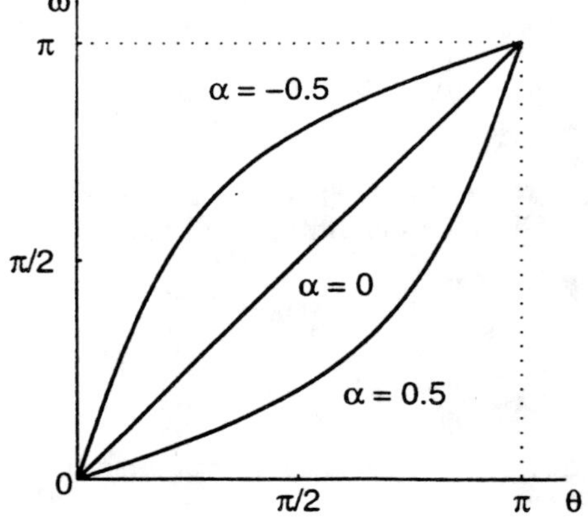

Next, an equation for α is found in terms of θ_p and ω_p. Starting with $G(z^{-1})$,

$$\begin{aligned}
Z^{-1} &= \frac{z^{-1}-\alpha}{1-\alpha z^{-1}} \\
e^{-j\theta_p} &= \frac{e^{-j\omega_p}-\alpha}{1-\alpha e^{-j\omega_p}} \\
e^{-j\theta_p} - \alpha e^{-j\theta_p}e^{-j\omega_p} &= e^{-j\omega_p}-\alpha \\
e^{-j\theta_p} - e^{-j\omega_p} &= \alpha(e^{-j(\theta_p+\omega_p)}-1) \\
\alpha &= \frac{e^{-j\theta_p} - e^{-j\omega_p}}{e^{-j(\theta_p+\omega_p)}-1} \\
&= \frac{e^{-j(\theta_p+\omega_p)/2}(e^{-j(\theta_p-\omega_p)/2}-e^{j(\theta_p-\omega_p)/2})}{e^{-j(\theta_p+\omega_p)/2}(e^{-j(\theta_p+\omega_p)/2}-e^{j(\theta_p+\omega_p)/2})} \\
&= \frac{-2j\sin[(\theta_p-\omega_p)/2]}{-2j\sin[(\theta_p+\omega_p)/2]} \\
&= \frac{\sin[(\theta_p-\omega_p)/2]}{\sin[(\theta_p+\omega_p)/2]}
\end{aligned}$$

(d) Using the equation for ω found in part c, with $\theta_p = \pi/2$,

$$\omega_p = \tan^{-1}\left[\frac{1-\alpha^2}{2\alpha}\right]$$

(i)

$$\begin{aligned}
\omega_p &= \tan^{-1}\left[\frac{1-(-0.2679)^2}{2(-0.2679)}\right] \\
&= \tan^{-1}\left(\frac{0.9282}{-0.5358}\right) \\
&= 2\pi/3
\end{aligned}$$

(ii)

$$\begin{aligned}
\omega_p &= \tan^{-1}\left[\frac{1-(0)^2}{2(0)}\right] \\
&= \tan^{-1}(\infty) \\
&= \pi/2
\end{aligned}$$

(iii)

$$\begin{aligned}
\omega_p &= \tan^{-1}\left[\frac{1-(0.4142)^2}{2(0.4142)}\right] \\
&= \tan^{-1}(1) \\
&= \pi/4
\end{aligned}$$

(e) The first-order allpass system

$$G(z^{-1}) = -\frac{z^{-1}+\alpha}{1+\alpha z^{-1}}$$

satisfies the criteria that the unit circle in the Z-plane maps to the unit circle in the z-plane, and that $\theta = 0$ maps to $\omega = \pi$. Next, α is found in terms of θ_p and ω_p.

$$Z^{-1} = -\frac{z^{-1}+\alpha}{1+\alpha z^{-1}}$$

$$\begin{aligned}
e^{-j\theta_p} &= -\frac{e^{-j\omega_p}+\alpha}{1+\alpha e^{-j\omega_p}} \\
-e^{-j\theta_p} - \alpha e^{-j(\omega_p+\theta)} &= e^{-j\omega_p}+\alpha \\
\alpha(1+e^{-j(\omega_p+\theta_p)}) &= -e^{-j\theta_p} - e^{-j\omega_p} \\
\alpha &= -\frac{e^{-j\theta_p}+e^{-j\omega_p}}{1+e^{-j(\omega_p+\theta_p)}} \\
&= -\frac{e^{-j(\omega_p+\theta_p)/2}(e^{-j(-\omega_p+\theta_p)/2}+e^{-j(\omega_p-\theta_p)/2})}{e^{-j(\omega_p+\theta_p)/2}(e^{j(\omega_p+\theta_p)/2}+e^{-j(\omega_p+\theta_p)/2})} \\
&= -\frac{\cos[(\omega_p-\theta_p)/2]}{\cos[(\omega_p+\theta_p)/2]}
\end{aligned}$$

(f) First, an equation for ω is found in terms of θ and α.

$$\begin{aligned}
Z^{-1} &= -\frac{z^{-1}+\alpha}{1+\alpha z^{-1}} \\
e^{-j\theta} &= -\frac{e^{-j\omega}+\alpha}{1+\alpha e^{-j\omega}} \\
-e^{-j\theta} - \alpha e^{-j(\omega+\theta)} &= e^{-j\omega}+\alpha \\
e^{-j\omega}(1+\alpha e^{-j\theta}) &= -e^{-j\theta}-\alpha \\
-e^{-j\omega} &= \frac{e^{-j\theta}+\alpha}{1+\alpha e^{-j\theta}} \\
e^{-j(\omega-\pi)} &= \frac{e^{-j\theta}+\alpha}{1+\alpha e^{-j\theta}}\cdot\frac{1+\alpha e^{j\theta}}{1+\alpha e^{j\theta}} \\
&= \frac{e^{-j\theta}+2\alpha+\alpha^2 e^{j\theta}}{1+2\alpha\cos\theta+\alpha^2} \\
&= \frac{\cos\theta - j\sin\theta + 2\alpha + \alpha^2\cos\theta + j\alpha^2\sin\theta}{1+2\alpha\cos\theta+\alpha^2} \\
&= \frac{\cos\theta + 2\alpha + \alpha^2\cos\theta + j(-\sin\theta + \alpha^2\sin\theta)}{1+2\alpha\cos\theta+\alpha^2}
\end{aligned}$$

Therefore,

$$\begin{aligned}
-\omega+\pi &= \tan^{-1}\left[\frac{(\alpha^2-1)\sin\theta}{2\alpha+(1+\alpha^2)\cos\theta}\right] \\
\omega &= \tan^{-1}\left[\frac{(1-\alpha^2)\sin\theta}{2\alpha+(1+\alpha^2)\cos\theta}\right]+\pi
\end{aligned}$$

Note that this lowpass to highpass expression is the similar to the lowpass to lowpass expression for ω found in part (c). The only difference is the additive π term, which shifts the lowpass filter into a highpass filter. The frequency warping is plotted below.

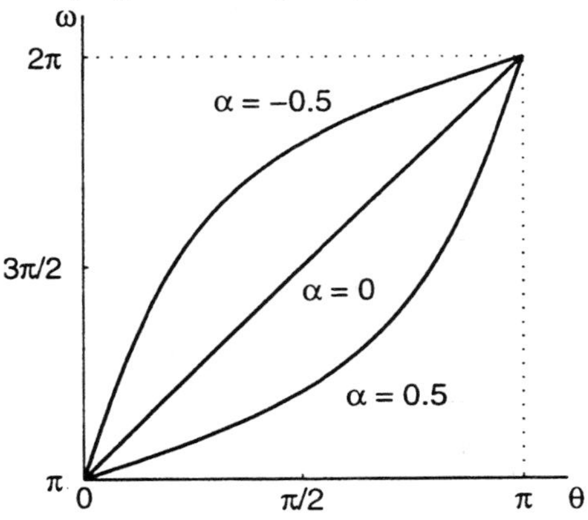

For $\theta_p = \pi/2$, this becomes

$$\omega = \tan^{-1}\left[\frac{(1-\alpha^2)}{2\alpha}\right] + \pi$$

(i)

$$\begin{aligned}\omega_p &= \tan^{-1}\left[\frac{1-(-0.2679)^2}{2(-0.2679)}\right] + \pi \\ &= \tan^{-1}\left(\frac{0.9282}{-0.5358}\right) + \pi \\ &= 2\pi/3 + \pi \\ &= 5\pi/3\end{aligned}$$

The right edge of the low pass filter gets warped to $5\pi/3$, which is equivalent to $-\pi/3$. The frequency response of this filter appears below.

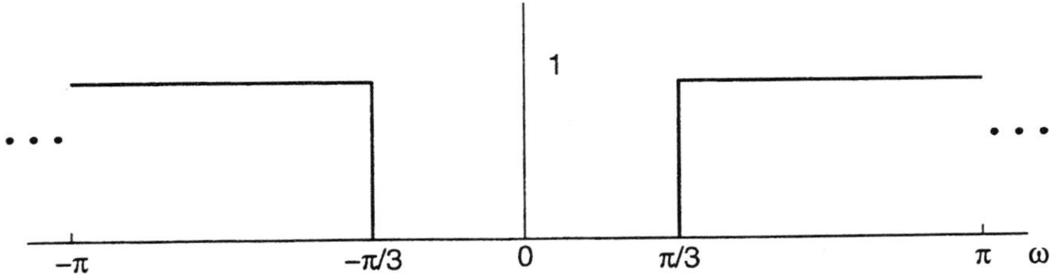

(ii)

$$\begin{aligned}\omega_p &= \tan^{-1}\left[\frac{1-(0)^2}{2(0)}\right] + \pi \\ &= \tan^{-1}(\infty) + \pi \\ &= \pi/2 + \pi \\ &= 3\pi/2\end{aligned}$$

The right edge of the low pass filter gets warped to $3\pi/2$, which is equivalent to $-\pi/2$. The frequency response of this filter appears below.

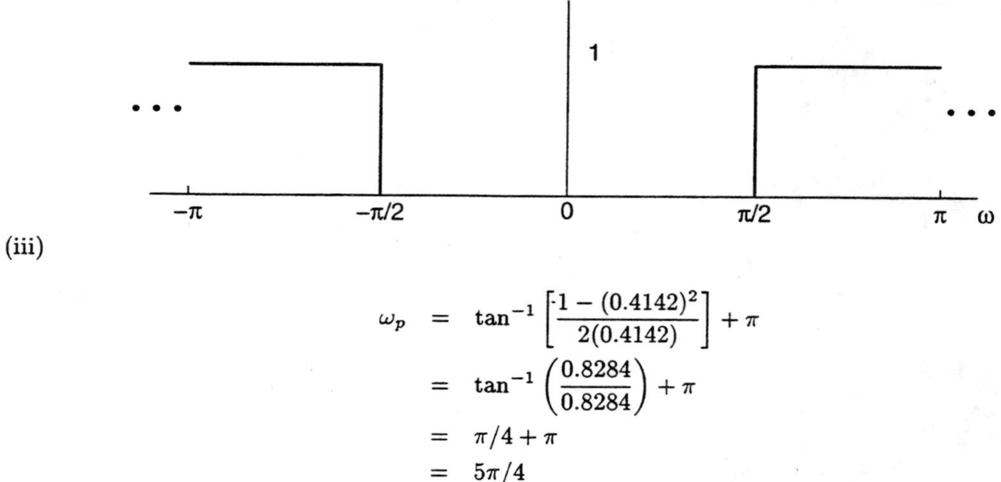

(iii)

$$\begin{aligned}\omega_p &= \tan^{-1}\left[\frac{1-(0.4142)^2}{2(0.4142)}\right]+\pi \\ &= \tan^{-1}\left(\frac{0.8284}{0.8284}\right)+\pi \\ &= \pi/4+\pi \\ &= 5\pi/4\end{aligned}$$

The right edge of the low pass filter gets warped to $5\pi/4$, which is equivalent to $-3\pi/4$. The frequency response of this filter appears below.

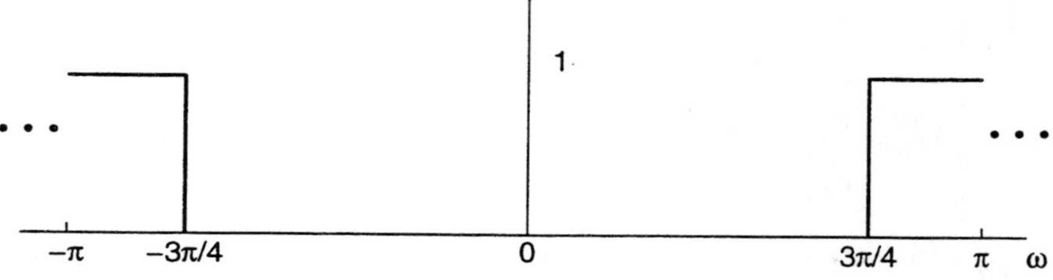

Solutions – Chapter 8

The Discrete-Time Fourier Transform

8.1. We sample a periodic continuous-time signal with a sampling rate:

$$F_s = \frac{\Omega s}{2\pi} = \frac{1}{T} = \frac{6}{10^{-3}}\text{Hz}$$

(a) The sampled signal is given by:

$$x[n] = x_c(nT)$$

Expressed as a Discrete Fourier Series:

$$x[n] = \sum_{k=-9}^{9} a_k e^{j\frac{2\pi}{6}kn}$$

We note that, in accordance with the discussion of Section 8.1, the sampled signal is represented by the summation of harmonically-related complex exponentials. The fundamental frequency of this set of exponentials is $2\pi/N$, where $N = 6$.

Therefore, the sequence $x[n]$ is periodic with period 6.

(b) For any bandlimited continuous-time signal, the Nyquist Criterion may be stated from Eq. (4.14b) as:

$$F_s \geq 2F_N,$$

where F_s is the sampling rate (Hz), and F_N corresponds to the highest frequency component in the signal (also Hz).

As evident by the finite Fourier series representation of $x_c(t)$, this continuous-time signal is, indeed, bandlimited with a maximum frequency of $F_n = \frac{9}{10^{-3}}$ Hz.

Therfore, by sampling at a rate of $F_s = \frac{6}{10^{-3}}$ Hz, the Nyquist Criterion is violated, and aliasing results.

(c) We use the analysis equation of Eq. (8.11):

$$\tilde{X}[k] = \sum_{n=0}^{N-1} \tilde{x}[n] e^{-j\frac{2\pi}{N}kn}$$

From part (a), $\tilde{x}[n]$ is periodic with $N = 6$.

Substitution yields:

$$\begin{aligned}\tilde{X}[k] &= \sum_{n=0}^{5}\left(\sum_{m=-9}^{9} a_m e^{j\frac{2\pi}{6}mn}\right)e^{-j\frac{2\pi}{6}kn} \\ &= \sum_{n=0}^{5}\sum_{m=-9}^{9} a_m e^{j(2\pi/6)(m-k)n}\end{aligned}$$

We reverse the order of the summations, and use the orthogonality relationship from Example 8.1:

$$\tilde{X}[k] = 6\sum_{m=-9}^{9} a_m \sum_{r=-\infty}^{\infty} \delta[m-k+rN]$$

Taking the infinite summation to the outside, we recognize the convolution between a_m and shifted impulses (Recall $a_m = 0$ for $|m| > 9$). Thus,

$$\tilde{X}[k] = 6\sum_{r=-\infty}^{\infty} a_{k-6r}$$

Note that from $\tilde{X}[k]$, the aliasing is apparent.

8.2. (a) Using the analysis equation of Eq. (8.11)

$$\tilde{X}[k] = \sum_{n=0}^{N-1} \tilde{x}[n] W_N^{kn}$$

Since $\tilde{x}[n]$ is also periodic with period $3N$,

$$\begin{aligned}\tilde{X}_3[k] &= \sum_{n=0}^{3N-1} \tilde{x}[n] W_{3N}^{kn} \\ &= \sum_{n=0}^{N-1} \tilde{x}[n] W_{3N}^{kn} + \sum_{n=N}^{2N-1} \tilde{x}[n] W_{3N}^{kn} + \sum_{n=2N}^{3N-1} \tilde{x}[n] W_{3N}^{kn}\end{aligned}$$

Performing a change of variables in the second and third summations of $\tilde{X_3}[k]$,

$$\tilde{X}_3[k] = \sum_{n=0}^{N-1} \tilde{x}[n] W_{3N}^{kn} + W_{3N}^{kN} \sum_{n=0}^{N-1} \tilde{x}[n+N] W_{3N}^{kn} + W_{3N}^{2kN} \sum_{n=0}^{N-1} \tilde{x}[n+2N] W_{3N}^{kn}$$

Since $\tilde{x}[n]$ is periodic with period N, and $W_{3N}^{kn} = W_N^{(\frac{k}{3})n}$,

$$\begin{aligned}\tilde{X}_3[k] &= \left(1 + e^{-j2\pi(\frac{k}{3})} + e^{-j2\pi(\frac{2k}{3})}\right) \sum_{n=0}^{N-1} \tilde{x}[n] W_N^{(\frac{k}{3}n)} \\ &= \left(1 + e^{-j2\pi(\frac{k}{3})} + e^{-j2\pi(\frac{2k}{3})}\right) \tilde{X}[k] \\ &= \begin{cases} 3\tilde{X}[k/3], & k = 3\ell \\ 0, & \text{otherwise} \end{cases}\end{aligned}$$

(b) Using $N = 2$ and $\tilde{x}[n]$ as in Fig P8.2-1:

$$\begin{aligned}\tilde{X}[k] &= \sum_{n=0}^{N-1} \tilde{x}[n] W_N^{kn} \\ &= \sum_{n=0}^{1} \tilde{x}[n] e^{-j\frac{2\pi}{2}kn} \\ &= \tilde{x}[0] + \tilde{x}[1] e^{-j\pi k} \\ &= 1 + 2(-1)^k \\ &= \begin{cases} 3, & k = 0 \\ -1, & k = 1 \end{cases}\end{aligned}$$

Observe, from Fig. P8.2-1, that $\tilde{x}[n]$ is also periodic with period $3N = 6$:

$$\begin{aligned}\tilde{X}_3[k] &= \sum_{n=0}^{3N-1} \tilde{x}[n] W_{3N}^{kn} \\ &= \sum_{n=0}^{5} \tilde{x}[n] e^{-j\frac{\pi}{3}kn} \\ &= (1 + e^{-j\frac{2\pi}{3}k} + e^{-j\frac{4\pi}{3}k})(1 + 2(-1)^{\frac{k}{3}}) \\ &= (1 + e^{-j\frac{2\pi}{3}k} + e^{-j\frac{4\pi}{3}k})\tilde{X}[k/3] \\ &= \begin{cases} 9, & k = 0 \\ -3, & k = 3 \\ 0, & k = 1, 2, 4, 5. \end{cases}\end{aligned}$$

8.3. (a) The DFS coefficients will be real if $\tilde{x}[n]$ is even. Only signal B can be even (i.e., $\tilde{x}_B[n] = \tilde{x}_B[-n]$; if the origin is selected as the midpoint of either the nonzero block, or the zero block).

(b) The DFS coefficients will be imaginary if $\tilde{x}[n]$ is even. None of the sequences in Fig P8.3-1 can be odd.

(c) We use the analysis equation, Eq. (8.11) and the closed form expression for a geometric series. Assuming unit amplitudes and discarding DFS points which are zero:

$$\begin{aligned}
\tilde{X}_A[k] &= \sum_{n=0}^{3} e^{j\frac{2\pi}{8}kn} \\
&= \frac{1 - e^{j\frac{\pi}{4}4k}}{1 - e^{j\frac{\pi}{4}k}} \\
&= \frac{1-(-1)^k}{1 - e^{j\frac{\pi}{4}k}} = 0, k = \pm 2, \pm 4, \ldots \\
\tilde{X}_B[k] &= \sum_{n=0}^{2} e^{j\frac{2\pi}{8}kn} \\
&= \frac{1 - e^{j\frac{\pi}{4}3k}}{1 - e^{j\frac{\pi}{4}k}} \\
\tilde{X}_C[k] &= \sum_{n=0}^{3} e^{j\frac{2\pi}{8}kn} - \sum_{n=4} 7e^{j\frac{2\pi}{8}kn} \\
&= \sum_{n=0}^{3} \left(e^{j\frac{\pi}{4}kn} - e^{j\frac{\pi}{4}k(n+4)}\right) \\
&= \left(1 - e^{j\pi k}\right) \frac{1 - e^{j\pi k}}{1 - e^{j\frac{\pi}{4}k}} \\
&= 0, \quad k = \pm 2, \pm 4, \ldots
\end{aligned}$$

8.4. A periodic sequence is constructed from the sequence:

$$x[n] = \alpha^n u[n] \ , \ |\alpha| < 1$$

as follows:

$$\tilde{x}[n] = \sum_{r=-\infty}^{\infty} x[n + rN] \ , \ |\alpha| < 1$$

(a) The Fourier transform of $x[n]$:

$$\begin{aligned}
X(e^{j\omega}) &= \sum_{n=-\infty}^{\infty} x[n]e^{-j\omega n} \\
&= \sum_{n=0}^{\infty} \alpha^n e^{-j\omega n} \\
&= \frac{1}{1 - \alpha e^{-j\omega}}, \qquad |\alpha| < 1
\end{aligned}$$

(b) The DFS of $\tilde{x}[n]$:

$$\tilde{X}[k] = \sum_{n=0}^{N-1} \tilde{x}[n] W_N^{kn}$$

$$= \sum_{n=0}^{N-1} \sum_{r=-\infty}^{\infty} x[n+rN] W_N^{kn}$$

$$= \sum_{n=0}^{N-1} \sum_{r=-\infty}^{\infty} \alpha^{n+rN} u[n+rN] W_N^{kn}$$

$$= \sum_{n=0}^{N-1} \sum_{r=0}^{\infty} \alpha^{n+rN} W_N^{kn}$$

Rearranging the summations gives:

$$\begin{aligned}
\tilde{X}[k] &= \sum_{r=0}^{\infty} \alpha^{rN} \sum_{n=0}^{N-1} \alpha^n W_N^{kn} \\
&= \sum_{r=0}^{\infty} \alpha^{rN} \left(\frac{1-\alpha^N e^{-j2\pi k}}{1-\alpha e^{-j\frac{2\pi k}{N}}} \right) , \ |\alpha| < 1 \\
&= \frac{1}{1-\alpha^N} \left(\frac{1-\alpha^N e^{-j2\pi k}}{1-\alpha e^{-j\frac{2\pi k}{N}}} \right) , \ |\alpha| < 1 \\
\tilde{X}[k] &= \frac{1}{1-\alpha e^{-j(2\pi k/N)}} , \ |\alpha| < 1
\end{aligned}$$

(c) Comparing the results of part (a) and part (b):

$$\tilde{X}[k] = X(e^{j\omega})\big|_{\omega=2\pi k/N}.$$

8.5. (a)

$$\begin{aligned}
x[n] &= \delta[n] \\
X[k] &= \sum_{n=0}^{N-1} \delta[n] W_N^{kn}, \qquad 0 \le k \le (N-1) \\
&= 1
\end{aligned}$$

(b)

$$\begin{aligned}
x[n] &= \delta[n-n_0], \qquad 0 \le n_0 \le (N-1) \\
X[k] &= \sum_{n=0}^{N-1} \delta[n-n_0] W_N^{kn}, \qquad 0 \le k \le (N-1) \\
&= W_N^{kn_0}
\end{aligned}$$

(c)

$$\begin{aligned}
x[n] &= \begin{cases} 1, & n \text{ even} \\ 0, & n \text{ odd} \end{cases} \\
X[k] &= \sum_{n=0}^{N-1} x[n] W_N^{kn}, \qquad 0 \le k \le (N-1) \\
&= \sum_{n=0}^{(N/2)-1} W_N^{2kn} \\
&= \frac{1-e^{-j2\pi k}}{1-e^{-j(\pi k/N)}} \\
X[k] &= \begin{cases} N/2, & k = 0, N/2 \\ 0, & \text{otherwise} \end{cases}
\end{aligned}$$

(d)

$$\begin{aligned}
x[n] &= \begin{cases} 1, & 0 \le n \le ((N/2)-1) \\ 0, & N/2 \le n \le (N-1) \end{cases} \\
X[k] &= \sum_{n=0}^{N-1} x[n] W_N^{kn}, \qquad 0 \le k \le (N-1) \\
&= \sum_{n=0}^{(N/2)-1} W_N^{kn} \\
&= \frac{1 - e^{-j\pi k}}{1 - e^{-j(2\pi k)/N}} \\
X[k] &= \begin{cases} N/2, & k = 0 \\ \dfrac{2}{1 - e^{-j(2\pi k/N)}}, & k \text{ odd} \\ 0, & k \text{ even}, 0 \le k \le (N-1) \end{cases}
\end{aligned}$$

(e)

$$\begin{aligned}
x[n] &= \begin{cases} a^n, & 0 \le n \le (N-1) \\ 0, & \text{otherwise} \end{cases} \\
X[k] &= \sum_{n=0}^{N-1} a^n W_N^{kn}, \qquad 0 \le k \le (N-1) \\
&= \frac{1 - a^N e^{-j2\pi k}}{1 - a e^{-j(2\pi k)/N}} \\
X[k] &= \frac{1 - a^N}{1 - a e^{-j(2\pi k)/N}}
\end{aligned}$$

8.6. Consider the finite-length sequence

$$x[n] = \begin{cases} e^{j\omega_0 n}, & 0 \le n \le (N-1) \\ 0, & \text{otherwise} \end{cases}$$

(a) The Fourier transform of $x[n]$:

$$\begin{aligned}
X(e^{j\omega}) &= \sum_{n=-\infty}^{\infty} x[n] e^{-j\omega n} \\
&= \sum_{n=0}^{N-1} e^{j\omega_0 n} e^{-j\omega n} \\
X(e^{j\omega}) &= \frac{1 - e^{-j(\omega-\omega_0)N}}{1 - e^{-j(\omega-\omega_0)}} \\
&= \frac{e^{-j(\omega-\omega_0)(N/2)}}{e^{-j(\omega-\omega_0)/2}} \left(\frac{\sin[(\omega-\omega_0)(N/2)]}{\sin[(\omega-\omega_0)/2]} \right) \\
X(e^{j\omega}) &= e^{-j(\omega-\omega_0)((N-1)/2)} \left(\frac{\sin[(\omega-\omega_0)(N/2)]}{\sin[(\omega-\omega_0)/2]} \right)
\end{aligned}$$

(b) N-point DFT:

$$X[k] = \sum_{n=0}^{N-1} x[n] W_N^{kn}, \qquad 0 \le k \le (N-1)$$

$$= \sum_{n=0}^{N-1} e^{j\omega_0 n} W_N^{kn}$$

$$= \frac{1 - e^{-j((2\pi k/N)-\omega_0)N}}{1 - e^{-j((2\pi k/N)-\omega_0)}}$$

$$= e^{-j(\frac{2\pi k}{N}-\omega_0)(\frac{N-1}{2})} \frac{\sin\left[\left(\frac{2\pi k}{N} - \omega_0\right)\frac{N}{2}\right]}{\sin\left[\left(\frac{2\pi k}{N} - \omega_0\right)/2\right]}$$

Note that $X[k] = X(e^{j\omega})|_{\omega=(2\pi k)/N}$

(c) Suppose $\omega_0 = (2\pi k_0)/N$, where k_0 is an integer:

$$X[k] = \frac{1 - e^{-j(k-k_0)2\pi}}{1 - e^{-j(k-k_0)(2\pi)/N}}$$

$$= e^{-j(2\pi/N)(k-k_0)((N-1)/2)} \frac{\sin \pi(k - k_0)}{\sin(\pi(k - k_0)/N)}$$

8.7. We have a six-point uniform sequence, $x[n]$, which is nonzero for $0 \le n \le 5$. We sample the Z-transform of $x[n]$ at four equally-spaced points on the unit circle.

$$X[k] = X(z)|_{z=e^{(2\pi k/4)}}$$

We seek the sequence $x_1[n]$ which is the inverse DFT of $X[k]$. Recall the definition of the Z-transform:

$$X(z) = \sum_{n=-\infty}^{\infty} x[n]z^{-n}$$

Since $x[n]$ is zero for all n outside $0 \le n \le 5$, we may replace the infinite summation with a finite summation. Furthermore, after substituting $z = e^{j(2\pi k/4)}$, we obtain

$$X[k] = \sum_{n=0}^{5} x[n]W_4^{kn}, \qquad 0 \le k \le 4$$

Note that we have taken a 4-point DFT, as specified by the sampling of the Z-transform; however, the original sequence was of length 6. As a result, we can expect some aliasing when we return to the time domain via the inverse DFT.

Performing the DFT,

$$X[k] = W_4^{0k} + W_4^{k} + W_4^{2k} + W_4^{3k} + W_4^{4k} + W_4^{5k}, \qquad 0 \le k \le 4$$

Taking the inverse DFT by inspection, we note that there are six impulses (one for each value of n above). However,

$$W_4^{4k} = W_4^{0k} \text{ and } W_4^{5k} = W_4^{k},$$

so two points are aliased. The resulting time-domain signal is

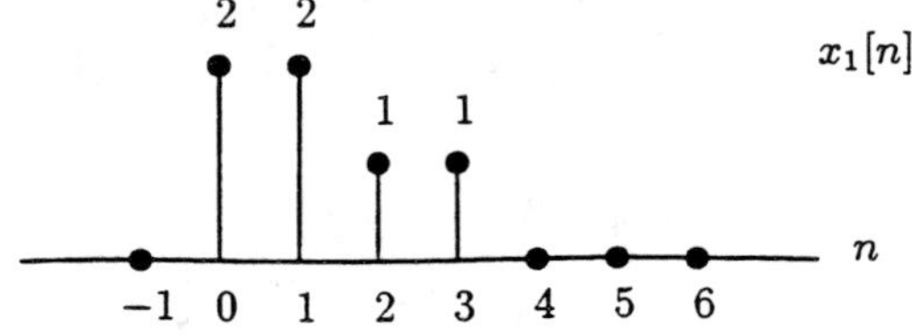

8.8. Fourier transform of $x[n] = (1/2)^n u[n]$:

$$\begin{aligned} X(e^{j\omega}) &= \sum_{n=-\infty}^{\infty} x[n]e^{-j\omega n} \\ &= \sum_{n=0}^{\infty} \left(\frac{1}{2}\right)^n e^{-j\omega n} \\ &= \frac{1}{1-\frac{1}{2}e^{-j\omega}} \end{aligned}$$

Now, sample the frequency spectra of $x[n]$:

$$Y[k] = X(e^{j\omega})|_{\omega=2\pi k/10}, \qquad 0 \le k \le 9$$

We have the 10-pt DFT:

$$\begin{aligned} Y[k] &= \frac{1}{1-\frac{1}{2}e^{-j(2\pi k/10)}}, \qquad 0 \le k \le 9 \\ &= \sum_{n=0}^{9} y[n]W_{10}^{kn} \end{aligned}$$

Recall:

$$\left(\frac{1}{2}\right)^n \xrightarrow[\text{N-pt}]{\text{DFT}} \frac{1-(\frac{1}{2})^N}{1-\frac{1}{2}e^{-j(2\pi k/N)}}$$

So, we may infer:

$$y[n] = \frac{(\frac{1}{2})^n}{1-(\frac{1}{2})^{10}}, \qquad 0 \le n \le 9$$

8.9. Given a 20-pt finite-duration sequence $x[n]$:

(a) We wish to obtain $X(e^{j\omega})|_{\omega=4\pi/5}$ using the smallest DFT possible. A possible size of the DFT is evident by the periodicity of $e^{j\omega}|_{\omega=4\pi/5}$. Suppose we choose the size of the DFT to be $M = 5$. The data sequence is 20 points long, so we use the time-aliasing technique derived in the previous problem. Specifically, we alias $x[n]$ as:

$$x_1[n] = \sum_{r=-\infty}^{\infty} x[n+5r]$$

This aliased version of $x[n]$ is periodic with period 5 now. The 5-pt DFT is computed. The desired value occurs at a frequency corresponding to:

$$\frac{2\pi k}{N} = \frac{4\pi}{5}$$

For $N = 5$, $k = 2$, so the desired value may be obtained as $X[k]|_{k=2}$.

(b) Next, we wish to obtain $X(e^{j\omega})|_{\omega=10\pi/27}$.
The smallest DFT is of size $L = 27$. Since the DFT is larger than the data block size, we pad $x[n]$ with 7 zeros as follows:

$$x_2[n] = \begin{cases} x[n], & 0 \le n \le 19 \\ 0, & 20 \le n \le 26 \end{cases}$$

We take the 27-pt DFT, and the desired value corresponds to $X[k]$ evaluated at $k = 5$.

8.10. From Fig P8.10-1, the two 8-pt sequences are related through a circular shift. Specifically,

$$x_2[n] = x_1[((n-4))_8]$$

From property 5 in Table 8.2,

$$\text{DFT}\{x_1[((n-4))_8]\} = W_8^{4k} X_1[k]$$

Thus,

$$\begin{aligned} X_2[k] &= W_8^{4k} X_1[k] \\ &= e^{-j\pi k} X_1[k] \\ X_2[k] &= (-1)^k X_1[k] \end{aligned}$$

8.11. We wish to perform the circular convolution between two 6-pt sequences. Since $x_2[n]$ is just a shifted impulse, the circular-convolution coincides with a circular shift of $x_1[n]$ by two points.

$$\begin{aligned} y[n] &= x_1[n] \textcircled{6} x_2[n] \\ &= x_1[n] \textcircled{6} \delta[n-2] \\ &= x_1[((n-2))_6] \end{aligned}$$

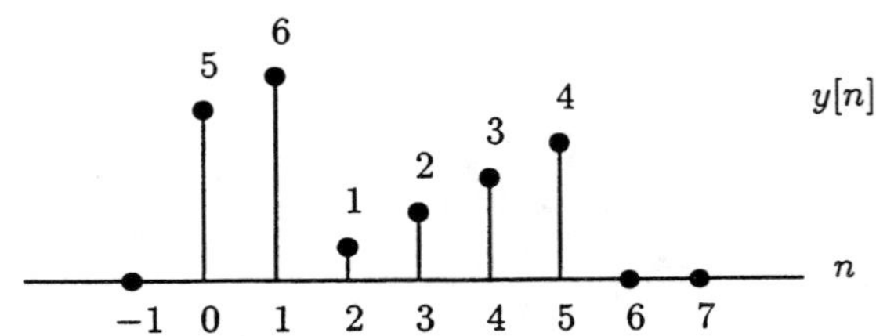

8.12. (a)

$$x[n] = \cos(\frac{\pi n}{2}), \qquad 0 \le n \le 3$$

transforms to

$$X[k] = \sum_{n=0}^{3} \cos(\frac{\pi n}{2}) W_4^{kn}, \qquad 0 \le k \le 3$$

The cosine term contributes only two non-zero values to the summation, giving:

$$\begin{aligned} X[k] &= 1 - e^{-j\pi k}, \qquad 0 \le k \le 3 \\ &= 1 - W_4^{2k} \end{aligned}$$

(b)

$$h[n] = 2^n, \qquad 0 \le n \le 3$$

$$\begin{aligned} H[k] &= \sum_{n=0}^{3} 2^n W_4^{kn}, \qquad 0 \le k \le 3 \\ &= 1 + 2W_4^k + 4W_4^{2k} + 8W_4^{3k} \end{aligned}$$

(c) Remember, circular convolution equals linear convolution plus aliasing. We need $N \geq 3+4-1=6$ to avoid aliasing. Since $N=4$,we expect to get aliasing here. First, find $y[n]=x[n]*h[n]$:

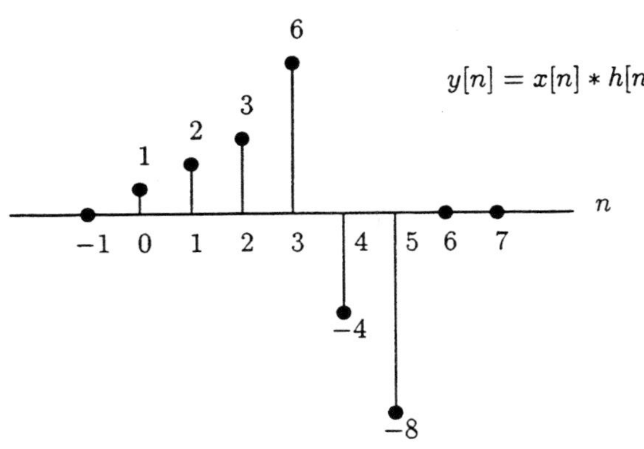

For this problem, aliasing means the last three points $(n=4,5,6)$ will wrap-around on top of the first three points, giving $y[n]=x[n]④h[n]$:

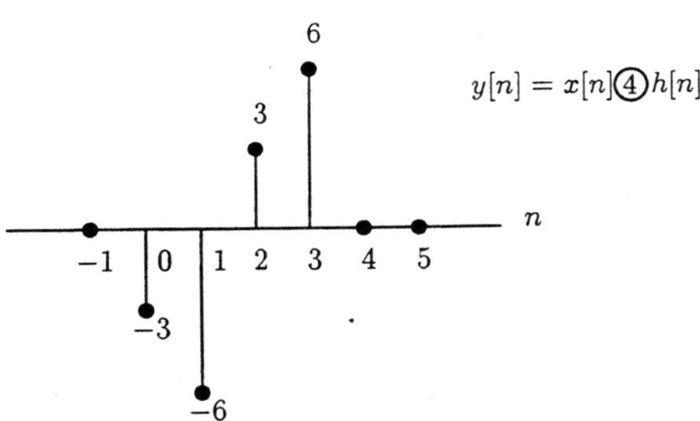

(d) Using the DFT values we calculated in parts (a) and (b):

$$\begin{aligned} Y[k] &= X[k]H[k] \\ &= 1+2W_4^k+4W_4^{2k}+8W_4^{3k}-W_4^{2k}-2W_4^{3k}-4W_4^{4k}-8W_4^{5k} \end{aligned}$$

Since $W_4^{4k}=W_4^{0k}$ and $W_4^{5k}=W_4^k$

$$Y[k] = -3-6W_4^k+3W_4^{2k}+6W_4^{3k}, \quad 0 \leq k \leq 3$$

Taking the inverse DFT:

$$y[n]=-3\delta[n]-6\delta[n-1]+3\delta[n-2]+6\delta[n-3], \quad 0 \leq n \leq 3$$

8.13. Using the properties of the DFT, we get $y[n] = x[((n-2))_5]$, that is $y[n]$ is equal to $x[n]$ circularly shifted by 2. We get:

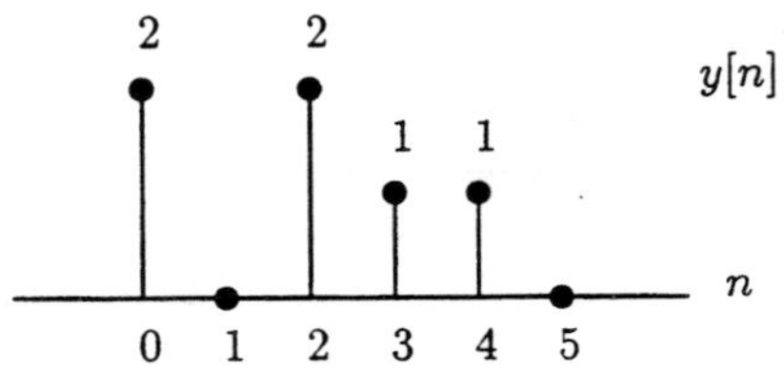

8.14. $x_3[n]$ is the linear convolution of $x_1[n]$ and $x_2[n]$ time-aliased to $N = 8$. Carrying out the 8-point circular convolution, we get:

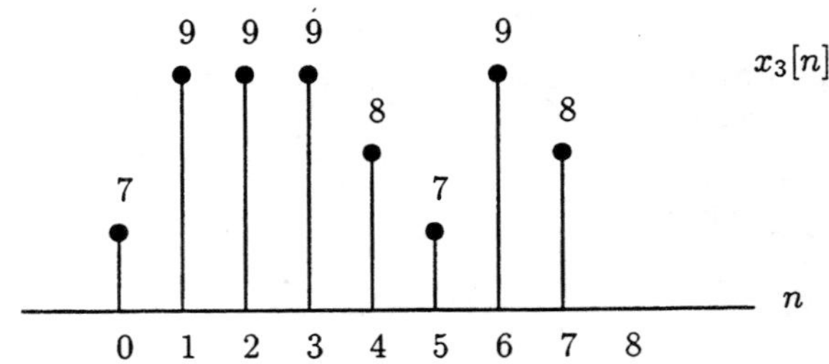

We thus conclude $x_3[2] = 9$.

8.15. $y[n]$ is the linear convolution of $x_1[n]$ and $x_2[n]$ time-aliased to $N = 4$. Carrying out the 4-point circular convolution, we get:

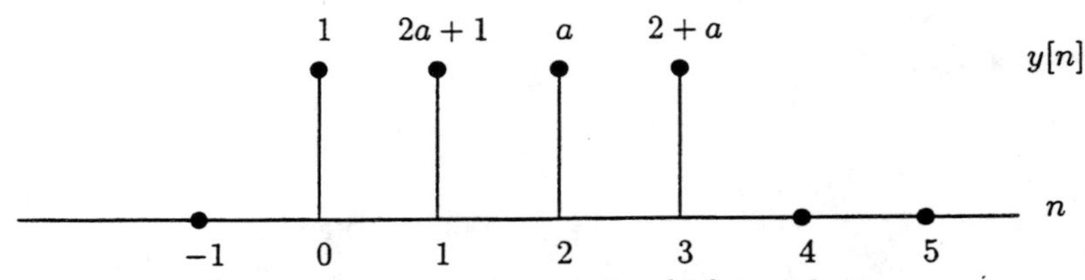

Matching the above sequence to the one given, we get $a = -1$, which is unique.

8.16. $X_1[k]$ is the 4-point DFT of $x[n]$ and $x_1[n]$ is the 4-point inverse DFT of $X_1[k]$, therefore $x_1[n]$ is $x[n]$ time aliased to $N = 4$. In other words, $x_1[n]$ is one period of $\tilde{x}[n] = x[((n))_4]$. We thus have:

$$4 = b + 1.$$

Therefore, $b = 3$. This is clearly unique.

8.17. Looking at the sequences, we see that $x_1[n] * x_2[n]$ is non-zero for $1 \leq n \leq 8$. The smallest N such that $x_1[n] \circledN x_2[n] = x_1[n] * x_2[n]$ is therefore $N = 9$.

8.18. Taking the inverse DFT of $X_1[k]$ and using the properties of the DFT, we get:

$$x_1[n] = x[((n+3))_5].$$

Therefore:

$$x_1[0] = x[3] = c.$$

We thus conclude that $c = 2$.

8.19. $x_1[n]$ and $x[n]$ are related by a circular shift as can be seen from the plots. Using the properties of the DFT and the relationship between $X_1[k]$ and $X[k]$, we have:

$$x_1[n] = x[((n-m))_6].$$

$m = 2$ works, clearly this choice is not unique, any $m = 2 + 6l$, where l is an integer, would work.

8.20.

$$X_1[k] = X[k]e^{+j(2\pi k2/N)}.$$

Using the properties of the DFT, we get:

$$x_1[n] = x[((n+2))_N].$$

From the figures, we conclude that:

$$N = 5.$$

This choice of N is unique.

8.21. (a) We seek a sequence $\tilde{y}_1[n]$ such that

$$\tilde{Y}_1[k] = \tilde{X}_1[k]\tilde{X}_2[k]$$

From the discussion of Section 8.2.5, $\tilde{y}[n]$ is the result of the periodic convolution between $\tilde{x}_1[n]$ and $\tilde{x}_2[n]$.

$$\tilde{y}_1[n] = \sum_{m=0}^{N-1} \tilde{x}_1[m]\tilde{x}_2[n-m]$$

Since $\tilde{x}_2[n]$ is a periodic impulse, shifted by two, the resultant sequence will be a shifted (by two) replica of $\tilde{x}_1[n]$.

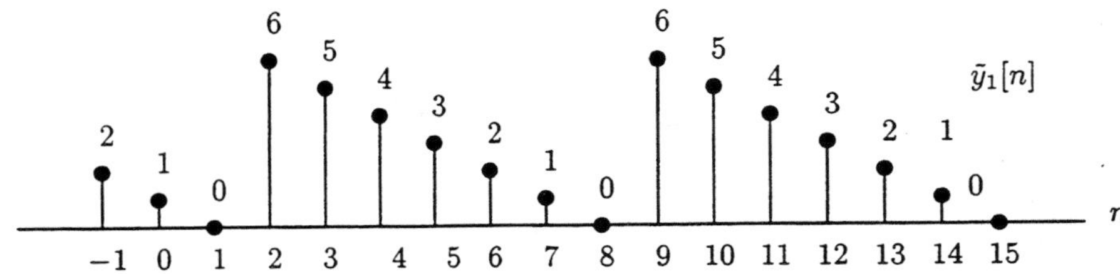

Using the analysis equation of Eq. (8.11), we may rigorously derive $\tilde{y}_1[n]$:

$$\tilde{X}_1[k] = \sum_{n=0}^{6} \tilde{x}_1[n]W_7^{kn}$$

$$
\begin{aligned}
&= 6 + 5W_7^k + 4W_7^{2k} + 3W_7^{3k} + 2W_7^{4k} + W_7^{5k} \\
\tilde{X}_2[k] &= \sum_{n=0}^{6} \tilde{x}_2[n]W_7^{kn} \\
&= W_7^{2k} \\
\tilde{Y}_1[k] &= \tilde{X}_1[k]\tilde{X}_2[k] \\
&= 6W_7^{2k} + 5W_7^{3k} + 4W_7^{4k} + 3W_7^{5k} + 2W_7^{6k} + W_7^{7k}
\end{aligned}
$$

Noting that $W_7^{7k} = e^{j\frac{2\pi}{7}(7k)} = 1 = W_7^{0k}$, we use the synthesis equation of Eq. (8.12) to construct $\tilde{y}_1[n]$. The result is identical to the sequence depicted above.

(b) The DFS of the signal illustrated in Fig. P8.21-2.is given by:

$$
\begin{aligned}
\tilde{X}_3[k] &= \sum_{n=0}^{6} \tilde{x}_3[n]W_7^{kn} \\
&= 1 + W_7^{4k}
\end{aligned}
$$

Therefore:

$$
\begin{aligned}
\tilde{Y}_2[k] &= \tilde{X}_1[k]\tilde{X}_3[k] \\
&= \tilde{X}_1[k] + W_7^{4k}\tilde{X}_1[k]
\end{aligned}
$$

Since the DFS is linear, the inverse DFS of $\tilde{Y}_2[k]$ is given by:

$$\tilde{y}_2[n] = \tilde{x}_1[n] + \tilde{x}_1[n-4].$$

8.22. For a finite-length sequence $x[n]$, with length equal to N, the periodic repetition of $x[-n]$ is represented by

$$x[((-n))_N] = x[((-n+\ell N))_N], \qquad \ell\text{: integer}$$

where the right side is justified since $x[n]$ (and $x[-n]$) is periodic with period N.

The above statement holds true for any choice of ℓ. Therefore, for $\ell = 1$:

$$x[((-n))_n] = x[((-n+N))_N]$$

8.23. We have $x[n]$ for $0 \le n \le P$.

We desire to compute $X(z)|_{z=e^{-j(2\pi k/N)}}$ using one N-pt DFT.

(a) Suppose $N > P$ (the DFT size is larger than the data segment). The technique used in this case is often referred to as zero-padding. By appending zeros to a small data block, a larger DFT may be used. Thus the frequency spectra may be more finely sampled. It is a common misconception to believe that zero-padding enhances spectral resolution. The addition of a larger block of data to a larger DFT would enhance this quality.

So, we append $N_z = N - P$ zeros to the end of the sequence as follows:

$$
x'[n] = \begin{cases} x[n], & 0 \le n \le (P-1) \\ 0, & P \le n \le N \end{cases}
$$

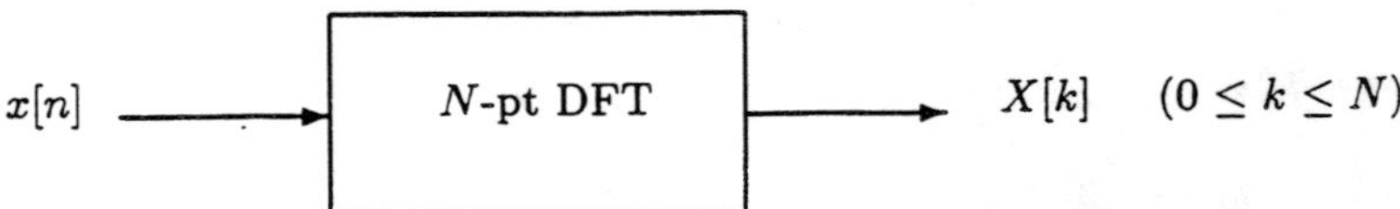

(b) Suppose $N > P$, consider taking a DFT which is smaller than the data block. Of course, some aliasing is expected. Perhaps we could introduce time aliasing to offset the effects.

Consider the N-pt inverse DFT of $X[k]$,

$$x[n] = \frac{1}{N}\sum_{k=0}^{N-1} X[k]W_N^{-kn}, \qquad 0 \le n \le (N-1)$$

Suppose $X[k]$ was obtained as the result of an infinite summation of complex exponents:

$$x[n] = \frac{1}{N}\sum_{k=0}^{N-1}\left(\sum_{m=0}^{\infty} x[m]e^{-j(2\pi k/N)m}\right)W_N^{-kn}$$

Rearrange to get:

$$x[n] = \sum_{m=-\infty}^{\infty} x[m]\left(\frac{1}{N}\sum_{k=0}^{N-1} e^{-j(2\pi/N)(m-n)k}\right)$$

Using the orthogonality relationship of Example 8.1:

$$\begin{aligned} x[n] &= \sum_{m=-\infty}^{\infty} x[m]\sum_{r=-\infty}^{\infty}\delta[m-n+rN] \\ x[n] &= \sum_{r=-\infty}^{\infty} x[n-rN] \end{aligned}$$

So, we should alias $x[n]$ as above. Then we take the N-pt DFT to get $X[k]$.

8.24. No. Recall that the DFT merely samples the frequency spectra. Therefore, the fact the $Im\{X[k]\} = 0$ for $0 \le k \le (N-1)$ does not guarantee that the imaginary part of the continuous frequency spectra is also zero.

For example, consider a signal which consists of an impulse centered at $n = 1$.

$$x[n] = \delta[n-1], \qquad 0 \le n \le 1$$

The Fourier transform is:

$$\begin{aligned} X(e^{j\omega}) &= e^{-j\omega} \\ Re\{X(e^{j\omega})\} &= \cos(\omega) \\ Im\{X(e^{j\omega})\} &= -\sin(\omega) \end{aligned}$$

Note that neither is zero for all $0 \le \omega \le 2$. Now, suppose we take the 2-pt DFT:

$$\begin{aligned} X[k] &= W_2^k, \qquad 0 \le k \le 1 \\ &= \begin{cases} 1, & k = 0 \\ -1, & k = 1 \end{cases} \end{aligned}$$

So, $Im\{X[k]\} = 0, \quad \forall k$. However, $Im\{X(e^{j\omega})\} \neq 0$.

Note also that the size of the DFT plays a large role. For instance, consider taking the 3-pt DFT of

$$\begin{aligned} x[n] &= \delta[n-1], \qquad 0 \le n \le 2 \\ X[k] &= W_3^k, \qquad 0 \le k \le 2 \\ &= \begin{cases} 1, & k = 0 \\ e^{-j(2\pi/3)}, & k = 1 \\ e^{-j(4\pi/3)}, & k = 2 \end{cases} \end{aligned}$$

Now, $Im\{X[k]\} \neq 0$, for $k = 1$ or $k = 2$.

8.25. Both sequences $x[n]$ and $y[n]$ are of finite-length ($N = 4$).

Hence, no aliasing takes place. From Section 8.6.2, multiplication of the DFT of a sequence by a complex exponential corresponds to a circular shift of the time-domain sequence.

Given $Y[k] = W_4^{3k}X[k]$, we have

$$y[n] = x[((n-3))_4]$$

We use the technique suggested in problem 8.28. That is, we temporarily extend the sequence such that a periodic sequence with period 4 is formed.

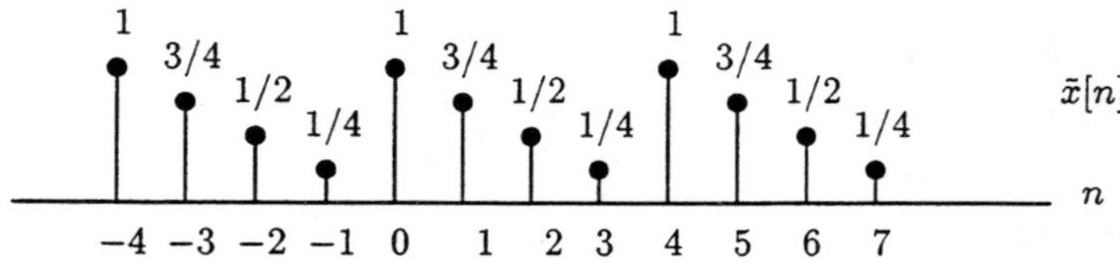

Now, we shift by three (to the right), and set all values outside $0 \le n \le 3$ to zero.

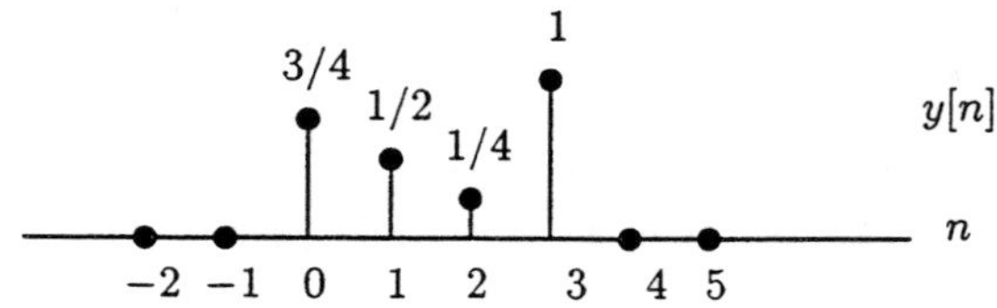

8.26. (a) When multiplying the DFT of a sequence by a complex exponential, the time-domain signal undergoes a circular shift.

For this case,

$$Y[k] = W_6^{4k}X[k], \qquad 0 \le k \le 5$$

Therefore,

$$y[n] = x[((n-4))_6], \qquad 0 \le n \le 5$$

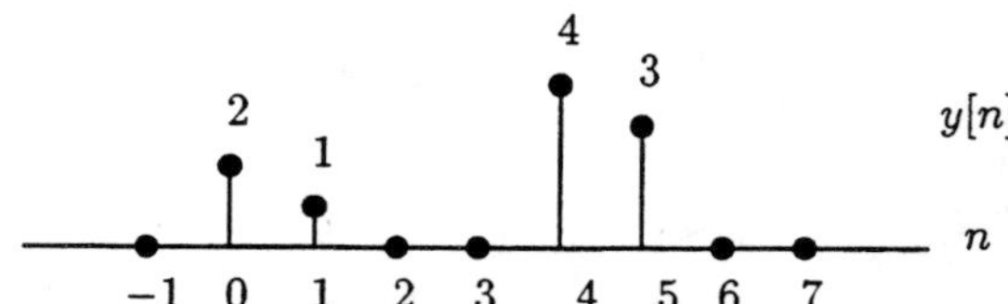

(b) There are two ways to approach this problem. First, we attempt a solution by brute force.

$$\begin{aligned}
X[k] &= 4 + 3W_6^k + 2W_6^{2k} + W_6^{3k}, \qquad W_6^k = e^{-j(2\pi k/6)} \text{ and } 0 \le k \le 5 \\
W[k] &= \mathcal{R}e\{X[k]\} \\
&= \frac{1}{2}(X[k] + X^*[k]) \\
&= \frac{1}{2}(4 + 3W_6^k + 2W_6^{2k} + W_6^{3k} + 4 + 3W_6^{-k} + 2W_6^{-2k} + W_6^{-3k})
\end{aligned}$$

Notice that

$$\begin{aligned}
W_N^k &= e^{-j(2\pi k/N)} \\
W_N^{-k} &= e^{j(2\pi k/N)} = e^{-j(2\pi/N)(N-k)} = W_N^{N-k} \\
W[k] &= 4 + \frac{3}{2}\left[W_6^k + W_6^{6-k}\right] + \left[W_6^{2k} + W_6^{6-2k}\right] + \frac{1}{2}\left[W_6^{3k} + W_6^{6-3k}\right], \qquad 0 \le k \le 5
\end{aligned}$$

So,

$$\begin{aligned}
w[n] &= 4\delta[n] + \frac{3}{2}\Big(\delta[n-1] + \delta[n-5]\Big) + \delta[n-2] + \delta[n-4] \\
&\quad + \frac{1}{2}\Big(\delta[n-3] + \delta[n-3]\Big) \\
w[n] &= 4\delta[n] + \frac{3}{2}\delta[n-1] + \delta[n-2] + \delta[n-3] + \delta[n-4] + \frac{3}{2}\delta[n-5], \qquad 0 \le n \le 5
\end{aligned}$$

Sketching $w[n]$:

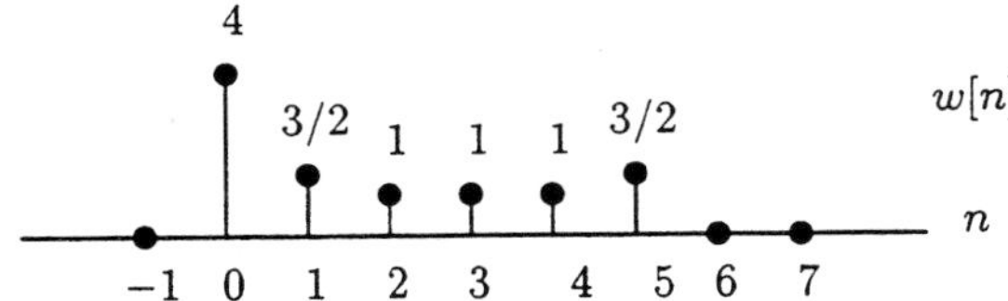

As an alternate approach, suppose we use the properties of the DFT as listed in Table 8.2.

$$\begin{aligned}
W[k] &= \mathcal{R}e\{X[k]\} \\
&= \frac{X[k] + X^*[k]}{2} \\
w[n] &= \frac{1}{2}\ \text{IDFT}\{X[k]\} + \frac{1}{2}\ \text{IDFT}\{X^*[k]\} \\
&= \frac{1}{2}\Big(x[n] + x^*[((-n))_N]\Big)
\end{aligned}$$

For $0 \le n \le N-1$ and $x[n]$ real:

$$w[n] = \frac{1}{2}\Big(x[n] + x[N-n]\Big)$$

4 3 2 1 $x[N-n]$, for $N = 6$

n

−1 0 1 2 3 4 5 6 7

So, we observe that $w[n]$ results as above.

(c) The DFT is decimated by two. By taking alternate points of the DFT output, we have half as many points. The influence of this action in the time domain is, as expected, the appearance of aliasing. For the case of decimation by two, we shall find that an additional replica of x[n] surfaces, since the sequence is now periodic with period 3.

From part (b):

$$X[k] = 4 + 3W_6^k + 2W_6^{2k} + W_6^{3k}, \qquad 0 \le k \le 5$$

Let $Q[k] = X[2k]$,

$$Q[k] = 4 + 3W_3^k + 2W_3^{2k} + W_3^{3k}, \qquad 0 \le k \le 2$$

Noting that $W_3^{3k} = W_3^{0k}$

$$q[n] = 5\delta[n] + 3\delta[n-1] + 2\delta[n-2], \qquad 0 \le n \le 2$$

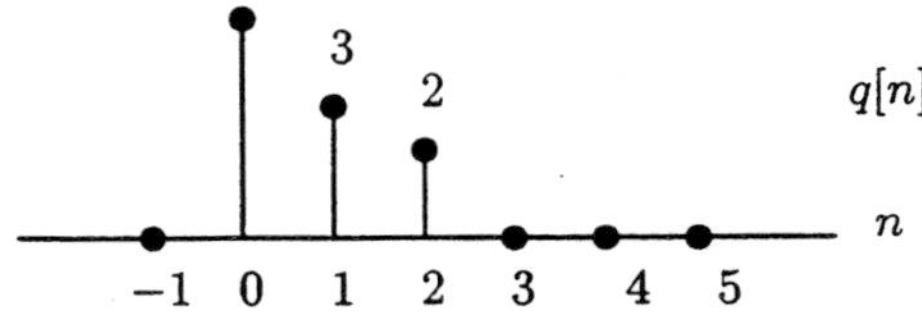

8.27. (a) The linear convolution, $x_1[n] * x_2[n]$ is a sequence of length $100 + 10 - 1 = 109$.

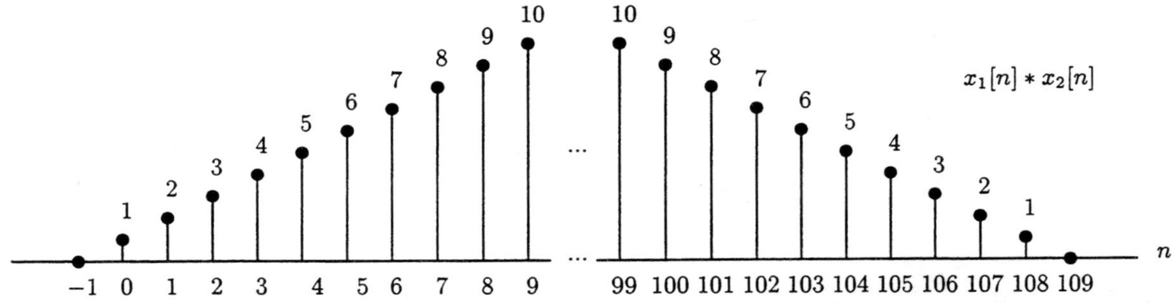

(b) The circular convolution, $x_1[n] \, \textcircled{\scriptsize 100} \, x_2[n]$, can be obtained by aliasing the first 9 points of the linear convolution above:

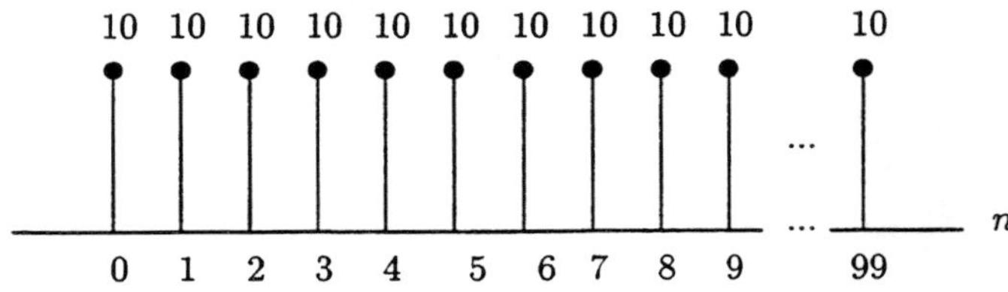

(c) Since $N \ge 109$, the circular convolution $x_1[n] \, \textcircled{\scriptsize 110} \, x_2[n]$ will be equivalent to the linear convolution of part (a).

8.28. We may approach this problem in two ways. First, the notion of modulo arithmetic may be simplified if we utilize the implied periodic extension. That is, we redraw the original signal as if it were periodic with period $N = 4$. A few periods are sufficient:

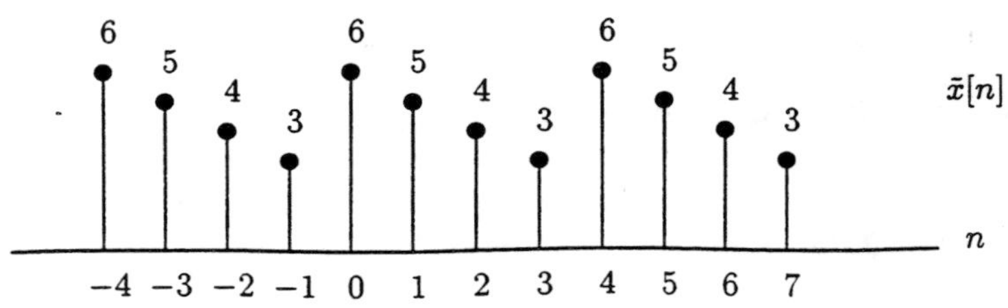

To obtain $x_1[n] = x[((n-2))_4]$, we shift by two (to the right) and only keep those points which lie in the original domain of the signal (i.e. $0 \leq n \leq 3$):

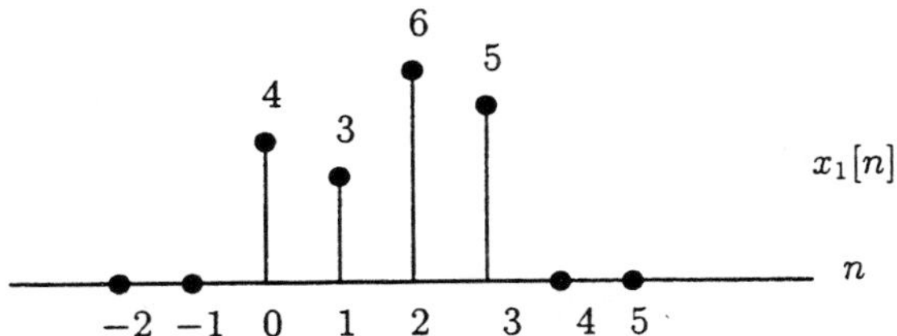

To obtain $x_2[n] = x[((-n))_4]$, we fold the pseudo-periodic version of $x[n]$ over the origin (time-reversal), and again we set all points outside $0 \leq n \leq 3$ equal to zero. Hence,

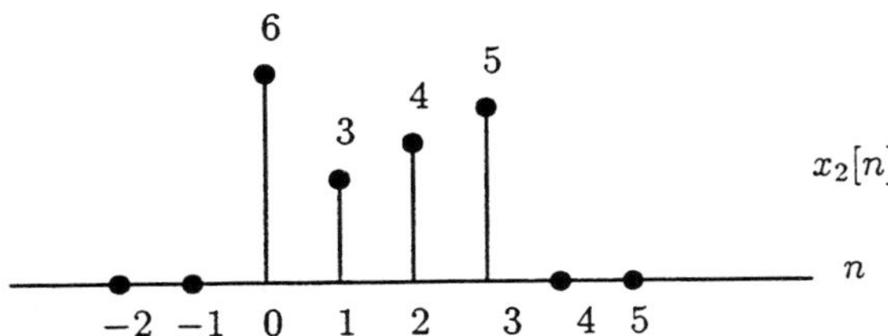

Note that $x[((0))_4] = x[0]$, etc.

In the second approach, we work with the given signal. The signal is confined to $0 \leq n \leq 3$; therefore, the circular nature must be maintained by picturing the signal on the circumference of a cylinder.

8.29. Circular convolution equals linear convolution plus aliasing. First, we find $y[n] = x_1[n] * x_2[n]$:

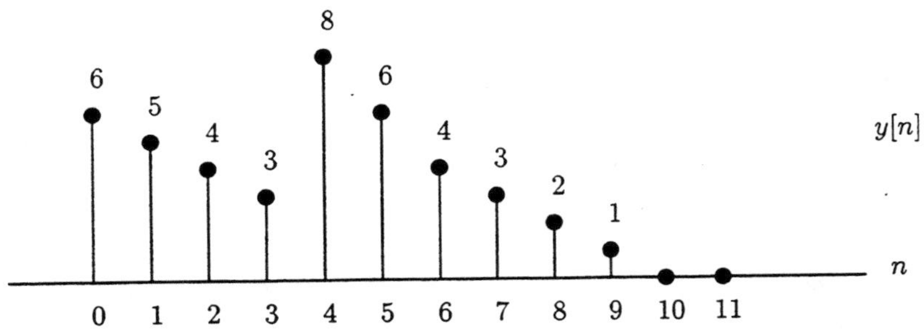

Note that $y[n]$ is a ten point sequence ($N = 6 + 5 - 1$).

(a) For $N = 6$, the last four non-zero point ($6 \leq n \leq 9$) will alias to the first four points, giving us $y_1[n] = x_1[n] \circledast_6 x_2[n]$

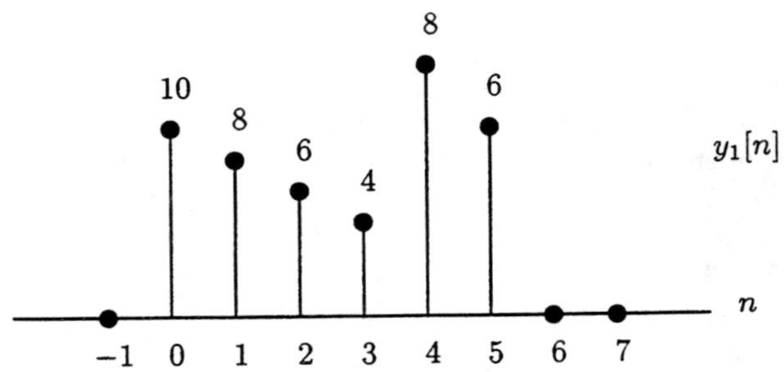

(b) For $N = 10, N \geq 6 + 5 - 1$, so no aliasing occurs, and circular convolution is identical to linear convolution.

8.30. We have a finite length sequence, whose 64-pt DFT contains only one nonzero point (for $k = 32$).

(a) Using the synthesis equation Eq. (8.68):

$$x[n] = \frac{1}{N}\sum_{k=0}^{N-1} X[k]W_N^{-kn}, \qquad 0 \leq n \leq (N-1)$$

Substitution yields:

$$\begin{aligned} x[n] &= \frac{1}{64}X[32]W_{64}^{-32n} \\ &= \frac{1}{64}e^{j\frac{2\pi}{64}(32)n} \\ &= \frac{1}{64}e^{j\pi n} \\ x[n] &= \frac{1}{64}(-1)^n, \qquad 0 \leq n \leq (N-1) \end{aligned}$$

The answer is unique because we have taken the 64-pt DFT of a 64-pt sequence.

(b) The sequence length is now $N = 192$.

$$\begin{aligned} x[n] &= \frac{1}{192}\sum_{k=0}^{191} X[k]W_{192}^{-kn}, \; 0 \leq n \leq 191 \\ x[n] &= \begin{cases} \frac{1}{64}(-1)^n & 0 \leq n \leq 63 \\ 0 & 64 \leq n \leq 191 \end{cases} \end{aligned}$$

This solution is not unique. By taking only 64 spectral samples, $x[n]$ will be aliased in time. As an alternate sequence, consider

$$x'[n] = \frac{1}{64}\left(\frac{1}{3}\right)(-1)^n, \qquad 0 \leq n \leq 191$$

8.31. We have a 10-point sequence, $x[n]$. We want a modified sequence, $x_1[n]$, such that the 10-pt. DFT of $x_1[n]$ corresponds to

$$X_1[k] = X(z)|_{z=\frac{1}{2}e^{j[(2\pi k/10)+(\pi/10)]}}$$

Recall the definition of the Z-transform of $x[n]$:

$$X(z) = \sum_{n=-\infty}^{\infty} x[n]z^{-n}$$

Since $x[n]$ is of finite duration ($N = 10$), we assume:

$$x[n] = \begin{cases} \text{nonzero}, & 0 \le n \le 9 \\ 0, & \text{otherwise} \end{cases}$$

Therefore,

$$X(z) = \sum_{n=0}^{9} x[n] z^{-n}$$

Substituting in $z = \frac{1}{2}e^{j[(2\pi k/10)+(\pi/10)]}$:

$$X(z)\big|_{z=\frac{1}{2}e^{j[(2\pi k/10)+(\pi/10)]}} = \sum_{n=0}^{9} x[n] \left(\frac{1}{2}e^{j[(2\pi k/10)+(\pi/10)]}\right)^{-n}$$

We seek the signal $x_1[n]$, whose 10-pt. DFT is equivalent to the above expression. Recall the analysis equation for the DFT:

$$X_1[k] = \sum_{n=0}^{9} x_1[n] W_{10}^{kn}, \qquad 0 \le k \le 9$$

Since $W_{10}^{kn} = e^{-j(2\pi/10)kn}$, by comparison

$$x_1[n] = x[n] \left(\frac{1}{2}e^{j(\pi/10)}\right)^{-n}$$

8.32. We have a finite-length sequence, $x[n]$ with $N = 8$. Suppose we interpolate by a factor of two. That is, we wish to double the size of $x[n]$ by inserting zeros at all odd values of n for $0 \le n \le 15$.

Mathematically,

$$y[n] = \begin{cases} x[n/2], & n \text{ even}, \quad 0 \le n \le 15 \\ 0; & n \text{ odd}, \end{cases}$$

The 16-pt. DFT of $y[n]$:

$$\begin{aligned} Y[k] &= \sum_{n=0}^{15} y[n] W_{16}^{kn}, \qquad 0 \le k \le 15 \\ &= \sum_{n=0}^{7} x[n] W_{16}^{2kn} \end{aligned}$$

Recall, $W_{16}^{2kn} = e^{j(2\pi/16)(2k)n} = e^{-j(2\pi/8)kn} = W_8^{kn}$,

$$Y[k] = \sum_{n=0}^{7} x[n] W_8^{kn}, \qquad 0 \le k \le 15$$

Therefore, the 16-pt. DFT of the interpolated signal contains two copies of the 8-pt. DFT of $x[n]$. This is expected since $Y[k]$ is now periodic with perood 8 (see problem 8.1). Therefore, the correct choice is C.

As a quick check, $Y[0] = X[0]$.

8.33. (a) Since

$$x_2[n] = \begin{cases} x[n], & 0 \le n \le N-1 \\ -x[n-N], & N \le n \le 2N-1 \\ 0, & \text{otherwise} \end{cases}$$

If $X[k]$ is known, $x_2[n]$ can be constructed by :

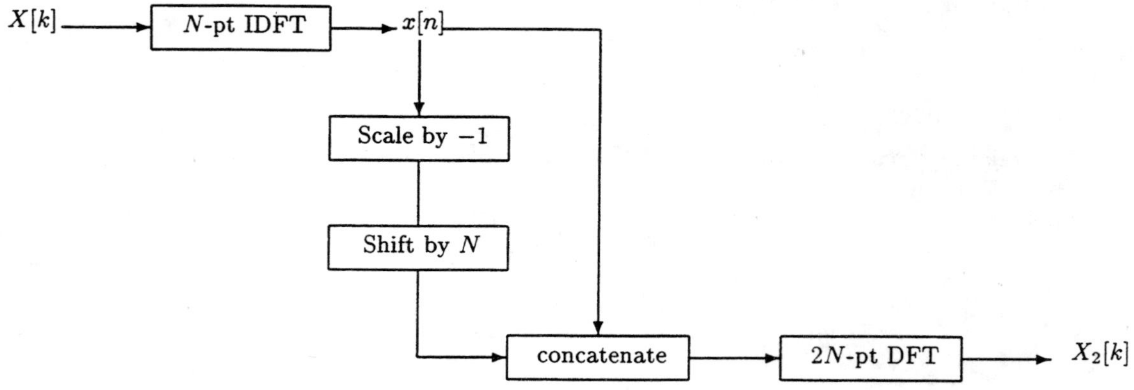

(b) To obtain $X[k]$ from $X_1[k]$, we might try to take the inverse DFT (2N-pt) of $X_1[k]$, then take the N-pt DFT of $x_1[n]$ to get $X[k]$.
However, the above approach is highly inefficient. A more reasonable approach may be achieved if we examine the DFT analysis equations involved. First,

$$\begin{aligned} X_1[k] &= \sum_{n=0}^{2N-1} x_1[n] W_{2N}^{kn}, \qquad 0 \le k \le (2N-1) \\ &= \sum_{n=0}^{N-1} x[n] W_{2N}^{kn} \\ &= \sum_{n=0}^{N-1} x[n] W_N^{(k/2)n}, \qquad 0 \le k \le (N-1) \\ X_1[k] &= X[k/2], \qquad 0 \le k \le (N-1) \end{aligned}$$

Thus, an easier way to obtain $X[k]$ from $X_1[k]$ is simply to decimate $X_1[k]$ by two.

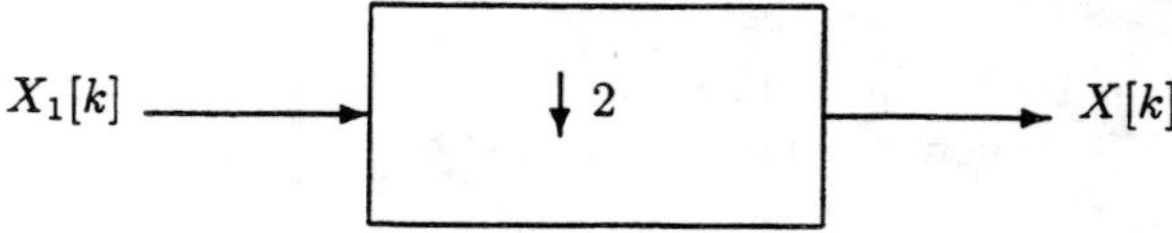

8.34. (a) The DFT of the even part of a real sequence:
If $x[n]$ is of length N, then $x_e[n]$ is of length $2N-1$:

$$x_e[n] = \begin{cases} \dfrac{x[n]+x[-n]}{2}, & (-N+1) \le n \le (N-1) \\ 0 & \text{otherwise} \end{cases}$$

$$X_e[k] = \sum_{n=-N+1}^{N-1} \left(\frac{x[n]+x[-n]}{2}\right) W_{2N-1}^{kn}, \qquad (-N+1) \le k \le (N-1)$$

$$= \sum_{n=-N+1}^{0} \frac{x[-n]}{2} W_{2N-1}^{kn} + \sum_{n=0}^{N-1} \frac{x[n]}{2} W_{2N-1}^{kn}$$

Let $m=-n$,

$$X_e[k] = \sum_{n=0}^{N-1} \frac{x[n]}{2} W_{2N-1}^{-kn} + \sum_{n=0}^{N-1} \frac{x[n]}{2} W_{2N-1}^{kn}$$

$$X_e[k] = \sum_{n=0}^{N-1} x[n] \cos\left(\frac{2\pi kn}{2N-1}\right)$$

Recall

$$X[k] = \sum_{n=0}^{N-1} x[n] W_N^{kn}, \qquad 0 \le k \le (N-1)$$

and

$$Re\{X[k]\} = \sum_{n=0}^{N-1} x[n] \cos\left(\frac{2\pi kn}{N}\right)$$

So: DFT$\{x_e[n]\} \neq Re\{X[k]\}$

(b)

$$Re\{X[k]\} = \frac{X[k]+X^*[k]}{2}$$

$$= \frac{1}{2}\sum_{n=0}^{N-1} x[n]W_N^{kn} + \frac{1}{2}\sum_{n=0}^{N-1} x[n]W_N^{-kn}$$

$$= \frac{1}{2}\sum_{n=0}^{N-1} (x[n]+x[N-n])W_N^{kn}$$

So,

$$Re\{X[k]\} = \text{DFT}\left\{\frac{1}{2}(x[n]+x[N-n])\right\}$$

8.35. From condition 1, we can determine that the sequence is of finite length ($N=5$). Given:

$$X(e^{j\omega}) = 1 + A_1\cos\omega + A_2\cos 2\omega$$

$$= 1 + \frac{A_1}{2}(e^{j\omega}+e^{-j\omega}) + \frac{A_2}{2}(e^{j2\omega}+e^{-j2\omega})$$

From the Fourier analysis equation, we can see by matching terms that:

$$x[n] = \delta[n] + \frac{A_1}{2}(\delta[n-1]+\delta[n+1]) + \frac{A_2}{2}(\delta[n-2]+\delta[n+2])$$

Condition 2 yields one of the values for the amplitude constants of condition 1. Since $x[n] * \delta[n-3] = x[n-3] = 5$ for $n = 2$, we know $x[-1] = 5$, and also that $x[1] = x[-1] = 5$. Knowing both these values tells us that $A_1 = 10$.

For condition 3, we perform a circular convolution between $x[((n-3))_8]$ and $w[n]$, a three-point sequence. For this case, linear convolution is the same as circular convolution since $N = 8 \geq 6 + 3 - 1$.

We know $x[((n-3))_8] = x[n-3]$, and convolving this with $w[n]$ from Fig P8.35-1 gives:

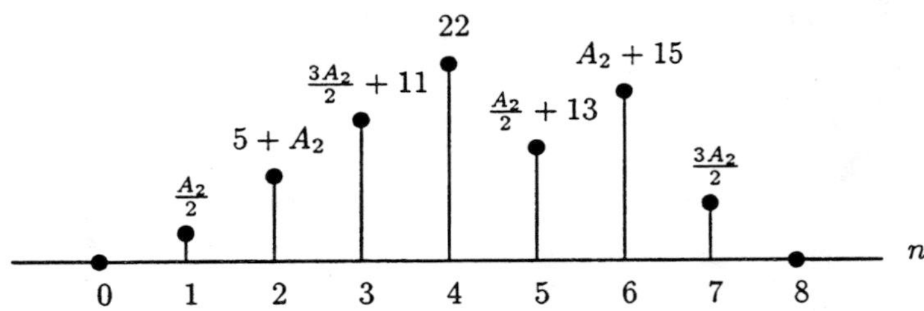

For $n = 2, w[n] * x[n-3] = 11$ so $A_2 = 6$. Thus, $x[2] = x[-2] = 3$, and we have fully specified $x[n]$:

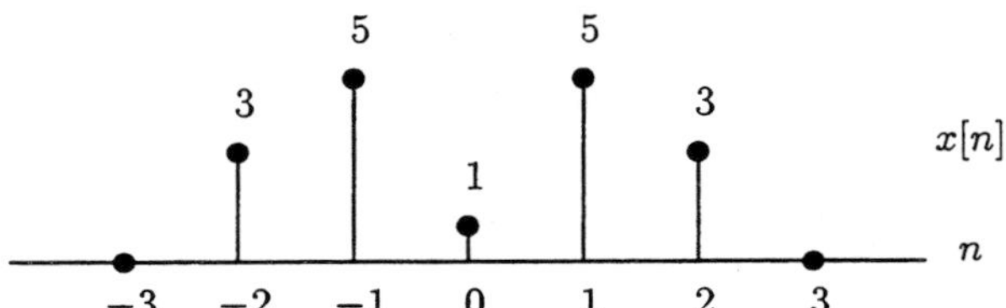

8.36. We have the finite-length sequence:

$$x[n] = 2\delta[n] + \delta[n-1] + \delta[n-3]$$

(i) Suppose we perform the 5-pt DFT:

$$X[k] = 2 + W_5^k + W_5^{3k}, \qquad 0 \leq k \leq 5$$

where $W_5^k = e^{-j(\frac{2\pi}{5})k}$.

(ii) Now, we square the DFT of $x[n]$:

$$\begin{aligned} Y[k] &= X^2[k] \\ &= 2 + 2W_5^k + 2W_5^{3k} \\ &\quad + 2W_5^k + W_5^{2k} + W_5^{5k} \\ &\quad + 2W_5^{3k} + W_5^{4k} + W_5^{6k}, \qquad 0 \leq k \leq 5 \end{aligned}$$

Using the fact $W_5^{5k} = W_5^0 = 1$ and $W_5^{6k} = W_5^k$

$$Y[k] = 3 + 5W_5^k + W_5^{2k} + 4W_5^{3k} + W_5^{4k}, \qquad 0 \leq k \leq 5$$

(a) By inspection,

$$y[n] = 3\delta[n] + 5\delta[n-1] + \delta[n-2] + 4\delta[n-3] + \delta[n-4], \qquad 0 \le n \le 5$$

(b) This procedure performs the autocorrelation of a real sequence. Using the properties of the DFT, an alternative method may be achieved with convolution:

$$y[n] = \text{IDFT}\{X^2[k]\} = x[n] * x[n]$$

The IDFT and DFT suggest that the convolution is circular. Hence, to ensure there is no aliasing, the size of the DFT must be $N \ge 2M - 1$ where M is the length of $x[n]$. Since $M = 3, N \ge 5$.

8.37. (a)

$$g_1[n] = x[N-1-n], \qquad 0 \le n \le (N-1)$$

$$G_1[k] = \sum_{n=0}^{N-1} x[N-1-n]W_N^{kn}, \qquad 0 \le k \le (N-1)$$

Let $m = N - 1 - n$,

$$\begin{aligned} G_1[k] &= \sum_{m=0}^{N-1} x[m]W_N^{k(N-1-m)} \\ &= W_N^{k(N-1)} \sum_{m=0}^{N-1} x[m]W_N^{-km} \end{aligned}$$

Using $W_N^k = e^{-j(2\pi k/N)}, W_N^{k(N-1)} = W_N^{-k} = e^{j(2\pi k/N)}$

$$\begin{aligned} G_1[k] &= e^{j(2\pi k/N)} \sum_{m=0}^{N-1} x[m]e^{j(2\pi km/N)} \\ &= e^{j(2\pi k/N} X(e^{j\omega})|_{\omega=(2\pi k/N)} \\ G_1[k] &= H_7[k] \end{aligned}$$

(b)

$$g_2[n] = (-1)^n x[n], \qquad 0 \le n \le (N-1)$$

$$\begin{aligned} G_2[k] &= \sum_{n=0}^{N-1} (-1)^n x[n]W_N^{kn}, \qquad 0 \le k \le (N-1) \\ &= \sum_{n=0}^{N-1} x[n]W_N^{(\frac{N}{2})n}W_N^{kn} \\ &= \sum_{n=0}^{N-1} x[n]W_N^{(k+\frac{N}{2})n} \\ &= X(e^{j\omega})|_{\omega=2\pi(k+\frac{N}{2})/N} \\ G_2[k] &= H_8[k] \end{aligned}$$

(c)

$$g_3[n] = \begin{cases} x[n], & 0 \le n \le (N-1) \\ x[n-N], & N \le n \le (2N-1) \\ 0, & \text{otherwise} \end{cases}$$

$$\begin{aligned}
G_3[k] &= \sum_{n=0}^{2N-1} x[n] W_{2N}^{kn}, \qquad 0 \le k \le (N-1) \\
&= \sum_{n=0}^{N-1} x[n] W_{2N}^{kn} + \sum_{n=N}^{2N-1} x[n-N] W_{2N}^{kn} \\
&= \sum_{n=0}^{N-1} x[n] W_{2N}^{kn} + \sum_{m=0}^{N-1} x[m] W_{2N}^{k(m+N)} \\
&= \sum_{n=0}^{N-1} x[n] \left(1 + W_{2N}^{kN}\right) W_{2N}^{kn} \\
&= \left(1 + W_N^{(kN/2)}\right) \sum_{n=0}^{N-1} x[n] W_N^{(kn/2)} \\
&= \left(1 + (-1)^k\right) X(e^{j\omega})|_{\omega=(\pi k/N)} \\
G_3[k] &= H_3[k]
\end{aligned}$$

(d)

$$g_4[n] = \begin{cases} x[n] + x[n+N/2], & 0 \le n \le (N/2-1) \\ 0, & \text{otherwise} \end{cases}$$

$$\begin{aligned}
G_4[k] &= \sum_{n=0}^{N/2-1} \left(x[n] + x[n + \frac{N}{2}]\right) W_{N/2}^{kn}, \qquad 0 \le k \le (N-1) \\
&= \sum_{n=0}^{N/2-1} x[n] W_{N/2}^{kn} + \sum_{n=0}^{N/2-1} x[n+N/2] W_{N/2}^{kn} \\
&= \sum_{n=0}^{N/2-1} x[n] W_{N/2}^{kn} + \sum_{m=N/2}^{N-1} x[m] W_{N/2}^{k(m-N/2)} \\
&= \sum_{n=0}^{N-1} x[n] W_N^{2kn} \\
&= X(e^{j\omega})|_{\omega=(4\pi k/N)} \\
G_4[k] &= H_6[k]
\end{aligned}$$

(e)

$$g_5[n] = \begin{cases} x[n], & 0 \le n \le (N-1) \\ 0, & N \le n \le (2N-1) \\ 0, & \text{otherwise} \end{cases}$$

$$
\begin{aligned}
G_5[k] &= \sum_{n=0}^{2N-1} x[n]W_{2N}^{kn}, \qquad 0 \le k \le (N-1) \\
&= \sum_{n=0}^{N-1} x[n]W_{2N}^{kn} \\
&= X(e^{j\omega})|_{\omega=(\pi k/N)} \\
G_5[k] &= H_2[k]
\end{aligned}
$$

(f)

$$
g_6[n] = \begin{cases} x[n/2], & n \text{ even}, \quad 0 \le n \le (2N-1) \\ 0, & n \text{ odd} \end{cases}
$$

$$
\begin{aligned}
G_6[k] &= \sum_{n=0}^{2N-1} x[n/2]W_{2N}^{kn}, \qquad 0 \le k \le (N-1) \\
&= \sum_{n=0}^{N-1} x[n]W_{N}^{kn} \\
&= X(e^{j\omega})|_{\omega=(2\pi k/N)} \\
G_6[k] &= H_1[k]
\end{aligned}
$$

(g)

$$
g_7[n] = x[2n], \qquad 0 \le n \le (N/2-1)
$$

$$
\begin{aligned}
G_7[k] &= \sum_{n=0}^{\frac{N}{2}-1} x[2n]W_{N/2}^{kn}, \qquad 0 \le k \le (N-1) \\
&= \sum_{n=0}^{N-1} x[n]\left(\frac{1+(-1)^n}{2}\right)W_N^{kn} \\
&= \sum_{n=0}^{N-1} x[n]\left(\frac{1+W_N^{(N/2)n}}{2}\right)W_N^{kn} \\
&= \frac{1}{2}\sum_{n=0}^{N-1} x[n]\left(W_N^{nk}+W_N^{n(k+N/2)}\right) \\
&= \frac{1}{2}\left[X(e^{j(2\pi/N)}) + X(e^{j(2\pi/N)(k+N/2)})\right] \\
G_7[k] &= H_5[k]
\end{aligned}
$$

8.38. From Table 8.2, the N-pt DFT of an N-pt sequence will be real-valued if

$$
x[n] = x[((-n))_N].
$$

For $0 \le n \le (N-1)$, this may be stated as,

$$
x[n] = x[N-n], \qquad 0 \le n \le (N-1)
$$

For this case, N = 10, and

$$\begin{aligned} x[1] &= x[9] \\ x[2] &= x[8] \\ &\vdots \end{aligned}$$

The Fourier transform of $x[n]$ displays generalized linear phase (see Section 5.7.2). This implies that for $x[n] \neq 0$, $0 \leq n \leq (N-1)$:

$$x[n] = x[N-1-n]$$

For $N = 10$,

$$\begin{aligned} x[0] &= x[9] \\ x[1] &= x[8] \\ x[2] &= x[7] \\ &\vdots \end{aligned}$$

To satify both conditions, $x[n]$ must be a constant for $0 \leq n \leq 9$.

8.39. We have two 100-pt sequences which are nonzero for the interval $0 \leq n \leq 99$.
If $x_1[n]$ is nonzero for $10 \leq n \leq 39$ only, the linear convolution

$$x_1[n] * x_2[n]$$

is a sequence of length $40 + 100 - 1 = 139$, which is nonzero for the range $10 \leq n \leq 139$.

A 100-pt circular convolution is equivalent to the linear convolution with the first 40 points aliased by the values in the range $100 \leq n \leq 139$.

Therefore, the 100-pt circular convolution will be equivalent to the linear convolution only in the range $40 \leq n \leq 99$.

8.40. (a) Since $x[n]$ is 50 points long, and $h[n]$ is 10 points long, the linear convolution $y[n] = x[n] * h[n]$ must be $50 + 10 - 1 = 59$ pts long.

(b) Circular convolution = linear convolutin + aliasing.
If we let $y[n] = x[n] * h[n]$, a more mathematical statement of the above is given by

$$x[n] \circledN h[n] = \sum_{r=-\infty}^{\infty} y[n + rN], \qquad 0 \leq n \leq (N-1)$$

For $N = 50$,

$$x[n] \text{(50)} h[n] = y[n] + y[n+50], \qquad 0 \leq n \leq 49$$

We are given: $x[n] \text{(50)} h[n] = 10$
Hence,

$$y[n] + y[n+50] = 10, \qquad 0 \leq n \leq 49$$

Also, $y[n] = 5, \quad 0 \leq n \leq 4.$
Using the above information:

$$
\begin{array}{llcl}
n=0 & y[0]+y[50] & = & 10 \\
\vdots & y[50] & = & 5 \\
n=4 & y[4]+y[54] & = & 10 \\
 & y[54] & = & 5 \\
n=5 & y[5]+y[55] & = & 10 \\
\vdots & y[55] & = & ? \\
n=8 & y[8]+y[58] & = & 10 \\
 & y[58] & = & ? \\
n=9 & y[9] & = & 10 \\
\vdots & & & \\
n=49 & y[49] & = & 10
\end{array}
$$

To conclude, we can determine $y[n]$ for $9 \leq n \leq 55$ only. (Note that $y[n]$ for $0 \leq n \leq 4$ is given.)

8.41. We have

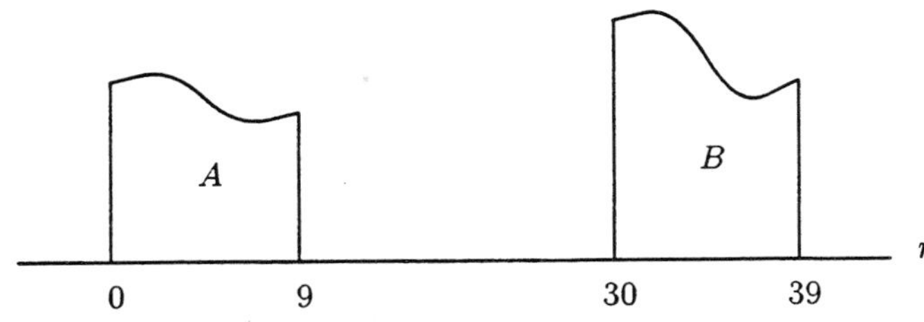

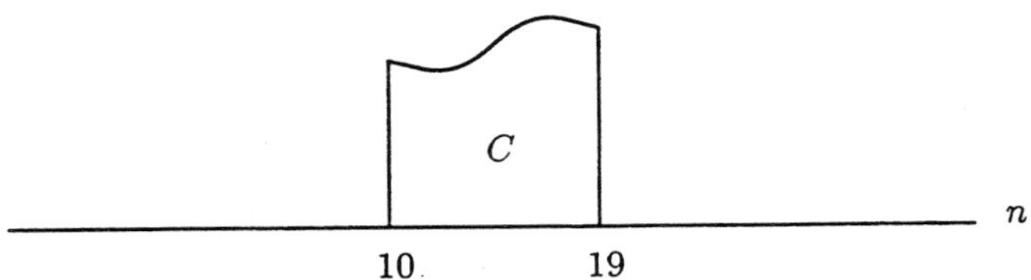

(a) The linear convolution $x[n] * y[n]$ is a $40 + 20 - 1 = 59$ point sequence:

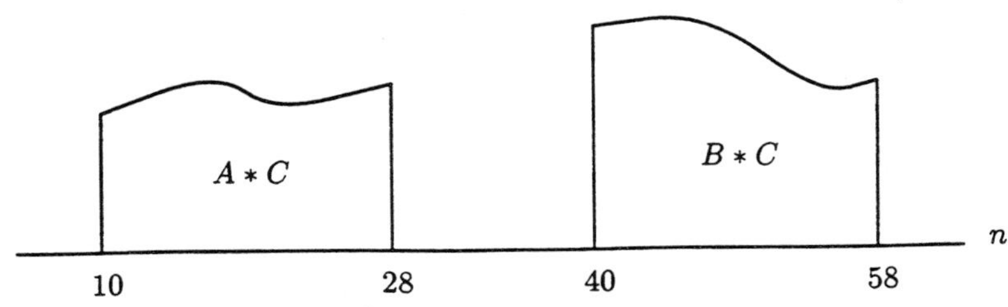

Thus, $x[n] * y[n] = w[n]$ is nonzero for $10 \leq n \leq 28$ and $40 \leq n \leq 58$.

(b) The 40-pt circluar convolution can be obtained by aliasing the linear convolution. Specifically, we alias the points in the range $40 \leq n \leq 58$ to the range $0 \leq n \leq 18$.
Since $w[n] = x[n] * y[n]$ is zero for $0 \leq n \leq 9$, the circular convolution $g[n] = x[n] \textcircled{40} y[n]$ consists of only the (aliased) values:

$$w[n] = x[n] * y[n], \qquad 40 \leq n \leq 49$$

Also, the points of $g[n]$ for $18 \leq n \leq 39$ will be equivalent to the points of $w[n]$ in this range.
To conclude,

$$\begin{aligned} w[n] &= g[n], \quad 18 \leq n \leq 39 \\ w[n+40] &= g[n], \quad 0 \leq n \leq 9 \end{aligned}$$

8.42. (a) The two sequences are related by the circular shift:

$$h_2[n] = h_1[((n+4))_8]$$

Thus,

$$H_2[k] = W_8^{-4k} H_1[k]$$

and

$$|H_2[k]| = |W_8^{-4k} H_1[k]| = |H_1[k]|$$

So, yes the magnitudes of the 8-pt DFTs are equal.

(b) $h_1[n]$ is nearly like $(\sin x)/x$.
Since $H_2[k] = e^{j\pi k} H_1[k]$, $h_1[n]$ is a better lowpass filter.

8.43. (a) Overlap add:
If we divide the input into sections of length L, each section will have an output length:

$$L + 100 - 1 = L + 99$$

Thus, the required length is

$$L = 256 - 99 = 157$$

If we had 63 sections, $63 \times 157 = 9891$, there will be a remainder of 109 points. Hence, we must pad the remaining data to 256 and use another DFT.
Therefore, we require 64 DFTs and 64 IDFTs. Since $h[n]$ also requires a DFT, the total:

65 DFTs and 64 IDFTs

(b) Overlap save:
We require 99 zeros to be padded in from of the sequence. The first 99 points of the output of each section will be discarded. Thus the length after padding is 10099 points. The length of each section overlap is $256 - 99 = 157 = L$.
We require $65 \times 157 = 10205$ to get all 10099 points. Because $h[n]$ also requires a DFT:

66 DFTs and 65 IDFTs

(c) Ignoring the transients at the beginning and end of the direct convolution, each output point requires 100 multiplies and 99 adds.
overlap add:

$$\begin{aligned} \#\ \text{mult} &= 129(1024) = 132096 \\ \#\ \text{add} &= 129(2048) = 264192 \end{aligned}$$

overlap save:

$$\begin{aligned}
\#\text{ mult} &= 131(1024) &= 134144 \\
\#\text{ add} &= 131(2048) &= 268288
\end{aligned}$$

direct convolution:

$$\begin{aligned}
\#\text{ mult} &= 100(10000) &= 1000000 \\
\#\text{ add} &= 99(10000) &= 990000
\end{aligned}$$

8.44. First we need to compute the values $Q[0]$ and $Q[3]$:

$$\begin{aligned}
Q[0] &= X_1(1) = X_1(e^{jw})|_{w=0} \\
&= \sum_{n=0}^{\infty} x_1[n] = \frac{1}{1-\frac{1}{4}} \\
&= \frac{4}{3} \\
Q[3] &= X_1(-1) = X_1(e^{jw})|_{w=\pi} \\
&= \sum_{n=0}^{\infty} x_1[n](-1)^n \\
&= \frac{4}{3}
\end{aligned}$$

One possibility for $Q[k]$, the six-point DFT, is:

$$Q[k] = \frac{4}{3}\delta[k] + \frac{4}{3}\delta[k-3].$$

We then find $q[n]$, for $0 \le n < 6$:

$$\begin{aligned}
q[n] &= \frac{1}{6}\sum_{k=0}^{5} Q[k]e^{\frac{2\pi}{6}kn} \\
&= \frac{1}{6}(\frac{4}{3} + \frac{4}{3}(-1)^n) \\
&= \frac{2}{9}(1 + (-1)^n)
\end{aligned}$$

otherwise it's 0. Here's a sketch of q[n]:

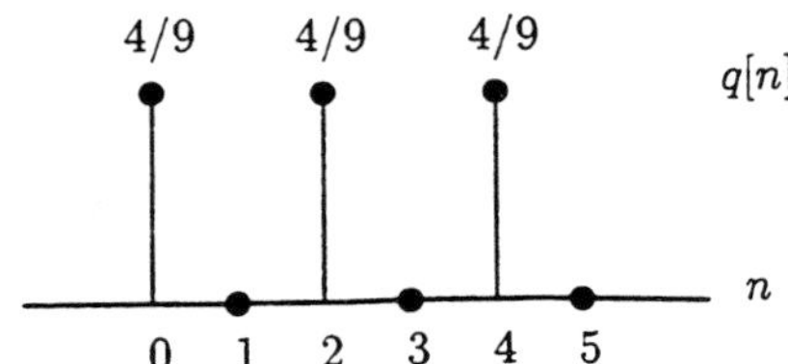

8.45. We have:

$$DFT_7\{x_2[n]\} = X_2[k] = \sum_0^4 x_2[n]e^{-j\frac{2\pi}{7}kn}.$$

Then:

$$\begin{aligned}
x_2[0] &= \frac{1}{7}\sum_{k=0}^{6} X_2[k] \\
&= \frac{1}{7}\sum_{k=0}^{6}(Re\{X_2[k]\} + jIm\{X_2[k]\}) \\
&= \frac{1}{7}\sum_{k=0}^{6} Re\{X_2[k]\} \text{ , since } x_2[0] \text{ is real.} \\
&= g[0].
\end{aligned}$$

To determine the relationship between $x_2[1]$ and g[1], we first note that since $x_2[n]$ is real:

$$X(e^{jw}) = X^*(e^{-jw}).$$

Therefore:

$$X[k] = X^*[N-k] \text{ , } k = 0, ..., 6.$$

We thus have:

$$\begin{aligned}
g[1] &= \frac{1}{7}\sum_{k=0}^{6} Re\{X_2[k]\}W_7^{-k} \\
&= \frac{1}{7}\sum_{k=0}^{6} \frac{X_2[k] + X_2^*[k]}{2}W_7^{-k} \\
&= \frac{1}{7}\sum_{k=0}^{6} \frac{X_2[k]}{2}W_7^{-k} + \frac{1}{7}\sum_{k=0}^{6} \frac{X_2[N-k]}{2}W_7^{-k} \\
&= \frac{1}{2}x_2[1] + \frac{1}{14}\sum_{k=0}^{6} X_2[k]W_7^{k} \\
&= \frac{1}{2}x_2[1] + \frac{1}{14}\sum_{k=0}^{6} X_2[k]W_7^{-6k} \\
&= \frac{1}{2}(x_2[1] + x_2[6]) \\
&= \frac{1}{2}(x_2[1] + 0) \\
&= \frac{1}{2}x_2[1].
\end{aligned}$$

8.46. (i) This corresponds to $x_i[n] = x_i^*[((-n))_N]$, where $N = 5$. Note that this is only true for $x_2[n]$.

(ii) $X_i(e^{jw})$ has linear phase corresponds to $x_i[n]$ having some internal symmetry, this is only true for $x_1[n]$.

(iii) The DFT has linear phase corresponds to $\tilde{x}_i[n]$ (the periodic sequence obtained from $x_i[n]$) being symmetric, this is true for $x_1[n]$ and $x_2[n]$ only.

8.47. (a)

$$\frac{1}{8}\sum_{k=0}^{7} X[k]e^{j\frac{2\pi}{8}k9} = \frac{1}{8}\sum_{k=0}^{7} X[k]e^{j\frac{2\pi}{8}k} = x[1].$$

(b)

$$\begin{aligned} V[k] &= X(z)\big|_{z=2e^{j(\frac{2\pi k+\pi}{8})}} \\ &= \sum_{n=-\infty}^{n=\infty} x[n]z^{-n}\big|_{z=2e^{j(\frac{2\pi k+\pi}{8})}} \\ &= \sum_{n=0}^{n=8} x[n]z^{-n}\big|_{z=2e^{j(\frac{2\pi k+\pi}{8})}} \\ &= \sum_{n=0}^{n=8} x[n](2e^{j\frac{\pi}{8}})^{-n}e^{-j\frac{2\pi k}{8}n} \\ &= \sum_{n=0}^{n=8} v[n]e^{-j\frac{2\pi k}{8}n}. \end{aligned}$$

We thus conclude that

$$v[n] = x[n](2e^{j\frac{\pi}{8}})^{-n}.$$

(c)

$$\begin{aligned} w[n] &= \frac{1}{4}\sum_{k=0}^{3} W[k]W_4^{-kn} \\ &= \frac{1}{4}\sum_{k=0}^{3}(X[k] + X[k+4])e^{+j\frac{2\pi}{4}kn} \\ &= \frac{1}{4}\sum_{k=0}^{3} X[k]e^{+j\frac{2\pi}{4}kn} + \frac{1}{4}\sum_{k=0}^{3} X[k+4]e^{+j\frac{2\pi}{4}kn} \\ &= \frac{1}{4}\sum_{k=0}^{3} X[k]e^{+j\frac{2\pi}{4}kn} + \frac{1}{4}\sum_{k=4}^{7} X[k]e^{+j\frac{2\pi}{4}kn} \\ &= \frac{1}{4}\sum_{k=0}^{7} X[k]e^{+j\frac{2\pi}{8}k2n} \\ &= 2x[2n]. \end{aligned}$$

We thus conclude that

$$w[n] = 2x[2n].$$

(d) Note that $Y[k]$ can be written as:

$$\begin{aligned} Y[k] &= X[k] + (-1)^k X[k] \\ &= X[k] + W_8^{4k} X[k]. \end{aligned}$$

Using the DFT properties, we thus conclude that

$$y[n] = x[n] + x[((n-4))_8].$$

8.48. (a) No. x[n] only has N degrees of freedom and we have $M \geq N$ constraints which can only be satisfied if $x[n] = 0$. Specifically, we want

$$X(e^{j\frac{2\pi k}{M}}) = DFT_M\{x[n]\} = 0.$$

Since $M \geq N$, there is no aliasing and x[n] can be expressed as:

$$x[n] = \frac{1}{M}\sum_{k=0}^{M-1} X[k]W_M^{kn}\ ,\ n = 0, ..., M-1.$$

Where $X[k]$ is the M-point DFT of $x[n]$, since $X[k] = 0$, we thus conclude that $x[n] = 0$, and therefore the answer is NO.

(b) Here, we only need to make sure that when time-aliased to M samples, $x[n]$ is all zeros. For example, let

$$x[n] = \delta[n] - \delta[n-2]$$

then,

$$X(e^{jw}) = 1 - e^{-2jw}.$$

Let $M = 2$, then we have

$$\begin{aligned} X(e^{j\frac{2\pi}{2}0}) &= 1 - 1 = 0 \\ X(e^{j\frac{2\pi}{2}1}) &= 1 - 1 = 0 \end{aligned}$$

8.49. $x_2[n]$ is $x_1[n]$ time aliased to have only N samples. Since

$$x_1[n] = (\frac{1}{3})^n u[n],$$

We get:

$$x_2[n] = \begin{cases} \frac{(\frac{1}{3})^n}{1-(\frac{1}{3})^N} & ,\quad n = 0, ..., N-1 \\ 0 & ,\quad \text{otherwise} \end{cases}$$

8.50. (a) Let $n = 0, ..., 7$, we can write $x[n]$ as:

$$\begin{aligned} x[n] &= 1 + \frac{1}{2}(e^{j\frac{\pi}{4}n} + e^{-j\frac{\pi}{4}n}) - \frac{1}{4}(e^{j\frac{3\pi}{4}n} + e^{-j\frac{3\pi}{4}n}) \\ &= 1 + \frac{1}{2}e^{j\frac{2\pi}{8}n} + \frac{1}{2}e^{j\frac{2\pi}{8}n7} - \frac{1}{4}e^{j\frac{2\pi}{8}n3} - \frac{1}{4}e^{j\frac{2\pi}{8}n5} \\ &= \frac{1}{8}(8 + 4e^{j\frac{2\pi}{8}n} + 4e^{j\frac{2\pi}{8}n7} - 2e^{j\frac{2\pi}{8}n3} - 2e^{j\frac{2\pi}{8}n5}) \\ &= \frac{1}{8}\sum_{k=0}^{7} X_8[k]e^{j\frac{2\pi k}{8}n} \end{aligned}$$

We thus get the following plot for $X_8[k]$:

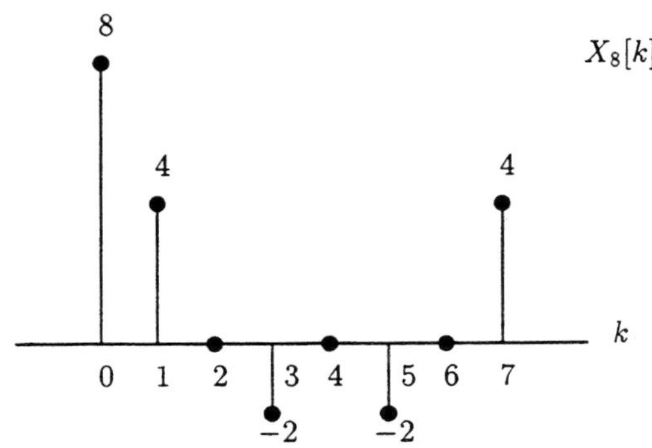

(b) Now let $n = 0, ..., 15$, we can write $v[n]$ as:

$$\begin{aligned} v[n] &= 1 + \frac{1}{2}(e^{j\frac{\pi}{4}n} + e^{-j\frac{\pi}{4}n}) - \frac{1}{4}(e^{j\frac{3\pi}{4}n} + e^{-j\frac{3\pi}{4}n}) \\ &= 1 + \frac{1}{2}e^{j\frac{2\pi}{16}n2} + \frac{1}{2}e^{j\frac{2\pi}{16}n14} - \frac{1}{4}e^{j\frac{2\pi}{16}n6} - \frac{1}{4}e^{j\frac{2\pi}{16}n10} \\ &= \frac{1}{16}(16 + 8e^{j\frac{2\pi}{16}n2} + 8e^{j\frac{2\pi}{16}n14} - 4e^{j\frac{2\pi}{16}n6} - 4e^{j\frac{2\pi}{16}n10}) \\ &= \frac{1}{16}\sum_{k=0}^{15} V_{16}[k]e^{j\frac{2\pi k}{16}n} \end{aligned}$$

We thus get the following plot for $V_{16}[k]$:

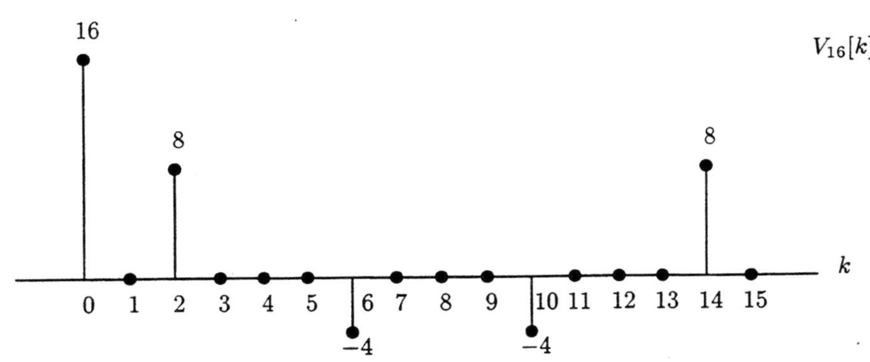

(c)

$$|X_{16}[k]| = X(e^{j\omega})|_{\omega=\frac{2\pi}{16}k} \qquad 0 \le k \le 15$$

where $X(e^{j\omega})$ is the Fourier transform of $x[n]$.
Note that $x[n]$ can be expressed as:

$$x[n] = y[n]w[n]$$

where:

$$y[n] = 1 + \cos(\frac{\pi n}{4}) - \frac{1}{2}\cos(\frac{3\pi n}{4})$$

and $w[n]$ is an eight-point rectangular window.
$|X_{16}[k]|$ will therefore have as its even points the sequence $|X_8[k]|$ .The odd points will correspond to the bandlimited interpolation between the even-point samples. The values that we can find exactly by inspection are thus:

$$|X_{16}[k]| = |X_8[k/2]| \qquad k = 0, 2, 4, ..., 14.$$

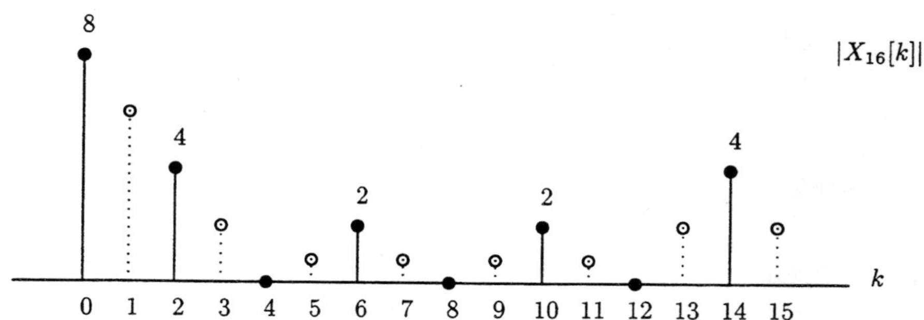

8.51. We wish to verify the identity of Eq. (8.7):

$$\frac{1}{N}\sum_{n=0}^{N-1} e^{j\frac{2\pi}{N}(k-r)n} = \begin{cases} 1, & k-r = mN,\ m:\ \text{integer} \\ 0, & \text{otherwise} \end{cases}$$

(a) For $k - r = mN$,

$$\begin{aligned} e^{j\frac{2\pi}{N}(k-r)n} &= e^{j\frac{2\pi}{N}(mN)n} \\ & e^{j2\pi mn} \\ & (1)^{mn} \end{aligned}$$

Since m and n are integers;

$$e^{j\frac{2\pi}{N}(k-r)n} = 1 \text{ , for } k - r = mN$$

So,

$$\begin{aligned} \frac{1}{N}\sum_{n=0}^{N-1} e^{j\frac{2\pi}{N}(k-r)n} &= \frac{1}{N}\sum_{n=0}^{N-1} 1 \\ &= 1 \text{ , for } k - r = mN \end{aligned}$$

(b)

$$\frac{1}{N}\sum_{n=0}^{N-1} e^{j\frac{2\pi}{N}ln} = \frac{1 - e^{j\frac{2\pi}{N}lN}}{1 - e^{j\frac{2\pi}{N}l}}$$

This closed form solution is indeterminate for $l = mN$ only.
For the case when $l = mN$, we use L'Hôpital's Rule to find:

$$\begin{aligned} \lim_{l \to mN} \frac{1 - e^{j2\pi l}}{1 - e^{j\frac{2\pi}{N}l}} &= \left[\frac{-j2\pi e^{j2\pi l}}{-j\frac{2\pi}{N} e^{j\frac{2\pi}{N}l}} \right]_{l=mN} \\ &= N \end{aligned}$$

(c) For the case when $k - r \neq mN$:

$$\begin{aligned}\frac{1}{N}\sum_{n=0}^{N-1} e^{j\frac{2\pi}{N}(k-r)n} &= \frac{1-e^{j2\pi(k-r)}}{1-e^{j\frac{2\pi}{N}(k-r)}} \\ &= 0\end{aligned}$$

Note that the denominator is nonzero, while the numerator will always be zero for $k - r \neq mN$.

8.52. (a) We know from Eq. (8.11) that if $\tilde{x}_1[n] = \tilde{x}[n-m]$, we have:

$$\tilde{X}_1[k] = \sum_{n=0}^{N-1} \tilde{x}[n-m] W_N^{kn}$$

If we substitute $r = n - m$ into this equation, we get:

$$\begin{aligned}\tilde{X}_1[k] &= \sum_{r=-m}^{N-1-m} \tilde{x}[r] W_N^{k(r+m)} \\ &= W_N^{km} \sum_{r=-m}^{N-1-m} \tilde{x}[r] W_N^{kr}\end{aligned}$$

(b) We can decompose the summation from part (a) into

$$\tilde{X}_1[k] = W_N^{km}\left[\sum_{r=-m}^{-1} \tilde{x}[r] W_N^{kr} + \sum_{r=0}^{N-1-m} \tilde{x}[r] W_N^{kr}\right]$$

Using the fact that $\tilde{x}[r]$ and W_N^{kr} are periodic with period N:

$$\sum_{r=-m}^{-1} \tilde{x}[r] W_N^{kr} = \sum_{r=-m}^{-1} \tilde{x}[r+N] W_N^{k(r+N)}$$

Substituting $\ell = r + N$

$$\sum_{r=-m}^{-1} \tilde{x}[r] W_N^{kr} = \sum_{\ell=N-m}^{N-1} \tilde{x}[\ell] W_N^{k\ell}$$

(c) Using the result from part (b):

$$\begin{aligned}\tilde{X}_1[k] &= W_N^{km}\left[\sum_{r=N-m}^{N-1} \tilde{x}[r] W_N^{kr} + \sum_{r=0}^{N-m-1} \tilde{x}[r] W_N^{kr}\right] \\ &= W_N^{km} \sum_{r=0}^{N-1} \tilde{x}[r] W_N^{kr} \\ &= W_N^{km} \tilde{X}[k]\end{aligned}$$

Hence, if $\tilde{x}_1[n] = \tilde{x}[n-m]$, then $\tilde{X}_1[k] = W_N^{km}\tilde{X}[k]$.

8.53. (a) 1. The DFS of $\tilde{x}^*[n]$ is given by:

$$\begin{aligned}\sum_{n=0}^{N-1} \tilde{x}^*[n] W_N^{kn} &= \left(\sum_{n=0}^{N-1} \tilde{x}[n] W_N^{-kn}\right)^* \\ &= \tilde{X}^*[-k]\end{aligned}$$

2. The DFS of $\tilde{x}^*[-n]$:

$$\begin{aligned}\sum_{n=0}^{N-1} \tilde{x}^*[-n] W_N^{kn} &= \left(\sum_{l=-N+1}^{0} \tilde{x}[l] W_N^{kl}\right)^* \\ &= X^*[k]\end{aligned}$$

3. The DFS of $Re\{\tilde{x}[n]\}$:

$$\begin{aligned}\sum_{n=0}^{N-1} \frac{\tilde{x}[n] + \tilde{x}^*[n]}{2} W_N^{kn} &= \frac{1}{2}\left(\tilde{X}[k] + \tilde{X}^*[-k]\right) \\ &\dot{=} \tilde{X}_e[k]\end{aligned}$$

4. The DFS of $jIm\{\tilde{x}[n]\}$:

$$\begin{aligned}\sum_{n=0}^{N-1} \frac{\tilde{x}[n] - \tilde{x}^*[n]}{2} W_N^{kn} &= \frac{1}{2}\left(\tilde{X}[k] - \tilde{X}^*[-k]\right) \\ &= \tilde{X}_0[k]\end{aligned}$$

(b) Consider $\tilde{x}[n]$ real:

1.

$$Re\{\tilde{X}[k]\} = \frac{\tilde{X}[k] + \tilde{X}^*[k]}{2}$$

From part (a), if $\tilde{x}[n]$ is real,

$$\begin{aligned}\text{DFS } \{\tilde{x}[n]\} &= \text{DFS } \{\tilde{x}^*[n]\} \\ \text{DFS } \{\tilde{x}[-n]\} &= \text{DFS } \{\tilde{x}^*[-n]\}\end{aligned}$$

So,

$$\begin{aligned}\tilde{X}[k] &= \tilde{X}^*[-k] \\ \tilde{X}[-k] &= \tilde{X}^*[k] \\ Re\{\tilde{X}[k]\} &= \frac{X^*[k] + X[-k]}{2} \\ &= Re\{\tilde{X}[-k]\}\end{aligned}$$

(i.e. the real part of $\tilde{X}[k]$ is even.)

2.

$$\begin{aligned}Im\{\tilde{X}[k]\} &= \frac{\tilde{X}[k] - \tilde{X}^*[k]}{2} \\ &= \frac{\tilde{X}^*[-k] - \tilde{X}[-k]}{2} \\ &= Im\{\tilde{X}[-k]\}\end{aligned}$$

(i.e., the imaginary part of $\tilde{X}[k]$ is odd.)

3.

$$\begin{aligned}|\tilde{X}[k]| &= \sqrt{\tilde{X}[k]\tilde{X}^*[k]} \\ &= \sqrt{\tilde{X}^*[-k]\tilde{X}[-k]} \\ &= |\tilde{X}[-k]|\end{aligned}$$

(i.e., the magnitude of $\tilde{X}[k]$ is even)

4.

$$\begin{aligned}\angle\tilde{X}[k] &= \arctan\left(\frac{\mathcal{I}m\{\tilde{X}[k]\}}{\mathcal{R}e\{\tilde{X}[k]\}}\right) \\ &= \arctan\left(\frac{\mathcal{I}m\{\tilde{X}[-k]\}}{\mathcal{R}e\{\tilde{X}[-k]\}}\right) \\ &= -\angle\tilde{X}[-k]\end{aligned}$$

(i.e., the angle of $\tilde{X}[k]$ is odd.)

8.54. 1. Let $x[n]$ $(0 \le n \le N-1)$ be one period of the periodic sequence $\tilde{x}[n]$. The Fourier transform of this periodic sequence can be expressed as:

$$\tilde{X}(e^{j\omega}) = \sum_{n=-\infty}^{\infty} \tilde{x}[n]e^{-j\omega n}$$

Recall the synthesis equation, Eq. (8.12):

$$\tilde{x}[n] = \frac{1}{N}\sum_{k=0}^{N-1} \tilde{X}[k]W_N^{-kn}$$

Substitution yields:

$$\tilde{X}(e^{jw}) = \sum_{n=-\infty}^{\infty}\left(\frac{1}{N}\sum_{k=0}^{N-1}\tilde{X}[k]W_N^{-kn}\right)e^{-j\omega n}$$

Rearranging the summations and combining terms:

$$\tilde{X}(e^{j\omega}) = \sum_{k=0}^{N-1}\tilde{X}[k]\left(\frac{1}{N}\sum_{n=-\infty}^{\infty} e^{j(\frac{2\pi k}{N}-\omega)n}\right)$$

The infinite summation is recognized as an impulse at $\omega = (2\pi k/N)$:

$$\tilde{X}(e^{j\omega}) = \frac{1}{N}\sum_{k=0}^{N-1}\tilde{X}[k]\delta\left(\omega - \frac{2\pi k}{N}\right)$$

2. Since $x[n]$ corresponds to one period of $\tilde{x}[n]$, we must apply a rectangular window (unit amplitude and length N) to the periodic sequence. Thus, to extract one period from $\tilde{x}[n]$:

$$x[n] = \tilde{x}[n]w[n]$$

where,

$$w[n] = \begin{cases} 1, & 0 \le n \le (N-1) \\ 0, & \text{otherwise}\end{cases}$$

The window has a Fourier transform:

$$\begin{aligned}W(e^{j\omega}) &= \sum_{n=-\infty}^{\infty} w[n]e^{-j\omega n} \\ &= \sum_{n=0}^{N-1} e^{-j\omega n} \\ &= \frac{1-e^{-j\omega N}}{1-e^{-j\omega}} \quad = \frac{e^{-j\omega\frac{N}{2}}}{e^{-j\frac{\omega}{2}}}\,\frac{e^{j\frac{\omega N}{2}} - e^{-j\frac{\omega N}{2}}}{e^{j\frac{\omega}{2}} - e^{-j\frac{\omega}{2}}} \\ &\qquad\qquad\qquad\quad = e^{-j\omega\left(\frac{N-1}{2}\right)}\frac{\sin\left(\omega\frac{N}{2}\right)}{\sin\left(\frac{\omega}{2}\right)}\end{aligned}$$

3. Since $x[n] = \tilde{x}[n]w[n]$, the Fourier transform of $x[n]$ can be represented by the periodic convolution (see Eq. (8.28)).

$$X(e^{j\omega}) = \frac{1}{2\pi}\int_{-\pi}^{\pi} d\theta \frac{1}{N}\sum_{k=0}^{N-1} \tilde{X}[k]\delta\left(\theta - \frac{2\pi k}{N}\right)\frac{\sin\left[\frac{N}{2}(w-\theta)\right]}{\sin\left(\frac{\omega-\theta}{2}\right)}e^{-j\left(\frac{N-1}{2}\right)(\omega-\theta)}$$

Integration over $-\pi \le \theta \le \pi$ reduces to the summation (note the impulse train):

$$\tilde{X}(e^{j\omega}) = \frac{1}{N}\sum_{k=0}^{N-1}\tilde{X}[k]\frac{\sin\left[(N\omega - 2\pi k)/2\right]}{\sin\left[\left(\omega - \frac{2\pi k}{N}\right)/2\right]}e^{-j\left(\frac{N-1}{2}\right)\left(\omega - \frac{2\pi k}{N}\right)}$$

Hence, the Fourier transform is obtained from the DFS via an interpolation formula.

8.55. The N-point DFT of the N-pt sequence, $x[n]$ is given by

$$\begin{aligned} X[k] &= \sum_{n=0}^{N-1} x[n]W_N^{kn}, \qquad 0 \le k \le (N-1) \\ X[0] &= \sum_{n=0}^{N-1} x[n] \end{aligned}$$

(a) Suppose $x[n] = -x[N-1-n]$. For N even, all elements of $x[n]$ will cancel with an antisymmetric component. For N odd, all elements have a counterpart with opposite sign. However, $x[(N-1)/2]$ must also be zero.
Therefore, for $x[n] = -x[N-1-n]$, $X[0] = 0$.

(b) Suppose $x[n] = x[N-1-n]$ and N even.

$$\begin{aligned} X[N/2] &= \sum_{n=0}^{N-1} x[n]W_N^{(N/2)n} \\ &= \sum_{n=0}^{N-1} x[n](-1)^n \\ &= x[0] - x[1] + x[2] - x[3] + \cdots + x[N-2] - x[N-1] \end{aligned}$$

Since $x[n] = x[N-1-n]$, then

$$\begin{aligned} x[0] &= x[N-1] \\ x[1] &= x[N-2] \\ &\vdots \end{aligned}$$

Therefore, $X[N/2] = 0$.

8.56. (a) The conjugate-symmetric part of a sequence:

$$x_e[n] = \frac{1}{2}\left(x[n] + x^*[-n]\right)$$

The periodic conjugate-symmetric part:

$$x_{ep}[n] = \frac{1}{2}\left(x[((n))_N] + x^*[((-n))_N]\right), \qquad 0 \le n \le (N-1)$$

Note that:

$$\begin{aligned} x[((n))_N] &= x[n], \quad 0 \le n \le (N-1) \\ x^*[((-n))_N] &= x^*[-n+N] + x^*[0]\delta[n] - x^*[0]\delta[n-N] \end{aligned}$$

Substituting into $x_{ep}[n]$:

$$x_{ep}[n] = \frac{1}{2}\left[x[n] + x^*[-n+N] + x^*[0]\delta[n] - x^*[0]\delta[n-N]\right], \qquad 0 \le n \le (N-1)$$

Since,

$$\begin{aligned} x_e[n] &= \frac{1}{2}\Big(x[n] + x^*[-n]\Big) \\ &= \frac{1}{2}\Big(x[n] + x^*[0]\delta[n]\Big), \qquad 0 \le n \le (N-1) \\ \text{and } x_e[n-N] &= \frac{1}{2}\Big(x[n-N] + x^*[N-n]\Big) \\ &= \frac{1}{2}\Big(-x^*[0]\delta[n-N] + x^*[N-n]\Big) \qquad 0 \le n \le (N-1) \end{aligned}$$

We can combine to get:

$$x_{ep}[n] = x_e[n] + x_e[n-N] \qquad 0 \le n \le (N-1)$$

The periodic conjugate-antisymmetric part is given as

$$x_{op}[n] = (x_o[n] + x_o[n-N]), \qquad 0 \le n \le (N-1)$$

Recall that the odd part can be expressed as

$$x_o[n] = \frac{1}{2}\Big(x[n] - x^*[-n]\Big)$$

So,

$$x_o[n-N] = \frac{1}{2}\Big(x[n-N] - x^*[N-n]\Big)$$

For $0 \le n \le (N-1)$:

$$\begin{aligned} x_o[n] &= \frac{1}{2}\Big(x[n] - x^*[0]\delta[n]\Big), \qquad 0 \le n \le N-1 \\ x_o[n-N] &= \frac{1}{2}\Big(x[0]\delta[n-N] - x^*[N-n]\Big) \end{aligned}$$

From the definition of $x_{op}[n]$:

$$\begin{aligned} x_{op}[n] &= \frac{1}{2}\Big(x[((n))_N] - x^*[((-n))_N]\Big), \qquad 0 \le n \le (N-1) \\ &= \frac{1}{2}\Big(x[n] - x^*[0]\delta[n] + x^*[0]\delta[n-N] - x^*[N-n]\Big), \qquad 0 \le n \le (N-1) \end{aligned}$$

Recognizing the expressions for $x_o[n]$ and $x_o[n-N]$ in $x_{op}[n]$, we have

$$x_{op}[n] = x_o[n] + x_o[n-N], \qquad 0 \le n \le (N-1)$$

(b) $x[n]$ is a sequence of length N; however,

$$x[n] = \begin{cases} x_1[n], & 0 \le n \le N/2 \\ 0, & N/2 \le n \le N-1 \end{cases}$$

The even part: (assume N is even)

$$x_e[n] = \begin{cases} \frac{x[n]}{2} + \frac{x^*[0]\delta[n]}{2}, & 0 \le n \le N/2 \\ \frac{x^*[-n]}{2}, & -N/2 \le n \le -1 \\ 0, & \text{otherwise} \end{cases}$$

From part (a):

$$x_{ep}[n] = x_e[n] + x_e[n-N], \quad 0 \le n \le (N-1)$$

Because $x[n] = 0$ for $|n| \ge N/2$,

$$x_{ep}[n] = x_e[n], \quad 0 \le n \le (N/2 - 1)$$

Also, since $x_e[n] = x_e^*[-n]$,

$$x_e[n] = x_{ep}^*[-n], \quad -N/2 < n \le -1$$

To conclude:

$$x_e[n] = \begin{cases} x_{ep}[n], & 0 \le n \le N/2 \\ \frac{x_{ep}[n]}{2}, & n = N/2 \\ x_{ep}^*[-n], & -N/2 < n \le -1 \\ \frac{x_{ep}^*[-n]}{2}, & n = -N/2 \end{cases}$$

8.57.

$$\sum_{n=0}^{N-1} |x[n]|^2 = \sum_{n=0}^{N-1} x[n]x^*[n]$$

From the synthesis equation:

$$x[n] = \frac{1}{N}\sum_{k=0}^{N-1} X[k]W_N^{-kn}$$

Hence,

$$x^*[n] = \frac{1}{N}\sum_{k=0}^{N-1} X^*[k]W_N^{kn}$$

substituting:

$$\sum_{n=0}^{N-1} |x[n]|^2 = \sum_{n=0}^{N-1} x[n]\left(\frac{1}{N}\sum_{k=0}^{N-1} X^*[k]W_N^{kn}\right)$$

$$
\begin{aligned}
&= \frac{1}{N}\sum_{k=0}^{N-1} X^*[k]\left(\sum_{n=0}^{N-1} x[n]W_N^{kn}\right) \\
&= \frac{1}{N}\sum_{k=0}^{N-1} X^*[k]X[k] \\
\sum_{n=0}^{N-1} |x[n]|^2 &= \frac{1}{N}\sum_{k=0}^{N-1} |X[k]|^2
\end{aligned}
$$

8.58. (a) This statement is TRUE:

$$
\begin{aligned}
X[k] &= X(e^{j\omega})|_{\omega=2\pi k/N} \\
&= B\left(\frac{2\pi k}{N}\right) e^{j(2\pi/N)k\alpha} \\
A[k] &= B\left(\frac{2\pi k}{N}\right) \\
\gamma &= \frac{2\pi\alpha}{N}
\end{aligned}
$$

(b) This statement is FALSE:
Suppose $x[n] = \delta[n] + \frac{1}{2}\delta[n-1]$,

$$
\begin{aligned}
X[k] &= 1 + \frac{1}{2}e^{-j\pi k} \\
&= 1 + \frac{1}{2}(-1)^k
\end{aligned}
$$

Expressed in the form

$$
\begin{aligned}
X[k] &= A[k]e^{j\gamma k}, \\
A[k] &= 1 + \frac{1}{2}(-1)^k \\
\text{and } \gamma &= 0
\end{aligned}
$$

The Fourier transform of $x[n]$ is $X(e^{j\omega}) = 1 + \frac{1}{2}e^{j\omega}$, which cannot be expressed in the form $X(e^{-j\omega}) = B(\omega)e^{j\alpha\omega}$.

8.59. We desire 128 samples of $X(e^{j\omega})Y(e^{j\omega})$.

Since $x[n]$ and $y[n]$ are 256 points long, the linear convolution, $x[n] * y[n]$, will be 512 points long.

We are given a 128-pt DFT only. Therefore, we must time-alias to get 128 samples. The most efficient implementation is:

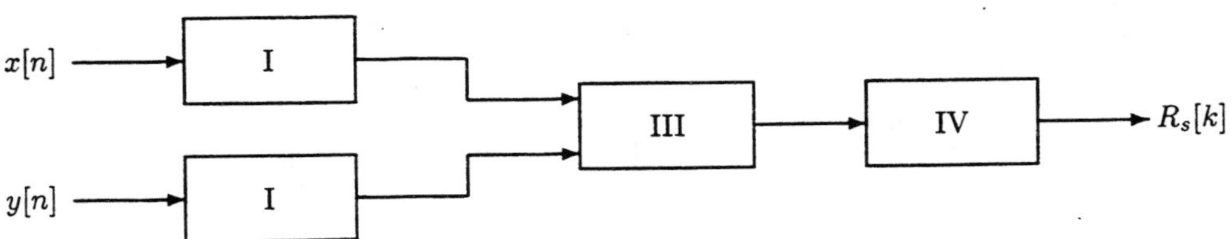

Total cost = 110.

8.60. Ideally, the inverse system would be:

$$H_i(z) = z - bz^{-1}$$

Hence,

$$X(z) = (z - bz^{-1})Y(z)$$

and

$$x[n] = y[n+1] - by[n-1], \qquad -\infty \le n \le \infty$$

If we use an N-pt block of $y[n]$:

$$y[n]: \qquad 0 \le n \le N,$$

then

$$V[k] = (W_N^{-k} - bW_N^{k})Y[k]$$

and

$$v[n] = y[((n+1))_N] - by[((n-1))_N]$$

Because the shift is circular, the points at $n = 0$ and $n = (N-1)$ will not be correct. Therefore, only the points in the range $1 \le n \le (N-2)$ are valid.

8.61. (a)

$$\begin{aligned}
X[k] &= \sum_{n=0}^{N-1} x[n]e^{-j(2\pi/N)kn}, \qquad 0 \le k \le (N-1) \\
X_M[k] &= \sum_{n=0}^{N-1} x[n]e^{-j(2\pi k/N+\pi/N)n} \\
&= \sum_{n=0}^{N-1} x[n]e^{-j(\pi n/N)}e^{-j(2\pi/N)kn}
\end{aligned}$$

So, $x_M[n] = x[n]e^{-j(\pi n/N)}$.

(b)

$$\begin{aligned}
X_M[N-k] &= \sum_{n=0}^{N-1} x[n]e^{-j(\pi n/N)}e^{-j(2\pi/N)(N-k)n}, \qquad 0 \le k \le (N-1) \\
&= \sum_{n=0}^{N-1} x[n]e^{-j(\pi n/N)}e^{j(2\pi/N)k} \\
X_M[N-(k+1)] &= \sum_{n=0}^{N-1} x[n]e^{-j(\pi n/N)}e^{-j(2\pi/N)(N-k-1)n} \\
&= \sum_{n=0}^{N-1} x[n]e^{-j(\pi n/N)}e^{-j(2\pi/N)(N-1)n}e^{j(2\pi/N)kn} \\
&= \sum_{n=0}^{N-1} x[n]e^{j(\pi n/N)}e^{j(2\pi/N)kn} \\
&= X_M^*[k]
\end{aligned}$$

So,

$$X_M[k] = X_M^*[N-(k+1)] \text{ , for } 0 \le k \le (N-1) \text{ and } x[n] \text{ real.}$$

(c) (i) $N-k-1$ is odd when k is even. If $R[k] = X_M[2k]$, we may obtain $X_M[k]$ from $R[k]$ as follows:

$$G[k] = \begin{cases} R[k/2], & \text{k even} \\ R^*[(N-(k+1))/2], & \text{k odd} \end{cases}$$

where we note that

$$R^*[(N-(k+1))/2] = X_M^*[N-(k+1)]$$

for k odd.

(ii)

$$\begin{aligned} R[k] &= X_M[2k] \\ &= \sum_{n=0}^{(N/2)-1} x[n]e^{-j(4\pi k/N+\pi/N)n} \\ &= \sum_{n=0}^{N-1} x[n]e^{-j(\pi n/N)}e^{-j\left(\frac{2\pi kn}{N/2}\right)} \\ &= \sum_{n=0}^{(N/2)-1} x[n]e^{-j(\pi n/N)}e^{-j\left(\frac{2\pi kn}{N/2}\right)} + \sum_{n=N/2}^{N-1} x[n]e^{-j(\pi n/N)}e^{-j\left(\frac{2\pi kn}{N/2}\right)} \\ &= \sum_{n=0}^{(N/2)-1} \left(x[n]e^{-j(\pi n/N)} + x[n+N/2]e^{-j(\pi n/N)}e^{-j(\pi/2)}\right) e^{-j\left(\frac{2\pi kn}{N/2}\right)} \end{aligned}$$

So,

$$r[n] = (x[n] - jx[n+N/2])e^{-j(\pi n/N)}, \quad 0 \le n \le \left(\frac{N}{2}-1\right)$$

(d)

$$\begin{aligned} X_{3M}[k] &= X_{1M}[k]X_{2M}[k] \\ X_{3M}[n] &= \sum_{r=0}^{N-1} x_{1M}[r]x_{2M}[((n-r))_N] \end{aligned}$$

From part (a):

$$\begin{aligned} x_{1M}[n] &= x_1[n]e^{-j(\pi n/N)} \\ x_{2M}[n] &= x_2[n]e^{-j(\pi n/N)} \\ x_{3M}[n] &= x_3[n]e^{-j(\pi n/N)} \end{aligned}$$

So,

$$\begin{aligned} x_3[n] &= e^{j(\pi n/N)} \sum_{r=0}^{N-1} x_1[r]x_2[((n-r))_N]e^{-j(\pi/N)[((n-r))_N+r]} \\ &= \sum_{r=0}^{N-1} x_1[r]x_2[((n-r))_N]e^{-j(\pi/N)[((n-r))_N-(n-r)]} \end{aligned}$$

Since,

$$((n-r))_N = \begin{cases} n-r, & n \ge r \\ N+n-r, & n < r \end{cases}$$

$$((n-r))_N - (n-r) = \begin{cases} 0, & n \ge r \\ N, & n < r \end{cases}$$

then

$$e^{-j(\pi/N)[((n-r))_N-(n-r)]} = \text{sgn}\,[n-r] = \begin{cases} 1, & n \geq r \\ -1, & n < r \end{cases}$$

and

$$x_3 = \sum_{r=0}^{N-1} x_1[r]x_2[((n-r))_N]\text{sgn}\,[n-r]$$

(e) Suppose, that for $n \geq N/2$:

$$\begin{aligned} x_{1M}[n] &= x_1[n]e^{-j(\pi n/N)} = 0 \\ x_{2M}[n] &= x_2[n]e^{-j(\pi n/N)} = 0 \end{aligned}$$

then the modified circular convolution is equivalent to the modified linear convolution:

$$x_{1M}[n] \circledN x_{2M}[n] = x_{1M}[n] * x_{2M}[n]$$

(i.e. no aliasing occurs.)

$$\begin{aligned} x_{3M}[n] &= x_{1M}[n] * x_{2M}[n] \\ &= \sum_{r=0}^{N-1} x_{1M}[r]x_{2M}[n-r] \end{aligned}$$

Thus,

$$\begin{aligned} x_3[n] &= e^{j(\pi n/N)} \sum_{r=0}^{N-1} x_1[n]x_2[n-r]e^{-j(\pi n/N)}e^{-j(\pi n/N)(n-r)} \\ &= \sum_{r=0}^{N-1} x_1[r]x_2[n-r]e^{-j(\pi/N)(n-r)} \end{aligned}$$

So,

$$x_3[n] = \sum_{r=0}^{N-1} x_1[r]x_2[n-r]e^{-j(\pi/N)(n-r)} = x_1[n] * x_2[n]$$

8.62. (a) We wish to compute $x[n] \textcircled{63} h[n]$:

$$\begin{aligned} \text{let } x_1[n] &= x[n], & 0 \leq n \leq 31 \\ x_2[n] &= x[n+32], & 0 \leq n \leq 30 \\ h_1[n] &= h[n], & 0 \leq n \leq 31 \\ h_2[n] &= h[n+32], & 0 \leq n \leq 30 \end{aligned}$$

$$\begin{aligned} x[n] * h[n] = {} & x_1[n] * h_1[n] + x_1[n] * h_2[n] * \delta[n-32] + x_2[n] * h_1[n] * \delta[n-32] \\ & + x_2[n] * h_2[n] * \delta[n-32] * \delta[n-32] \end{aligned}$$

Let

$$\begin{aligned} y_1[n] &= x_1[n] * h_1[n] &= x_1[n] \textcircled{64} h_1[n] \\ y_2[n] &= x_1[n] * h_2[n] &= x_1[n] \textcircled{64} h_2[h] \\ y_3[n] &= x_2[n] * h_1[n] &= x_2[n] \textcircled{64} h_1[n] \\ y_4[n] &= x_2[n] * h_2[n] &= x_2[n] \textcircled{64} h_2[n] \end{aligned}$$

We can compute each of the above circular convolutions with two 64-pt DFTs and one 64-pt inverse DFT.

$$\begin{aligned} y[n] &= x[n] * h[n] \\ &= y_1[n] + y_2[n-32] + y_3[n-32] + y_4[n-64] \end{aligned}$$

So

$$x[n] \circledast_{63} h[n] = y[n] + y[n+63], \qquad 0 \le n \le 62$$

The total computational cost is 12 DFTs of size $N = 64$.

(b) Using two 128-pt DFTs and one 128-pt inverse DFT:

$$y[n] = x[n] \circledast_{128} h[n] = x[n] * h[n]$$

The 63-pt circular convolution:

$$x[n] \circledast_{63} h[n] = y[n] + y[n+63], \qquad 0 \le n \le 62$$

(c) Using the 64-pt DFT method of part (a):

$$\#\text{mult} = 4(12)(64 \log_2(64)) = 18432$$

Using 128-pt DFTs:

$$\#\text{mult} = 4(3)(128 \log_2(128)) = 10752$$

Direct convolution:

$$\#\text{mult} = 2 \sum_{n=1}^{63} n - 63 = 3969$$

8.63. From each circular convolution, the first 49 points will be incorrect. Therefore, we get 51 good points and the input must be overlapped by $100 - 51 = 49$ points.

(a) $V = 49$

(b) $M = 51$

(c) The points extracted correspond to the range $49 \le n \le 99$.

Distorting filter: $h[n] = \delta[n] - \frac{1}{2}\delta[n - n_0]$

8.64. (a) The Z-transform of $h[n]$

$$\begin{aligned} H(z) &= \sum_{n=-\infty}^{\infty} h[n] z^{-n} \\ H(z) &= 1 - \frac{1}{2} z^{-n_0} \end{aligned}$$

The N-pt DFT of $h[n]$: $(N = 4n_0)$

$$\begin{aligned} H[k] &= \sum_{n=0}^{4n_0-1} h[n] W_{4n}^{kn_0}, \qquad 0 \le k \le (4n_0 - 1) \\ &= 1 - \frac{1}{2} W_{4n_0}^{kn_0} \\ H[k] &= 1 - \frac{1}{2} e^{-j(\pi/2)k} \end{aligned}$$

(b)

$$H_i(z) = \frac{1}{1+1/2z^{-n_0}}, \qquad |z| > \left(\frac{1}{2}\right)^{-n_0} \text{ for causality}$$

$$h_i[n] = \sum_{k=0}^{\infty} \left(\frac{1}{2}\right)^{n/n_0} \delta[n-kn_0]$$

The filter is IIR.

(c)

$$G[k] = \frac{1}{H[k]} = \frac{1}{1-e^{-j(\pi/2)k}}, \qquad 0 \le k \le (4n_0-1)$$

The impulse response, $g[n]$, is just $h_i[n]$ time-aliased by $4n_0$ points:

$$\begin{aligned} g[n] &= \left(1+\frac{1}{16}+\frac{1}{256}+\cdots\right)\delta[n] + \left(\frac{1}{2}+\frac{1}{32}+\frac{1}{512}+\cdots\right)\delta[n-n_0] \\ &+ \left(\frac{1}{4}+\frac{1}{64}+\frac{1}{1024}+\cdots\right)\delta[n-2n_0] + \left(\frac{1}{8}+\frac{1}{128}+\frac{1}{2048}+\cdots\right)\delta[n-3n_0] \\ g[n] &= \frac{16}{15}\delta[n] + \frac{8}{15}\delta[n-n_0] + \frac{4}{15}\delta[n-2n_0] + \frac{2}{15}\delta[n-3n_0] \end{aligned}$$

(d) Indeed,

$$G[k]H[k] = 1, \qquad 0 \le k \le (4n_0-1)$$

However, this relationship is only true at $4n_0$ distinct frequencies. This fact does not imply that for all ω:

$$G(e^{j\omega})H(e^{j\omega}) = 1$$

(e)

$$\begin{aligned} y[n] &= g[n] * h[n] \\ &= \frac{16}{15}\delta[n] + \frac{8}{15}\delta[n-n_0] + \frac{4}{15}\delta[n-2n_0] + \frac{2}{15}\delta[n-3n_0] - \frac{8}{15}\delta[n-n_0] \\ &\quad -\frac{4}{15}\delta[n-2n_9] - \frac{2}{15}\delta[n-3n_0] - \frac{1}{15}\delta[n-4n_0] \\ y[n] &= \frac{16}{15}\delta[n] - \frac{1}{15}\delta[n-4n_0] \end{aligned}$$

8.65. (a) We start by computing $\tilde{X}_H[k+N]$:

$$\begin{aligned} \tilde{X}_H[k+N] &= \sum_{n=0}^{N-1} \tilde{x}[n] H_N[n(k+N)] \\ &= \sum_{n=0}^{N-1} \tilde{x}[n](\cos(\frac{2\pi(nk+nN)}{N}) + \sin(\frac{2\pi(nk+nN)}{N}) \\ &= \sum_{n=0}^{N-1} \tilde{x}[n](\cos(\frac{2\pi nk}{N}) + \sin(\frac{2\pi nk}{N})) \\ &= \sum_{n=0}^{N-1} \tilde{x}[n] H_N[nk] \\ &= \tilde{X}_H[k]. \end{aligned}$$

We thus conclude that the DHS coefficients form a sequence that is also periodic with period N.

(b) We have:

$$\begin{aligned}\frac{1}{N}\sum_{k=0}^{N-1}\tilde{X}_H[k]H_N[nk] &= \frac{1}{N}\sum_{k=0}^{N-1}(\sum_{m=0}^{N-1}\tilde{x}[m]H_N[mk])H_N[nk]\\ &= \frac{1}{N}\sum_{m=0}^{N-1}\tilde{x}[m]\sum_{k=0}^{N-1}H_N[mk]H_N[nk]\\ &= \frac{1}{N}\tilde{x}[n]N\\ &= \tilde{x}[n].\end{aligned}$$

Where we have used the fact that $\sum_{k=0}^{N-1} H_N[mk]H_N[nk] = N$ only if $((m))_N = ((n))_N$, otherwise it's 0.
This completes the derivation of the DHS synthesis formula.

(c) We have:

$$\begin{aligned}H_N[a+N] &= \cos(\frac{2\pi(a+N)}{N}) + \sin(\frac{2\pi(a+N)}{N})\\ &= \cos(\frac{2\pi a}{N}+2\pi) + \sin(\frac{2\pi a}{N}+2\pi)\\ &= \cos(\frac{2\pi a}{N}) + \sin(\frac{2\pi a}{N})\\ &= H_N[a].\end{aligned}$$

And:

$$\begin{aligned}H_N[a+b] &= \cos(\frac{2\pi(a+b)}{N}) + \sin(\frac{2\pi(a+b)}{N})\\ &= (C_N[a]C_N[b] - S_N[a]S_N[b]) + (S_N[a]C_N[b] + C_N[a]S_N[b])\\ &= C_N[b](C_N[a] + S_N[a]) + S_N[b](-S_N[a] + C_N[a])\\ &= C_N[b](C_N[a] + S_N[a]) + S_N[b](S_N[-a] + C_N[-a])\\ &= C_N[b]H_N[a] + S_N[b]H_N[-a]\\ &= C_N[a]H_N[b] + S_N[a]H_N[-b] \text{ (since } H_N[a+b] = H_N[b+a] \text{)}\end{aligned}$$

Where we have used trigonometric properties.

(d) We have:

$$\begin{aligned}DHS(\tilde{x}[n-n_0]) &= \sum_{n=0}^{N-1}\tilde{x}[n-n_0]H_N[nk]\\ &= \sum_{n=-n_0}^{N-1-n_0}\tilde{x}[n]H_N[(n+n_0)k]\end{aligned}$$

$$
\begin{aligned}
&= \sum_{n=-n_0}^{N-1-n_0} \tilde{x}[n](H_N[nk]C_N[n_0k] + H_N[-nk]S_N[n_0k]) \\
&= C_N[n_0k] \sum_{n=-n_0}^{N-1-n_0} \tilde{x}[n]H_N[nk] + S_N[n_0k] \sum_{n=-n_0}^{N-1-n_0} \tilde{x}[n]H_N[-nk] \\
&= C_N[n_0k] \sum_{n=0}^{N-1} \tilde{x}[n]H_N[nk] + S_N[n_0k] \sum_{n=0}^{N-1} \tilde{x}[n]H_N[-nk] \\
&= C_N[n_0k]\tilde{X}_H[k] + S_N[n_0k]\tilde{X}_H[-k]
\end{aligned}
$$

Where we have used the periodicity of $H_N[nk]$ and $\tilde{x}[n]$.

(e) We have:

$$
\begin{aligned}
DHT\{\tilde{x}_3[n]\} &= DHT\{\sum_{m=0}^{N-1} x_1[m]x_2[((n-m))_N]\} \\
X_{H3}[k] &= \sum_{n=0}^{N-1}(\sum_{m=0}^{N-1} x_1[m]x_2[((n-m))_N])H_N[nk] \\
&= \sum_{m=0}^{N-1} x_1[m] \sum_{n=0}^{N-1} x_2[((n-m))_N]H_N[nk] \\
&= \sum_{m=0}^{N-1} x_1[m]DHT\{x_2[((n-m))_N]\} \\
&= \sum_{m=0}^{N-1} x_1[m](X_{H2}[k]C_N[mk] + X_{H2}[((-k))_N]S_N[mk]) \text{ (using P8.65-7)} \\
&= \sum_{m=0}^{N-1} x_1[m]X_{H2}[k]C_N[mk] + \sum_{m=0}^{N-1} x_1[m]X_{H2}[((-k))_N]S_N[mk] \\
&= \sum_{m=0}^{N-1} x_1[m]X_{H2}[k](\frac{H_N[mk] + H_N[-mk]}{2}) \\
&\quad + \sum_{m=0}^{N-1} x_1[m]X_{H2}[((-k))_N](\frac{H_N[mk] - H_N[-mk]}{2}) \\
&= \frac{1}{2}X_{H2}[k](X_{H1}[k] + X_{H1}[((-k))_N]) + \frac{1}{2}X_{H2}[((-k))_N](X_{H1}[k] - X_{H1}[((-k))_N]) \\
&= \frac{1}{2}X_{H1}[k](X_{H2}[k] + X_{H2}[((-k))_N]) + \frac{1}{2}X_{H1}[((-k))_N](X_{H2}[k] - X_{H2}[((-k))_N])
\end{aligned}
$$

This is the desired convolution property.

(f) Since the DFT of $x[n]$ is given by:

$$
\begin{aligned}
X[k] &= \sum_{n=0}^{N-1} x[n]e^{-j\frac{2\pi kn}{N}} \\
&= \sum_{n=0}^{N-1} x[n](\cos(-\frac{2\pi kn}{N}) + j\sin(-\frac{2\pi kn}{N}))
\end{aligned}
$$

$$\begin{aligned} &= \sum_{n=0}^{N-1} x[n](\cos(\frac{2\pi kn}{N}) - j\sin(\frac{2\pi kn}{N})) \\ &= \sum_{n=0}^{N-1} x[n](C_N[kn] - jS_N[kn]) \end{aligned}$$

then:

$$\begin{aligned} \sum_{n=0}^{N-1} x[n]C_N[kn] &= \frac{1}{2}(X[k] + X[((-k))_N]) \\ \sum_{n=0}^{N-1} x[n]S_N[kn] &= -\frac{1}{2j}(X[k] - X[((-k))_N]) \end{aligned}$$

We thus get:

$$\begin{aligned} X_H[k] &= \sum_{n=0}^{N-1} x[n](C_N[kn] + S_N[kn]) \\ &= \frac{1}{2}(X[k] + X[((-k))_N]) - \frac{1}{2j}(X[k] - X[((-k))_N]) \\ &= (\frac{1}{2} - \frac{1}{2j})X[k] + (\frac{1}{2} + \frac{1}{2j})X[((-k))_N] \end{aligned}$$

This allows us to obtain $X_H[k]$ from $X[k]$.

(g) We have:

$$X_H[k] = \sum_{n=0}^{N-1} x[n](C_N[kn] + S_N[kn])$$

Therefore:

$$\begin{aligned} \sum_{n=0}^{N-1} x[n]C_N[kn] &= \frac{1}{2}(X_H[k] + X_H[((-k))_N]) \\ \sum_{n=0}^{N-1} x[n]S_N[kn] &= \frac{1}{2}(X_H[k] - X_H[((-k))_N]) \end{aligned}$$

We thus get:

$$\begin{aligned} X[k] &= \sum_{n=0}^{N-1} x[n]e^{-j\frac{2\pi kn}{N}} \\ &= \sum_{n=0}^{N-1} x[n](C_N[kn] - jS_N[kn]) \end{aligned}$$

$$
\begin{aligned}
&= \frac{1}{2}(X_H[k] + X_H[((-k))_N]) - j\frac{1}{2}(X_H[k] - X_H[((-k))_N]) \\
&= (\frac{1}{2} - \frac{j}{2})X_H[k] + (\frac{1}{2} + \frac{j}{2})X_H[((-k))_N]
\end{aligned}
$$

This allows us to obtain $X[k]$ from $X_H[k]$.

8.66. (a) The DTFT is given by:

$$
\begin{aligned}
\tilde{X}(e^{jw}) &= X(e^{jw}) + X(e^{jw})e^{-jwN} \\
&= X(e^{jw})(1 + e^{-jwN})
\end{aligned}
$$

The DFT is just samples of the DTFT:

$$
\begin{aligned}
\tilde{X}[k] &= \tilde{X}(e^{jw})|_{w=\frac{2\pi k}{2N}} \\
&= X(e^{j2\pi k2N})(1 + (-1)^k)
\end{aligned}
$$

Therefore:

$$
\tilde{X}[k] = \begin{cases} 2X[\frac{k}{2}] & , \quad k \text{ even} \\ 0 & , \quad k \text{ odd} \end{cases}
$$

(b) The original system computes the following:

$$
\tilde{X}[k]H[k] = \begin{cases} 2X[\frac{k}{2}]H[k] & , \quad k \text{ even} \\ 0 & , \quad k \text{ odd} \end{cases}
$$

We thus want:

$$
\begin{aligned}
X[k]G[k] &= 2X[k]H[2k] & k = 0, ..., N-1 \\
G[k] &= 2H[2k] \\
&= 2\sum_{n=0}^{2N-1} h[n]e^{-j\frac{2\pi 2kn}{2N}} & k = 0, ..., N-1 \\
g[n] &= 2(h[n] + h[n+N])
\end{aligned}
$$

System A time aliases and multiplies by 2.

For system B, we need:

$$
Y[k] = \begin{cases} W[\frac{k}{2}] & , \quad k \text{ even} \\ 0 & , \quad k \text{ odd} \end{cases}
$$

Thus:

$$y[n] = \begin{cases} w[n] & , \quad 0 \le n \le N-1 \\ w[n-N] & , \quad N \le n \le 2N-1 \\ 0 & , \quad \text{otherwise} \end{cases}$$

System B regenerates the $2N-$point sequence by repeating w[n].

8.67. (a) We have:

$$|H(e^{jw})| = \begin{cases} 1 & , \quad |w| \le \frac{\pi}{4} \\ 0 & , \quad \text{otherwise} \end{cases}$$

Since $h[n]$ is FIR, we assume it is non-zero over $0 \le n \le N$. The phase of $H(e^{jw})$ should be set such that $h[n]$ is symmetric about the center of its range, i.e. $\frac{N}{2}$. Therefore, the phase of $H(e^{jw})$ should be $e^{j\frac{wN}{2}}$. So one possible $H[k]$ may be:

$$H[k] = \begin{cases} e^{j\frac{2\pi}{4N}\frac{N}{2}k} & , \quad 0 \le k \le \frac{1}{8}4N \\ 0 & , \quad \text{otherwise} \\ e^{j\frac{2\pi}{4N}\frac{N}{2}k} & , \quad 4N - \frac{N}{2} \le k \le 4N \end{cases}$$

that is:

$$H[k] = \begin{cases} e^{j\frac{\pi}{4}k} & , \quad 0 \le k \le \frac{N}{2} \\ 0 & , \quad \text{otherwise} \\ e^{j\frac{\pi}{4}k} & , \quad 4N - \frac{N}{2} \le k \le 4N \end{cases}$$

(b) System A needs to perform the following operations:

$$Y_2[k] = \begin{cases} X[k]H'[k] & , \quad 0 \le k \le \frac{N}{2} \\ 0 & , \quad \text{otherwise} \\ X[k-3N]H'[k-3N] & , \quad 4N - \frac{N}{2} \le k \le 4N \end{cases}$$

Where $H'[k]$ is the $N-$point DFT of $h[n]$.

(c) It is cheaper to implement $N-$point DFTs than $4N-$point DFTs, therefore the implementation in Figure P8.67-2 is usually preferable to the one in Figure P8.67-1.

8.68. Substituting the expression for $X_1[k]$ from equation (8.164) into equation (8.165), we get:

$$\begin{aligned} x_1[n] &= \frac{1}{2N-2}\sum_{k=0}^{2N-3} X_1[k]e^{j2\pi kn/(2N-2)} \\ &= \frac{1}{2N-2}\Big(\sum_{k=0}^{N-1} X^{c1}[k]e^{j2\pi kn/(2N-2)} + \sum_{k=N}^{2N-3} X^{c1}[2N-2-k]e^{j2\pi kn/(2N-2)}\Big) \end{aligned}$$

Note that:

$$\begin{aligned}\sum_{k=N}^{2N-3} X^{c1}[2N-2-k]e^{j2\pi kn/(2N-2)} &= \sum_{r=1}^{N-2} X^{c1}[r]e^{j2\pi(2N-2-r)n/(2N-2)} \\ &= \sum_{k=1}^{N-2} X^{c1}[k]e^{-j2\pi kn/(2N-2)}\end{aligned}$$

therefore:

$$\begin{aligned}x_1[n] &= \frac{1}{2N-2}(\sum_{k=0}^{N-1} X^{c1}[k]e^{j2\pi kn/(2N-2)} + \sum_{k=1}^{N-2} X^{c1}[k]e^{-j2\pi kn/(2N-2)}) \\ &= \frac{1}{2N-2}(X^{c1}[0] + X^{c1}[N-1]e^{j2\pi n} + \sum_{k=1}^{N-2} X^{c1}[k](e^{j2\pi kn/(2N-2)} + e^{-j2\pi kn/(2N-2)})) \\ &= \frac{1}{2N-2}(X^{c1}[0] + X^{c1}[N-1]e^{j\pi n} + \sum_{k=1}^{N-2} X^{c1}[k]2\cos(\frac{\pi kn}{N-1}))\end{aligned}$$

and:

$$\begin{aligned}x[n] &= x_1[n] & \text{for } n = 0, 1, ..., N-1 \\ &= \frac{1}{N-1}(\sum_{k=0}^{N-1} \alpha[k]X^{c1}[k]\cos(\frac{\pi kn}{N-1})) & 0 \le n \le N-1\end{aligned}$$

where $\alpha[k]$ is given by:

$$\alpha[k] = \begin{cases} \frac{1}{2} &, \quad k = 0 \text{ and } N-1 \\ 1 &, \quad 1 \le k \le N-2. \end{cases}$$

This completes the derivation.

8.69.

$$v[n] = x_2[2n]$$

therefore, for $k = 0, 1, ..., N-1$:

$$V[k] = \frac{1}{2}(X_2[k] + X_2[k+N]).$$

Using equation (8.168), we have:

$$\begin{aligned}V[k] &= \frac{1}{2}(X_2[k] + X_2[k+N]) \\ &= e^{j\frac{\pi k}{2N}}Re\{X[k]e^{-j\frac{\pi k}{2N}}\} + e^{j\frac{\pi(k+N)}{2N}}Re\{X[k+N]e^{-j\frac{\pi(k+N)}{2N}}\} \\ &= e^{j\frac{\pi k}{2N}}Re\{X[k]e^{-j\frac{\pi k}{2N}}\} + e^{j\frac{\pi}{2}}e^{j\frac{\pi k}{2N}}Re\{X[k+N]e^{-j\frac{\pi k}{2N}}e^{-j\frac{\pi}{2}}\} \\ &= e^{j\frac{\pi k}{2N}}Re\{X[k]e^{-j\frac{\pi k}{2N}}\} + je^{j\frac{\pi k}{2N}}Re\{-jX[k+N]e^{-j\frac{\pi k}{2N}}\} \\ &= e^{j\frac{\pi k}{2N}}(Re\{X[k]e^{-j\frac{\pi k}{2N}}\} + jIm\{X[k+N]e^{-j\frac{\pi k}{2N}}\}.\end{aligned}$$

Using the above expression, we get:

$$\begin{aligned}
2Re\{e^{-j\frac{2\pi k}{4N}}V[k]\} &= 2Re\{e^{-j\frac{\pi k}{2N}}e^{j\frac{\pi k}{2N}}(Re\{X[k]e^{-j\frac{\pi k}{2N}}\} + jIm\{X[k+N]e^{-j\frac{\pi k}{2N}}\})\} \\
&= 2Re\{X[k]e^{-j\frac{\pi k}{2N}}\} \\
&= X^{c2}[k] \qquad \text{where we used equation (8.170).}
\end{aligned}$$

Furthermore, we have:

$$\begin{aligned}
2Re\{e^{-j\frac{2\pi k}{4N}}V[k]\} &= 2Re\{e^{-j\frac{2\pi k}{4N}}\sum_{n=0}^{N-1} v[n]e^{-j\frac{2\pi kn}{N}}\} \\
&= 2Re\{\sum_{n=0}^{N-1} v[n]e^{-j(\frac{2\pi k}{N}(n+\frac{1}{4}))}\} \\
&= 2\sum_{n=0}^{N-1} Re\{v[n]e^{-j(\frac{2\pi k}{N}(n+\frac{1}{4}))}\} \\
&= 2\sum_{n=0}^{N-1} v[n]\cos(\frac{2\pi k}{N}(n+\frac{1}{4})) \\
&= 2\sum_{n=0}^{N-1} v[n]\cos(\frac{\pi k(4n+1)}{2N}).
\end{aligned}$$

and:

$$\begin{aligned}
2Re\{e^{-j\frac{2\pi k}{4N}}V[k]\} &= 2Re\{X[k]e^{-j\frac{\pi k}{2N}}\} \\
&= 2Re\{\sum_{n=0}^{2N-1} x[n]e^{-j\frac{2\pi kn}{2N}}e^{-j\frac{\pi k}{2N}}\} \\
&= 2Re\{\sum_{n=0}^{N-1} x[n]e^{-j\frac{\pi k}{2N}(2n+1)}\} \\
&= 2\sum_{n=0}^{N-1} Re\{x[n]e^{-j\frac{\pi k}{2N}(2n+1)}\} \\
&= 2\sum_{n=0}^{N-1} x[n]\cos(\frac{\pi k(2n+1)}{2N}).
\end{aligned}$$

From the results above, we conclude, for $k = 0, 1, ..., N-1$:

$$\begin{aligned}
X^{c2}[k] &= 2Re\{e^{-j\frac{2\pi k}{4N}}V[k]\} \\
&= 2\sum_{n=0}^{N-1} v[n]\cos(\frac{\pi k(4n+1)}{2N}) \\
&= 2\sum_{n=0}^{N-1} x[n]\cos(\frac{\pi k(2n+1)}{2N}).
\end{aligned}$$

8.70. Substituting the expression for $X_2[k]$ from equation (8.174) into equation (8.175), we get:

$$
\begin{aligned}
x_2[n] &= \frac{1}{2N}\sum_{k=0}^{2N-1} X_2[k]e^{j2\pi kn/(2N)} \\
&= \frac{1}{2N}(X^{c2}[0] + \sum_{k=1}^{N-1} X^{c2}[k]e^{j\pi k/(2N)}e^{j2\pi kn/(2N)} - \sum_{k=N+1}^{2N-1} X^{c2}[2N-k]e^{j\pi k/(2N)}e^{j2\pi kn/(2N)}) \\
&= \frac{1}{2N}(X^{c2}[0] + \sum_{k=1}^{N-1} X^{c2}[k]e^{j\pi k(2n+1)/(2N)} - \sum_{k=N+1}^{2N-1} X^{c2}[2N-k]e^{j\pi k(2n+1)/(2N)}) \\
&= \frac{1}{2N}(X^{c2}[0] + \sum_{k=1}^{N-1} X^{c2}[k]e^{j\pi k(2n+1)/(2N)} - \sum_{k=1}^{N-1} X^{c2}[k]e^{j\pi(2N-k)(2n+1)/(2N)}) \\
&= \frac{1}{2N}(X^{c2}[0] + \sum_{k=1}^{N-1} X^{c2}[k]e^{j\pi k(2n+1)/(2N)} + \sum_{k=1}^{N-1} X^{c2}[k]e^{-j\pi k(2n+1)/(2N)}) \\
&= \frac{1}{2N}(X^{c2}[0] + \sum_{k=1}^{N-1} X^{c2}[k](e^{j\pi k(2n+1)/(2N)} + e^{-j\pi k(2n+1)/(2N)})) \\
&= \frac{1}{2N}(X^{c2}[0] + \sum_{k=1}^{N-1} X^{c2}[k]\cos(\frac{\pi k(2n+1)}{2N})).
\end{aligned}
$$

Furthermore:

$$
\begin{aligned}
x[n] &= x_2[n] && \text{for } n = 0, 1, ..., N-1 \\
&= \frac{1}{N}\sum_{k=0}^{N-1} \beta[k]X^{c2}[k]\cos(\frac{\pi k(2n+1)}{2N}) && 0 \le n \le N-1
\end{aligned}
$$

where $\beta[k]$ is given by:

$$
\beta[k] = \begin{cases} \frac{1}{2} \ , & k = 0 \\ 1 \ , & 1 \le k \le N-1. \end{cases}
$$

This completes the derivation.

8.71. First we derive Parseval's theorem for the DFT.
Let $x[n]$ be an N point sequence and define $y[n]$ as follows:

$$
y[n] = x[n] \textcircled{N} \, x^*[((-n))_N].
$$

Using the properties of the DFT, we have:

$$
Y[k] = X[k]X^*[k] = |X[k]|^2.
$$

Note that:

$$
y[0] = \sum_n |x[n]|^2
$$

and using the DFT synthesis equation, we get:

$$
y[0] = \frac{1}{N}\sum_{k=0}^{N-1} Y[k].
$$

Parseval's Theorem for the DFT is therefore:

$$\sum_n |x[n]|^2 = \frac{1}{N}\sum_{k=0}^{N-1} |X[k]|^2.$$

(a) Note that:

$$\sum_{n=0}^{N-1} |X^{c1}[k]|^2 = \sum_{n=0}^{N-1} |X_1[k]|^2$$

and, using equation (8.164):

$$\sum_{n=0}^{2N-3} |X_1[k]|^2 = 2\sum_{n=0}^{N-1} |X^{c1}[k]|^2 - |X^{c1}[0]|^2 - |X^{c1}[N-1]|^2.$$

Using the DFT properties:

$$\sum_n |x_1[n]|^2 = \frac{1}{2N-2}\sum_{k=0}^{2N-3} |X_1[k]|^2$$

and, using equation (8.161):

$$\sum_{n=0}^{2N-3} |x_1[n]|^2 = 2\sum_{n=0}^{N-1} |x[n]|^2 - |x[0]|^2 - |x[N-1]|^2.$$

We thus conclude:

$$\frac{1}{2N-2}(2\sum_{n=0}^{N-1} |X^{c1}[k]|^2 - |X^{c1}[0]|^2 - |X^{c1}[N-1]|^2) = 2\sum_{n=0}^{N-1} |x[n]|^2 - |x[0]|^2 - |x[N-1]|^2.$$

(b) Using equation (8.171),

$$\sum_{n=0}^{N-1} |X^{c2}[k]|^2 = \sum_{n=0}^{N-1} |X_2[k]|^2.$$

Note that, using equation (8.167):

$$\sum_{k=0}^{2N-1} |X_2[k]|^2 = 2\sum_{k=0}^{N-1} |X[k]|^2 - |X[0]|^2,$$

and, using equation (8.166):

$$\sum_{n=0}^{2N-1} |x_2[n]|^2 = 2\sum_{n=0}^{N-1} |x[n]|^2.$$

Using the DFT properties:

$$\sum_{n=0}^{2N-1} |x_2[n]|^2 = \frac{1}{2N}\sum_{k=0}^{2N-1} |X_2[k]|^2.$$

We thus conclude:

$$\frac{1}{2N}(2\sum_{k=0}^{N-1} |X[k]|^2 - |X[0]|^2) = 2\sum_{n=0}^{N-1} |x[n]|^2.$$

Solutions – Chapter 9

Computation of the Discrete-Time Fourier Transform

9.1. There are several possible approaches to this problem. Two are presented below.

Solution #1: Use the program to compute the DFT of $X[k]$, yielding the sequence $g[n]$.

$$g[n] = \sum_{k=0}^{N-1} X[k]e^{-j2\pi kn/N}$$

Then, compute

$$x[n] = \frac{1}{N} g[((N-n))_N]$$

for $n = 0, \ldots, N-1$. We demonstrate that this solution produces the inverse DFT below.

$$\begin{aligned} x[n] &= \frac{1}{N} g[((N-n))_N] \\ &= \frac{1}{N} \sum_{k=0}^{N-1} X[k]e^{-j2\pi k(N-n)/N} \\ &= \frac{1}{N} \sum_{k=0}^{N-1} X[k]e^{j2\pi kn/N} \end{aligned}$$

Solution #2: Take the complex conjugate of $X[k]$, and then compute its DFT using the program, yielding the sequence $f[n]$.

$$f[n] = \sum_{k=0}^{N-1} X^*[k]e^{-j2\pi kn/N}$$

Then, compute

$$x[n] = \frac{1}{N} f^*[n]$$

We demonstrate that this solution produces the inverse DFT below.

$$\begin{aligned} x[n] &= \frac{1}{N} f^*[n] \\ &= \frac{1}{N} \sum_{k=0}^{N-1} X[k]e^{j2\pi kn/N} \end{aligned}$$

9.2. (a) The "gain" along the emphasized path is $-W_N^2$.

(b) In general, there is only one path between each input sample and each output sample.

(c) $x[0]$ to $X[2]$: The gain is 1.
$x[1]$ to $X[2]$: The gain is W_N^2.
$x[2]$ to $X[2]$: The gain is $-W_N^0 = -1$.
$x[3]$ to $X[2]$: The gain is $-W_N^0 W_N^2 = -W_N^2$.
$x[4]$ to $X[2]$: The gain is $W_N^0 = 1$.
$x[5]$ to $X[2]$: The gain is $W_N^0 W_N^2 = W_N^2$.
$x[6]$ to $X[2]$: The gain is $-W_N^0 W_N^0 = -1$.
$x[7]$ to $X[2]$: The gain is $-W_N^0 W_N^0 W_N^2 = -W_N^2$, as in Part (a).
Now

$$\begin{aligned} X[2] &= \sum_{n=0}^{7} x[n]W_8^{2n} \\ &= x[0] + x[1]W_8^2 + x[2]W_8^4 + x[3]W_8^6 + x[4]W_8^8 + x[5]W_8^{10} + x[6]W_8^{12} \\ &\quad + x[7]W_8^{14} \\ &= x[0] + x[1]W_8^2 + x[2](-1) + x[3](-W_8^2) + x[4](1) + x[5]W_8^2 \\ &\quad + x[6](-1) + x[7](-W_8^2) \end{aligned}$$

Each input sample contributes the proper amount to the output DFT sample.

9.3. (a) The input should be placed into A[r] in bit-reversed order.

$$\begin{aligned} A[0] &= x[0] \\ A[1] &= x[4] \\ A[2] &= x[2] \\ A[3] &= x[6] \\ A[4] &= x[1] \\ A[5] &= x[5] \\ A[6] &= x[3] \\ A[7] &= x[7] \end{aligned}$$

The output should then be extracted from D[r] in sequential order.

$$X[k] = D[k], \quad k = 0, \ldots, 7$$

(b) First, we find the DFT of $(-W_N)^n$ for $N = 8$.

$$\begin{aligned} X[k] &= \sum_{n=0}^{7} (-W_8)^n W_8^{nk} \\ &= \sum_{n=0}^{7} (-1)^n W_8^n W_8^{nk} \\ &= \sum_{n=0}^{7} (W_8^{-4})^n W_8^n W_8^{nk} \\ &= \sum_{n=0}^{7} W_8^{n(k-3)} \\ &= \frac{1 - W^{k-3}}{1 - W_8^{k-3}} \\ &= 8\delta[k-3] \end{aligned}$$

A sketch of D[r] wis provided below.

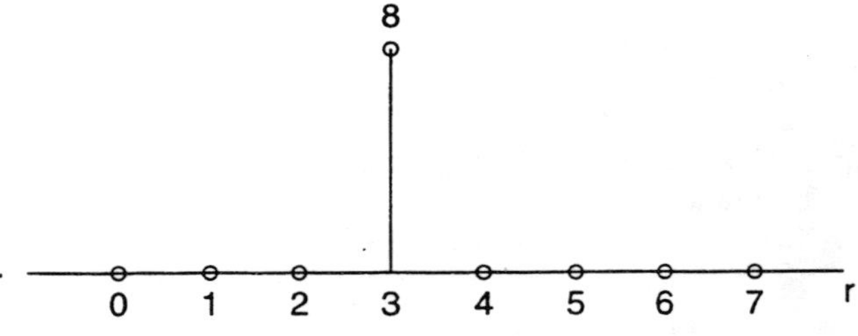

(c) First, the array $D[r]$ is expressed in terms of $C[r]$.

$$\begin{aligned} D[0] &= C[0] + C[4] \\ D[1] &= C[1] + C[5]W_8^1 \\ D[2] &= C[2] + C[6]W_8^2 \\ D[3] &= C[3] + C[7]W_8^3 \end{aligned}$$

$$\begin{aligned} D[4] &= C[0] - C[4] \\ D[5] &= C[1] - C[5]W_8^1 \\ D[6] &= C[2] - C[6]W_8^2 \\ D[7] &= C[3] - C[7]W_8^3 \end{aligned}$$

Solving this system of equations for $C[r]$ gives

$$\begin{aligned} C[0] &= (D[0] + D[4])/2 \\ C[1] &= (D[1] + D[5])/2 \\ C[2] &= (D[2] + D[6])/2 \\ C[3] &= (D[3] + D[7])/2 \\ C[4] &= (D[0] - D[4])/2 \\ C[5] &= (D[1] - D[5])W_8^{-1}/2 \\ C[6] &= (D[2] - D[6])W_8^{-2}/2 \\ C[7] &= (D[3] - D[7])W_8^{-3}/2 \end{aligned}$$

for $r = 0, 1, ..., 7$. A sketch of C[r] is provided below.

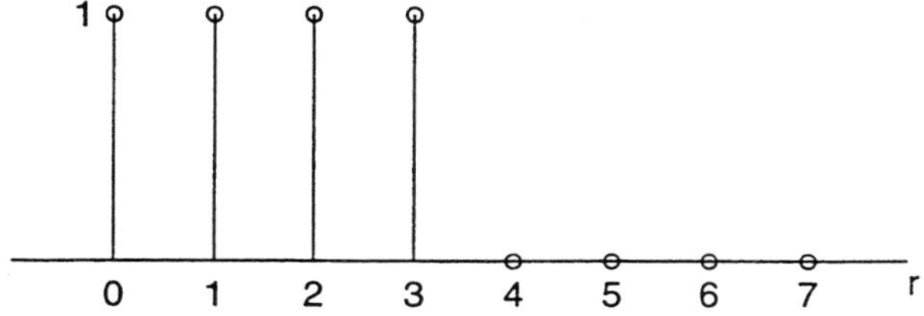

9.4. (a) In any stage, $N/2$ butterflies must be computed. In the mth stage, there are 2^{m-1} different coefficients.

(b) Looking at figure 9.10, we notice that the coefficients are

1st stage:	W_8^0
2nd stage:	W_8^0, W_8^2
3rd stage:	$W_8^0, W_8^1, W_8^2, W_8^3$

Here we have listed the *different* coefficients only. The values above correspond to the impulse response

$$h[n] = W_{2^m}^n u[n]$$

which can be generated by the recursion

$$y[n] = W_{2^m} y[n-1] + x[n]$$

Using this recursion, we only generate a sequence of length $L = 2^{m-1}$, which consists of the different coefficients. Then, the remaining $\frac{N}{2} - L$ coefficients are found by repeating these L coefficients.

(c) The difference equation from Part (b) is periodic, since

$$\begin{aligned} h[n] &= W_{2^m}^n u[n] \\ &= e^{-j2\pi n/2^m} u[n] \end{aligned}$$

has a period $R = 2^m$. Thus, the frequency of this oscillator is

$$\omega = \frac{2\pi}{2^m}$$

9.5. Multiplying out the terms, we find that

$$(A-B)D+(C-D)A = AD-BD+AC-AD = AC-BD = X$$

$$(A-B)D+(C+D)B = AD-BD+BC+BD = AD+BC = Y$$

Thus, the algorithm is verified.

9.6. *Answer 3*

Decimation in Time: The figure is the basic butterfly with $r=2$.

Decimation in Frequency: The figure is the end of one butterfly and the start of a second with $r=2$.

9.7. The figure corresponds to the flow graph of a second-order recursive system implementing Goertzel's algorithm. This system finds $X[k]$ for $k=7$, which corresponds to a frequency of

$$\omega_k = \frac{14\pi}{32} = \frac{7\pi}{16}$$

9.8. This is an application of the causal version of the chirp transform with

$$\begin{aligned} N &= 20 && \text{The length of } x[n] \\ M &= 10 && \text{The number of desired samples} \\ \omega_0 &= \tfrac{2\pi}{7} && \text{The starting frequency} \\ \Delta\omega &= \tfrac{2\pi}{21} && \text{The frequency spacing between samples} \end{aligned}$$

We therefore have

$$y[n+19] = X(e^{j\omega_n}), \quad n = 0,\ldots,9$$

for $\omega_n = \omega_0 + n\Delta\omega$ or

$$y[n] = X(e^{j\omega_n}), \quad n = 19,\ldots,28$$

for $\omega_n = \omega_0 + (n-19)\Delta\omega$.

9.9. In this problem, we are using butterfly flow graphs to compute a DFT. These computations are done in place, in an array of registers. An example flow graph for a $N=8$, (or $v = \log_2 8 = 3$), decimation-in-time DFT is provided below.

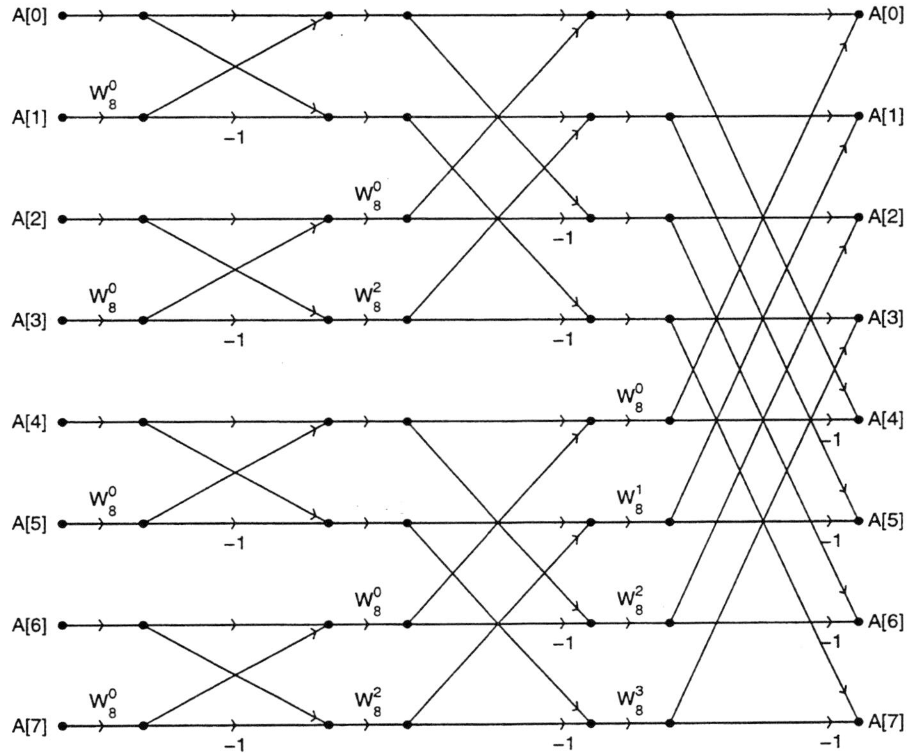

(a) The difference between ℓ_1 and ℓ_0 can be found by using the figure above. For example, in the first stage, the array elements $A[4]$ and $A[5]$ comprise a butterfly. Thus, $\ell_1 - \ell_0 = 5 - 4 = 1$. This difference of 1 holds for all the other butterflies in the first stage. Looking at the other stages, we find

$$\text{stage m} = 1: \quad \ell_1 - \ell_0 = 1$$
$$\text{stage m} = 2: \quad \ell_1 - \ell_0 = 2$$
$$\text{stage m} = 3: \quad \ell_1 - \ell_0 = 4$$

From this we find that the difference, in general, is

$$\ell_1 - \ell_0 = 2^{m-1}, \qquad \text{for } m = 1, \ldots, v$$

(b) Again looking at the figure, we notice that for stage 1, there are 4 butterflies with the same twiddle factor. The ℓ_0 for these butterflies are 0, 2, 4, and 6, which we see differ by 2. For stage 2, there are two butterflies with the same twiddle factor. Consider the butterflies with the W_8^0 twiddle factor. The ℓ_0 for these two butterflies are 0 and 4, which differ by 4. Note that in the last stage, there are no butterflies with the same twiddle factor, as the four twiddle factors are unique. Thus, we found

$$\text{stage m} = 1: \quad \Delta\ell_0 = 2$$
$$\text{stage m} = 2: \quad \Delta\ell_0 = 4$$
$$\text{stage m} = 3: \quad \text{n/a}$$

From this, we can generalize the result

$$\Delta\ell_0 = 2^m, \qquad \text{for } m = 1, \ldots, v - 1$$

9.10. This is an application of the causal version of the chirp transform with

$$\begin{aligned} N &= 12 && \text{The length of } x[n] \\ M &= 5 && \text{The number of desired samples} \\ \omega_0 &= \tfrac{2\pi}{19} && \text{The starting frequency} \\ \Delta\omega &= \tfrac{2\pi}{10} && \text{The distance in frequency between samples} \end{aligned}$$

Letting $W = e^{-j\Delta\omega}$ we must have

$$r[n] = e^{-j\omega_0 n} W^{n^2/2} = e^{-j\frac{2\pi}{19}n} e^{-j\frac{2\pi}{10}n^2/2}$$

9.11. Reversing the bits (denoted by $\rightarrow$) gives

$$\begin{aligned}
0 &= 0000 \rightarrow 0000 = 0 \\
1 &= 0001 \rightarrow 1000 = 8 \\
2 &= 0010 \rightarrow 0100 = 4 \\
3 &= 0011 \rightarrow 1100 = 12 \\
4 &= 0100 \rightarrow 0010 = 2 \\
5 &= 0101 \rightarrow 1010 = 10 \\
6 &= 0110 \rightarrow 0110 = 6 \\
7 &= 0111 \rightarrow 1110 = 14 \\
8 &= 1000 \rightarrow 0001 = 1 \\
9 &= 1001 \rightarrow 1001 = 9 \\
10 &= 1010 \rightarrow 0101 = 5 \\
11 &= 1011 \rightarrow 1101 = 13 \\
12 &= 1100 \rightarrow 0011 = 3 \\
13 &= 1101 \rightarrow 1011 = 11 \\
14 &= 1110 \rightarrow 0111 = 7 \\
15 &= 1111 \rightarrow 1111 = 15
\end{aligned}$$

The new sample order is 0, 8, 4, 12, 2, 10, 6, 14, 1, 9, 5, 13, 3, 11, 7, 15.

9.12. *False.* It is possible by rearranging the order in which the nodes appear in the signal flow graph. However, the computation cannot be carried out in-place.

9.13. Only the $m = 1$ stage will have this form. No other stage of a $N = 16$ radix-2 decimation-in-frequency FFT will have a W_{16} term raised to an odd power.

9.14. The possible values of r for each of the four stages are

$$\begin{aligned}
m &= 1, && r = 0 \\
m &= 2, && r = 0, 4 \\
m &= 3, && r = 0, 2, 4, 6 \\
m &= 4, && r = 0, 1, 2, 3, 4, 5, 6, 7
\end{aligned}$$

9.15. Plugging in some values of N for the two programs, we find

N	Program A	Program B
2	4	20
4	16	80
8	64	240
16	256	640
32	1024	1600
64	4096	3840

Thus, we see that a sequence with length $N = 64$ is the shortest sequence for which Program B runs faster than Program A.

9.16. The possible values for r for each of the four stages are

$$\begin{aligned} m &= 1, \quad & r &= 0 \\ m &= 2, & r &= 0, 4 \\ m &= 3, & r &= 0, 2, 4, 6 \\ m &= 4, & r &= 0, 1, 2, 3, 4, 5, 6, 7 \end{aligned}$$

where W_N^r is the twiddle factor for each stage. Since the particular butterfly shown has $r = 2$, the stages which have this butterfly are

$$m = 3, 4$$

9.17. The FFT is a decimation-in-time algorithm, since the decimation-in-frequency algorithm has only W_{32}^0 terms in the last stage.

9.18. If the $N_1 = 1021$ point DFT was calculated using the convolution sum directly it would take N_1^2 multiplications. If the $N_2 = 1024$ point DFT was calculated using the FFT it would take $N_2 \log_2 N_2$ multiplications. Assuming that the number of multiplications is proportional to the calculation time the ratio of the two times is

$$\frac{N_1^2}{N_2 \log_2 N_2} = \frac{1021^2}{1024 \log_2 1024} = 101.8 \approx 100$$

which would explain the results.

9.19. $X(e^{j6\pi/8})$ corresponds to the $k = 3$ index of a length $N = 8$ DFT. Using the flow graph of the second-order recursive system for Goertzel's algorithm,

$$\begin{aligned} a &= 2\cos\left(\frac{2\pi k}{N}\right) \\ &= 2\cos\left(\frac{2\pi(3)}{8}\right) \\ &= -\sqrt{2} \\ b &= -W_N^k \\ &= -e^{-j6\pi/8} \\ &= \frac{1+j}{\sqrt{2}} \end{aligned}$$

9.20. First, we derive a relationship between the $X_1(e^{j\omega})$ and $X(e^{j\omega})$ using the shift and time reversal properties of the DTFT.

$$\begin{aligned} x_1[n] &= x[32-n] \\ X_1(e^{j\omega}) &= X(e^{-j\omega})e^{-j32\omega} \end{aligned}$$

Looking at the figure we see that calculating $y[32]$ is just an application of the Goertzel algorithm with $k=7$ and $N=32$. Therefore,

$$\begin{aligned} y[32] &= X_1[7] \\ &= X_1(e^{j\omega})\big|_{\omega=\frac{2\pi 7}{32}} \\ &= X(e^{-j\omega})e^{-j\omega 32}\big|_{\omega=\frac{7\pi}{16}} \\ &= X(e^{-j\frac{7\pi}{16}})e^{-j(\frac{7\pi}{16})32} \\ &= X(e^{-j\frac{7\pi}{16}}) \end{aligned}$$

Note that if we put $x[n]$ through the system directly, we would be evaluating $X(z)$ at the conjugate location on the unit circle, i.e., at $\omega = +7\pi/16$.

9.21. (a) Assume $x[n]=0$, for $n<0$ and $n>N-1$. From the figure, we see that

$$y_k[n] = x[n] + W_N^k y_k[n-1]$$

Starting with $n=0$, and iterating this recursive equation, we find

$$\begin{aligned} y_k[0] &= x[0] \\ y_k[1] &= x[1] + W_N^k x[0] \\ y_k[2] &= x[2] + W_N^k x[1] + W_N^{2k} x[0] \\ &\vdots \\ y_k[N] &= x[N] + W_N^k x[N-1] + \cdots + W_N^{k(N-1)} x[1] + W_N^{kN} x[0] \\ &= 0 + \sum_{\ell=0}^{N-1} W_N^{k(N-\ell)} x[\ell] \\ &= \sum_{\ell=0}^{N-1} W_N^{-k\ell} x[\ell] \\ &= \sum_{\ell=0}^{N-1} x[\ell] W_N^{(N-k)\ell} \\ &= X[N-k] \end{aligned}$$

(b) Using the figure, we find the system function $Y_k(z)$.

$$\begin{aligned} Y_k(z) &= X(z)\frac{1-W_N^{-k}z^{-1}}{1-2z^{-1}\cos(\frac{2\pi k}{N})+z^{-2}} \\ &= X(z)\frac{1-W_N^{-k}z^{-1}}{(1-W_N^{-k}z^{-1})(1-W_N^{k}z^{-1})} \\ &= \frac{X(z)}{1-W_N^k z^{-1}} \end{aligned}$$

Therefore, $y_k[n] = x[n] + W_N^k y_k[n-1]$. This is the same difference equation as in part (a).

9.22. The flow graph for 16 point radix-2 decimation-in-time FFT algorithm is shown below.

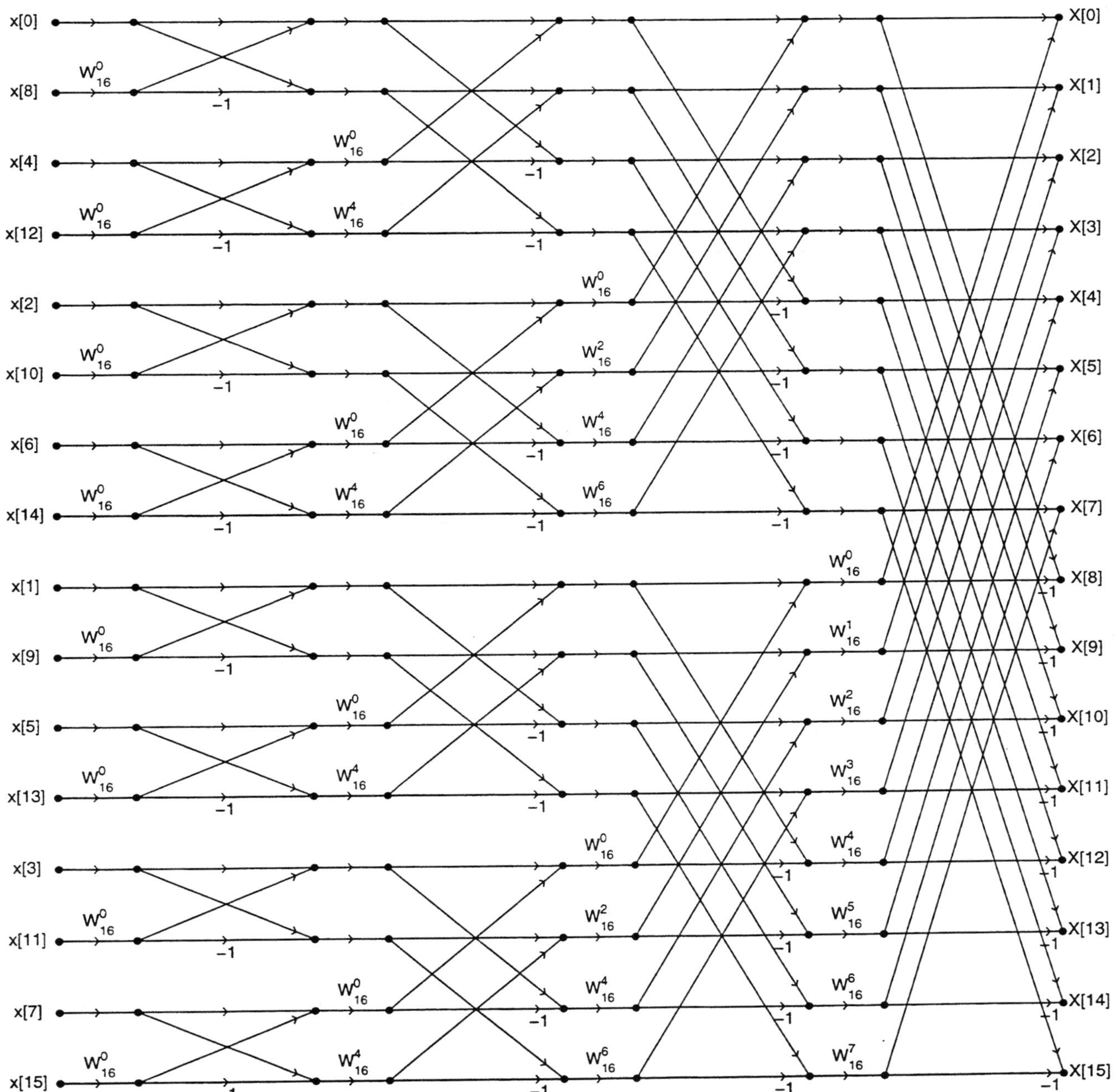

To determine the number of real multiplications and additions required to implement the flow graph, consider the number of real multiplications and additions introduced by each of the coefficients W_N^k:

$$\begin{array}{lll}
W_{16}^0: & 0 \text{ real multiplications} + 0 \text{ real additions} & (W_{16}^0 = 1) \\
W_{16}^4: & 0 \text{ real multiplications} + 0 \text{ real additions} & (W_{16}^4(a+jb) = b - aj) \\
W_{16}^2: & 2 \text{ real multiplications} + 2 \text{ real additions} & (W_{16}^2(a+jb) = \frac{\sqrt{2}}{2}(a+b) + j\frac{\sqrt{2}}{2}(b-a)) \\
W_{16}^6: & 2 \text{ real multiplications} + 2 \text{ real additions} & \text{similarly} \\
W_{16}^1: & 4 \text{ real multiplications} + 2 \text{ real additions} & \\
W_{16}^3: & 4 \text{ real multiplications} + 2 \text{ real additions} & \\
W_{16}^5: & 4 \text{ real multiplications} + 2 \text{ real additions} & \\
W_{16}^7: & 4 \text{ real multiplications} + 2 \text{ real additions} &
\end{array}$$

The contribution of all the W_N^k's on the flow graph is 28 real multiplications and 20 real additions. The butterflies contribute 0 real multiplications and 32 real additions per stage. Since there are four stages, the butterflies contribute 0 real multiplications and 128 real additions. In total, 28 real multiplications and 148 real additions are required to implement the flow graph.

9.23. (a) Setting up the butterfly's system of equations in matrix form gives

$$\begin{bmatrix} 1 & 1 \\ W_N^r & -W_N^r \end{bmatrix} \begin{bmatrix} X_{m-1}[p] \\ X_{m-1}[q] \end{bmatrix} = \begin{bmatrix} X_m[p] \\ X_m[q] \end{bmatrix}$$

Solving for

$$\begin{bmatrix} X_{m-1}[p] \\ X_{m-1}[q] \end{bmatrix}$$

gives

$$\begin{bmatrix} X_{m-1}[p] \\ X_{m-1}[q] \end{bmatrix} = \begin{bmatrix} \frac{1}{2} & \frac{1}{2}W_N^{-r} \\ \frac{1}{2} & -\frac{1}{2}W_N^{-r} \end{bmatrix} \begin{bmatrix} X_m[p] \\ X_m[q] \end{bmatrix}$$

which is consistent with Figure P9.6-2.

(b) The flow graph appears below.

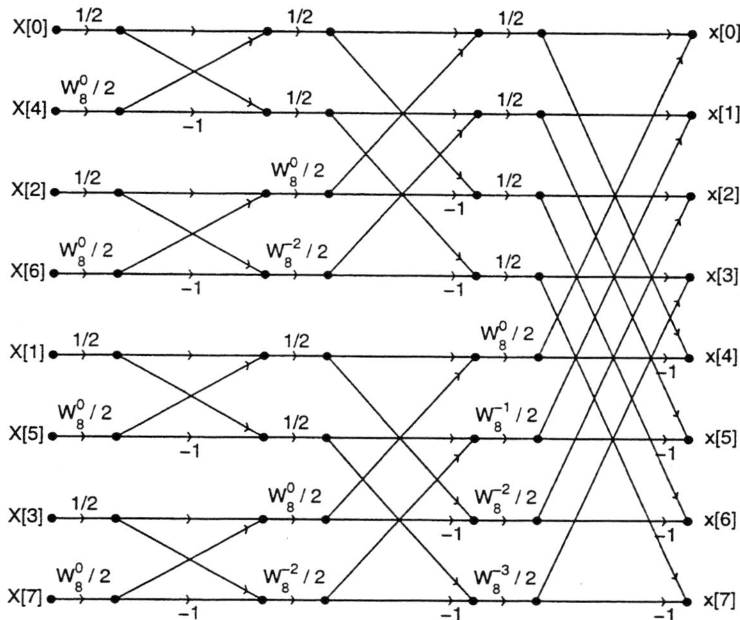

(c) The modification is made by removing all factors of $1/2$, changing all W_N^{-r} to W_N^r, and relabeling the input and the output, as shown in the flow graph below.

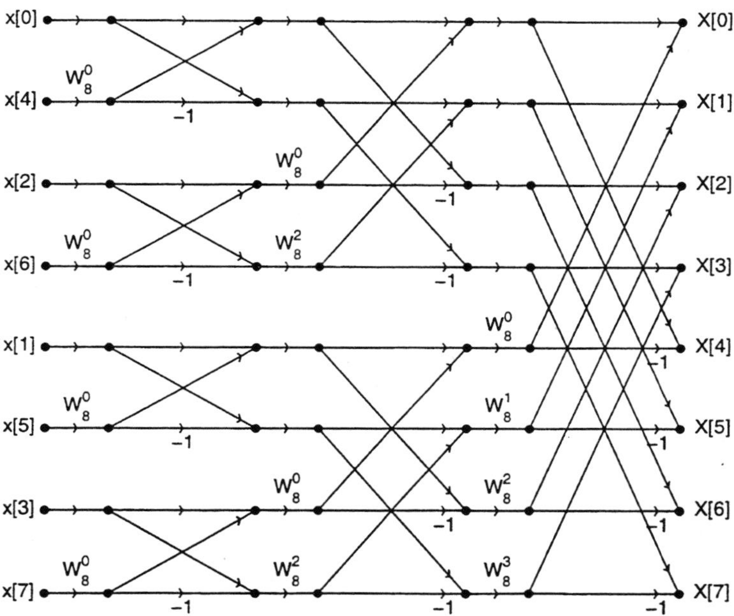

(d) *Yes.* In general, for each decimation-in-time FFT algorithm there exists a decimation-in-frequency FFT algorithm that corresponds to interchanging the input and output and reversing the direction of all the arrows in the flow graph.

9.24. (a) Using the figure, it is observed that each output $Y[k]$ is a scaled version of $X[k]$. The scaling factor is $W[k]$, which is found to be

$$\begin{array}{lcllllllll} k & = & 0 & 1 & 2 & 3 & 4 & 5 & 6 & 7 \\ W[k] & = & 1 & G & G & G^2 & G & G^2 & G^2 & G^3 \end{array}$$

Using this $W[k]$, $Y[k] = W[k]X[k]$.

(b) $W[k] = G^{p[k]}$, where $p[k]$ = the number of ones in the binary representation of index k.

(c) A procedure for finding $\hat{x}[n]$ is as follows.

step 1: Form $W'[k] = 1/W[k]$.

step 2: Take the inverse DFT of $W'[k]$, yielding $w'[n]$.

step 3: Let $\hat{x}[n]$ be the circular convolution of $x[n]$ and $w'[n]$.

If $\hat{x}[n]$ is input to the modified FFT algorithm, then the output will be $X[k]$, as shown below.

$$\begin{aligned} Y[k] &= W[k]\hat{X}[k] \\ &= W[k]X[k]W'[k] \\ &= X[k] \end{aligned}$$

9.25. Let z_k be the z-plane locations of the 25 points uniformly spaced on an arc of a circle of radius 0.5 from $-\pi/6$ to $2\pi/3$. Then

$$z_k = 0.5e^{j(\omega_0 + k\Delta\omega)}, \quad k = 0, 1, \ldots, 24$$

where

$$\begin{aligned} \omega_0 &= -\frac{\pi}{6} \\ \Delta\omega &= \left(\frac{5\pi}{6}\right)\left(\frac{1}{24}\right) \\ &= \frac{5\pi}{144} \end{aligned}$$

From the definition of the z-transform,

$$X(z_k) = \sum_{n=0}^{N-1} x[n] z_k^{-n}$$

Plugging in z_k, and setting $W = e^{-j\Delta\omega}$,

$$X(z_k) = \sum_{n=0}^{N-1} x[n](0.5)^{-n} e^{-j\omega_0 n} W^{nk}$$

This is similar to the expression for $X(e^{jw})$ using the chirp transform algorithm. The only difference is the $(0.5)^{-n}$ term. Setting

$$g[n] = x[n](0.5)^{-n} e^{-j\omega_0 n} W^{n^2/2}$$

we get

$$X(z_k) = W^{k^2/2} \sum_{n=0}^{N-1} g[n] W^{-(k-n)^2/2}$$

using the result of the chirp transform algorithm. A procedure for computing $X(z)$ at the points z_k is then

- Multiply the sequence x[n] by the sequence $(0.5)^{-n}e^{-j\omega_0 n}W^{n^2/2}$ to form $g[n]$.
- Convolve $g[n]$ with the sequence $W^{-n^2/2}$.
- Multiply this result by the sequence $W^{n^2/2}$ to form $X(z_k)$.

A block diagram of this system appears below.

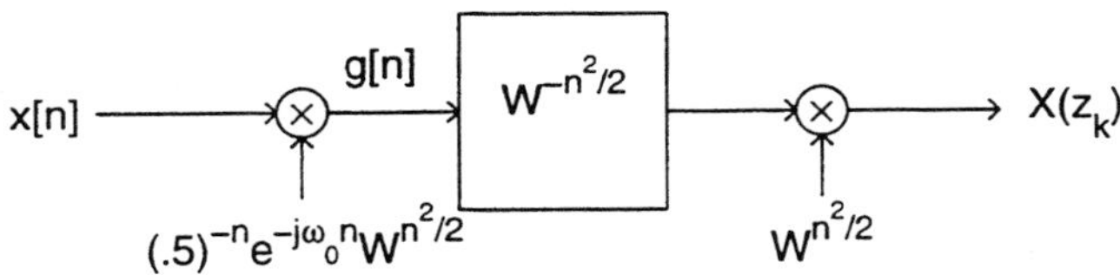

9.26.

$$
\begin{aligned}
Y[k] &= \sum_{n=0}^{2N-1} y[n]e^{-j(\frac{2\pi}{2N})kn} \\
&= \sum_{n=0}^{N-1} e^{-j(\pi/N)n^2}e^{-j(2\pi/N)(k/2)n} + \sum_{n=N}^{2N-1} e^{-j(\pi/N)n^2}e^{-j(2\pi/N)(k/2)n} \\
&= \sum_{n=0}^{N-1} e^{-j(\pi/N)n^2}e^{-j(2\pi/N)(k/2)n} + \sum_{l=0}^{N-1} e^{-j(\pi/N)(l+N)^2}e^{-j(2\pi/N)(k/2)(l+N)} \\
&= \sum_{n=0}^{N-1} e^{-j(\pi/N)n^2}e^{-j(2\pi/N)(k/2)n} + e^{-j\pi k}\sum_{l=0}^{N-1} e^{-j(\pi/N)(l^2+2Nl+N^2)}e^{-j(2\pi/N)(k/2)l} \\
&= \sum_{n=0}^{N-1} e^{-j(\pi/N)n^2}e^{-j(2\pi/N)(k/2)n} + (-1)^k\sum_{l=0}^{N-1} e^{-j(\pi/N)l^2}e^{-j(2\pi/N)(k/2)l} \\
&= (1+(-1)^k)\sum_{n=0}^{N-1} e^{-j(\pi/N)n^2}e^{-j(2\pi/N)(k/2)n} \\
&= \begin{cases} 2X[k/2], & k \text{ even} \\ 0, & k \text{ odd} \end{cases}
\end{aligned}
$$

Thus,

$$
Y[k] = \begin{cases} 2\sqrt{N}e^{-j\pi/4}e^{j(\pi/N)k^2/4}, & k \text{ even} \\ 0, & k \text{ odd} \end{cases}
$$

9.27. Let

$$y[n] = e^{-j2\pi n/627}x[n]$$

Then

$$Y(e^{j\omega}) = X(e^{j(\omega+\frac{2\pi}{627})})$$

Let $y'[n] = \sum_{m=-\infty}^{\infty} y[n+256m], \quad 0 \le n \le 255$, and let $Y'[k]$ be the 256 point DFT of $y'[n]$. Then

$$Y'[k] = X\left(e^{j(\frac{2\pi k}{256}+\frac{2\pi}{627})}\right)$$

See problem 9.30 for a more in-depth analysis of this technique.

9.28. (a) The problem states that the effective frequency spacing, Δf, should be 50 Hz or less. This constrains N such that

$$\begin{aligned}\Delta f &= \frac{1}{NT} \leq 50 \\ N &\geq \frac{1}{50T} \\ &\geq 200\end{aligned}$$

Since the sequence length L is 500, and N must be a power of 2, we might conclude that the minimum value for N is 512 for computing the desired samples of the z-transform.

However, we can compute the samples with N equal to 256 by using time aliasing. In this technique, we would zero pad $x[n]$ to a length of 512, then form the 256 point sequence

$$y[n] = \begin{cases} x[n] + x[n+256], & 0 \leq n \leq 255 \\ 0, & \text{otherwise} \end{cases}$$

We could then compute 256 samples of the z-transform of $y[n]$. The effective frequency spacing of these samples would be $1/(NT) \approx 39$ Hz which is lower than the 50 Hz specification.
Note that these samples also correspond to the *even*-indexed samples of a length 512 sampled z-transform of $x[n]$. Problem 9.30 discusses this technique of time aliasing in more detail.

(b) Let

$$y[n] = (1.25)^n x[n]$$

Then, using the modulation property of the z-transform, $Y(z) = X(0.8z)$ and so $Y[k] = X(0.8e^{j2\pi k/N})$.

9.29. (a) We offer two solutions to this problem.

Solution #1: Looking at the DFT of the sequence, we find

$$\begin{aligned}X[k] &= \sum_{n=0}^{N-1} x[n]e^{-j2\pi kn/N} \\ &= \sum_{n=0}^{(N/2)-1} x[n]e^{-j2\pi kn/N} + \sum_{n=N/2}^{N-1} x[n]e^{-j2\pi kn/N} \\ &= \sum_{n=0}^{(N/2)-1} x[n]e^{-j2\pi kn/N} + \sum_{r=0}^{(N/2)-1} x[r+(N/2)]e^{-j2\pi k[r+(N/2)]/N} \\ &= \sum_{n=0}^{(N/2)-1} x[n][1-(-1)^k]e^{-j2\pi kn/N} \\ &= 0, \quad k \text{ even}\end{aligned}$$

Solution #2: Alternatively, we can use the circular shift property of the DFT to find

$$\begin{aligned}X[k] &= -X[k]e^{-j(\frac{2\pi}{N})k(\frac{N}{2})} \\ &= -(-1)^k X[k] \\ &= (-1)^{k+1} X[k]\end{aligned}$$

When k is even, we have $X[k] = -X[k]$ which can only be true if $X[k] = 0$.

(b) Evaluating the DFT at the odd-indexed samples gives us

$$
\begin{aligned}
X[2k+1] &= \sum_{n=0}^{N-1} x[n]e^{-j(2\pi/N)(2k+1)n} \\
&= \sum_{n=0}^{N/2-1} x[n]e^{-j2\pi n/N}e^{-j2\pi kn/(N/2)} + \sum_{n=N/2}^{N-1} x[n]e^{-j2\pi n/N}e^{-j2\pi kn/(N/2)} \\
&= \mathrm{DFT}_{N/2}\left\{x[n]e^{-j(2\pi/N)n}\right\} + \sum_{l=0}^{N/2-1} x[l+(N/2)]e^{-j2\pi[l+(N/2)]/N}e^{-j2\pi k[l+(N/2)]/(N/2)} \\
&= \mathrm{DFT}_{N/2}\left\{x[n]e^{-j(2\pi/N)n}\right\} + (-1)(-1)\sum_{l=0}^{N/2-1} x[l]e^{-j2\pi l/N}e^{-j2\pi kl/(N/2)} \\
&= \mathrm{DFT}_{N/2}\left\{2x[n]e^{-j(2\pi/N)n}\right\}
\end{aligned}
$$

for $k = 0, \ldots, N/2 - 1$. Thus, we can compute the odd-indexed DFT values using one $N/2$ point DFT plus a small amount of extra computation.

9.30. (a) Note that we can write the even-indexed values of $X[k]$ as $X[2k]$ for $k = 0, \ldots, (N/2) - 1$. From the definition of the DFT, we find

$$
\begin{aligned}
X[2k] &= \sum_{n=0}^{N-1} x[n]e^{-j2\pi(2k)n/N} \\
&= \sum_{n=0}^{N/2-1} x[n]e^{-j\frac{2\pi}{(N/2)}kn} \\
&\quad + \sum_{n=0}^{N/2-1} x[n+(N/2)]e^{-j\frac{2\pi}{(N/2)}kn}e^{-j\frac{2\pi}{(N/2)}(N/2)k} \\
&= \sum_{n=0}^{N/2-1} (x[n]+x[n+(N/2)])e^{-j\frac{2\pi}{(N/2)}kn} \\
&= Y[k]
\end{aligned}
$$

Thus, the algorithm produces the desired results.

(b) Taking the M-point DFT $Y[k]$, we find

$$
\begin{aligned}
Y[k] &= \sum_{n=0}^{M-1}\sum_{r=-\infty}^{\infty} x[n+rM]e^{-j2\pi kn/M} \\
&= \sum_{r=-\infty}^{\infty}\sum_{n=0}^{M-1} x[n+rM]e^{-j2\pi k(n+rM)/M}e^{j2\pi(rM)k/M}
\end{aligned}
$$

Let $l = n + rM$. This gives

$$
\begin{aligned}
Y[k] &= \sum_{l=-\infty}^{\infty} x[l]e^{-j2\pi kl/M} \\
&= X(e^{j2\pi k/M})
\end{aligned}
$$

Thus, the result from Part (a) is a special case of this result if we let $M = N/2$. In Part (a), there are only two r terms for which $y[n]$ is nonzero in the range $n = 0, \ldots, (N/2) - 1$.

(c) We can write the odd-indexed values of $X[k]$ as $X[2k+1]$ for $k = 0, \ldots, (N/2) - 1$. From the definition of the DFT, we find

$$\begin{aligned}
X[2k+1] &= \sum_{n=0}^{N-1} x[n]e^{-j2\pi(2k+1)n/N} \\
&= \sum_{n=0}^{N-1} x[n]e^{-j2\pi n/N}e^{-j2\pi(2k)n/N} \\
&= \sum_{n=0}^{(N/2)-1} x[n]e^{-j2\pi n/N}e^{-j\frac{2\pi}{(N/2)}kn} + \sum_{n=0}^{(N/2)-1} x[n+(N/2)]e^{-j2\pi[n+(N/2)]/N}e^{-j\frac{2\pi}{N/2}k[n+(N/2)]} \\
&= \sum_{n=0}^{(N/2)-1} \left[(x[n] - x[n+(N/2)])e^{-j\frac{2\pi}{N}n}\right] e^{-j\frac{2\pi}{(N/2)}kn}
\end{aligned}$$

Let

$$y[n] = \begin{cases} (x[n] - x[n+(N/2)])e^{-j(2\pi/N)n}, & 0 \le n \le (N/2) - 1 \\ 0, & \text{otherwise} \end{cases}$$

Then $Y[k] = X[2k+1]$. Thus, The algorithm for computing the odd-indexed DFT values is as follows.

step 1: Form the sequence

$$y[n] = \begin{cases} (x[n] - x[n+(N/2)])e^{-j(2\pi/N)n}, & 0 \le n \le (N/2) - 1 \\ 0, & \text{otherwise} \end{cases}$$

step 2: Compute the $N/2$ point DFT of $y[n]$, yielding the sequence $Y[k]$.

step 3: The odd-indexed values of $X[k]$ are then $X[k] = Y[(k-1)/2]$, $k = 1, 3, \ldots, N-1$.

9.31. (a) Since $x[n]$ is real, $x[n] = x^*[n]$, and $X[k]$ is conjugate symmetric.

$$\begin{aligned}
X[k] &= \sum_{n=0}^{N-1} x^*[n]e^{-j\frac{2\pi}{N}kn} \\
&= \left(\sum_{n=0}^{N-1} x[n]e^{j\frac{2\pi}{N}kn}e^{-j\frac{2\pi}{N}Nn}\right)^* \\
&= X^*[N-k]
\end{aligned}$$

Hence, $X_R[k] = X_R[N-k]$ and $X_I[k] = -X_I[N-k]$.

(b) In Part (a) it was shown that the DFT of a real sequence $x[n]$ consists of a real part that has even symmetry, and an imaginary part that has odd symmetry. We use this fact in the DFT of the sequence $g[n]$ below.

$$\begin{aligned}
G[k] &= X_1[k] + jX_2[k] \\
&= (X_{1ER}[k] + jX_{1OI}[k]) + j(X_{2ER}[k] + jX_{2OI}[k]) \\
&= \underbrace{X_{1ER}[k] - X_{2OI}[k]}_{\text{real part}} + j\,\underbrace{(X_{1OI}[k] + X_{2ER}[k])}_{\text{imaginary part}}
\end{aligned}$$

In these expressions, the subscripts "E" and "O" denote even and odd symmetry, respectively, and the subscripts "R" and "I" denote real and imaginary parts, respectively.

Therefore, the even and real part of $G[k]$ is

$$G_{ER}[k] = X_{1ER}[k]$$

the odd and real part of $G[k]$ is

$$G_{OR}[k] = -X_{2OI}[k]$$

the even and imaginary part of $G[k]$ is

$$G_{EI}[k] = X_{2ER}[k]$$

and the odd and imaginary part of $G[k]$ is

$$G_{OI}[k] = X_{1OI}[k]$$

Having established these relationships, it is easy to come up with expressions for $X_1[k]$ and $X_2[k]$.

$$\begin{aligned} X_1[k] &= X_{1ER}[k] + jX_{1OI}[k] \\ &= G_{ER}[k] + jG_{OI}[k] \\ X_2[k] &= X_{2ER}[k] + jX_{2OI}[k] \\ &= G_{EI}[k] - jG_{OR}[k] \end{aligned}$$

(c) An $N = 2^\nu$ point FFT requires $(N/2)\log_2 N$ complex multiplications and $N\log_2 N$ complex additions. This is equivalent to $2N\log_2 N$ real multiplications and $3N\log_2 N$ real additions.

(i) The two N-point FFTs, $X_1[k]$ and $X_2[k]$, require a total of $4N\log_2 N$ real multiplications and $6N\log_2 N$ real additions.

(ii) Computing the N-point FFT, $G[k]$, requires $2N\log_2 N$ real multiplications and $3N\log_2 N$ real additions. Then, the computation of $G_{ER}[k]$, $G_{EI}[k]$, $G_{OI}[k]$, and $G_{OR}[k]$ from $G[k]$ requires approximately $4N$ real multiplications and $4N$ real additions. Then, the formation of $X_1[k]$ and $X_2[k]$ from $G_{ER}[k]$, $G_{EI}[k]$, $G_{OI}[k]$, and $G_{OR}[k]$ requires no real additions or multiplications. So this technique requires a total of approximately $2N\log_2 N + 4N$ real multiplications and $3N\log_2 N + 4N$ real additions.

(d) Starting with

$$X[k] = \sum_{n=0}^{N-1} x[n]e^{-j2\pi kn/N}$$

and separating $x[n]$ into its even and odd numbered parts, we get

$$X[k] = \sum_{n \text{ even}} x[n]e^{-j2\pi kn/N} + \sum_{n \text{ odd}} x[n]e^{-j2\pi kn/N}$$

Substituting $n = 2\ell$ for n even, and $n = 2\ell + 1$ for n odd, gives

$$\begin{aligned} X[k] &= \sum_{\ell=0}^{(N/2)-1} x[2\ell]e^{-j2\pi k\ell/(N/2)} + \sum_{\ell=0}^{(N/2)-1} x[2\ell+1]e^{-j2\pi k(2\ell+1)/N} \\ &= \sum_{\ell=0}^{(N/2)-1} x[2\ell]e^{-j2\pi k\ell/(N/2)} + e^{-j2\pi k/N}\sum_{\ell=0}^{(N/2)-1} x[2\ell+1]e^{-j2\pi k\ell/(N/2)} \\ &= \begin{cases} X_1[k] + e^{-j2\pi k/N}X_2[k], & 0 \le k < \frac{N}{2} \\ X_1[k-(N/2)] - e^{-j2\pi k/N}X_2[k-(N/2)], & \frac{N}{2} \le k < N \end{cases} \end{aligned}$$

(e) The algorithm is then

step 1: Form the sequence $g[n] = x[2n] + jx[2n+1]$, which has length $N/2$.
step 2: Compute $G[k]$, the $N/2$ point DFT of $g[n]$.
step 3: Separate $G[k]$ into the four parts, for $k = 1, \ldots, (N/2) - 1$

$$\begin{aligned} G_{OR}[k] &= \frac{1}{2}(G_R[k] - G_R[(N/2) - k]) \\ G_{ER}[k] &= \frac{1}{2}(G_R[k] + G_R[(N/2) - k]) \\ G_{OI}[k] &= \frac{1}{2}(G_I[k] - G_I[(N/2) - k]) \\ G_{EI}[k] &= \frac{1}{2}(G_I[k] + G_I[(N/2) - k]) \end{aligned}$$

which each have length $N/2$.
step 4: Form

$$\begin{aligned} X_1[k] &= G_{ER}[k] + jG_{OI}[k] \\ X_2'[k] &= e^{-j2\pi k/N}(G_{EI}[k] - jG_{OR}[k]) \end{aligned}$$

which each have length $N/2$.
step 5: Then, form

$$X[k] = X_1[k] + X_2'[k], \qquad 0 \le k < \frac{N}{2}$$

step 6: Finally, form

$$X[k] = X^*[N-k], \qquad \frac{N}{2} \le k < N$$

Adding up the computational requirements for each step of the algorithm gives (approximately)
step 1: 0 real multiplications and 0 real additions.
step 2: $2\frac{N}{2}\log_2\frac{N}{2}$ real multiplications and $3\frac{N}{2}\log_2\frac{N}{2}$ real additions.
step 3: $2N$ real multiplications and $2N$ real additions.
step 4: $2N$ real multiplications and N real additions.
step 5: 0 real multiplications and N real additions.
step 6: 0 real multiplications and 0 real additions.
In total, approximately $N\log_2\frac{N}{2} + 4N$ real multiplications and $\frac{3}{2}N\log_2\frac{N}{2} + 4N$ real additions are required by this technique.
The number of real multiplications and real additions required if $X[k]$ is computed using one N-point FFT computation with the imaginary part set to zero is $2N\log_2 N$ real multiplications and $3N\log_2 N$ real additions.

9.32. (a) The length of the sequence is $L + P - 1$.

(b) In evaluating $y[n]$ using the convolution sum, each nonzero value of $h[n]$ is multiplied once with every nonzero value of $x[n]$. This can be seen graphically using the flip and slide view of convolution. The total number of real multiplies is therefore LP.

(c) To compute $y[n] = h[n] * x[n]$ using the DFT, we use the procedure described below.
step 1: Compute N point DFTs of $x[n]$ and $h[n]$.
step 2: Multiply them together to get $Y[k] = H[k]X[k]$.
step 3: Compute the inverse DFT to get $y[n]$.
Since $y[n]$ has length $L + P - 1$, N must be greater than or equal to $L + P - 1$ so the circular convolution implied by step 2 is equivalent to linear convolution.

(d) For these signals, N is large enough so that circular convolution of $x[n]$ and $h[n]$ and the linear convolution of $x[n]$ and $h[n]$ produce the same result. Counting the number of complex multiplications for the procedure in part (b) we get

DFT of $x[n]$	$(N/2)\log_2 N$
DFT of $h[n]$	$(N/2)\log_2 N$
$Y[k] = X[k]H[k]$	N
Inverse DFT of $Y[k]$	$(N/2)\log_2 N$
	$(3N/2)\log_2 N + N$

Since there are 4 real multiplications for every complex multiplication we see that the procedure takes $6N\log_2 N + 4N$ real multiplications. Using the answer from part (a), we see that the direct method requires $(N/2)(N/2) = N^2/4$ real multiplications.

The following table shows that the smallest $N = 2^\nu$ for which the FFT method requires fewer multiplications than the direct method is 256.

N	Direct Method	FFT method
2	1	20
4	4	64
8	16	176
16	64	448
32	256	1088
64	1024	2560
128	4096	5888
256	16384	13312

9.33. (a) For each L point section, $P-1$ samples are discarded, leaving $L-P+1$ output samples. The complex multiplications are:

L point FFT of input:	$(L/2)\log_2 L = \nu 2^\nu/2$
Multiplication of filter and section DFT:	$L = 2^\nu$
L point inverse FFT:	$(L/2)\log_2 L = \nu 2^\nu/2$
Total per section:	$2^\nu(\nu+1)$

Therefore,

$$\frac{\text{Complex Multiplications}}{\text{Output Sample}} = \frac{2^\nu(\nu+1)}{2^\nu - P + 1}$$

Note we assume here that $H[k]$ has been precalculated.

(b) The figure below plots the number of complex multiplications per sample versus ν. For $\nu = 12$, the number of multiplies per sample reaches a minimum of 14.8. In comparison, direct evaluation of the convolution sum would require 500 complex multiplications per output sample.

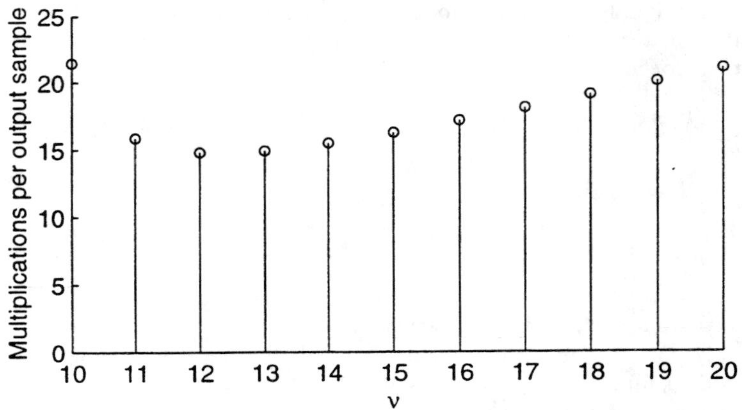

Although $\nu = 9$ is the first valid choice for overlap-save method, it is not plotted since the value is so large (in the hundreds) it would obscure the graph.

(c)

$$\begin{aligned}\lim_{\nu\to\infty} \frac{2^\nu(\nu+1)}{2^\nu - P + 1} &= \lim_{\nu\to\infty} \frac{\nu+1}{1+\frac{-P+1}{2^\nu}} \\ &= \nu\end{aligned}$$

Thus, for $P = 500$ the direct method will be more efficient for $\nu > 500$.

(d) We want

$$\frac{2^\nu(\nu+1)}{2^\nu - P + 1} \leq P.$$

Plugging in $P = L/2 = 2^{\nu-1}$ gives

$$\frac{2^\nu(\nu+1)}{2^\nu - 2^{\nu-1} + 1} \leq 2^{\nu-1}.$$

As seen in the table below, the FFT will require fewer complex multiplications than the direct method when $\nu = 5$ or $P = 2^4 = 16$.

	Overlap/Save	Direct
ν	$\frac{2^\nu(\nu+1)}{2^\nu-2^{\nu-1}+1}$	$2^{\nu-1}$
1	2	1
2	4	2
3	6.4	4
4	8.9	8
5	11.3	16

9.34. This problem asks that we find eight equally spaced *inverse* DFT coefficients using the chirp transform algorithm. The book derives the algorithm for the forward DFT. However, with some minor tweaking, it is easy to formulate an inverse DFT. First, we start with the inverse DFT relation

$$\begin{aligned}x[n] &= \frac{1}{N}\sum_{k=0}^{N-1} X[k]e^{j2\pi nk/N} \\ x[n_\ell] &= \frac{1}{N}\sum_{k=0}^{N-1} X[k]e^{j2\pi n_\ell k/N}\end{aligned}$$

Next, we define

$$\begin{aligned} \Delta n &= 1 \\ n_\ell &= n_0 + \ell \Delta n \end{aligned}$$

where $\ell = 0, \ldots, 7$. Substituting this into the equation above gives

$$x[n_\ell] = \frac{1}{N} \sum_{k=0}^{N-1} X[k] e^{j2\pi n_0 k/N} e^{j2\pi \ell \Delta n k/N}$$

Defining

$$W = e^{-j2\pi \Delta n/N}$$

we find

$$x[n_\ell] = \frac{1}{N} \sum_{k=0}^{N-1} X[k] e^{j2\pi n_0 k/N} W^{-\ell k}$$

Using the relation

$$\ell k = \frac{1}{2}[\ell^2 + k^2 - (k - \ell)^2]$$

we get

$$x[n_\ell] = \frac{1}{N} \sum_{k=0}^{N-1} X[k] e^{j2\pi n_0 k/N} W^{-\ell^2/2} W^{-k^2/2} W^{(k-\ell)^2/2}$$

Let

$$G[k] = X[k] e^{j2\pi n_0 k/N} W^{-k^2/2}$$

Then,

$$x[n_\ell] = \frac{1}{N} W^{-\ell^2/2} \left(\sum_{k=0}^{N-1} G[k] W^{(k-\ell)^2/2} \right)$$

From this equation, it is clear that the inverse DFT can be computed using the chirp transform algorithm. All we need to do is replace n by k, change the sign of each of the exponential terms, and divide by a factor of N. Therefore,

$$\begin{aligned} m_1[k] &= e^{j2\pi k n_0/N} W^{-k^2/2} \\ m_2[k] &= W^{-k^2/2} \\ h[k] &= \frac{1}{N} W^{k^2/2} \end{aligned}$$

Using this system with $n_0 = 1020$, and $\ell = 0, \ldots, 7$ will result in a sequence $y[n]$ which will contain the desired samples, where

$$\begin{aligned} y[0] &= x[1020] \\ y[1] &= x[1021] \\ y[2] &= x[1022] \\ y[3] &= x[1023] \\ y[4] &= x[0] \\ y[5] &= x[1] \\ y[6] &= x[2] \\ y[7] &= x[3] \end{aligned}$$

9.35. First note that

$$\begin{aligned} x_i[n] &= \begin{cases} x[n], & iL \le n \le iL + 127, \\ 0, & \text{otherwise} \end{cases} \\ &= \begin{cases} x[n + iL], & 0 \le n \le 127, \\ 0, & \text{otherwise} \end{cases} \end{aligned}$$

Using the above we can implement the system with the following block diagram.

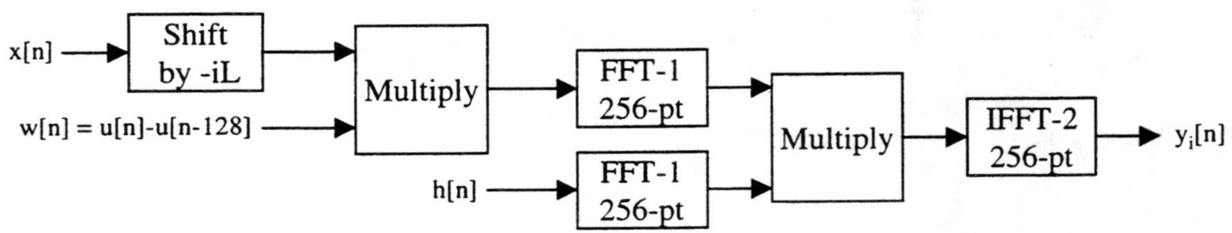

The FFT size was chosen as the next power of 2 higher than the length of the linear convolution. This insures the circular convolution implied by multiplying DFTs corresponds to linear convolution as well.

$$\begin{aligned} N_{\text{Conv}} &= N_{x_i} + N_{\text{h}} - 1 \\ &= 128 + 64 - 1 \\ &= 191 \end{aligned}$$

$$N_{\text{FFT}} = 256$$

9.36. (a) The flow graph of a decimation-in-frequency radix-2 FFT algorithm for N = 16 is shown below.

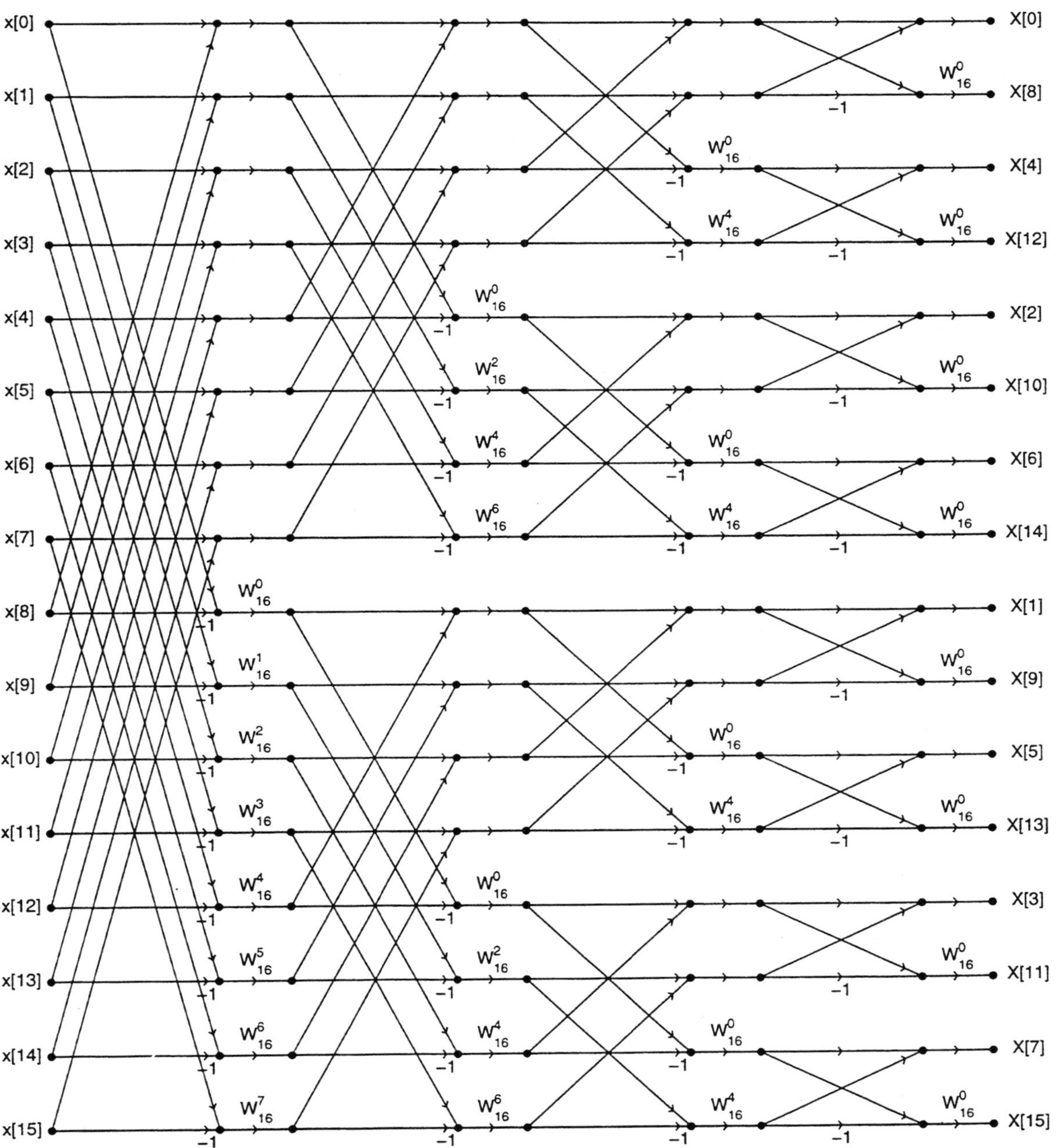

(b) The pruned flow graph is shown below.

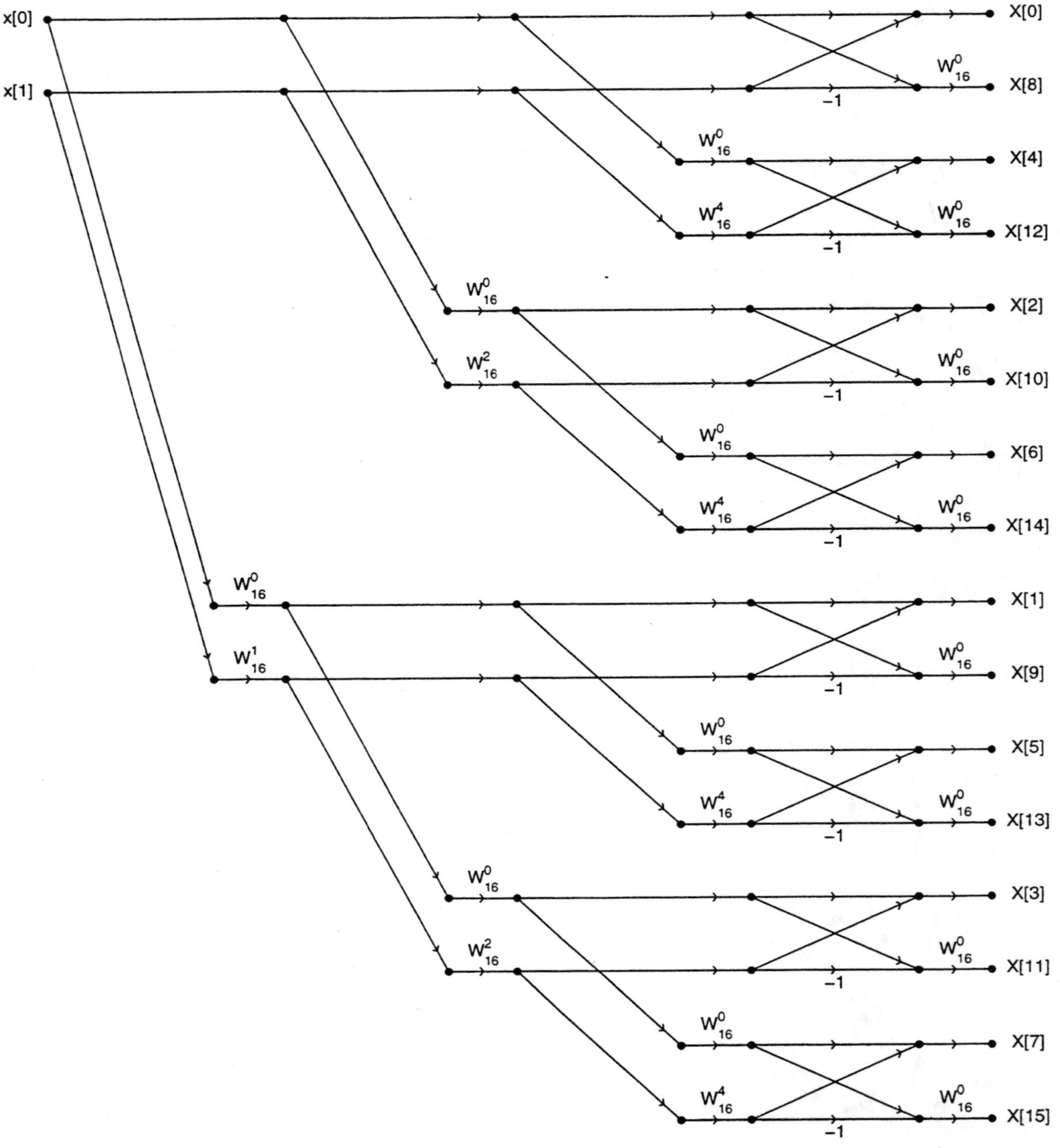

(c) The pruned butterflies can be used in $(\nu - \mu)$ stages. For simplicity, assume that $N/2$ complex multiplies are required in each unpruned stage. Counting all W_N^k terms gives

$$\begin{aligned}\text{Number of multiplications} &= (\text{Unpruned multiplications}) + (\text{Pruned multiplications}) \\ &= \mu \cdot \frac{N}{2} + \sum_{k=1}^{\nu-\mu} 2^k\end{aligned}$$

$$\begin{aligned} &= \mu \cdot \frac{2^\nu}{2} + \sum_{k=0}^{\nu-\mu} 2^k - 1 \\ &= \mu \cdot 2^{\nu-1} + \frac{1 - 2^{\nu-\mu+1}}{1-2} - 1 \\ &= \mu \cdot 2^{\nu-1} + 2^{\nu-\mu+1} - 2 \end{aligned}$$

9.37. (a) Starting with the equation

$$f[n] = x[2n+1] - x[2n-1] + Q, \quad n = 0, 1, \ldots, \frac{N}{2} - 1,$$

where

$$Q = \frac{2}{N} \sum_{n=0}^{\frac{N}{2}-1} x[2n+1],$$

we note that $x[2n+1] = h[n]$, and $x[2n-1] = h[n-1]$ for $n = 0, 1, \ldots, \frac{N}{2} - 1$. We then get

$$f[n] = h[n] - h[n-1] + Q, \quad n = 0, 1, \ldots, \frac{N}{2} - 1.$$

Taking the $N/2$ point DFT of both sides gives

$$\begin{aligned} F[k] &= H[k] - W_{N/2}^k H[k] + Q \sum_{n=0}^{\frac{N}{2}-1} W_{N/2}^{kn} \\ &= H[k](1 - W_N^{2k}) + \frac{N}{2} Q\delta[k] \end{aligned}$$

So

$$\begin{aligned} F[0] &= \frac{N}{2} Q \\ &= \frac{N}{2} \frac{2}{N} \sum_{n=0}^{\frac{N}{2}-1} x[2n+1] \\ &= \sum_{n=0}^{\frac{N}{2}-1} x[2n+1] \\ &= H[0] \end{aligned}$$

Therefore,

$$\begin{aligned} X[k] &= G[k] + W_N^k H[k] \\ X[0] &= G[0] + H[0] = G[0] + F[0] \\ X[N/2] &= G[N/2] + W_N^{N/2} H[N/2] \\ &= G[0] + W_N^{N/2} H[0] \\ &= G[0] - H[0] = G[0] - F[0] \end{aligned}$$

(b) The equation,

$$F[k] = H[k](1 - W_N^{2k}) + \frac{N}{2} Q\delta[k]$$

for $k \neq 0$ becomes

$$\begin{aligned} F[k] &= H[k](1 - W_N^{2k}) \\ &= H[k] W_N^k (W_N^{-k} - W_N^k) \end{aligned}$$

So

$$H[k] = \frac{F[k]}{W_N^k(W_N^{-k} - W_N^k)}$$

Therefore,

$$\begin{aligned} X[k] &= G[k] + W_N^k H[k] \\ &= G[k] + \frac{F[k]}{W_N^{-k} - W_N^k} \\ &= G[k] - \frac{j}{2}\frac{F[k]}{\sin(2\pi k/N)} \end{aligned}$$

Clearly, we need to compute $X[0]$ and $X[N/2]$ with a separate formula since the $\sin(2\pi k/N) = 0$ for $k = 0$ and $k = N/2$.

(c) For each stage of the FFT, the equations

$$\begin{aligned} X[0] &= G[0] + F[0] \\ X[N/2] &= G[0] - F[0] \end{aligned}$$

require 2 real additions each, since the values $G[0]$ and $F[0]$ may be complex. We therefore require a total of 4 real additions to implement these two equations per stage.

For a single stage, the equation

$$X[k] = G[k] - \frac{1}{2}j\frac{F[k]}{\sin(2\pi k/N)} \quad k \neq 0, N/2$$

requires $(N-2)/2$ multiplications of the purely imaginary "twiddle factor" terms by the complex coefficents of $F[k]$ for $k \neq 0, N/2$. The number of multiplications were halved using the symmetry $\sin(2\pi(k + N/2)/N) = -\sin(2\pi k/N)$ and the fact that $F[k]$ is periodic with period $N/2$. Since multiplying a complex number by a purely imaginary number takes 2 real multiplies, we see that the equation requires a total of $(N-2)$ real multiplies per stage.

We also need $(N-2)$ complex additions to add the $G[k]$ and modified $F[k]$ terms for $k \neq 0, N/2$. Since a complex addition requires two real additions, we see that the equation takes a total of $2(N-2)$ real additions per stage.

Putting this all together with the fact that there are $\log_2 N$ stages gives us the totals

$$\begin{aligned} \text{Real Multiplications} &= (N-2)\log_2 N \\ \text{Real Additions} &= 2N\log_2 N \end{aligned}$$

Note that this is approximately half the computation of that of the standard FFT.

(d) The division by $\sin(2\pi k/N)$ for k near 0 and $N/2$ can cause $X[k]$ to get quite large at these values of k. Imagine a signal $x_1[n]$, and signal $x_2[n]$ formed from $x_1[n]$ by adding a small amount of white noise. Using this FFT algorithm, the two FFTs $X_1[k]$ and $X_2[k]$ can vary greatly at such values of k.

9.38. (a)

$$\begin{aligned} X[2k] &= \sum_{n=0}^{N-1} x[n]W_N^{2kn} \\ &= \sum_{n=0}^{(N/2)-1} \left(x[n]W_N^{2kn} + x[n+(N/2)]W_N^{2k(n+(N/2))}\right) \\ &= \sum_{n=0}^{(N/2)-1} \left(x[n] + x[n+(N/2)]\right) W_N^{2kn} \end{aligned}$$

In the derivation above, we used the fact that $W_N^{kN} = 1$. Since $W_N^{2kn} = W_{N/2}^{kn}$, $X[2k]$ has been expressed as an $N/2$ point DFT of the sequence $x[n] + x[n + (N/2)]$, $n = 0, 1, \ldots, (N/2) - 1$.

(b)

$$\begin{aligned}
X[4k+1] &= \sum_{n=0}^{N-1} x[n] W_N^{(4k+1)n} \\
&= \sum_{n=0}^{(N/4)-1} \Big(x[n] W_N^n W_N^{4kn} + x[n + (N/4)] W_N^{n+(N/4)} W_N^{4k(n+(N/4))} \\
&\quad + x[n + (N/2)] W_N^{n+(N/2)} W_N^{4k(n+(N/2))} + x[n + (3N/4)] W_N^{n+(3N/4)} W_N^{4k(n+(3N/4))} \Big) \\
&= \sum_{n=0}^{(N/4)-1} \{(x[n] - x[n + (N/2)]) - j(x[n + (N/4)] - x[n + (3N/4)])\} W_N^n W_N^{4kn}
\end{aligned}$$

In the derivation above, we used the fact that $W_N^{N/4} = -j$, $W_N^{3N/4} = j$, $W_N^{N/2} = -1$, and $W_N^{kN} = 1$. Since $W_N^{4kn} = W_{N/4}^{kn}$, $X[4k+1]$ has been expressed as a $N/4$ point DFT. But we need to multiply the sequence $(x[n] - x[n + (N/2)]) - j(x[n + (N/4)] - x[n + (3N/4)])$ by the twiddle factor W_N^n, $0 \le n \le (N/4) - 1$ *before* we compute the $N/4$ point DFT.

The other odd-indexed terms can be shown in the same way to be

$$\begin{aligned}
X[4k+3] &= \sum_{n=0}^{(N/4)-1} \{(x[n] - x[n + (N/2)]) \\
&\quad + j(x[n + (N/4)] - x[n + (3N/4)])\} W_N^{3n} W_N^{4kn}, \quad k = 0, 1, \ldots, (N/4) - 1.
\end{aligned}$$

Parts (a) and (b) show that we can replace the computation of an N point DFT with the computation of one $N/2$ point DFT, two $N/4$ point DFTs, and some extra complex arithmetic.

(c) Assume $N = 16$ and define

$$\begin{aligned}
g[n] &= x[n] + x[n + (N/2)], \quad n = 0, 1, \ldots, (N/2) - 1 \\
f_1[n] &= x[n] - x[n + (N/2)], \quad n = 0, 1, \ldots, (N/4) - 1 \\
f_2[n] &= x[n + (N/4)] - x[n + (3N/4)], \quad n = 0, 1, \ldots, (N/4) - 1
\end{aligned}$$

A diagram for computing the values of $X[k]$ looks like:

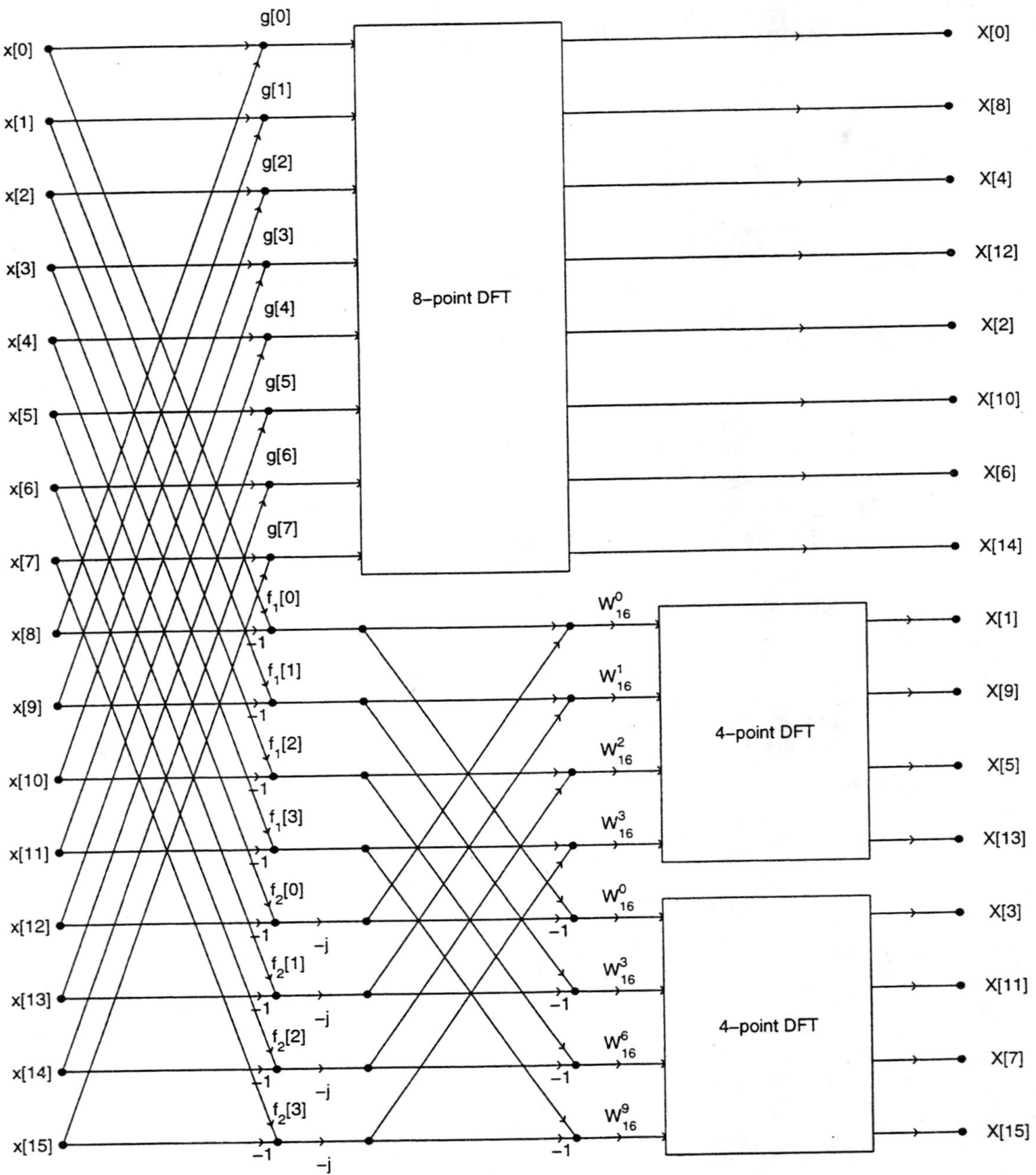

If we carry on applying the split-radix principle, we get the next diagram:

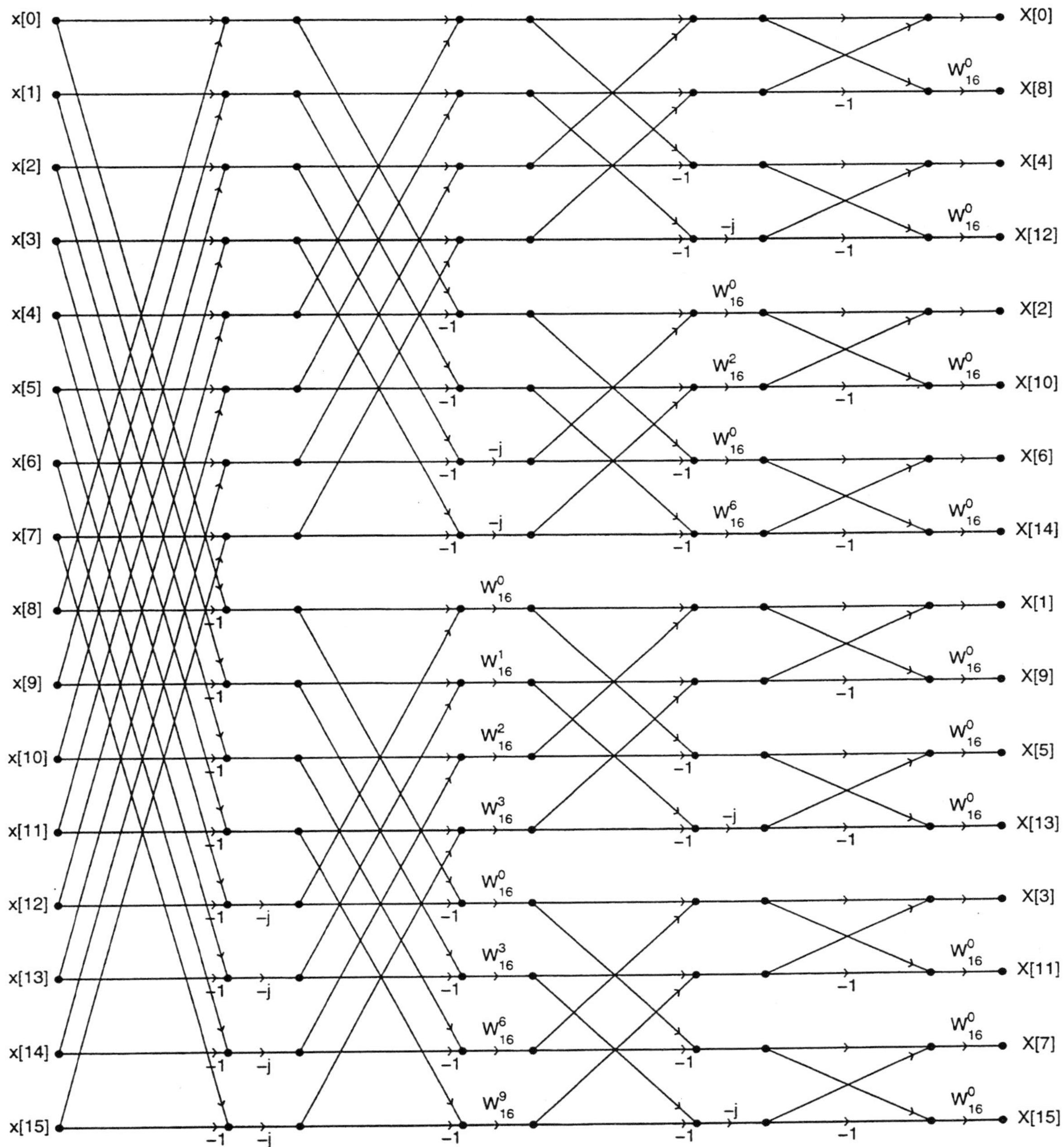

(d) The flow diagram for the regular radix-2 decimation-in-frequency algorithm is shown in the next figure for $N = 16$. Not counting trivial multiplications by W_N^0, we find that there are 17 complex multiplications total. Of these 17 complex multiplications, 7 are multiplications by $W_{16}^4 = -j$. Since a multiplication by $-j$ can be done with zero real multiplications, and a complex multiplication requires 4 real multiplications, we find that the total number of real multiplications for the decimation-in-frequency algorithm to be $(10)(4) = 40$.

Taking a look at the split-radix algorithm, we find again that there are 17 complex multiplications.

In this case, however, 9 of these are by $W_{16}^4 = -j$. Thus, it takes a total of $(8)(4) = 32$ real multiplications to implement this flow graph.

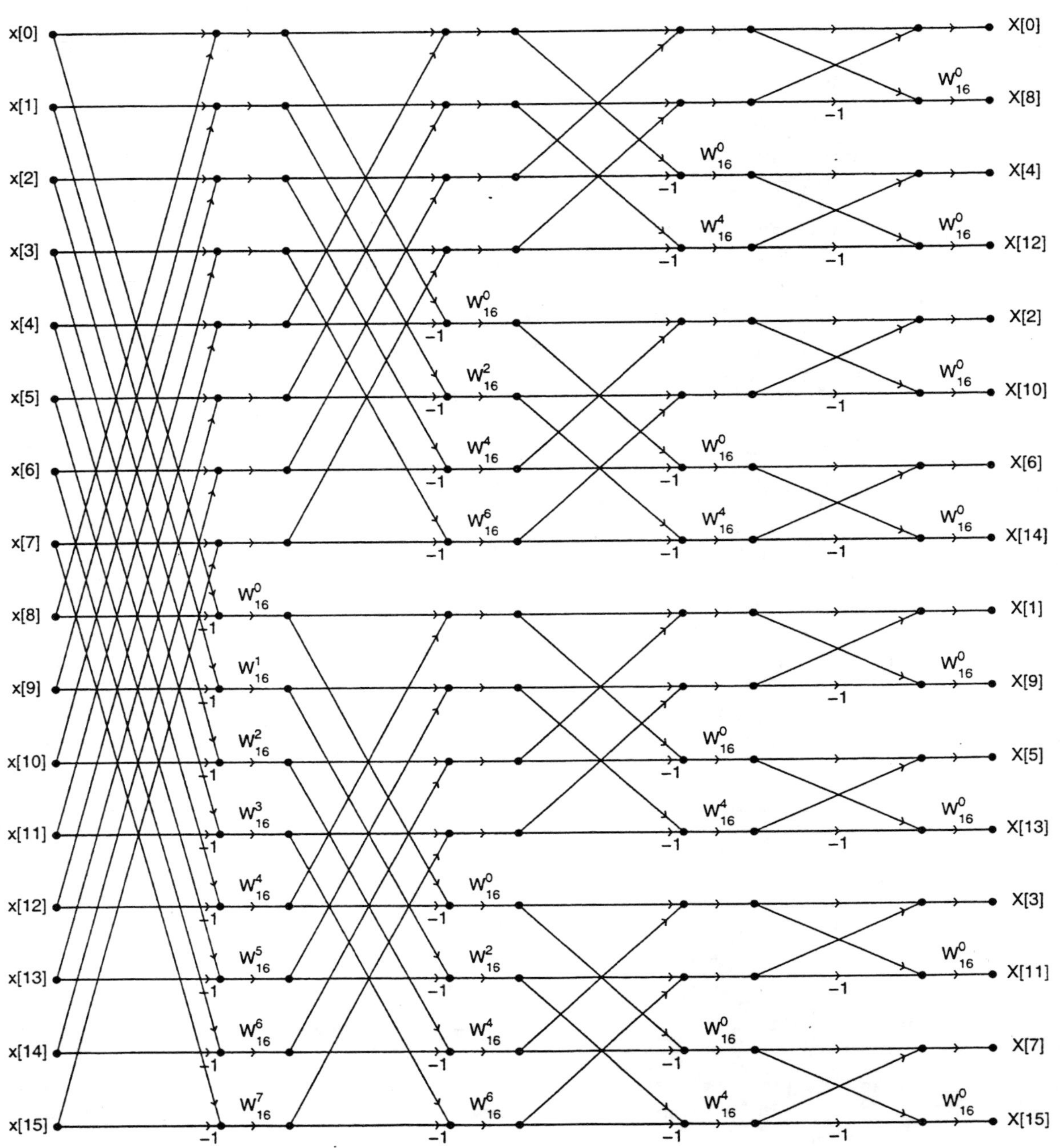

9.39. (a) Noting that

$$\arctan(x) = x - \frac{x^3}{3} + \frac{x^5}{5} - \frac{x^7}{7} + \ldots \qquad |x| < 1$$

$$\theta_i = \arctan(2^{-i}) = 2^{-i} - \frac{2^{-3i}}{3} + \frac{2^{-5i}}{5} - \frac{2^{-7i}}{7} + \ldots$$

we notice that, to first order, the θ_i and θ_{i+1} differ by a factor of 2. (Note that these formulae are in radians). This approximate factor of 2 for sucessive θ_i is confirmed by looking at some values of θ_i: $\theta_0 = 45°$, $\theta_1 = 26.6°$, $\theta_2 = 14.0°$, $\theta_3 = 7.1°$. So we have a set of angles whose values are decreasing by about a factor of 2.

You can add and subtract these θ_i angles to form any angle $0 < \theta < \pi/2$. The error is bound by $\theta_M = \arctan(2^{-M})$, the angle that would be included next in the sum. If the error were greater than θ_M, then one of the α_i terms must have been incorrect. The inclusion of the Mth term must bring the sum closer to θ.

(b) An algorithm to compute θ_i is described below.

$\alpha_0 = +1$
$\hat{\theta} = \alpha_0\theta_0$
for $i = 1$ to $M - 1$
  if $(\hat{\theta} > \theta)$
    $\alpha_i = -1$
  else
    $\alpha_i = +1$
  endif
  $\hat{\theta} = \alpha_i\theta_i + \hat{\theta}$
end for

Using this algorithm, the sequence α_i is found to be

i	0	1	2	3	4	5	6	7	8	9	10
α_i	1	-1	1	1	-1	-1	1	1	-1	-1	-1

(c) Note that $(X + jY)(1 + j\alpha_i 2^{-i}) = (X - \alpha_i Y 2^{-i}) + j(Y + \alpha_i X 2^{-i})$. Hence, the recursion is simply multiplying by M complex numbers of the form $(1 + j\alpha_i 2^{-i})$. These can be represented in polar form:

$$\begin{aligned}(1 + j\alpha_i 2^{-i}) &= \sqrt{1 + 2^{-2i}}e^{j\alpha_i \arctan(2^{-i})} \\ &= G_i e^{j\alpha_i\theta_i}\end{aligned}$$

Multiplication of polar numbers produces a sum of the phases, $\alpha_i\theta_i$.

$$\hat{\theta} = \sum_{i=0}^{M-1} \alpha_i\theta_i$$

(d) Multiplication of polar numbers produces a product of the magnitudes, G_i.

$$G_M = \prod_{i=0}^{M-1} \sqrt{1 + 2^{-2i}}$$

9.40. (a) Starting with the definition of the DFT,

$$X[k] = \sum_{n=0}^{N-1} x[n]W_N^{nk}$$

$$\begin{aligned}
X[3k] &= \sum_{n=0}^{N-1} x[n]W_N^{3nk} \\
&= \sum_{n=0}^{N/3-1} x[n]W_N^{3nk} + \sum_{n=N/3}^{2N/3-1} x[n]W_N^{3nk} + \sum_{n=2N/3}^{N-1} x[n]W_N^{3nk}
\end{aligned}$$

Substituting $m = n - N/3$ into the second summation, and $m = n - 2N/3$ into the third summation gives

$$\begin{aligned}
X[3k] &= \sum_{n=0}^{N/3-1} x[n]W_N^{3nk} + \sum_{m=0}^{N/3-1} x[m+N/3]W_N^{3mk}W_N^{Nk} + \sum_{m=0}^{N/3-1} x[m+2N/3]W_N^{3mk}W_N^{2Nk} \\
&= \sum_{n=0}^{N/3-1} (x[n] + x[n+N/3] + x[n+2N/3])W_N^{3nk} \\
&= \sum_{n=0}^{N/3-1} (x[n] + x[n+N/3] + x[n+2N/3])W_{N/3}^{nk}
\end{aligned}$$

Define the sequence

$$x_1[n] = x[n] + x[n+N/3] + x[n+2N/3]$$

The 3-point DFT of $x_1[n]$ is $X_1[k] = X[3k]$.

(b) This part is similar to part (a). First, $x_2[n]$ is found. Starting again with the definition of the DFT,

$$\begin{aligned}
X[k] &= \sum_{n=0}^{N-1} x[n]W_N^{nk} \\
X[3k+1] &= \sum_{n=0}^{N-1} x[n]W_N^{n(3k+1)} \\
&= \sum_{n=0}^{N/3-1} x[n]W_N^{n(3k+1)} + \sum_{n=N/3}^{2N/3-1} x[n]W_N^{n(3k+1)} + \sum_{n=2N/3}^{N-1} x[n]W_N^{n(3k+1)}
\end{aligned}$$

Substituting $m = n - N/3$ into the second summation, and $m = n - 2N/3$ into the third summation gives

$$\begin{aligned}
X[3k+1] &= \sum_{n=0}^{N/3-1} x[n]W_N^{n(3k+1)} + \sum_{m=0}^{N/3-1} x[m+N/3]W_N^{(m+N/3)(3k+1)} \\
&\quad + \sum_{m=0}^{N/3-1} x[m+2N/3]W_N^{(m+2N/3)(3k+1)} \\
&= \sum_{n=0}^{N/3-1} x[n]W_N^{n(3k+1)} + \sum_{m=0}^{N/3-1} x[m+N/3]W_N^{m(3k+1)}W_N^{Nk}W_N^{N/3} \\
&\quad + \sum_{m=0}^{N/3-1} x[m+2N/3]W_N^{m(3k+1)}W_N^{2Nk}W_N^{2N/3} \\
&= \sum_{n=0}^{N/3-1} (x[n] + x[n+N/3]W_N^{N/3} + x[n+2N/3]W_N^{2N/3})W_N^{n(3k+1)}
\end{aligned}$$

$$= \sum_{n=0}^{N/3-1} (x[n] + x[n+N/3]W_N^{N/3} + x[n+2N/3]W_N^{2N/3})W_N^n W_{N/3}^{kn}$$

Define the sequence

$$x_2[n] = (x[n] + x[n+N/3]W_N^{N/3} + x[n+2N/3]W_N^{2N/3})W_N^n$$

The 3-point DFT of $x_2[n]$ is $X_2[k] = X[3k+1]$. Next, $x_3[n]$ is found in a similar manner. Starting with the definition of the DFT,

$$\begin{aligned}
X[k] &= \sum_{n=0}^{N-1} x[n]W_N^{nk} \\
X[3k+2] &= \sum_{n=0}^{N-1} x[n]W_N^{n(3k+2)} \\
&= \sum_{n=0}^{N/3-1} x[n]W_N^{n(3k+2)} + \sum_{n=N/3}^{2N/3-1} x[n]W_N^{n(3k+2)} + \sum_{n=2N/3}^{N-1} x[n]W_N^{n(3k+2)}
\end{aligned}$$

Substituting $m = n - N/3$ into the second summation, and $m = n - 2N/3$ into the third summation gives

$$\begin{aligned}
X[3k+2] &= \sum_{n=0}^{N/3-1} x[n]W_N^{n(3k+2)} + \sum_{m=0}^{N/3-1} x[m+N/3]W_N^{(m+N/3)(3k+2)} \\
&\quad + \sum_{m=0}^{N/3-1} x[m+2N/3]W_N^{(m+2N/3)(3k+2)} \\
&= \sum_{n=0}^{N/3-1} x[n]W_N^{n(3k+2)} + \sum_{m=0}^{N/3-1} x[m+N/3]W_N^{m(3k+2)}W_N^{Nk}W_N^{2N/3} \\
&\quad + \sum_{m=0}^{N/3-1} x[m+2N/3]W_N^{m(3k+2)}W_N^{2Nk}W_N^{4N/3} \\
&= \sum_{n=0}^{N/3-1} (x[n] + x[n+N/3]W_N^{2N/3} + x[n+2N/3]W_N^{4N/3})W_N^{n(3k+2)} \\
&= \sum_{n=0}^{N/3-1} (x[n] + x[n+N/3]W_N^{2N/3} + x[n+2N/3]W_N^{4N/3})W_N^{2n}W_{N/3}^{kn}
\end{aligned}$$

Define the sequence

$$x_3[n] = (x[n] + x[n+N/3]W_N^{2N/3} + x[n+2N/3]W_N^{4N/3})W_N^{2n}$$

The 3-point DFT of $x_3[n]$ is $X_3[k] = X[3k+2]$.

(c) To draw the radix-3 butterfly, it helps to derive the output of the butterfly first. From the definition of the DFT,

$$\begin{aligned}
X[k] &= \sum_{n=0}^{2} x[n]W_3^{nk} \\
X[0] &= x[0] + x[1] + x[2] \\
X[1] &= x[0] + x[1]W_3^1 + x[2]W_3^2 \\
X[2] &= x[0] + x[1]W_3^2 + x[2]W_3^4 = x[0] + x[1]W_3^2 + x[2]W_3^1
\end{aligned}$$

The butterfly for the 3 point DFT is drawn below.

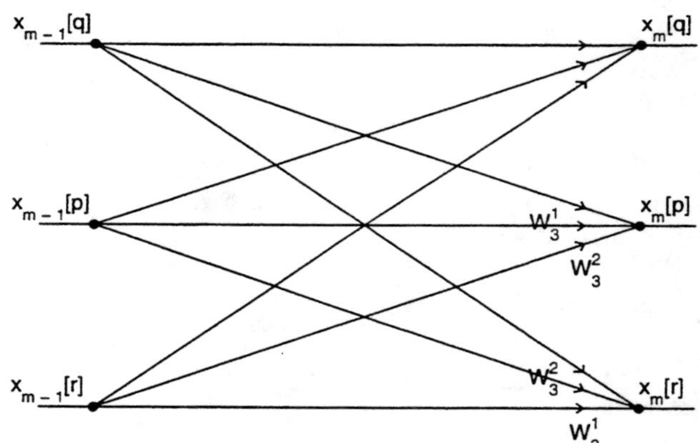

(d) Using the results from parts (a) and (b), the flow graph is drawn below.

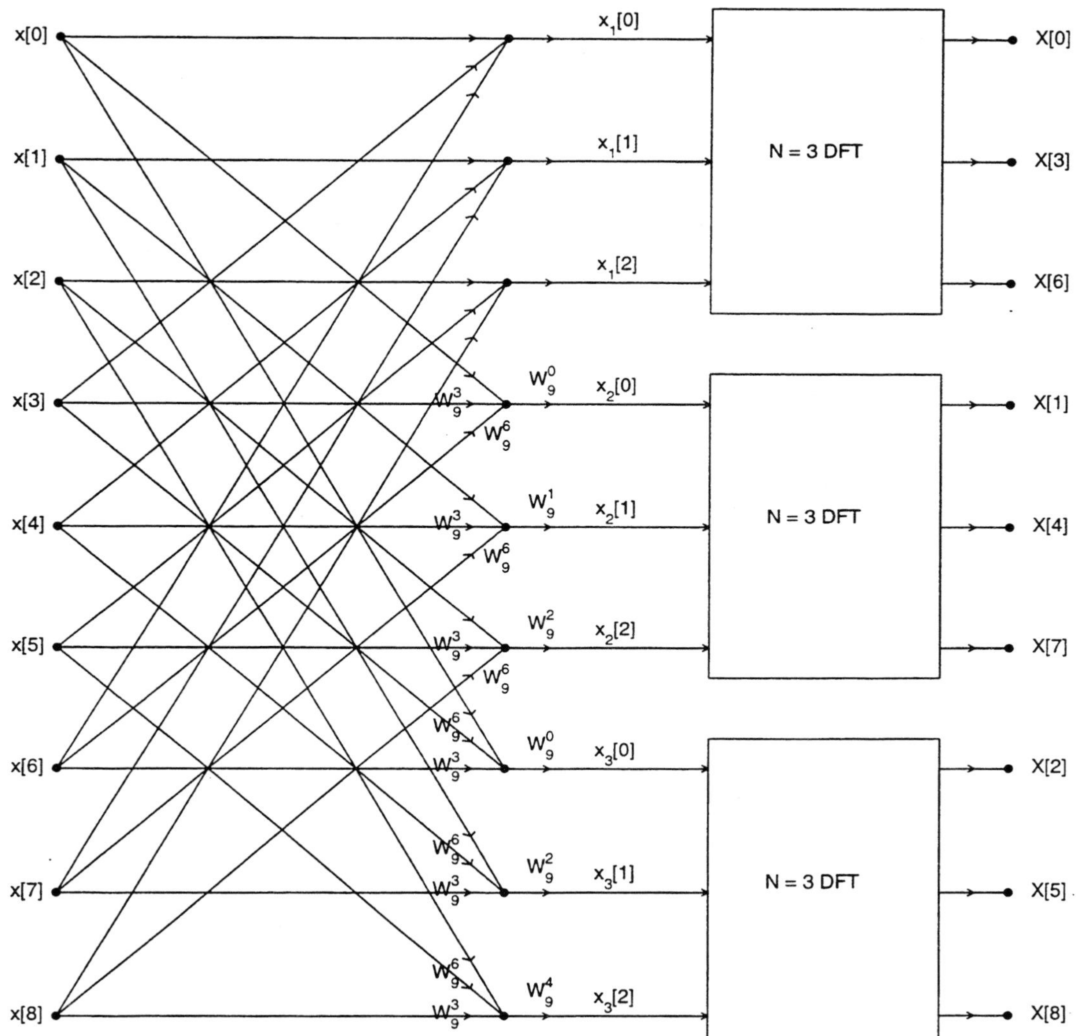

(e) The system consisting entirely of $N = 3$ DFTs is drawn below.

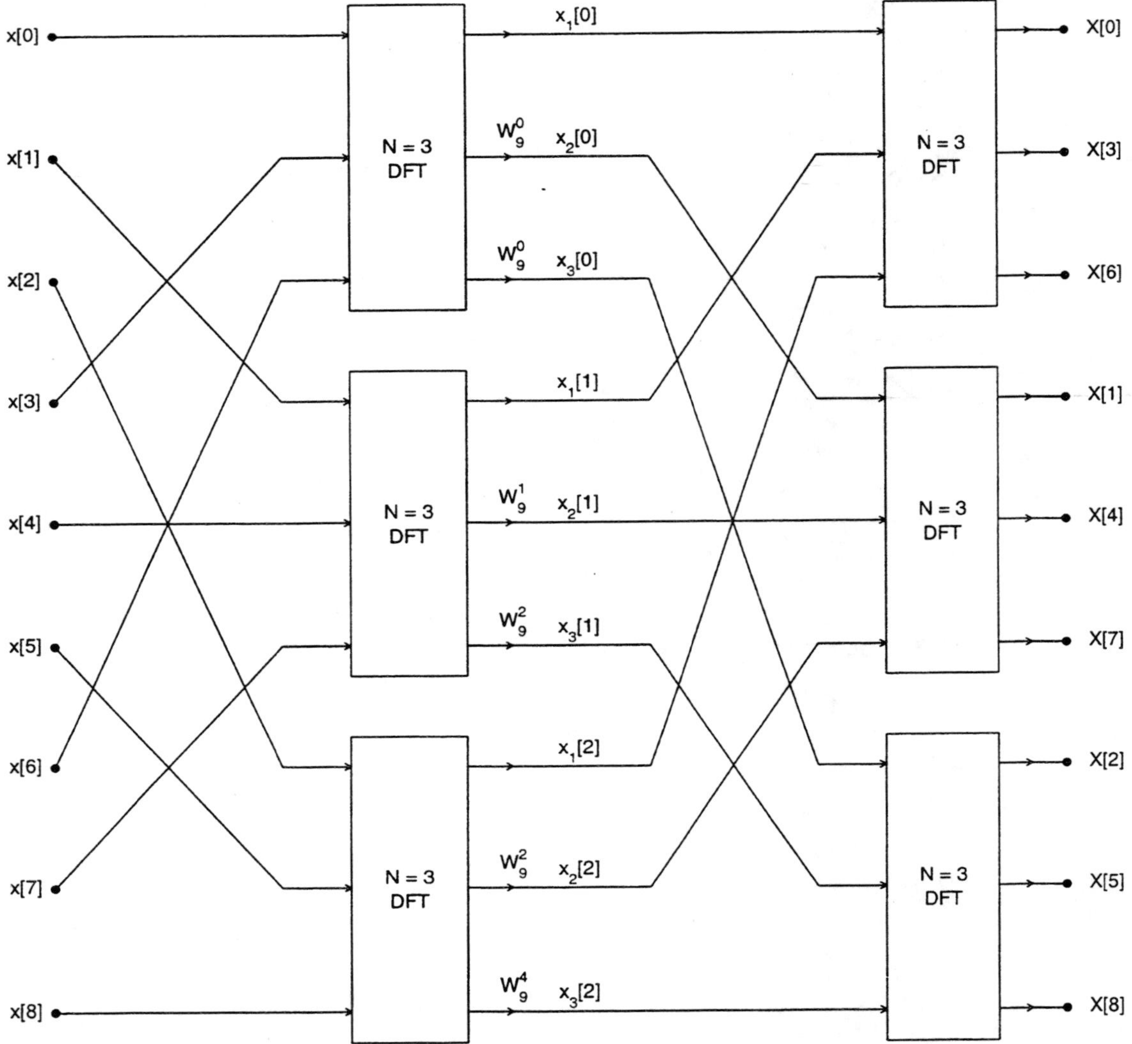

(f) A direct implementation of the 9 point DFT equation requires $9^2 = 81$ complex multiplications. The system in part (e), in constrast, requires 4 complex multiplications for each 3 point DFT, and an additional 4 from the twiddle factors, if we do not count the trival W_N^0 multiplications. In total, the system in part (e) requires 28 complex multiplications. In general, a radix-3 FFT of a sequence of length $N = 3^\nu$ requires *approximately*

$$\text{Number of complex multiplications} = \left(4\frac{\text{complex multiplications}}{\text{3-pt DFT}}\right)\left(\frac{N}{3}\frac{\text{3-pt DFTs}}{\text{stage}}\right)(\nu \text{ stages}) + \left(\frac{\text{N twiddle factors}}{\text{stage with twiddle factors}}\right)(\nu - 1 \text{ stages with twiddle factors})$$

Replacing ν with $\log_3 N$, and simplifying this formula gives

$$\text{Number of complex multiplications} = \frac{7}{3} N \log_3 N - N$$

Note that this formula for a radix-3 FFT is of the form $N \log_3 N$. The constant multiplier, $\frac{7}{3}$, is significantly larger than that of a radix-2 FFT. This is because a radix-2 butterfly has no complex multiplications, while in part (c) we found that a radix-3 butterfly has 4 complex multiplications. Also note that this formula is an upper bound, since some of the N twiddle factors in the $\nu - 1$ stages will be trivial. However, the formula is a good estimate.

9.41. (a)

$$\begin{aligned} X[k] &= h^*[k] \sum_{n=0}^{N-1} (x[n]h^*[n])h[k-n] \\ &= e^{-j\pi k^2/N} \sum_{n=0}^{N-1} x[n] e^{-j\pi n^2/N} e^{j\pi(k^2-2kn+n^2)/N} \\ &= \sum_{n=0}^{N-1} x[n] e^{-j2\pi nk/N} \end{aligned}$$

(b)

$$X[k+N] = h^*[k+N] \sum_{n=0}^{N-1} x[n]h^*[n]h[k+N-n]$$

$$\begin{aligned} h^*[k+N] &= e^{-j\pi(k+N)^2/N} \\ &= e^{-j\pi(k^2+2kN+N^2)/N} \\ &= e^{-j\pi k^2/N} e^{-j\pi N} \\ &= h^*[k] e^{-j\pi N} \end{aligned}$$

So

$$\begin{aligned} X[k+N] &= h^*[k] e^{-j\pi N} \sum_{n=0}^{N-1} x[n]h^*[n]h[k-n] e^{j\pi N} \\ &= X[k] \end{aligned}$$

(c) From the figure

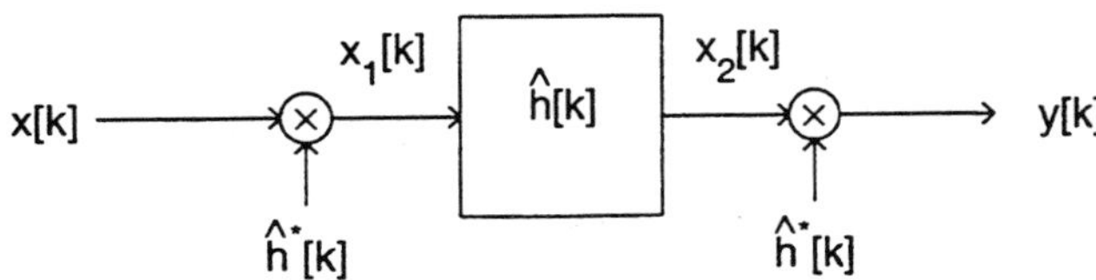

we define the signals $x_1[k]$ and $x_2[k]$ to be

$$x_1[k] = x[k]\hat{h}^*[k]$$

$$
\begin{aligned}
x_2[k] &= \sum_{\ell=-\infty}^{\infty} x_1[\ell]\hat{h}[k-\ell] \\
&= \sum_{\ell=0}^{N-1} x[\ell]e^{-j\pi\ell^2/N}e^{j\pi(k-\ell)^2/N} \\
&\quad k \in [0,\ldots,2N-1]
\end{aligned}
$$

Therefore,

$$
\begin{aligned}
y[k] &= \hat{h}^*[k]x_2[k] \qquad k \in [N,\ldots,2N-1] \\
&= e^{-j\pi k^2/N}\sum_{\ell=0}^{N-1} x[\ell]e^{-j\pi\ell^2/N}e^{j\pi(k-\ell)^2/N} \qquad k \in [N,\ldots,2N-1] \\
&= \sum_{\ell=0}^{N-1} x[\ell]e^{-j2\pi k\ell/N} \qquad k \in [N,\ldots,2N-1] \\
&= X[k+N] \qquad k \in [0,\ldots,N-1] \\
&= X[k]
\end{aligned}
$$

(d)

$$
\begin{aligned}
\hat{H}(z) &= \sum_{k=0}^{2N-1} e^{j\pi k^2/N}z^{-k} \\
&= \sum_{r=0}^{M-1}\sum_{\ell=0}^{2M-1} e^{j\pi(r+\ell M)^2/N}z^{-(r+\ell M)} \\
&= \sum_{r=0}^{M-1}\sum_{\ell=0}^{2M-1} e^{j\pi r^2/N}e^{j2\pi r\ell/M}e^{j\pi\ell^2}z^{-r}z^{-\ell M} \\
&= \sum_{r=0}^{M-1} e^{j\pi r^2/N}z^{-r}\left[\sum_{\ell=0}^{2M-1}(e^{j2\pi r/M}z^{-M})^{\ell}(-1)^{\ell^2}\right] \\
&= \sum_{r=0}^{M-1} e^{j\pi r^2/N}z^{-r}\left[\sum_{\ell=0}^{2M-1}(e^{j2\pi r/M}z^{-M})^{\ell}(-1)^{\ell}\right] \\
&= \sum_{r=0}^{M-1} e^{j\pi r^2/N}z^{-r}\left[\sum_{\ell=0}^{2M-1}(-e^{j2\pi r/M}z^{-M})^{\ell}\right] \\
&= \sum_{r=0}^{M-1} e^{j\pi r^2/N}z^{-r}\left[\frac{1-e^{j2\pi r(2M)/M}z^{-2M^2}}{1+e^{j2\pi r/M}z^{-M}}\right] \\
&= \sum_{r=0}^{M-1} e^{j\pi r^2/N}z^{-r}\left[\frac{1-z^{-2M^2}}{1+e^{j(2\pi/M)r}z^{-M}}\right]
\end{aligned}
$$

(e) The flow graph for the system,

$$
\hat{H}(z) = (1-z^{-2M^2})\sum_{r=0}^{M-1}\frac{z^{-r}e^{j\pi r^2/M}}{1+e^{j2\pi r/M}z^{-M}}
$$

is drawn below.

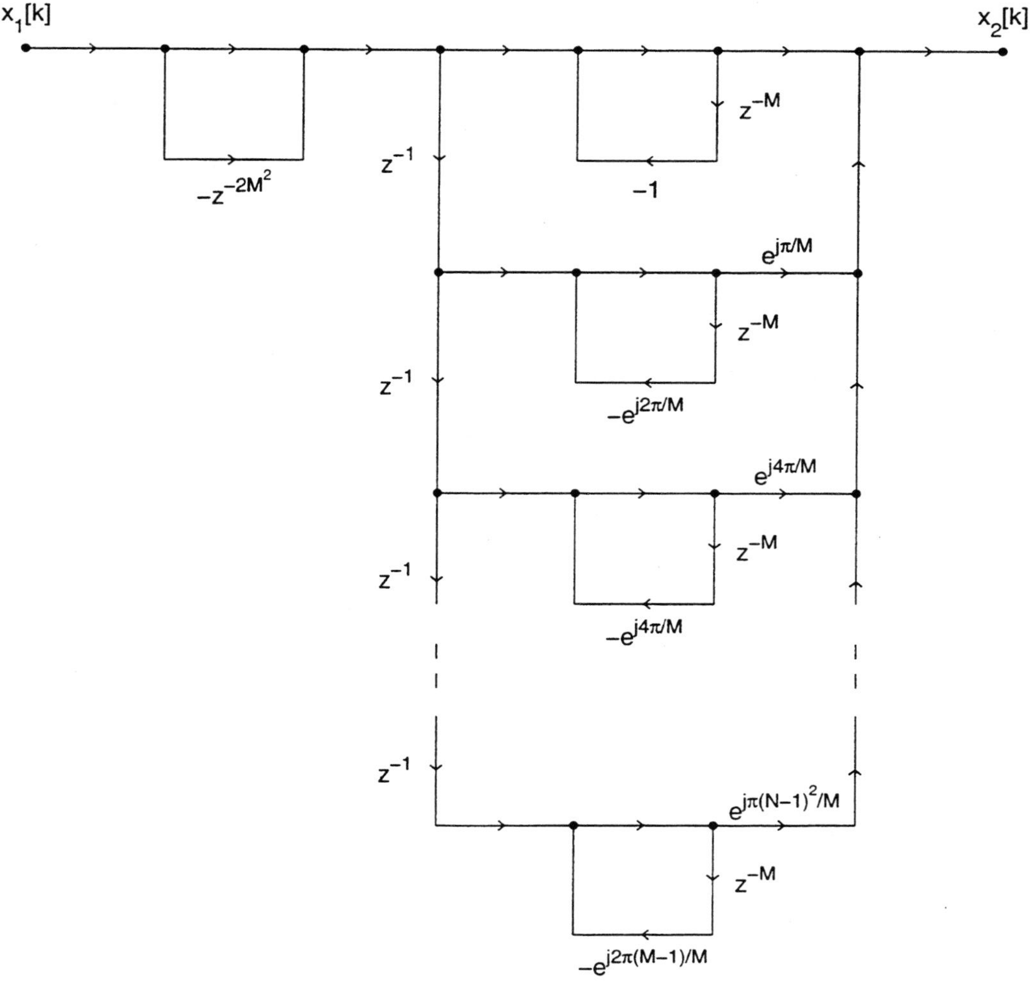

(f) **Complex multiplications:** Since we are only interested in $y[k]$ for $k = N, N+1, \ldots, 2N-1$ we do not need to calculate the complex multiplications on the output side of each parallel branch until $k \geq N$. Thus,

Operation	Complex Multiplications
$x_1[k] = x[k]\hat{h}^*[k]$	N
Poles of $\hat{H}(z)$ for $k = 0, \ldots, N-1$	NM
Poles and branch exponentials of $\hat{H}(z)$ for $k = N, \ldots, 2N-1$	$2NM$
$y[k] = x_2[k]\hat{h}^*[k]$	N

$$= 3MN + 2N$$
$$= 3M^3 + 2M^2$$

We are including the multiplication of -1 and 1 from the first branch here for simplicity. Direct evaluation requires $N^2 = M^4$ complex multiplications.
Note that since we are only interested in $y[k]$ for $k = N, N+1, \ldots, 2N-1$, the initial delay of $2M^2$ is unneccessary; we have obtained all interesting output before the first delayed sample appears.

Complex additions: The complex additions on the output side of each parallel branch do not need to be computed until $k \geq N$. Thus,

Operation	Complex Additions
Poles of $\hat{H}(z)$ for $k = 0, \ldots, N-1$	NM
Poles and branch exponentials of $\hat{H}(z)$ for $k = N, \ldots, 2N-1$	$2NM$
	$= 3MN$
	$= 3M^3$

Direct evaluation requires $N(N-1) = M^2(M^2-1)$ complex additions.

9.42. (a) We separate the system function $H(z)$ into two pieces; one corresponding to $h_R[n] = Re\{h[n]\}$ and another corresponding to $h_I[n] = Im\{h[n]\}$.

$$\begin{aligned} H(z) &= \frac{1 - W_N^k z^{-1}}{1 - 2\cos(2\pi k/N)z^{-1} + z^{-2}} \\ H_R(z) &= \frac{1 - \cos(2\pi k/N)z^{-1}}{1 - 2\cos(2\pi k/N)z^{-1} + z^{-2}} \\ h_R[n] &= \cos(2\pi kn/N)u[n] \\ H_I(z) &= \frac{\sin(2\pi k/N)z^{-1}}{1 - 2\cos(2\pi k/N)z^{-1} + z^{-2}} \\ h_I[n] &= \sin(2\pi kn/N)u[n] \end{aligned}$$

Since $x[n]$ is real, the real and imaginary parts of $X[k] = y_k[N]$ are computed using the following flowgraph.

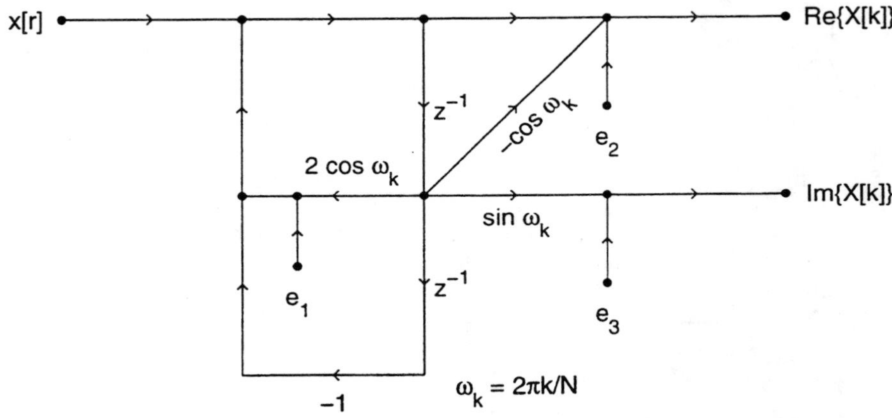

(b)

$$\begin{aligned} \text{Re}\{X[k]\} &= \text{Re}\{y_k[N]\} \\ \text{Im}\{X[k]\} &= \text{Im}\{y_k[N]\} \end{aligned}$$

Since the output of interest is the Nth sample, we need only consider the variance at time N. The noise $e_1[n]$ is input to both $h_R[n]$ and $h_I[n]$. Using the techniques from chapter 6, we find the variance of the noise is

$$\sigma_R^2[N] = \sigma_{e_2}^2 + \sigma_{e_1}^2 \sum_{n=0}^{N} h_R^2[n]$$

$$\sigma_I^2[N] = \sigma_{e_3}^2 + \sigma_{e_1}^2 \sum_{n=0}^{N} h_I^2[n].$$

Let $\theta = 2\pi k/N$.

$$\begin{aligned}
\sum_{n=0}^{N} h_R^2[n] &= \sum_{n=0}^{N} \cos^2 \theta n \\
&= \frac{1}{4}\sum_{n=0}^{N}(e^{j\theta n} + e^{-j\theta n})^2 \\
&= \frac{1}{4}\sum_{n=0}^{N}(e^{j\theta 2n} + 2 + e^{-j\theta 2n}) \\
&= \frac{1}{4}\left(\frac{1 - e^{j2\theta(N+1)}}{1 - e^{j2\theta}} + 2(N+1) + \frac{1 - e^{-j2\theta(N+1)}}{1 - e^{-j2\theta}}\right) \\
&= \frac{1}{4}(1 + 2(N+1) + 1) \\
&= \frac{N}{2} + 1
\end{aligned}$$

Similarly, $\sum_{n=0}^{N} h_I^2[n] = N/2$.
Therefore,

$$\begin{aligned}
\sigma_R^2[n] &= \frac{2^{-2B}}{12}(1 + (N/2) + 1) \\
&= \frac{2^{-2B}}{12}(N+4)/2 \\
\sigma_I^2[n] &= \frac{2^{-2B}}{12}(1 + (N/2)) \\
&= \frac{2^{-2B}}{12}(N+2)/2
\end{aligned}$$

9.43.

$$X[k] = \sum_{n=0}^{N-1} x[n]\cos(2\pi kn/N) - j\sum_{n=0}^{N-1} x[n]\sin(2\pi kn/N).$$

For $k \neq 0$, there are $N-1$ multiplies in the computation of the real part and the imaginary part:

$$\sigma_R^2 = (N-1)\sigma^2 = \sigma_I^2,$$

where $\sigma^2 = 2^{-2B}/12$. For $k = 0$ there are no multiplies, and therefore $\sigma_R^2 = 0 = \sigma_I^2$.

$$\sigma_R^2 = \sigma_I^2 = \begin{cases} 0 & k = 0 \\ (N-1)\sigma^2 & k \neq 0 \end{cases}$$

9.44. (a)

$$|X_{m-1}[q]W_N^r| = |X_{m-1}[q]||W_N^r| = |X_{m-1}[q]|$$

$$|X_m[p]| \leq |X_{m-1}[p]| + |X_{m-1}[q]| < \frac{1}{2} + \frac{1}{2} = 1$$

implies that $|\text{Re}\{X_m[p]\}| < 1$ and $|\text{Im}\{X_m[p]\}| < 1$. A similar argument holds for $|X_m[q]|$.

(b) The conditions are not sufficient to guarantee that overflow cannot occur.

$$\begin{aligned}|\text{Re}\{X_m[p]\}| &\le |\text{Re}\{X_m[p]\}| + |\text{Re}\{W_N^r X_{m-1}[q]\}| \\ &\le \frac{1}{2} + \left|\cos\left(\frac{2\pi r}{N}\right)\text{Re}\{X_{m-1}[q]\} - \sin\left(\frac{2\pi r}{N}\right)\text{Im}\{X_{m-1}[q]\}\right|\end{aligned}$$

Consider the worst case, when $r = 3N/8$. Then,

$$\begin{aligned}|\text{Re}\{X_m[p]\}| &\le \frac{1}{2} + \left|\frac{1}{\sqrt{2}}\text{Re}\{X_{m-1}[q]\} + \frac{1}{\sqrt{2}}\text{Im}\{X_{m-1}[q]\}\right| \\ &\le \frac{1}{2} + \frac{1}{\sqrt{2}} \not< 1.\end{aligned}$$

Therefore, overflow can occur.

9.45. (a) First, note that each stage has $N/2$ butterflies. In the first stage, all the multiplications are $W_N^0 = +1$. In the second stage, half are $+1$ and the other half are $W_N^{N/4} = -j$. Successive stages have half the number of the previous stage. In general,

$$\text{Number of } +1 \text{ multiplications in stage } m = \frac{N}{2^m}, \qquad m = 1, \ldots, v$$

and

$$\text{Number of } -j \text{ multiplications in stage } m = \begin{cases} 0, & m = 1 \\ N/2^m, & m = 2, \ldots, v \end{cases}$$

(b) If we assume that all the $+1$ and $-j$ multiplications are done noiselessly, then the noise variance will be different at each output node. This is easily seen by looking at Figure 9.10, where we see for example that $X[0]$ will be noise-free, while $X[1]$ will not be noise-free. Thus, a noise analysis would be required for each output node separately. A somewhat simpler approach would be to assume that since the first two stages consist of only $+1$ and $-j$ multiplications, these two stages can be performed noiselessly. Each output node is connected to all $N/2$ butterflies in the first stage and to $N/4$ butterflies in the second stage. Thus, if the first two stages are performed noiselessly, a better estimate of the number of independent noise sources contributing to the output is

$$N - 1 - \frac{N}{2} - \frac{N}{4} = \frac{N}{4} - 1.$$

Note that all the odd indexed outputs will have exactly $(N/4) - 1$ of these noise sources, while the even indexed outputs will have less. In fact, $X[0]$, $X[N/4]$, $X[N/2]$, $X[3N/4]$ will be noiseless. $X[N/8]$, $X[3N/8]$, $X[5N/8]$, and $X[7N/8]$ will have one noise source. It is possible to continue this analysis for all $X[k]$, but clearly, a complicated formula would be required to describe the number of noise sources for all even k. We have shown that

$$\begin{aligned}\text{Number of noise sources} &= (N/4) - 1, \qquad k \text{ odd} \\ \text{Number of noise sources} &< (N/4) - 1, \qquad k \text{ even}\end{aligned}$$

Thus, the number of noise sources is upper bounded $(N/4) - 1$. Using this bound, we can get a more optimistic output noise variance.

$$\begin{aligned}\mathcal{E}[|F[k]|^2] &\le (\frac{N}{4} - 1)\sigma_B^2 \\ &\lesssim \frac{N}{4}\sigma_B^2 \quad \text{for large } N\end{aligned}$$

When the scaling is done at the input, an upper bound on the noise-to-signal ratio is found to be

$$\frac{\mathcal{E}[|F[k]|^2]}{\mathcal{E}[|X[k]|^2]} \lesssim \frac{\frac{N}{4}\sigma_B^2}{\frac{1}{3N}} = \frac{3}{4}N^2\sigma_B^2 = \frac{N^2 2^{-2B}}{4}$$

This equation is similar to Eq. 9.65, but scaled by $\frac{1}{4}$. This implies that Eq. 9.65 is about 1 bit too pessimistic. However, note that the N^2 dependence is still present.

Another approach to this noise analysis is to compute the average noise at the output by using the average number of noisy butterflies connected to an output node. This style of analysis is used in Weinstein.

(c) Now assume as before that the first two stages are noiseless. Thus, equation 9.67 would not include the first two stages.

$$\begin{aligned}
\mathcal{E}[|F[k]|^2] &\leq \sigma_B^2 \sum_{m=2}^{\nu-1} 2^{(\nu-m)}(\frac{1}{2})^{2\nu-2m-2} \\
&= \sigma_B^2 \sum_{m=2}^{\nu-1} (\frac{1}{2})^{\nu-m-2} \\
&= 2\sigma_B^2 \sum_{k=0}^{\nu-3} (\frac{1}{2})^k \\
&= 2\sigma_B^2 \left(\frac{1-(\frac{1}{2})^{\nu-2}}{1-\frac{1}{2}}\right) \\
&= 4\sigma_B^2(1-(\frac{1}{2})^{\nu-2}) \\
&= 4\sigma_B^2(1-\frac{4}{N})
\end{aligned}$$

Thus,

$$\begin{aligned}
\frac{\mathcal{E}[|F[k]|^2]}{\mathcal{E}[|X[k]|^2]} &\leq 12N\sigma_B^2\frac{N-4}{N} \\
&\lesssim 12(N-4)\sigma_B^2
\end{aligned}$$

9.46. The butterfly for decimation-in-frequency is drawn below.

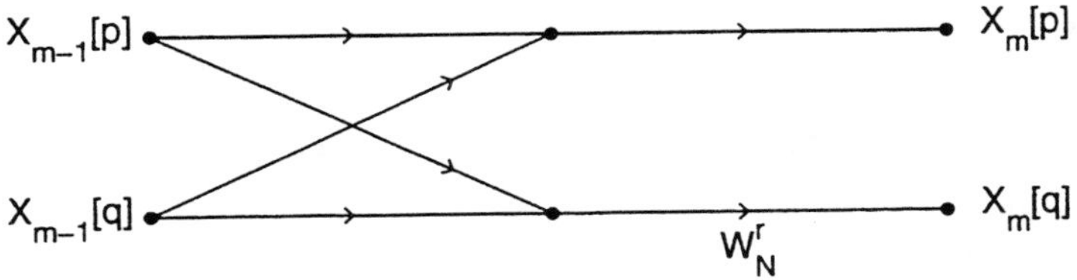

where

$$\begin{aligned}
X_m[p] &= X_{m-1}[p] + X_{m-1}[q] \\
X_m[q] &= (X_{m-1}[p] - X_{m-1}[q])W_N^r
\end{aligned}$$

The statistical model is drawn below.

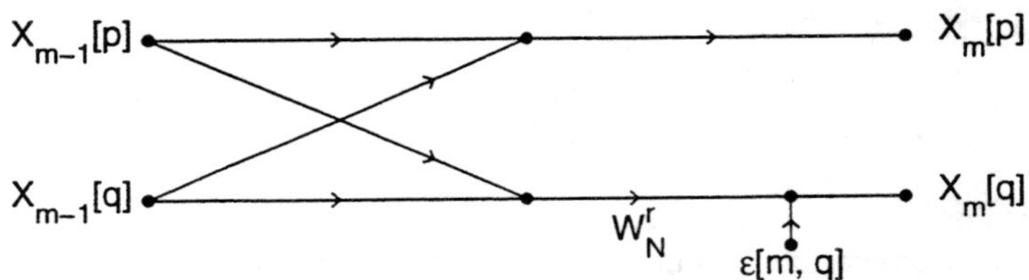

As in a decimation-in-time FFT, each output node connects to $N-1$ butterflies in a decimation-in-frequency FFT, each of which introduces a noise source whose variance is

$$\mathcal{E}[|\epsilon[m,q]|^2] = \sigma_B^2 = \frac{1}{3}2^{-2B}.$$

Thus the output noise propagated through the flowgraph is

$$\mathcal{E}[|F[k]|^2] = (N-1)\sigma_B^2$$

since each noise source propagates along a unity gain path to the output nodes.

Thus, the results for the decimation-in-frequency FFT are identical to those for the decimation-in-time FFT. This is true for both cases of scaling either at the input of the FFT by $1/N$, or at the input of each stage of the FFT by $1/2$.

9.47. Recall the following symmetry properties of the DFT:

$$\begin{aligned}
x[n] \text{ real} \quad &\Longleftrightarrow \quad X[k] = X^*[N-k] \\
x[n] = x^*[N-n] \quad &\Longleftrightarrow \quad \mathrm{Im}\{X[k]\} = 0 \\
x[n] = -x^*[N-n] \quad &\Longleftrightarrow \quad \mathrm{Re}\{X[k]\} = 0
\end{aligned}$$

Thus, $x[n]$ real and even $\Longleftrightarrow$ $X[k]$ real and even; and $x[n]$ real and odd $\Longleftrightarrow$ $X[k]$ imaginary and odd.

(a)

$$y_1[n] = x_1[n] + x_3[n]$$

$x_1[n]$ is real and even; $x_3[n]$ is real and odd.

$$Y_1[k] = \mathrm{Re}\{Y_1[k]\} + j\mathrm{Im}\{Y_1[k]\} = X_1[k] + X_3[k]$$

$\mathrm{Re}\{Y_1[k]\}$ is real and even; $j\mathrm{Im}\{Y_1[k]\}$ is imaginary and odd; $X_1[k]$ is real and even; $X_3[k]$ is imaginary and odd. It follows that

$$\begin{aligned}
X_1[k] &= \mathrm{Re}\{Y_1[k]\} \\
X_3[k] &= j\mathrm{Im}\{Y_1[k]\}
\end{aligned}$$

(b)

$$y_3[n] = y_1[n] + jy_2[n]$$

$$\begin{aligned}
Y_3[k] &= Y_1[k] + jY_2[k] = [\mathrm{Re}\{Y_1[k]\} + j\mathrm{Im}\{Y_1[k]\}] + j[\mathrm{Re}\{Y_2[k]\} + j\mathrm{Im}\{Y_2[k]\}] \\
&= \underbrace{\mathrm{Re}\{Y_1[k]\}}_{\text{real}} - \underbrace{\mathrm{Im}\{Y_2[k]\}}_{\text{odd}} + j[\underbrace{\mathrm{Re}\{Y_2[k]\}}_{\text{even}} + \underbrace{\mathrm{Im}\{Y_1[k]\}}_{\text{odd}}] \\
Y_3[k] &= [\mathrm{Ev}\{\mathrm{Re}\{Y_3[k]\}\} + \mathrm{Od}\{\mathrm{Re}\{Y_3[k]\}\}] + j[\mathrm{Ev}\{\mathrm{Im}\{Y_3[k]\}\} + \mathrm{Od}\{\mathrm{Im}\{Y_3[k]\}\}]
\end{aligned}$$

Thus we have

$$\begin{aligned}\mathrm{Re}\{Y_1[k]\} &= \mathrm{Ev}\{\mathrm{Re}\{Y_3[k]\}\}\\ \mathrm{Re}\{Y_2[k]\} &= \mathrm{Ev}\{\mathrm{Im}\{Y_3[k]\}\}\\ \mathrm{Im}\{Y_1[k]\} &= \mathrm{Od}\{\mathrm{Im}\{Y_3[k]\}\}\\ \mathrm{Im}\{Y_2[k]\} &= -\mathrm{Od}\{\mathrm{Re}\{Y_3[k]\}\}\end{aligned}$$

and so

$$\begin{aligned}Y_1[k] &= \frac{1}{2}[\mathrm{Re}\{Y_3[k]\} + \mathrm{Re}\{Y_3[N-k]\}]\\ &\quad + \frac{j}{2}[\mathrm{Im}\{Y_3[k]\} - \mathrm{Im}\{Y_3[N-k]\}]\\ Y_2[k] &= \frac{1}{2}[\mathrm{Im}\{Y_3[k]\} + \mathrm{Im}\{Y_3[N-k]\}]\\ &\quad - \frac{j}{2}[\mathrm{Re}\{Y_3[k]\} - \mathrm{Re}\{Y_3[N-k]\}]\end{aligned}$$

and from part (a)

$$\begin{aligned}X_1[k] &= \frac{1}{2}[\mathrm{Re}\{Y_3[k]\} + \mathrm{Re}\{Y_3[N-k]\}]\\ X_2[k] &= \frac{1}{2}[\mathrm{Im}\{Y_3[k]\} + \mathrm{Im}\{Y_3[N-k]\}]\\ X_3[k] &= \frac{j}{2}[\mathrm{Im}\{Y_3[k]\} - \mathrm{Im}\{Y_3[N-k]\}]\\ X_4[k] &= \frac{-j}{2}[\mathrm{Re}\{Y_3[k]\} - \mathrm{Re}\{Y_3[N-k]\}]\end{aligned}$$

(c)

$$u_3[n] = x_3[((n+1))_N] - x_3[((n-1))_N]$$

$$u_3[((N-n))_N] = x_3[((N-n+1))_N] - x_3[((N-n-1))_N]$$

Since $x_3[n] = x_3[((N-n))_N]$,

$$u_3[((N-n))_N] = x_3[((n-1))_N] - x_3[((n+1))_N] = -u_3[n]$$

For $n = 0$, we have $u_3[0] = -u_3[0]$, which is only satisfied for $u_3[0] = 0$.

(d) Using the circular shift property of the DFT we have

$$\begin{aligned}U_3[k] &= X_3[k]e^{j(2\pi/N)k} - X_3[k]e^{-j(2\pi/N)k}\\ &= 2j\sin(2\pi k/N)X_3[k]\end{aligned}$$

(e) From part (a), since $u_3[n]$ is antisymmetric,

$$X_1[k] = \mathrm{Re}\{Y_1[k]\}$$

$$U_3[k] = j\mathrm{Im}\{Y_1[k]\}$$

and so

$$X_3[k] = \frac{\mathrm{Im}\{Y_1[k]\}}{2\sin\frac{2\pi k}{N}} \quad k \neq 0, \ \frac{N}{2}$$

Note that $X_3[0]$ cannot be recovered using this technique, and if N is even, neither can $X_3[N/2]$.

(f) In part (b) replace X_3 and X_4 with U_3 and U_4 and use the result of (d) to give

$$\begin{aligned}
X_1[k] &= \frac{1}{2}[\text{Re}\{Y_3[k]\} + \text{Re}\{Y_3[N-k]\}] \\
X_2[k] &= \frac{1}{2}[\text{Im}\{Y_3[k]\} + \text{Im}\{Y_3[N-k]\}] \\
X_3[k] &= \frac{1}{4}[\text{Im}\{Y_3[k]\} - \text{Im}\{Y_3[N-k]\}]/\sin(2\pi k/N), \quad k \neq 0, N/2 \\
X_4[k] &= -\frac{1}{4}[\text{Re}\{Y_3[k]\} - \text{Re}\{Y_3[N-k]\}]/\sin(2\pi k/N), \quad k \neq 0, N/2
\end{aligned}$$

9.48. First, we find an expression for samples of the system function $H(z)$.

$$H(z) = \frac{\sum_{r=0}^{M} b_r z^{-r}}{1 - \sum_{\ell=1}^{N} a_\ell z^{-\ell}}$$

$$H(e^{j2\pi k/N}) = \frac{\sum_{r=0}^{M} b_r e^{-j2\pi kr/N}}{1 - \sum_{\ell=1}^{N} a_\ell e^{-j2\pi k\ell/N}}$$

Now assume $N,\ M \leq 511$. Let $b[n] = b_n$ and

$$a[n] = \begin{cases} 1, & n = 0 \\ a_n, & 1 \leq n \leq N \end{cases}$$

Let $B[k]$, $A[k]$ be the 512 pt DFTs of $b[n]$, and $a[n]$. Then

$$H(e^{j2\pi k/512}) = \frac{B[k]}{A[k]}$$

9.49. (a) It is interesting to note that (linear) convolution and polynomial multiplication are the same operation. Many mathematical software tools, like Matlab, perform polynomial multiplication using convolution. Here, we replace

$$p(x) = \sum_{i=0}^{L-1} a_i x^i, \qquad q(x) = \sum_{i=0}^{M-1} b_i x^i$$

with

$$p[n] = \sum_{i=0}^{L-1} a_i \delta[n-i], \qquad q[n] = \sum_{i=0}^{M-1} b_i \delta[n-i]$$

Then,

$$r[n] = p[n] * q[n].$$

The coefficients in $r[n]$ will be identically equal to those of $r(x)$. We can compute $r[n]$ with circular convolution, instead of linear convolution, by zero padding $p[n]$ and $q[n]$ to a length $N = L+M-1$. This zero padding ensures that linear convolution and circular convolution will give the same result.

(b) We can implement the circular convolution of $p[n]$ and $q[n]$ using the following procedure.

step 1: Take the DFTs of $p[n]$ and $q[n]$ using the FFT program. This gives $P[k]$ and $Q[k]$.

step 2: Multiply to get $R[k] = P[k]Q[k]$.

step 3: Take the inverse DFT of $R[k]$ using the FFT program. This gives $r[n]$.

Here, we assumed that the FFT program also computes inverse DFTs. If not, it is a relatively simple matter to modify the input to the program so that its output is an inverse DFT. (See problem 9.1).

While it may seem that this procedure is more work, for long sequences, it is actually more efficient. The direct computation of $r[n]$ requires approximately $(L+M)^2$ real multiplications, since a_i and b_i are real. Assuming that a length $L+M$ FFT computation takes $[(L+M)/2]\log_2(L+M)$ complex multiplications, we count the complex multiplications required in the procedure described above to be

Operation	Complex Multiplications
FFTs of $p[n]$ and $q[n]$	$2[(L+M)/2]\log_2(L+M) = (L+M)\log_2(L+M)$
$R[k] = P[k]Q[k]$	$L+M$
Inverse FFT of $R[k]$	$[(L+M)/2]\log_2(L+M)$

$$= [3(L+M)/2]\log_2(L+M) + (L+M)$$

Since a complex multiplication is computed using 4 real multiplications, the number of real multiplications required by this technique is $6(L+M)\log_2(L+M)+4(L+M)$. Plugging in some values for $(L+M) = 2^\nu$, we find

$L+M$	Direct	FFT
2	4	20
4	16	64
8	64	176
16	256	448
32	1024	1088
64	4096	2560

Thus, for $(L+M) \geq 64$, the FFT approach is more efficient.

(c) The binary integers u and v have corresponding decimal values, which are

$$\begin{aligned} u_{\text{decimal}} &= \sum_{i=0}^{L-1} u_i 2^i \\ v_{\text{decimal}} &= \sum_{i=0}^{M-1} v_i 2^i \end{aligned}$$

Note the resemblance to $p(x)$ and $q(x)$ of part (a). We form the signals

$$\begin{aligned} u[n] &= \sum_{i=0}^{L-1} u_i \delta[n-i] \\ v[n] &= \sum_{i=0}^{M-1} v_i \delta[n-i] \end{aligned}$$

and use the procedure described in part (b). This computes the product $u \cdot v$ in binary. For $L = 8000$ and $M = 1000$, this procedure requires approximately

$$\begin{aligned} \#\text{ real multiplications} &= 6(8000+1000)\log_2(8000+1000) + 4(8000+1000) \\ &= 7.45 \times 10^5 \end{aligned}$$

In contrast, the direct computation requries 8.1×10^7 real multiplications.

(d) For the (forward and inverse) FFTs, the mean-square value of the output noise is $(L+M)\sigma_B^2$. While σ_B^2 will be small, as there are 16 bits, the noise can be significant, since $L+M$ is a large number.

9.50. (a) Using the definition of the discrete Hartley transform we get

$$\begin{aligned} H_N[a+N] &= C_N[a+N] + S_N[a+N] \\ &= \cos(2\pi a/N + 2\pi) + \sin(2\pi a/N + 2\pi) \\ &= \cos(2\pi a/N) + \sin(2\pi a/N) \\ &= C_N[a] + S_N[a] \\ &= H_N[a] \end{aligned}$$

$$\begin{aligned} H_N[a+b] &= C_N[a+b] + S_N[a+b] \\ &= \cos(2\pi a/N + 2\pi b/N) + \sin(2\pi a/N + 2\pi b/N) \\ &= \cos(2\pi a/N)\cos(2\pi b/N) - \sin(2\pi a/N)\sin(2\pi b/N) \\ &\quad + \sin(2\pi a/N)\cos(2\pi b/N) + \cos(2\pi a/N)\sin(2\pi b/N) \end{aligned}$$

Grouping the terms in the last equation one way gives us

$$\begin{aligned} H_N[a+b] &= [\cos(2\pi a/N) + \sin(2\pi a/N)]\cos(2\pi b/N) \\ &\quad + [\cos(-2\pi a/N) + \sin(-2\pi a/N)]\sin(2\pi b/N) \\ &= H_N[a]C_N[b] + H_N[-a]S_N[b] \end{aligned}$$

while grouping the terms another way gives us

$$\begin{aligned} H_N[a+b] &= [\cos(2\pi b/N) + \sin(2\pi b/N)]\cos(2\pi a/N) \\ &\quad + [\cos(-2\pi b/N) + \sin(-2\pi b/N)]\sin(2\pi a/N) \\ &= H_N[b]C_N[a] + H_N[-b]S_N[a] \end{aligned}$$

(b) To obtain a fast algorithm for computation of the discrete Hartley transform, we can proceed as in the decimation-in-time FFT algorithm; i.e.,

$$\begin{aligned} X_H[k] &= \sum_{r=0}^{(N/2)-1} x[2r]H_N[2rk] + \sum_{r=0}^{(N/2)-1} x[2r+1]H_N[(2r+1)k] \\ &= \sum_{r=0}^{(N/2)-1} x[2r]H_N[2rk] + \sum_{r=0}^{(N/2)-1} x[2r+1]H_N[2rk]C_N[k] \\ &\quad + \sum_{r=0}^{(N/2)-1} x[2r+1]H_N[((-2rk))_N]S_N[k] \end{aligned}$$

Now since $H_N[2rk] = H_{N/2}[rk]$, we have

$$\begin{aligned} X_H[k] &= \sum_{r=0}^{(N/2)-1} x[2r]H_{N/2}[rk] + \sum_{r=0}^{(N/2)-1} x[2r+1]H_{N/2}[rk]C_N[k] \\ &\quad + \sum_{r=0}^{(N/2)-1} x[2r+1]H_{N/2}[((-rk))_{N/2}]S_N[k] \\ &= F[k] + G[k]C_N[k] + G[((-k))_{N/2}]S_N[k] \end{aligned}$$

where

$$F[k] = \sum_{r=0}^{(N/2)-1} x[2r]H_{N/2}[rk]$$

is the $N/2$-point DHT of the even-indexed points and

$$G[k] = \sum_{r=0}^{(N/2)-1} x[2r+1]H_{N/2}[rk]$$

is the $N/2$-point DHT of the odd-indexed points. As in the derivation of the decimation-in-time FFT algorithm, we can continue to divide the sequences in half if N is a power of 2. Thus the indexing will be exactly the same except that we have to access $G[((-k))_{N/2}]$ as well as $G[k]$ and $F[k]$; i.e., the "butterfly" is slightly more complicated. The fast Hartley transform will require $N \log_2 N$ operations as in the case of the DFT, but the multiplies and adds will be real instead of complex.

9.51. (a)

$$\mathbf{F}_1 = \begin{bmatrix} 1 & 1 & 0 & 0 & 0 & 0 & 0 & 0 \\ 1 & -1 & 0 & 0 & 0 & 0 & 0 & 0 \\ 0 & 0 & 1 & 1 & 0 & 0 & 0 & 0 \\ 0 & 0 & 1 & -1 & 0 & 0 & 0 & 0 \\ 0 & 0 & 0 & 0 & 1 & 1 & 0 & 0 \\ 0 & 0 & 0 & 0 & 1 & -1 & 0 & 0 \\ 0 & 0 & 0 & 0 & 0 & 0 & 1 & 1 \\ 0 & 0 & 0 & 0 & 0 & 0 & 1 & -1 \end{bmatrix} \quad \mathbf{T}_1 = \begin{bmatrix} 1 & 0 & 0 & 0 & 0 & 0 & 0 & 0 \\ 0 & 1 & 0 & 0 & 0 & 0 & 0 & 0 \\ 0 & 0 & W_8^0 & 0 & 0 & 0 & 0 & 0 \\ 0 & 0 & 0 & W_8^2 & 0 & 0 & 0 & 0 \\ 0 & 0 & 0 & 0 & 1 & 0 & 0 & 0 \\ 0 & 0 & 0 & 0 & 0 & 1 & 0 & 0 \\ 0 & 0 & 0 & 0 & 0 & 0 & W_8^0 & 0 \\ 0 & 0 & 0 & 0 & 0 & 0 & 0 & W_8^2 \end{bmatrix}$$

$$\mathbf{F}_2 = \begin{bmatrix} 1 & 0 & 1 & 0 & 0 & 0 & 0 & 0 \\ 0 & 1 & 0 & 1 & 0 & 0 & 0 & 0 \\ 1 & 0 & -1 & 0 & 0 & 0 & 0 & 0 \\ 0 & 1 & 0 & -1 & 0 & 0 & 0 & 0 \\ 0 & 0 & 0 & 0 & 1 & 0 & 1 & 0 \\ 0 & 0 & 0 & 0 & 0 & 1 & 0 & 1 \\ 0 & 0 & 0 & 0 & 1 & 0 & -1 & 0 \\ 0 & 0 & 0 & 0 & 0 & 1 & 0 & -1 \end{bmatrix} \quad \mathbf{T}_2 = \begin{bmatrix} 1 & 0 & 0 & 0 & 0 & 0 & 0 & 0 \\ 0 & 1 & 0 & 0 & 0 & 0 & 0 & 0 \\ 0 & 0 & 1 & 0 & 0 & 0 & 0 & 0 \\ 0 & 0 & 0 & 1 & 0 & 0 & 0 & 0 \\ 0 & 0 & 0 & 0 & W_8^0 & 0 & 0 & 0 \\ 0 & 0 & 0 & 0 & 0 & W_8^1 & 0 & 0 \\ 0 & 0 & 0 & 0 & 0 & 0 & W_8^2 & 0 \\ 0 & 0 & 0 & 0 & 0 & 0 & 0 & W_8^3 \end{bmatrix}$$

$$\mathbf{F}_3 = \begin{bmatrix} 1 & 0 & 0 & 0 & 1 & 0 & 0 & 0 \\ 0 & 1 & 0 & 0 & 0 & 1 & 0 & 0 \\ 0 & 0 & 1 & 0 & 0 & 0 & 1 & 0 \\ 0 & 0 & 0 & 1 & 0 & 0 & 0 & 1 \\ 1 & 0 & 0 & 0 & -1 & 0 & 0 & 0 \\ 0 & 1 & 0 & 0 & 0 & -1 & 0 & 0 \\ 0 & 0 & 1 & 0 & 0 & 0 & -1 & 0 \\ 0 & 0 & 0 & 1 & 0 & 0 & 0 & -1 \end{bmatrix}$$

(b)

$$\begin{aligned} \mathbf{Q}^H &= \mathbf{F}_1^H \mathbf{T}_1^H \mathbf{F}_2^H \mathbf{T}_2^H \mathbf{F}_3^H \\ &= \mathbf{F}_1 \mathbf{T}_1^* \mathbf{F}_2 \mathbf{T}_2^* \mathbf{F}_3 \end{aligned}$$

where $*$ denotes conjugation. Drawing the flow graph, we get

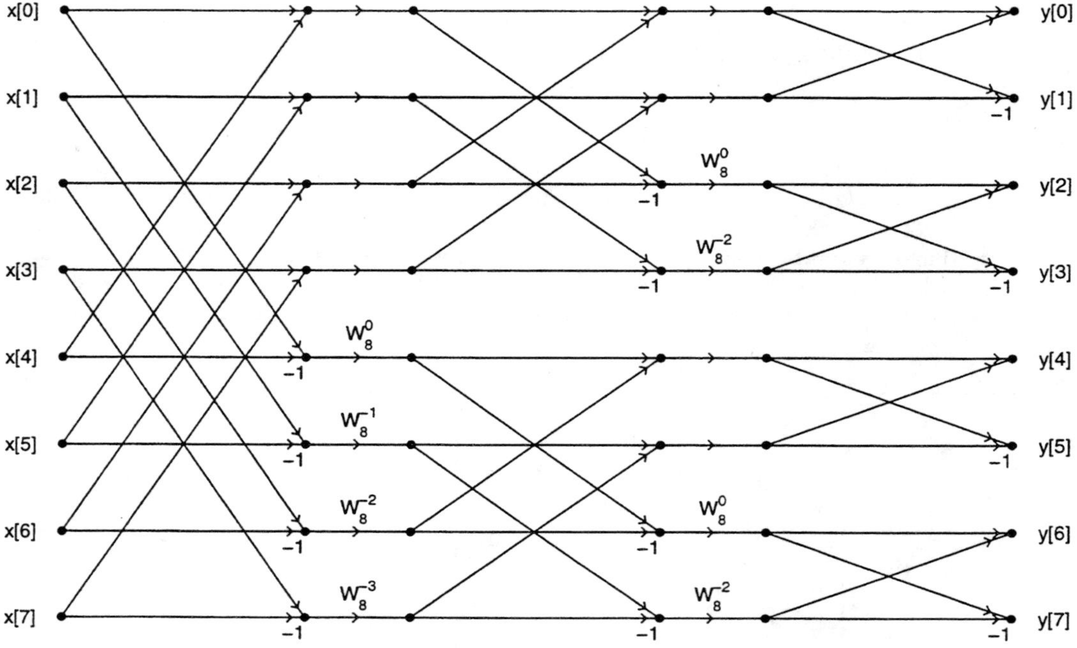

This structure is the decimation in frequency FFT with the twiddle factors conjugated and therefore calculates

$$N \cdot \text{IDFT}\{x[n]\}$$

(c) Knowing that $\mathbf{Q}$ calculates the DFT and $\frac{1}{N}\mathbf{Q}^H$ calculates the IDFT, we should realize that cascading the two should just return the original signal. More formally we have

$$\mathbf{F}_1^H\mathbf{F}_1 = 2\mathbf{I} \quad \mathbf{F}_2^H\mathbf{F}_2 = 2\mathbf{I} \quad \mathbf{F}_3^H\mathbf{F}_3 = 2\mathbf{I}$$

$$\mathbf{T}_1^H\mathbf{T}_1 = \mathbf{I} \quad \mathbf{T}_2^H\mathbf{T}_2 = \mathbf{I}$$

$$\begin{aligned}(1/N)\mathbf{Q}^H\mathbf{Q} &= (1/N)\left(\mathbf{F}_1^H\mathbf{T}_1^H\mathbf{F}_2^H\mathbf{T}_2^H\mathbf{F}_3^H\right)\left(\mathbf{F}_3\mathbf{T}_2\mathbf{F}_2\mathbf{T}_1\mathbf{F}_1\right) \\ &= (1/N)(N\mathbf{I}) \\ &= \mathbf{I}\end{aligned}$$

where $N = 8$ in this case.

9.52. (a) First, we derive the circular convolution property of the DFT. We start with the circular convolution of $x[n]$ and $h[n]$.

$$y[n] = \sum_{m=0}^{N-1} x[m]h[((n-m))_N]$$

Taking the DFT of both sides gives

$$\begin{aligned}Y[k] &= \sum_{n=0}^{N-1}\sum_{m=0}^{N-1} x[m]h[((n-m))_N]W^{nk} \\ &= \sum_{m=0}^{N-1} x[m] \sum_{n=0}^{N-1} h[((n-m))_N]W^{nk}\end{aligned}$$

Using the circular shift property of the DFT,

$$\begin{aligned} Y[k] &= \sum_{m=0}^{N-1} x[m]H[k]W_N^{mk} \\ &= H[k]\sum_{m=0}^{N-1} x[m]W_N^{mk} \\ &= H[k]X[k] \end{aligned}$$

Next, the orthogonality of the basis vectors is shown to be a necessary requirement for the circular convolution property. We start again with the circular convolution of $x[n]$ and $h[n]$

$$y[n] = \sum_{m=0}^{N-1} x[m]h[((n-m))_N]$$

Substituting the inverse DFT for $x[m]$ and $h[((n-m))_N]$ gives

$$\begin{aligned} y[n] &= \sum_{m=0}^{N-1}\left(\frac{1}{N}\sum_{k_1=0}^{N-1} X[k_1]W_N^{-k_1 m}\right)\left(\frac{1}{N}\sum_{k_2=0}^{N-1} H[k_2]W_N^{-k_2((n-m))_N}\right) \\ &= \sum_{m=0}^{N-1}\left(\frac{1}{N}\sum_{k_1=0}^{N-1} X[k_1]W_N^{-k_1 m}\right)\left(\frac{1}{N}\sum_{k_2=0}^{N-1} H[k_2]W_N^{-k_2(n-m)}\right) \\ &= \frac{1}{N^2}\sum_{k_1=0}^{N-1}\sum_{k_2=0}^{N-1}\left(X[k_1]H[k_2]W_N^{-k_2 n}\sum_{m=0}^{N-1} W_N^{-k_1 m}W_N^{k_2 m}\right) \end{aligned}$$

With orthogonal basis vectors,

$$\sum_{n=0}^{N-1} W_N^{nk} = \begin{cases} N, & k=0 \\ 0, & k \neq 0 \end{cases}$$

so the right-most summation becomes

$$\begin{aligned} \sum_{m=0}^{N-1} W_N^{-k_1 m}W_N^{k_2 m} &= \sum_{m=0}^{N-1} W_N^{(k_2-k_1)m} \\ &= N\delta[k_1-k_2] \end{aligned}$$

Therefore,

$$\begin{aligned} y[n] &= \frac{1}{N^2}\sum_{k_1=0}^{N-1}\sum_{k_2=0}^{N-1}\left(X[k_1]H[k_2]W_N^{-k_2 n}N\delta[k_1-k_2]\right) \\ &= \frac{1}{N}\sum_{k_1=0}^{N-1} X[k_1]H[k_1]W_N^{-k_1 n} \\ &= \sum_{m=0}^{N-1} x[m]h[((n-m))_N] \end{aligned}$$

Therefore, the circular convolution property holds as long as the basis vectors are orthogonal.

(b)

$$\left(\left(\sum_{n=0}^{3} 4^{nk}\right)\right)_{17} = \left((1+4^k+16^k+64^k)\right)_{17}$$

$$
\begin{aligned}
k &= 0: \ ((1+1+1+1))_{17} &&= ((4))_{17} &&= 4 \\
k &= 1: \ ((1+4+16+64))_{17} &&= ((85))_{17} &&= 0 \\
k &= 2: \ ((1+16+256+4096))_{17} &&= ((4369))_{17} &&= 0 \\
k &= 3: \ ((1+64+4096+262144))_{17} &&= ((266305))_{17} &&= 0
\end{aligned}
$$

The relation holds for $P = 17$, $N = 4$, and $W_N = 4$.

(c)

$$
\begin{aligned}
X[k] &= \left(\left(\sum_{n=0}^{3} x[n]4^{nk}\right)\right)_{17} \\
&= ((1 \cdot 1 + 2 \cdot 4^k + 3 \cdot 16^k + 0 \cdot 64^k))_{17} \\
&= ((1 + 2 \cdot 4^k + 3 \cdot 16^k))_{17}
\end{aligned}
$$

Using this formula for $X[k]$,

$$
\begin{aligned}
X[0] &= ((1+2+3))_{17} &&= ((6))_{17} &&= 6 \\
X[1] &= ((1+2\cdot 4+3\cdot 16))_{17} &&= ((57))_{17} &&= 6 \\
X[2] &= ((1+2\cdot 16+3\cdot 256))_{17} &&= ((801))_{17} &&= 2 \\
X[3] &= ((1+2\cdot 64+3\cdot 4096))_{17} &&= ((12417))_{17} &&= 7
\end{aligned}
$$

$$
\begin{aligned}
H[k] &= \left(\left(\sum_{n=0}^{3} h[n]4^{nk}\right)\right)_{17} \\
&= ((3 \cdot 1 + 1 \cdot 4^k + 0 \cdot 16^k + 0 \cdot 64^k))_{17} \\
&= ((3 + 4^k))_{17}
\end{aligned}
$$

Using this formula for $H[k]$,

$$
\begin{aligned}
H[0] &= ((3+1))_{17} &&= ((4))_{17} &&= 4 \\
H[1] &= ((3+4))_{17} &&= ((7))_{17} &&= 7 \\
H[2] &= ((3+16))_{17} &&= ((19))_{17} &&= 2 \\
H[3] &= ((3+64))_{17} &&= ((67))_{17} &&= 16
\end{aligned}
$$

Multiplying terms $Y[k] = X[k]H[k]$ gives

$$
\begin{aligned}
Y[0] &= ((24))_{17} &&= 7 \\
Y[1] &= ((42))_{17} &&= 8 \\
Y[2] &= ((4))_{17} &&= 4 \\
Y[3] &= ((112))_{17} &&= 10
\end{aligned}
$$

(d) By trying out different values,

$$
\begin{aligned}
N^{-1} &= 13 \\
W_N^{-1} &= 13
\end{aligned}
$$

$$
((N^{-1}N))_{17} = ((W_N^{-1}W_N))_{17} = ((13 \cdot 4))_{17} = ((52))_{17} = 1
$$

(e)

$$
\begin{aligned}
y[n] &= \left(\left(13\sum_{k=0}^{3} Y[k]13^{nk}\right)\right)_{17} \\
&= ((13[7\cdot 1+8\cdot 13^n+4\cdot 169^n+10\cdot 2197^n]))_{17}
\end{aligned}
$$

Using this formula for $y[n]$,

$$
\begin{aligned}
y[0] &= ((13[7+8+4+10]))_{17} &&= ((377))_{17} &&= 3 \\
y[1] &= ((13[7\cdot 1+8\cdot 13+4\cdot 169+10\cdot 2197]))_{17} &&= ((295841))_{17} &&= 7 \\
y[2] &= ((13[7\cdot 1+8\cdot 169+4\cdot 28561+10\cdot 4826809]))_{17} &&= ((628988009))_{17} &&= 11 \\
y[3] &= ((13[7\cdot 1+8\cdot 2197+4\cdot 4826809+10\cdot 10604499373]))_{17} &&= ((1378836141137))_{17} &&= 3
\end{aligned}
$$

Performing manual convolution $y[n] = x[n] * h[n]$ gives

$$
\begin{aligned}
y[0] &= 3 \\
y[1] &= 7 \\
y[2] &= 11 \\
y[3] &= 3
\end{aligned}
$$

The results agree.

9.53. (a) The tables below list the values for n and k obtained with the index maps.

n_1 \ n_2	0	1	2
0	0	1	2
1	3	4	5

k_1 \ k_2	0	1	2
0	0	2	4
1	1	3	5

As shown, the index maps only produce $n = 0, \ldots, 5$ and $k = 0, \ldots, 5$.

(b) Making the substitution we get

$$
\begin{aligned}
X[k] &= X[k_1+2k_2] \\
&= \sum_{n=0}^{5} x[n]W_6^{(k_1+2k_2)n} \\
&= \sum_{n_2=0}^{2}\sum_{n_1=0}^{1} x[3n_1+n_2]W_6^{(k_1+2k_2)(3n_1+n_2)}
\end{aligned}
$$

(c) Expanding out the W_6 terms we get

$$
\begin{aligned}
W_6^{(k_1+2k_2)(3n_1+n_2)} &= W_6^{3k_1n_1}W_6^{6k_2n_1}W_6^{k_1n_2}W_6^{2k_2n_2} \\
&= W_2^{k_1n_1}W_6^{k_1n_2}W_3^{k_2n_2}
\end{aligned}
$$

(d) Grouping the terms we get

$$
X[k_1+2k_2] = \sum_{n_2=0}^{2}\left[\left(\sum_{n_1=0}^{1} x[3n_1+n_2]W_2^{k_1n_1}\right)W_6^{k_1n_2}\right]W_3^{k_2n_2}
$$

The interpretation of this equation is as follows

(i) Let $G[k_1, n_2]$ be the $N = 2$ point DFTs of the inner parenthesis; i.e.,

$$G[k_1, n_2] = \sum_{n_1=0}^{1} x[3n_1 + n_2] W_2^{k_1 n_1}, \qquad \begin{cases} 0 \le k_1 \le 1, \\ 0 \le n_2 \le 2. \end{cases}$$

This calculates 3 DFTs, one for each column of the index map associated with n. Since the DFT size is 2, we can perform these with simple butterflies and use no multiplications.

(ii) Let $\tilde{G}[k_1, n_2]$ be the set of 3 column DFTs multiplied by the twiddle factors.

$$\tilde{G}[k_1, n_2] = W_6^{k_1 n_2} G[k_1, n_2], \qquad \begin{cases} 0 \le k_1 \le 1, \\ 0 \le n_2 \le 2. \end{cases}$$

(iii) The outer sum calculates two $N = 3$ point DFTs, one for each of the two values of k_1.

$$X[k_1 + 2k_2] = \sum_{n_2=0}^{2} \tilde{G}[k_1, n_2] W_3^{k_2 n_2}, \qquad \begin{cases} 0 \le k_1 \le 1, \\ 0 \le k_2 \le 2. \end{cases}$$

(e) The signal flow graph looks like

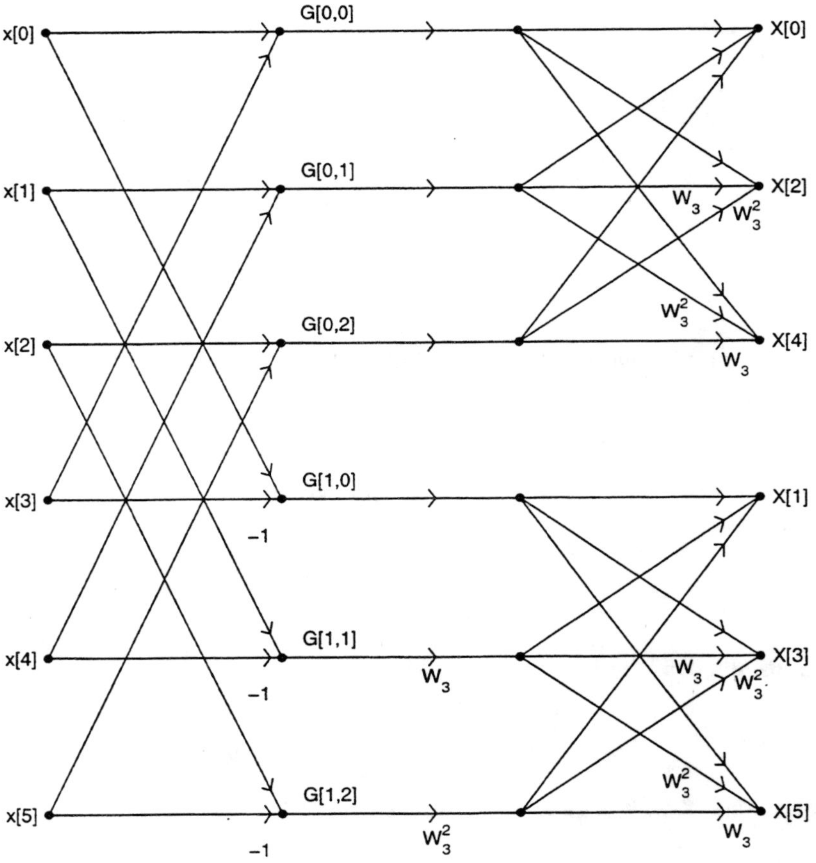

The only complex multiplies are due to the twiddle factors. Therefore, there are 10 complex multiplies. The direct implementation requires $N^2 = 6^2 = 36$ complex multiplies (a little less if you do not count multiplies by 1 or -1).

(f) The alternate index map can be found be reversing the roles of n and k; i.e.,

$$\begin{aligned} n &= n_1 + 2n_2 \qquad \text{for } n_1 = 0, 1;\ n_2 = 0, 1, 2 \\ k &= 3k_1 + k_2 \qquad \text{for } k_1 = 0, 1;\ k_2 = 0, 1, 2 \end{aligned}$$

Solutions – Chapter 10

Fourier Analysis of Signals

Using the Discrete Fourier Transform

10.1. (a) Using the relation

$$\Omega_k = \frac{2\pi k}{NT},$$

we find that the index $k = 150$ in $X[k]$ corresponds to a continuous time frequency of

$$\begin{aligned} \Omega_{150} &= \frac{2\pi(150)}{(1000)(10^{-4})} \\ &= 2\pi(1500) \text{ rad/s} \end{aligned}$$

(b) For this part, it is important to realize that the $k = 800$ index corresponds to a *negative* continuous-time frequency. Since the DFT is periodic in k with period N,

$$\begin{aligned} \Omega_{800} &= \frac{2\pi(800 - 1000)}{1000(10^{-4})} \\ &= -2\pi(2000) \text{ rad/s} \end{aligned}$$

10.2. Using the relation

$$\Omega_k = \frac{2\pi k}{NT}$$

or

$$f_k = \frac{k}{NT}$$

we find that the equivalent analog spacing between frequencies is

$$\Delta f = \frac{1}{NT}$$

Thus, in addition to the constraint that N is a power of 2, there are two conditions which must be met:

$$\begin{aligned} \tfrac{1}{T} &> 10,000 \text{ Hz} \quad \text{(to avoid aliasing)} \\ \tfrac{1}{NT} &< 5 \text{ Hz} \quad \text{(given)} \end{aligned}$$

These conditions can be expressed in the form

$$10,000 < \frac{1}{T} < 5N$$

The minimal $N = 2^{\nu}$ that satisfies the relationship is

$$N = 2048$$

for which

$$10,000 \text{ Hz} < \frac{1}{T} < 10,240 \text{ Hz}$$

Thus, $F_{\text{min}} = 10,000$ Hz, and $F_{\text{max}} = 10,240$ Hz.

10.3. (a) The length of a window is

$$\begin{aligned} L &= \left(16,000 \, \frac{\text{samples}}{\text{sec}}\right)(20 \times 10^{-3} \text{ sec}) \\ &= 320 \text{ samples} \end{aligned}$$

(b) The *frame rate* is the number of frames of data processed per second, or equivalently, the number of DFT computations done per second. Since the window is advanced 40 samples between computations of the DFT, the frame rate is

$$\begin{aligned} \text{frame rate} &= \left(16,000 \, \frac{\text{samples}}{\text{sec}}\right)\left(\frac{1 \text{ frame processed}}{40 \text{ samples}}\right) \\ &= 400 \, \frac{\text{frames}}{\text{sec}} \end{aligned}$$

(c) The most straightforward solution to this problem is to say that since the window length L is 320, we need $N \geq L$ in order to do the DFT. Therefore, a value of $N = 512$ meets the criteria of $N \geq L$, $N = 2^{\nu}$. However, since the windows overlap, we can find a smaller N.

Since the window advances 40 samples between computations, we really only need 40 *valid* samples for each DFT in order to reconstruct the original input signal. If we time alias the windowed data, we can use a smaller DFT length than the window length. With $N = 256$, 64 samples will be time aliased, and remaining 192 samples will be valid. However, with $N = 128$, all the samples will be aliased. Therefore, the minimum size of N is 256.

(d) Using the relation

$$\Delta f = \frac{1}{NT},$$

the frequency spacing for $N = 512$ is

$$\Delta f = \frac{16,000}{512} = 31.25 \text{ Hz}$$

and for $N = 256$ is

$$\Delta f = \frac{16,000}{256} = 62.5 \text{ Hz}$$

10.4. (a) Since $x[n]$ is real, $X[k]$ must be conjugate symmetric.

$$X[k] = X^*[((-k))_N]$$

We can use this conjugate symmetry property to find $X[k]$ for $k = 200$.

$$\begin{aligned} X[((-k))_N] &= X^*[k] \\ X[((-800))_{1000}] &= (1+j)^* \\ X[200] &= 1-j \end{aligned}$$

(b) Since an N-point DFT is periodic in k with period N, we know that

$$X[800] = 1 + j$$

implies that

$$X[-200] = 1 + j$$

Using the relation

$$\Omega_k = \frac{2\pi k}{NT},$$

we find

$$\begin{aligned} \Omega_{-200} &= \frac{-2\pi(200)}{(1000)(1/20,000)} \\ &= -2\pi(4000) \text{ rad/s} \\ \Omega_{200} &= \frac{2\pi(200)}{(1000)(1/20,000)} \\ &= 2\pi(4000) \text{ rad/s} \end{aligned}$$

Consequently,

$$\begin{aligned} X_c(j\Omega)\,|_{\Omega=-2\pi(4000)} &= \frac{1+j}{20,000} \\ X_c(j\Omega)\,|_{\Omega=2\pi(4000)} &= \frac{1-j}{20,000} \end{aligned}$$

Note that both expressions for $X_c(j\Omega)$ have been multiplied by the sampling period $T = 1/20,000$ because sampling the continuous-time signal $x_c(t)$ involves multiplication by $1/T$.

10.5. (a) After windowing, we have

$$\begin{aligned} x[n] &= \cos(\Omega_0 T n) \\ &= \frac{1}{2}\left[e^{j\Omega_0 T n} + e^{-j\Omega_0 T n}\right] \\ &= \frac{1}{2}\left[e^{j\frac{2\pi}{N}(\frac{N\Omega_0 T}{2\pi})n} + e^{-j\frac{2\pi}{N}(\frac{N\Omega_0 T}{2\pi})n}\right] \end{aligned}$$

for $n = 0, \ldots, N-1$ and $x[n] = 0$ outside this range. Using the DFT properties we get

$$X[k] = \frac{N}{2}\delta[((k - \tfrac{N\Omega_0 T}{2\pi}))_N] + \frac{N}{2}\delta[((k + \tfrac{N\Omega_0 T}{2\pi}))_N]$$

If we choose

$$T = \frac{2\pi}{N\Omega_0}k_0$$

then

$$X[k] = \frac{N}{2}\delta[k - k_0] + \frac{N}{2}\delta[k - (N - k_0)],$$

which is nonzero for $X[k_0]$ and $X[N - k_0]$, but zero everywhere else.

(b) *No*, the choice for T is not unique since we can choose the integer k_0.

10.6. Since $x[n]$ is real, $X[k]$ must be conjugate symmetric.

$$\begin{aligned} X[k] &= X^*[((-k))_N] \\ X[((-k))_N] &= X^*[k] \end{aligned}$$

Therefore,

$$\begin{aligned} X[((-900))_{1000}] &= (1)^* \\ X[100] &= 1 \\ X[((-420))_{1000}] &= (5)^* \\ X[580] &= 5 \end{aligned}$$

Note that the $k = 900$ and $k = 580$ correspond to negative frequencies of Ω. Since the DFT is periodic in k with period N, we use $k = 900 - 1000 = -100$ and $k = 580 - 1000 = -420$, respectively, in the equations below.

Starting with

$$\Omega_k = \frac{2\pi k}{NT},$$

we find

$$\begin{aligned} \Omega_{-100} &= \frac{2\pi(-100)}{(1000)(1/10,000)} \\ &= -2\pi(1000) \text{ rad/s} \\ \Omega_{100} &= \frac{2\pi(100)}{(1000)(1/10,000)} \\ &= 2\pi(1000) \text{ rad/s} \\ \Omega_{-420} &= \frac{2\pi(-420)}{(1000)(1/10,000)} \\ &= -2\pi(4200) \text{ rad/s} \\ \Omega_{420} &= \frac{2\pi(420)}{(1000)(1/10,000)} \\ &= 2\pi(4200) \text{ rad/s} \end{aligned}$$

Consequently,

$$
\begin{aligned}
X_c(j\,\Omega)\,\big|_{\Omega=-2\pi(1000)} &= \frac{1}{10,000} \\
X_c(j\,\Omega)\,\big|_{\Omega=2\pi(1000)} &= \frac{1}{10,000} \\
X_c(j\,\Omega)\,\big|_{\Omega=-2\pi(4200)} &= \frac{1}{2,000} \\
X_c(j\,\Omega)\,\big|_{\Omega=2\pi(4200)} &= \frac{1}{2,000}
\end{aligned}
$$

Note that all expressions for $X_c(j\,\Omega)$ have been multiplied by the sampling period $T = 1/10,000$ because sampling the continuous-time signal $x_c(t)$ involves multiplication by $1/T$.

10.7. The Hamming window's mainlobe is $\Delta\omega_{ml} = \frac{8\pi}{L-1}$ radians wide. We want

$$
\begin{aligned}
\Delta\omega_{ml} &\leq \frac{\pi}{100} \\
\frac{8\pi}{L-1} &\leq \frac{\pi}{100} \\
L &\geq 801
\end{aligned}
$$

Because the window length is constrained to be a power of 2, we see that

$$L_{\text{min}} = 1024$$

10.8. *All windows expect the Blackman satisfy the criteria.* Using the table, and noting that the window length $N = M + 1$, we find

Rectangular:

$$
\begin{aligned}
\Delta w_{ml} &= \frac{4\pi}{M+1} \\
&= \frac{4\pi}{256} \\
&= \frac{\pi}{64} \leq \frac{\pi}{25} \text{ rad}
\end{aligned}
$$

The resolution of the rectangular window satisfies the criteria.

Bartlett, Hanning, Hamming:

$$
\begin{aligned}
\Delta w_{ml} &= \frac{8\pi}{M} \\
&= \frac{8\pi}{255} \\
&= \frac{\pi}{31.875} \leq \frac{\pi}{25} \text{ rad}
\end{aligned}
$$

The resolution of the Bartlett, Hanning, and Hamming windows satisfies the criteria.

Blackman:

$$
\begin{aligned}
\Delta w_{ml} &= \frac{12\pi}{M} \\
&= \frac{12\pi}{255} \\
&= \frac{\pi}{21.25} \nleq \frac{\pi}{25} \text{ rad}
\end{aligned}
$$

The Blackman window does not have a frequency resolution of at least $\pi/25$ radians. Therefore, this window does not satisfy the criteria.

10.9. The rectangular window's mainlobe is

$$\Delta\omega_{ml} = \frac{4\pi}{L} = \frac{4\pi}{64}$$

radians wide. The difference in frequency between each cosine must be greater than this amount to be resolved. If they are not separated enough, the mainlobes from each cosine will overlap too much and only a single peak will be seen. The separation of the cosines for each signal is

$$\begin{aligned}
\Delta\omega_1 &= \left|\frac{\pi}{4} - \frac{17\pi}{64}\right| = \frac{\pi}{64} \\
\Delta\omega_2 &= \left|\frac{\pi}{4} - \frac{21\pi}{64}\right| = \frac{5\pi}{64} \\
\Delta\omega_3 &= \left|\frac{\pi}{4} - \frac{21\pi}{64}\right| = \frac{5\pi}{64}
\end{aligned}$$

Clearly, the cosines in $x_1[n]$ are too closely spaced in frequency to produce distinct peaks.

In $x_3[n]$, we have a small amplitude cosine which will be obscurred by the large sidelobes from the rectangular window. The peak will therefore not be visible.

The only signal from which we would expect to see two distinct peaks is $x_2[n]$.

10.10. The equivalent continuous-time frequency spacing is

$$\Delta f = \frac{1}{NT}$$

Thus, to satisfy the criterion that the frequency spacing between consecutive DFT samples is 1 Hz or less we must have

$$\begin{aligned}
\Delta f &\leq 1 \\
\frac{1}{NT} &\leq 1 \\
T &\geq \frac{1}{N} \\
T &\geq \frac{1}{1024} \text{ sec}
\end{aligned}$$

However, we must also satisfy the Sampling Theorem to avoid aliasing. We therefore have the addition restriction that,

$$\begin{aligned}
\frac{1}{T} &\geq 200 \text{ Hz} \\
T &\leq \frac{1}{200} \text{ sec}
\end{aligned}$$

Putting the two constraints together we find

$$\frac{1}{1024} \leq T \leq \frac{1}{200}$$

$$T_{\min} = \frac{1}{1024} \text{ sec}$$

10.11. The equivalent frequency spacing is

$$\Delta\Omega = \frac{2\pi}{NT} = \frac{2\pi}{(8192)(50\mu s)} = 15.34 \text{ rad/s}$$

or

$$\Delta f = \frac{\Delta\Omega}{2\pi} = 2.44 \text{ Hz}$$

10.12. The equivalent frequency spacing is

$$\Delta f = \frac{1}{NT}$$

Thus, the minimum DFT length N such that adjacent samples of $X[k]$ correspond to a frequency spacing of 5 Hz or less in the original continuous-time signal is

$$\begin{aligned}
\Delta f &\leq 5 \\
\frac{1}{NT} &\leq 5 \\
N &\geq \frac{1}{5T} \\
&\geq \frac{8000}{5} \\
&\geq 1600 \text{ samples}
\end{aligned}$$

10.13. Since $w[n]$ is the rectangular window and we are using $N = 36$ we have

$$\begin{aligned}
X_r[k] &= \sum_{m=0}^{35} x[rR+m]e^{-j(2\pi/36)km} \\
&= \text{DFT}\{x[rR+n]\}
\end{aligned}$$

Because $x[n]$ is zero outside the range $0 \leq n \leq 71$, $X_r[k]$ will be zero except when $r = 0$ or $r = 1$. When $r = 0$, the 36 points in the sum of the DFT only include the section

$$\cos(\pi n/6) = \frac{e^{j(\frac{2\pi}{36})3n} + e^{-j(\frac{2\pi}{36})3n}}{2}$$

of $x[n]$. Therefore, we can use the properties of the DFT to find

$$\begin{aligned}
X_0[k] &= \tfrac{36}{2}\delta[((k-3))_{36}] + \tfrac{36}{2}\delta[((k+3))_{36}] \\
&= 18\delta[k-3] + 18\delta[k-33]
\end{aligned}$$

When $r = 1$, the 36 points in the sum of the DFT only include the section

$$\cos(\pi n/2) = \frac{e^{j(\frac{2\pi}{36})9n} + e^{-j(\frac{2\pi}{36})9n}}{2}$$

of $x[n]$. Therefore, we can use the properties of the DFT to find

$$\begin{aligned}
X_1[k] &= \tfrac{36}{2}\delta[((k-9))_{36}] + \tfrac{36}{2}\delta[((k+9))_{36}] \\
&= 18\delta[k-9] + 18\delta[k-27]
\end{aligned}$$

Putting it all together we get

$$X_r[k] = \begin{cases} 18(\delta[k-3] + \delta[k-33]), & r = 0 \\ 18(\delta[k-9] + \delta[k-27]), & r = 1 \\ 0, & \text{otherwise} \end{cases}$$

10.14. *The signals $x_2[n]$, $x_3[n]$, and $x_6[n]$ could be $x[n]$,* as described below.

Looking at the figure, it is clear that there are two nonzero DFT coefficients at $k = 8$, and $k = 16$. These correspond to frequencies

$$\begin{aligned}\omega_1 &= \frac{(2\pi)(8)}{128} \\ &= \frac{\pi}{8} \text{ rad} \\ \omega_2 &= \frac{(2\pi)(16)}{128} \\ &= \frac{\pi}{4} \text{ rad}\end{aligned}$$

Also notice that the magnitude of the DFT coefficient at $k = 16$ is about 3 times that of the DFT coefficient at $k = 8$.

- $x_1[n]$: The second cosine term has a frequency of $.26\pi$ rad, which is neither $\pi/8$ rad or $\pi/4$ rad. Consequently, $x_1[n]$ is not consistent with the information shown in the figure.
- $x_2[n]$: This signal is consistent with the information shown in the figure. The peaks occur at the correct locations, and are scaled properly.
- $x_3[n]$: This signal is consistent with the information shown in the figure. The peaks occur at the correct locations, and are scaled properly.
- $x_4[n]$: This signal has a cosine term with frequency $\pi/16$ rad, which is neither $\pi/8$ rad or $\pi/4$ rad. Consequently, $x_4[n]$ is not consistent with the information shown in the figure.
- $x_5[n]$: This signal has sinusoids with the correct frequencies, but the scale factors on the two terms are not consistent with the information shown in the figure.
- $x_6[n]$: This signal is consistent with the information shown in the figure. Note that phase information is not represented in the DFT magnitude plot.

10.15. The instantaneous frequency of the chirp signal is

$$\omega_i[n] = \omega_0 + \lambda n$$

This describes a line with slope λ and intercept ω_0. Thus,

$$\lambda = \frac{\Delta y}{\Delta x} = \frac{(0.5\pi - 0.25\pi)}{(19000 - 0)} = 41.34 \times 10^{-6} \text{ rad}$$

$$\omega_0 = 0.25\pi \text{ rad}$$

10.16. Using

$$\Delta f = \frac{1}{NT}$$

and assuming no aliasing occured when the continuous-time signal was sampled, we find that the frequency spacing between spectral samples is

$$\begin{aligned}\Delta f &= \frac{1}{(1024)(1/10,000)} \\ &= 9.77 \text{ Hz}\end{aligned}$$

or

$$\Delta\Omega = 2\pi\Delta f = 61.4 \text{ rad/s}$$

10.17. We should choose *Method 2.*

Method 1: This doubles the number of samples we take of the frequency variable, but does not change the frequency resolution. The size of the main lobe from the window remains the same.

Method 2: *This improves the frequency resolution since the main lobe from the window gets smaller.*

Method 3: This increases the time resolution (the ability to distinguish events in time), but does not affect the frequency resolution.

Method 4: This will decrease the frequency resolution since the main lobe from the window increases. This is a strange thing to do since there are samples of x[n] that do not get used in the transform.

Method 5: This will only improve the resolution if we can ignore any problems due to sidelobe leakage. For example, changing to a rectangular window will improve our ability to resolve two equal amplitude sinusoids. In most cases, however, we need to worry about sidelobe levels. A large sidelobe might mask the presence of a low amplitude signal. Since we do not know ahead of time the nature of the signal we are trying to analyze, changing to a rectangular window may actually make things worse. Thus, in general, changing to a rectangular window will not necessarily increase the frequency resolution.

10.18. *No*, the peaks will not have the same height. The peaks in $V_2(e^{j\omega})$ will be larger than those in $V_1(e^{j\omega})$.

First, note that the Fourier transform of the rectangular window has a higher peak than that of the Hamming window. If this is not obvious, consider Figure 7.21, and recall that the Fourier transform of an L-point window $w[n]$, evaluated at DC ($\omega = 0$), is

$$W(e^{j0}) = \sum_{n=0}^{L-1} w[n]$$

Let the rectangular window be $w_R[n]$, and the Hamming window be $w_H[n]$. It is clear from the figure (where M = L+1) that

$$\sum_{n=0}^{L-1} w_R[n] > \sum_{n=0}^{L-1} w_H[n]$$

Therefore,

$$W_R(e^{j0}) > W_H(e^{j0})$$

Thus, the Fourier transform of the rectangular window has a higher peak than that of the Hamming window.

Now recall that the multiplication of two signals in the time domain corresponds to a periodic convolution in the frequency domain. So in the frequency domain, $V_1(e^{j\omega})$ is the convolution of two scaled impulses from the sinusoid, with the Fourier transform of the L-point Hamming window, $W_H(e^{j\omega})$. This results in two scaled copies of $W_H(e^{j\omega})$, centered at the frequencies of the sinusoid. Similarly, $V_2(e^{j\omega})$ consists of two scaled copies of $W_R(e^{j\omega})$, also centered at the frequencies of the sinusoid. The scale factor is the same in both cases, resulting from the Fourier transform of the sinusoid.

Since the peaks of the Fourier transform of the rectangular window are higher than those of the Hamming window, the peaks in $V_2(e^{j\omega})$ will be larger than those in $V_1(e^{j\omega})$.

10.19. Using the approximation given in the chapter

$$L \simeq \frac{24\pi(A_{sl}+12)}{155\Delta_{ml}} + 1$$

we find for $A_{sl} = 30$ dB and $\Delta_{ml} = \frac{\pi}{40}$ rad,

$$\begin{aligned} L &\simeq \frac{24\pi(30+12)}{155(\pi/40)} + 1 \\ &\simeq 261.1 \rightarrow 262 \end{aligned}$$

10.20. (a) The best sidelobe attenuation expected under these constraints is

$$\begin{aligned} L &\simeq \frac{24\pi(A_{sl}+12)}{155\Delta_{ml}}+1 \\ 512 &\simeq \frac{24\pi(A_{sl}+12)}{155(\pi/100)}+1 \\ A_{sl} &\simeq 21 \text{ dB} \end{aligned}$$

(b) The two sinusoidal components are separated by at least $\pi/50$ radians. Since the largest allowable mainlobe width is $\pi/100$ radians, we know that the peak of the DFT magnitude of the weaker sinusoidal component will not be located in the mainlobe of the DFT magnitude of the stronger sinusoidal component. Thus, we only need to consider the sidelobe height of the stronger component.

Converting 21 dB attenuation back from dB gives

$$\begin{aligned} -21 \text{ dB} &= 20\log_{10} m \\ m &= 0.0891 \end{aligned}$$

Since the amplitude of the stronger sinusoidal component is 1, the amplitude of the weaker sinusoidal component must be greater than 0.0891 in order for the weaker sinusoidal component to be seen over the sidelobe of the stronger sinusoidal component.

10.21. We have

$$\begin{aligned} v[n] &= \cos(2\pi n/5)w[n] \\ &= \left[\frac{e^{j2\pi n/5}+e^{-j2\pi n/5}}{2}\right]w[n] \\ V(e^{j\omega}) &= \frac{1}{2}W(e^{j(\omega-2\pi/5)})+\frac{1}{2}W(e^{j(\omega+2\pi/5)}) \end{aligned}$$

The rectangular window's transform is

$$W(e^{j\omega}) = \frac{\sin(16\omega)}{\sin(\omega/2)}e^{-j\omega 31/2}$$

In order to label $V(e^{j\omega})$ correctly, we must find the mainlobe height, strongest sidelobe height, and the first nulls of $W(e^{j\omega})$.

Mainlobe Height of $W(e^{j\omega})$: The peak height is at $\omega = 0$ for which we can use l'hôpital's rule to find

$$W(e^{j0}) = 32\frac{\cos(16\omega)}{\cos(\omega/2)}\bigg|_{\omega=0} = 32$$

Strongest Sidelobe height of $W(e^{j\omega})$: The strongest sidelobe height for the rectangular window is 13 dB below the main peak height. Therefore, since 13 dB = 0.2239 we have

$$\text{Strongest Sidelobe height} = 0.2239(32) \approx 7.2$$

First Nulls of $W(e^{j\omega})$: The first nulls can be found be noting that $W(e^{j\omega}) = 0$ when $\sin(16\omega) = 0$ Thus, the first nulls occur at

$$\omega = \pm\frac{2\pi}{32}$$

Therefore, $|V(e^{j\omega})|$ looks like

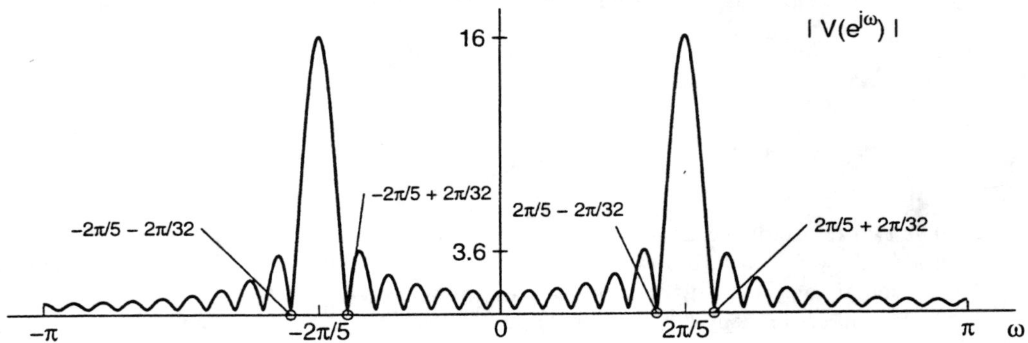

Note that the numbers used above for the heights are not exact because we are adding two copies of $W(e^{j\omega})$ to get $V(e^{j\omega})$ and the exact values for the heights will depend on relative phase and location of the two copies. However, they are a very good approximation and the error is small.

10.22. The 'instantaneous frequency' of $x[n]$, denoted as $\lambda[n]$, can be determined by taking the derivative with respect to n of the argument of the cosine term. This gives

$$\begin{aligned}\lambda[n] &= \frac{d}{dn}\left[\frac{\pi n}{4} + 1000\sin\left(\frac{\pi n}{8000}\right)\right] \\ &= \frac{\pi}{4} + \frac{\pi}{8}\cos\left(\frac{\pi n}{8000}\right) \\ \frac{\lambda[n]}{2\pi} &= \frac{1}{8} + \frac{1}{16}\cos\left(\frac{\pi n}{8000}\right)\end{aligned}$$

Once $\lambda[n]/2\pi$ is known, it is simple to sketch the spectrogram, shown below.

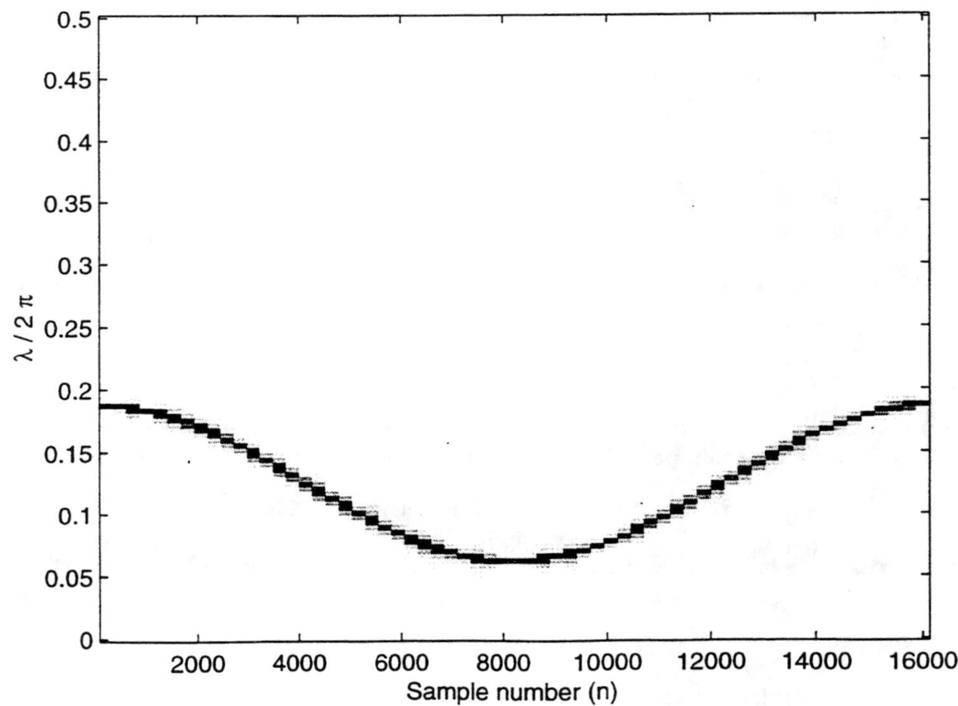

Here, we see a cosine plot shifted up the frequency $(\lambda/2\pi)$ axis by a constant. As is customary in a spectrogram, only the frequencies $0 \leq \lambda/2\pi \leq 0.5$ are plotted.

10.23. In this problem, we relate the DFT $X[k]$ of a discrete-time signal $x[n]$ to the continuous-time Fourier transform $X_c(j\Omega)$ of the continuous-time signal $x_c(t)$. Since $x[n]$ is obtained by sampling $x_c(t)$,

$$\begin{aligned} x[n] &= x_c(nT) \\ X(e^{j\omega}) &= \frac{1}{T}\sum_{r=-\infty}^{\infty} X_c\left(j\frac{\omega}{T} + j\frac{2\pi r}{T}\right) \end{aligned}$$

Over one period, assuming no aliasing, this is

$$X(e^{j\omega}) = \frac{1}{T}X_c\left(j\frac{\omega}{T}\right) \qquad \text{for } -\pi \leq \omega \leq \pi$$

which is equivalent to

$$X(e^{j\omega}) = \begin{cases} \frac{1}{T}X_c\left(j\frac{\omega}{T}\right), & \text{for } 0 \leq \omega < \pi \\ \frac{1}{T}X_c\left(j\frac{\omega-2\pi}{T}\right), & \text{for } \pi \leq \omega < 2\pi \end{cases}$$

Since the DFT is a sampled version of $X(e^{j\omega})$,

$$X[k] = X(e^{j\omega})\big|_{\omega=2\pi k/N} \qquad \text{for } 0 \leq k \leq N-1$$

we find

$$X[k] = \begin{cases} \frac{1}{T}X_c\left(j\frac{2\pi k}{NT}\right), & \text{for } 0 \leq k < \frac{N}{2} \\ \frac{1}{T}X_c\left(j\frac{2\pi(k-N)}{NT}\right), & \text{for } \frac{N}{2} \leq k \leq N-1 \end{cases}$$

Breaking up the DFT into two terms like this is necessary to relate the negative frequencies of $X_c(j\Omega)$ to the proper indicies $\frac{N}{2} \leq k \leq N-1$ in $X[k]$.

Method 1: Using the above equation for $X[k]$, and plugging in values of $N = 4000$, and $T = 25\mu$s, we find

$$X_1[k] = \begin{cases} 40{,}000X_c(j2\pi \cdot 10 \cdot k), & \text{for } 0 \leq k \leq 1999 \\ 40{,}000X_c(j2\pi \cdot 10 \cdot (k-4000)), & \text{for } 2000 \leq k \leq 3999 \end{cases}$$

Therefore, we see this does not provide the desired samples. A sketch is provided below, for a triangular-shaped $X_c(j\Omega)$.

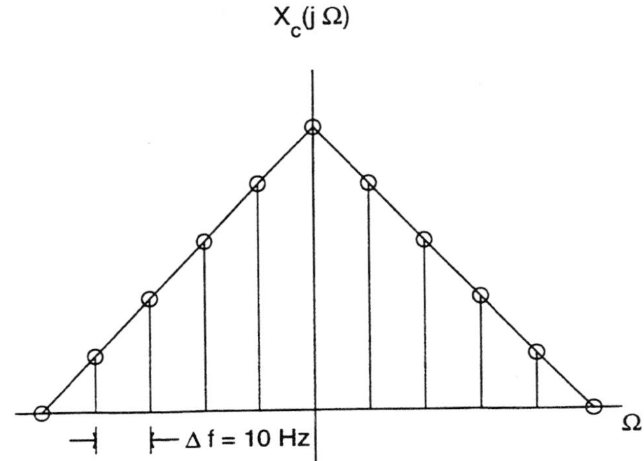

Method 2: This time we plug in values of $N = 4000$, and $T = 50\mu s$ to find

$$X_2[k] = \begin{cases} 20,000 X_c\left(j2\pi \cdot 5 \cdot k\right), & \text{for } 0 \leq k \leq 1999 \\ 20,000 X_c\left(j2\pi \cdot 5 \cdot (k - 4000)\right), & \text{for } 2000 \leq k \leq 3999 \end{cases}$$

Therefore, we see this *does* provide the desired samples. A sketch is provided below.

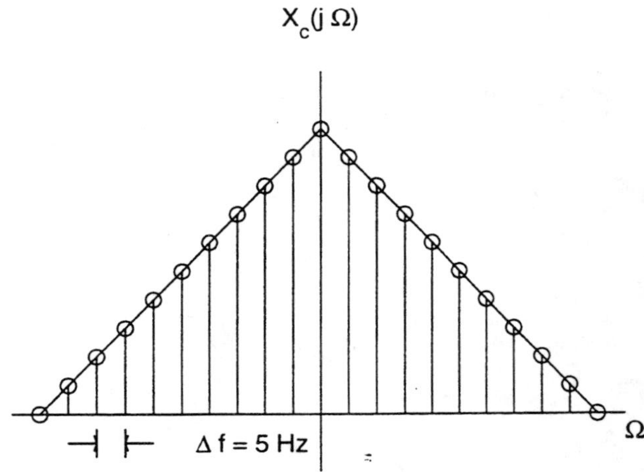

Method 3: Noting that $x_3[n] = x_2[n] + x_2\left[n - \frac{N}{2}\right]$, we get

$$X_3[k] = X_2[k] + (-1)^k X_2[k]$$

$$X_3[k] = \begin{cases} 2X_2[k], & \text{for } k \text{ even} \\ 0, & \text{otherwise} \end{cases}$$

$$X_3[k] = \begin{cases} 40,000 X_c\left(j2\pi \cdot 5 \cdot k\right), & \text{for } k \text{ even, and } 0 \leq k \leq 1999 \\ 40,000 X_c\left(j2\pi \cdot 5 \cdot (k - 4000)\right), & \text{for } k \text{ even, and } 2000 \leq k \leq 3999 \\ 0, & \text{otherwise} \end{cases}$$

This system provides the desired samples only for k an even integer. A sketch is provided below.

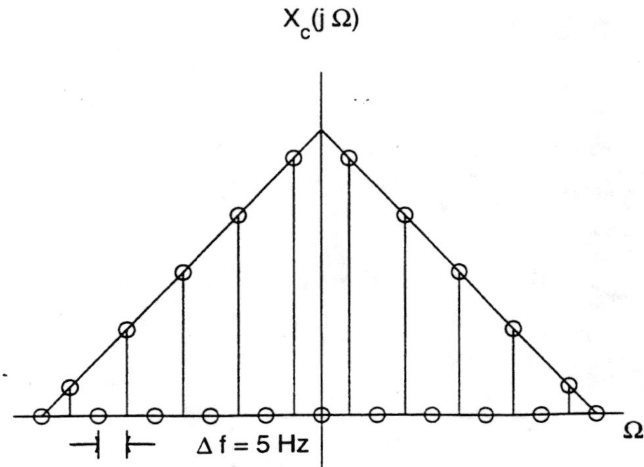

10.24. (a) In this problem, we relate the DFT $X[k]$ of a discrete-time signal $x[n]$ to the continuous-time Fourier tranform $X_c(j\Omega)$ of the continuous-time signal $x_c(t)$. Since $x[n]$ is obtained by sampling $x_c(t)$,

$$\begin{aligned} x[n] &= x_c(nT) \\ X(e^{j\omega}) &= \frac{1}{T}\sum_{r=-\infty}^{\infty} X_c\left(j\frac{\omega}{T} + j\frac{2\pi r}{T}\right) \end{aligned}$$

Over one period, assuming no aliasing, this is

$$X(e^{j\omega}) = \frac{1}{T}X_c\left(j\frac{\omega}{T}\right) \qquad \text{for } -\pi \le \omega \le \pi$$

which is equivalent to

$$X(e^{j\omega}) = \begin{cases} \frac{1}{T}X_c\left(j\frac{\omega}{T}\right), & \text{for } 0 \le \omega < \pi \\ \frac{1}{T}X_c\left(j\frac{\omega-2\pi}{T}\right), & \text{for } \pi \le \omega < 2\pi \end{cases}$$

Since the DFT is a sampled version of $X(e^{j\omega})$,

$$X[k] = X(e^{j\omega})\big|_{\omega=2\pi k/N} \qquad \text{for } 0 \le k \le N-1$$

we find

$$X[k] = \begin{cases} \frac{1}{T}X_c\left(j\frac{2\pi k}{NT}\right), & \text{for } 0 \le k < \frac{N}{2} \\ \frac{1}{T}X_c\left(j\frac{2\pi(k-N)}{NT}\right), & \text{for } \frac{N}{2} \le k \le N-1 \end{cases}$$

Breaking up the DFT into two terms like this is necessary to relate the negative frequencies of $X_c(j\Omega)$ to the proper indicies $\frac{N}{2} \le k \le N-1$ in $X[k]$.

The effective frequency spacing is

$$\begin{aligned} \Delta\Omega &= \frac{2\pi}{NT} \\ &= \frac{2\pi}{(1000)(1/20,000)} \\ &= 2\pi(20) \text{ rad/s} \end{aligned}$$

(b) Next, we determine if the designer's assertion that

$$Y[k] = \alpha X_c(j2\pi \cdot 10 \cdot k)$$

is correct. To understand the effect of each step in the procedure, it helps to draw some frequency domain plots. Assume the spectrum of the original signal $x_c(t)$ looks like

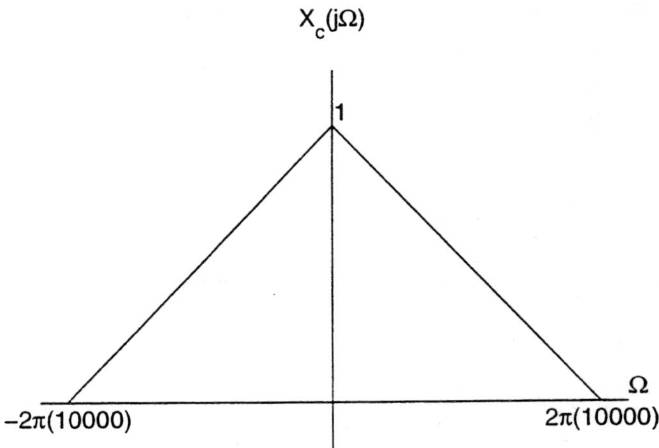

Sampling this continuous-time signal will produce the discrete-time signal $x[n]$, with a spectrum

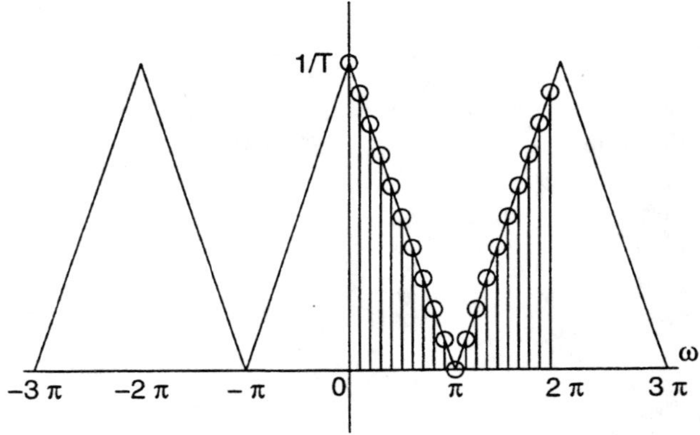

Next, we form

$$W[k] = \begin{cases} X[k], & 0 \le k \le 250 \\ 0, & 251 \le k \le 749 \\ X[k], & 750 \le k \le 999 \end{cases}$$

and find $w[n]$ as the inverse DFT of $W[k]$.

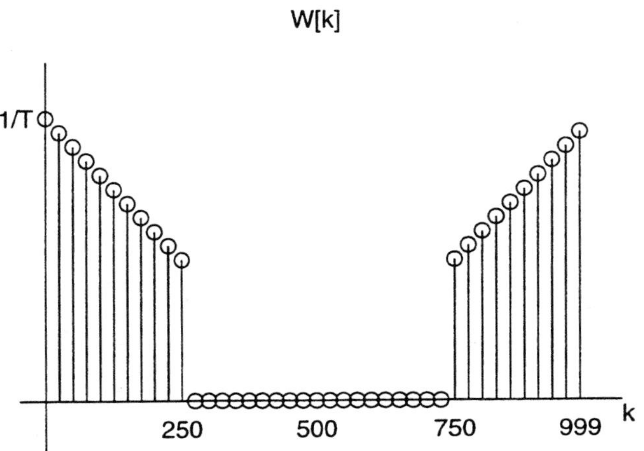

Before going on, we should plot the Fourier transform, $W(e^{j\omega})$, of $w[n]$. It will look like

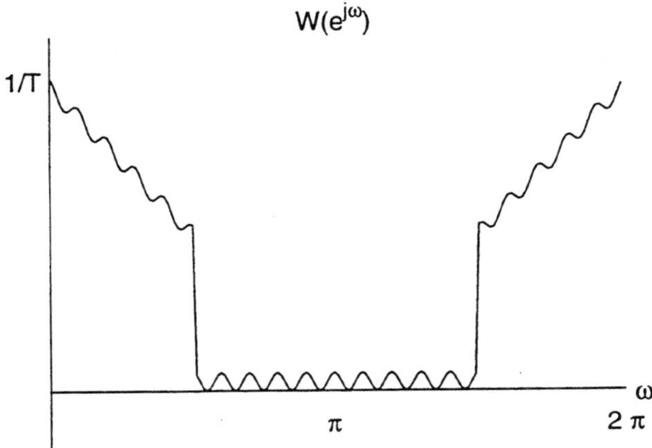

$W(e^{j\omega})$ goes through the DFT points and therefore is equal to samples of $X_c(j\Omega)$ at these points for $0 \leq k \leq 250$ and $750 \leq k \leq 999$, but it is *not equal* to $X_c(j\Omega)$ between those frequencies. Furthermore, $W(e^{j\omega}) = 0$ at the DFT frequencies for $251 \leq k \leq 749$, but it is not zero between those frequencies; i.e. we can not do ideal lowpass filtering using the DFT.

Now we define

$$y[n] = \begin{cases} w[2n], & 0 \leq n \leq 499 \\ 0, & 500 \leq n \leq 999 \end{cases}$$

and let $Y[k]$ be the DFT of $y[n]$. First note that $Y(e^{j\omega})$ is

$$Y(e^{j\omega}) = \frac{1}{2}W(e^{j\omega/2}) + \frac{1}{2}W(e^{j(\omega-2\pi)/2})$$

which looks like

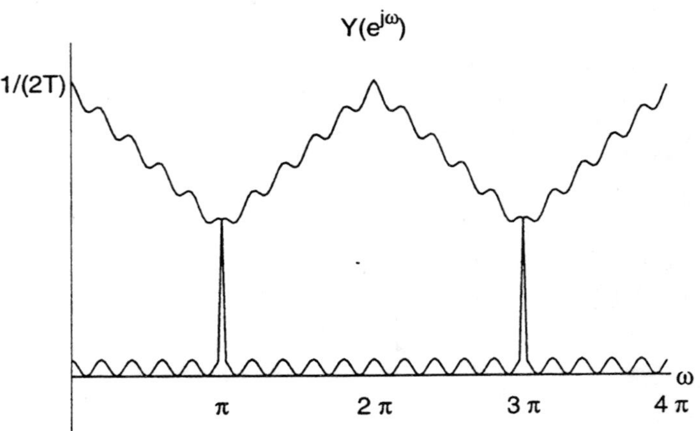

$Y[k]$ is equal to samples of the $Y(e^{j\omega})$

$$\begin{aligned} Y[k] &= Y(e^{j\omega})|_{\omega=2\pi k/N} \\ &= \frac{1}{2}W\left(e^{j\frac{2\pi}{N}\frac{k}{2}}\right) + \frac{1}{2}W\left(e^{j\frac{2\pi}{N}\left(\frac{k-N}{2}\right)}\right) \end{aligned}$$

Now putting all that we know together, we see that for $k = 0, 1, \ldots, 500$, $Y[k]$ is related to $X_c(j\Omega)$ as follows.

$$Y[k] = \begin{cases} \frac{1}{2T}X_c(j2\pi \cdot 10 \cdot k), & k \text{ even, } k \neq 500 \\ \frac{1}{T}X_c(j2\pi \cdot 10 \cdot k), & k = 500 \\ \frac{1}{2T}W(e^{j\pi k/N}) + \frac{1}{2T}W(e^{j\pi(k-N)/N}) & k \text{ odd} \end{cases}$$

In other words, the even indexed DFT samples are not aliased, but the odd indexed values (and $k = 500$) are aliased. The designer's assertion is not correct.

10.25. (a) Starting with definition of the time-dependent Fourier transform,

$$Y[n, \lambda) = \sum_{m=-\infty}^{\infty} y[n+m]w[m]e^{-j\lambda m}$$

we plug in

$$y[n+m] = \sum_{k=0}^{M} h[k]x[n+m-k]$$

to get

$$\begin{aligned} Y[n, \lambda) &= \sum_{m=-\infty}^{\infty}\sum_{k=0}^{M} h[k]x[n+m-k]w[m]e^{-j\lambda m} \\ &= \sum_{k=0}^{M} h[k] \sum_{m=-\infty}^{\infty} x[n+m-k]w[m]e^{-j\lambda m} \\ &= \sum_{k=0}^{M} h[k]X[n-k, \lambda) \\ &= h[n] * X[n, \lambda) \end{aligned}$$

where the convolution is for the variable n.

(b) Starting with

$$\check{Y}[n,\lambda) = e^{-j\lambda n}Y[n,\lambda)$$

we find

$$\begin{aligned}
\check{Y}[n,\lambda) &= e^{-j\lambda n}\left[\sum_{k=0}^{M} h[k]X[n-k,\lambda)\right] \\
&= e^{-j\lambda n}\left[\sum_{k=0}^{M} h[k]e^{j(n-k)\lambda}\check{X}[n-k,\lambda)\right] \\
&= \sum_{k=0}^{M} h[k]e^{-j\lambda k}\check{X}[n-k,\lambda)
\end{aligned}$$

If the window is long compared to M, then a small time shift in $\check{X}[n,\lambda)$ won't radically alter the spectrum, and

$$\check{X}[n-k,\lambda) \simeq \check{X}[n,\lambda)$$

Consequently,

$$\begin{aligned}
\check{Y}[n,\lambda) &\simeq \sum_{k=0}^{M} h[k]e^{-j\lambda k}\check{X}[n,\lambda) \\
&\simeq H(e^{j\lambda})\check{X}[n,\lambda)
\end{aligned}$$

10.26. Plugging in the relation for $c_{vv}[m]$ into the equation for $I(\omega)$ gives

$$\begin{aligned}
I(\omega) &= \frac{1}{LU}\sum_{m=-(L-1)}^{L-1}\left[\sum_{n=0}^{L-1} v[n]v[n+m]\right] e^{-j\omega m} \\
&= \frac{1}{LU}\sum_{n=0}^{L-1} v[n] \sum_{m=-(L-1)}^{L-1} v[n+m]e^{-j\omega m}
\end{aligned}$$

Let $\ell = n+m$ in the second summation. This gives

$$\begin{aligned}
I(\omega) &= \frac{1}{LU}\sum_{n=0}^{L-1} v[n] \sum_{\ell=n-(L-1)}^{n+(L-1)} v[\ell]e^{-j\omega(\ell-n)} \\
&= \frac{1}{LU}\sum_{n=0}^{L-1} v[n]e^{j\omega n} \sum_{\ell=n-(L-1)}^{n+(L-1)} v[\ell]e^{-j\omega \ell}
\end{aligned}$$

Note that for all values of $0 \le n \le L-1$, the second summation will be over *all* non-zero values of $v[\ell]$ in the range $0 \le \ell \le L-1$. As a result,

$$\begin{aligned}
I(\omega) &= \frac{1}{LU}\sum_{n=0}^{L-1} v[n]e^{j\omega n}\sum_{\ell=0}^{L-1} v[\ell]e^{-j\omega\ell} \\
&= \frac{1}{LU}V^*(e^{j\omega})V(e^{j\omega}) \\
&= \frac{1}{LU}|V(e^{j\omega})|^2
\end{aligned}$$

Note that in this analysis, we have assumed that $v[n]$ is a real sequence.

10.27. (a) Since $x[n]$ has length L, the aperiodic function, $c_{xx}[m]$, will be $2L-1$ points long. Therefore, in order for the aperiodic correlation function to equal the periodic correlation fuction, $\tilde{c}_{xx}[m]$, for $0 \le m \le L-1$, we require that the inverse DFT is not time aliased. So, the minimum inverse DFT length N_{min} is

$$N_{\text{min}} = 2L - 1$$

(b) If we require M points to be unaliased, we can have $L-M$ aliased points. Therefore, for $\tilde{c}_{xx}[m] = c_{xx}[m]$ for $0 \le m \le M-1$, the minimum inverse DFT length N_{min} is

$$\begin{aligned} N_{\text{min}} &= 2L - 1 - (L - M) \\ &= L + M - 1 \end{aligned}$$

10.28. (a) Let

$$w_R[m] = \frac{1}{\sqrt{M}}(u[n] - u[n-M])$$

be a scaled rectangular pulse. Then we can write the aperiodic autocorrelation as,

$$\begin{aligned} w_B[m] &= \sum_{n=-\infty}^{\infty} w_R[n]w_R[n+m] \\ &= \sum_{k=-\infty}^{\infty} w_R[k-m]w_R[k] \\ &= \sum_{k=-\infty}^{\infty} w_R[k]w_R[-(m-k)] \\ &= w_R[m] * w_R[-m] \end{aligned}$$

The convolution above is the triangular signal described by the symmetric Bartlett window formula. This is shown graphically below for a few critical cases of m.
Consider $m = -(M-1)$. This is first value of m for which the two signals overlap.

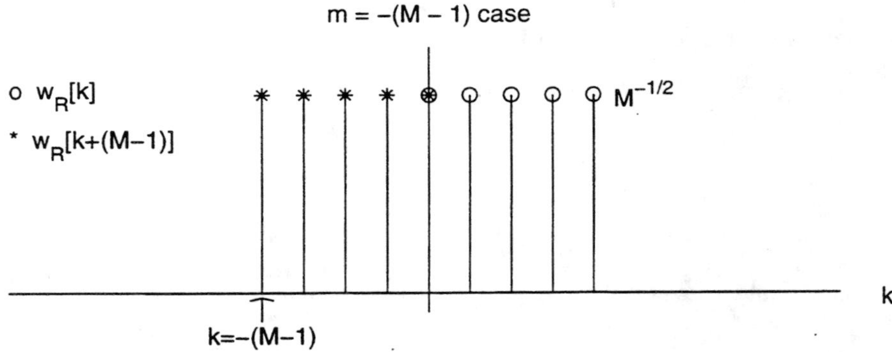

At $m = 0$, all non-zero samples overlap.

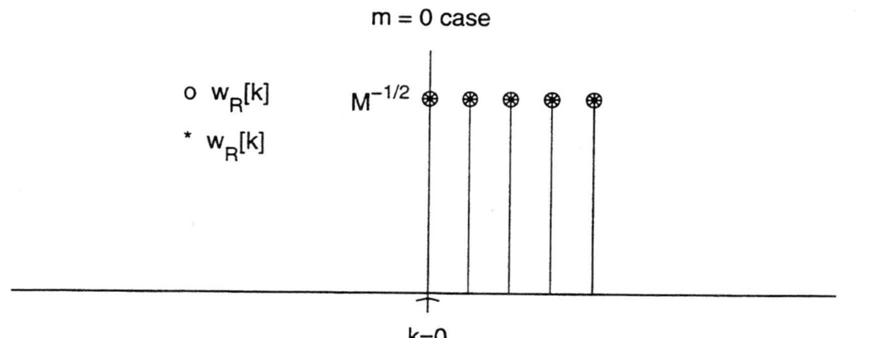

Consider $m = (M-1)$. This is last value of m for which the two signals overlap.

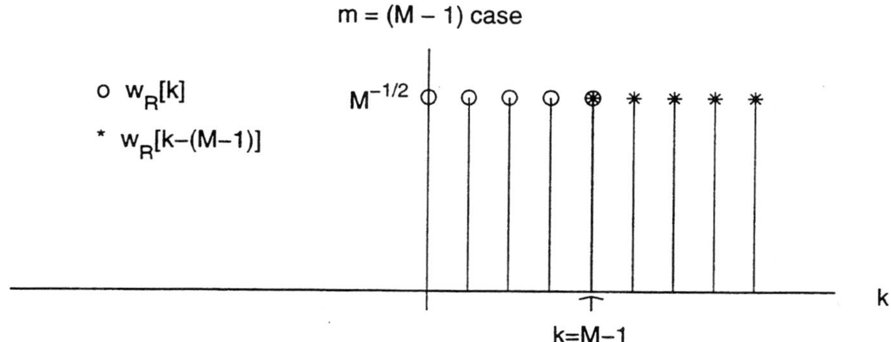

The final result of the aperiodic autocorrelation is

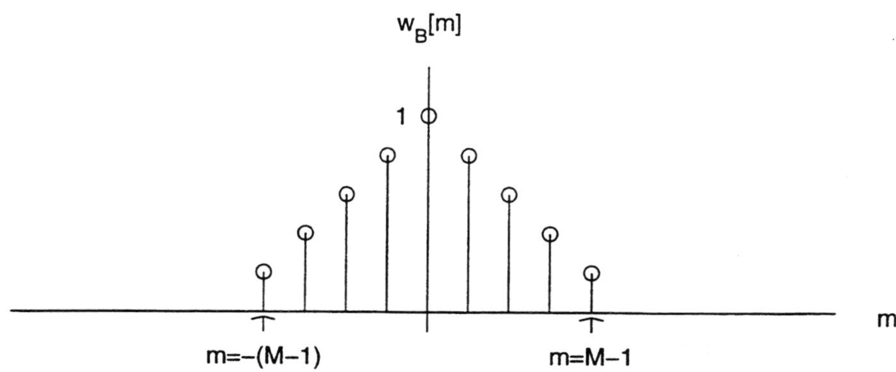

Stated mathematically, this is

$$w_B[m] = \begin{cases} 1 - |m|/M, & |m| \leq M-1 \\ 0, & \text{otherwise} \end{cases}$$

(b) The transform of the causal scaled rectangular pulse $w_R[n]$ is

$$W_R(e^{j\omega}) = \frac{1}{\sqrt{M}} \frac{\sin(\omega M/2)}{\sin(\omega/2)} e^{-j\omega(M-1)/2}$$

From part (a), we know that the Bartlett window can be found by convolving $w_R[m]$ with $w_R[-m]$. In the frequency domain, we therefore have,

$$\begin{aligned} W_B(e^{j\omega}) &= W_R(e^{j\omega})W_R(e^{-j\omega}) \\ &= \left[\frac{1}{\sqrt{M}}\frac{\sin(\omega M/2)}{\sin(\omega/2)}e^{-j\omega(M-1)/2}\right]\left[\frac{1}{\sqrt{M}}\frac{\sin(-\omega M/2)}{\sin(-\omega/2)}e^{j\omega(M-1)/2}\right] \\ &= \frac{1}{M}\left[\frac{\sin(\omega M/2)}{\sin(\omega/2)}\right]^2 \end{aligned}$$

(c) The power spectrum, defined as the Fourier transform of the aperiodic autocorrelation sequence, is always nonnegative. Thus, any window that can be represented as an aperiodic autocorrelation sequence will have a nonnegative Fourier transform. So to generate other finite-length window sequences, $w[n]$, that have nonnegative Fourier transforms, simply take the aperiodic autocorrelation of an input sequence, $x[n]$.

$$w[n] = \sum_{m=-\infty}^{\infty} x[m]x[n+m]$$

The signal $w[n]$ will have a nonnegative Fourier transform.

10.29. (a) **Rectangular:** The Fourier transform of the rectangular window is given by

$$W_R(e^{j\omega}) = \sum_{m=-(M-1)}^{M-1} (1)e^{-j\omega m}$$

Let $n = m + (M-1)$. Then, $m = n - (M-1)$, and

$$\begin{aligned} W_R(e^{j\omega}) &= \sum_{n=0}^{2(M-1)} e^{-j\omega[n-(M-1)]} \\ &= e^{j\omega(M-1)}\sum_{n=0}^{2(M-1)} e^{-j\omega n} \end{aligned}$$

Using the relation

$$\sum_{n=0}^{M-1} a^n = \frac{1-a^M}{1-a}$$

we find

$$\begin{aligned} W_R(e^{j\omega}) &= e^{j\omega(M-1)}\frac{1-e^{-j\omega[2(M-1)+1]}}{1-e^{-j\omega}} \\ &= e^{j\omega(M-1)}\frac{1-e^{-j\omega(2M-1)}}{1-e^{-j\omega}} \\ &= \frac{e^{j\omega(M-1)} - e^{-j\omega M}}{1-e^{-j\omega}} \\ &= \frac{e^{-j\omega/2}[e^{j\omega(M-1/2)} - e^{-j\omega(M-1/2)}]}{e^{-j\omega/2}[e^{j\omega/2} - e^{-j\omega/2}]} \\ &= \frac{e^{j\omega(M-1/2)} - e^{-j\omega(M-1/2)}}{e^{j\omega/2} - e^{-j\omega/2}} \\ &= \frac{2j\sin[\omega(M-\frac{1}{2})]}{2j\sin(\omega/2)} \\ &= \frac{\sin[\omega(M-\frac{1}{2})]}{\sin(\omega/2)} \end{aligned}$$

or

$$W_R(e^{j\omega}) = \frac{\sin[\omega\frac{2M-1}{2}]}{\sin(\omega/2)}$$

where $2M - 1$ is the window length. A sketch of $W_R(e^{j\omega})$ appears below.

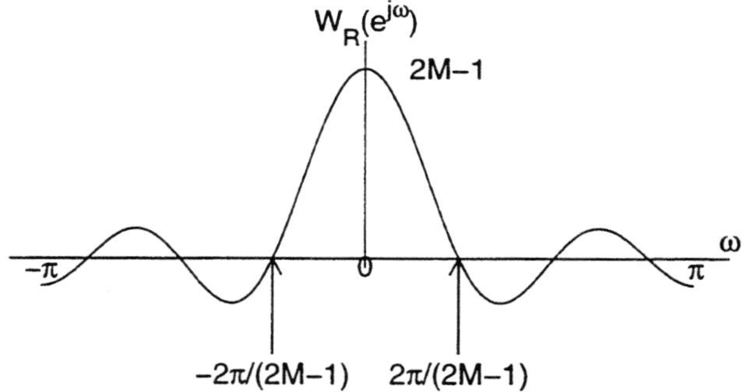

Bartlett (triangular): $W_B(e^{j\omega})$ is the Fourier transform of a triangular signal,

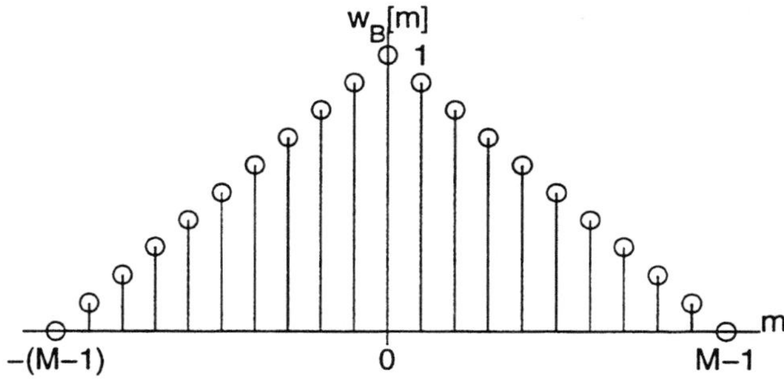

which is the convolution of a rectangular signal,

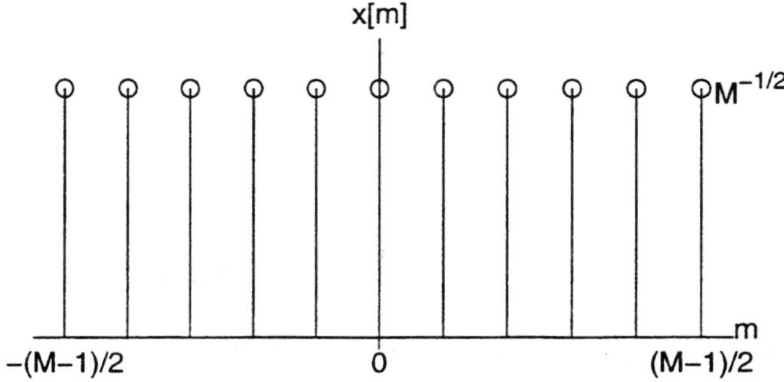

with itself. That is, $w_B[m] = x[m] * x[m]$.
Above, we found the Fourier tranform of a rectangular window, as

$$W_R(e^{j\omega}) = \frac{\sin[\omega\frac{2M-1}{2}]}{\sin(\omega/2)}$$

where $2M - 1$ was the length of the window. We can use this result to find the Fourier transform of $x[m]$. The signal $x[m]$ is similar to the rectangular window, the difference being that it is scaled by $\frac{1}{\sqrt{M}}$ and has a length $2\frac{M-1}{2}+1=M$. Therefore,

$$X(e^{j\omega}) = \frac{1}{\sqrt{M}} \frac{\sin(\omega M/2)}{\sin(\omega/2)}$$

The time domain convolution, $w_B[m] = x[m]*x[m]$ corresponds to a multiplication, $W_B(e^{j\omega}) = [X(e^{j\omega})]^2$ in the frequency domain. As a result,

$$\begin{aligned} W_B(e^{j\omega}) &= \left[X(e^{j\omega})\right]^2 \\ &= \frac{1}{M}\left[\frac{\sin(\omega M/2)}{\sin(\omega/2)}\right]^2 \end{aligned}$$

A sketch of $W_B(e^{j\omega})$ appears below.

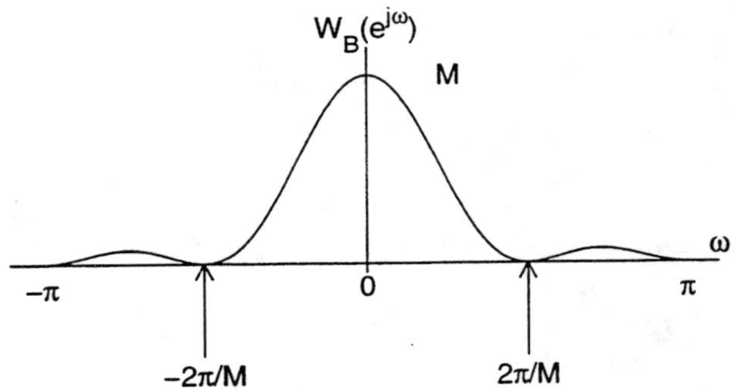

Hanning/Hamming: Starting with

$$\begin{aligned} w_H[m] &= (\alpha + \beta\cos[\pi m/(M-1)])\, w_R[m] \\ w_H[m] &= \left(\alpha + \frac{\beta}{2}e^{j\pi m/(M-1)} + \frac{\beta}{2}e^{-j\omega m/(M-1)}\right) w_R[m] \end{aligned}$$

We take the Fourier transform to find

$$\begin{aligned} W_H(e^{j\omega}) &= \alpha W_R(e^{j\omega}) + \frac{\beta}{2}\left(W_R(e^{j[\omega-\pi/(M-1)]}) + W_R(e^{j[\omega+\pi/(M-1)]})\right) \\ &= \alpha\frac{\sin[\omega\,(M-\frac{1}{2})]}{\sin(\omega/2)} + \frac{\beta}{2}\left[\frac{\sin[(\omega-\frac{\pi}{M-1})(M-\frac{1}{2})]}{\sin[(\omega-\frac{\pi}{M-1})/2]}\right] \\ &+ \frac{\beta}{2}\left[\frac{\sin[(\omega+\frac{\pi}{M-1})(M-\frac{1}{2})]}{\sin[(\omega+\frac{\pi}{M-1})/2]}\right] \end{aligned}$$

A sketch of $W_H(e^{j\omega})$ appears below.

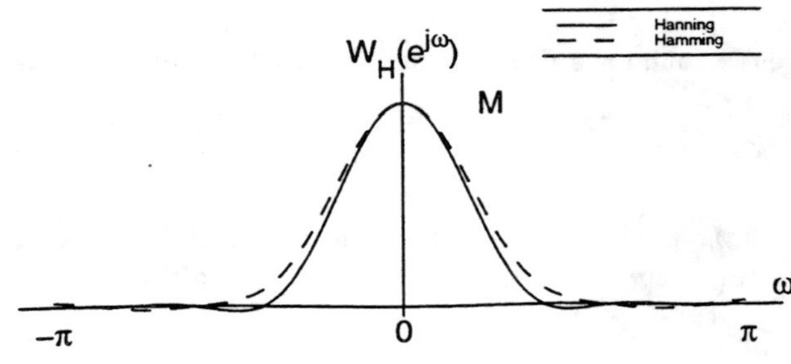

(b) **Rectangular:** The approximate mainlobe width, and the approximate variance ratio, F, for the rectangular window are found below for large M.
In part (a), we found the Fourier transform of the rectangular window as

$$W_R(e^{j\omega}) = \frac{\sin[\omega(M-\frac{1}{2})]}{\sin(\omega/2)}$$

The numerator becomes zero when the argument of its sine term equals πn.

$$\begin{aligned} \frac{(2M-1)\omega}{2} &= \pi n \\ \omega &= \frac{2\pi n}{2M-1} \end{aligned}$$

Plugging in $n = 1$ gives us half the mainlobe bandwidth.

$$\begin{aligned} \frac{1}{2}\text{Mainlobe bandwidth} &= \frac{2\pi}{2M-1} \\ \text{Mainlobe bandwidth} &= \frac{4\pi}{2M-1} \\ \text{Mainlobe bandwidth} &\simeq \frac{2\pi}{M} \end{aligned}$$

$$\begin{aligned} \text{F} &= \frac{1}{Q}\sum_{m=-(M-1)}^{(M-1)} w^2[m] \\ &= \frac{1}{Q}(2M-1) \\ &\simeq \frac{2M}{Q} \end{aligned}$$

Bartlett (triangular): The approximate mainlobe width, and the approximate variance ratio, F, for the Bartlett window are found below for large M.

In part (a), we found the Fourier transform of the Bartlett window as

$$W_B(e^{j\omega}) = \frac{1}{M}\left[\frac{\sin(\omega M/2)}{\sin(\omega/2)}\right]^2$$

The numerator becomes zero when the argument of its sine term equals πn.

$$\begin{aligned} \frac{\omega M}{2} &= \pi n \\ \omega &= \frac{2\pi n}{M} \end{aligned}$$

Plugging in $n = 1$ gives us half the mainlobe bandwidth.

$$\begin{aligned} \frac{1}{2}\text{Mainlobe bandwidth} &= \frac{2\pi}{M} \\ \text{Mainlobe bandwidth} &= \frac{4\pi}{M} \end{aligned}$$

To compute F, we use the relations

$$\begin{aligned} \sum_{m=0}^{M-1} m &= \frac{M(M-1)}{2} \\ \sum_{m=0}^{M-1} m^2 &= \frac{M(M-1)(2M-1)}{6} \end{aligned}$$

$$
\begin{aligned}
\mathrm{F} &= \frac{1}{Q}\sum_{m=-(M-1)}^{(M-1)}\left(1-\frac{|m|}{M}\right)^2 \\
&= \frac{1}{Q}\left[2\sum_{m=0}^{M-1}\left(1-\frac{m}{M}\right)^2-1\right] \\
&= \frac{1}{Q}\left[2\sum_{m=0}^{M-1}1-\frac{4}{M}\sum_{m=0}^{M-1}m+\frac{2}{M^2}\sum_{m=0}^{M-1}m^2-1\right] \\
&= \frac{1}{Q}\left[2M-\frac{4(M-1)M}{2M}+\frac{2(M-1)M(2M-1)}{6M^2}-1\right] \\
&\simeq \frac{1}{Q}\left[2M-2M+\frac{2M}{3}\right] \\
&\simeq \frac{2M}{3Q}
\end{aligned}
$$

Hanning/Hamming: We can approximate the mainlobe bandwidth by analyzing the Fourier transform derived in Part (a). Looking at one of the terms from this expression,

$$\frac{\beta}{2}\left[\frac{\sin[(\omega-\frac{\pi}{M-1})(M-\frac{1}{2})]}{\sin[(\omega-\frac{\pi}{M-1})/2]}\right]$$

we note that the numerator is zero whenever the its argument equals πn, or

$$
\begin{aligned}
\left(\omega-\frac{\pi}{M-1}\right)\left(M-\frac{1}{2}\right) &= \pi n \\
\omega &= \frac{n\pi}{M-(1/2)}+\frac{\pi}{M-1} \\
&\simeq \frac{n\pi}{M}+\frac{\pi}{M} \\
&\simeq \frac{\pi(n+1)}{M}
\end{aligned}
$$

So the mainlobe bandwidth for this term is

$$
\begin{aligned}
\frac{1}{2}\text{Mainlobe bandwidth} &\simeq \frac{\pi}{M} \\
\text{Mainlobe bandwidth} &\simeq \frac{2\pi}{M}
\end{aligned}
$$

Note that the peak value for this term occurs at a frequency $\omega \simeq \pi/M$.

A similar analysis can be applied to the other terms in Fourier transform derived in Part (a). The mainlobe bandwidth for the term

$$\frac{\beta}{2}\left[\frac{\sin[(\omega+\frac{\pi}{M-1})(M-\frac{1}{2})]}{\sin[(\omega+\frac{\pi}{M-1})/2]}\right]$$

is also $2\pi/M$. Note that the peak value for this term occurs at a frequency $\omega \simeq -\pi/M$.

Finally, the mainlobe bandwidth for the term

$$\alpha\frac{\sin[\omega\,(M-\frac{1}{2})]}{\sin(\omega/2)}$$

is also $2\pi/M$. Note that the peak value for this term occurs at a frequency $\omega = 0$.

A sample plot of these three terms, for $\beta = 2\alpha$ and large M is shown below.

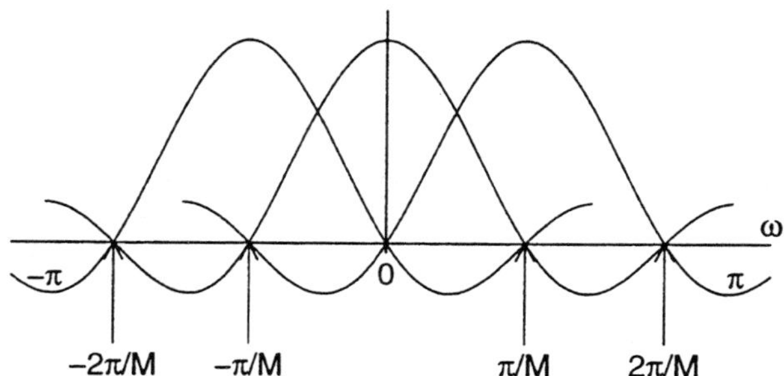

Thus, for large M, the mainlobe bandwidth is bounded by

$$\frac{2\pi}{M} < \text{Mainlobe bandwidth} < \frac{4\pi}{M}$$

Therefore, a reasonable approximation for the mainlobe bandwidth is

$$\text{Mainlobe bandwidth} \simeq \frac{3\pi}{M}$$

$$\begin{aligned}
\mathrm{F} &= \frac{1}{Q}\sum_{m=-(M-1)}^{M-1}\left(\alpha+\beta\cos\left(\frac{\pi m}{M-1}\right)\right)^2 \\
&= \frac{1}{Q}\left[\sum_{m=-(M-1)}^{M-1}\alpha^2 + 2\alpha\beta\sum_{m=-(M-1)}^{M-1}\cos\left(\frac{\pi m}{M-1}\right) + \beta^2\sum_{m=-(M-1)}^{M-1}\cos^2\left(\frac{\pi m}{M-1}\right)\right]
\end{aligned}$$

Using the relation

$$\cos^2\theta = \frac{1}{2}+\frac{1}{2}\cos 2\theta$$

we get

$$\begin{aligned}
\mathrm{F} = \frac{1}{Q}\Bigg[&\sum_{m=-(M-1)}^{M-1}\alpha^2 + 2\alpha\beta\sum_{m=-(M-1)}^{M-1}\cos\left(\frac{\pi m}{M-1}\right) \\
&+\frac{\beta^2}{2}\sum_{m=-(M-1)}^{M-1}(1) + \frac{\beta^2}{2}\sum_{m=-(M-1)}^{M-1}\cos\left(\frac{2\pi m}{M-1}\right)\Bigg].
\end{aligned}$$

Noting that

$$\begin{aligned}
\sum_{m=-(M-1)}^{M-1}\cos\left(\frac{\pi m}{M-1}\right) &= -1 \\
\sum_{m=-(M-1)}^{M-1}\cos\left(\frac{2\pi m}{M-1}\right) &= 1
\end{aligned}$$

we conclude

$$\begin{aligned} \mathrm{F} &= \frac{1}{Q}\left[(2M-1)\alpha^2 - 2\alpha\beta + \frac{\beta^2}{2}(2M-1) + \frac{\beta^2}{2}\right] \\ &\simeq \frac{2M}{Q}\left(\alpha^2 + \frac{\beta^2}{2}\right) \end{aligned}$$

10.30. (a) Using the definition of the time-dependent Fourier transform we find

$$\begin{aligned} X[0,k] &= \sum_{m=0}^{13} x[m]e^{-j(2\pi/7)km} \\ &= \sum_{m=0}^{6} x[m]e^{-j(2\pi/7)km} + \sum_{l=7}^{13} x[l]e^{-j(2\pi/7)kl} \\ &= \sum_{m=0}^{6} x[m]e^{-j(2\pi/7)km} + \sum_{m=0}^{6} x[m+7]e^{-j(2\pi/7)km}e^{-j2\pi k} \\ &= \sum_{m=0}^{6} (x[m] + x[m+7])e^{-j(2\pi/7)km} \end{aligned}$$

By plotting $x[m]$

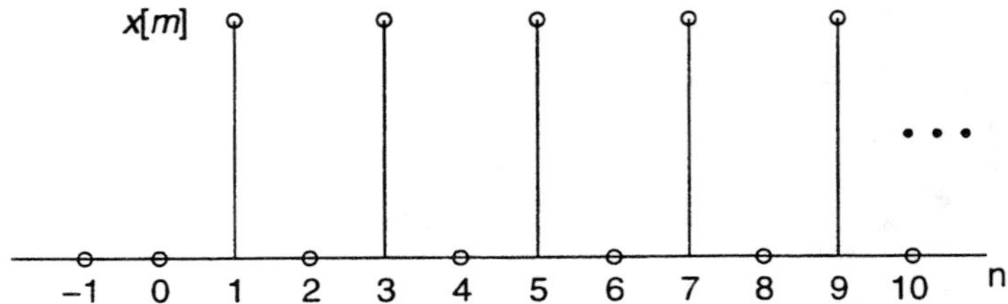

we see that $x[m] + x[m+7] = 1$ for $0 \le m \le 6$. Thus,

$$\begin{aligned} X[0,k] &= \sum_{m=0}^{6} (1)e^{-j(2\pi/7)km} \\ &= \mathcal{DFT}\{1\} \\ &= 7\delta[k] \end{aligned}$$

(b) If we follow the same procedure we used in part (a) we find

$$\begin{aligned} X[n,k] &= \sum_{m=0}^{13} x[n+m]e^{-j(2\pi/7)km} \\ &= \sum_{m=0}^{6} x[n+m]e^{-j(2\pi/7)km} + \sum_{l=7}^{13} x[n+l]e^{-j(2\pi/7)kl} \\ &= \sum_{m=0}^{6} (x[n+m] + x[n+m+7])e^{-j(2\pi/7)km} \end{aligned}$$

With $n \ge 0$ we have $x[n+m] + x[n+m+7] = 1$ for $0 \le m \le 6$, and so

$$\begin{aligned} X[n,k] &= \mathcal{DFT}\{1\} \\ &= 7\delta[k] \end{aligned}$$

Therefore, for $0 \leq n \leq \infty$ we have

$$\sum_{k=0}^{6} X[n,k] = \sum_{k=0}^{6} 7\delta[k] = 7$$

10.31. (a) Sampling the continuous-time input signal

$$x(t) = e^{j(3\pi/8)10^4 t}$$

with a sampling period $T = 10^{-4}$ yields a discrete-time signal

$$x[n] = x(nT) = e^{j3\pi n/8}$$

In order for $X_w[k]$ to be nonzero at exactly one value of k, it is necessary for the frequency of the complex exponential of $x[n]$ to correspond to that of a DFT coefficent, $w_k = 2\pi k/N$. Thus,

$$\frac{3\pi}{8} = \frac{2\pi k}{N}$$
$$N = \frac{16k}{3}$$

The smallest value of k for which N is an integer is $k = 3$. Thus, the smallest value of N such that $X_w[k]$ is nonzero at exactly one value of k is

$$N = 16$$

(b) The rectangular windows, $w_1[n]$ and $w_2[n]$, differ only in their lengths. $w_1[n]$ has length 32, and $w_2[n]$ has length 8. Recall that compared to that of a longer window, the Fourier transform of a shorter window has a larger mainlobe width and higher sidelobes. Since the DFT is a sampled version of the Fourier transform, we might try to look for these features in the two plots. We notice that the second plot, Figure P10.31-3, appears to have a larger mainlobe width and higher sidelobes. As a result, we conclude that Figure P10.31-2 corresponds to $w_1[n]$, and P10.31-3 corresponds to $w_2[n]$.

(c) A simple technique to estimate the value of ω_0 is to find the value of k at which the peak of $|X_w[k]|$ occurs. Then, the estimate, is

$$\hat{\omega}_0 = \frac{2\pi k}{N}$$

The corresponding value of $\hat{\Omega}_0$ is

$$\hat{\Omega}_0 = \frac{2\pi k}{NT}$$

This estimate is not exact, since the peak of the Fourier transform magnitude $|X_w(e^{j\omega})|$ might occur between two values of the DFT magnitude $|X_w[k]|$, as shown below.

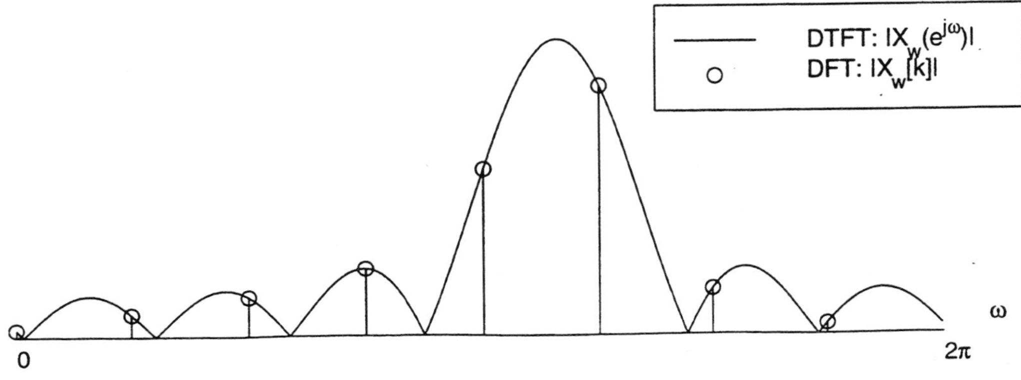

The maximum possible error, $\Omega_{\text{max error}}$, of the frequency estimate is one half of the frequency resolution of the DFT.

$$\begin{aligned}\Omega_{\text{max error}} &= \frac{1}{2}\frac{2\pi}{NT} \\ &= \frac{\pi}{NT}\end{aligned}$$

For the system parameters of $N = 32$, and $T = 10^{-4}$, this is

$$\Omega_{\text{max error}} = 982 \text{ rad/s}$$

(d) To develop a procedure to get an exact estimate of Ω_0, it helps to derive $X_w[k]$. First, let's find the Fourier transform of $x_w[n] = x[n]w[n]$, where $w[n]$ is an N-point rectangular window.

$$\begin{aligned}X_w(e^{j\omega}) &= \sum_{n=0}^{N-1} e^{j\omega_0 n} e^{-j\omega n} \\ &= \sum_{n=0}^{N-1} e^{-j(\omega-\omega_0)n}\end{aligned}$$

Let $\omega' = \omega - \omega_0$. Then,

$$\begin{aligned}X_w(e^{j\omega}) &= \sum_{n=0}^{N-1} e^{-j\omega' n} \\ &= \frac{1-e^{-j\omega' N}}{1-e^{-j\omega'}} \\ &= \frac{(e^{j\omega' N/2} - e^{-j\omega' N/2})e^{-j\omega' N/2}}{(e^{-j\omega'/2} - e^{-j\omega'/2})e^{-j\omega'/2}} \\ &= \frac{\sin(\omega' N/2)}{\sin(\omega'/2)} e^{-j\omega'(N-1)/2} \\ &= \frac{\sin[(\omega-\omega_0)N/2]}{\sin[(\omega-\omega_0)/2]} e^{-j(\omega-\omega_0)(N-1)/2}\end{aligned}$$

Note that $X_w(e^{j\omega})$ has generalized linear phase. Having established this equation for $X_w(e^{j\omega})$, we now find $X_w[k]$. Recall that $X_w[k]$ is simply the Fourier transform $X_w(e^{j\omega})$ evaluated at the frequencies $\omega = 2\pi k/N$, for $k = 0, \ldots, N-1$. Thus,

$$X_w[k] = \frac{\sin[(2\pi k/N - \omega_0)N/2]}{\sin[(2\pi k/N - \omega_0)/2]} e^{-j(2\pi k/N - \omega_0)(N-1)/2}$$

Note that the phase of $X_w[k]$, using the above equation, is

$$\angle X_w[k] = -\frac{(2\pi k/N - \omega_0)(N-1)}{2} + m\pi$$

where the $m\pi$ term comes from the fact that the term

$$\frac{\sin[(2\pi k/N - \omega_0)N/2]}{\sin[(2\pi k/N - \omega_0)/2]}$$

can change sign (i.e. become negative or positive), and thereby offset the phase by π radians. In addition, this term accounts for wrapping the phase, so that the phase stays in the range $[-\pi, \pi]$.

Re-expressing the equation for $\angle X_w[k]$, we find

$$\omega_0 = \frac{2(\angle X_w[k] - m\pi)}{N-1} + \frac{2\pi k}{N}$$

Let $X_{1w}[k]$ be the DFT of the 32-point sequence $x_{1w}[n] = x[n]w_1[n]$, and let $X_{2w}[k]$ be the DFT of the 8-point sequence $x_{2w}[n] = x[n]w_2[n]$. Note that the kth DFT coefficient of $X_{2w}[k]$ corresponds to $X_{1w}[4k]$. Thus, we can relate the 8 DFT coeffients of $X_{2w}[k]$ to 8 of the DFT coefficients in $X_{1w}[k]$. Using the $k = 0$th DFT coefficient for simplicity, we find

$$\begin{aligned}\omega_0 &= \frac{2(\angle X_{w1}[0] - m\pi)}{32-1} = \frac{2(\angle X_{w2}[0] - p\pi)}{8-1} \\ &= \frac{\angle X_{w1}[0] - m\pi}{15.5} = \frac{\angle X_{w2}[0] - p\pi}{3.5}\end{aligned}$$

A solution that satisfies these equations, with m and p integers, will yield a precise estimate of ω_0. We can accelerate solving these equations by determining which values of m and p to check. This is done by looking at the peak of $|X_w[k]|$ in a procedure similar to Part (c). Suppose that the indices for two largest values of $|X_w[k]|$ are k_{min} and k_{max}. Then, we know that the peak of $|X(e^{j\omega})|$ will occur in the range

$$\frac{2\pi k_{min}}{N} \leq \omega_0 \leq \frac{2\pi k_{max}}{N}$$

By re-expressing the equation for $\angle X_w[k]$, we see that

$$\begin{aligned}m_{min} &= \frac{1}{\pi}\left[2\angle X_{w1}[k_{min}] + \left(\frac{2\pi k_{min}}{N} - \hat{\omega}_0\right)(N-1)\right] \\ m_{max} &= \frac{1}{\pi}\left[2\angle X_{w1}[k_{max}] + \left(\frac{2\pi k_{max}}{N} - \hat{\omega}_0\right)(N-1)\right]\end{aligned}$$

In these equations, $\hat{\omega}_0$ is the estimate found in Part (c). So we would look for values of m in the range $[\lfloor m_{min} \rfloor, \lceil m_{max} \rceil]$. Similar expressions hold for p.

Once ω_0 is known, we can find Ω_0 using the relation $\Omega_0 = \omega_0/T$.

10.32. For each part, we use the definition of the time-dependent Fourier transform,

$$X[n,\lambda) = \sum_{m=-\infty}^{\infty} x[n+m]w[m]e^{-j\lambda m}.$$

(a) *Linearity*: using $x[n] = ax_1[n] + bx_2[n]$,

$$\begin{aligned}X[n,\lambda) &= \sum_{m=-\infty}^{\infty} x[n+m]w[m]e^{-j\lambda m} \\ &= \sum_{m=-\infty}^{\infty} (ax_1[n+m] + bx_2[n+m])\, w[m]e^{-j\lambda m} \\ &= a\sum_{m=-\infty}^{\infty} x_1[n+m]w[m]e^{-j\lambda m} + b\sum_{m=-\infty}^{\infty} x_2[n+m]w[m]e^{-j\lambda m} \\ &= aX_1[n,\lambda) + bX_2[n,\lambda)\end{aligned}$$

(b) *Shifting*: using $y[n] = x[n - n_0]$,

$$Y[n,\lambda) = \sum_{m=-\infty}^{\infty} y[n+m]w[m]e^{-j\lambda m}$$

$$
\begin{aligned}
&= \sum_{m=-\infty}^{\infty} x[n-n_0+m]w[m]e^{-j\lambda m} \\
&= X[n-n_0,\lambda)
\end{aligned}
$$

(c) *Modulation:* using $y[n] = e^{j\omega_0 n}x[n]$,

$$
\begin{aligned}
y[n+m] &= e^{j\omega_0(n+m)}x[n+m] \\
Y[n,\lambda) &= \sum_{m=-\infty}^{\infty} y[n+m]w[m]e^{-j\lambda m} \\
&= \sum_{m=-\infty}^{\infty} e^{j\omega_0(n+m)}x[n+m]w[m]e^{-j\lambda m} \\
&= \sum_{m=-\infty}^{\infty} e^{j\omega_0 n}x[n+m]w[m]e^{-j(\lambda-\omega_0)m} \\
&= e^{j\omega_0 n}X[n,\lambda-\omega_0)
\end{aligned}
$$

(d) *Conjugate Symmetry:* for $x[n]$ and $w[n]$ real,

$$
\begin{aligned}
X[n,\lambda) &= \sum_{m=-\infty}^{\infty} x[n+m]w[m]e^{-j\lambda m} \\
&= \left[\sum_{m=-\infty}^{\infty} x[n+m]w[m]e^{j\lambda m}\right]^* \\
&= [X[n,-\lambda)]^* \\
&= X^*[n,-\lambda)
\end{aligned}
$$

10.33. (a) We are given that $\phi_c(\tau) = \mathcal{E}\{x_c(t)x_c(t+\tau)\}$. Since $x[n] = x_c(nT)$,

$$
\begin{aligned}
\phi[m] &= \mathcal{E}\{x[n]x[n+m]\} \\
&= \mathcal{E}\{x_c(nT)x_c(nT+mT)\} \\
&= \phi_c(mT)
\end{aligned}
$$

(b) $P(\omega)$ and $P_c(\Omega)$ are the transforms of $\phi[m]$ and $\phi_c(\tau)$ respectively. Since $\phi[m]$ is a sampled version of $\phi_c(\tau)$, $P(\omega)$ and $P_c(\Omega)$ are related by

$$
P(\omega) = \frac{1}{T}\sum_{k=-\infty}^{\infty} P_c\left(\frac{\omega-2\pi k}{T}\right)
$$

(c) The condition is that no aliasing occurs when sampling. Thus, we require that $P_c(\Omega) = 0$ for $|\Omega| \geq \frac{\pi}{T}$ so that

$$
P(\omega) = \frac{1}{T}P_c\left(\frac{\omega}{T}\right), \qquad |\omega| < \pi
$$

10.34. In this problem, we are given

- $x[n] = A\cos(\omega_0 n + \theta) + e[n]$
- θ is a uniform random variable on 0 to 2π
- $e[n]$ is an independent, zero mean random variable

(a) Computing the autocorrelation function,

$$\begin{aligned}
\phi_{xx}[m] &= \mathcal{E}\{x[n]x[n+m]\} \\
&= \mathcal{E}\{(A\cos(\omega_0 n+\theta)+e[n])\,(A\cos(\omega_0(n+m)+\theta)+e[n+m])\} \\
&= \mathcal{E}\{A^2\cos(\omega_0 n+\theta)\cos(\omega_0(n+m)+\theta)\} \\
&\quad + \mathcal{E}\{Ae[n]\cos(\omega_0(n+m)+\theta)\} + \mathcal{E}\{Ae[n+m]\cos(\omega_0 n+\theta)\} \\
&\quad + \mathcal{E}\{e[n]e[n+m]\} \\
&= A^2\mathcal{E}\{\cos(\omega_0 n+\theta)\cos(\omega_0(n+m)+\theta)\} \\
&\quad + A\mathcal{E}\{e[n]\}\,\mathcal{E}\{\cos(\omega_0(n+m)+\theta)\} + A\mathcal{E}\{e[n+m]\}\,\mathcal{E}\{\cos(\omega_0 n+\theta)\} \\
&\quad + \mathcal{E}\{e[n]e[n+m]\}
\end{aligned}$$

First, note that

$$\cos(a)\cos(b) = \frac{1}{2}\cos(a+b) + \frac{1}{2}\cos(a-b)$$

Therefore, the first term can be re-expressed as

$$A^2\mathcal{E}\left\{\frac{1}{2}\cos\left(2\omega_0 n+\omega_0 m+2\theta\right)+\frac{1}{2}\cos(\omega_0 m)\right\}$$

Next, note that

$$\mathcal{E}\{e[n]\} = 0$$

As a result, the two middle terms drop out. Finally, note that since $e[n]$ is a sequence of zero-mean variables that are uncorrelated with each other,

$$\mathcal{E}\{e[n]e[n+m]\} = \sigma_e^2\delta[m], \qquad \text{where } \sigma_e^2 = \mathcal{E}\left\{e^2[n]\right\}$$

Putting this together, we get

$$\phi_{xx}[m] = A^2\mathcal{E}\left\{\frac{1}{2}\cos\left(2\omega_0 n+\omega_0 m+2\theta\right)+\frac{1}{2}\cos(\omega_0 m)\right\} + \sigma_e^2\delta[m]$$

Since $\frac{1}{2\pi}\int_0^{2\pi}\cos(2\omega_0 n+\omega_0 m+2\theta)d\theta = 0$, we have

$$\phi_{xx}[m] = \frac{A^2}{2}\cos(\omega_0 m) + \sigma_e^2\delta[m]$$

(b) Since the Fourier transform of $\cos(\omega_0 m)$ is $\pi\delta(\omega-\omega_0)+\pi\delta(\omega+\omega_0)$ for $|\omega|\le\pi$,

$$\Phi_{xx}(e^{j\omega}) = P_{xx}(\omega) = \frac{A^2\pi}{2}\left[\delta(\omega-\omega_0)+\delta(\omega+\omega_0)\right] + \sigma_e^2$$

10.35. (a) Plugging in the equation

$$I[k] = I(\omega_k) = \frac{1}{L}|V[k]|^2$$

into the relation

$$\text{var}[I(\omega)] \simeq P_{xx}^2(\omega)$$

we find that

$$\begin{aligned}
\text{var}\left[\frac{1}{L}|V[k]|^2\right] &\simeq P_{xx}^2(\omega) \\
\text{var}\left[|V[k]|^2\right] &\simeq L^2P_{xx}^2(\omega)
\end{aligned}$$

This equation can be used to find the approximate variance of $|X[k]|^2$. We substitute the signal $X[k]$ for $V[k]$, the DFT length N for L, and use the power spectrum

$$P_{xx}(w) = \sigma_x^2$$

This gives

$$\text{var}\left[|X[k]|^2\right] = N^2\sigma_x^4$$

(b) The cross-correlation is found below.

$$\begin{aligned}
\mathcal{E}\{X[k]X^*[r]\} &= \sum_{n_1=0}^{N-1}\sum_{n_2=0}^{N-1} \mathcal{E}\{x[n_1]x[n_2]\} W_N^{kn_1} W_N^{-rn_2} \\
&= \sum_{n_1=0}^{N-1}\sum_{n_2=0}^{N-1} \sigma_x^2 \delta[n_1 - n_2] W_N^{kn_1} W_N^{-rn_2} \\
&= \sum_{n=0}^{N-1} \sigma_x^2 W_N^{(k-r)n} \\
&= \sigma_x^2 \left[\frac{1 - W_N^{N(k-r)}}{1 - W_N^{(k-r)}}\right] \\
&= N\sigma_x^2 \delta[k-r]
\end{aligned}$$

Note that the cross-correlation is zero everywhere except when $k = r$. This is what one would expect for white noise, since samples for which $k \neq r$ are completely uncorrelated.

10.36. (a) The length of the data record is

$$\begin{aligned}
Q &= 10 \text{ seconds} \cdot \frac{20,000 \text{ samples}}{\text{second}} \\
Q &= 200,000 \text{ samples}
\end{aligned}$$

(b) To achieve a 10 Hz or less spacing between samples of the power spectrum, we require

$$\begin{aligned}
\frac{1}{NT} &\leq 10 \text{ Hz} \\
N &\geq \frac{1}{10T} \\
&\geq \frac{20,000}{10} \\
&\geq 2,000 \text{ samples}
\end{aligned}$$

Since N must also be a power of 2, we choose $N = 2048$.

(c)

$$\begin{aligned}
K &= \frac{Q}{L} \\
&= \frac{200,000}{2048} \\
&= 97.66 \text{ segments}
\end{aligned}$$

If we zero-pad the last segment so that it contains 2048 samples, we will have $K = 98$ segments.

(d) The key to reducing the variance is to use more segments. Two methods are discussed below. Note that in both methods, we want the segments to be length $L = 2048$ so that we maintain the frequency spacing.

(i) Decreasing the length of the segments to $\frac{1}{10}$th their length, and then zero-padding them to $L = 2048$ samples will increase K by a factor of 10. Accordingly, the variance will decrease by a factor of 10. However, the frequency resolution will be reduced.

(ii) If we increase the data record to 2,000,000 samples, we can keep the window length the same and increase K by a factor of 10.

10.37. (a) Taking the expected value of

$$\overline{\phi}[m] = \frac{1}{2\pi}\int_{-\pi}^{\pi} \overline{I}(\omega)e^{j\omega m}d\omega$$

gives

$$\begin{aligned}\mathcal{E}\left\{\overline{\phi}[m]\right\} &= \mathcal{E}\left\{\frac{1}{2\pi}\int_{-\pi}^{\pi} \overline{I}(\omega)e^{j\omega m}d\omega\right\} \\ &= \frac{1}{2\pi}\int_{-\pi}^{\pi} \mathcal{E}\left\{\overline{I}(\omega)\right\}e^{j\omega m}d\omega\end{aligned}$$

Using the relation

$$\mathcal{E}\left\{\overline{I}(w)\right\} = \frac{1}{2\pi LU}\int_{-\pi}^{\pi} P_{xx}(\theta)C_{ww}(e^{j(\omega-\theta)})d\theta$$

we find

$$\begin{aligned}\mathcal{E}\left\{\overline{\phi}[m]\right\} &= \frac{1}{2\pi}\int_{-\pi}^{\pi}\left[\frac{1}{2\pi LU}\int_{-\pi}^{\pi} P_{xx}(\theta)C_{ww}(e^{j(\omega-\theta)})d\theta\right]e^{j\omega m}d\omega \\ &= \frac{1}{2\pi LU}\int_{-\pi}^{\pi} P_{xx}(\theta)\left[\frac{1}{2\pi}\int_{-\pi}^{\pi} C_{ww}(e^{j(\omega-\theta)})e^{j\omega m}d\omega\right]d\theta\end{aligned}$$

Substituting $\omega' = \omega - \theta$ in the inner integral yields

$$\begin{aligned}\mathcal{E}\left\{\overline{\phi}[m]\right\} &= \frac{1}{2\pi LU}\int_{-\pi}^{\pi} P_{xx}(\theta)\left[\frac{1}{2\pi}\int_{-\pi-\theta}^{\pi-\theta} C_{ww}(e^{j\omega'})e^{j(\omega'+\theta)m}d\omega'\right]d\theta \\ &= \frac{1}{2\pi LU}\int_{-\pi}^{\pi} P_{xx}(\theta)e^{j\theta m}\left[\frac{1}{2\pi}\int_{-\pi-\theta}^{\pi-\theta} C_{ww}(e^{j\omega'})e^{j\omega' m}d\omega'\right]d\theta\end{aligned}$$

Note we can change the limits of integration of the inner integral to be $[-\pi, \pi]$ because we are integrating over the whole period. Doing this gives

$$\begin{aligned}\mathcal{E}\left\{\overline{\phi}[m]\right\} &= \frac{1}{2\pi LU}\int_{-\pi}^{\pi} P_{xx}(\theta)e^{j\theta m}\left[\frac{1}{2\pi}\int_{-\pi}^{\pi} C_{ww}(e^{j\omega'})e^{j\omega' m}d\omega'\right]d\theta \\ &= \frac{1}{2\pi LU}\int_{-\pi}^{\pi} P_{xx}(\theta)e^{j\theta m}\left\{c_{ww}[m]\right\}d\theta \\ &= \frac{1}{LU}c_{ww}[m]\left[\frac{1}{2\pi}\int_{-\pi}^{\pi} P_{xx}(\theta)e^{j\theta m}d\theta\right] \\ &= \frac{1}{LU}c_{ww}[m]\phi_{xx}[m]\end{aligned}$$

(b)

$$\overline{\phi}_p[m] = \frac{1}{N}\sum_{k=0}^{N-1}\overline{I}[k]e^{j2\pi km/N}$$

By applying the sampling theorem to Fourier transforms, we see that

$$\begin{aligned}
\overline{\phi}_p[m] &= \sum_{r=-\infty}^{\infty} \overline{\phi}_{xx}[m+rN] \\
\mathcal{E}\left\{\overline{\phi}_p[m]\right\} &= \sum_{r=-\infty}^{\infty} \mathcal{E}\left\{\overline{\phi}_{xx}[m+rN]\right\} \\
&= \frac{1}{LU}\sum_{r=-\infty}^{\infty} c_{ww}[m+rN]\phi_{xx}[m+rN]
\end{aligned}$$

which is a time aliased version of $\mathcal{E}\left\{\overline{\phi}_{xx}[m]\right\}$.

(c) N should be chosen so that no time aliasing occurs. Since $\overline{\phi}_{xx}[m]$ is $2L-1$ points long, we should choose $N \geq 2L$.

10.38. (a) For $0 \leq m \leq M$,

$$\begin{aligned}
\hat{\phi}_{xx}[m] &= \frac{1}{Q}\sum_{n=0}^{Q-m-1} x[n]x[n+m] \\
&= \frac{1}{Q}\left[\sum_{n=0}^{M-1} x[n]x[n+m] + \sum_{n=M}^{2M-1} x[n]x[n+m] + \ldots + \sum_{n=(K-1)M}^{KM-1} x[n]x[n+m]\right] \\
&= \frac{1}{Q}\left[\sum_{n=0}^{M-1} x[n]x[n+m]\right. \\
&\qquad \left. + \sum_{n=0}^{M-1} x[n+M]x[n+M+m] + \ldots + \sum_{n=0}^{M-1} x[n+(K-1)M]x[n+(K-1)M+m]\right] \\
&= \frac{1}{Q}\sum_{i=0}^{K-1}\sum_{n=0}^{M-1} x[n+iM]x[n+iM+m] \\
&= \frac{1}{Q}\sum_{i=0}^{K-1} c_i[m]
\end{aligned}$$

where

$$c_i[m] = \sum_{n=0}^{M-1} x[n+iM]x[n+iM+m] \qquad \text{for } 0 \leq m \leq M-1$$

(b) We can rewrite the expression for $c_i[m]$ from part (a) as

$$\begin{aligned}
c_i[m] &= \sum_{n=0}^{M-1} x[n+iM]x[n+iM+m] \\
&= \sum_{n=0}^{M-1} x[n+iM]x[n+iM+m] + \sum_{n=M}^{N-1} 0 \cdot x[n+iM+m] \\
&= \sum_{n=0}^{N-1} x_i[n]y_i[n+m]
\end{aligned}$$

where

$$x_i[n] = \begin{cases} x[n+iM], & 0 \leq n \leq M-1 \\ 0, & M \leq n \leq N-1 \end{cases}$$

and

$$y_i[n] = x[n + iM] \qquad \text{for } 0 \le n \le N-1$$

Thus, the correlations $c_i[m]$ can be obtained by computing N-point *linear* correlations. Next, we show that for $N \ge 2M - 1$, circular correlation is equivalent to linear correlation.

Note that the circular correlation of $x_i[n]$ with $y_i[n]$,

$$\tilde{c}_{yx}[m] = \sum_{n=0}^{N-1} x_i[n]y_i[((n+m))_N]$$

can be expressed as

$$\begin{aligned}
\tilde{c}_{yx}[m] &= \tilde{c}_{xy}[-m] \\
&= \sum_{n=0}^{N-1} x_i[((n-m))_N]y_i[n] \\
&= \sum_{n=0}^{N-1} x_i'[((m-n))_N]y_i[n]
\end{aligned}$$

where $x'[n] = x[-n]$. Note that this is a circular *convolution* of $x_i[-n]$ with $y_i[n]$. Thus, we have expressed the circular correlation of $x_i[n]$ with $y_i[n]$ as a circular convolution of $x_i[-n]$ with $y_i[n]$. Now recall from chapter 8 that the circular convolution of two M point signals is equivalent to their linear convolution when $N \ge 2M - 1$. Since we can express the circular correlation in terms of a circular convolution, this result applies to circular correlation as well. Therefore, we see that if $N \ge 2M - 1$,

$$c_i[m] = \tilde{c}_i[m] \qquad \text{for } 0 \le m \le M-1$$

Thus, the minimum value of N is $2M - 1$.

(c) A procedure for computing $\hat{\phi}_{xx}[m]$ is described below.

step 1: Compute $X_i[k]$ and $Y_i[k]$, which are the $N \ge 2M - 1$ point DFTs of $x_i[n]$ and $y_i[n]$.

step 2: Multiply $X_i[k]$ and $Y_i^*[k]$ point by point, yielding $C_i[k] = \tilde{C}_i[k] = X_i[k]Y_i^*[k]$.

step 3: Repeat the above two steps for all data (K times), then compute

$$\hat{\Phi}_{xx}[k] = \frac{1}{Q}\sum_{i=0}^{K-1} C_i[k] \qquad \text{for } 0 \le k \le N-1$$

step 4: Take the N point inverse DFT of $\hat{\Phi}_{xx}[k]$ to get $\hat{\phi}_{xx}[m]$.

Assuming that a radix-2 FFT, requiring $\frac{N}{2}\log_2 N$ complex multiplications is used to compute the forward and inverse DFTS, the number of complex multiplications is

$2 \cdot \frac{N}{2}\log_2 N \cdot K = KN\log_2 N,$	for step 1
$KN,$	for step 2
$N,$	for divide by Q operation in step 3
$\frac{N}{2}\log_2 N$	for step 4

So the total number of complex multiplications is $(K + \frac{1}{2})N\log_2 N + (K+1)N$.

(d) The procedure developed in part (c) would compute the cross-correlation estimate $\hat{\phi}_{xy}$ without any major modifications. All we need to do is redefine $y_i[n]$ as

$$y_i[n] = y[n + iM], \qquad 0 \le n \le N-1$$

and $x_i[n]$ is the same as it was before, namely

$$x_i[n] = \begin{cases} x[n+iM], & 0 \le n \le M-1 \\ 0, & M \le n \le N-1 \end{cases}$$

Note that for $m < 0$, $\hat{\phi}_{xy}[m] = \hat{\phi}_{yx}[-m]$.

(e) For $N = 2M$,

$$\begin{aligned} y_i[n] &= x[n+iM], \qquad \text{for } 0 \le n \le 2M-1 \\ &= x[n+iM](u[n]-u[n-M]) + x[n+iM](u[n-M]-u[n-2M]) \\ &= x[n+iM](u[n]-u[n-M]) + x[n-M+(i+1)M](u[n-M]-u[n-2M]) \\ &= x_i[n] + x_{i+1}[n-M] \end{aligned}$$

Taking the DFT of this expression yields

$$Y_i[k] = X_i[k] + (-1)^k X_{i+1}[k]$$

A procedure for computing $\hat{\phi}_{xx}$ for $0 \le m \le M-1$ is described below.

step 1: Compute the N point DFT $X_i[k]$ for $i = 0, 1, \ldots, K$.

step 2: Compute $Y_i[k] = X_i[k] + (-1)^k X_{i+1}[k]$ for $i = 0, 1, \ldots, K-1$.

step 3: Let $A_0[k] = 0$ and compute

$$A_i[k] = A_{i-1}[k] + X_i[k]Y_i^*[k], \quad i = 1, \ldots, K-1$$

step 4: Define $V[k] = A_{K-1}[k]$. Compute $v[m]$, the N point inverse DFT of $V[k]$.

step 5: Compute

$$\hat{\phi}_{xx}[m] = \frac{1}{Q} v[m]$$

Assuming that a radix-2 FFT, requiring $\frac{N}{2}\log_2 N$ complex multiplications is used to compute the forward and inverse DFTs, the number of complex multiplications is

$(K+1)\frac{N}{2}\log_2 N$,	for step 1
0,	for step 2
$(K-1)N$,	for step 3
$\frac{N}{2}\log_2 N$,	for step 4
N,	for the divide by Q in step 5

So the total number of complex multiplications is $\frac{K+2}{2}N\log_2 N + KN$. Note that for large N and K, this procedure requires roughly half the number of complex multiplications as the procedure described in part (c).

10.39. (a) Using the relations,

$$\begin{aligned} c[n,m] &= \frac{1}{2\pi}\int_{-\pi}^{\pi} |X[n,\lambda)|^2 e^{j\lambda m} d\lambda \\ X[n,\lambda) &= \sum_{m=-\infty}^{\infty} x[n+m]w[m]e^{-j\lambda m} d\lambda \end{aligned}$$

we find

$$\begin{aligned}
c[n,m] &= \frac{1}{2\pi}\int_{-\pi}^{\pi}|X[n,\lambda)|^2 e^{j\lambda m}d\lambda \\
&= \frac{1}{2\pi}\int_{-\pi}^{\pi}X[n,\lambda)X[n,-\lambda)e^{j\lambda m}d\lambda \\
&= \frac{1}{2\pi}\int_{-\pi}^{\pi}\left(\sum_{l=-\infty}^{\infty}x[n+l]w[l]e^{-j\lambda l}\right)\left(\sum_{r=-\infty}^{\infty}x[n+r]w[r]e^{j\lambda r}\right)e^{j\lambda m}d\lambda \\
&= \sum_{l=-\infty}^{\infty}\sum_{r=-\infty}^{\infty}x[n+l]w[l]x[n+r]w[r]\left(\frac{1}{2\pi}\int_{-\pi}^{\pi}e^{-j\lambda l}e^{j\lambda r}e^{j\lambda m}d\lambda\right) \\
&= \sum_{l=-\infty}^{\infty}\sum_{r=-\infty}^{\infty}x[n+l]w[l]x[n+r]w[r]\left(\frac{1}{2\pi}\int_{-\pi}^{\pi}e^{-j\lambda(-l+r)}e^{j\lambda m}d\lambda\right)
\end{aligned}$$

Using the Fourier transform relation,

$$\delta[n-n_0] \longleftrightarrow e^{-j\omega n_0}$$

we find

$$c[n,m] = \sum_{l=-\infty}^{\infty}\sum_{r=-\infty}^{\infty}x[n+l]w[l]x[n+r]w[r]\delta[m-l+r]$$

The $\delta[m-l+r]$ term is zero everwhere except when $m-l+r=0$. Therefore, we can replace the two sums of l and r with one sum over r, by substituting $l=m+r$.

$$\begin{aligned}
c[n,m] &= \sum_{r=-\infty}^{\infty}x[n+m+r]w[m+r]x[n+r]w[r] \\
&= \sum_{r=-\infty}^{\infty}x[n+r]w[r]x[n+m+r]w[m+r]
\end{aligned}$$

(b) First, note that

$$\begin{aligned}
|X[n,\lambda)|^2 &= X[n,-\lambda)X[n,\lambda) \\
&= |X[n,-\lambda)|^2
\end{aligned}$$

Starting with the definition of $c[n,m]$,

$$c[n,m] = \frac{1}{2\pi}\int_{-\pi}^{\pi}|X[n,\lambda)|^2 e^{j\lambda m}d\lambda$$

$$c[n,-m] = \frac{1}{2\pi}\int_{-\pi}^{\pi}|X[n,\lambda)|^2 e^{-j\lambda m}d\lambda$$

we substitute $\lambda' = -\lambda$ to get

$$\begin{aligned}
c[n,-m] &= -\frac{1}{2\pi}\int_{\pi}^{-\pi}|X[n,-\lambda')|^2 e^{j\lambda' m}d\lambda' \\
&= \frac{1}{2\pi}\int_{-\pi}^{\pi}|X[n,-\lambda')|^2 e^{j\lambda' m}d\lambda' \\
&= \frac{1}{2\pi}\int_{-\pi}^{\pi}|X[n,\lambda')|^2 e^{j\lambda' m}d\lambda' \\
&= c[n,m]
\end{aligned}$$

Thus, the time-dependent autocorrelation function is an even function of m for n fixed. Next, we use this fact to obtain the equivalent expression for $c[n, m]$.

$$\begin{aligned} c[n,m] &= \sum_{r=-\infty}^{\infty} x[n+r]w[r]x[m+n+r]w[m+r] \\ &= \sum_{r=-\infty}^{\infty} x[n+r]w[r]x[-m+n+r]w[-m+r] \end{aligned}$$

Substituting $r' = n + r$ gives

$$\begin{aligned} &= \sum_{r'=-\infty}^{\infty} x[r']w[r'-n]x[r'-m]w[(r'-m)-n] \\ &= \sum_{r'=-\infty}^{\infty} x[r']x[r'-m]w[r'-n]w[-(m+n-r')] \\ &= \sum_{r'=-\infty}^{\infty} x[r']x[r'-m]h_m[n-r'] \end{aligned}$$

where

$$h_m[r] = w[-r]w[-(m+r)]$$

(c) To compute $c[n, m]$ by causal operations, we see that

$$h_m[r] = w[-r]w[-(m+r)]$$

requires that $w[r]$ must be zero for

$$\begin{aligned} -r &< 0 \\ r &> 0 \end{aligned}$$

and $w[r]$ must be zero for

$$\begin{aligned} -(m+r) &< 0 \\ m+r &> 0 \\ r &> -m \end{aligned}$$

Thus, $w[r]$ must be zero for $r > \min(0, -m)$. If m is positive, then $w[r]$ must be zero for $r > 0$. This is equivalent to the requirement that $w[-r]$ must be zero for $r < 0$.

(d) Plugging in

$$w[-r] = \begin{cases} a^r, & r \geq 0 \\ 0, & r < 0 \end{cases}$$

into $h_m[r] = w[-r]w[-(m+r)]$, we find

$$h_m[r] = \begin{cases} a^{2r+m}, & r \geq 0, r \geq -m \\ 0, & \text{otherwise} \end{cases}$$

Taking the z-transform of this expression gives

$$\begin{aligned} H_m(z) &= \sum_{r=-\infty}^{\infty} h_m[r]z^{-r} \\ &= \sum_{r=0}^{\infty} a^{2r+m}z^{-r} \\ &= a^m \sum_{r=0}^{\infty} (a^2z^{-1})^r \end{aligned}$$

Again we have assumed that m is positive. If $|z| > a^2$, then

$$\begin{aligned} H_m(z) &= \frac{a^m}{1 - a^2 z^{-1}} \\ h_m[r] &= a^m \delta[r] + a^2 h_m[r-1] \end{aligned}$$

Using this in the equation for $c[n, m]$ gives

$$\begin{aligned} c[n,m] &= \sum_{r=-\infty}^{\infty} x[r]x[r-m]h_m[n-r] \\ &= \sum_{r=-\infty}^{\infty} x[r]x[r-m]\left(a^m \delta[n-r] + a^2 h_m[n-r-1]\right) \\ &= a^m x[n]x[n-m] + a^2 \sum_{r=-\infty}^{\infty} x[r]x[r-m]h_m[n-r-1] \\ &= a^m x[n]x[n-m] + a^2 c[n-1, m] \end{aligned}$$

A block diagram of this system appears below.

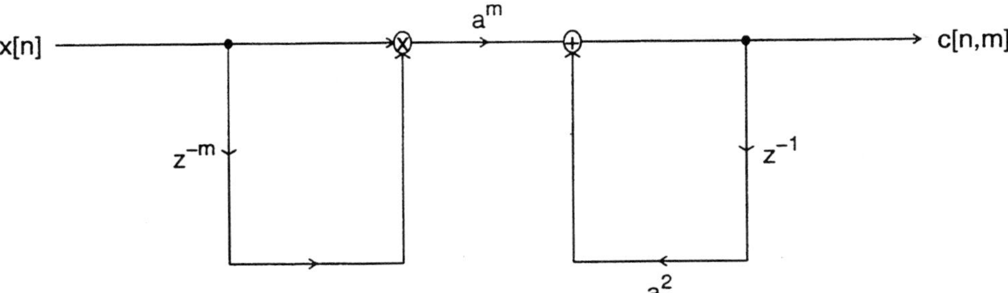

(e) Next, consider the system

$$w[-r] = \begin{cases} ra^r, & r \geq 0 \\ 0, & r < 0 \end{cases}$$

$$\begin{aligned} h_m[r] &= \{ra^r u[r]\}\{(r+m)a^{r+m}u[r+m]\} \\ &= a^m r^2 a^{2r} + a^m m r a^{2r} \qquad r \geq 0; r \geq -m \end{aligned}$$

To get the z-transform $H_m(z)$, recall the z-transform property: $rx[r] \leftrightarrow -z\frac{dX(z)}{dz}$. Using this property, we find

$$\begin{aligned} ra^{2r}u[r] &\Longleftrightarrow \frac{a^2 z^{-1}}{(1-a^2z^{-1})^2} \\ r^2 a^{2r} u[r] &\Longleftrightarrow \frac{a^2 z^{-1}(1+a^2 z^{-1})}{(1-a^2 z^{-1})^3} \end{aligned}$$

Again we have assumed that m is positive. Thus,

$$\begin{aligned} H_m(z) &= a^m \left[\frac{a^2 z^{-1}(1+a^2z^{-1})}{(1-a^2z^{-1})^3}\right] + ma^m \left[\frac{a^2 z^{-1}}{(1-a^2z^{-1})^2}\right] \\ &= \frac{a^{m+2}z^{-1}(1+a^2z^{-1}) + ma^m(a^2z^{-1})(1-a^2z^{-1})}{(1-a^2z^{-1})^3} \end{aligned}$$

$$= \frac{a^{m+2}z^{-1}(1 + a^2z^{-1} + m - ma^2z^{-1})}{(1 - a^2z^{-1})^3}$$
$$= \frac{a^{m+2}(1+m)z^{-1} + a^{m+4}(1-m)z^{-2}}{1 - 3a^2z^{-1} + 3a^4z^{-2} - a^6z^{-3}}$$

Cross-multiplying and taking the inverse z-transform gives

$$h_m[r] - 3a^2h_m[r-1] + 3a^4h_m[r-2] - a^6h_m[r-3] = a^{m+2}(1+m)\delta[r-1] + a^{m+4}(1-m)\delta[r-2]$$
$$h_m[r] = 3a^2h_m[r-1] - 3a^4h_m[r-2] + a^6h_m[r-3] + a^{m+2}(1+m)\delta[r-1] + a^{m+4}(1-m)\delta[r-2]$$

Using this relation for $h_m[r]$ in

$$c[n,m] = \sum_{r=-\infty}^{\infty} x[r]x[r-m]h_m[n-r]$$

we get

$$\begin{aligned} c[n,m] &= \sum_{r=-\infty}^{\infty} x[r]x[r-m]\left(3a^2h_m[n-r-1] - 3a^4h_m[n-r-2] + a^6h_m[n-r-3]\right) \\ &\quad + \sum_{r=-\infty}^{\infty} x[r]x[r-m]\left(a^{m+2}(1+m)\delta[n-r-1] + a^{m+4}(1-m)\delta[n-r-2]\right) \\ &= 3a^2c[n-1,m] - 3a^4c[n-2,m] + a^6c[n-3,m] \\ &\quad + a^{m+2}(1+m)x[n-1]x[n-1-m] + a^{m+4}(1-m)x[n-2]x[n-2-m] \end{aligned}$$

A block diagram of this system appears below.

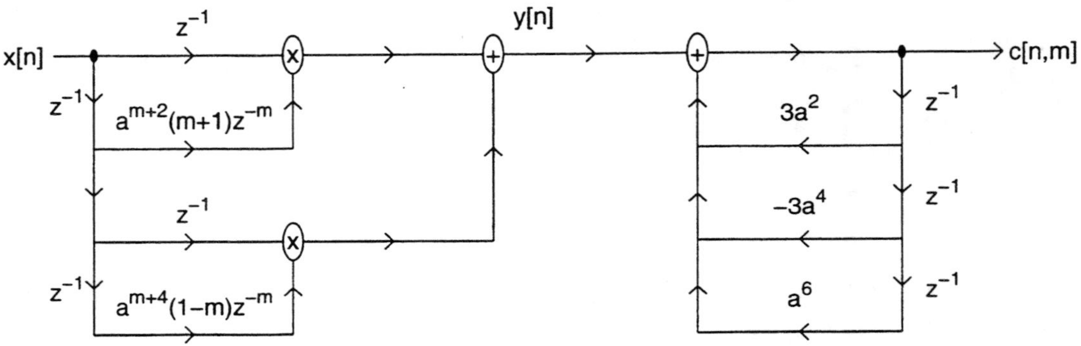

10.40. (a) Looking at the figure, we see that

$$\begin{aligned} X[n,\lambda) &= \left\{\left(x[n]e^{-j\lambda n}\right) * h_0[n]\right\} e^{j\lambda n} \\ &= \left[\sum_{m=-\infty}^{\infty} x[n-m]e^{-j\lambda(n-m)}h_0[m]\right] e^{j\lambda n} \\ &= \sum_{m=-\infty}^{\infty} x[n-m]h_o[m]e^{j\lambda m} \end{aligned}$$

Let $m' = -m$. Then,

$$X[n,\lambda) = \sum_{m'=\infty}^{-\infty} x[n+m']h_0[-m']e^{-j\lambda m'}$$

$$= \sum_{m'=-\infty}^{\infty} x[n+m']h_0[-m']e^{-j\lambda m'}$$
$$= X[n,\lambda)$$

if $h_0[-m] = w[m]$. Next, we show that for λ fixed, $X[n,\lambda)$ behaves as a linear, time-invariant system.

Linear: Inputting the signal $ax_1[n] + bx_2[n]$ into the system yields

$$\sum_{m=-\infty}^{\infty} (ax_1[n+m] + bx_2[n+m])\, h_0[-m]e^{-j\lambda m} =$$
$$\sum_{m=-\infty}^{\infty} ax_1[n+m]h_0[-m]e^{-j\lambda m} + \sum_{m=-\infty}^{\infty} bx_2[n+m]h_0[-m]e^{-j\lambda m} = aX_1[n,\lambda) + bX_2[n,\lambda)$$

The system is linear.

Time invariant: Shifting the input $x[n]$ by an amount l yields

$$\sum_{m=-\infty}^{\infty} x[n+m+l]h_0[-m]e^{-j\lambda m} = X[n+l,\lambda)$$

which is the output shifted by l samples. The system is time-invariant.

Next, we find the impulse response and frequency response of the system. To find the impulse response, denoted as $h[n]$, we let $x[n] = \delta[n]$.

$$h[n] = \sum_{m=-\infty}^{\infty} \delta[n+m]w[m]e^{-j\lambda m}$$
$$= w[-n]e^{j\lambda n}$$
$$= h_0[n]e^{j\lambda n}$$

Taking the DTFT gives the frequency response, denoted as $H(e^{j\omega})$.

$$H(e^{j\omega}) = H_0(e^{j(\omega-\lambda)})$$

(b) We find $S(e^{j\omega})$ to be

$$s[n] = \left(x[n]e^{-j\lambda n}\right) * w[-n]$$
$$S(e^{j\omega}) = X\left(e^{j(\omega+\lambda)}\right) W(e^{-j\omega})$$
$$S(e^{j\omega}) = X\left(e^{j(\omega+\lambda)}\right) H_0(e^{j\omega})$$

Note that most typical window sequences are lowpass in nature, and are centered around a frequency of $\omega = 0$. Since $H_0(e^{j\omega}) = W(e^{-j\omega})$ is the Fourier transform of a window which is lowpass in nature, the signal $S(e^{j\omega})$ is also lowpass.

The signal $s[n] = \check{X}[n,\lambda)$ is multiplied by a complex exponential $e^{j\lambda n}$. This modulation shifts the frequency response of $S(e^{j\omega})$ so that it is centered at $\omega = \lambda$.

$$h[n] = s[n]e^{j\lambda n}$$
$$H(e^{j\omega}) = S\left(e^{j(\omega-\lambda)}\right)$$

Since $S(e^{j\omega})$ is lowpass filter centered at $\omega = 0$, the overall system is a bandpass filter centered at $\omega = \lambda$.

(c) First, it is shown that the individual outputs $y_k[n]$ are samples (in the λ dimension) of the time-dependent Fourier transform.

$$\begin{aligned} y_k[n] &= \sum_{m=-\infty}^{\infty} x[n+m]w[m]e^{-j\lambda_k m} \\ &= \sum_{m=-\infty}^{\infty} x[n+m]w[m]e^{-j2\pi km/N} \\ &= X[n,\lambda)|_{\lambda=2\pi k/N} \end{aligned}$$

Next, it is shown that the overall output is $y[n] = Nw[0]x[n]$.

$$\begin{aligned} y[n] &= \sum_{k=0}^{N-1} y_k[n] \\ &= \sum_{k=0}^{N-1} \sum_{m=-\infty}^{\infty} x[n+m]w[m]e^{-j2\pi km/N} \\ &= \sum_{m=-\infty}^{\infty} \sum_{k=0}^{N-1} x[n+m]w[m]e^{-j2\pi km/N} \\ &= \sum_{m=-\infty}^{\infty} x[n+m]w[m] \underbrace{\sum_{k=0}^{N-1} e^{-j2\pi km/N}}_{N\delta[m]} \\ &= Nw[0]x[n] \end{aligned}$$

(d) Consider a single channel,

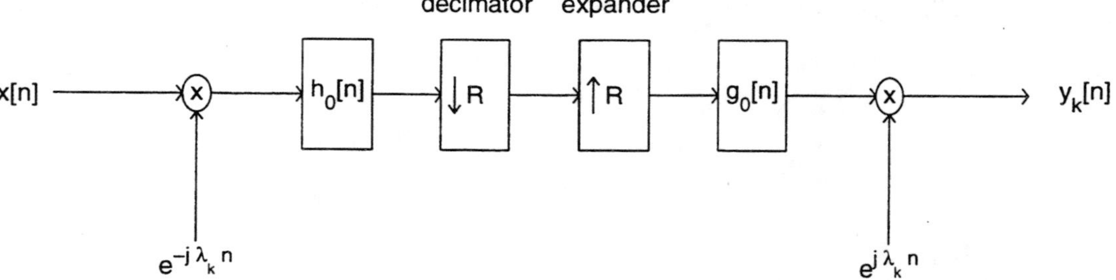

In the frequency domain, the input to the decimator is

$$X\left(e^{j(\omega+\lambda_k)}\right) H_0(e^{j\omega})$$

so the output of the decimator is

$$\frac{1}{R}\sum_{l=0}^{R-1} X\left(e^{j((\omega-2\pi l)/R+\lambda_k)}\right) H_0\left(e^{j(\omega-2\pi l)/R}\right)$$

The output of the expander is

$$\frac{1}{R}\sum_{l=0}^{R-1} X\left(e^{j(\omega+\lambda_k-2\pi l/R)}\right) H_0\left(e^{j(\omega-2\pi l/R)}\right)$$

The output $Y_k(e^{j\omega})$ is then

$$Y_k(e^{j\omega}) = \frac{1}{R}\sum_{l=0}^{R-1} G_0\left(e^{j(\omega-\lambda_k)}\right) X\left(e^{j(\omega-2\pi l/R)}\right) H_0\left(e^{j(\omega-\lambda_k-2\pi l/R)}\right)$$

The overall system output is formed by summing these terms over k.

$$\begin{aligned} Y(e^{j\omega}) &= \sum_{k=0}^{N-1} Y_k(e^{j\omega}) \\ &= \frac{1}{R}\sum_{l=0}^{R-1}\sum_{k=0}^{N-1} G_0\left(e^{j(\omega-\lambda_k)}\right) X\left(e^{j(\omega-2\pi l/R)}\right) H_0\left(e^{j(\omega-\lambda_k-2\pi l/R)}\right) \end{aligned}$$

To cancel the aliasing, we rewrite the equation as follows:

$$\begin{aligned} Y(e^{j\omega}) &= X(e^{j\omega})\frac{1}{R}\sum_{k=0}^{N-1} H_0\left(e^{j(\omega-\lambda_k)}\right) G_0\left(e^{j(\omega-\lambda_k)}\right) \\ &+ \underbrace{\sum_{l=1}^{R-1} X\left(e^{j(\omega-2\pi l/R)}\right)\frac{1}{R}\sum_{k=0}^{N-1} G_0\left(e^{j(\omega-\lambda_k)}\right) H_0\left(e^{j(\omega-\lambda_k-2\pi l/R)}\right)}_{\text{Aliasing Component}} \end{aligned}$$

Therefore, we require the following relations to be satisfied so that $y[n] = x[n]$:

$$\begin{aligned} \sum_{k=0}^{N-1} G_0\left(e^{j(\omega-\lambda_k)}\right) H_0\left(e^{j(\omega-\lambda_k-2\pi l/R)}\right) &= 0, \qquad \forall\, \omega, \text{ and } l = 1, \ldots, R-1 \\ \sum_{k=0}^{N-1} H_0\left(e^{j(\omega-\lambda_k)}\right) G_0\left(e^{j(\omega-\lambda_k)}\right) &= R, \qquad \forall\, \omega \end{aligned}$$

(e) *Yes*, it is possible. $G_o(e^{j\omega}) = NH_0(e^{j\omega})$ will yield exact reconstruction.

(f) See chapter 7 in "Multirate Digital Signal Processing" by Crochiere and Rabiner, 1983.

(g) Once again, we consider a single channel,

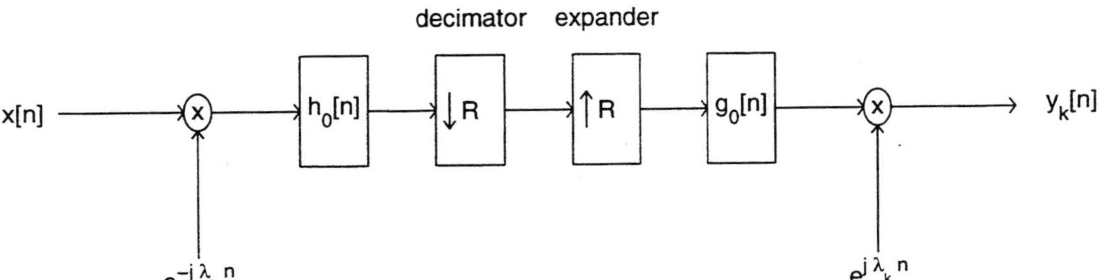

From Part (a), we know that the output of the filter $h_0[n]$ is

$$\check{X}[n,\lambda_k) = \sum_{m=-\infty}^{\infty} x[m]h_0[n-m]e^{-j\lambda_k m}$$

or, using $\lambda_k = 2\pi k/N$,

$$\check{X}[n,k] = \sum_{m=-\infty}^{\infty} x[m]h_0[n-m]e^{-j2\pi km/N}$$

Therefore, the output of the decimator is

$$\check{X}[Rn,k] = \sum_{m=-\infty}^{\infty} x[m]h_0[Rn-m]e^{-j2\pi km/N}$$

Recall that in general, the output of an expander with expansion factor R is

$$x_e[n] = \sum_{\ell=-\infty}^{\infty} x[\ell]\delta[n-\ell R]$$

This relation is given in chapter 3. Therefore, the output of the expander is

$$\sum_{\ell=-\infty}^{\infty} \check{X}[R\ell,k]\delta[n-\ell R]$$

This signal is then convolved with $g_0[n]$, giving

$$\sum_{m=-\infty}^{\infty}\sum_{\ell=-\infty}^{\infty} \check{X}[R\ell,k]\delta[m-\ell R]g_0[n-m] = \sum_{\ell=-\infty}^{\infty} \check{X}[R\ell,k]g_0[n-\ell R]$$

Therefore,

$$\begin{aligned}
y_k[n] &= \sum_{\ell=-\infty}^{\infty} g_0[n-\ell R]\left(\sum_{m=-\infty}^{\infty} x[m]h_0[Rl-m]e^{-j2\pi km/N}\right)e^{j2\pi kn/N} \\
y[n] &= \sum_{k=0}^{N-1}\sum_{\ell=-\infty}^{\infty} g_0[n-\ell R]\left(\sum_{m=-\infty}^{\infty} x[m]h_0[Rl-m]e^{-j2\pi km/N}\right)e^{j2\pi kn/N} \\
&= \sum_{k=0}^{N-1}\sum_{\ell=-\infty}^{\infty} g_0[n-\ell R]\sum_{m=-\infty}^{\infty} x[m]h_0[Rl-m]e^{-j2\pi k(m-n)/N} \\
&= \sum_{\ell=-\infty}^{\infty}\sum_{m=-\infty}^{\infty} g_0[n-\ell R]h_0[Rl-m]x[m]\sum_{k=0}^{N-1} e^{j2\pi k(n-m)/N}
\end{aligned}$$

Now recall that $\sum_{k=0}^{N-1} e^{j2\pi k(n-m)/N} = N\delta\left[((n-m))_N\right]$, by considering it as a Fourier series expansion, or as an inverse DFT of $Ne^{-j2\pi mk/N}$. Thus,

$$\sum_{k=0}^{N-1} e^{j2\pi k(n-m)/N} = N\sum_{r=-\infty}^{\infty}\delta[n-m-rN]$$

where r is an integer. Therefore,

$$\begin{aligned}
y[n] &= \sum_{\ell=-\infty}^{\infty}\sum_{m=-\infty}^{\infty} g_0[n-\ell R]h_0[\ell R-m]x[m]N\sum_{r=-\infty}^{\infty}\delta[n-m-rN] \\
&= N\sum_{\ell=-\infty}^{\infty}\sum_{r=-\infty}^{\infty} g_0[n-\ell R]h_0[\ell R-n+rN]x[n-rN] \\
&= N\sum_{r=-\infty}^{\infty} x[n-rN]\sum_{\ell=-\infty}^{\infty} g_0[n-\ell R]h_0[\ell R+rN-n]
\end{aligned}$$

Therefore, if we want $y[n] = x[n]$, we require

$$\sum_{\ell=-\infty}^{\infty} g_0[n - \ell R]h_0[\ell R + rN - n] = \delta[r]$$

for all values n.

(h) Intuitively, we see that it is possible since we are keeping the necessary number of samples. If $g_0[n] = \delta[n]$ find that

$$\begin{aligned}\sum_{\ell=-\infty}^{\infty} \delta[n - \ell R]h_0[\ell R + rN - n] &= h_0[rN] \\ &= \delta[r]\end{aligned}$$

since $h_0[rN]$ is zero for all values of r, except $r = 0$, where it is equal to 1. Thus, the condition derived in Part (g) is satisfied.

(i) See Rabiner and Crochiere or Portnoff. (Hint: consider an overlap and add FFT algorithm.)

10.41. Note that $h[n]$ is real in this problem.

(a) First, we express $y[n]$ as the convolution of $h[n]$ and $x[n]$.

$$y[n] = \sum_{k=-\infty}^{\infty} h[k]x[n-k]$$

The autocorrelation of $y[n]$ is then

$$\begin{aligned}\phi_{yy}[m] &= \mathcal{E}\{y[n+m]y[n]\} \\ &= \mathcal{E}\left\{\sum_{k=-\infty}^{\infty} h[k]x[n+m-k]\sum_{l=-\infty}^{\infty} h[l]x[n-l]\right\} \\ &= \sum_{k=-\infty}^{\infty}\sum_{l=-\infty}^{\infty} h[k]h[l]\mathcal{E}\{x[n+m-k]x[n-l]\} \\ &= \sum_{k=-\infty}^{\infty}\sum_{l=-\infty}^{\infty} h[k]h[l]\phi_{xx}[l+m-k]\end{aligned}$$

Since $x[n]$ is white noise, it has the autocorrelation function

$$\phi_{xx}[l+m-k] = \sigma_x^2\delta[l+m-k]$$

Substituting this into the expression for $\phi_{yy}[m]$ gives

$$\begin{aligned}\phi_{yy}[m] &= \sigma_x^2\sum_{k=-\infty}^{\infty}\sum_{l=-\infty}^{\infty} h[k]h[l]\delta[l+m-k] \\ &= \sigma_x^2\sum_{l=-\infty}^{\infty} h[l+m]h[l]\end{aligned}$$

Note that

$$\phi_{yy}[m] = \sigma_x^2\sum_{l=-\infty}^{\infty} h[l-m]h[l]$$

is also a correct answer, since $\phi_{yy}[m] = \phi_{yy}[-m]$.

(b) Taking the DTFT of $\phi_{yy}[m]$ will give the power density spectrum $\Phi_{yy}(\omega)$.

$$\begin{aligned}\Phi_{yy}(\omega) &= \sum_{m=-\infty}^{\infty}\left\{\sigma_x^2 \sum_{l=-\infty}^{\infty} h[l+m]h[l]\right\} e^{-j\omega m} \\ &= \sigma_x^2 \sum_{l=-\infty}^{\infty} h[l] \sum_{m=-\infty}^{\infty} h[l+m]e^{-j\omega m}\end{aligned}$$

Substituting $k = l + m$ into the second summation gives

$$\begin{aligned}\Phi_{yy}(\omega) &= \sigma_x^2 \sum_{l=-\infty}^{\infty} h[l] \sum_{k=-\infty}^{\infty} h[k]e^{-j\omega(k-l)} \\ &= \sigma_x^2 \sum_{l=-\infty}^{\infty} h[l]e^{j\omega l} \sum_{k=-\infty}^{\infty} h[k]e^{-j\omega k} \\ &= \sigma_x^2 \sum_{l=-\infty}^{\infty} h[-l]e^{-j\omega l} \sum_{k=-\infty}^{\infty} h[k]e^{-j\omega k} \\ &= \sigma_x^2 H^*(e^{j\omega})H(e^{j\omega}) \\ &= \sigma_x^2 \left|H(e^{j\omega})\right|^2\end{aligned}$$

(c) This problem can be approached either in the time domain or the z-transform domain.

Time domain: Since all the a_k's are zero for a MA process,

$$y[n] = \sum_{k=0}^{M} b_k x[n-k]$$

so $y[n]$ is nonzero for $0 \le n \le M$. Note that the autocorrelation sequence,

$$\phi_{yy}[m] = \sum_{n=-\infty}^{\infty} y[n+m]y[n]$$

can be re-written as a convolution

$$\phi_{yy}[m] = \sum_{n=-\infty}^{\infty} g[m-n]y[n]$$

where $g[n] = y[-n]$. Therefore,

$$\phi_{yy}[n] = y[-n] * y[n]$$

Since $y[-n]$ is nonzero for $-M \le n \le 0$, and $y[n]$ is nonzero for $0 \le n \le M$, we see that their convolution $\phi_{yy}[m]$ is nonzero only in the interval $|m| \le M$.

Z-transform domain: Note that

$$\Phi_{yy}(z) = \sigma_x^2 H(z)H^*(z)$$

If all the a_k's $= 0$, then

$$\begin{aligned}H(z) &= \sum_{k=0}^{M} b_k z^{-k} \\ \Phi_{yy}(z) &= \sum_{k=0}^{M} b_k z^{-k} \sum_{\ell=0}^{M} b_\ell^* z^{\ell}\end{aligned}$$

The relation for $\Phi_{yy}(z)$ above is found by multiplying two polynomials in z. The highest power of z in $\Phi_{yy}(z)$ is z^M which arises from the multiplication of the $k = 0$ and $l = M$ coefficients. The smallest power of z in $\Phi_{yy}(z)$ is z^{-M} which arises from the multiplication of the $k = M$ and $l = 0$ coefficents. Thus, $\phi_{yy}[m]$ is nonzero only in the interval $|m| \leq M$.

(d) For an AR process,

$$\begin{aligned} H(z) &= \frac{b_0}{1 - \sum_{k=1}^{N} a_k z^{-k}} \\ &= \frac{b_0}{\prod_{k=1}^{N}(1 - \alpha_k z^{-1})} \end{aligned}$$

Since

$$\Phi_{yy}(z) = \sigma_x^2 H(z) H^*(z)$$

$$\Phi_{yy}(z) = \frac{b_0^2}{\prod_{k=1}^{N}(1 - \alpha_k z^{-1})(1 - \alpha_k^* z)}$$

Thus, the poles for $\Phi_{yy}(z)$ come in conjugate reciprocal pairs. A sample pole-zero diagram appears below.

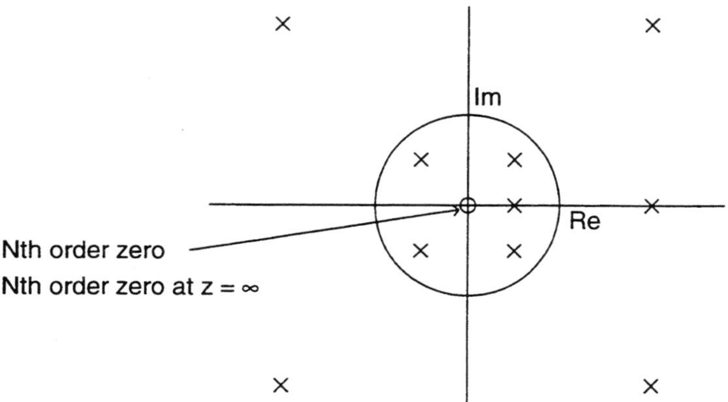

By performing a partial fraction expansion on $\Phi_{yy}(z)$ we find that each pole pair contributes a sequence of the form $A_k \alpha_k^{|m|}$

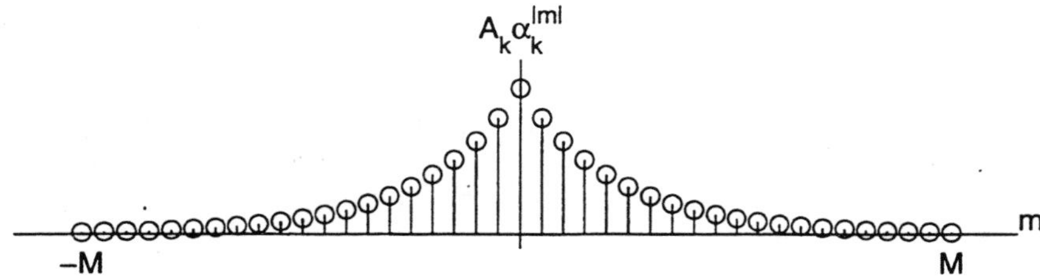

and therefore

$$\phi_{yy}[m] = \sum_{k=1}^{N} A_k \alpha_k^{|m|}$$

(e) For an AR process, with $b_0 = 1$,

$$H(z) = \frac{Y(z)}{X(z)} = \frac{1}{1 - \sum_{k=1}^{N} a_k z^{-k}}$$

which means that

$$y[n] = \sum_{k=1}^{N} a_k y[n-k] + x[n]$$

The autocorrelation function is then

$$\begin{aligned}
\phi_{yy}[m] &= \phi_{yy}[-m] \\
&= \mathcal{E}\{y[n-m]y[n]\} \\
&= \mathcal{E}\left\{ y[n-m] \left(\sum_{k=1}^{N} a_k y[n-k] + x[n] \right) \right\} \\
&= \sum_{k=1}^{N} a_k \mathcal{E}\{y[n-m]y[n-k]\} + \mathcal{E}\{y[n-m]x[n]\} \\
&= \sum_{k=1}^{N} a_k \phi_{yy}[m-k] + \phi_{yx}[-m] \\
&= \sum_{k=1}^{N} a_k \phi_{yy}[m-k] + \phi_{xy}[m]
\end{aligned}$$

For $m = 0$,

$$\phi_{yy}[0] = \sum_{k=1}^{N} a_k \phi_{yy}[-k] + \phi_{xy}[0]$$

The $\phi_{xy}[0]$ term is

$$\begin{aligned}
\phi_{xy}[0] &= \mathcal{E}\{x[n]y[n]\} \\
&= \mathcal{E}\left\{ x[n] \left(\sum_{k=1}^{N} a_k y[n-k] + x[n] \right) \right\} \\
&= \sum_{k=1}^{N} a_k \mathcal{E}\{x[n]y[n-k]\} + \mathcal{E}\{x[n]x[n]\} \\
&= \sum_{k=1}^{N} a_k \mathcal{E}\{x[n]y[n-k]\} + \sigma_x^2
\end{aligned}$$

Note that $x[n]$ is uncorrelated with the $y[n-k]$, for $k = 1, \ldots, N$. Therefore,

$$\phi_{xy}[0] = \sigma_x^2$$

Thus,

$$\begin{aligned}
\phi_{yy}[0] &= \sum_{k=1}^{N} a_k \phi_{yy}[-k] + \sigma_x^2 \\
&= \sum_{k=1}^{N} a_k \phi_{yy}[k] + \sigma_x^2
\end{aligned}$$

since $\phi_{yy}[k] = \phi_{yy}[-k]$. For $m \geq 1$,

$$\begin{aligned}
\phi_{yy}[m] &= \sum_{k=1}^{N} a_k \phi_{yy}[m-k] + \phi_{xy}[m] \\
&= \sum_{k=1}^{N} a_k \phi_{yy}[m-k]
\end{aligned}$$

since $\phi_{xy}[m]$ is zero for all $m \geq 1$.

(f) By symmetry of the autocorrelation sequence, we know that

$$\begin{aligned}
\phi_{yy}[m-k] &= \phi_{yy}[k-m] \\
&= \phi_{yy}[|m-k|]
\end{aligned}$$

Thus,

$$\sum_{k=1}^{N} a_k \phi_{yy}[|m-k|] = \sum_{k=1}^{N} a_k \phi_{yy}[m-k]$$

Using the result from part (e), we get

$$\sum_{k=1}^{N} a_k \phi_{yy}[|m-k|] = \phi_{yy}[m]$$

for $m = 1, 2, \ldots, N$.

10.42. (a) Sampling $x_c(t)$ we get

$$\begin{aligned}
x[n] &= x_c(nT) \\
&= \frac{1}{16} \sum_{k=-4}^{4} \left(\frac{1}{2}\right)^{|k|} e^{j(2\pi/16)kn}
\end{aligned}$$

Define the periodic sequence $X[k]$ to be

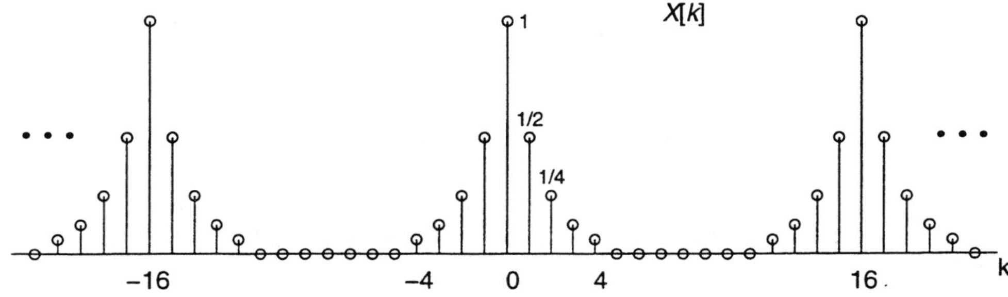

Then we see that we can write $x[n]$ in terms of $X[k]$:

$$\begin{aligned}
x[n] &= \frac{1}{16} \sum_{k=-4}^{4} X[k] e^{j(2\pi/16)kn} \\
&= \frac{1}{16} \sum_{k=-8}^{7} X[k] e^{j(2\pi/16)kn} \\
&= \text{IDFS}\{X[k]\}
\end{aligned}$$

However, since the period we use in the sum of the IDFS is unimportant we can also write

$$\begin{aligned} x[n] &= \frac{1}{16}\sum_{k=0}^{15} X[k]e^{j(2\pi/16)kn} \\ &= \text{IDFS}\{X[k]\} \\ &= \text{IDFT}\{X_0[k]\} \end{aligned}$$

where $X_0[k]$ is the period of $X[k]$ starting at zero, i.e.,

$$X_0[k] = \begin{cases} X[k], & k = 0, \ldots, 15 \\ 0, & \text{otherwise} \end{cases}$$

Using this information we can now find $G[k]$

$$\begin{aligned} G[k] &= \text{DFT}\{g[n]\} \\ &= \text{DFT}\{x[n](u[n] - u[n-16])\} \\ &= \text{DFT}\{x[n]\} \\ &= \text{DFT}\{\text{IDFT}\{X_0[k]\}\} \\ &= X_0[k] \end{aligned}$$

Thus, $G[k]$ looks like

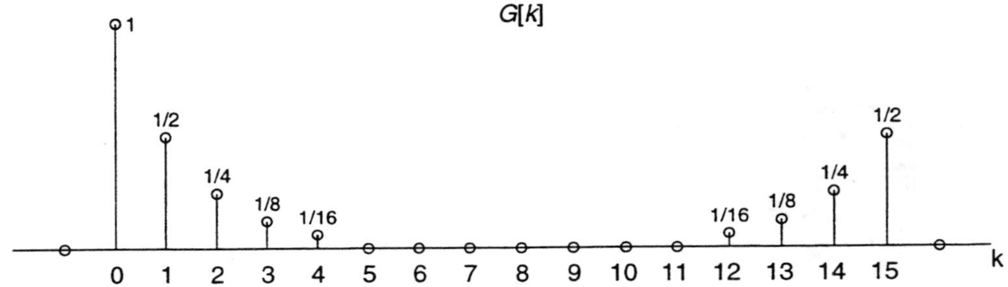

(b) We want to find a sequence $Q[k]$ such that

$$\begin{aligned} q[n] &= \alpha x_c\left(\frac{n2\pi}{32}\right) \\ &= \frac{\alpha}{16}\sum_{k=-4}^{4}\left(\frac{1}{2}\right)^{|k|} e^{j(2\pi/32)kn} \end{aligned}$$

We can apply the same idea as we did in part (a), except now the DFS and DFT size should be 32 instead of 16. Going through the same steps will lead us to the sequence $Q[k]$ that looks like:

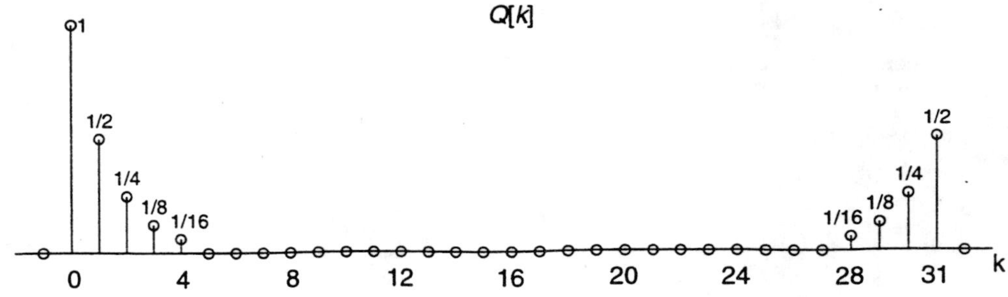

(Here we have assumed $\alpha = 1$). We see that we can interpolate in the time domain by zero padding in the *middle* of the DFT samples.

10.43. (a) Using the relation,

$$f_k = \begin{cases} \frac{k}{NT}, & 0 \le k \le N/2 \\ \frac{k-N}{NT}, & N/2 \le k \le N \end{cases}$$

where N is the DFT length and T is the sampling period, the continuous-time frequencies corresponding to the DFT indices $k = 32$ and $k = 231$ are

$$\begin{aligned} f_{32} &= \frac{32}{(256)(1/20,000)} \\ &= 2500 \text{ Hz} \\ f_{231} &= \frac{231 - 256}{(256)(1/20,000)} \\ &= -1953 \text{ Hz} \end{aligned}$$

(b) Since

$$\hat{x}[n] = x[n]w_R[n]$$

the DTFT of $\hat{x}[n]$ is simply the periodic convolution of $X(e^{j\omega})$ with $W_R(e^{j\omega})$.

$$\hat{X}(e^{j\omega}) = \frac{1}{2\pi}\int_{-\pi}^{\pi} X(e^{j\theta})W_R(e^{j(\omega-\theta)})d\theta$$

(c) Multiplication in the time domain corresponds to periodic convolution in the frequency domain, as shown in part (b). To evaluate this periodic convolution at the frequency $\omega_{32} = 2\pi(32)/L$, (where $L = N = 256$) corresponding to the $k = 32$ DFT coefficient, we first shift the window $W_{avg}(e^{j\omega})$ to ω_{32}. Then, we multiply the shifted window with $X(e^{j\omega})$, and integrate the result. In order for

$$X_{avg}[32] = \alpha\hat{X}[31] + \hat{X}[32] + \alpha\hat{X}[33]$$

we must therefore have

$$W_{avg}(e^{j\omega}) = \begin{cases} 1, & \omega = 0 \\ \alpha, & \omega = \pm 2\pi/L \\ 0, & 2\pi k/L, \qquad \text{for } k = 2, 3, \ldots, L-2 \end{cases}$$

Note that we are only specifying $W_{avg}(e^{j\omega})$ at the DFT frequencies $\omega = 2\pi k/L$, for $k = 0, \ldots, L-1$.

(d) Note that the L point DFT of a rectangular window of length L is

$$\begin{aligned} W_R[k] &= \sum_{n=0}^{L-1}(1)e^{-j2\pi k/L} \\ &= \frac{1 - e^{-j2\pi k}}{1 - e^{-j2\pi kL}} \\ &= L\delta[k] \end{aligned}$$

$W_{avg}(e^{j\omega})$ is only specified at DFT frequencies $\omega = 2\pi k/L$, and it can take on other values between these frequencies. Therefore, the DTFT of $W_{avg}(e^{j\omega})$ can be written in terms of $W_R(e^{j\omega})$ and two shifted versions of $W_R(e^{j\omega})$.

$$W_{avg}(e^{j\omega}) = \frac{\alpha}{L}W_R\left(e^{j(\omega+2\pi/L)}\right) + \frac{1}{L}W_R(e^{j\omega}) + \frac{\alpha}{L}W_R\left(e^{j(\omega-2\pi/L)}\right)$$

(e) Taking the inverse DTFT of $W_{avg}(e^{j\omega})$ gives $w_{avg}[n]$.

$$\begin{aligned} w_{avg}[n] &= \frac{\alpha}{L}w_R[n]e^{-j2\pi n/L} + \frac{1}{L}w_R[n] + \frac{\alpha}{L}w_R[n]e^{j2\pi n/L} \\ &= \left[\frac{1}{L} + \frac{2\alpha}{L}\cos\left(\frac{2\pi n}{L}\right)\right] w_R[n] \end{aligned}$$

A sketch of $w_{avg}[n]$ is provided below.

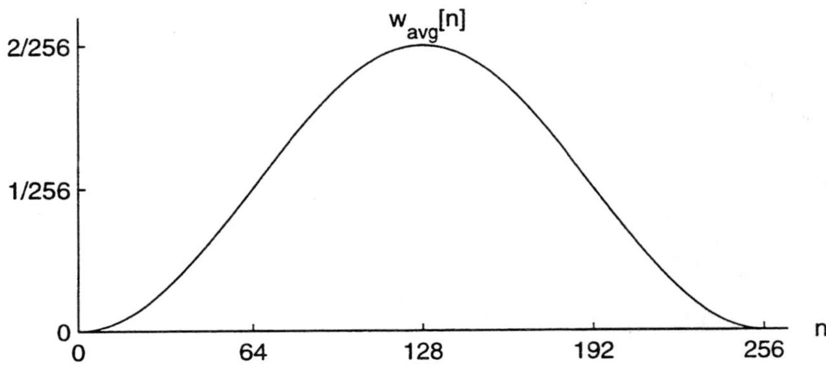

10.44. (a) After the lowpass filter, the highest frequency in the signal is $\Delta\omega$. To avoid aliasing in the downsampler we must have

$$\begin{aligned} \Delta\omega M &\leq \pi \\ M &\leq \frac{\pi}{\Delta\omega} \\ &\leq \frac{N}{2k_\Delta} \end{aligned}$$

$$M\text{max} = \frac{N}{2k_\Delta}$$

(b) The fourier transform of $x_l[n]$ looks like

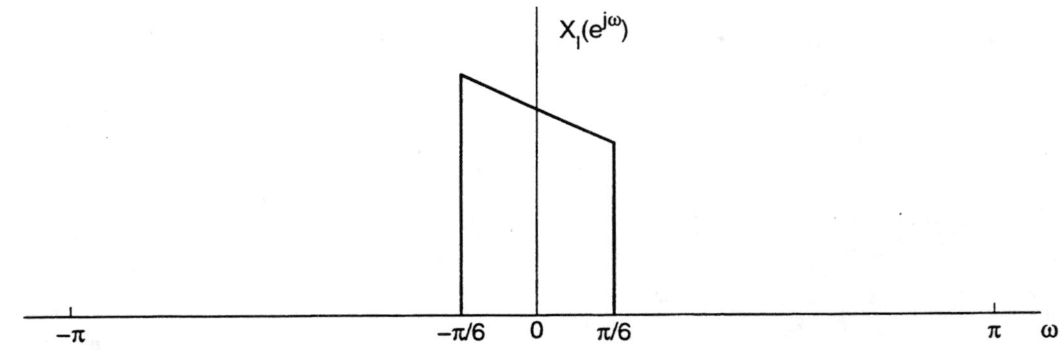

so $M = 6$ is the largest M we can use that avoids aliasing. With this choice of M the fourier transform of $x_z[n]$ looks like

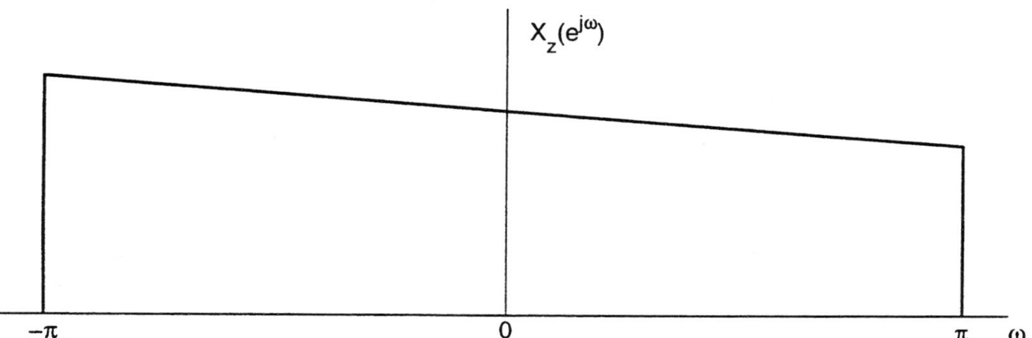

Taking the DFT of $x_z[n]$ gives us N samples of $X_z(e^{j\omega})$ spaced $2\pi/N$ apart in frequency. By examining the figures above we see that these samples correspond to the desired samples of $X(e^{j\omega})$ which will be spaced $2\Delta\omega/N$ apart inside the region $-\Delta\omega < \omega < \Delta\omega$.

Note that after downsampling the endpoints of the region alias. Therefore, we cannot trust the values our new DFT provides at those points. However, the way the problem is set up we already know the values at the endpoints from the original DFT.

(c) The system $p[n]$ periodically replicates $X_N[n]$ to create $\tilde{X}_N[n]$. Then, the upsampler inserts $M-1$ zeros in betweeen each sample of $\tilde{X}_N[n]$. Thus, the samples $k_c - k_\Delta$ and $k_c + k_\Delta$ which border the zoom region in the original DFT map to $M(k_c - k_\Delta)$ and $M(k_c + k_\Delta)$. The system $h[n]$ then interpolates between the nonzero points filling in the "missing" samples. Since the linear phase filter is length 513 it adds a delay of $M/2 = 512/2 = 256$ samples so the desired samples of $\tilde{X}_{NM}[n]$ now lie in the region

$$\begin{aligned} M(k_c - k_\Delta) + 256 \quad &\leq n \leq \quad M(k_c + k_\Delta) + 256 \\ k_c' - k_\Delta' \quad &\leq n \leq \quad k_c' + k_\Delta' \end{aligned}$$

where

$$\begin{aligned} k_c' &= Mk_c + 256 \\ k_\Delta' &= Mk_\Delta \end{aligned}$$

(d) A typical sketch of $X(e^{j\omega})$ and $X_N[k]$ look like.

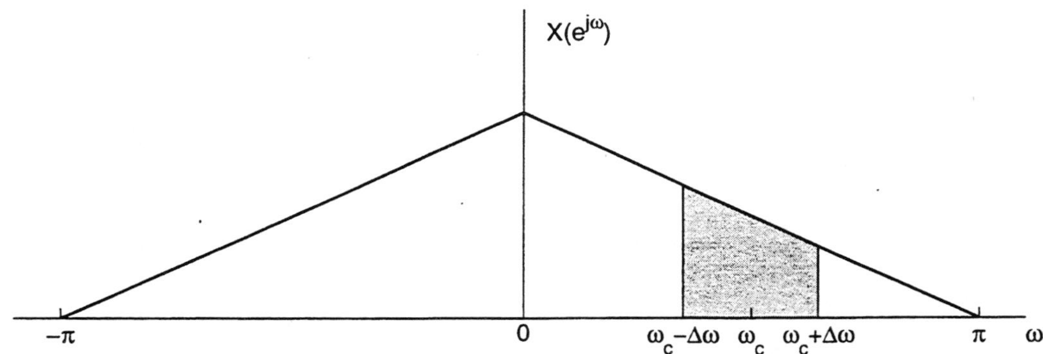

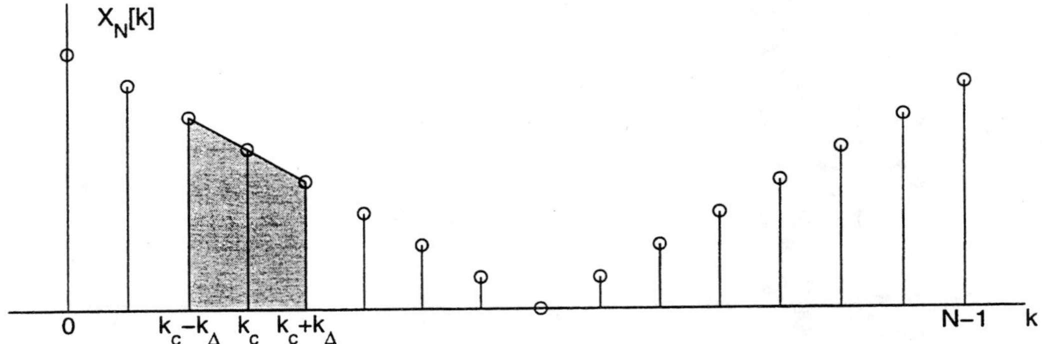

After periodically replicating and upsampling by M we have a signal that looks like

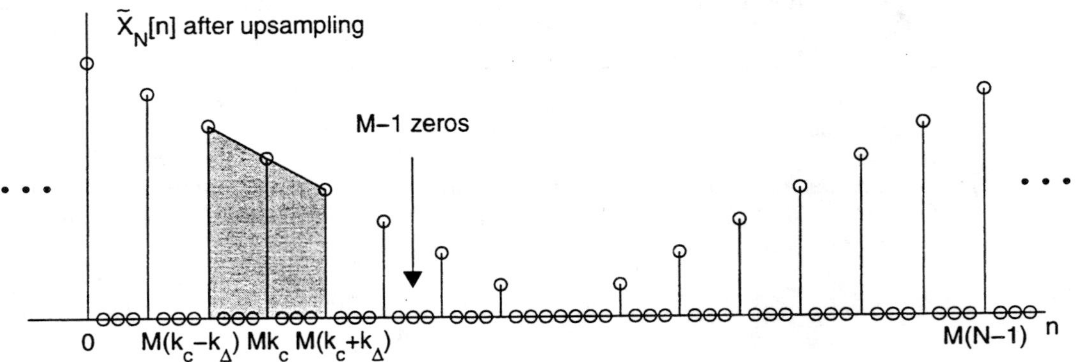

Filtering by $h[n]$ then interpolates between the samples. $\tilde{X}_{NM}[n]$ is shown below if we assume that $h[n]$ is the ideal zero phase filter. The points with an x correspond to the interpolated points.

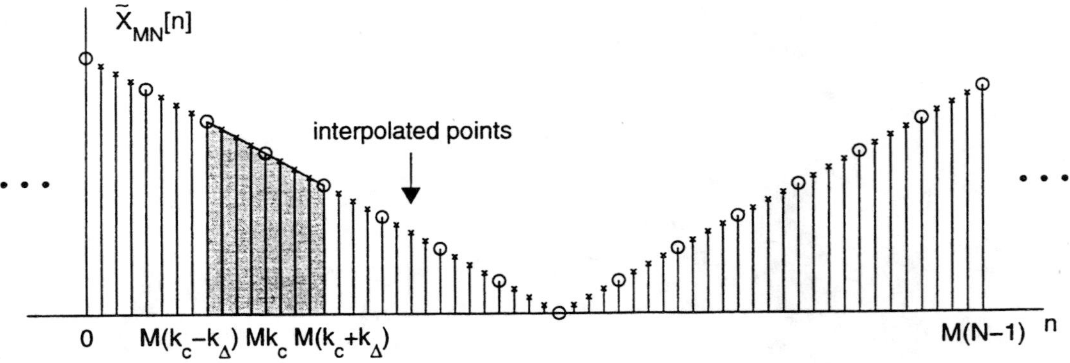

Thus, we need to extract the points

$$\begin{aligned} M(k_c - k_\Delta) \quad &\leq n \leq \quad M(k_c + k_\Delta) \\ k_c' - k_\Delta' \quad &\leq n \leq \quad k_c' + k_\Delta' \end{aligned}$$

where

$$\begin{aligned} k'_c &= Mk_c \\ k'_\Delta &= Mk_\Delta \end{aligned}$$

Solutions – Chapter 11

Discrete Hilbert Transforms

11.1. Using the fact that $x_e[n]$ is the inverse transform of $\mathcal{R}e$ we get

$$\begin{aligned}\mathcal{R}e\{X(e^{j\omega})\} &= 2 - ae^{j\omega} - ae^{-j\omega} \\ x_e[n] &= 2\delta[n] - a\delta[n+1] - a\delta[n-1]\end{aligned}$$

Since $x[n]$ is causal, we can recover it from $x_e[n]$

$$x[n] = 2x_e[n]u[n] - x_e[0]\delta[n] = 2\delta[n] - 2a\delta[n-1]$$

This implies that

$$x_o[n] = \frac{x[n] - x[-n]}{2} = a\delta[n+1] - a\delta[n-1]$$

and since $j\mathcal{I}m\{X(e^{j\omega})\}$ is the transform of $x_o[n]$ we find

$$\mathcal{I}m\{X(e^{j\omega})\} = 2a\sin\omega$$

11.2. Taking the inverse transform of $\mathcal{R}e\{X(e^{j\omega})\} = 5/4 - \cos\omega$, we get

$$x_e[n] = \frac{5}{4}\delta[n] - \frac{1}{2}\delta[n+1] - \frac{1}{2}\delta[n-1]$$

Since $x[n]$ is causal, we can recover it from $x_e[n]$

$$x[n] = 2x_e[n]u[n] - x_e[0]\delta[n] = \frac{5}{4}\delta[n] - \delta[n-1],$$

11.3. Note that

$$\begin{aligned}|X(e^{j\omega})|^2 &= \frac{5}{4} - \cos\omega \\ &= \left(1 - \frac{1}{2}e^{-j\omega}\right)\left(1 - \frac{1}{2}e^{j\omega}\right) \\ &= X(e^{j\omega})X^*(e^{j\omega})\end{aligned}$$

If $X(e^{j\omega}) = (1 - \frac{1}{2}e^{-j\omega})$ we get

$$x[n] = \delta[n] - \frac{1}{2}\delta[n-1]$$

but this does not satisfy the conditions on $x[n]$ given in the problem statement.
However, if we let $X(e^{j\omega}) = (1 - \frac{1}{2}e^{-j\omega})e^{-j\omega}$ we get

$$x[n] = \delta[n-1] - \frac{1}{2}\delta[n-2]$$

which satisfies all the constraints. The idea behind this choice is that cascading a signal with an allpass system does not change the magnitude squared response.
Another choice that works is $X(e^{j\omega}) = \frac{1}{2}(1 - 2e^{-j\omega})e^{-j\omega}$ for which we get

$$x[n] = \frac{1}{2}\delta[n-1] - \delta[n-2]$$

The idea behind this choice was to flip the zero to its reciprocal location outside the unit circle. This has the same magnitude squared response up to a scaling factor; hence, the $\frac{1}{2}$ term.

11.4. Take the DTFT of $x_r[n]$ to get

$$x_r[n] = \frac{1}{2}\delta[n] - \frac{1}{4}\delta[n+2] - \frac{1}{4}\delta[n-2]$$

$$X_r(e^{j\omega}) = \frac{1}{2} - \frac{1}{2}\cos 2\omega.$$

where $X_r(e^{j\omega}) = \frac{1}{2}[X(e^{j\omega}) + X^*(e^{j\omega})]$ is the *conjugate symmetric* part of $X(e^{j\omega})$. Since $X(e^{j\omega}) = 0$ for $-\pi \leq \omega < 0$ we have

$$\begin{aligned} X(e^{j\omega}) &= \begin{cases} 2X_r(e^{j\omega}), & 0 \leq \omega < \pi \\ 0, & \text{otherwise} \end{cases} \\ &= \begin{cases} 1 - \cos 2\omega, & 0 \leq \omega < \pi \\ 0, & \text{otherwise} \end{cases} \end{aligned}$$

Thus,

$$\mathcal{Re}\{X(e^{j\omega})\} = \begin{cases} 1 - \cos 2\omega, & 0 \leq \omega < \pi \\ 0, & \text{otherwise} \end{cases}$$

and

$$\mathcal{Im}\{X(e^{j\omega})\} = 0.$$

About Notation: $X_R(e^{j\omega})$ with a capital R is the real part of $X(e^{j\omega})$. $X_r(e^{j\omega})$ with a small r is the conjugate symmetric part of $X(e^{j\omega})$ which is complex-valued in general.

11.5. The Hilbert transform can be viewed as a filter with frequency response

$$H(e^{j\omega}) = \begin{cases} -j, & 0 < \omega < \pi, \\ j, & -\pi < \omega < 0. \end{cases}$$

(a) First, take the transform of $x_r[n]$

$$X_r(e^{j\omega}) = \pi\delta(\omega - \omega_0) + \pi\delta(\omega + \omega_0).$$

Now, filter with $H(e^{j\omega})$ and take the inverse transform to get $x_i[n]$

$$\begin{aligned} X_i(e^{j\omega}) &= H(e^{j\omega})X_r(e^{j\omega}) \\ &= -j\pi\delta(\omega - \omega_0) + j\pi\delta(\omega + \omega_0) \end{aligned}$$

$$x_i[n] = \sin \omega_0 n$$

(b) Similarly, $x_i[n] = -\cos \omega_0 n$.

(c) $x_r[n]$ is the ideal low pass filter

$$x_r[n] = \frac{\sin(\omega_c n)}{\pi n} \longleftrightarrow \begin{cases} 1, & |\omega| \leq \omega_c \\ 0, & \omega_c < |\omega| \leq \pi \end{cases}$$

After filtering with the Hilbert tranformer we get

$$X_i(e^{j\omega}) = \begin{cases} -j, & 0 \leq \omega \leq \omega_c \\ j, & -\omega_c \leq \omega \leq 0 \\ 0, & \omega_c \leq |\omega| \leq \pi \end{cases}$$

Taking the inverse transform yields

$$x_i[n] = \frac{1}{2\pi}\int_{-\omega_c}^{0} je^{j\omega n}\,d\omega - \frac{1}{2\pi}\int_0^{\omega_c} je^{j\omega n}\,d\omega = \frac{1 - \cos \omega_c n}{\pi n}$$

11.6. Using Euler's identity,

$$\begin{aligned} jX_I(e^{j\omega}) &= j(2\sin\omega - 3\sin 4\omega) \\ &= 2\left(\frac{e^{j\omega} - e^{-j\omega}}{2}\right) - 3\left(\frac{e^{j4\omega} - e^{-j4\omega}}{2}\right) \\ &= -\frac{3}{2}e^{j4\omega} + e^{j\omega} - e^{-j\omega} + \frac{3}{2}e^{-j4\omega} \end{aligned}$$

Since $x_o[n]$ is the inverse transform of $jX_I(e^{j\omega})$ we get

$$x_o[n] = -\frac{3}{2}\delta[n+4] + \delta[n+1] - \delta[n-1] + \frac{3}{2}\delta[n-4]$$

Because $x[n]$ is real and causal we can recover most of x[n], i.e.,

$$\begin{aligned} x[n] &= 2x_o[n]u[n] + x[0]\delta[n] \\ &= x[0]\delta[n] - 2\delta[n-1] + 3\delta[n-4] \end{aligned}$$

The extra information given to us allows us to find $x[0]$,

$$\begin{aligned} 6 &= X(e^{j\omega})\big|_{\omega=0} \\ &= \sum_{n=-\infty}^{\infty} x[n]e^{j\omega(0)} \\ &= x[0] - 2 + 3 \end{aligned}$$

Plugging this into our equation for $x[n]$ we find

$$x[n] = 5\delta[n] - 2\delta[n-1] + 3\delta[n-4]$$

11.7. (a) Given the imaginary part of $X(e^{j\omega})$, we can take the inverse DTFT to find the odd part of $x[n]$, denoted $x_o[n]$.

$$\begin{aligned} \mathcal{Im}\left\{X(e^{j\omega})\right\} &= \sin\omega + 2\sin 2\omega \\ &= \frac{1}{2j}e^{j\omega} - \frac{1}{2j}e^{-j\omega} + \frac{1}{j}e^{j2\omega} - \frac{1}{j}e^{-j2\omega} \\ &= \frac{1}{j}e^{j2\omega} + \frac{1}{2j}e^{j\omega} - \frac{1}{2j}e^{-j\omega} - \frac{1}{j}e^{-j2\omega} \end{aligned}$$

$$\begin{aligned} x_o[n] &= \mathcal{DFT}^{-1}\left[j\mathcal{Im}\left\{X(e^{j\omega})\right\}\right] \\ &= \mathcal{DFT}^{-1}\left[e^{j2\omega} + \frac{1}{2}e^{j\omega} - \frac{1}{2}e^{-j\omega} - e^{-j2\omega}\right] \\ &= \delta[n+2] + \frac{1}{2}\delta[n+1] - \frac{1}{2}\delta[n-1] - \delta[n-2] \end{aligned}$$

Using the formula $x[n] = 2x_o[n]u[n] + x[0]\delta[n]$, we find

$$x[n] = -\delta[n-1] - 2\delta[n-2] + x[0]\delta[n]$$

Any $x[0]$ will result in a correct solution to this problem. Setting $x[0] = 0$ gives the result

$$x[n] = -\delta[n-1] - 2\delta[n-2]$$

(b) No, the answer to part (a) is not unique, since any choice for $x[0]$ will result in a correct solution.

11.8. Using Euler's identity and the fact that $x_o[n]$ is the inverse transform of $jX_I(e^{j\omega})$ we find

$$\begin{aligned} jX_I(e^{j\omega}) &= 3j\sin 2\omega \\ &= 3\left(\frac{e^{j2\omega}-e^{-j2\omega}}{2}\right) \\ x_o[n] &= \frac{3}{2}(\delta[n+2]-\delta[n-2]) \end{aligned}$$

Because $x[n]$ is real and causal we can recover all of $x[n]$ except at $n=0$,

$$\begin{aligned} x[n] &= 2x_o[n]u[n] + x[0]\delta[n] \\ &= -3\delta[n-2] + x[0]\delta[n] \end{aligned}$$

Therefore,

$$\begin{aligned} x_e[n] &= \frac{x[n]+x[-n]}{2} \\ &= \frac{(-3\delta[n-2]+x[0]\delta[n]) + (-3\delta[n+2]+x[0]\delta[n])}{2} \\ &= -\frac{3}{2}\delta[n+2] + x[0]\delta[n] - \frac{3}{2}\delta[n-2] \end{aligned}$$

Using the fact that $X_R(e^{j\omega})$ is the transform of $x_e[n]$ we find

$$\begin{aligned} X_R(e^{j\omega}) &= -\frac{3}{2}e^{j2\omega} + x[0] - \frac{3}{2}e^{-j2\omega} \\ &= x[0] - 3\cos 2\omega \end{aligned}$$

Thus, $X_{R2}(e^{j\omega})$ and $X_{R3}(e^{j\omega})$ are possible if $x[0]=-1$ and $x[0]=0$ respectively.

11.9. (a) Given the imaginary part of $X(e^{j\omega})$, we can take the inverse DTFT to find the odd part of $x[n]$, denoted $x_o[n]$.

$$\begin{aligned} \mathcal{Im}\left\{X(e^{j\omega})\right\} &= 3\sin\omega + \sin 3\omega \\ &= \frac{3}{2j}e^{j\omega} - \frac{3}{2j}e^{-j\omega} + \frac{1}{2j}e^{j3\omega} - \frac{1}{2j}e^{-j3\omega} \\ &= \frac{1}{2j}e^{j3\omega} + \frac{3}{2j}e^{j\omega} - \frac{3}{2j}e^{-j\omega} - \frac{1}{2j}e^{-j3\omega} \end{aligned}$$

$$\begin{aligned} x_o[n] &= \mathcal{DFT}^{-1}\left[j\mathcal{Im}\left\{X(e^{j\omega})\right\}\right] \\ &= \mathcal{DFT}^{-1}\left[\frac{1}{2}e^{j3\omega} + \frac{3}{2}e^{j\omega} - \frac{3}{2}e^{-j\omega} - \frac{1}{2}e^{-j3\omega}\right] \\ &= \frac{1}{2}\delta[n+3] + \frac{3}{2}\delta[n+1] - \frac{3}{2}\delta[n-1] - \frac{1}{2}\delta[n-3] \end{aligned}$$

Using the formula $x[n] = 2x_o[n]u[n] + x[0]\delta[n]$, we find

$$x[n] = -3\delta[n-1] - \delta[n-3] + x[0]\delta[n]$$

Taking the DTFT of $x[n]$ gives

$$X(e^{j\omega}) = -3e^{-j\omega} - e^{-j3\omega} + x[0]$$

Evaluating this at $\omega = \pi$ gives

$$X(e^{j\omega})\big|_{\omega=\pi} = -3e^{-j\pi} - e^{-j3\pi} + x[0] = 3$$

$$\begin{aligned} 3 + 1 + x[0] &= 3 \\ x[0] &= -1 \end{aligned}$$

Therefore,

$$x[n] = -3\delta[n-1] - \delta[n-3] - \delta[n]$$

(b) Yes, the answer to part (a) is unique. The specification of $X(e^{j\omega})$ at $\omega = \pi$ allowed us to find a unique $x[n]$.

11.10. Factoring the magnitude squared response we get

$$\left|H(e^{j\omega})\right|^2 = \frac{\frac{5}{4} - \cos\omega}{5 + 4\cos\omega} = \frac{1 - \cos\omega + \frac{1}{4}}{1 + 4\cos\omega + 4} = \frac{(1 - \frac{1}{2}e^{-j\omega})(1 - \frac{1}{2}e^{j\omega})}{(1 + 2e^{-j\omega})(1 + 2e^{j\omega})}$$

$$\begin{aligned} |H(z)|^2 &= \frac{(1 - \frac{1}{2}z^{-1})(1 - \frac{1}{2}z)}{(1 + 2z^{-1})(1 + 2z)} \\ &= H(z)H^*(1/z^*) \end{aligned}$$

Since $h[n]$ is stable and causal and has a stable and causal inverse, it must be a minimum phase system. It therefore has all its poles and zeros inside the unit circle which allows us to uniquely identify $H(z)$ from $|H(z)|^2$.

$$\begin{aligned} H(z) &= \frac{1 - \frac{1}{2}z^{-1}}{1 + 2z} \\ &= \frac{1}{2}z^{-1}\left(\frac{1 - \frac{1}{2}z^{-1}}{1 + \frac{1}{2}z^{-1}}\right) \\ &= \frac{1}{2}z^{-1}\left(-1 + \frac{2}{1 + \frac{1}{2}z^{-1}}\right), \qquad |z| > \tfrac{1}{2} \end{aligned}$$

$$h[n] = -\frac{1}{2}\delta[n-1] + \left(-\frac{1}{2}\right)^{(n-1)} u[n-1]$$

11.11. Note that $x_i[n]$ can be written as

$$x_i[n] = -4\delta[n+3] + 4\delta[n-3]$$

Taking the DTFT of $x_i[n]$ gives

$$\begin{aligned} X_i(e^{jw}) &= -4e^{j3\omega} + 4e^{-j3\omega} \\ &= -4(2j\sin 3\omega) \\ &= -8j\sin 3\omega \end{aligned}$$

Since $X(e^{jw}) = 0$ for $-\pi \le \omega < 0$, we can find $X(e^{jw})$ using the relation

$$X(e^{jw}) = \begin{cases} 2jX_i(e^{jw}), & 0 < \omega < \pi \\ 0, & -\pi \le \omega < 0 \end{cases}$$

Thus,

$$X(e^{jw}) = \begin{cases} 16\sin 3\omega, & 0 < \omega < \pi \\ 0, & -\pi \leq \omega < 0 \end{cases}$$

Therefore, the real part of $X(e^{j\omega})$ is

$$\begin{aligned} X_r(e^{j\omega}) &= \frac{1}{2}\left[X(e^{j\omega}) + X^*(e^{-j\omega})\right] \\ &= \begin{cases} 8\sin 3\omega, & 0 < \omega < \pi \\ -8\sin 3\omega, & -\pi \leq \omega < 0 \end{cases} \end{aligned}$$

11.12. (a) Factoring the magnitude squared response we get

$$\begin{aligned} |H(e^{j\omega})|^2 &= \frac{10}{9} - \frac{2}{3}\cos\omega = 1 - \frac{2}{3}\cos\omega + \frac{1}{9} = \left(1 - \frac{1}{3}e^{-j\omega}\right)\left(1 - \frac{1}{3}e^{j\omega}\right) \\ &= H(e^{j\omega})H^*(e^{j\omega}) \end{aligned}$$

Thus, one choice for $H(e^{j\omega})$ and $h[n]$ is

$$H(e^{j\omega}) = 1 - \frac{1}{3}e^{-j\omega}$$

$$h[n] = \delta[n] - \frac{1}{3}\delta[n-1]$$

(b) *No.* We can find a new system by taking the zero from the original system and flipping it to its reciprocal location. This only changes the magnitude squared response by a scaling factor. If we compensate for the scaling factor the two magnitude squared responses will be the same. Thus, we find

$$\begin{aligned} H(e^{j\omega}) &= \frac{1}{3}(1 - 3e^{-j\omega}) \\ h[n] &= \frac{1}{3}\delta[n] - 3\delta[n-1] \end{aligned}$$

satisifies the given conditions.

11.13. Expressing $X_R(e^{j\omega})$ in terms of complex exponentials gives

$$\begin{aligned} X_R(e^{j\omega}) &= 1 + \cos\omega + \sin\omega - \sin 2\omega \\ &= 1 + \frac{1}{2}e^{j\omega} + \frac{1}{2}e^{-j\omega} + \frac{1}{2j}e^{j\omega} - \frac{1}{2j}e^{-j\omega} - \frac{1}{2j}e^{j2\omega} + \frac{1}{2j}e^{-j2\omega} \\ &= -\frac{1}{2j}e^{j2\omega} + \frac{1}{2}e^{j\omega} + \frac{1}{2j}e^{j\omega} + 1 + \frac{1}{2}e^{-j\omega} - \frac{1}{2j}e^{-j\omega} + \frac{1}{2j}e^{-j2\omega} \end{aligned}$$

Taking the inverse DTFT of $X_R(e^{j\omega})$ gives the conjugate-symmetric part of $x[n]$, denoted as $x_e[n]$.

$$x_e[n] = -\frac{1}{2j}\delta[n+2] + \frac{1}{2}\delta[n+1] + \frac{1}{2j}\delta[n+1] + \delta[n] + \frac{1}{2}\delta[n-1] - \frac{1}{2j}\delta[n-1] + \frac{1}{2j}\delta[n-2]$$

Using the relation $x[n] = 2x_e[n]u[n] - x_e[0]\delta[n]$,

$$x[n] = \delta[n] + \delta[n-1] + j\delta[n-1] - j\delta[n-2]$$

We then find the conjugate-antisymmetric part, $x_o[n]$ as

$$\begin{aligned}
x_o[n] &= \frac{1}{2}\left(x[n] - x^*[-n]\right) \\
&= \frac{1}{2}\left(\delta[n] + \delta[n-1] + j\delta[n-1] - j\delta[n-2] - \delta[n] - \delta[-n-1] + j\delta[-n-1] - j\delta[-n-2]\right) \\
&= \frac{1}{2}\left(\delta[n-1] + j\delta[n-1] - j\delta[n-2] - \delta[n+1] + j\delta[n+1] - j\delta[n+2]\right) \\
&= -\frac{1}{2}\left(\delta[n+1] - \delta[n-1]\right) + \frac{j}{2}\left(\delta[n+1] + \delta[n-1]\right) - \frac{j}{2}\left(\delta[n+2] + \delta[n-2]\right)
\end{aligned}$$

Taking the DTFT of $x_o[n]$ gives $jX_I(e^{jw})$.

$$\begin{aligned}
jX_I(e^{jw}) &= -\frac{1}{2}\left(e^{j\omega} - e^{-j\omega}\right) + \frac{j}{2}\left(e^{j\omega} + e^{-j\omega}\right) - \frac{j}{2}\left(e^{j2\omega} + e^{-j2\omega}\right) \\
&= -j\sin\omega + j\cos\omega - j\cos 2\omega
\end{aligned}$$

So

$$X_I(e^{jw}) = -\sin\omega + \cos\omega - \cos 2\omega$$

11.14. First note that,

(a) The inverse transform of $X_R(e^{j\omega})$ is $x_e[n]$, the even part of $x[n]$. This is true for any sequence whether it is causal, anticausal, or neither.

(b) $jX_I(e^{j\omega})$ is the transform of $x_o[n]$, the odd part of $x[n]$. This is true for any sequence whether it is causal, anticausal, or neither.

(c) For an anticausal sequence

$$x[n] = 2x_e[n]u[-n] - x_e[0]\delta[n]$$

Using Euler's identity and (a),

$$\begin{aligned}
X_R(e^{j\omega}) &= \sum_{k=0}^{\infty}\left(\frac{1}{2}\right)^k \cos(k\omega) \\
&= 1 + \frac{1}{2}\sum_{k=1}^{\infty}\left(\frac{1}{2}\right)^k \left(e^{jk\omega} + e^{-jk\omega}\right)
\end{aligned}$$

$$x_e[n] = \delta[n] + \frac{1}{2}\sum_{k=1}^{\infty}\left(\frac{1}{2}\right)^k \left(\delta[n+k] + \delta[n-k]\right)$$

Using (c) and then taking the odd part we get,

$$\begin{aligned}
x[n] &= 2x_e[n]u[-n] - x_e[0]\delta[n] \\
&= \delta[n] + \sum_{k=1}^{\infty}\left(\frac{1}{2}\right)^k \delta[n+k]
\end{aligned}$$

$$\begin{aligned}
x_o[n] &= \frac{x[n] - x[-n]}{2} \\
&= \frac{1}{2}\sum_{k=1}^{\infty}\left(\frac{1}{2}\right)^k \left(\delta[n+k] - \delta[n-k]\right)
\end{aligned}$$

Now taking the DTFT and using (b),

$$\begin{aligned} jX_I(e^{j\omega}) &= \frac{1}{2}\sum_{k=1}^{\infty}\left(\frac{1}{2}\right)^k (e^{jk\omega} - e^{-jk\omega}) \\ &= j\sum_{k=1}^{\infty}\left(\frac{1}{2}\right)^k \sin(k\omega) \\ &= j\sum_{k=0}^{\infty}\left(\frac{1}{2}\right)^k \sin(k\omega) \end{aligned}$$

Thus,

$$X_I(e^{j\omega}) = \sum_{k=0}^{\infty}\left(\frac{1}{2}\right)^k \sin(k\omega)$$

11.15. Given $X_i(e^{j\omega})$, we can take the inverse DTFT of $jX_i(e^{j\omega})$ to find the odd part of $x[n]$, denoted $x_o[n]$.

$$\begin{aligned} \mathcal{Im}\left\{X(e^{j\omega})\right\} &= \sin\omega \\ &= \frac{1}{2j}e^{j\omega} - \frac{1}{2j}e^{-j\omega} \end{aligned}$$

$$\begin{aligned} x_o[n] &= \mathcal{DFT}^{-1}\left[j\mathcal{Im}\left\{X(e^{j\omega})\right\}\right] \\ &= \mathcal{DFT}^{-1}\left[\frac{1}{2}e^{j\omega} - \frac{1}{2}e^{-j\omega}\right] \\ &= \frac{1}{2}\delta[n+1] - \frac{1}{2}\delta[n-1] \end{aligned}$$

Using the formula $x[n] = 2x_o[n]u[n] + x[0]\delta[n]$,

$$x[n] = -\delta[n-1] + x[0]\delta[n]$$

Since

$$\sum_{n=-\infty}^{\infty} x[n] = 3$$

$$\begin{aligned} -1 + x[0] &= 3 \\ x[0] &= 4 \end{aligned}$$

Therefore,

$$x[n] = 4\delta[n] - \delta[n-1]$$

11.16. Using Euler's identity and the fact that $x_e[n]$ is the inverse transform of $X_R(e^{j\omega})$ we have

$$\begin{aligned} X_R(e^{j\omega}) &= 2 - 4\cos(3\omega) \\ &= 2 - 2(e^{j\omega} + e^{-j\omega}) \end{aligned}$$

$$x_e[n] = -2\delta[n+3] + 2\delta[n] - 2\delta[n-3]$$

Since $x[n]$ is real and causal, it is fully determined by its even part $x_e[n]$,

$$\begin{aligned} x[n] &= 2x_e[n]u[n] - x_e[0]\delta[n] \\ &= 4\delta[n] - 4\delta[n-3] - 2\delta[n] \\ &= 2\delta[n] - 4\delta[n-3] \end{aligned}$$

Using this information in the second condition we find

$$\begin{aligned} X(e^{j\omega})|_{\omega=\pi} &= \sum_{n=-\infty}^{\infty} x[n]e^{j\pi n} \\ &= \sum_{n=-\infty}^{\infty} x[n](-1)^n \\ &= 2+4 \\ &\neq 7 \end{aligned}$$

Thus, there is no real, causal sequence that satisfies both conditions.

11.17. There is more than one way to solve this problem. Two solutions are presented below.

Solution 1: Yes, it is possible to determine $x[n]$ uniquely. Note that $X[k]$, the 2 point DFT of a real signal $x[n]$, is also real, as demonstrated below.

$$\begin{aligned} X[k] &= \sum_{n=0}^{1} x[n]e^{-j2\pi nk/2} \\ X[k] &= \sum_{n=0}^{1} x[n](-1)^{nk} \end{aligned}$$

Thus,

$$\begin{aligned} X[0] &= x[0]+x[1] \\ X[1] &= x[0]-x[1] \end{aligned}$$

Clearly, if $x[n]$ is real, then $X[k]$ is real. Therefore, we can conclude that the imaginary part $X_I[k]$ is zero.

Therefore, the inverse DFT of $X_R[k]$ is $x[n]$, computed below.

$$\begin{aligned} x[n] &= \frac{1}{2}\sum_{k=0}^{1} X_R[k]e^{j2\pi nk/2} \\ x[n] &= \frac{1}{2}\sum_{k=0}^{1} X_R[k](-1)^{nk} \end{aligned}$$

$$\begin{aligned} x[0] &= \frac{1}{2}(X_R[0]+X_R[1]) \\ &= -1 \\ x[1] &= \frac{1}{2}(X_R[0]-X_R[1]) \\ &= 3 \end{aligned}$$

Thus,

$$x[n] = -\delta[n] + 3\delta[n-1]$$

Solution 2: Start by making the assumption that $X[k]$ is complex, i.e., $X_I[k]$ is nonzero and $X_R[k] = 2\delta[k] - 4\delta[k-1]$. Then, because $x_{ep}[n]$ is the inverse DFT of $X_R[k]$ we find

$$\begin{aligned} x_{ep}[n] &= \frac{1}{2}\sum_{k=0}^{1} X_R[k]e^{j2\pi nk/2} \\ &= \frac{1}{2}\sum_{k=0}^{1} X_R[k](-1)^{nk} \end{aligned}$$

and

$$\begin{aligned} x_{ep}[0] &= \frac{1}{2}(X_R[0] + X_R[1]) \\ &= -1 \\ x_{ep}[1] &= \frac{1}{2}(X_R[0] - X_R[1]) \\ &= 3 \end{aligned}$$

$$x_{ep}[n] = -\delta[n] + 3\delta[n-1]$$

Because $x[n]$ is real and causal, we can determine it from $x_{ep}[n]$

$$x[n] = \begin{cases} x_{ep}[n], & n = 0 \\ 2x_{ep}[n], & 0 < n < N/2 \\ x_{ep}[N/2], & n = N/2 \\ 0, & \text{otherwise} \end{cases}$$

With $N = 2$ we have

$$x[n] = -\delta[n] + 3\delta[n-1]$$

If we began by making the assumption that $X[k]$ was real, i.e., $X_I[k] = 0$ and $X[k] = X_R[k] = 2\delta[k] - 4\delta[k-1]$ than by taking the inverse transform we find that

$$x[n] = x_{ep}[n] = -\delta[k] + 3\delta[k-1]$$

This is the same answer we got before. Since there was no ambiguities in our determination of $x[n]$, we conclude that $x[n]$ can be uniquely determined.
The next problem shows that when $N > 2$, we cannot necessarily uniquely determine $x[n]$ from $X_R[k]$ unless we make additional assumptions about $x[n]$ such as periodic causality. When $N > 2$ the two assumptions we used above leads to two different sequences with the same $X_R[k]$.

11.18. Sequence 1: For $k = 0, 1, 2$ we have

$$X_R[k] = 9\delta[k] + 6\delta[k-1] + 6\delta[((k+1))_3]$$

and $X_R[k] = 0$ for any other k. Using the DFT properties and taking the inverse DFT we find for $n = 1, 2, 3$

$$\begin{aligned} x_{ep}[n] &= 3 + 2\left(e^{j(2\pi/3)n} + e^{-j(2\pi/3)n}\right) \\ &= 3 + 4\cos(2\pi n/3) \\ &= 7\delta[n] + \delta[n-1] + \delta[n-2] \end{aligned}$$

If we let $x[n] = x_{ep}[n]$ we have the desired sequence.

Sequence 2: If we assume $x[n]$ is periodically causal, we can use the following property to solve for $x[n]$ from $x_{ep}[n]$:

$$x[n] = \begin{cases} x_{ep}[0], & n = 0 \\ 2x_{ep}[n], & 0 < n < \frac{N}{2} \\ 0, & \text{otherwise} \end{cases}$$

Note that this is only true for odd N. For even N, we would also need to handle the $n = N/2$ point as shown in the chapter. We have

$$\begin{aligned} x[n] &= \begin{cases} x_{ep}[0], & n = 0 \\ 2x_{ep}[n], & n = 1 \\ 0, & \text{otherwise} \end{cases} \\ &= 7\delta[n] + 2\delta[n-1] \end{aligned}$$

11.19. Given the real part of $X[k]$, we can take the inverse DFT to find the even periodic part of $x[n]$, denoted $x_{ep}[n]$.

Using the inverse DFT relation,

$$x_{ep}[n] = \frac{1}{N}\sum_{k=0}^{N-1} X_R[k]W^{-nk}$$

we find

$$\begin{aligned} x_{ep}[0] &= \frac{1}{4}(4+1+2+1) = 2 \\ x_{ep}[1] &= \frac{1}{4}(4+j-2-j) = \frac{1}{2} \\ x_{ep}[2] &= \frac{1}{4}(4-1+2-1) = 1 \\ x_{ep}[3] &= \frac{1}{4}(4-j-2+j) = \frac{1}{2} \end{aligned}$$

Thus,

$$x_{ep}[n] = 2\delta[n] + \frac{1}{2}\delta[n-1] + \delta[n-2] + \frac{1}{2}\delta[n-3]$$

Next, we can relate the odd periodic and even periodic parts of $x[n]$ using

$$x_{op}[n] = \begin{cases} x_{ep}[n], & 0 < n < N/2 \\ -x_{ep}[n], & N/2 < n \leq N-1 \\ 0, & \text{otherwise} \end{cases}$$

Performing this operation gives

$$x_{op}[n] = \frac{1}{2}\delta[n-1] - \frac{1}{2}\delta[n-3]$$

Taking the DFT of $x_{op}[n]$ yields $jX_I[k]$. Using the DFT relation,

$$jX_I[k] = \sum_{n=0}^{N-1} x_{op}[n]W^{nk}$$

we find

$$\begin{aligned} jX_I[0] &= \left(0 + \frac{1}{2} + 0 - \frac{1}{2}\right) = 0 \\ jX_I[1] &= \left(0 - \frac{j}{2} + 0 - \frac{j}{2}\right) = -j \\ jX_I[2] &= \left(0 + \frac{1}{2} + 0 - \frac{1}{2}\right) = 0 \\ jX_I[3] &= \left(0 + \frac{j}{2} + 0 + \frac{j}{2}\right) = j \end{aligned}$$

Thus,

$$jX_I[k] = -j\delta[k-1] + j\delta[k-3]$$

11.20. As the following shows, the second condition implies $x[0] = 1$.

$$\begin{aligned} x[0] &= \left.\frac{1}{6}\sum_{k=0}^{5} X[k]e^{j(2\pi/6)kn}\right|_{n=0} \\ &= \frac{1}{6}\sum_{k=0}^{5} X[k] \\ &= 1 \end{aligned}$$

This condition eliminates all choices except $x_2[n]$ and $x_3[n]$.

The odd periodic parts of $x_2[n]$ and $x_3[n]$ for $n = 0, \ldots, 5$ are

$$\begin{aligned} x_{op_2}[n] &= \frac{x_2[n] - x_2^*[((-n))_6]}{2} \\ &= \frac{1}{3}\left(\delta[n-4] - \delta[((n+4))_6]\right) - \frac{1}{3}\left(\delta[n-5] - \delta[((n+5))_6]\right) \end{aligned}$$

$$\begin{aligned} x_{op_3}[n] &= \frac{x_3[n] - x_3^*[((-n))_6]}{2} \\ &= \frac{1}{3}\left(\delta[n-1] - \delta[((n+1))_6]\right) - \frac{1}{3}\left(\delta[n-2] - \delta[((n+2))_6]\right) \end{aligned}$$

For $n < 0$ or $n > 5$, these sequences are zero. Since the transform of $x_{op}[n]$ is $jX_I[k]$ we find for $k = 0, \ldots, 5$

$$\begin{aligned} jX_{I_2}[k] &= \frac{1}{3}\left(e^{-j(2\pi/6)4k} - e^{j(2\pi/6)4k}\right) - \frac{1}{3}\left(e^{-j(2\pi/6)5k} - e^{j(2\pi/6)5k}\right) \\ &= -\frac{2}{3}j\sin(4\pi k/3) + \frac{2}{3}j\sin(5\pi k/3) \\ &= j\frac{2}{\sqrt{3}}\left(-\delta[k-2] + \delta[k-4]\right) \end{aligned}$$

$$\begin{aligned} jX_{I_3}[k] &= \frac{1}{3}\left(e^{-j(2\pi/6)k} - e^{j(2\pi/6)k}\right) - \frac{1}{3}\left(e^{-j(2\pi/6)2k} - e^{j(2\pi/6)2k}\right) \\ &= -\frac{2}{3}j\sin(\pi k/3) + \frac{2}{3}j\sin(2\pi k/3) \\ &= j\frac{2}{\sqrt{3}}\left(-\delta[k-2] + \delta[k-4]\right) \end{aligned}$$

Thus, both $x_2[n]$ and $x_3[n]$ are consistent with the information given.

11.21. (a) *Method 1*:

We are given

$$\begin{aligned} X_R(\rho e^{j\omega}) &= U(\rho, \omega) \\ &= 1 + \rho^{-1}\alpha\cos\omega \end{aligned}$$

Since $\frac{\partial U}{\partial \rho} = \frac{1}{\rho}\frac{\partial V}{\partial \omega}$ we have,

$$\begin{aligned} \frac{\partial V}{\partial \omega} &= -\alpha\rho^{-1}\cos\omega \\ V &= -\alpha\rho^{-1}\sin\omega + K(\rho) \end{aligned}$$

Since $\frac{\partial V}{\partial \rho} = -\frac{1}{\rho}\frac{\partial U}{\partial \omega}$ we have,

$$\overbrace{\alpha\rho^{-2}\sin\omega + K'(\rho)}^{\frac{\partial V}{\partial \rho}} = \overbrace{\alpha\rho^{-2}\sin\omega}^{-\frac{1}{\rho}\frac{\partial U}{\partial \omega}}$$

Thus,

$$\begin{aligned} K'(\rho) &= 0 \\ K(\rho) &= C \end{aligned}$$

Since $x[n]$ is real $V(\rho,\omega)$ is an odd function of ω. Hence, $V(\rho,0) = 0$, implying that $C = 0$. Therefore,

$$\begin{aligned} X(\rho e^{j\omega}) &= U(\rho,\omega) + jV(\rho,\omega) \\ &= 1 + \rho^{-1}\alpha\cos\omega - j\rho^{-1}\alpha\sin\omega \\ &= 1 + \alpha\rho^{-1}(\cos\omega - j\sin\omega) \\ &= 1 + \alpha\rho^{-1}e^{-j\omega} \\ X(z) &= 1 + \alpha z^{-1} \end{aligned}$$

(b) *Method 2*: Since $X_R(e^{j\omega})$ is the transform of $x_e[n]$ we have

$$\begin{aligned} X_R(e^{j\omega}) &= 1 + \alpha\cos\omega \\ &= 1 + \frac{\alpha}{2}e^{j\omega} + \frac{\alpha}{2}e^{-j\omega} \\ x_e[n] &= \delta[n] + \frac{\alpha}{2}\delta[n+1] + \frac{\alpha}{2}\delta[n-1] \end{aligned}$$

Because $x[n]$ is real and causal, we can recover $x_o[n]$ from $x_e[n]$ as follows

$$\begin{aligned} x_o[n] &= \begin{cases} x_e[n], & n > 0 \\ 0, & n = 0 \\ -x_e[n], & n < 0 \end{cases} \\ &= -\frac{\alpha}{2}\delta[n+1] + \frac{\alpha}{2}\delta[n-1] \end{aligned}$$

Thus,

$$\begin{aligned} x[n] &= x_e[n] + x_o[n] \\ &= \delta[n] + \alpha\delta[n-1] \\ X(z) &= 1 + \alpha z^{-1} \end{aligned}$$

Note that we could have obtained $x[n]$ directly from $x_e[n]$ as follows

$$\begin{aligned} x[n] &= 2x_e[n]u[n] - x_e[0]\delta[n] \\ &= (2\delta[n] + \alpha\delta[n+1] + \alpha\delta[n-1])u[n] - \delta[n] \\ &= \delta[n] + \alpha\delta[n-1] \end{aligned}$$

11.22. Taking the z-transform of $u_N[n]$ we get

$$\begin{aligned} U_N(z) &= \frac{2}{1-z^{-1}} - \frac{2z^{-N/2}}{1-z^{-1}} - 1 + z^{-N/2} \\ &= \frac{1 - z^{-N/2} + z^{-1} - z^{-1-N/2}}{1-z^{-1}}, \qquad |z| \neq 0 \end{aligned}$$

Sampling this we find

$$\begin{aligned} \tilde{U}_N[k] &= U_N(e^{2\pi k/N}) \\ &= \frac{1 - (-1)^k + e^{-j2\pi k/N} - e^{-j2\pi k/N}(-1)^k}{1 - e^{-j2\pi k/N}} \end{aligned}$$

When k is even but $k \neq 0$ we see that $\tilde{U}_N[k] = 0$. For k odd, we get

$$\begin{aligned}
\tilde{U}_N[k] &= \frac{2 + 2e^{-j2\pi k/N}}{1 - e^{-j2\pi k/N}} \\
&= \frac{2e^{-j\pi k/N}(e^{j\pi k/N} + e^{-j\pi k/N})}{e^{-j\pi k/N}(e^{j\pi k/N} - e^{-j\pi k/N})} \\
&= -2j\cot(\pi k/N)
\end{aligned}$$

When $k = 0$ we get $0/0$ which, if the function was continuous, you would use l'Hôpital's rule. In this case the function is discrete so that is not available to us. One route to the answer is to use the definition of the DFS

$$\begin{aligned}
\tilde{U}_N[0] &= \sum_{k=0}^{N} \tilde{u}_N[n]e^{-j\frac{2\pi}{N}kn}\Big|_{k=0} \\
&= \sum_{k=0}^{N} \tilde{u}_N[n] \\
&= N
\end{aligned}$$

Putting it all together gives us the desired answer

$$\tilde{U}_N[k] = \begin{cases} N, & k = 0, \\ -2j\cot(\pi k/N), & k \text{ odd}, \\ 0, & k \text{ even}, \ k \neq 0 \end{cases}$$

11.23. (a) Because $x_{ep}[n]$ is the inverse DFT of $X_R[k]$ we have for $n = 0, \ldots, N-1$ and $k = 0, \ldots, N-1$

$$\begin{aligned}
X_R[k] &= \frac{X[k] + X^*[k]}{2} \\
x_{ep}[n] &= \frac{x[n] + x^*[((-n))_N]}{2}
\end{aligned}$$

or equivalently, if we periodically extend these sequences with period N

$$\tilde{x}_e[n] = \frac{\tilde{x}[n] + \tilde{x}[-n]}{2}$$

Note that since the signal is real $\tilde{x}^*[-n] = \tilde{x}[-n]$.
The first period of $\tilde{x}[n]$ is zero from $n = M$ to $n = N-1$. If $N = 2(M-1)$ there is no overlap of $\tilde{x}[n]$ and $\tilde{x}[-n]$ except at $n = 0$ and $n = N/2$. We can therefore recover $\tilde{x}[n]$ from $\tilde{x}_e[n]$ with the following:

$$\tilde{x}[n] = \begin{cases} 2\tilde{x}_e[n], & n = 1, \ldots, N/2 - 1 \\ \tilde{x}_e[n], & n = 0, N/2 \\ 0, & n = M, \ldots, N-1 \end{cases}$$

If we tried to make N any smaller, the overlap of $\tilde{x}[n]$ and $\tilde{x}[-n]$ would prevent the recovery of $x[n]$. Consequently, the smallest value of N we can use to recover $X[k]$ from $X_R[k]$ is $N = 2(M-1)$.

(b) If $N = 2(M-1)$,

$$x[n] = x_{ep}[n]u_N[n] = \begin{cases} 2x_{ep}[n] & n = 1, \ldots, N/2 - 1 \\ x_{ep}[n], & n = 0, N/2 \\ 0, & \text{otherwise} \end{cases}$$

where

$$
\begin{aligned}
u_N[n] &= \begin{cases} 2, & n = 1, 2, \ldots, N/2-1 \\ 1, & n = 0, N/2 \\ 0, & \text{otherwise} \end{cases} \\
&= 2u[n] - 2u[n-N/2] - \delta[n] + \delta[n-N/2]
\end{aligned}
$$

Taking the DFT of $x[n]$ we find

$$X[k] = X_R[k] \otimes U_N[k]$$

where

$$
\begin{aligned}
U_N[k] &= DFT\{2u[n] - 2u[n-N/2] - \delta[n] + \delta[n-N/2]\} \\
&= \frac{1-(-1)^k + e^{-j2\pi k/N} - e^{-j2\pi k/N}(-1)^k}{1-e^{-j2\pi k/N}}, \qquad k = 0, \ldots, N-1 \\
U_N[k] &= \begin{cases} N, & k = 0, \\ -2j\cot(\pi k/N), & 0 < k < N-1,\ k \text{ odd} \\ 0, & \text{otherwise} \end{cases}
\end{aligned}
$$

11.24. We are given

$$
\begin{aligned}
H_R(e^{j\omega}) &= H_{ER}(e^{j\omega}) + H_{OR}(e^{j\omega}) \\
H_I(e^{j\omega}) &= H_{EI}(e^{j\omega}) + H_{OI}(e^{j\omega})
\end{aligned}
$$

$$
\begin{aligned}
h_r[n] &\longleftrightarrow H_r(e^{j\omega}) = H_A(e^{j\omega}) + jH_B(e^{j\omega}) \\
h_i[n] &\longleftrightarrow H_i(e^{j\omega}) = H_C(e^{j\omega}) + jH_D(e^{j\omega})
\end{aligned}
$$

where $h_r[n]$, $h_i[n]$, $H_R(e^{j\omega})$, $H_I(e^{j\omega})$, $H_{ER}(e^{j\omega})$, $H_{OR}(e^{j\omega})$, $H_{EI}(e^{j\omega})$, and $H_{OI}(e^{j\omega})$ are real. Begin by breaking $H(e^{j\omega})$ into its real and imaginary parts $H_R(e^{j\omega})$ and $H_I(e^{j\omega})$

$$
\begin{aligned}
H(e^{j\omega}) &= H_R(e^{j\omega}) + jH_I(e^{j\omega}) \\
&= [H_{ER}(e^{j\omega}) + H_{OR}(e^{j\omega})] + j[H_{EI}(e^{j\omega}) + H_{OI}(e^{j\omega})]
\end{aligned}
$$

Now solve for the conjugate symmetric and conjugate antisymmetric parts of $H(e^{j\omega})$

$$
\begin{aligned}
H_r(e^{j\omega}) &= \frac{H(e^{j\omega}) + H^*(e^{-j\omega})}{2} \\
&= \frac{[H_{ER}(e^{j\omega}) + H_{OR}(e^{j\omega})] + j[H_{EI}(e^{j\omega}) + H_{OI}(e^{j\omega})]}{2} \\
&\quad + \frac{[H_{ER}(e^{j\omega}) - H_{OR}(e^{j\omega})] - j[H_{EI}(e^{j\omega}) - H_{OI}(e^{j\omega})]}{2} \\
&= H_{ER}(e^{j\omega}) + jH_{OI}(e^{j\omega})
\end{aligned}
$$

$$
\begin{aligned}
H_i(e^{j\omega}) &= \frac{H(e^{j\omega}) - H^*(e^{-j\omega})}{2j} \\
&= \frac{[H_{ER}(e^{j\omega}) + H_{OR}(e^{j\omega})] + j[H_{EI}(e^{j\omega}) + H_{OI}(e^{j\omega})]}{2j} \\
&\quad - \frac{[H_{ER}(e^{j\omega}) - H_{OR}(e^{j\omega})] - j[H_{EI}(e^{j\omega}) - H_{OI}(e^{j\omega})]}{2j} \\
&= H_{EI}(e^{j\omega}) - jH_{OR}(e^{j\omega})
\end{aligned}
$$

Thus,

$$
\begin{aligned}
H_A(e^{j\omega}) &= H_{ER}(e^{j\omega}) \qquad & H_C(e^{j\omega}) &= H_{EI}(e^{j\omega}) \\
H_B(e^{j\omega}) &= H_{OI}(e^{j\omega}) \qquad & H_D(e^{j\omega}) &= -H_{OR}(e^{j\omega})
\end{aligned}
$$

11.25. (a) By inspection,

$$H(e^{j\omega}) = j(2H_{\text{lp}}(e^{j(\omega+\frac{\pi}{2})}) - 1)$$

$$H_{\text{lp}}(e^{j\omega}) = \frac{1 - jH(e^{j(\omega-\frac{\pi}{2})})}{2}$$

(b) **Find h[n]:**
Taking the inverse DTFT of $H(e^{j\omega})$ yields

$$\begin{aligned} h[n] &= j\left[2e^{-j(\pi/2)n}\, h_{\text{lp}}[n] - \delta[n]\right] \\ &= j\left[2\cos(\pi n/2)h_{\text{lp}}[n] - j2\sin(\pi n/2)h_{\text{lp}}[n] - \delta[n]\right] \\ &= 2\sin(\pi n/2)h_{\text{lp}}[n] \end{aligned}$$

The simplification in the last step used the fact that $h_{\text{lp}}[n] = \frac{\sin(\pi n/2)}{\pi n}$ is zero for even n and equals $1/2$ for $n = 0$.

Find $\mathbf{h_{lp}[n]}$:
Taking the inverse DTFT of $H_{\text{lp}}(e^{j\omega})$ yields

$$\begin{aligned} h_{\text{lp}}[n] &= \frac{\delta[n] - je^{j(\pi/2)n}\, h[n]}{2} \\ &= \frac{1}{2}\delta[n] - \frac{1}{2}(j)^{n+1}h[n] \end{aligned}$$

Using the fact that $h[n]$ is zero for $n = 0$ and n even we can reduce this to

$$h_{\text{lp}}[n] = \frac{\sin(\pi n/2)}{2}h[n] + \frac{1}{2}\delta[n]$$

(c) The linear phase causes a delay of $n_d = M/2$ in the responses. If n_d is not an integer, then we interpret $h_{\text{lp}}[n]$ and $h[n]$ as

$$\begin{aligned} h_{\text{lp}}[n - n_d] &= \frac{\sin(\pi(n - n_d)/2)}{\pi(n - n_d)} \\ h[n - n_d] &= \frac{2}{\pi}\frac{\sin^2(\pi(n - n_d)/2)}{(n - n_d)} \end{aligned}$$

Then,

$$\begin{aligned} \hat{h}[n] &= h[n - n_d]w[n] \\ &= 2\sin(\pi(n - n_d)/2)\, h_{\text{lp}}[n - n_d]w[n] \\ &= 2\sin(\pi(n - n_d)/2)\, \hat{h}_{\text{lp}}[n] \end{aligned}$$

where $\hat{h}[n]$ and $\hat{h}_{\text{lp}}[n]$ are the causal FIR approximations to $h[n]$ and $h_{\text{lp}}[n]$. Similarly,

$$\hat{h}_{\text{lp}}[n] = \begin{cases} \dfrac{\sin(\pi(n - n_d)/2)}{2}\hat{h}[n] + \dfrac{1}{2}\delta[n - n_d]w[n], & M \text{ even} \\ \sin(\pi(n - n_d)/2)\hat{h}[n], & M \text{ odd} \end{cases}$$

(d) The lowpass filter corresponding to the first filter in the example looks like

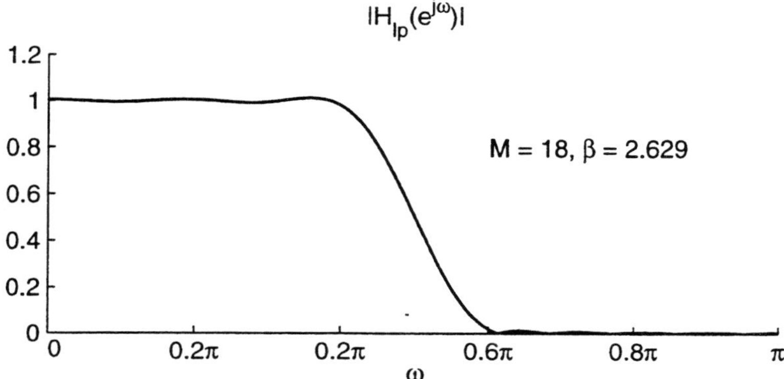

The lowpass filter corresponding to the second filter in the example looks like

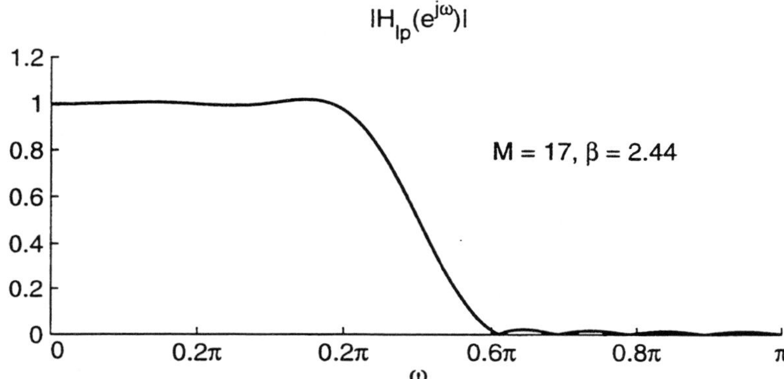

11.26. (a) The example shown here samples at the Nyquist rate of $T = \pi/(\Omega_c + \Delta\Omega)$ as in the chapter's example, but the bandpass signal is such that $\Delta\Omega/(\Omega_c + \Delta\Omega) = 3/5$. Then, $2\pi/(\Delta\Omega T) = 10/3$.

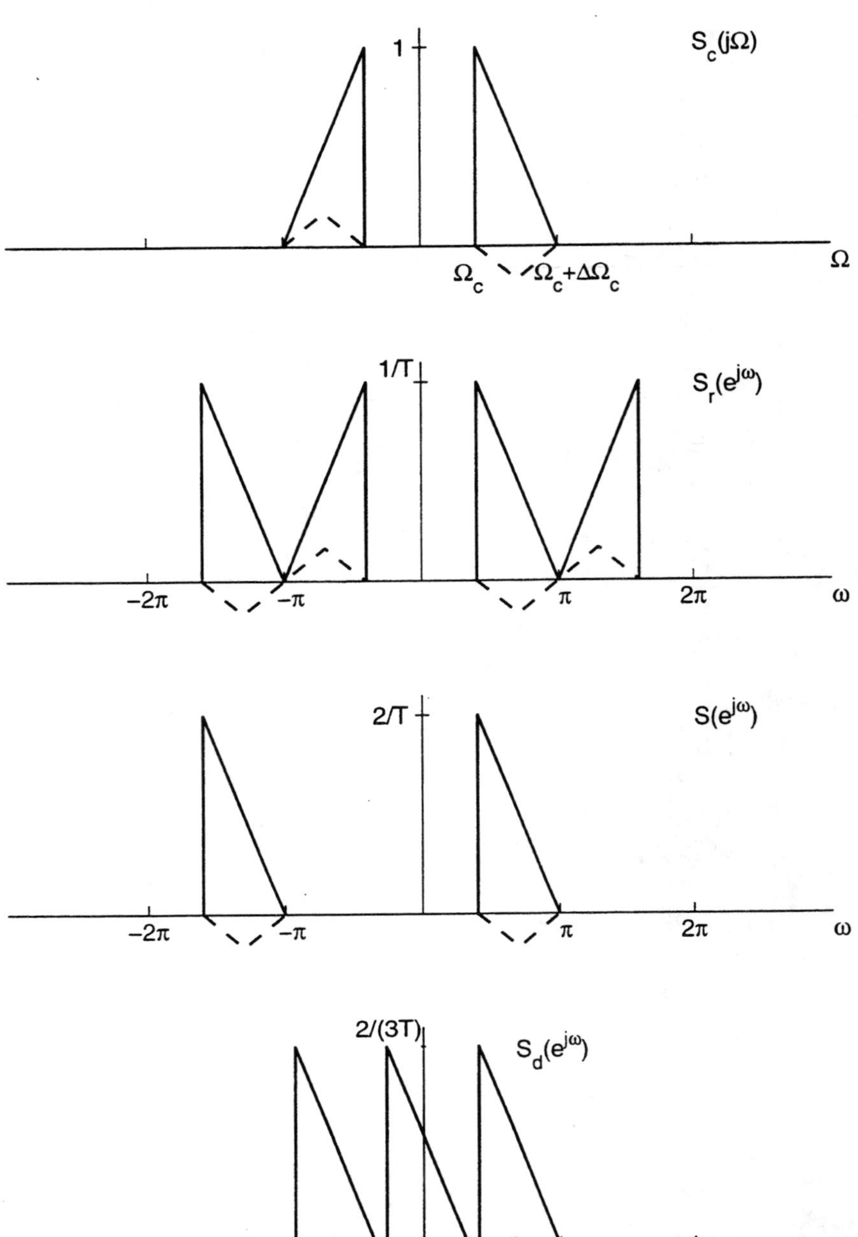

(b) If $2\pi/(\Delta\Omega T) = M + e$, where M is an integer and e some fraction, then using the Nyquist rate of $2\pi/T = 2(\Omega_c + \Delta\Omega)$ will force decimation by M. As just shown, this choice for T causes $S_d(e^{j\omega})$ to have intervals of zero. Instead, choose T such that $2\pi/(\Delta\Omega T)$ is the next highest integer

$$\frac{2\pi}{\Delta\Omega T} = M + 1.$$

Then decimating by $(M + 1)$ produces the desired result.

11.27. *Yes,* it is possible to always uniquely recover the system input from the system output. Although

$Y(e^{j\omega})$ contains roughly half the frequency spectrum as $X(e^{j\omega})$, we can reconstruct $X(e^{j\omega})$ from $Y(e^{j\omega})$. We can accomplish this by recognizing that since $x[n]$ is real, $X(e^{j\omega})$ must be conjugate symmetric.

The output of the system, $y[n]$, has a Fourier transform $Y(e^{j\omega})$ that is the product of $X(e^{j\omega})$ and $H(e^{j\omega})$. Therefore, $Y(e^{j\omega})$ will correspond to

$$Y(e^{j\omega}) = \begin{cases} X(e^{j\omega}), & 0 \le \omega \le \pi \\ 0, & \text{otherwise} \end{cases}$$

At first glance, it may seem like $X(e^{j\omega}) = Y(e^{j\omega}) + Y^*(e^{-j\omega})$. This is close to the right answer, but it doesn't take into consideration the fact that $Y(e^{j\omega})$ is non-zero at $\omega = 0$ and $\omega = \pi$. Thus, the solution $X(e^{j\omega}) = Y(e^{j\omega}) + Y^*(e^{-j\omega})$, will be incorrect at $\omega = 0$ and $\omega = \pi$, since $Y(e^{j\omega})$ and $Y^*(e^{j\omega})$ will overlap at these frequencies. It is necessary to pay special attention to these frequencies to get the right answer. Let

$$Z(e^{j\omega}) = \begin{cases} 0, & \omega = 0, \omega = \pi \\ Y(e^{j\omega}), & \text{otherwise} \end{cases}$$

Alternatively, we can express $Z(e^{j\omega})$ with the constants a and b defined as

$$\begin{aligned} a &= Y(e^{j\omega})\big|_{\omega=0} &= \sum_{n=-\infty}^{\infty} y[n] \\ b &= Y(e^{j\omega})\big|_{\omega=\pi} &= \sum_{n=-\infty}^{\infty} y[n](-1)^n \end{aligned}$$

$$Z(e^{j\omega}) = Y(e^{j\omega}) - a\delta(\omega) - b\delta(\omega - \pi)$$

We can construct a conjugate symmetric $X(e^{j\omega})$ from $Y(e^{j\omega})$ and $Z(e^{j\omega})$ as

$$X(e^{j\omega}) = Y(e^{j\omega}) + Z^*(e^{-j\omega})$$

In the time domain, this is

$$x[n] = y[n] + z^*[n]$$

Or, since

$$z[n] = y[n] - \frac{a}{2\pi} - \frac{b(-1)^n}{2\pi}$$

$$x[n] = y[n] + y^*[n] - \frac{a}{2\pi} - \frac{b(-1)^n}{2\pi}$$

11.28. Since $H(z)$ corresponds to a real anticausal sequence $h[n]$, $F(z) = H(1/z)$ corresponds to a real, stable, causal sequence $f[n]$. We can apply the equation developed in the book for causal sequences to $F(z)$.

$$F(z) = \frac{1}{2\pi j}\oint_C F_R(v)\left(\frac{z+v}{z-v}\right)\frac{dv}{v}, \quad |z| \ge 1.$$

where $v = e^{j\theta}$ is the integration variable; i.e., the closed contour C is the unit circle of the v-plane. Now find $H(z)$

$$\begin{aligned} H(z) &= F(1/z) \\ &= \frac{1}{2\pi j}\oint_C H_R(v^{-1})\left(\frac{z^{-1}+v}{z^{-1}-v}\right)\frac{dv}{v}, \quad |z| \le 1 \end{aligned}$$

where $H_R(v) = \mathcal{R}e\{H(e^{j\theta})\}$.

11.29. (a) We have

$$\mathcal{H}\{x[n]\} = x[n] * h[n]$$
$$\mathcal{H}\{\mathcal{H}\{x[n]\}\} = x[n] * h[n] * h[n]$$

We need to show that $h[n]*h[n] = -\delta[n]$. Alternatively, we need to show that $H(e^{j\omega})H(e^{j\omega}) = -1$, which is easily seen from

$$H(e^{j\omega}) = \begin{cases} -j & 0 < \omega < \pi \\ j & -\pi < \omega < 0 \end{cases}$$

(b) In Parseval's theorem,

$$\sum_{n=-\infty}^{\infty} f[n]g^*[n] = \frac{1}{2\pi}\int_{-\pi}^{\pi} F(e^{j\omega})G^*(e^{j\omega})\,d\omega$$

Let $f[n] = \mathcal{H}\{x[n]\}$ and $g^*[n] = x[n]$. Then

$$\sum_{n=-\infty}^{\infty} \mathcal{H}\{x[n]\}x[n] = \frac{1}{2\pi}\int_{-\pi}^{\pi} H(e^{j\omega})X(e^{j\omega})X(e^{-j\omega})\,d\omega$$

where

$$H(e^{j\omega}) = \begin{cases} -j & 0 < \omega < \pi \\ j & -\pi < \omega < 0 \end{cases}$$

but the integral $= 0$ since the integrand is an odd function over the symmetric interval.

(c) Since $\mathcal{H}\{x[n]\} = x[n] * h[n]$

$$\begin{aligned} \mathcal{H}\{x[n] * y[n]\} &= (x[n] * y[n]) * h[n] \\ &= (x[n] * h[n]) * y[n] \\ &= x[n] * (y[n] * h[n]) \end{aligned}$$

by the commutativity and associativity of convolution.

11.30.

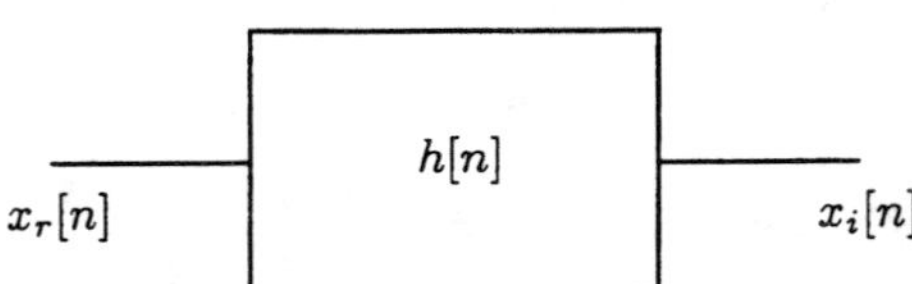

$h[n]$ is an ideal Hilbert Transformer:

$$h[n] = \begin{cases} \frac{2}{\pi}\frac{\sin^2(\pi n/2)}{n}, & n \neq 0 \\ 0, & n = 0 \end{cases}$$

$$H(e^{j\omega}) = \begin{cases} -j, & 0 < \omega < \pi \\ j, & -\pi < \omega < 0 \end{cases}$$

(a) In the frequency domain,

$$\begin{aligned} \Phi_{x_i x_i}(e^{j\omega}) &= |H(e^{j\omega})|^2 \Phi_{x_r x_r}(e^{j\omega}) \\ &= \Phi_{x_r x_r}(e^{j\omega}) \end{aligned}$$

Therefore, $\phi_{x_i x_i}[m] = \phi_{x_r x_r}[m]$.

(b) The cross-correlation between input and output is just the convolution of $\phi_{x_r x_r}[m]$ and $h[m]$,

$$\phi_{x_r x_i}[m] = \sum_{k=-\infty}^{\infty} h[k]\phi_{x_r x_r}[m-k]$$

The following shows that it is an odd function of m:

$$\begin{aligned}
\phi_{x_r x_i}[-m] &= \sum_{k=-\infty}^{\infty} h[k]\phi_{x_r x_r}[-m-k] \\
&= \sum_{\ell=-\infty}^{\infty} h[-\ell]\phi_{x_r x_r}[-m+\ell] \\
&= \sum_{\ell=-\infty}^{\infty} h[-\ell]\phi_{x_r x_r}[m-\ell] \\
&= -\sum_{\ell=-\infty}^{\infty} h[\ell]\phi_{x_r x_r}[m-\ell] \\
&= -\phi_{x_r x_i}[m]
\end{aligned}$$

since $h[n] = -h[-n]$ and $\phi_{x_r x_r}[m] = \phi_{x_r x_r}[-m]$.

(c) Starting from the definition of the autocorrelation and using the linearity of the expectation operator we get

$$\begin{aligned}
\phi_{xx}[m] &= \mathcal{E}[x[n]x^*[n+m]] \\
&= \mathcal{E}[(x_r[n] + jx_i[n])(x_r[n+m] - jx_i[n+m])] \\
&= \phi_{x_r x_r}[m] + \phi_{x_i x_i}[m] + j(\phi_{x_i x_r}[m] - \phi_{x_r x_i}[m]) \\
&= 2\phi_{x_r x_r}[m] - 2j\phi_{x_r x_i}[m]
\end{aligned}$$

The last line was found using the results from parts (a) and (b).

(d) Taking the transform of both sides of the equality from part (c) we find

$$\begin{aligned}
P_{xx}(\omega) &= 2\Phi_{x_r x_r}(e^{j\omega}) - 2j\Phi_{x_r x_i}(e^{j\omega}) \\
&= 2[\Phi_{x_r x_r}(e^{j\omega}) - jH(e^{j\omega})\Phi_{x_r x_r}(e^{j\omega})] \\
&= 2\Phi_{x_r x_r}(e^{j\omega})[1 - jH(e^{j\omega})]
\end{aligned}$$

Since

$$1 - jH(e^{j\omega}) = \begin{cases} 0, & 0 < \omega < \pi \\ 2, & -\pi < \omega < 0 \end{cases}$$

we get

$$P_{xx}(\omega) = \begin{cases} 0, & 0 < \omega < \pi \\ 4\Phi_{x_r x_r}(e^{j\omega}), & -\pi < \omega < 0 \end{cases}$$

11.31. (a) As shown in the figure below, the system reconstructs the original bandpass signal. As in the example, $T = \pi/(\Omega_c + \Delta\Omega)$ and $M = 5$.

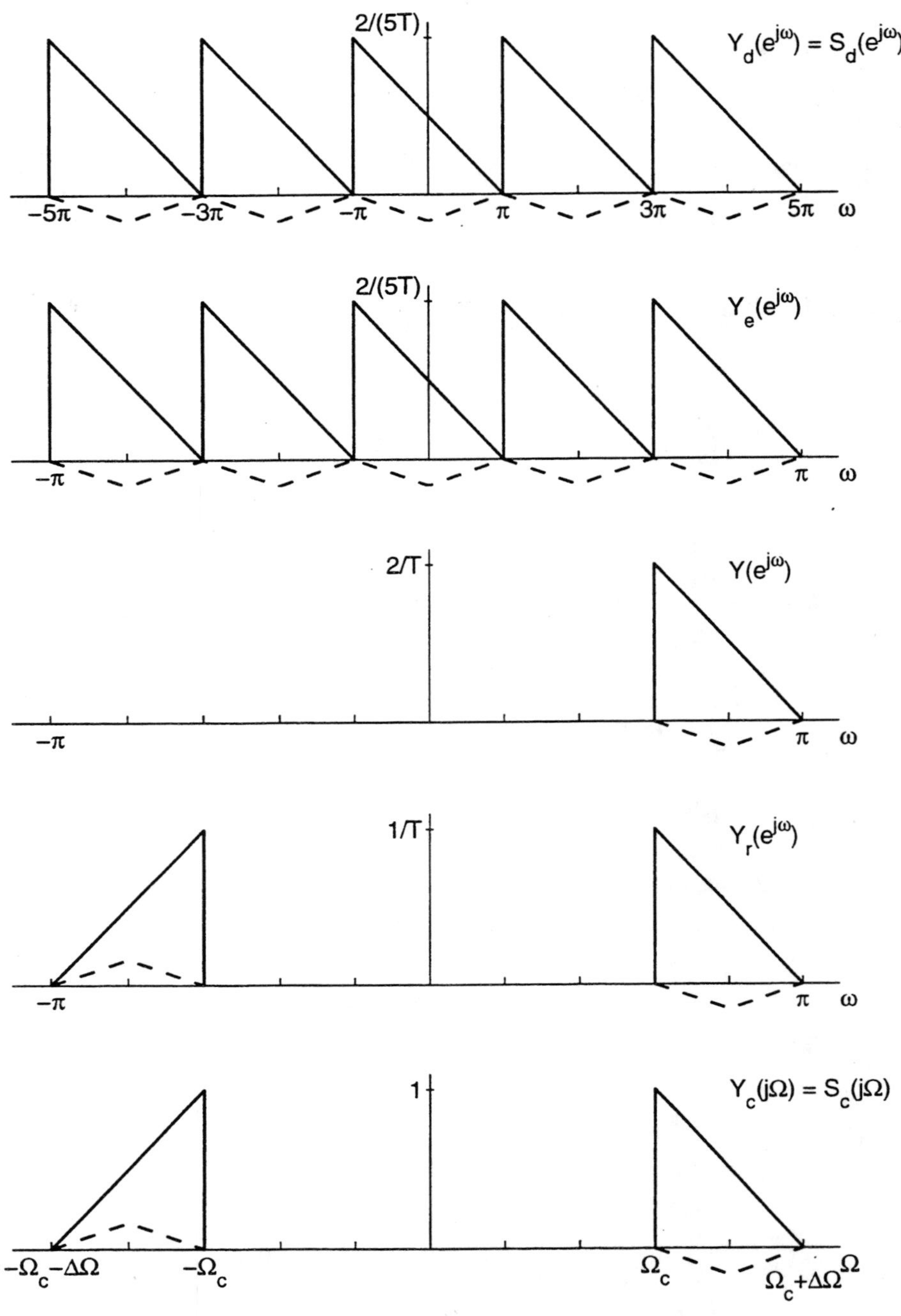

(b) In the frequency domain

$$H_i(e^{j\omega}) = \begin{cases} 5, & \frac{3\pi}{5} < \omega < \pi \\ 0, & \text{otherwise} \end{cases}$$

Note that $H_i(e^{j\omega}) = 5G(e^{j(\omega-4\pi/5)})$, where

$$G(e^{j\omega}) = \begin{cases} 1, & |\omega| < \frac{\pi}{5} \\ 0, & \text{otherwise} \end{cases}$$

$$g[n] = \frac{\sin(\pi n/5)}{\pi n}$$

We can therefore write $h_i[n]$ as

$$\begin{aligned} h_i[n] &= 5\frac{\sin(\frac{\pi}{5}n)}{\pi n} e^{j\frac{4\pi}{5}n} \\ &= \underbrace{\frac{5\cos(\frac{4\pi}{5}n)\sin(\frac{\pi}{5}n)}{\pi n}}_{h_{ri}[n]} + j\underbrace{\frac{5\sin(\frac{4\pi}{5}n)\sin(\frac{\pi}{5}n)}{\pi n}}_{h_{ii}[n]} \end{aligned}$$

(c) Using the information from part (b) we find

$$\begin{aligned} y[n] &= y_e[n] * h_i[n] \\ &= (y_{re}[n] + jy_{ie}[n]) * (h_{ri}[n] + jh_{ii}[n]) \\ &= \underbrace{(y_{re}[n] * h_{ri}[n] - y_{ie}[n] * h_{ii}[n])}_{y_r[n]} + j(y_{ie}[n] * h_{ri}[n] + y_{re}[n] * h_{ii}[n]) \end{aligned}$$

We can now redraw the figure using only real operations:

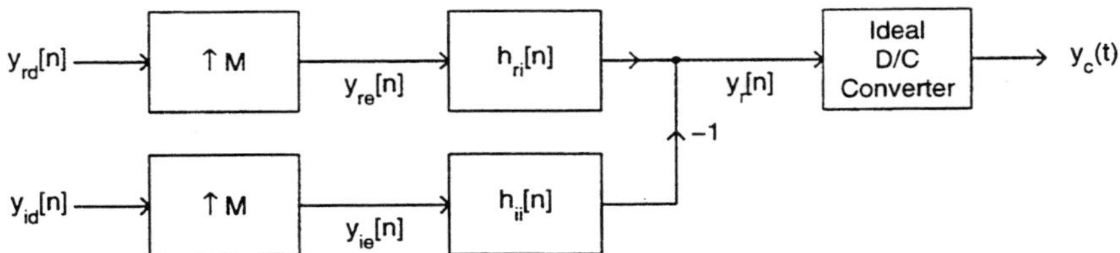

(d) From comparing the top and bottom figures in the answer to part (a), it is evident that the desired complex system response is given by:

$$H(e^{j\omega}) = \begin{cases} 1, & -\pi < \omega < 0 \\ 0, & 0 \le \omega \le \pi \end{cases}$$

11.32. (a) We know

$$\hat{X}(z) = \log[X(z)]$$

When $X(z)$ has a zero or a pole, the term $\log[X(z)]$ goes to negative infinity or infinity respectively. Therefore, $\hat{X}(z)$ has a pole at these locations.

If $\hat{x}[n]$ is causal, $\hat{X}(z)$ has a region of convergence that is the outside of a circle corresponding to its largest pole. However, we require the region of convergence to include the unit circle, i.e., $\hat{X}(e^{j\omega})$ is defined. These two conditions imply that the poles of $\hat{X}(z)$ must be inside the unit circle.

But the pole locations for $\hat{X}(z)$ correspond to the pole and zero locations for $X(z)$. We conclude the poles and zeros of $X(z)$ must be inside the unit circle, i.e., $x[n]$ must be minimum phase.

(b) This argument is similar to the last, but in reverse. Start with the fact that $x[n]$ is minimum phase and must have its poles and zeros inside the unit circle. Then, as shown in part (a), the poles of $\hat{X}(z)$ must also be inside the unit circle. Because the region of convergence must include the unit circle, we know it lies outside the circle defined by its largest pole. Thus, $\hat{x}[n]$ must be causal.

(c)

$$\hat{X}(z) = \log\left[A\frac{\prod_{k=1}^{M_i}(1-a_k z^{-1})\prod_{k=1}^{M_o}(1-b_k z)}{\prod_{k=1}^{N_i}(1-c_k z^{-1})\prod_{k=1}^{N_o}(1-d_k z)}\right]$$

$$
\begin{aligned}
&= \log(A) + \sum_{k=1}^{M_i} \log(1 - a_k z^{-1}) + \sum_{k=1}^{M_o} \log(1 - b_k z) \\
&\quad - \sum_{k=1}^{N_i} \log(1 - c_k z^{-1}) - \sum_{k=1}^{N_o} \log(1 - d_k z)
\end{aligned}
$$

(d) Using the power series expansion

$$\log(1 - x) = -\sum_{n=1}^{\infty} \frac{x^n}{n}$$

we find

$$
\begin{aligned}
\log(1 - \alpha z^{-1}) &= -\sum_{n=1}^{\infty} \frac{\alpha^n}{n} z^{-n}, \qquad |z| > |\alpha| \\
\log(1 - \beta z) &= -\sum_{n=1}^{\infty} \frac{\beta^n}{n} z^{n}, \qquad |z| > |\beta^{-1}| \\
&= \sum_{n=-\infty}^{-1} \frac{\beta^{-n}}{n} z^{-n}, \qquad |z| > |\beta^{-1}|
\end{aligned}
$$

From the equations above we can identify the following z-transform pairs

$$
\begin{aligned}
-\frac{\alpha^n}{n} u[n-1] &\longleftrightarrow \log(1 - \alpha z^{-1}), \qquad |z| > |\alpha| \\
\frac{\beta^{-n}}{n} u[-n-1] &\longleftrightarrow \log(1 - \beta z), \qquad |z| > |\beta^{-1}|
\end{aligned}
$$

We can now take the inverse transform of $\hat{X}(z)$.

$$
\hat{x}[n] = \begin{cases}
\log(A), & n = 0 \\
-\sum_{k=1}^{M_i} \frac{a_k^n}{n} + \sum_{k=1}^{N_i} \frac{c_k^n}{n}, & n > 0 \\
\sum_{k=1}^{M_o} \frac{b_k^{-n}}{n} - \sum_{k=1}^{N_o} \frac{d_k^{-n}}{n}, & n < 0
\end{cases}
$$

(e) From the results of part (d), we see if $\hat{x}[n]$ is causal, all the b_k and d_k terms must be zero. But the expression for $X(z)$ shows these terms correspond to the zeros and poles outside the unit circle. We conclude that all the zeros and poles of $X(z)$ are inside the unit circle, i.e., $x[n]$ is a minimum phase sequence.

Links to Matlab Projects

Matlab Links for Discrete-Time Signal Processing, Second Edition

We have found that MATLAB computer exercises are an important component in teaching signal processing at both the graduate and undergraduate levels. Based on our experiences with these computer projects, we have compiled this appendix as a resource for other instructors wishing to incorporate MATLAB exercises into a course using the second edition of *Discrete-time Signal Processing* as the primary textbook.

This appendix provides lists linking projects in the popular MATLAB supplements *Computer-Based Exercises in Signal Processing Using Matlab 5* by McClellan *et al.* and *Computer Explorations in Signals and Systems* by Buck, Daniel and Signer to specific sections, examples, and problems in *Discrete-Time Signal Processing, Second Edition.* Not every project in these books is listed, since for some of the projects there are no particularly germane problems, examples, or sections. The sections listed do not necessarily cover all the background necessary for a problem, but may be viewed as a minimum requirement to attempt the project. If the course has not covered the section listed with a project, the instructor should think very carefully before assigning that project. When specific examples in the text illustrate the same issues presented in the MATLAB project, we have attempted to identify those as well.

The textbook problems listed with projects may be there for several reasons. Some of the problems are analytic versions of the same problems posed in the MATLAB projects. In this case, the MATLAB projects can be viewed as a means for the students to confirm and expand the understanding they developed in solving the analytic "paper and pencil" problem. In other instances, the textbook problems listed are complementary to the MATLAB projects. These problems investigate the same issues as the MATLAB project, but from a different perspective. These problems might be assigned as "warm-up" exercises before tackling the more involved MATLAB project on these issues. Still other problems relate the MATLAB project to earlier or later material in *Discrete-Time Signal Processing, Second Edition*, illustrating a connection between the current topics and others presented elsewhere in the book.

Obviously, no list of this nature can replace the pedagogical instincts and judgment of an experienced instructor. We strongly recommend that instructors read and solve both the MATLAB project and textbook problems before assigning them. This will allow the instructor to verify that their students are suitably prepared for the issues and challenges in the problems and projects assigned. In our experience, appropriate MATLAB projects can spark considerable enthusiasm in the students, but inappropriately assigned projects leave the students disillusioned in short order.

In the interest of conserving space, the lists will abreviate *Discrete-Time Signal Process* as DTSP, *Discrete-time* as DT, *Continuous-time* as CT, and also use many other common abbreviations found in the textbook such as LTI, DTFT, DFS, DFT, etc ....

We hope you find these lists useful. Please send any suggestions for additions, corrections, or changes for these lists to

Prof. John R. Buck
ECE Dept., UMass Dartmouth
285 Old Westport Rd
N. Dartmouth, Ma 02747-2300
jbuck@umassd.edu

Links to *Computer Explorations in Signals and Systems*

Project	Project Subject	DTSP Sec.	DTSP Ex.	DTSP Problems
1.1	Tutorial: Signals	2.1		
1.2	Disrete-Time Sinusoids	2.1	2.2	2.7, 2.28
1.3	Trans. of DT Time Indices	2.1		2.29
1.4	Properties of DT Systems	2.2		2.1
1.5	1st Order LCCDE	2.5		2.20
2.1	Tutorial: `conv`	2.3		2.2, 2.3, 2.22, 2.24
2.2	Tutorial: `filter`	2.5		2.4, 2.22
2.4	DT LTI Systems	2.4		2.69
2.5	Linearity and Time-Inv.	2.4		2.1, 2.30
2.6	Noncausal FIR Filters	2.4		4.50
2.7	DT Convolution	2.3, 2.4, 8.7		
2.10	Echo Cancellation	5.2, 5.6.2		4.7, 5.33, 5.59, 8.64
3.1	Discrete Fourier Series	8.1		8.3
3.2	Tutorial `freqz`	2.6	2.18	2.6, 2.11
3.4	Eigenfunctions	2.6		2.11, 2.13, 2.26, 2.27
3.5	DFS Synthesis	8.1, 8.2	8.3	8.3
3.8	1st order IIR Filters	2.6	2.19	2.11
3.10	Computing the DFS	8.2.5, 8.7, 9.1, 9.3		8.43
5.1	Computing the DTFT	2.7, 8.4		2.17, 8.7, 8.8, 8.9, 8.23
5.2	Touch-tone	2.7, 8.5		
5.3	DT Allpass	2.6, 5.1.2, 5.5	5.1, 5.13	
5.4	Freq.-Sampling Filters	8.4		6.30, 6.37, 8.10, 8.24, 8.42
5.5	System ID	2.6, 8.5		3.16, 3.43, 8.64
6.2	Image Proc.	5.1		2.88
6.3	Filter Transformations	2.9, 4.6, 5.1		2.45, 5.21, 5.27
6.4	Phase Effects for LPF	5.1	5.1	5.57
6.5	FDMA			5.57
7.1	Aliasing	4.1, 4.2	4.1, 4.2, 4.3	4.1, 4.2, 4.3, 4.10 4.11, 4.19, 4.20
7.2	Reconstruction from Samples	4.3		4.19, 4.50
7.3	Sampling Rate Conversion	4.6		4.15, 4.16, 4.17, 4.18, 4.37, 4.44, 4.59
7.4	Bandpass Sampling	4.2		4.21
7.5	Half-Sample Delay	4.5		4.42
7.6	DT Differentiator	7.3.2	4.5, 4.6, 7.10	4.12, 4.30, 7.23
8.1	Hilbert Transform	2.9, 11.4.1, 11.4.2	11.4	2.58, 7.33, 11.25
8.2	AM Demodulator	2.9		
8.3	AM Synchronization	2.9		
10.1	DT Pole-zero Diagrams	3.1		3.3, 3.12, 3.16, 3.31, 3.32, 3.33, 5.2, 5.4, 5.7, 5.8
10.2	Geo. Interp. of $H(e^{j\omega})$	5.3	5.8, 5.9, 5.10	5.35, 5.60
10.3	Quant. of DT Struct.	6.7		6.33, 6.44
10.4	Back. & For. Diff.			7.42
10.5	Bilin. Transform	7.1.2, 7.1.3	7.3, 7.4	7.10, 7.14

Links to *Computer-Based Exercises for Signal Processing Using Matlab 5*

The titles given for the projects in the table below are not always those given in the book, but attempt to summarize the content of the project in two or three words. Depending on which was appropriate, some of the links below are for a group of projects in *Computer-Based Exercises*, and some are for a specific individual project.

Project Subject	Page	DTSP Sec.	DTSP Ex.	DTSP Problems
Basic Signals	2	2.0, 2.1		
Complex Signals	6	2.0, 2.1, 2.5		
LCCDEs	9	2.5		2.4, 2.5, 2.38
Steady-State Response	10	2.5, 2.6		
Freq. Resp. for LCCDEs	12	2.5, 2.6		2.47
Computing the DTFT	14	2.5, 2.7		2.17
DTFT Symmetries	17	2.7, 2.8, 2.9		2.17, 2.65
Computing Group Delay	25	5.1.2, 2.9		5.19
Effect of Group Delay	27	5.1.2	5.1	5.57
Negative Group Delay	28	5.1.2	5.1	5.25
Aliasing	29	4.1, 4.2	4.1, 4.2	4.1–4.4, 4.10
Freq. Domain View	31	4.2	4.1–4.3	4.23
Signal Reconstruction	33	4.3		4.25
Zero-Phase Filtering	35			2.66
Common DFTs	45	8.5, 8.6		8.5, 8.6
Difficult DFTs	47	8.5, 8.6		8.8, 8.49
DFT Symmetries	49	8.6.4		8.22, 8.34, 8.56
Inverse DFTs	52			9.1
Zero Padding	54	8.5, 8.6		8.32, 8.33, 8.37, 8.44
Real FFTs	55	9.3		9.31, 9.47
DFS	58	8.1, 8.2, 8.4	8.1, 8.3, 8.5, 8.6	8.2, 8.3
DFT Matrix	59			9.51
Circ. Index	67	8.6.5	8.10, 8.11	8.10, 8.13, 8.18, 8.19 8.20, 8.22, 8.28
Circ. Conv.	68	8.6.5	8.10, 8.11	8.11, 8.12, 8.14
Circ. & Lin. Conv.	70	8.7.2	8.12	8.17, 8.27, 8.29, 8.39, 8.40, 8.41
Block Conv.	73	8.7.3		8.43, 8.63
FFT Conv.	75			9.32, 9.33
DCT	77	8.8	8.13	8.69, 8.71
Disc. Hartley Trans.	81			8.65, 9.50
Window Types	85	10.2.1	10.3	10.28
Window Peformance	88			10.19, 10.20
Resolution	91	10.2.2	10.4–10.8	10.7, 10.8, 10.9, 10.14
Spectrogram	93	10.3		10.3, 10.13, 10.15, 10.17, 10.22

Project Subject	Page	DTSP Sec.	DTSP Ex.	DTSP Problems
Filtering Bandpass Pulse	105	10.3		
Freq. Samp. of DTFT	111		8.4	8.7, 8.9, 8.23
Interp. Filters	115	4.6		4.50
Zoom Transform	121	4.6, 10.1, 10.2		10.44
Decimation	124	4.6.1		4.14, 4.15
Rate Changing	127	4.6.3	4.11	4.16–4.18, 4.44, 4.59
Descriptions of Systems	131	2.3, 2.5, 2.7, 3.1, 5.3		
Measuring $H(e^{j\omega})$	137	2.7		9.48
Types of Systems	139	2.2, 2.6, 5.5, 5.6, 5.7		5.13, 5.15, 5.17–5.19, 5.38–5.40 5.45, 5.48, 5.53, 5.66, 5.70
Structres	148	6.3		6.23
Stochastic Signals	161	2.10		2.80–2.83, 2.87
Periodogram	178	10.6, 10.7		10.9, 10.14, 10.26, 10.28
Periodogram Avg.	182	10.6, 10.7		10.29, 10.37, 10.38
Narrowband Signals	185	10.6, 10.7		10.5, 10.9, 10.14, 10.31, 10.34
Quant. Signals	207	4.8, 4.9		4.57, 4.60–4.62
Multiplier Noise	213	6.6, 6.8		6.40, 6.42, 6.43, 6.45
Filter Struct.	216	6.6, 6.7		6.33, 6.43–6.45
Limit Cycles	225	6.9		
Quant. Noise	231	6.6–6.9		6.42–6.45
Freq. Samp. FIR Filters	249	8.4, 8.6		6.30, 6.37, 8.10, 8.24, 8.42
LSE FIR LPF Design	261	7.2		7.32, 7.37
Other LSE Filters	265			5.21, 7.27, 7.35
Windowed FIR Filters	267	7.2, 7.3		7.5, 7.6, 7.15, 7.16, 7.34
Parks-McClellan FIR	270	7.4, 7.4.1, 7.4.4, 7.5.1		7.8, 7.36, 7.38, 7.55, 7.56
Remez Exch. Alg.	272	7.4.3		7.39, 7.52
IIR Filters	280	7.0, App. B	7.1	
Bilin. Trans.	282	7.1.2, 7.1.3	7.3, 7.4	7.10, 7.12, 7.14, 7.21, 7.41, 7.43
Other IIR Filters	284			7.18, 7.27–7.29, 7.31, 7.45 7.58
Calculating the DFT	291	9.1		
Goertzel's Alg.	293	9.2		9.7, 9.19, 9.21
Deriv. of FFT	295	9.3, 9.4		9.17, 9.22, 9.30
Two-Factor FFT	298			9.40, 9.53
Split-Radix FFT	300			9.38
Prime-Factor FFT	302			9.53
Matlab FFT	312	9.3, 9.4		9.15, 9.18
Chirp z-Trans.	313	9.6.2		9.8, 9.10, 9.25, 9.27, 9.28, 9.34
Radar Simulation	318	10.5.2	10.11	
STFT of Speech	333	10.3, 10.5.1		10.3, 10.15
Vocal Tract Model	338			6.39
Uniform. Quant.	344	4.8		4.57
Mulaw Quant.	347	4.8		4.57

Additional Exam Problems

Problem 1

Let $x[n]$ be a purely real sequence. You are given the following information about $x[n]$ and must determine what it is. Even if you are unable to specify $x[n]$ fully, you may receive partial credit by describing which features of $x[n]$ are determined by each clue.

(a) $x[n]$ is a causal sequence.

(b) Let $v[n] = x[n+2]$. The discrete-time Fourier transform $V(e^{j\omega})$ is purely real.

(c)

$$\frac{1}{2\pi}\int_{-\pi}^{\pi} |X(e^{j\omega})|^2 d\omega = 9.$$

(d)

$$\lim_{z\to\infty} X(z) = 2$$

(e)

$$\frac{1}{2\pi}\int_{-\pi}^{\pi} X(e^{j\omega})e^{j\omega} d\omega = 0$$

(f)

$$x[2] > 0.$$

Problem 2

The signal $x[n]$ is real-valued. The plots in Figures 2.1 through 2.4 show the magnitude and phase of four different discrete-time Fourier transforms $X(e^{j\omega})$. **Note that the plots show the frequency interval $-2\pi \leq \omega \leq 2\pi$ since the frequency axis ω is normalized by π.**

For each of the four transforms, indicate if it could be $X(e^{j\omega})$, the Fourier transform of $x[n]$. If your answer is yes, indicate how the figure is consistent with the information given. If your answer is no, indicate why the figure is inconsistent with the information given. Note that it is possible that more than one of the figures is consistent with the information given about $x[n]$. **Answers without justification will be assumed to be guesses and receive no credit.**

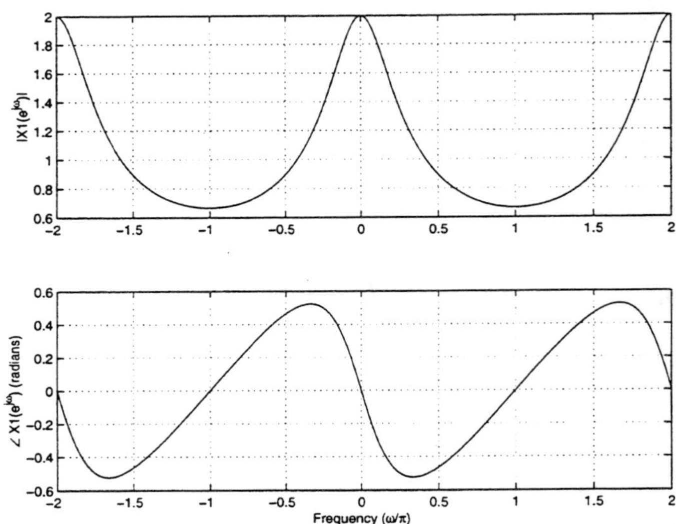

Figure 2.1. Magnitude and Phase of $X_1(e^{j\omega})$

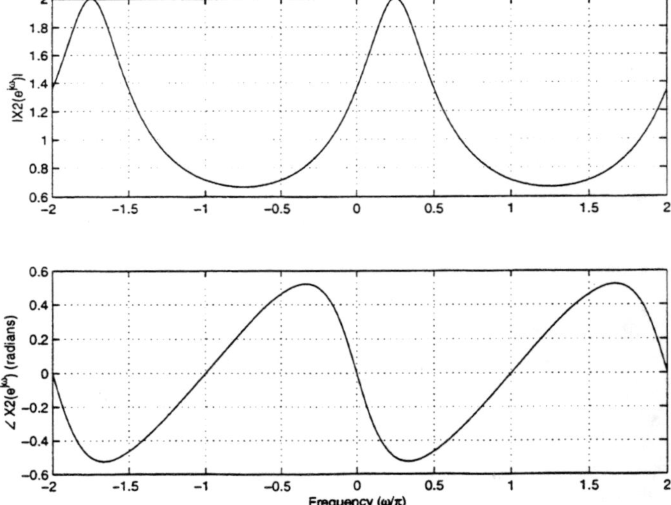

Figure 2.2. Magnitude and Phase of $X_2(e^{j\omega})$

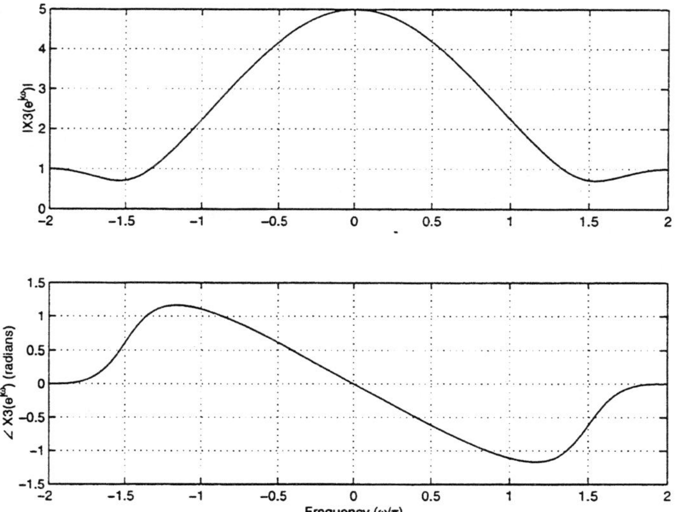

Figure 2.3. Magnitude and Phase of $X_3(e^{j\omega})$

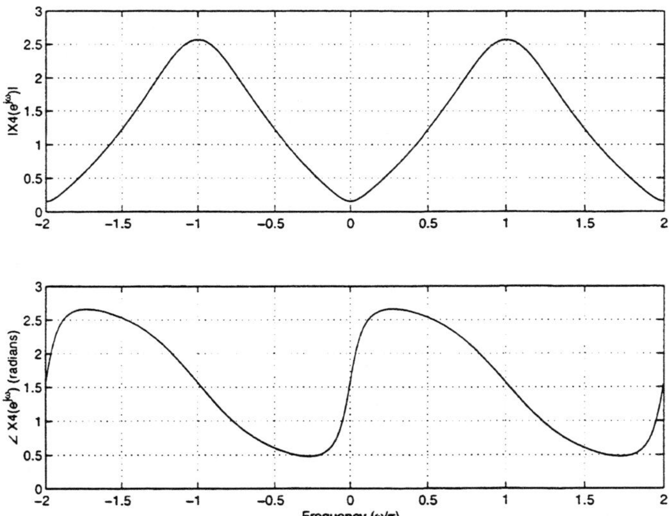

Figure 2.4. Magnitude and Phase of $X_4(e^{j\omega})$

Problem 3

A causal and stable LTI system has system function $H(z)$ with the pole-zero plot in Fig. 3.1. You are also told that $H(1) = 2$.

(a) What is the region of convergence (ROC) for $H(z)$?

(b) Is $h[n]$ real? Justify your answer.

(c) What is the pole-zero plot for the z-transform of $(\frac{1}{2})^n h[n]$?

(d) What is the pole-zero plot for the z-transform of $(\frac{j}{2})^n h[n]$?

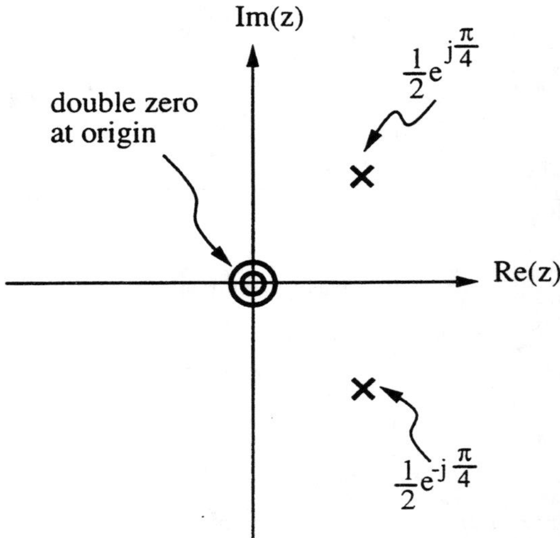

Figure 3.1. Pole-zero Plot for $H(z)$

Problem 4
Let the z-transform of the sequence $x[n]$ be denoted by $X(z)$. The pole-zero plot of $X(z)$ is shown in Fig. 4.1. There are 3 finite poles ($z = 1/2, \pm j/2$) and 2 finite zeros ($z = 0, 1$).

(a) Sketch the pole-zero plot of $Y_1(z)$ if $y_1[n] = x[n-2]$.

(b) Sketch the pole-zero plot of $Y_2(z)$ if $y_2[n] = x[1-n]$.

(c) Sketch the pole-zero plot of $Y_3(z)$ if $y_3[n] = (1/2)^n x[n]$.

(d) Sketch the pole-zero plot of $Y_4(z)$ if $y_4[n] = e^{(j\pi/4)n} x[n]$.

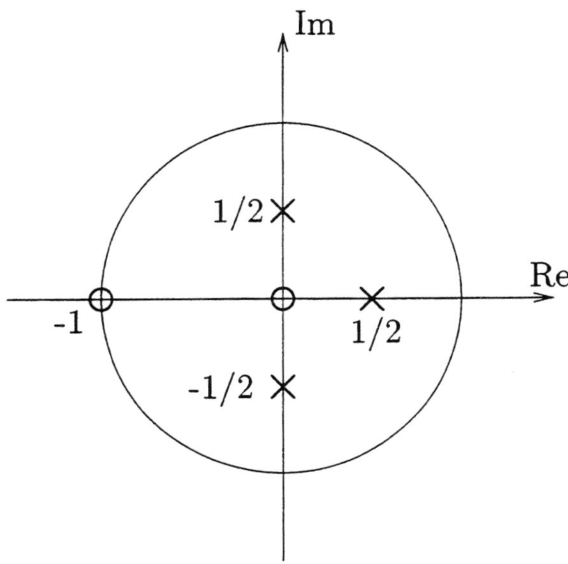

Figure 4.1. Pole-zero diagram for $X(z)$

Problem 5

(a) Consider the system shown in Fig. 5.1 with input $x[n]$ and output $y[n]$. Assume that $H(z)$ is causal. Is the overall system LTI? If so, determine $G(z)$, the z-transform of the overall system. If not, explain why.

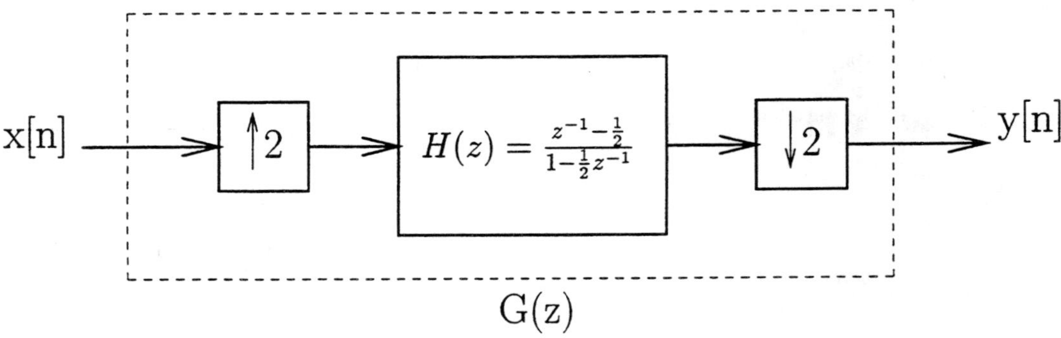

Figure 5.1. Overall system for Part (a)

(b) Consider the system shown in Fig. 5.2 with input $x[n]$ and output $y[n]$. Assume that $H(z)$ is causal. Is the overall system LTI? If so, determine $G(z)$, the z-transform of the overall system. If not, explain why.

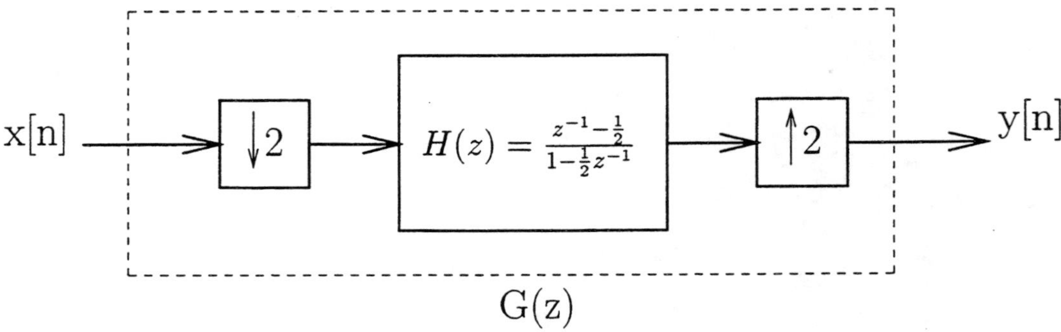

Figure 5.2. Overall system for Part (b)

Problem 6

Figures 6.1 and 6.2 depict a discrete-time signal $x[n]$ and its DTFT $X(e^{j\omega})$. Note that the discrete samples of $x[n]$ have been connected by straight lines using the MATLAB `plot` command. The signal $x[n]$ is used as the input to an LTI filter with the frequency response magnitude $|H(e^{j\omega})|$ shown in Figure 6.3. Note that this magnitude is plotted on a dB scale, i.e., $20\log_{10}|H(e^{j\omega})|$.

(a) Figure 6.4 shows five possible output signals $y_1[n]$ through $y_5[n]$. Which of these five signals could be the output of the filter in Figure 6.3 when the $x[n]$ in Figure 6.1 is the input? For each possible output you eliminate, justify your answer. **Choices eliminated without justification will be assumed to be guesses and receive no credit.**

(b) Figure 6.5 shows four different pole-zero plots. Which of these pole-zero plots could belong to the filter $|H(e^{j\omega})|$ shown in Figure 6.3. Again, justify your answer for each choice you eliminate. **Choices eliminated without justification will be assumed to be guesses and receive no credit.**

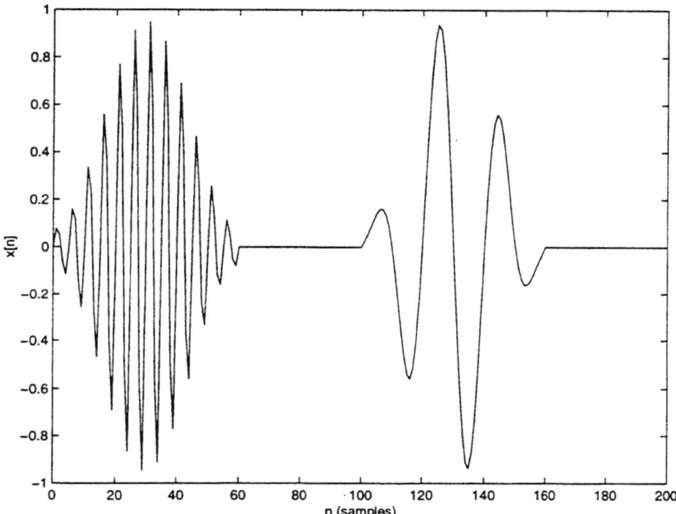

Figure 6.1. Input signal $x[n]$

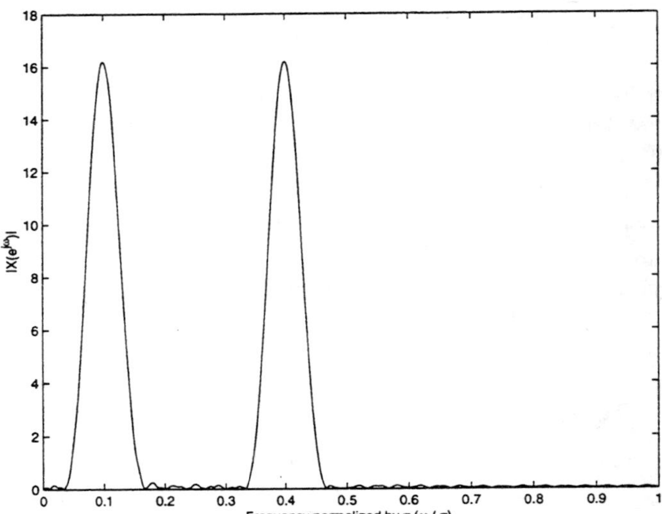

Figure 6.2. Input signal spectrum $X(e^{j\omega})$

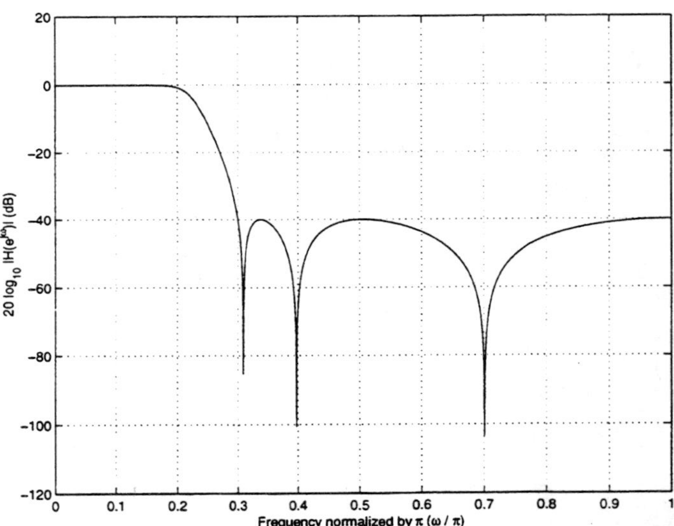

Figure 6.3. Filter Magnitude Response $|H(e^{j\omega})|$

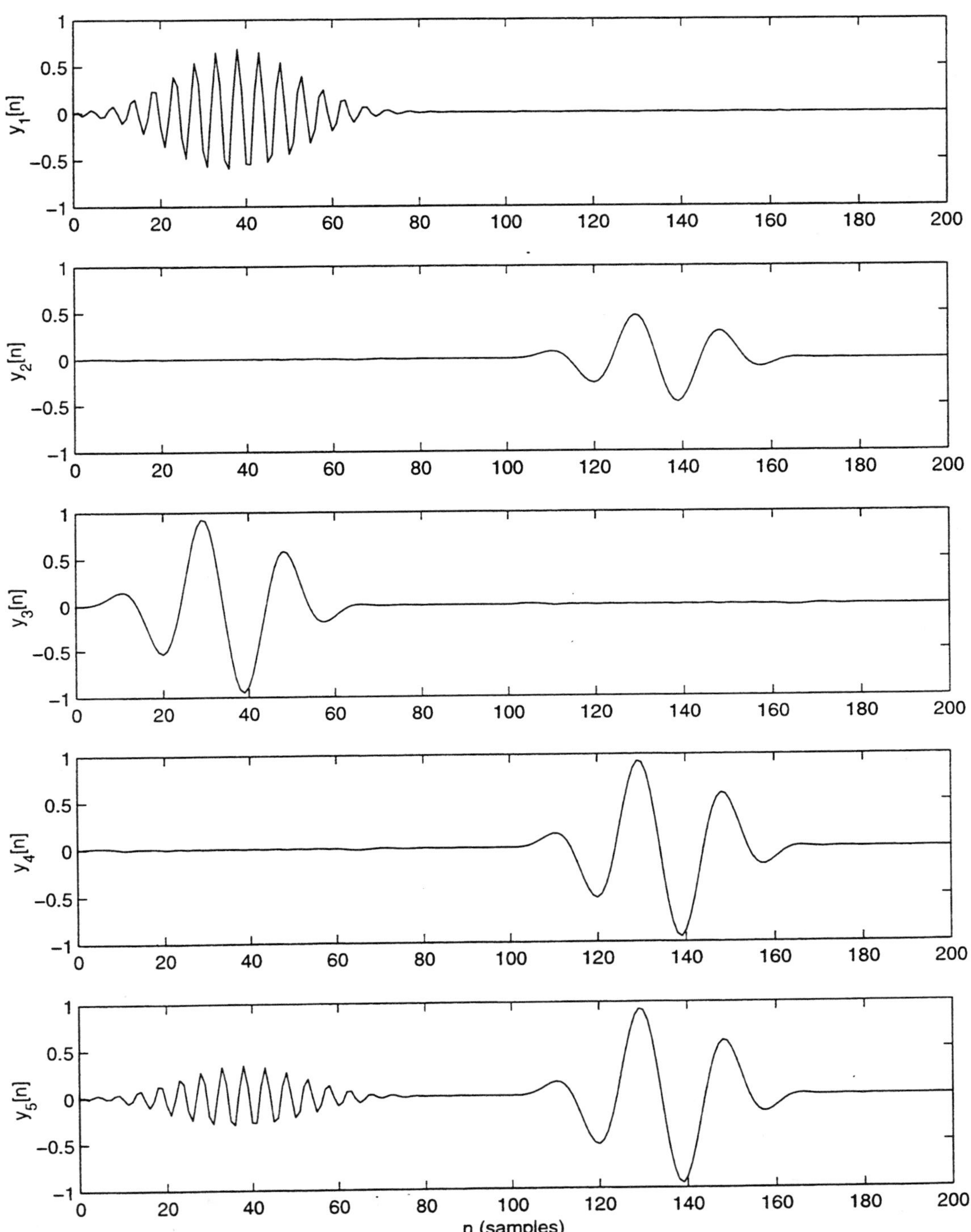

Figure 6.4. Output signals $y_1[n]$ through $y_5[n]$

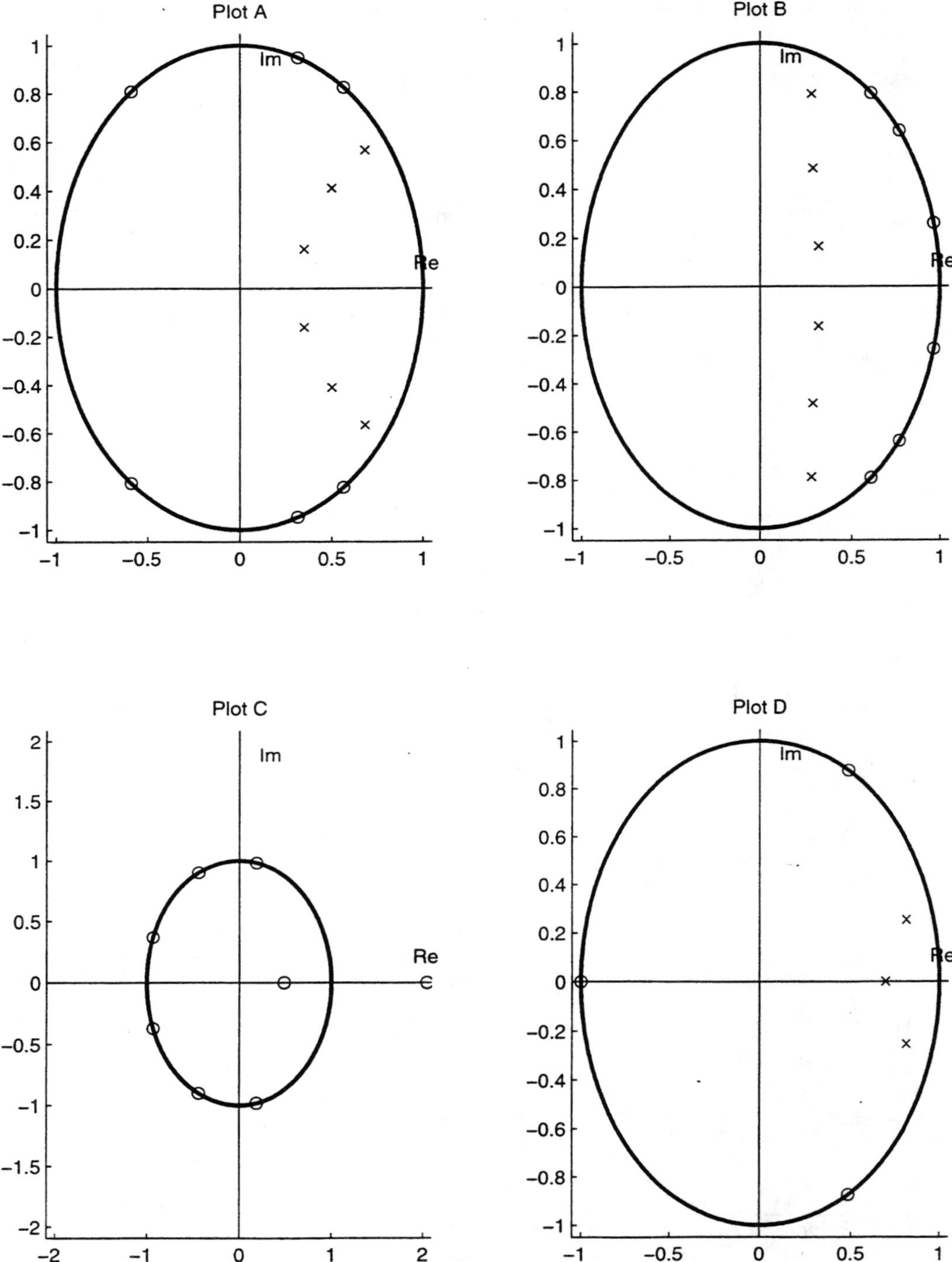

Figure 6.5. Pole-Zero Plots

Problem 7

Consider the LTI system represented by the system function

$$H(z) = \left(1 - \frac{1}{2}z^{-1}\right)\left(1 + \frac{3}{4}z^{-1}\right)\left(1 - 3z^{-1}\right).$$

This system function can be factored as

$$H(z) = H_{min}(z)H_{ap}(z),$$

where $H_{min}(z)$ is a minimum-phase system and $H_{ap}(z)$ is an allpass system.

(a) Sketch the pole-zero plot of this system function. You do **not** need to indicate the region of convergence. You **must** indicate any multiple order zeros or poles appropriately.

(b) Sketch pole-zero plots for $H_{min}(z)$ and $H_{ap}(z)$. Again, you do not need to indicate the region of convergence, but you must indicate all multiple order poles and zeros.

(c) Give expressions for $H_{min}(z)$ and $H_{ap}(z)$. Test that $|H_{ap}(e^{j\omega})| = 1$ as required by demonstrating that $H_{ap}(z)|_{z=1} = 1$.

Problem 8
Let $H(z)$ be the rational system function of a stable LTI system whose impulse response $h[n]$ is real. Suppose $C(z) = H(z)H^*(1/z^*)$ corresponds to the pole-zero plot in Fig. 8.1 with $C(1) = 1$.

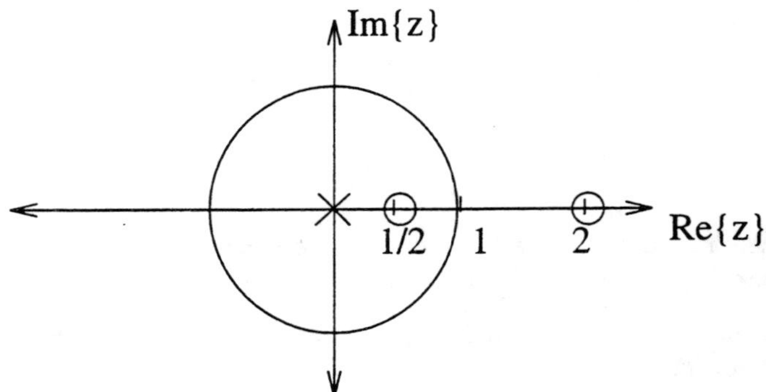

Figure 8.1. Pole-zero Plot for $C(z)$

(a) Make a fully labeled sketch of $|H(e^{j\omega})|$, the magnitude response of the system.

(b) Is it possible to construct an infinite-length impulse response $h[n]$ having the magnitude response you determine in (a)? If your answer is yes, construct an example $h[n]$ or $H(z)$. If your answer is no, explain.

(c) Identify all distinct finite-length impulse responses $h[n]$ with $h[0] > 0$ that could yield the pole-zero plot for $C(z)$ depicted in Fig. 8.1

Problem 9
Let $h[n]$ be a real-valued N-point sequence which is the impulse response of an FIR filter with generalized linear phase. We define the following three sequences:

$$
\begin{aligned}
g_1[n] &= h[2n] \\
g_2[n] &= \begin{cases} h[n/2], & n \text{ even}, \\ 0, & \text{otherwise}, \end{cases} \\
g_3[n] &= (-1)^n h[n]
\end{aligned}
$$

(a) Does $g_1[n]$ necessarily correspond to a filter with generalized linear phase? Justify your answer with a proof or counter-example.

(b) Does $g_2[n]$ necessarily correspond to a filter with generalized linear phase? Justify your answer with a proof or counter-example.

(c) Does $g_3[n]$ necessarily correspond to a filter with generalized linear phase? Justify your answer with a proof or counter-example. If your answer is "yes," does $g_3[n]$ necessarily correspond to the same *type*, i.e, Type I, Type II, Type III, or Type IV, for generalized linear phase filter as $h[n]$?

Problem 10

A causal LTI system has system function

$$H(z) = \frac{1 - 2.3z^{-1} - 1.7z^{-2}}{1 + 0.8z^{-1} - 0.25z^{-2} - 0.2z^{-3}} = \frac{(1 - 2.8885z^{-1})(1 + 0.5885z^{-1})}{(1 - 0.5z^{-1})(1 + 0.5z^{-1})(1 + 0.8z^{-1})}$$

(a) Write the single difference equation that is satisfied by the input $x[n]$ and the output $y[n]$.

(b) The system function can be expressed in the form

$$H(z) = \frac{-2}{1 - 0.5z^{-1}} + \frac{1}{1 + 0.5z^{-1}} + \frac{A}{1 + 0.8z^{-1}}.$$

Determine the value of A.

(c) Determine the impulse response of the system.

(d) The system can be implemented by the signal flow graph in Fig. 10.1. Fill in all the missing parameters *and symbols.*

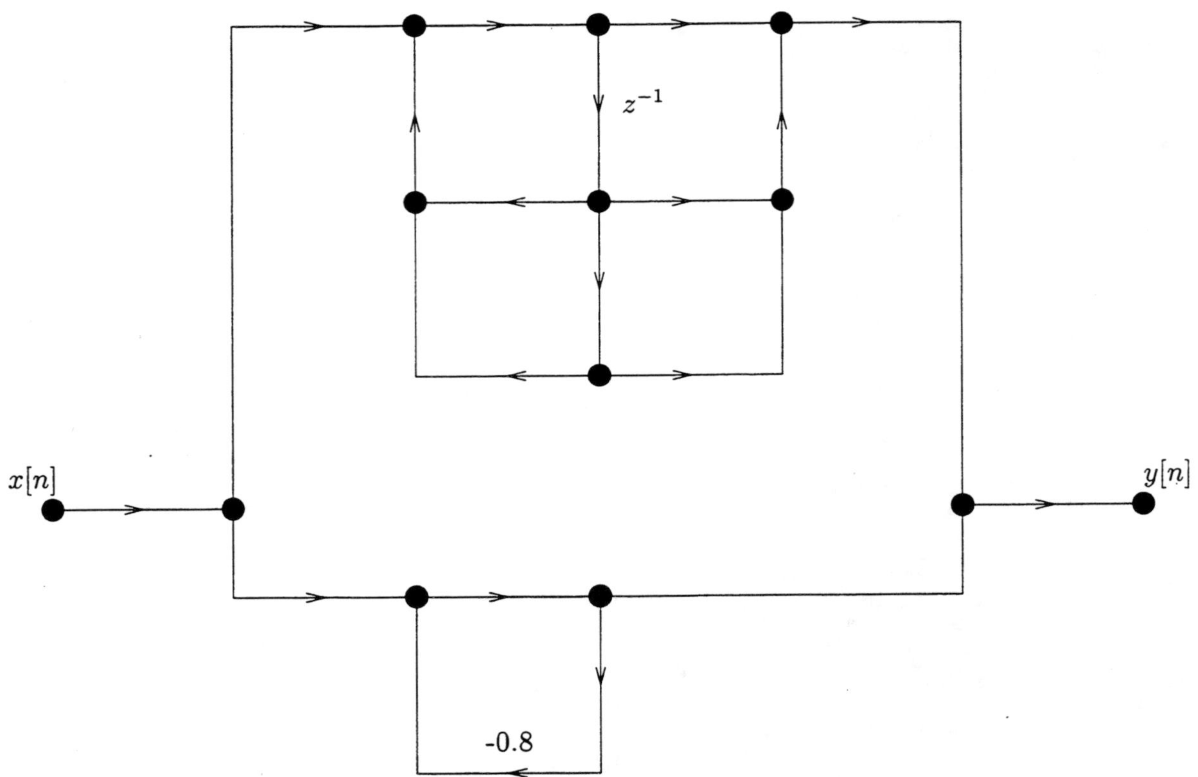

Figure 10.1. Signal flow graph for system

Problem 11

The signal flow graph in Fig. 11.1 represents a linear constant-coefficient difference equation. Determine the difference equation that relates the output $y[n]$ to the input $x[n]$.

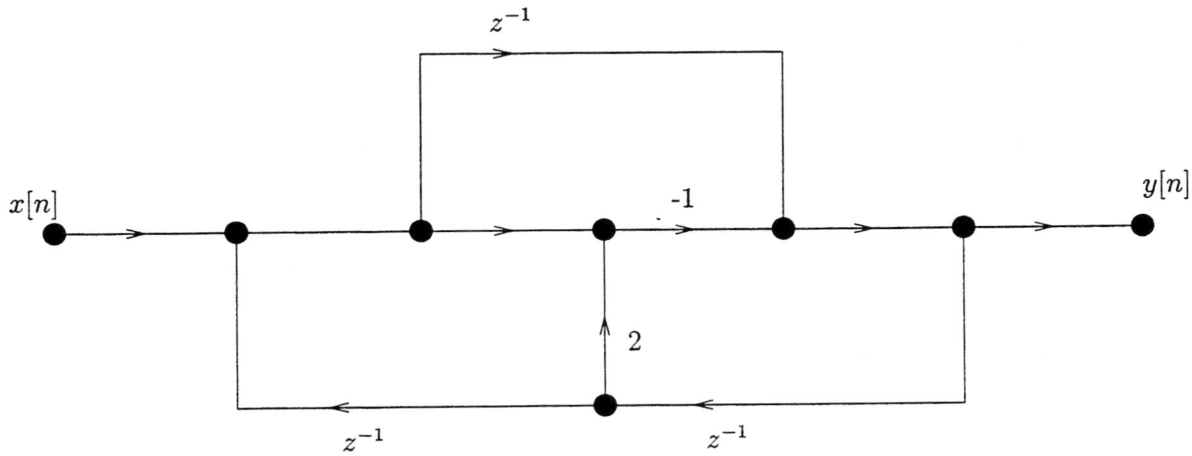

Figure 11.1. Signal flow graph for system

Problem 12
Figure 12.1 shows the signal flow graph for a causal, LTI system.

(a) Give the system function $H(z)$ for this system.

(b) Is the system stable?

(c) Draw the signal flow graph that results from applying the transposition theorem to the signal flow graph in Figure 12.1.

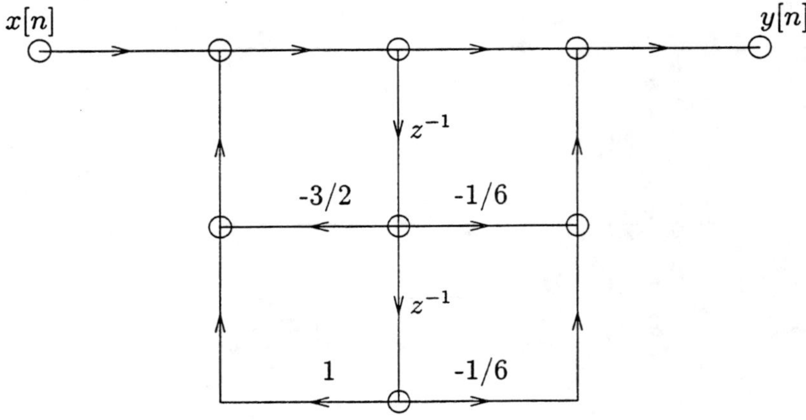

Figure 12.1. Signal Flow Graph of Causal, LTI System

Problem 13

For the system in Fig. 13.1

$$A(e^{j\omega}) = \begin{cases} 1, & |\omega| < \frac{\pi}{3} \\ 0, & \frac{\pi}{3} < |\omega| < \pi \end{cases} .$$

(a) Make a fully labeled sketch of $Y(e^{j\omega})$, the Fourier transform of the response of the system to an input $x[n]$ whose Fourier transform $X(e^{j\omega})$ is given in Fig. 13.2

(b) Is the system in Fig. 13.1 linear and time-invariant? Justify your answer clearly.

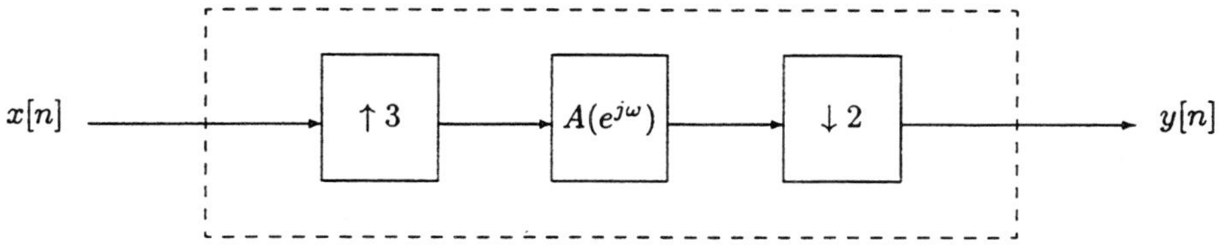

Figure 13.1. System

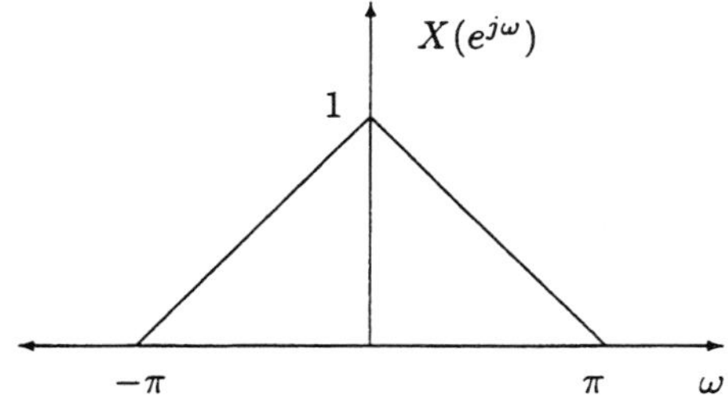

Figure 13.2. Fourier transform $X(e^{j\omega})$

Problem 14
Consider the discrete-time system shown in Fig 14.1, where

(i) M is a positive integer,

(ii) $x_e[n] = \begin{cases} x[n/M], & n = kM, \quad k \text{ any integer}, \\ 0, & \text{otherwise}, \end{cases}$

(iii) $y[n] = y_e[nM]$,

(iv) $H(e^{j\omega}) = \begin{cases} \text{M}, & |\omega| \le \pi/4, \\ 0, & \pi/4 < |\omega| \le \pi. \end{cases}$

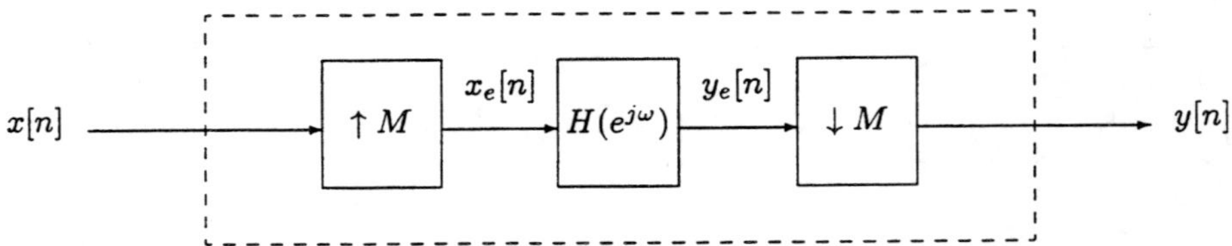

Figure 14.1. Signal processing system

(a) Assume that $M = 2$ and that $X(e^{j\omega})$, the discrete-time Fourier transform of $x[n]$, is real and as shown Fig. 14.2. Make an appropriately labeled sketch of $X_e(e^{j\omega})$, $Y_e(e^{j\omega})$ and $Y(e^{j\omega})$, the discrete-time Fourier transform. Be sure to label significant amplitudes and frequencies.

(b) For $M = 2$ and $X(e^{j\omega})$ as given in Fig. 14.2, find the value of

$$\epsilon = \sum_{n=-\infty}^{\infty} |x[n] - y[n]|^2$$

(c) For $M = 2$, the overall system is LTI. Determine and sketch the magnitude of the frequency response of the overall system, $|H_{eff}(e^{j\omega})|$.

(d) For $M = 6$, the overall system is *still* LTI. Determine and sketch the magnitude of the frequency response of the overall system, $|H_{eff}(e^{j\omega})|$.

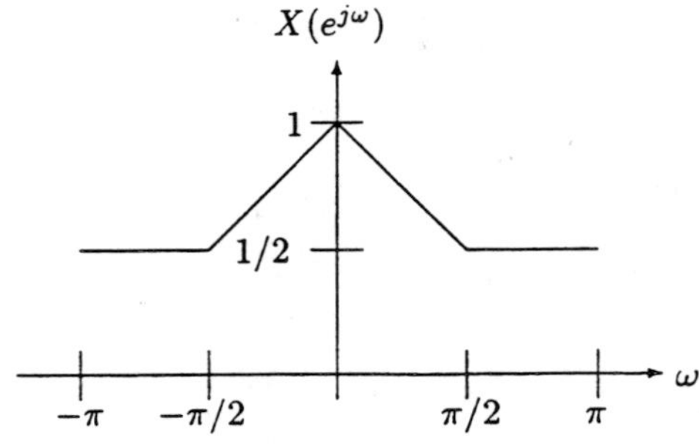

Figure 14.2. Input spectrum $X(e^{j\omega})$

Problem 15
Let $x_c(t)$ be a real-valued continuous-time signal with highest frequency $2\pi(250)$ rad/sec. Furthermore, let $y_c(t) = x_c(t - 1/1000)$.

(a) If $x[n] = x_c(n/500)$, is it theoretically possible to recover $x_c(t)$ from $x[n]$? Justify your answer.

(b) If $y[n] = y_c(n/500)$, is it theoretically possible to recover $y_c(t)$ from $y[n]$? Justify your answer.

(c) It is possible to obtain $y[n]$ from $x[n]$ as follows:

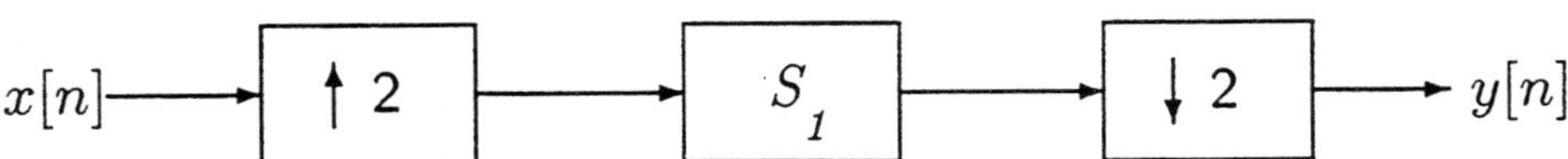

where S_1 is a digital filter with frequency response $H_1(e^{j\omega})$. Determine $H_1(e^{j\omega})$.

(d) It is also possible to obtain $y[n]$ from $x[n]$ as follows:

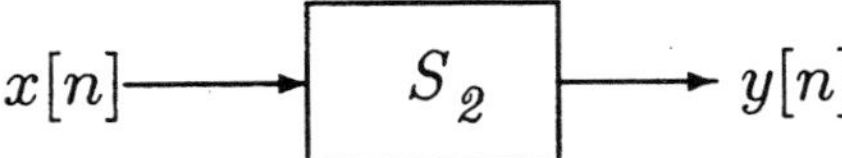

where S_2 is a digital filter with frequency response $H_2(e^{j\omega})$. Determine $H_2(e^{j\omega})$.

Problem 16
Consider the discrete-time system given in Fig. 16.1. Note that the second system is an LTI system whose impulse response is $h_2[n] = \delta[n-1]$.

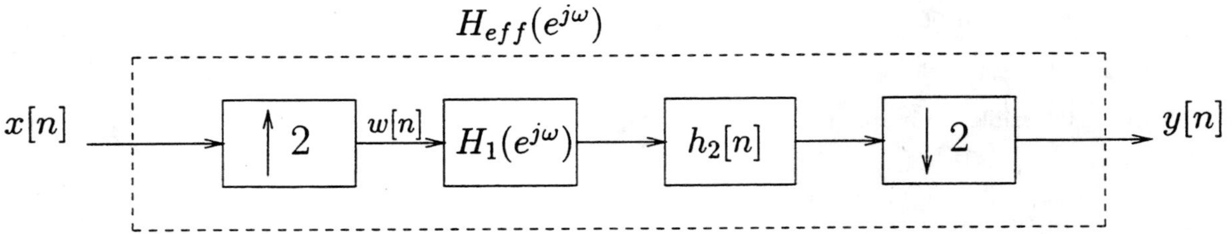

Figure 16.1. Discrete-time System

(a) For this part, $X(e^{j\omega})$ the Fourier transform of the input $x[n]$, is given in Fig. 16.2. Sketch $W(e^{j\omega})$, the Fourier transform of $w[n]$.

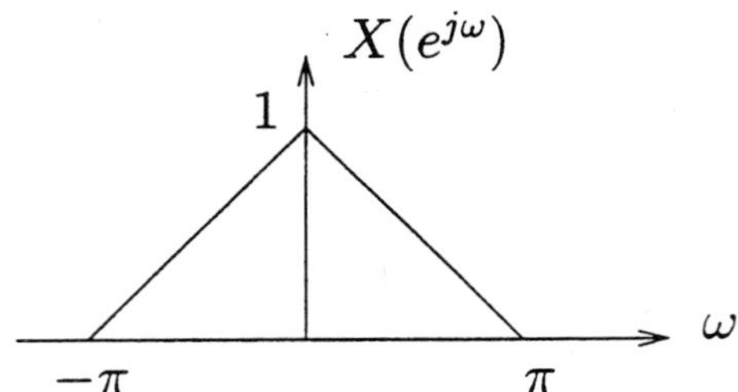

Figure 16.2. Input spectrum for Part (a)

(b) The overall system in Fig. 16.1 is an LTI system, i.e., $Y(e^{j\omega}) = H_{eff}(e^{j\omega})X(e^{j\omega})$. When $H_1(e^{j\omega})$ is as given in Fig. 16.3, determine $H_{eff}(e^{j\omega})$. Clearly justify your answer.

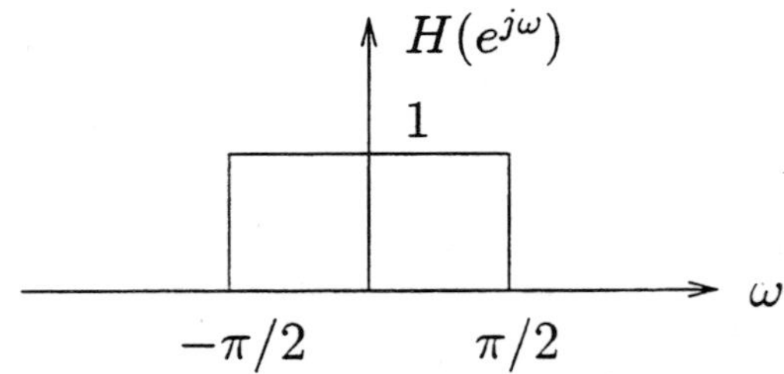

Figure 16.3. Frequency response $H_1(e^{j\omega})$

Problem 17
The system in Fig. 17.1 is proposed as a way of using "oversampling" to reduce the effect of quantization noise in sampling in an analog signal.

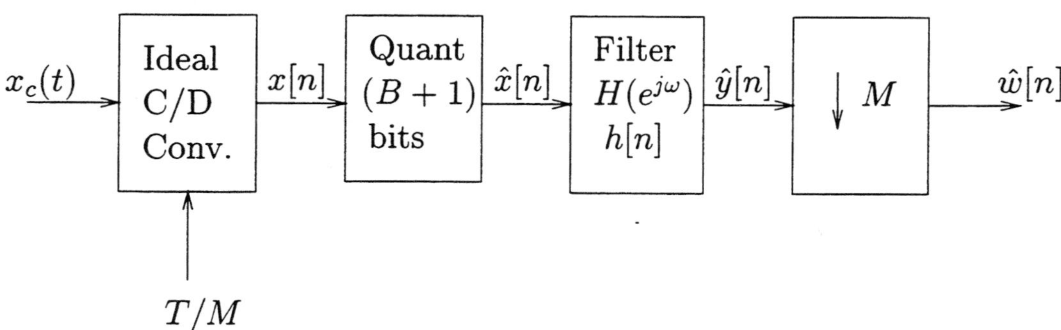

Figure 17.1. Oversampling system

The following information is known:

(1) The input is bandlimited so that $X_c(j\Omega) = 0$ for $|\Omega| \geq \pi/T$.

(2) The quantizer produces output samples rounded to $(B+1)$-bit precision (B bits and sign).

(3) M is an integer greater than one.

The sequences in Fig. 17.1 are represented as follows:

$$\begin{aligned} \hat{x}[n] &= x[n] + e[n] \\ \hat{y}[n] &= y[n] + f[n], \text{where } y[n] = x[n] * h[n] \\ \hat{w}[n] &= \hat{y}[Mn] = w[n] + g[n] \end{aligned}$$

The sequence $e[n]$ is a noise sequence with properties consistent with the linear noise model used to represent quantization error. The sequences $f[n]$ and $g[n]$ are the corresponding outputs due to the noise input $e[n]$.

The frequency response of the LTI filter is defined over one period by

$$H(e^{j\omega}) = \begin{cases} 1, & |\omega| < \pi/M \\ 0, & \pi/M \leq |\omega| \leq \pi \end{cases}$$

(a) Give an expression for $w[n]$ in terms of $x_c(t)$.

(b) Give expressions for the noise power at each point in the system, i.e., give expressions for σ_e^2, σ_f^2, σ_g^2.

(c) If possible, determine M so that the noise power σ_f^2 is "one bit bitter" than the noise power σ_e^2.

Problem 18

Consider the interconnection of systems shown in Fig. 18.1, where S_1 is a causal LTI system with system function

$$H_1(z) = \frac{1}{1 - \frac{1}{2}z^{-1}}$$

and S_2 is a causal LTI system.

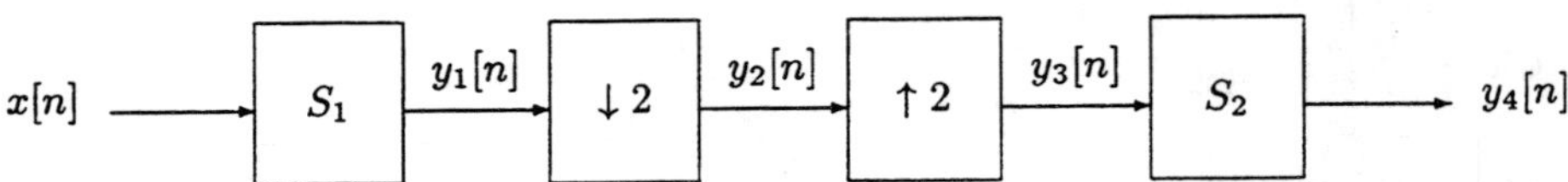

Figure 18.1. Interconnected Systems

(a) If $x[n] = \delta[n]$, show that $y_2[n] = \alpha^n u[n]$ and specify the value of α.

(b) If $x[n] = \delta[n]$, determine $Y_3(z)$ and its region of convergence.

(c) If $x[n] = \delta[n]$ and $y_4[n] = y_1[n]$, determine the impulse response of S_2.

(d) Is S_2 a minimum-phase system? Explain.

Problem 19

Let $H_{d1}(e^{j\omega})$ and $H_{d2}(e^{j\omega})$ correspond to ideal lowpass filters with real-valued impulse responses, $h_{d1}[n]$ and $h_{d2}[n]$, respectively.

$$H_{d1}(e^{j\omega}) = \begin{cases} 1, & 0 \le \omega < \pi/2, \\ 0, & \pi/2 < \omega \le \pi, \end{cases}$$

$$H_{d2}(e^{j\omega}) = \begin{cases} e^{-j4\omega}, & 0 \le \omega < \pi/2, \\ 0, & \pi/2 < \omega \le \pi. \end{cases}$$

A 9-point sequence, $h_1[n]$, restricted to be zero outside the interval $0 \le n \le 8$, is selected to minimize:

$$\epsilon_1^2 = \frac{1}{2\pi}\int_{-\pi}^{\pi} |H_1(e^{j\omega}) - H_{d1}(e^{j\omega})|^2 d\omega,$$

where $H_1(e^{j\omega})$ is the DTFT of $h_1[n]$. Let E_1^2 denote the minimized value of ϵ_1^2.

A 9-point sequence, $h_2[n]$, restricted to be zero outside the interval $0 \le n \le 8$, is selected to minimize:

$$\epsilon_2^2 = \frac{1}{2\pi}\int_{-\pi}^{\pi} |H_2(e^{j\omega}) - H_{d2}(e^{j\omega})|^2 d\omega,$$

where $H_2(e^{j\omega})$ is the DTFT of $h_2[n]$. Let E_2^2 denote the minimized value of ϵ_2^2.

A 9-point sequence, $h_3[n]$, restricted to be zero outside the interval $0 \le n \le 8$, is selected to minimize:

$$\epsilon_3^2 = \frac{1}{2\pi}\int_{-\pi}^{\pi} |H_3(e^{j\omega}) + H_{d1}(e^{j\omega}) - 1|^2 d\omega,$$

where $H_3(e^{j\omega})$ is the DTFT of $h_3[n]$. Let E_3^2 denote the minimized value of ϵ_3^2.

(a) Is $E_2^2 = E_1^2$? Justify your answer.

(b) Is $E_3^2 = E_1^2$? Justify your answer.

Problem 20

Shown in Fig. 20.1 is the frequency response of a zero-phase type I lowpass FIR filter, *i.e.*, $H(e^{j\omega})$ is of the form

$$H(e^{j\omega}) = \sum_{n=-L}^{L} h[n]e^{-j\omega n},$$

with $h[n] = h[-n]$. The filter was designed by the Parks-McClellan algorithm. Recall that the Parks-McClellan algorithm generates the filter which is optimal in terms of minimizing the maximum error.

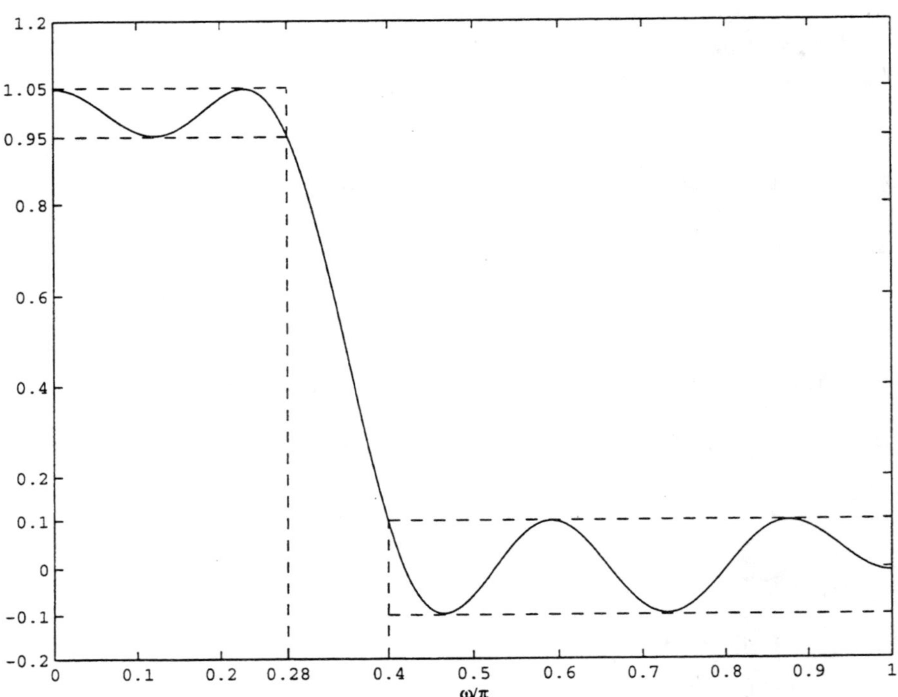

Figure 20.1. $H(e^{j\omega})$

You may make obvious assumptions about this computer-generated figure. For example, if a point "looks like" it has zero slope, assume it does. If two extrema "look like" they are of equal height, they are.

(a) Determine the possible value(s) of L from the given information.

(b) Given $h[n]$ from the previous part, you would like to design a zero-phase bandpass filter $h_B[n]$ whose impulse response extends from $n = -M$ to $n = M$ and which satisfies the specification shown in Fig. 20.2. You want $h_B[n]$ to be optimal in the sense of minimizing the maximum error of the filter from the desired response $D_p(\omega)$, shown in Fig. 20.3 and frequency domain error weighting function $W_p(\omega)$ shown in Fig. 20.4. Note that $D_p(\omega)$ and $W_p(\omega)$ are obtained from $D_p(x)$ and $W_p(x)$ of the alternation theorem using the substitution $x = \cos(\omega)$. $h_B[n]$ can be constructed directly from $h[n]$ for some particular value(s) of M without running the Parks-McClellan algorithm on the new specifications.

Specify how to construct $h_B[n]$ from $h[n]$, and for what value(s) of M this solution is optimal in the min-max sense. Justify these cases are optimal using the alternation theorem which is included below.

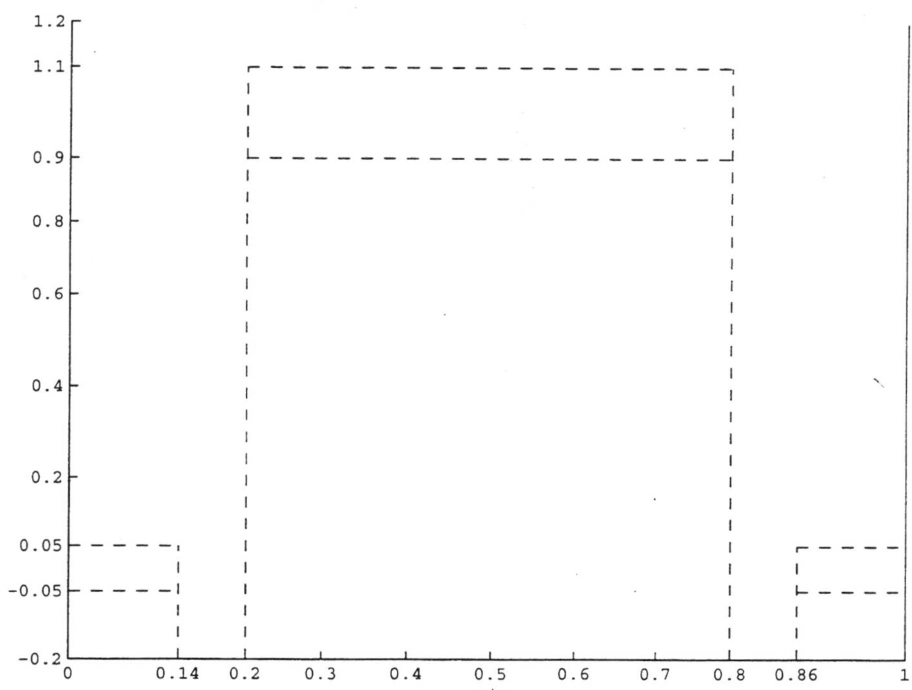

Figure 20.2. Specification of Desired Filter

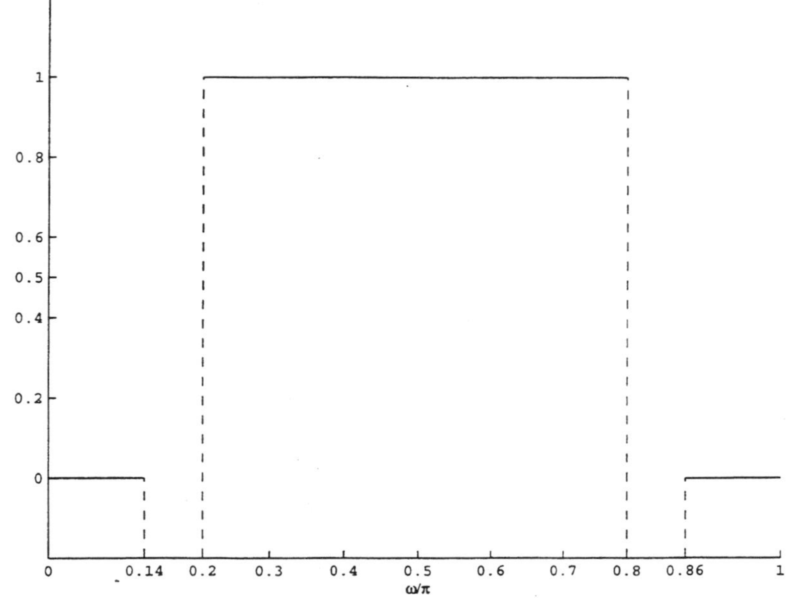

Figure 20.3. $D_p(\omega)$, Desired Frequency Response